Parametric Modeling

with I-DEAS 8®

Randy H. Shih
Oregon Institute of Technology

SDC
PUBLICATIONS
Mission, Kansas

Schroff Development Corporation
P.O. Box 1334
Mission KS 66222
(913) 262-2664
www.schroff.com

Shih, Randy H.
Parametric modeling with I-DEAS 8/
Randy H. Shih

ISBN: 1-58503-054-6

Printed and bound in the United States of America.

Preface

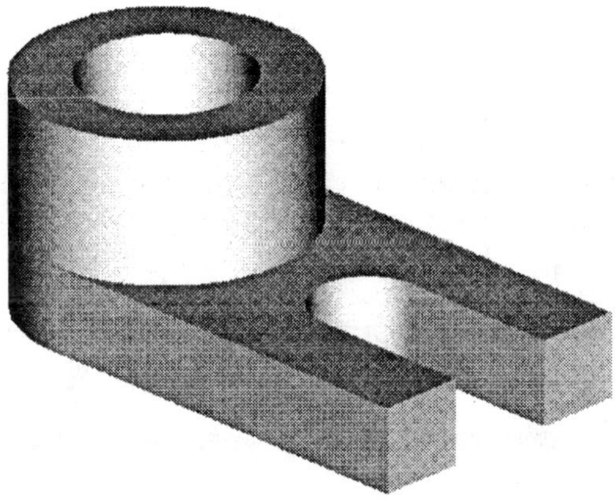

The primary goal of *Parametric Modeling with I-DEAS 8* is to introduce the important aspects of Solid Modeling and Parametric Modeling. This text is intended to be used as a training guide for students and professionals. This text covers *I-DEAS 8* and the chapters proceed in a pedagogical fashion to guide you from constructing basic shapes to building intelligent solid models, creating multi-view drawings and assemblies. This text takes a hands-on, exercise-intensive approach to all the important *Parametric Modeling* techniques and concepts. This text contains a series of tutorial style chapters illustrating the use of I-DEAS solid modeling modules for part design, part annotation, part drawings and part assembly. This text is designed to introduce beginning CAD users to I-DEAS. This text is also helpful to I-DEAS users upgrading from a previous release of the software. I-DEAS 8 provides many exciting tools for modeling, documenting and communicating product designs. This text also covers the most unique tool added in I-DEAS 8, the new three-dimensional-annotation and organizational tool. The solid modeling techniques and concepts discussed in this text are also applicable to other parametric feature-based CAD packages. The basic premise of this book is that the more designs you create using I-DEAS, the better you learn the software. With this in mind, each chapter introduces a new set of commands and concepts, building on previous chapters. This book does not attempt to cover all of the I-DEAS' features, only to provide an introduction to the software. It is intended to help you establish a good basis for exploring and growing in the exciting field of Computer Aided Engineering.

Acknowledgments

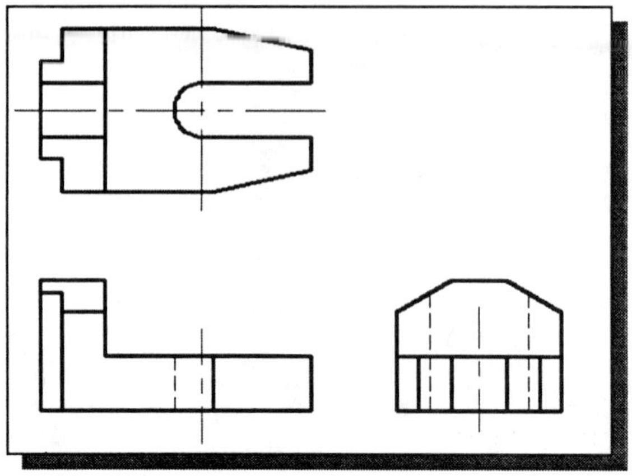

This book would not have been possible without a great deal of support. First, special thanks to two great teachers, Prof. George R. Schade of University of Nebraska-Lincoln and Mr. Denwu Lee, who taught me the fundamentals, the intrigue, and the sheer fun of Computer Aided Engineering.

The effort and support of the editorial and production staff of Schroff Development Corporation is gratefully acknowledged. I would especially like to thank Stephen Schroff and Mary Schmidt for their support and helpful suggestions during this project.

I am grateful that the Mechanical and Manufacturing Engineering Technology Department of Oregon Institute of Technology has provided me with an excellent environment in which to pursue my interests in teaching and research.

I would also like to thank Prof. John R. Steffen of Valparaiso University and Prof. Robert L. Mott of University of Dayton for helpful comments and suggestions; Mr. Mark H. Lawry of SDRC for his suggestions and encouragement.

Finally, truly unbounded thanks are due to my wife Hsiu-Ling and my daughter Cassandra for their understanding and encouragement throughout this project.

Randy H. Shih
Klamath Falls, Oregon

Table of Contents

Chapter 3
Constructive Solid Geometry Concept

Chapter 6
Geometric Construction Tools

Chapter 7
The BORN Technique and Work Features

Chapter 8
3-D Annotation and Associated Drawings

Chapter 9
Symmetrical Features in Designs

Chapter 10
Three-Dimensional Construction Tools

Chapter 11
Part Modeling - Finishing Touches

Chapter 12
Assembly Modeling - Putting It All Together

Index

Chapter 1
Introduction

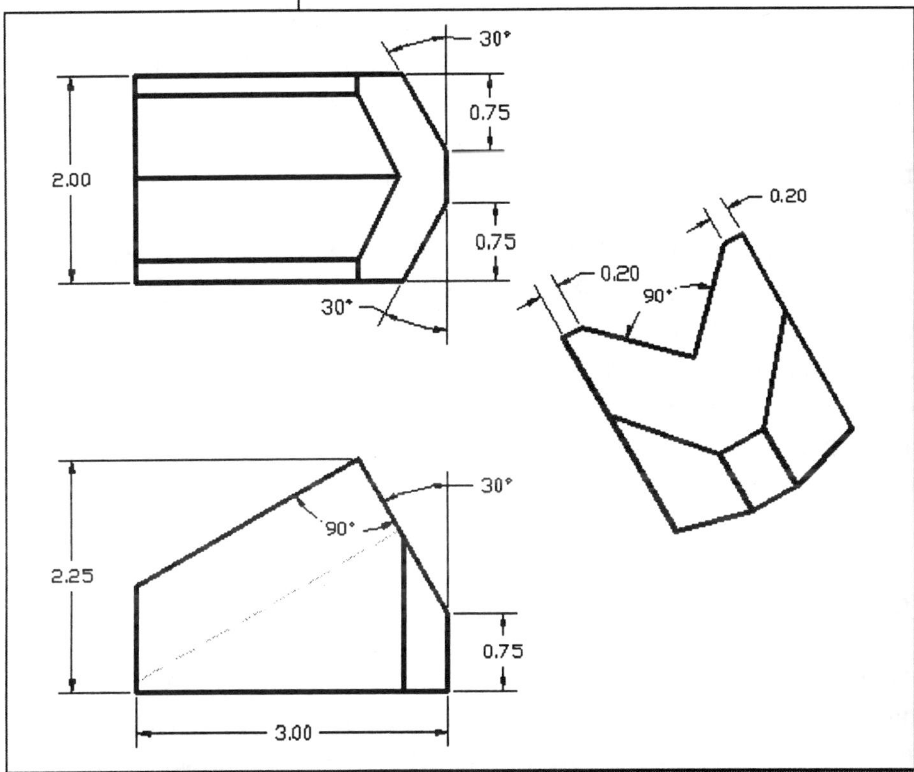

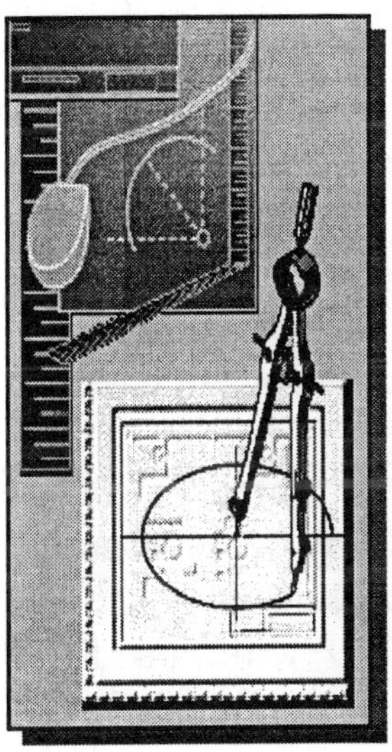

Learning Objectives

- ♦ Development of Computer Geometric Modeling
- ♦ Feature-Based Parametric Modeling
- ♦ Getting started with I-DEAS
- ♦ The I-DEAS Startup Window and Units Setup
- ♦ I-DEAS Screen Layout
- ♦ Mouse Buttons
- ♦ I-DEAS Data management concepts

Introduction

The rapid changes in the field of **Computer Aided Engineering** (CAE) have brought exciting advances in the engineering community. Recent advances have made the long-sought goal of **concurrent engineering** closer to a reality. CAE has become the core of concurrent engineering and is aimed at reducing design time, producing prototypes faster, and achieving higher product quality. **I-DEAS** (Integrated Design Engineering Analysis Software) is an integrated package of mechanical computer aided engineering software tools developed by Structural Dynamic Research Corporation (*SDRC*). **I-DEAS** is a tool that facilitates a concurrent engineering approach to the design, stress-analysis, simulation, and manufacturing of mechanical engineering products. The I-DEAS software allows us to quickly create three-dimensional solid models; the software greatly enhances and simplifies the design process. Real-life loads can also be simulated on the computer, using the I-DEAS simulation module, to predict the behaviors of the designs under a specific set of operating conditions. The computer models can also be used directly by manufacturing equipment such as machining centers, lathes, mills, or rapid prototyping machines to manufacture the product. In this text, we will be dealing only with the solid modeling modules used for part design, part drawings, and part assembly.

Development of Computer Geometric Modeling

Computer geometric modeling is a relatively new and rapidly expanding area. The transistor was invented in 1948, and general-purpose computers were invented soon after, in the 1950s and 1960s. One of the most important developments in computer graphics was the publication of Ivan Sutherland's ***Sketchpad*** (MIT doctoral dissertation) in 1963. This is considered the beginning of interactive computer graphics. During that time, several companies, such as General Motors, Boeing, and IBM, began development of interactive CAD programs. However, such developments were slowed by the high cost of computer hardware, the high programming cost, and the non-portability of software.

The 1970s were marked by significant progress in the development of microprocessors. It was in 1971 that Ted Hoff developed the first microprocessor. The era of the personal computer (PC) had begun through the development of large-scale integrated circuits (LSIC) in which all circuitry of the central processing unit (CPU) is on one chip. In the 1980s, improvements in computer hardware brought the power of mainframes to the desktop.

Computer modeling technology advanced along with computer hardware. CAD programs evolved into design tools rather than just drafting tools. During these years of development, modeling schemes progressed from two-dimensional (2-D) wireframe to three-dimensional (3-D) wireframe, to surface modeling and, finally, to solid modeling.

The development of three-dimensional modeling schemes started with three-dimensional (3-D) wireframes. Wireframe models are models consisting of locations of points and lines between appropriate pairs of points. The lines are used to represent transitions, such as from surface to surface. Lines are also a very economical way of representing geometry.
The first generation CAD packages were 2-D wireframe **Computer Aided Drafting** programs, basically the electronic equivalents of the drafting board. For typical models, this required that several to many views of the object be created individually as they would be on the drafting board. The 3-D model remained in the designer's mind, not in the computer database. Although such systems have some advantages over manual drafting, they are still tedious and labor intensive.

The development of the 3-D wireframe modeler was a major leap in the area of computer modeling. The computer database in the 3-D wireframe modeler contains the locations of all the points in space coordinates and it is sufficient to create just one model rather than multiple models. This single 3-D model can then be viewed from any direction as needed. The 3-D wireframe modelers require the least computer power and achieve reasonably good representation of 3-D models. However, because surface definition is not part of a wireframe model, all wireframe images have the inherent problem of ambiguity.

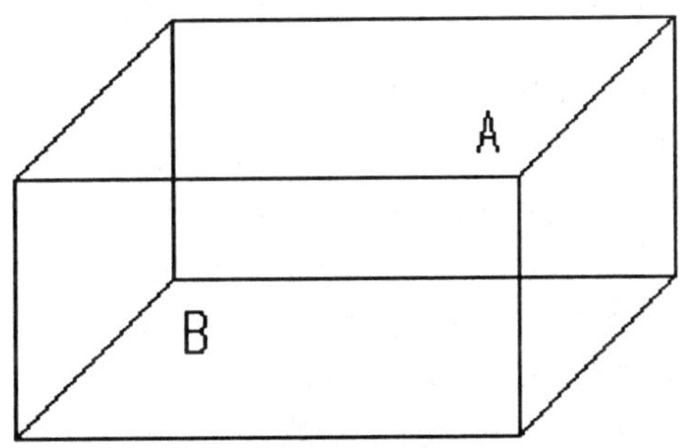

Wireframe Ambiguity: Which corner is in front, A or B?

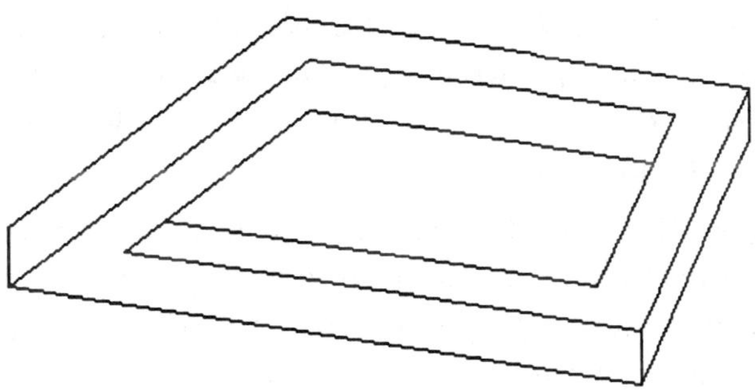

A non-realizable object: Wireframe models contain no surface definitions.

Surface modeling is the logical development in computer geometry modeling to follow the 3-D wireframe modeling scheme by organizing and grouping edges that define polygonal surfaces. Surface modeling describes the part's surfaces but not its interiors. Designers are still required to interactively examine surface models to insure that the various surfaces on a model are contiguous throughout. Many of the concepts used in 3-D wireframe and surface modelers are incorporated in the solid modeling scheme, but it is solid modeling that offers the most advantages as a design tool.
In the solid modeling presentation scheme, the solid definitions include nodes, edges, and surfaces, and it is a complete and unambiguous mathematical representation of a precisely enclosed and filled volume. Unlike the surface modeling method, solid modelers start with a solid or use topology rules to guarantee that all of the surfaces are stitched together properly. Two predominant methods for representing solid models are **constructive solid geometry** (CSG) representation and **boundary representation** (B-rep).

The CSG representation method can be defined as the combination of 3-D solid primitives. What constitutes a "primitive" varies somewhat with the software but typically includes a rectangular prism, a cylinder, a cone, a wedge, and a sphere. Most solid modelers allow the user to define additional primitives, which can be very complex.

In the B-rep representation method, objects are represented in terms of their spatial boundaries. This method defines the points, edges, and surfaces of a volume, and/or issues commands that sweep or rotate a defined face into a third dimension to form a solid. The object is then made up of the unions of these surfaces that completely and precisely enclose a volume.

By the 1980s, a new paradigm called *concurrent engineering* had emerged. With concurrent engineering, designers, design engineers, analysts, manufacturing engineers, and management engineers all work closely right from the initial stages of the design. In this way, all aspects of the design can be evaluated and any potential problems can be identified right from the start and throughout the design process. Using the principles of concurrent engineering, a new type of computer modeling technique appeared. The technique is known as the *feature-based parametric modeling technique*. The key advantage of the *feature-based parametric modeling technique* is its capability to produce very flexible designs. Changes can be made easily and design alternatives can be evaluated with minimum effort. Various software packages offer different approaches to feature-based parametric modeling, yet the end result is a flexible design defined by its design variables and parametric features.

Feature-Based Parametric Modeling

One of the key-elements in the I-DEAS solid modeling software is its use of the **feature-based parametric modeling technique**. The feature-based parametric modeling approach has elevated solid modeling technology to the level of a very powerful design tool. Parametric modeling automates the design and revision procedures by the use of parametric features. Parametric features control the model geometry by the use of design variables. The word ***Parametric*** means that the geometric definitions of the design, such as dimensions, can be varied at any time in the design process. Features are predefined parts or construction tools in which users define the key parameters. A part is described as a sequence of engineering features, which can be modified/changed at any time. The concept of parametric features makes modeling more closely match the actual design-manufacturing process than the mathematics of a solid modeling program. In parametric modeling, models and drawings are updated automatically when the design is refined.

Parametric modeling offers many benefits:

- **We begin with simple, conceptual models with minimal detail; this approach conforms to the design philosophy of "shape before size."**
- **Geometric constraints, dimensional constraints, and relational parametric equations can be used to capture design intent.**
- **We can quickly explore and evaluate different design variations and alternatives to determine the best design.**
- **Existing design data can be reused to create new designs.**

The feature-based parametric modeling technique enables the designer to incorporate the original **design intent** into construction of the model, and the individual features control the geometry in the event of a design change. As features are modified, the system updates the entire part by re-linking the individual features of the model.

The I-DEAS software is considered one of the easiest-to-use in the CAD/CAM industry. The unique user interfaces, such as the **Dynamic Navigator**, enable us to easily incorporate our design intent into the solid model. *I-DEAS*'s **Team Design Support** is a unique approach that assists product development teams to have the flexibility to manage and share data in a controlled, concurrent environment. I-DEAS also allows us to apply 3D-based annotation, in conjunction with engineering drawing conventions, directly to the solid model or assembly. We can document and communicate all production and manufacturing information in three-dimensional (3D) environment.

I-DEAS 8 is the eighth version, with many added features and enhancements, of the original I-DEAS software produced by Structural Dynamic Research Corporation (*SDRC*). The goal of using such a powerful package is to improve the design process and allows you, the product development team, to **Get There Faster** ™

Getting Started with *I-DEAS*

➢ I-DEAS is composed of a number of application software modules (called *applications* and *tasks*), all sharing a common database. In this text, we will be dealing only with the solid modeling modules used for part design, the tools necessary for the creation of models, and engineering drawings. You can select an application or a task when you start I-DEAS, or change applications/tasks using the pull-down menu within I-DEAS.

I-DEAS Applications

- Design
- Simulation
- Test
- Manufacturing
- Management
- Open Data/PCB

I-DEAS Design Tasks

- Master Modeler
- Master Assembly
- Master Drafting
- Mechanism Design
- Harness Design

◆ **I-DEAS Data Management Concepts**

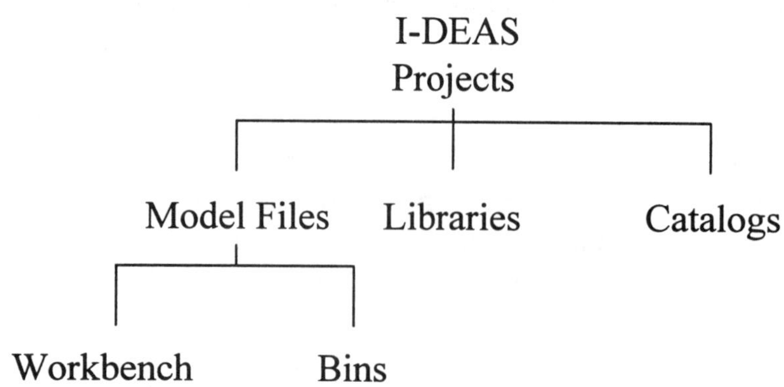

- **Model Files**

A model file is made up of a workbench and any number of bins. Think of a model file as a personal workspace, like a desk. Parts that are visible on the screen are described as being on the workbench. Parts in the model file can also be placed into bins in the model file, much like storing items in the drawers of a desk.

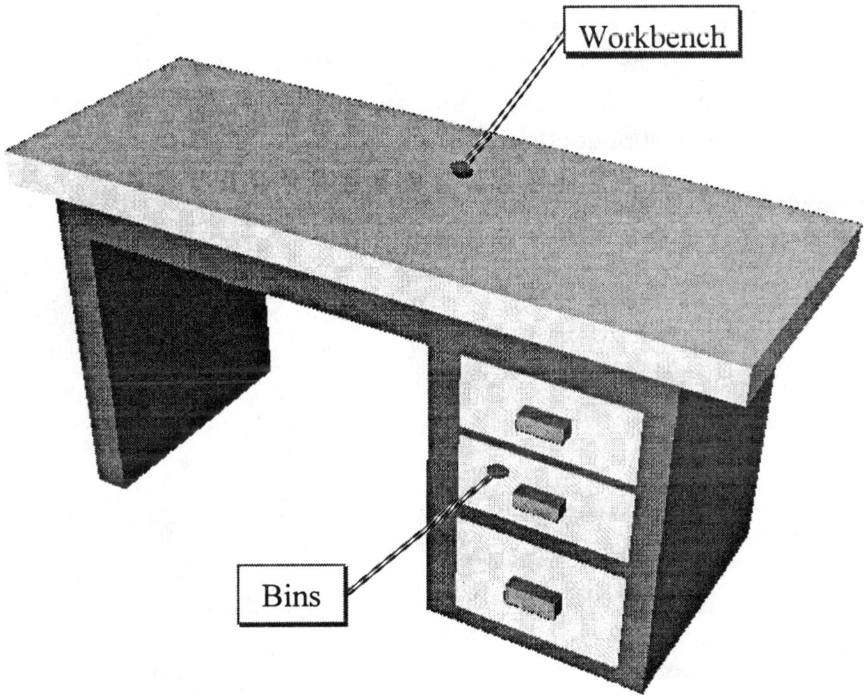

- **Libraries**

Libraries are used to share information among a project team. The libraries allow a project team to concurrently access parts. Libraries can also be used to automatically update your work, provide version control, and provide a central location to store models.

- **Catalogs**

Catalogs are used for standardized parts and features that would be referenced by the entire company. Information placed in catalogs is typically information that does not change very often.

Starting I-DEAS

- To start I-DEAS, select the *I-DEAS* icon or type "*ideas*" at your system prompt. Depending upon the type of workstation you are using, you may choose to use different display device options. Typical display device options are *X3D* and *OGL*. Choosing **X3D** will allow real-time rotation of wireframe models using the X11 protocol. Choosing **OGL** will use the Open-Graphics protocol and allow real-time rotation of shaded solid models. Several parameters are available at start-up, and you can type "*ideas -h*" at the system prompt to find out what other parameters are available. The program takes a while to load, so be patient. Eventually the *I-DEAS Start* window will appear on the screen, and you will be asked for a project name, a model file name, and the application and task you want to use.

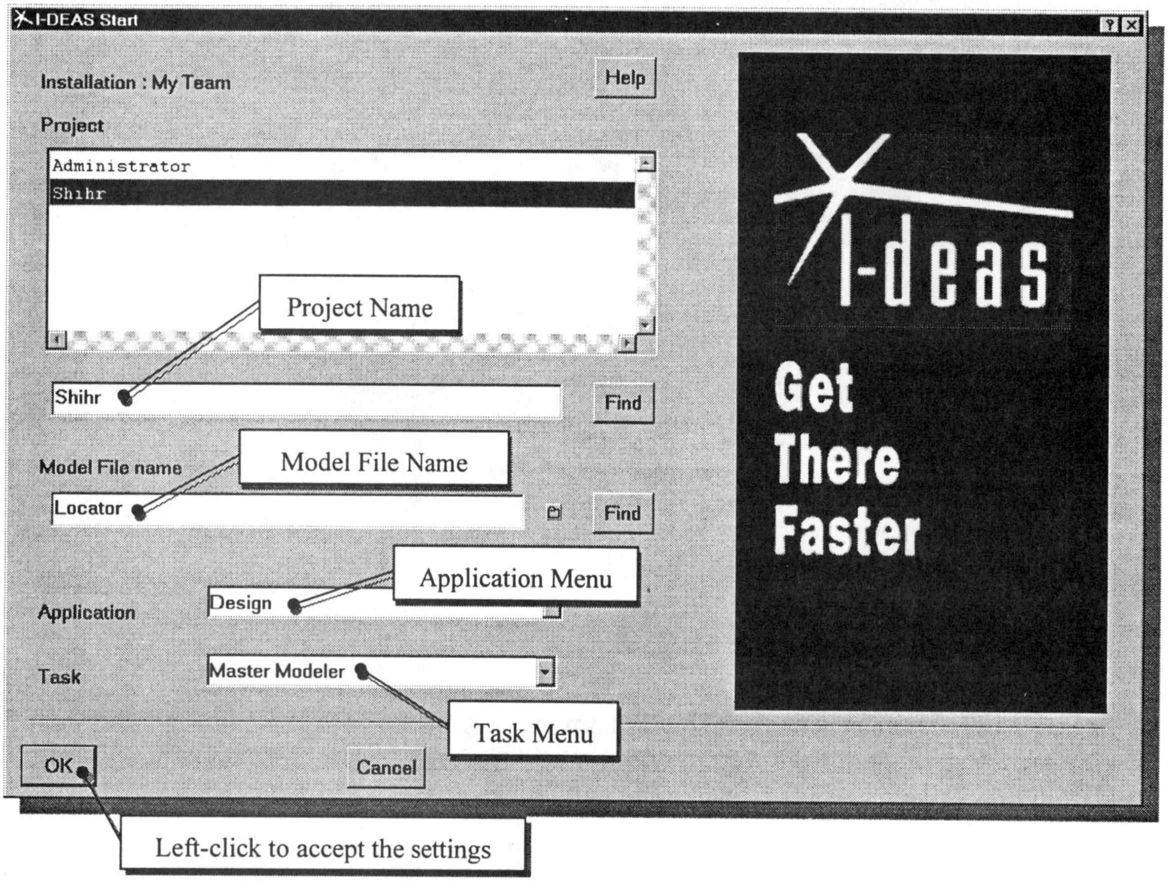

- **Project Name**
  The project name identifies the files associated with the project, allowing team members to easily locate the project files. Enter a project name by clicking with the left mouse button in the space provided and typing in a name, or select an existing project out of the list. The first time a new project name is entered, I-DEAS will alert you that a new project will be created. For a user not working on a team project, the user account name may be entered for simplicity.

- **Model File Name**
  The model file name identifies the part file that you want to work on. Enter a model file name by clicking with the left mouse button in the space provided and typing in a name, or select an existing model file name out of the folder. On some systems, the file name may not contain spaces or special characters, and the number of characters may be limited to 10 characters. The first time a new model file name is entered, I-DEAS will alert you that it is a new model file. A model file can contain many parts or assemblies, and actually consists of two files with the extension .MF1 and .MF2. One file contains model data and the other contains graphical data.

- **Application Menu**
  The application menu allows you to select the specific application you want. Click on the icon with the left mouse button to display the menu of choices. The *Design* application will be the first application we use in this text.

- **Task Menu**
  After selecting the application, select the particular *task* out of the task menu. *Master Modeler* is the basic task for creating solid models. Click and drag the left mouse button to make the selection from the menu of choices.

1. In the *Start Menu*, use your account name as the *project name* as shown.

2. Enter **Locator** as the *Model File name.*

3. Select **Design** in the *Application menu.*

4. Select **Master Modeler** in the *Task menu.*

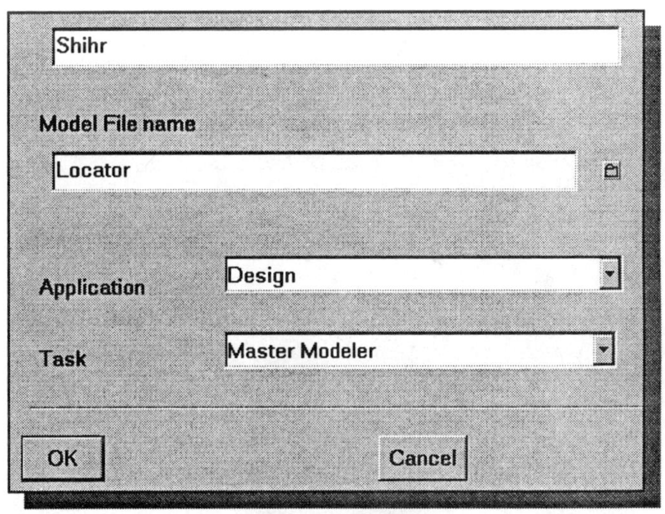

5. Click on the **OK** button to accept the settings and launch the selected application and task.

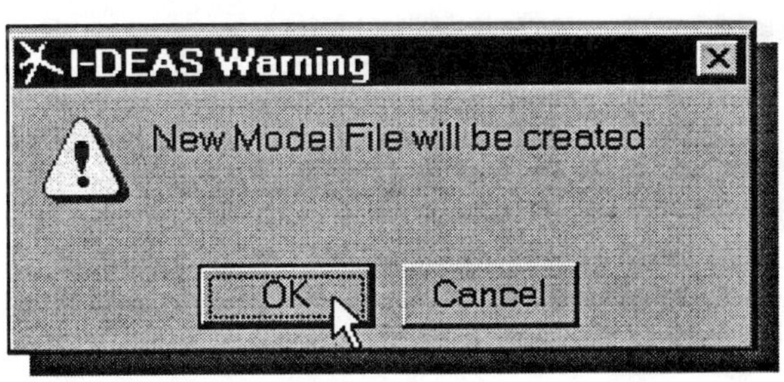

6. In the *I-DEAS warning dialogue box*, click on the **OK** button to acknowledge the creation of the new model file.

I-DEAS Screen Layout

➢ The four windows are the *graphics window*, the *prompt window*, the *list window*, and the *icon panel*. A line of *quick help* text appears at the bottom of the graphics window as you move the mouse cursor over the icons. You may resize by click and drag on the edges of the window or relocate these windows by click and drag on the window title area. If your computer system provides an icon or menu choice to close the window, DO NOT use it while in I-DEAS. If you close a window used for input or output, you run the risk of corrupting the I-DEAS model files. To leave I-DEAS, select *Exit* in the icon panel's *File* pull-down menu.

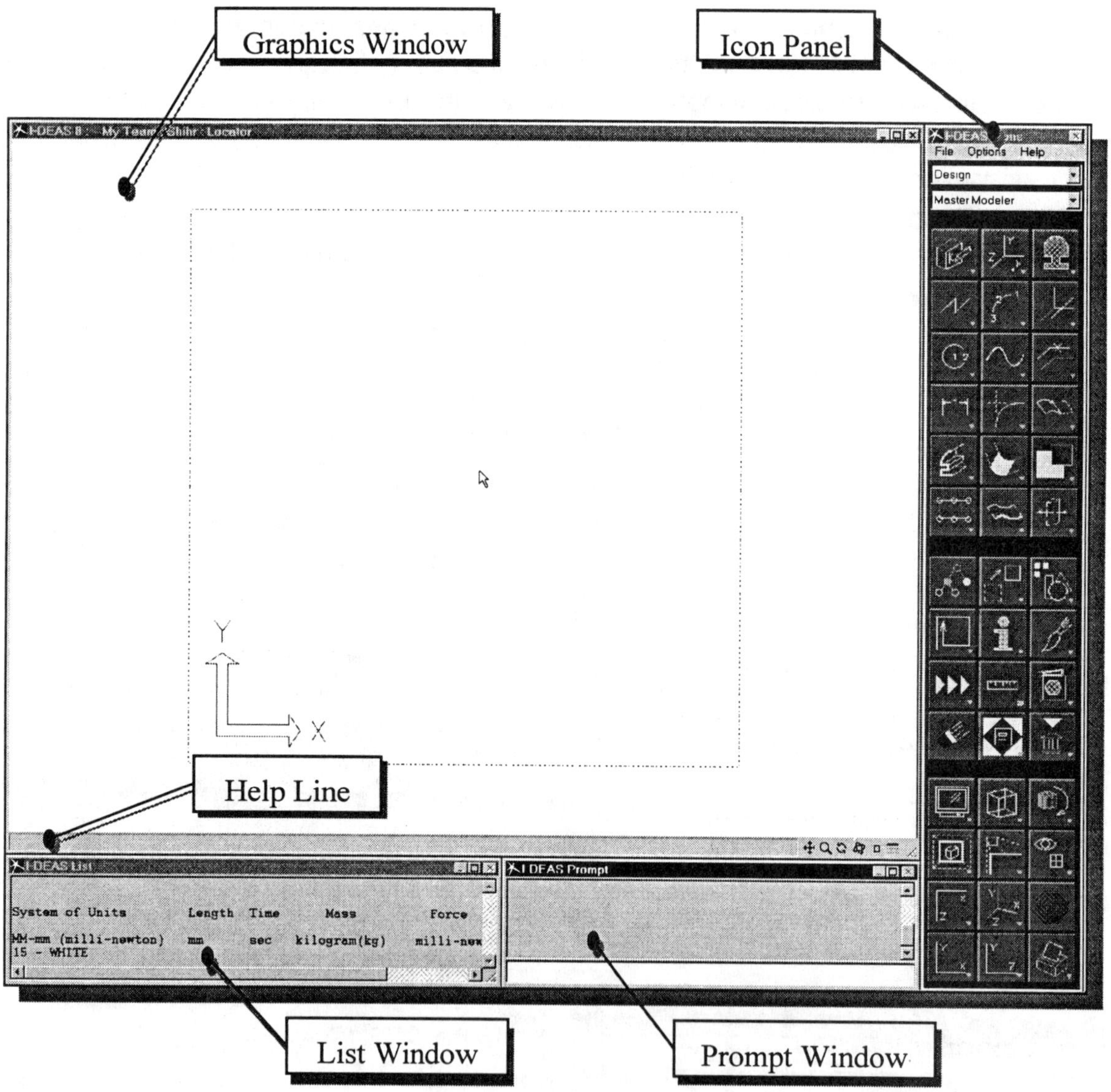

Mouse Buttons

➢ I-DEAS utilizes the mouse buttons extensively. In learning I-DEAS' interactive environment, it is important to understand the basic functions of the mouse buttons. It is highly recommended that you use a three-button mouse with I-DEAS since the package uses all three buttons for various functions.

- The **left-mouse-button** is used for most operations, such as selecting menus and icons, or picking graphic entities. *One click* of the button is used to select icons, menus and window entries, and to pick a graphic item. To pick multiple graphic items, hold down the SHIFT key and click on each item. The *press, hold, and drag* operation is used to bring up more pull-down menus and icon choices. Use the *double-click* operation in windows to open a listed item. *Multiple clicks* of the left button are used to access the part's History Tree hierarchy. The first click picks the *edge* or *face* (selection is highlighted), the second click picks the whole *part* (a white bounding box around the part), and the third click picks the *feature* (a yellow bounding box around the feature).

- The software utilizes the **middle-mouse-button** the same as the ENTER key, and is often used to accept the default setting to a prompt or to end a process. If you are using a two-button mouse, you can always hit the ENTER key to get the same result as clicking the middle button.

- The **right-mouse-button** brings up a pop-up option menu with different choices available. Press and hold down the right button then slide up and down to select the desired option.

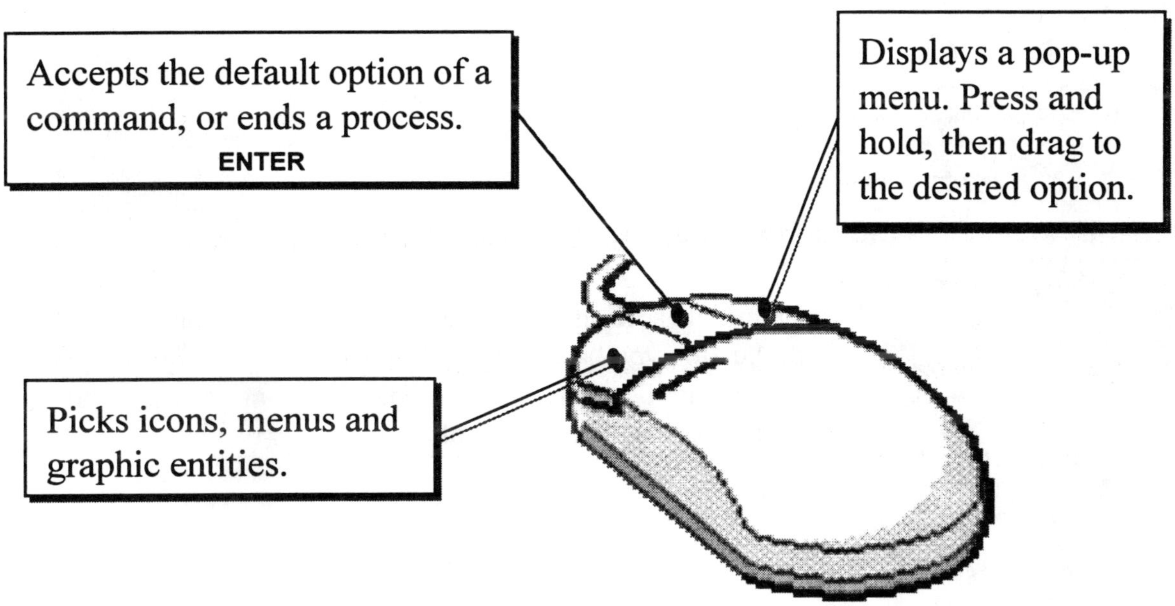

Icon Panel

Most of the command input in I-DEAS is made by picking icons in the icon panel. The icon panel is arranged in three icon sections, plus a set of pull down menu bars at the top.

♦ Top Menu Bars

The top menu bars contain the pull-down menus: File, Options, Help, Application, and Task. The File menu contains the I-DEAS input/output options such as *Open*, *Save*, *Plotting*, etc. This menu also contains the important *Exit* command. The Options menu contains option settings that allow you to set up units and other personal preferences. The Help menu contains options to access the I-DEAS Smart View Help System. This system contains the entire set of I-DEAS documentation with graphics and text. The Application and Task menus let you change to other I-DEAS applications and tasks.

♦ Task Specific Icon Panel

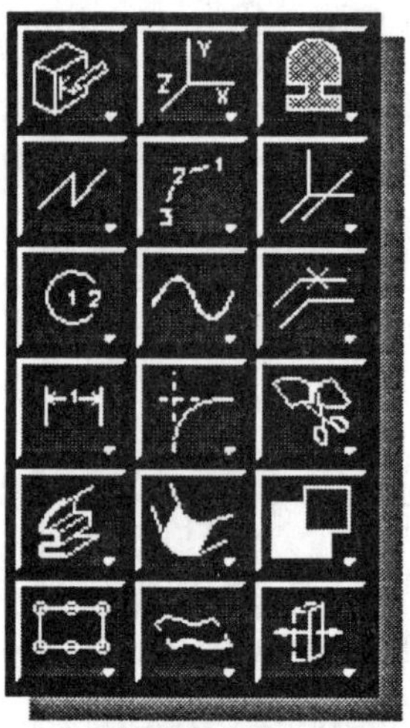

The top icon section contains icons that are specific to the Task you have chosen. The icons will change as different tasks are selected. The icons shown at the left are from the Master Modeler.

♦ Application Specific Icon Panel

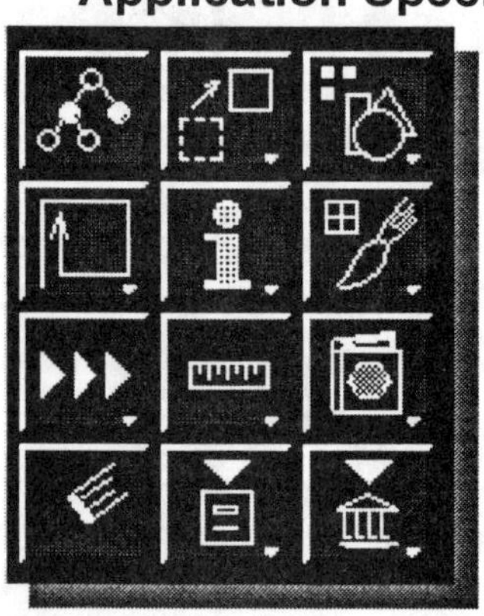

The middle section contains icons that are specific to the Application you have chosen. The icons will change as different applications are selected. The icons shown at the left are from the Design Application.

♦ Display Icon Panel

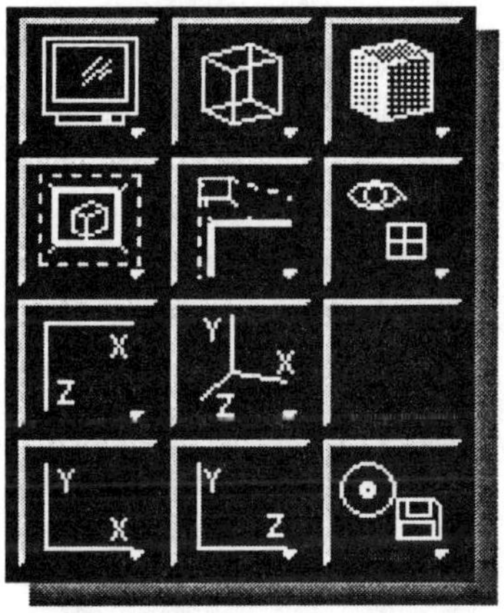

The bottom icon section contains icons that handle the various display operations. These icons control the screen display, such as the view scale, the view angle, redisplay, and shaded and hidden line displays.

Prompts

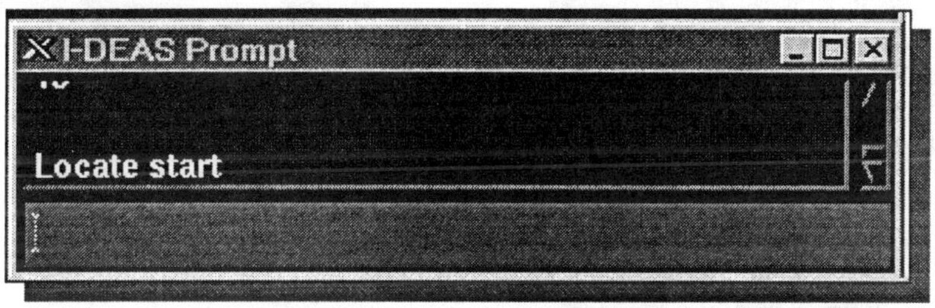

Some commands will require keyboard input in the prompt window. Prompts for keyboard input will usually start with the word "Enter" as opposed to "Pick," which implies picking model entities, or "Select," which is used to select an icon or menu command. If a default answer to a prompt is available, it is shown in parentheses ( ) at the end of the prompt. To abort a prompt, use the right-mouse-button and select *Cancel* from the pop-up menu, or type "*$*" on the keyboard.

Icon Operation

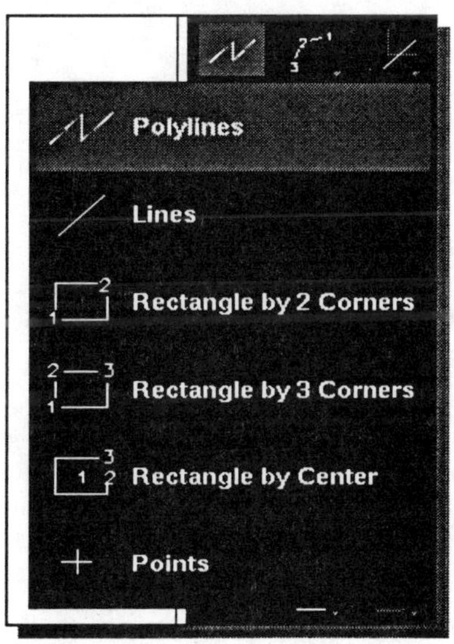

Most of the icons shown are actually a "stack" of related icons. The inverted triangle in the lower right corner of the icon indicates there are pull down selections. To select a different icon, hold down the left mouse button to pull down the list of icons and slide up and down to switch to other choices in the pull-down menu. The icon you used last will stay at the top of the "stack" of icons.

Leaving I-DEAS

To leave I-DEAS, use the left mouse button, click on File in the toolbar menu, and choose *Exit* from the pull-down menu. Do not take any short cuts in exiting. This may corrupt files and could cause system problems.

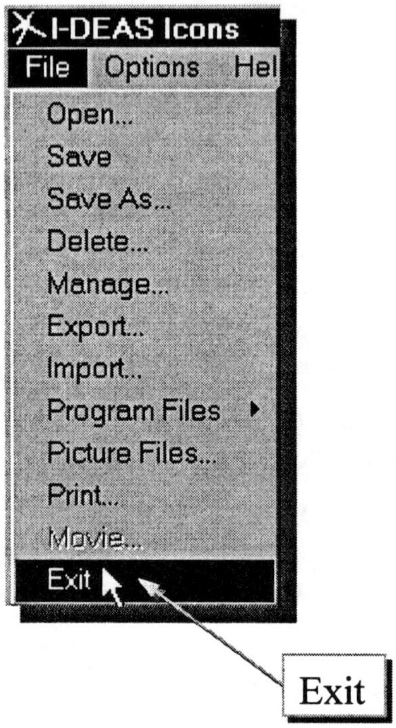

Chapter 2
Parametric Modeling Fundamentals

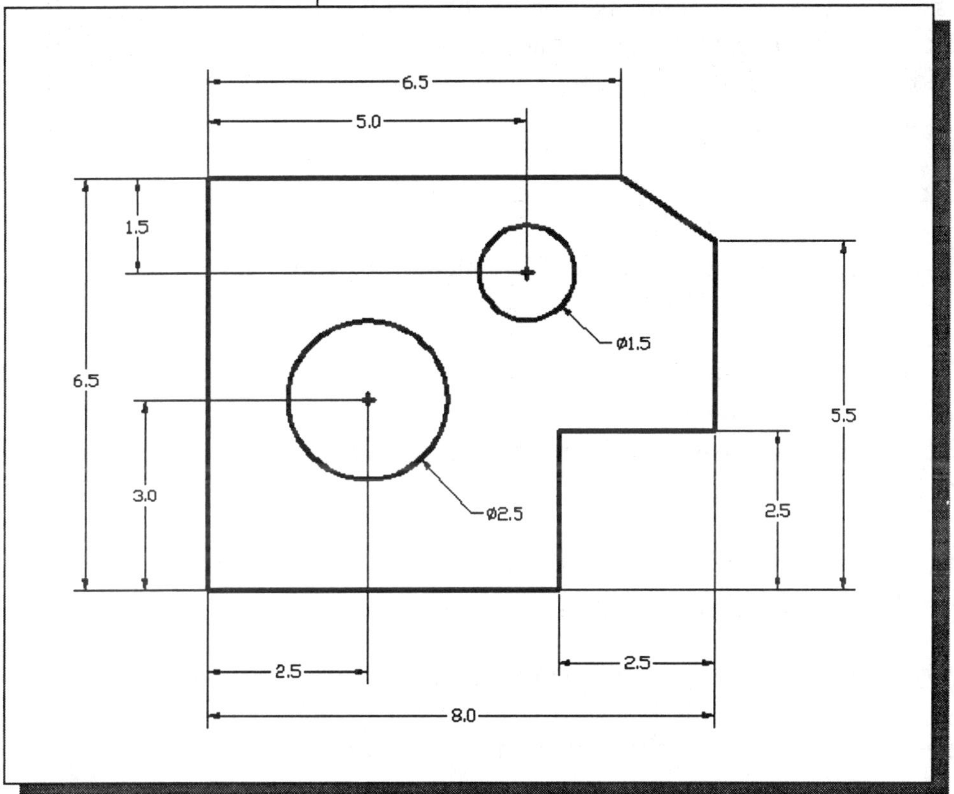

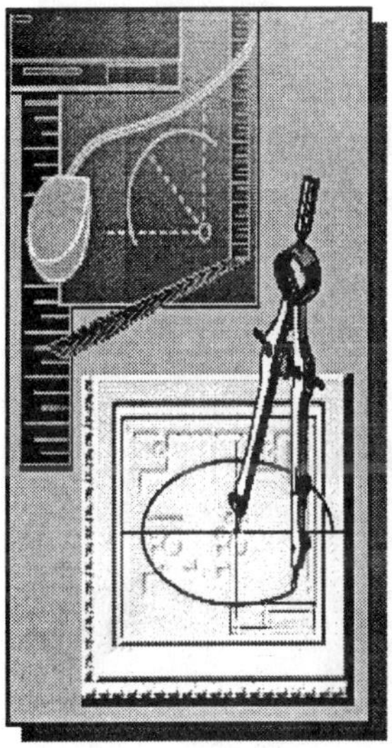

Learning Objectives

When you have completed this lesson, you will be able to:

- **Understanding the Parametric Part Modeling process**
- **Understand the basic functions of the Dynamic Navigator.**
- **Creating Rough Sketches**
- **Understand the "Shape before size" approach.**
- **Use the Dynamic Viewing commands.**
- **Using the Basic Modify commands.**

Introduction

The **feature-based parametric modeling** technique enables the designer to incorporate the original **design intent** into the construction of the model. The word ***parametric*** means the geometric definitions of the design, such as dimensions, can be varied at any time in the design process. Parametric modeling is accomplished by identifying and creating the key features of the design with the aid of computer software. The design variables, described in the sketches and described as parametric relations, can then be used to quickly modify/update the design.

In *I-DEAS*, the parametric part modeling process involves the following steps:

1. **Create a rough two-dimensional sketch of the basic shape of the base feature of the design.**

2. **Apply/delete/modify constraints and dimensions to the two-dimensional sketch.**

3. **Extrude, revolve, or sweep the parametric two-dimensional sketch to create the base solid feature of the design.**

4. **Add additional parametric features by identifying feature relations and complete the design.**

5. **Perform analyses on the computer model and refine the design as needed.**

6. **Create the desired drawing views to document the design.**

The approach of creating two-dimensional sketches of the three-dimensional features is an effective way to construct solid models. Many designs are in fact the same shape in one direction. Computer input and output devices we use today are largely two-dimensional in nature, which makes this modeling technique quite practical. This method also conforms to the design process that helps the designer with conceptual design along with the capability to capture the ***design intent***. Most engineers and designers can relate to the experience of making rough sketches on restaurant napkins to convey conceptual design ideas. *I-DEAS* provides many powerful modeling and design-tools, and there are many different approaches to accomplish modeling tasks. The basic principle of **feature-based modeling** is to build models by adding simple features one at a time. In this chapter, the general parametric part modeling procedure is illustrated; a very simple solid model with extruded features is used to introduce the *I-DEAS* user interface. The display viewing functions and the basic two-dimensional sketching tools are also demonstrated.

The L-Block design

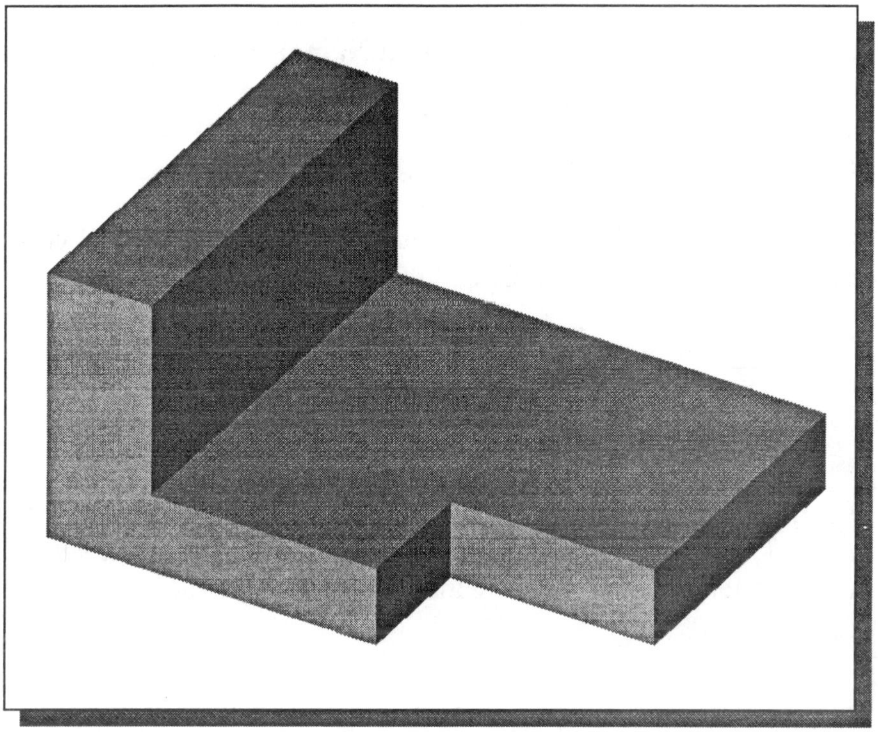

Starting I-DEAS

1. Select the *I-DEAS* icon or type "*ideas*" at your system prompt to start I-DEAS. The *I-DEAS Start* window will appear on the screen.

2. Fill in and select the items as shown below:

> Project Name: **(Your account Name)**
> Model File Name: **L_Block**
> Application: **Design**
> Task: **Master Modeler**

3. After you click **OK**, two *warning windows* will appear to tell you that a new model file will be created. Click **OK** on both windows as they come up.

> **I-DEAS Warning**
> **! New Model File will be created**
> **OK**

4. Next, I-DEAS will display four windows, the *graphics window*, the *prompt window*, the *list window* and the *icon panel*. A line of *quick help* text appears at the bottom of the graphics window as you move the mouse cursor over the icons.

Units Setup

❖ When starting a new model, the first thing we should do is determine the set of units we would like to use. I-DEAS displays the default set of units in the *list window*.

1. Use the left-mouse-button and select the **Options** menu in the icon panel as illustrated.

2. Select the **Units** option.

3. Inside the *graphics window*, pick **Inch (pound f)** from the pop-up menu. The set of units is stored with the model file when you save.

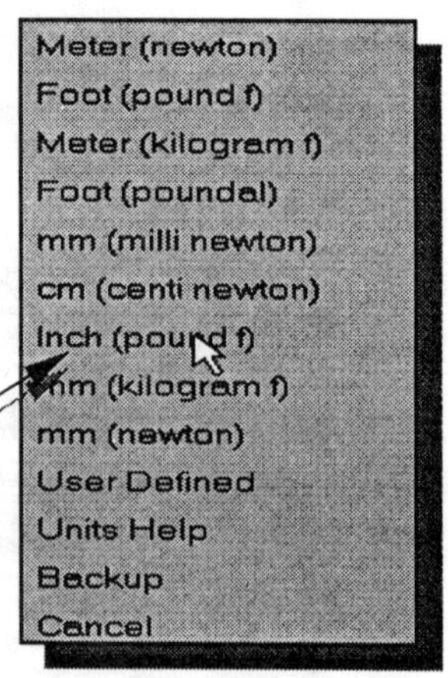

Creating Rough Sketches

Quite often during the early design stage, the shape of a design may not have any precise dimensions. Most conventional CAD systems require the user to input the precise lengths and locations of all geometric entities defining the design, which are not available during the early design stage. With *parametric modeling*, we can use the computer to elaborate and formulate the design idea further during the initial design stage. With *I-DEAS*, we can use the computer as an electronic sketchpad to help us concentrate on the formulation of forms and shapes for the design. This approach is the main advantage of *parametric modeling* over conventional solid-modeling techniques.

As the name implies, **rough sketches** are not precise at all. When sketching, we simply sketch the geometry so it closely resembles the desired shape. Precise scale or lengths are not needed. *I-DEAS* provides us with many tools to assist us in finalizing sketches. For example, geometric entities such as horizontal and vertical lines are set automatically. However, if the rough sketches are poor, it will require much more work to generate the desired parametric sketches. Here are some general guidelines for creating sketches in *I-DEAS*:

- **Create a sketch that is proportional to the desired shape.** Concentrate on the shapes and forms of the design.

- **Keep the sketches simple.** Leave out small geometry features such as fillets, rounds and chamfers. They can easily be placed using the *Fillet* and *Chamfer* commands after the parametric sketches have been established.

- **Exaggerate the geometric features of the desired shape.** For example, if the desired angle is 85 degrees, create an angle that is 50 or 60 degrees. Otherwise, *I-DEAS* might assume the intended angle to be a 90-degree angle.

- **Draw the geometry so that it does not overlap.** *Self-intersecting* geometry shapes and identical geometry placed at the same locations are not allowed.

- **The sketched geometric entities should form a closed region.** To create a solid feature such as an extruded solid, a closed region is required so that the extruded solid forms a 3D volume.

➢ **Note:** The concepts and principles involved in *parametric modeling* are very different, and sometimes they are totally opposite, those of conventional computer aided drafting. In order to understand and fully utilize *I-DEAS's* functionality, it will be helpful to take a *Zen* approach to learning the topics presented in this text: **Temporarily forget your knowledge and experiences of using conventional Computer Aided Drafting systems.**

Step 1: Creating a rough sketch

❖ In this lesson we will begin by building a 2-D sketch, as shown.

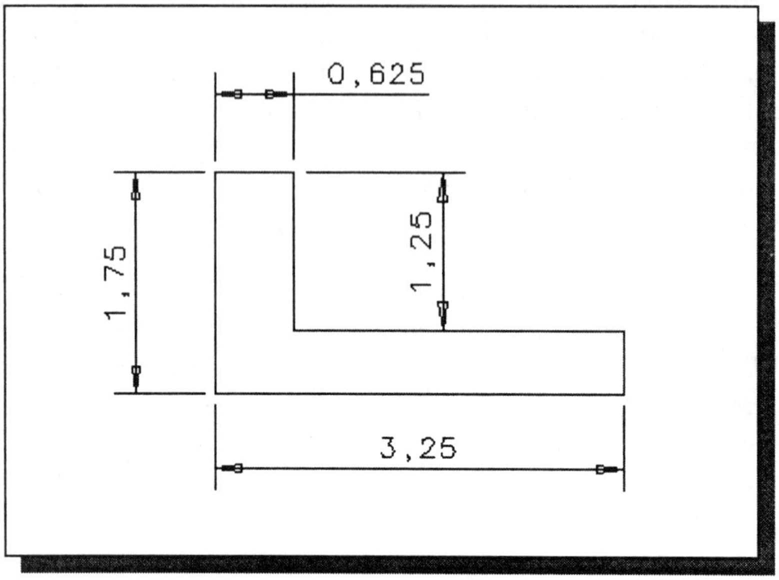

I-DEAS provides many powerful tools for sketching 2-D shapes. In the previous generation CAD programs, exact dimensional values were needed during construction, and adjustments to dimensional values were quite difficult once the model is built. In I-DEAS, we can now treat the sketch as if it is being done on a piece of napkin, and it was the general shape of the design that we are more interested in defining. The I-DEAS part model contains more than just the final geometry, it also contains the **design intent** that governs what will happen when geometry changes. The design philosophy of "shape before size" is implemented through the use of **I-DEAS Variational Geometry**. This allows the designer to construct solid models in a higher level and leave all the geometric details to I-DEAS. We will first create a rough sketch, by using some of the visual aids available, and then update the design through the associated control parameters.

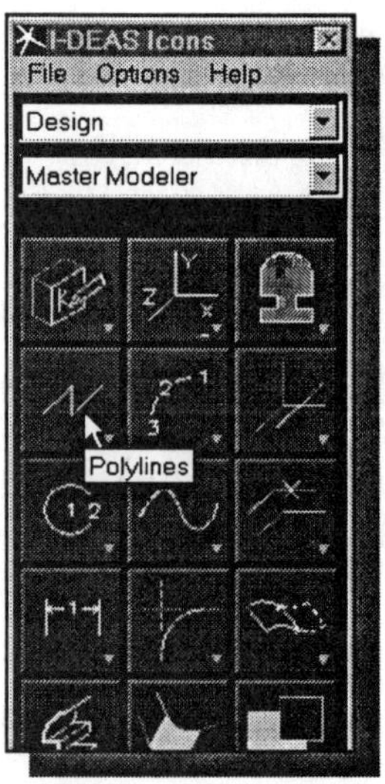

1. Pick **Polylines** in the icon panel. (The icon is located in the second row of the task specific icon panel. If the icon is not on top of the stack, press and hold down the left-mouse-button on the displayed icon to display all the choices. Select the desired icon by clicking with the left-mouse-button when the icon is highlighted.)

Graphics Cursors

Notice the cursor has changed from an arrow to a crosshair when graphical input is expected. Look in the prompt window for a description of what you are to choose. The cursor will change to a double crosshair when there is a possibly ambiguous choice. You can press the middle-mouse-button to accept the highlighted pick or choose a different item.

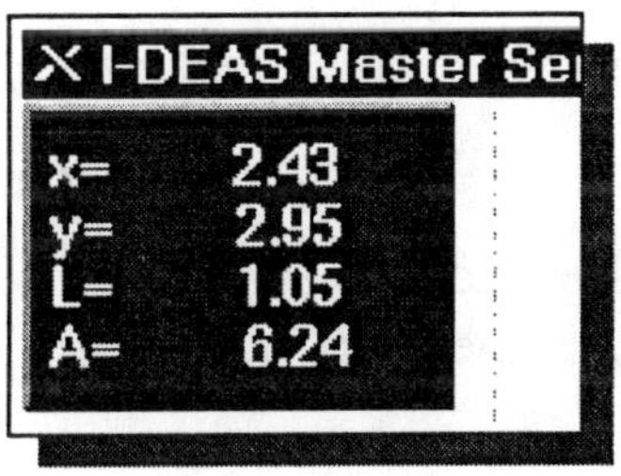

2. The message "*Locate start*" is displayed in the prompt window. Left-click a starting point of the shape, roughly at the center of the graphics window; it could be inside or outside of the displayed grids. In I-DEAS, the sketch plane actually extends into infinity. As you move the graphics cursor, you will see a digital readout in the upper left corner of the graphics window. The readout gives you the cursor location, the line length, and the angle of the line measured from horizontal. Move the cursor around and you will also notice different symbols appear along the line as it occupies different positions.

Dynamic Navigator

I-DEAS provides you with visual clues as the cursor is moved across the screen; this is the I-DEAS Dynamic Navigator. The Dynamic Navigator displays different symbols to show you alignments, perpendicularities, tangencies, etc. The Dynamic Navigator is also used to capture the *design intent* by creating constraints where they are recognized. The Dynamic Navigator displays the governing geometric rules as models are built.

	**Vertical**	indicates a line is vertical
	**Horizontal**	indicates a line is horizontal
------	**Dashed line**	indicates the alignment to the center point or endpoint of an entity
	**Parallel**	indicates a line is parallel to other entities
	**Perpendicular**	indicates a line is perpendicular to other entities
	**Endpoint**	indicates the cursor is at the endpoint of an entity

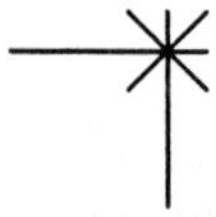	**Intersection**	indicates the cursor is at the intersection point of two entities
	**Center**	indicates the cursor is at the centers or midpoints of entities
	**Tangent**	indicates the cursor is at tangency points to curves

3. Move the graphics cursor directly below *point 1*. Pick the second point when the *vertical constraint* is displayed and the length of the line is about 2 inches.

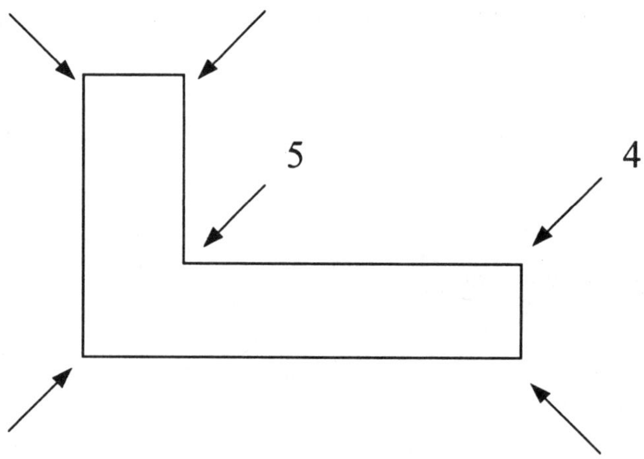

4. Move the graphics cursor horizontally to the right of *point 2*. The *perpendicular* symbol indicates when the line from *point 2* to *point 3* is perpendicular to the vertical line. Left-click to select the third point. Notice that dimensions are automatically created as you sketch the shape. These dimensions are also constraints, which are used to control the geometry. Different dimensions are added depending upon how the shape is sketched. Do not worry about the values not being exactly what we want. We will modify the dimensions later.

5. Move the graphics cursor directly above *point 3*. Do not place this point in alignment with the midpoint of the other vertical line. An additional constraint will be added if they are aligned. Left-click the fourth point directly above *point 3*.

6. Move the graphics cursor to the left of *point 4*. Again, watch the displayed symbol to apply the proper geometric rule that will match the design intent. A good rule of thumb is to exaggerate the features during the initial stage of sketching. For example, if you want to construct a line that is five degrees from horizontal, it would be easier to sketch a line that is 20 to 30 degrees from horizontal. We will be able to adjust the actual angle later. Left-click the fifth point horizontally from *point 4*.

7. Move the graphics cursor directly above the last point. Watch the different symbols displayed and place the point in alignment with *point 1*. Left-click the sixth point directly above *point 5*.

8. Move the graphics cursor near the starting point of the sketch. Notice the Dynamic Navigator will jump to the endpoints of entities. Left-click *point 1* again to end the sketch.

9. In the prompt window, you will see the message "*Locate start.*" By default, I-DEAS remains in the *Polylines* command and expects you to start a new sequence of lines.

10. Press the **ENTER** key or the middle-mouse-button to end the *Polylines* command.

Dynamic Viewing Functions

I-DEAS provides a special user interface called *Dynamic Viewing* that enables convenient viewing of the entities in the graphics window. The Dynamic Viewing functions are controlled with the function keys on the keyboard and the mouse.

❖ Panning – F1 and the mouse

Hold the **F1** function key down, and move the mouse to pan the display. This allows you to reposition the display while maintaining the same scale factor of the display. This function acts as if you are using a video camera. You control the display by moving the mouse.

Pan

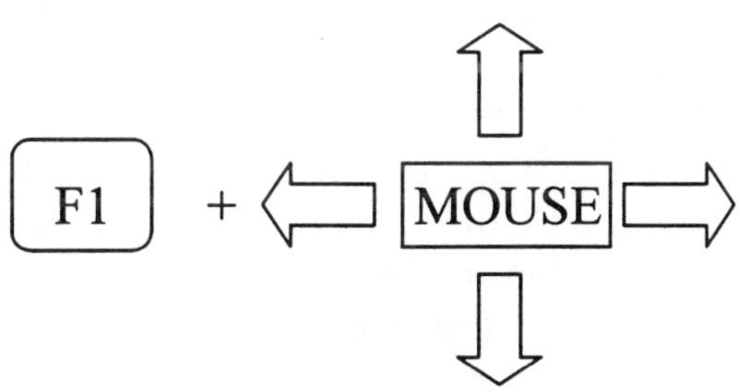

❖ Zooming – F2 and the mouse

Hold the **F2** function key down, and move the mouse vertically on the screen to adjust the scale of the display. Moving upward will reduce the scale of the display, making the entities display smaller on the screen. Moving downward will magnify the scale of the display.

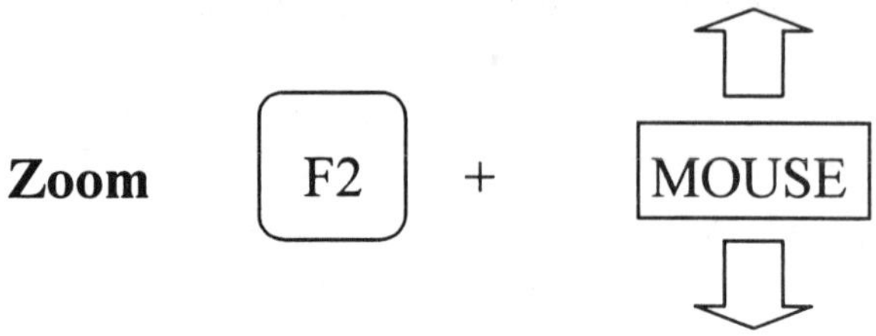

Basic Editing – Using the Eraser

One of the advantages of using a CAD system is the ability to remove entities without leaving any marks. We will delete one of the lines using the *Delete* command.

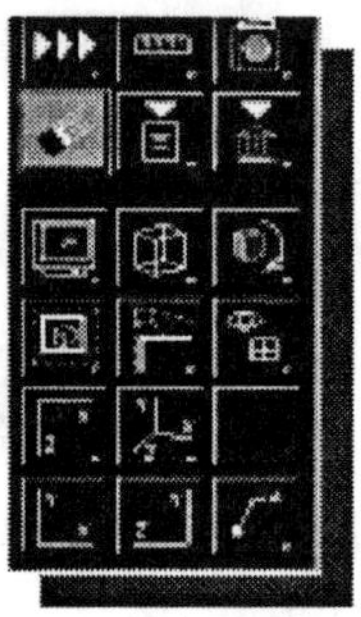

1. Pick **Delete** in the icon panel. (The icon is located in the last row of the *application icon panel*. The icon is a picture of an eraser at the end of a pencil.)

2. In the prompt window, the message "*Pick entity to delete*" appears. Pick the line as shown in the below figure.

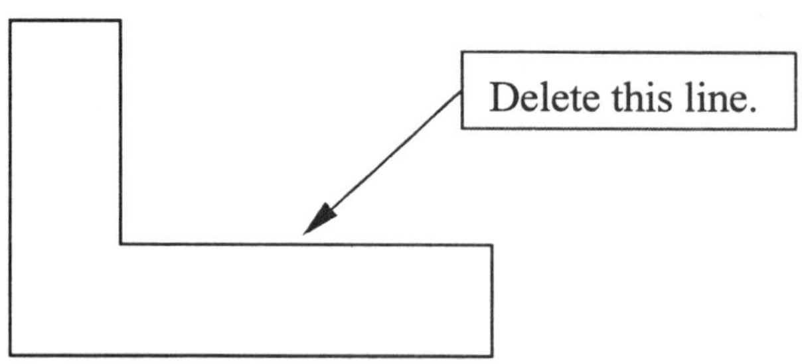

3. The prompt window now reads "*Pick entity to delete (done).*" Press the **ENTER** key of the **middle-mouse-button** to indicate you are done picking entities to be deleted.

4. In the prompt window, the message "*OK to delete 1 curve, 1 constraint and 1 dimension? (Yes)*" will appear. The "*1 constraint*" is the *parallel constraint* created by the **Dynamic Navigator**.

5. Press **ENTER**, or pick **Yes** in the pop-up menu to delete the selected line. The constraints and dimensions are used as geometric control variables. When the geometry is deleted, the associated control features are also removed.

6. In the *prompt window*, you will see the message "*Pick entity to delete*." By default, I-DEAS remains in the *Delete* command and expects you to select additional entities to be erased.

7. Press the **ENTER** key or the **middle-mouse-button** to end the *Delete* command.

Creating a Single Line

Now we will add another line at the same location by using the *Lines* command.

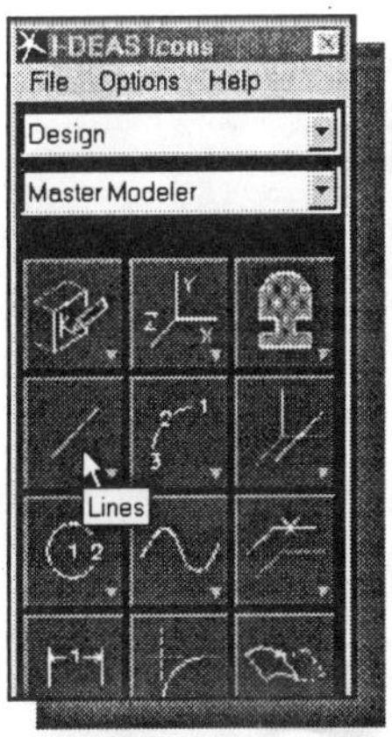

1. Pick **Lines** in the icon panel. (The icon is located in the same stack as the *Polylines* icon.) Press and hold down the left-mouse-button on the *Polylines* icon to display the available choices. Select the *Lines* command with the left-mouse-button when the option is highlighted.

2. The message "*Locate start*" is displayed in the prompt window. Move the graphics cursor near *point 1* and, as the *endpoint* symbol is displayed, pick with the left-mouse-button.

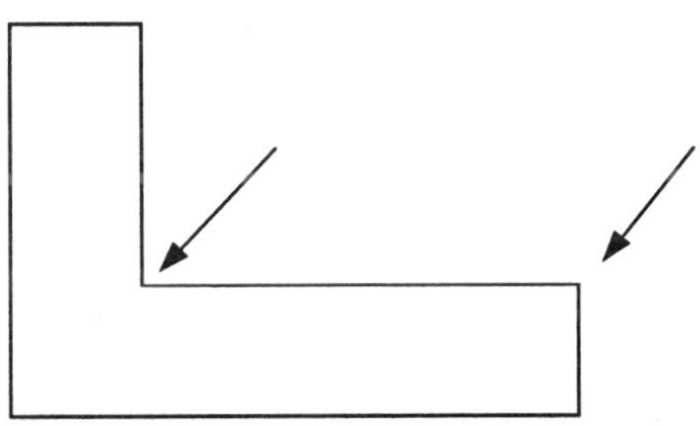

3. Move the graphics cursor near *point 2* and click the **left-mouse-button** when the *endpoint* symbol is displayed.

➢ Notice the Dynamic Navigator creates the parallel constraint and the dimension as the geometry is constructed.

4. The message "*Locate start*" is displayed in the prompt window. Press the **ENTER** key or use the middle-mouse-button to end the *Lines* command.

Consideration of Design Intent

While creating the sketch, it is very important to keep in mind the design intent. Always consider functionality of the part and key features of the design. Using I-DEAS, we can accomplish and maintain the design intent at all levels of the design process.

The dimensions automatically created by I-DEAS might not always match with the designer's intent. For example, in our current design, we may want to use the vertical distance between the top two horizontal lines as a key dimension. Even though it is a very simple calculation to figure out the corresponding length of the vertical dimension at the far-right, for more complex designs it might not be as simple, and to do additional calculations is definitely not desirable. The next section describes re-dimensioning the sketch.

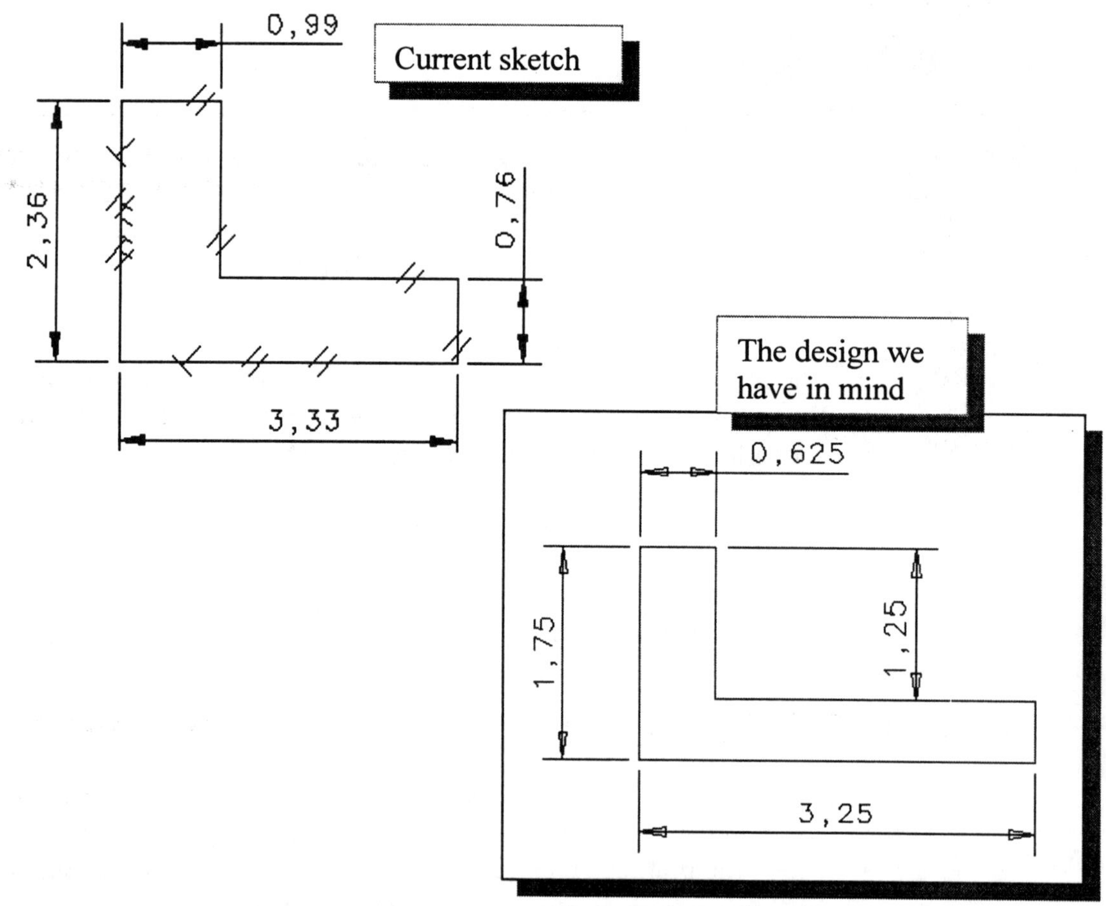

Step 2: Apply/Delete/Modify constraints and dimensions

As the sketch is made, *I-DEAS* automatically applies some of the geometric constraints (such as horizontal, parallel and perpendicular) to the sketched geometry. We can continue to modify the geometry, apply additional constraints, and/or define the size of the existing geometry. In this example, we will illustrate deleting existing dimensions and add new dimensions to describe the sketched entities.

To maintain our design intent, we will first remove the unwanted dimension and then create the desirable dimension.

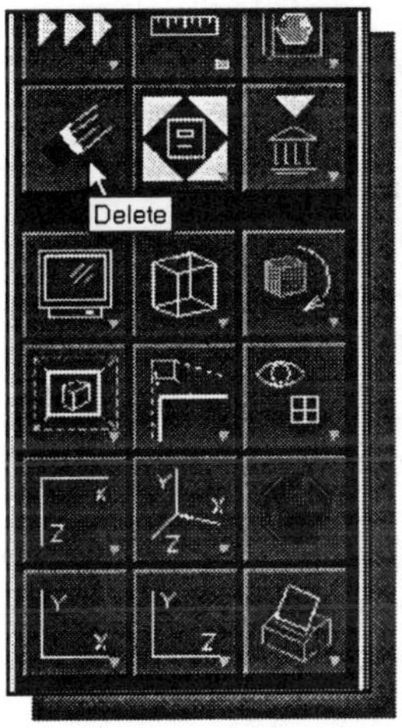

1. Pick **Delete** in the icon panel. (The icon is located in the last row of the application icon panel.)

2. Pick the dimension as shown.

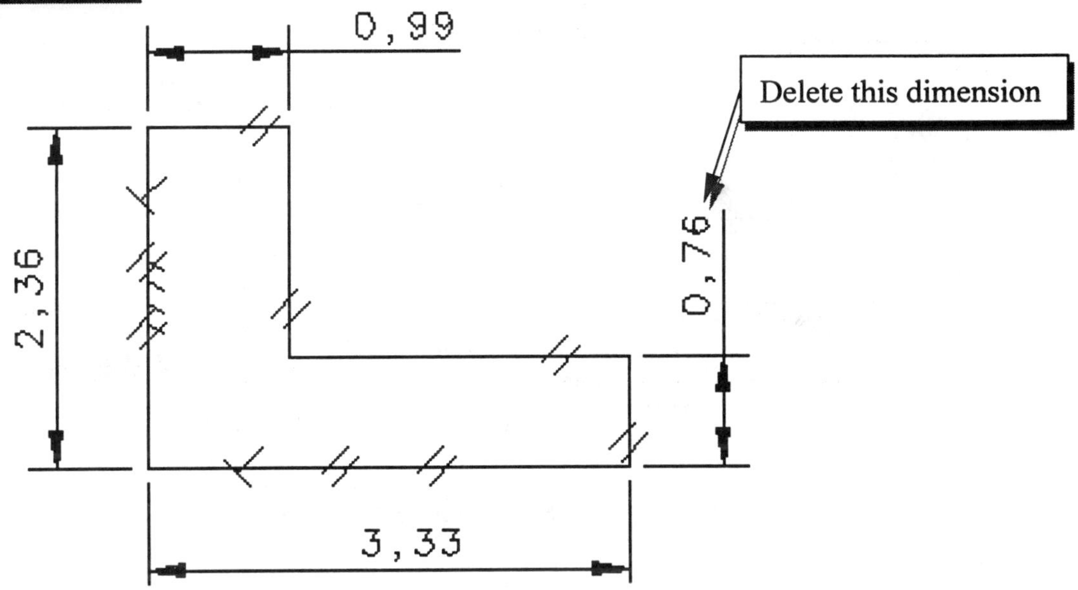

3. Press the **ENTER** key or the **middle-mouse-button** to accept the selection.

4. Pick **Yes** in the *popup menu* or press the **ENTER** key or the **middle-mouse-button** to delete the selected dimension and end the *Delete* command.

Creating Desired Dimensions

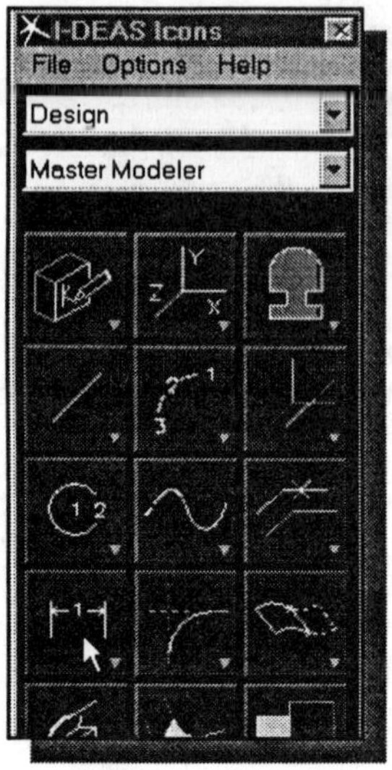

1. Choose **Dimension** in the icon panel. The message "*Pick the first entity to dimension*" is displayed in the prompt window.

2. Pick the **top-horizontal-line** as shown in the below figure.

3. Pick the **second horizontal line** as shown.

4. Place the text to the right of the model.

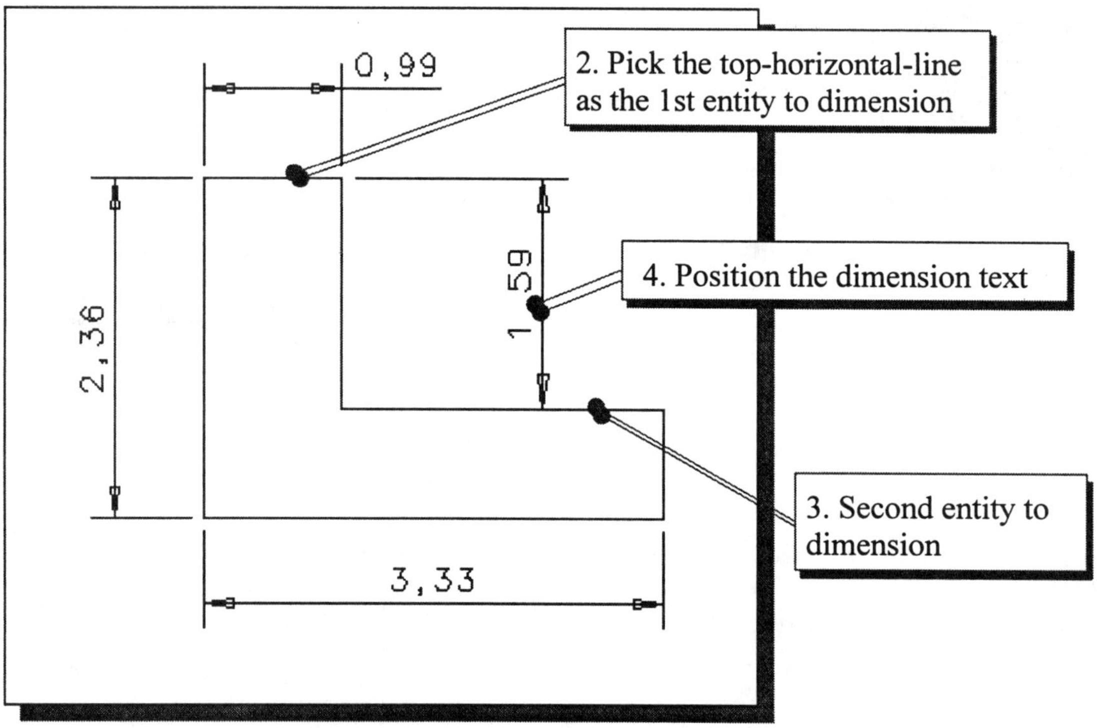

5. Press the **ENTER** key or the **middle-mouse-button** to end the *Dimension* command.

➢ In I-DEAS, the *Dimension* command will create a linear dimension (distance in between the two lines) if two parallel lines are selected. Selecting two lines that are not parallel will create an angular dimension (angle in between the two lines.)

Modifying Dimensional Values

Next we will adjust the dimensional values to the desired values. One of the main advantages of using a feature-based parametric solid modeler, such as I-DEAS, is the ability to easily modify existing entities. The operation of modifying dimensional values will demonstrate implementation of the design philosophy of "shape before size." In I-DEAS, several options are available to modify the dimensional values. In this lesson, we will demonstrate two of the options using the ***Modify*** command. The *Modify* command icon is located in the second row of the application icon panel; the icon is a picture of an arrowhead with a long tail.

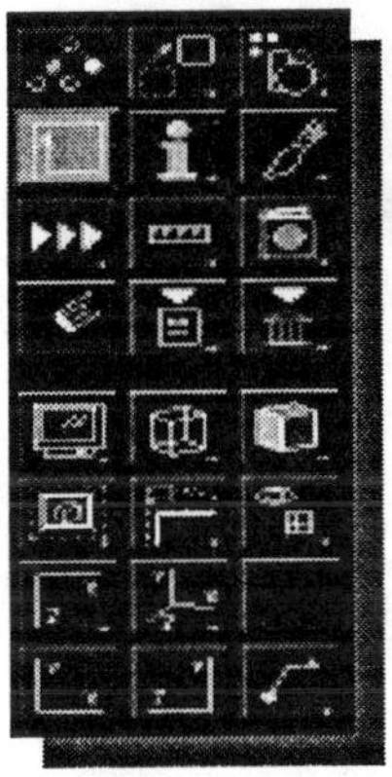

1. Choose **Modify** in the icon panel. (The icon is located in the second row of the application icon panel. If the icon is not on top of the stack, press and hold down the left-mouse-button on the displayed icon, then select the *Modify* icon.) The message "*Pick entity to modify*" is displayed in the prompt window.

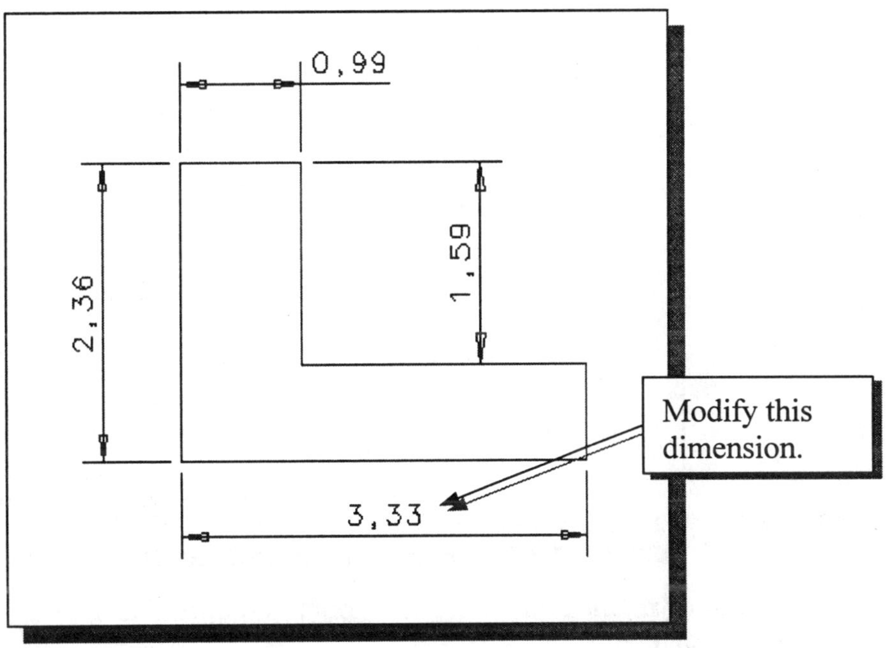

2. Pick the dimension as shown (the number might be different than displayed). The selected dimension will be highlighted. The *Modify Dimension* window appears.

❖ In the *Modify Dimension* window, the value of the selected dimension is displayed and also identified by a *Name* in the format of "Dxx," where the "D" indicates it is a dimension and the "xx" is a number incremented automatically as dimensions are added. You can change both the name and the value of the dimension by clicking and typing in the appropriate boxes.

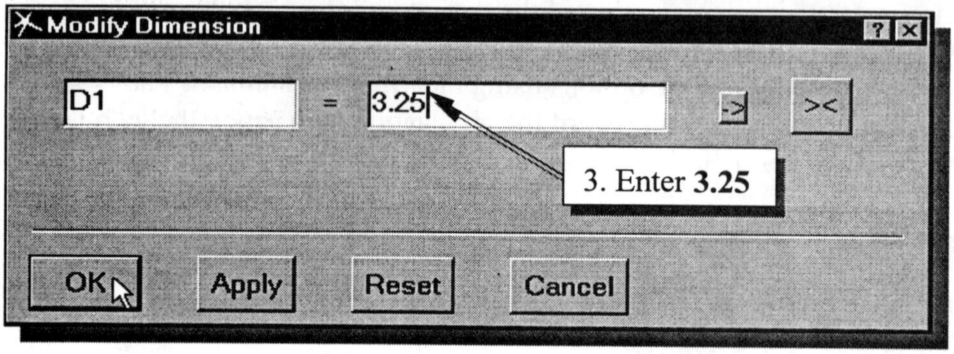

3. Modify the dimensional value to **3.25** as shown.

4. Click on the **OK** button to accept the value you have entered.

➢ I-DEAS will adjust the size of the object based on the new value entered.

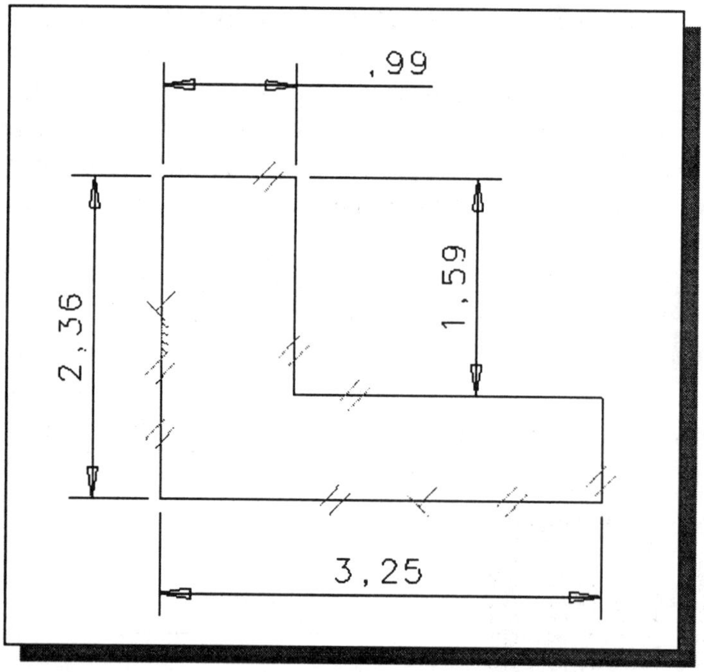

5. On your own, click on the top horizontal dimension and adjust the dimensional value to **0.625**.

6. Press the **ENTER** key or the **middle-mouse-button** to end the *Modify Dimension* command.

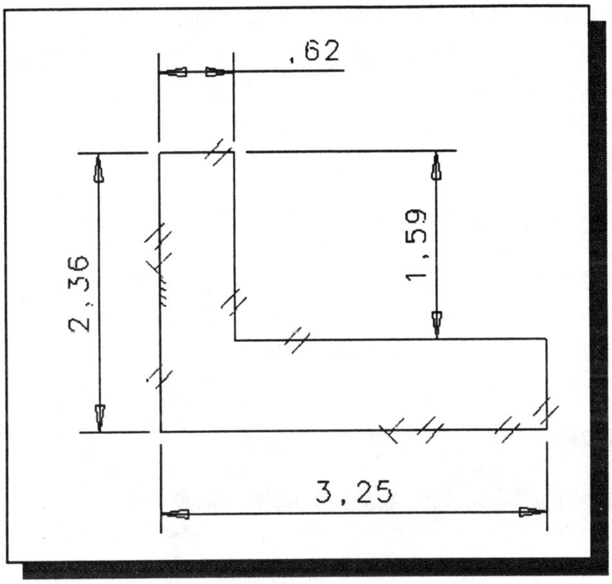

❖ The size of our design is automatically adjusted by I-DEAS based on the dimensions we have entered. I-DEAS uses the dimensional values as control variables and the geometric entities are modified accordingly. This approach of rough sketching the shape of the design first then finalizing the size of the design is known as the "Shape before size" approach.

Pre-selection of Entities

I-DEAS provides a flexible graphical user interface that allows users to select graphical entities BEFORE the command is selected (*Pre-selection*), or AFTER the command is selected (*Post-selection*). The procedure we have used so far is the *Post-selection* option. To pre-select one or more items to process, hold down the SHIFT key while you pick. Selected items will stay highlighted. You can *deselect* an item by selecting the item again. The item will be toggled on and off by each click. Another convenient feature of pre-selection is that the selected items remain selected after the command is executed.

1. Pre-select all of the dimensions by holding down the SHIFT key and clicking the left-mouse-button on each dimension value.

PRE-SELECT SHIFT + LEFT-mouse-button

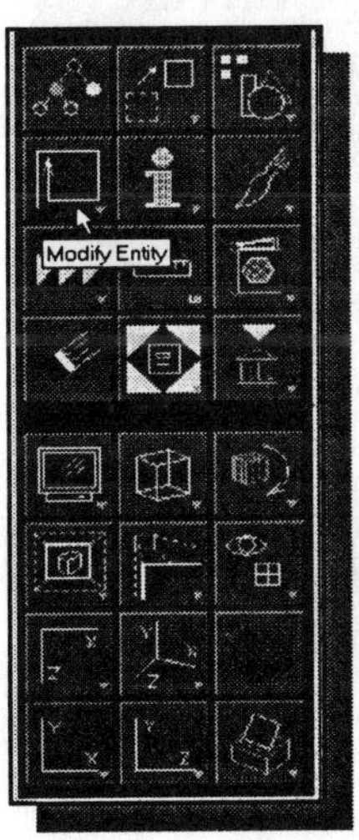

2. Select the **Modify** icon. The *Dimensions* window appears.

3. Move the *Dimensions* window around by "clicking and dragging" the window's title area with the left-mouse-button. You can also use the *Dynamic Viewing* functions (activate the graphics window first) to adjust the scale and location of the entities displayed in the graphics window (**F1** and the mouse, **F2** and the mouse).

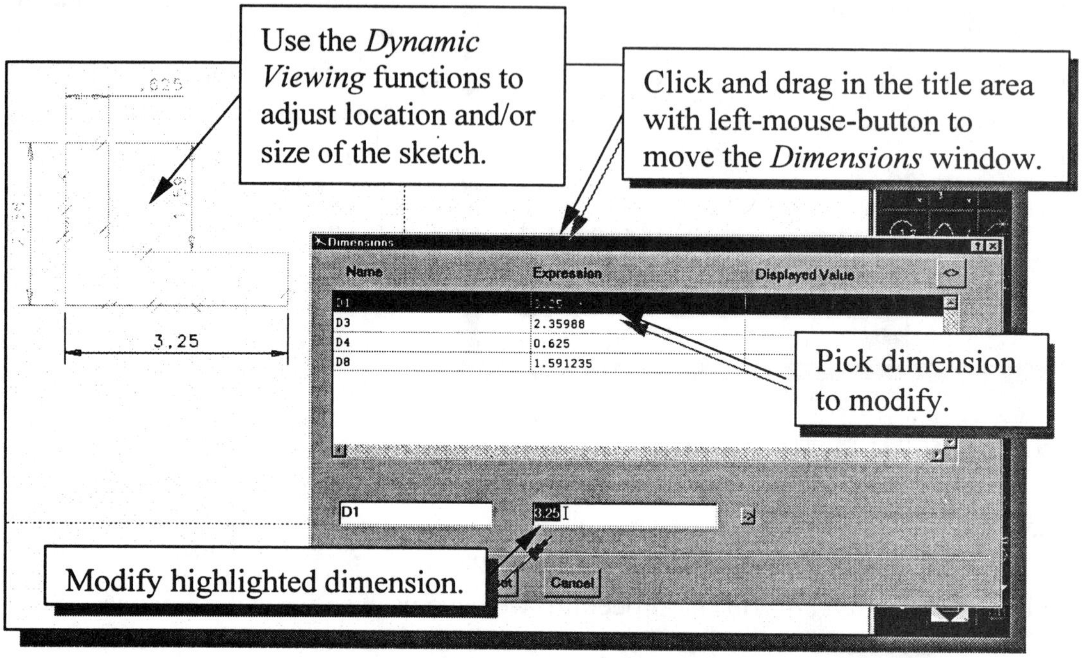

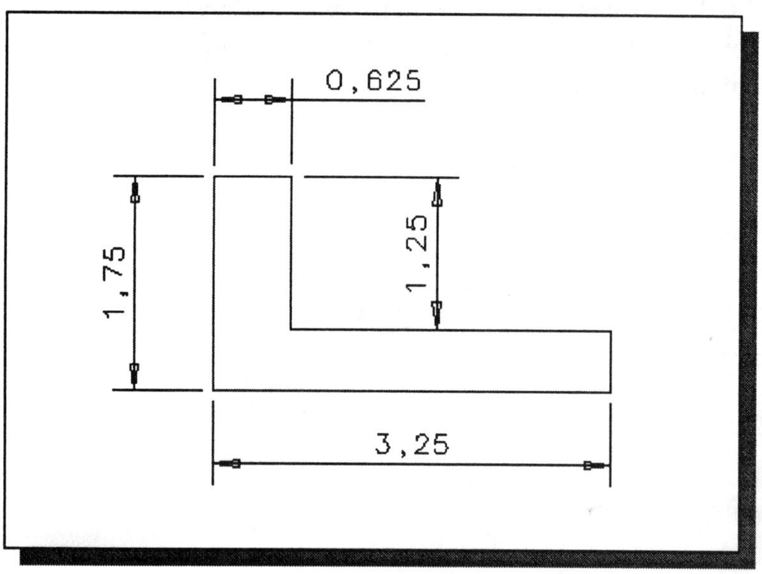

4. Click on one of the dimensions in the pop-up window. The selected dimension will be highlighted in the graphics window. Type in the desired value for the selected dimension. **DO NOT** hit the **ENTER** key. Select another dimension from the list to continue modifying. Modify all of the dimensional values to the values as shown.

5. Click the **OK** button to accept the values you have entered and close the *Dimensions* window.

➢ I-DEAS will now adjust the size of the shape to the desired dimensions. The design philosophy of "shape before size" is implemented quite easily. The geometric details are taken care of by I-DEAS.

Changing the Appearance of Dimensions

The top-horizontal-dimension we modified is displayed as 0.62, instead of the entered value (0.625.) We can adjust the appearance of dimensions by using the ***Appearance*** command.

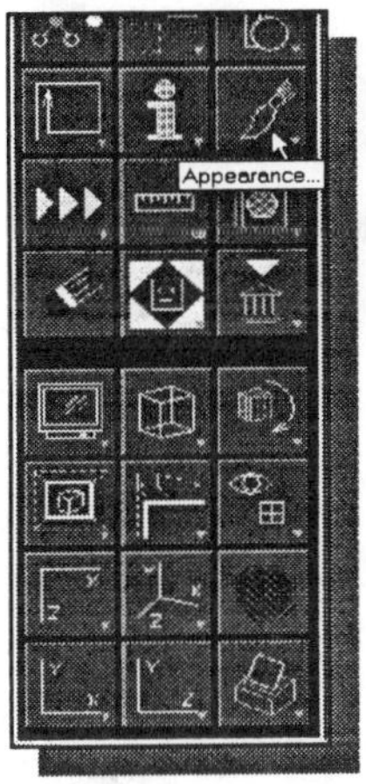

1. Choose **Appearance** in the icon panel. (The icon is located in the second row of the application icon panel. If the icon is not on top of the stack, press and hold down the left-mouse-button on the displayed icon, then select the *Appearance* icon.) The message "*Pick entity to modify*" is displayed in the prompt window.

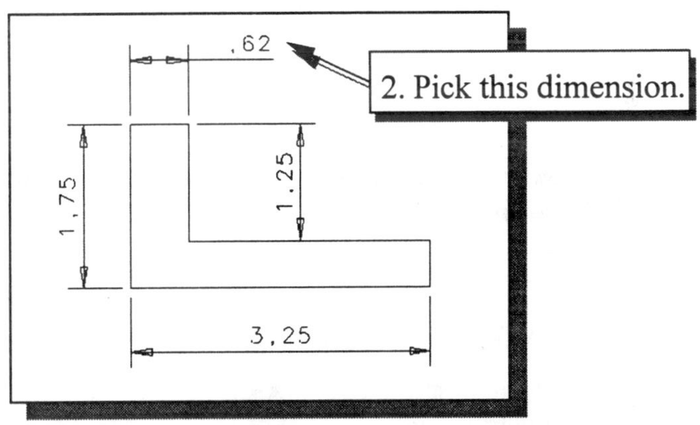

2. Pick the top horizontal dimension as shown in the figure.

3. The *message "Pick entity to modify (Done)"* is displayed in the prompt window. Press the **ENTER** key or use the **middle-mouse-button** to accept the selected object.

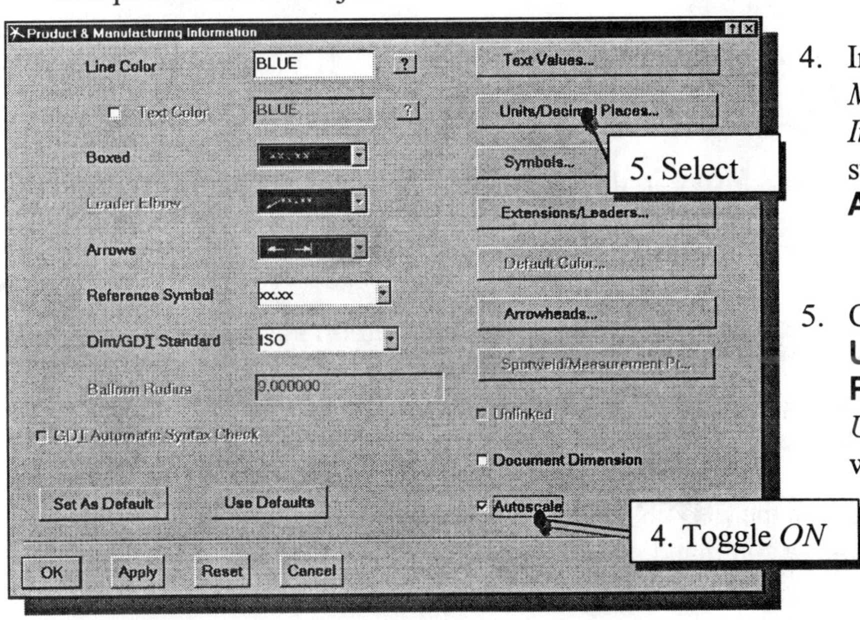

4. In the *Product & Manufacturing Information* window, switch **on** the **Autoscale** option.

5. Click on the **Units/Decimal Places...** button. The *Units & Decimal Places* window appears.

6. Set the decimal places to **3** to display three digits after the decimal point.

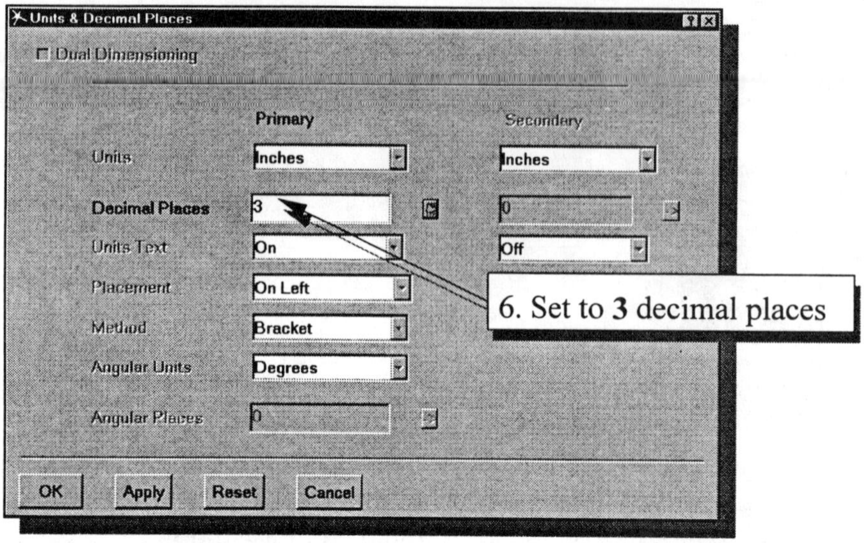

7. Click on the **OK** button to exit the *Units & Decimal Places* window.

8. Click on the **OK** icon to exit the *Product & Manufacturing Information* window.

9. Press the **ENTER** key or the **middle-mouse-button** to end the *Appearance* command.

Repositioning Dimensions

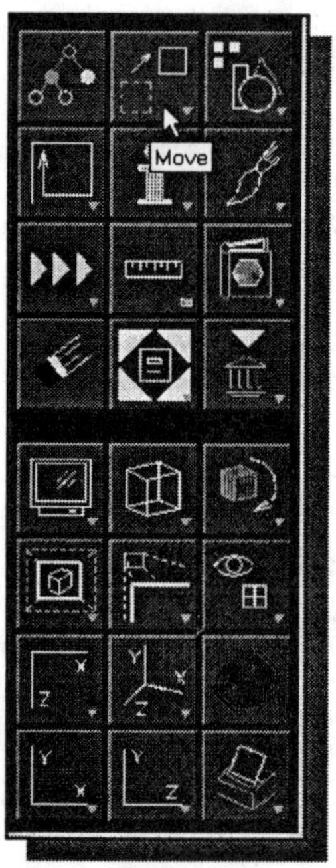

1. Choose **Move** in the icon panel. (The icon is located in the first row of the application icon panel.) The message "Pick entity to move" is displayed in the prompt window.

2. Select any of the dimensions displayed on the screen.

3. Move the cursor to position the dimension in a new location. Left-click once to accept the new location.

4. Press the **ENTER** key or the **middle-mouse-button** to end the *Move* command.

Step 3: Completing the Base Solid Feature

Now that the 2D sketch is completed, we will proceed to the next step: create a 3D part from the 2D profile. Extruding a 2D profile is one of the common methods that can be used to create 3D parts. We can extrude planar faces along a path. We can also specify a height value and a tapered angle. In *I-DEAS*, each face has a positive side and a negative side; the current face we're working on is set as the default positive side.

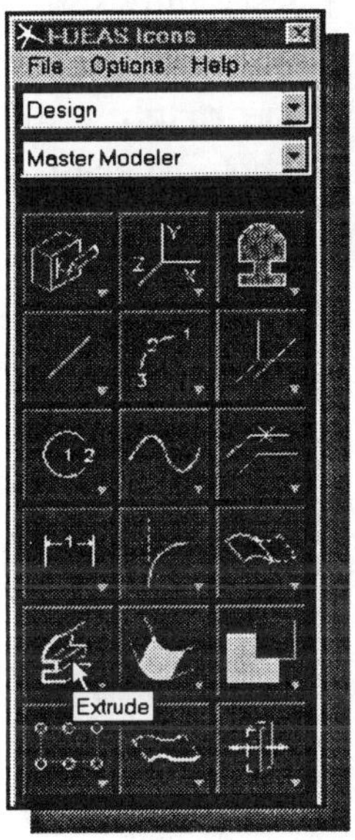

1. Choose **Extrude** in the icon panel. The *Extrude* icon is located in the fifth row of the task specific icon panel. Press and hold down the left-mouse-button on the icon to display all the choices and slide the mouse up and down to switch between different options. In the prompt window, the message "*Pick curve or section*" is displayed.

2. Pick any edge of the 2-D shape. By default, the *Extrude* command will automatically select all segments of the shape that form a closed region. Notice the different color signifying the selected segments.

3. Notice the I-DEAS prompt "*Pick curve to add or remove. (Done)*" We can select more geometry entities or deselect any entity that has been selected. Picking the same geometry entity will again toggle the selection of the entity "on" or "off" with each left-mouse-button click. Press the **ENTER** key to accept the selected entities.

4. The *Extrude Section* window will appear on the screen. Enter **2.5** as the *extrusion distance* and confirm that the ***New part*** option is switched on as shown.

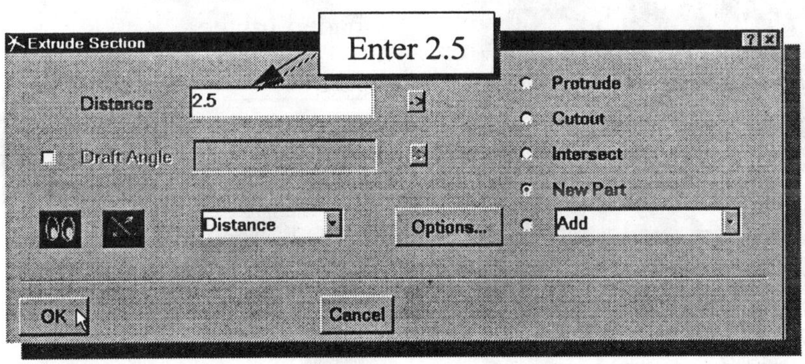

5. Click on the **OK** button to accept the settings and extrude the 2-D section into a 3D solid.

➢ Notice all of the dimensions disappeared from the screen. All of the dimensional values and geometric constraints are stored in the database by I-DEAS and they can be brought up at any time.

Display Viewing Commands

❖ 3-D Dynamic Rotation – F3 and the mouse

The I-DEAS *Dynamic Viewing* feature allows users to do "*Real-time*" rotation of the display. Hold the F3 function key down and move the mouse to rotate the display. This allows you to rotate the displayed model about the screen X (horizontal), Y (vertical), and Z (perpendicular to the screen) axes. Start with the cursor near the center of the screen and hold down F3; moving the cursor up or down will rotate about the screen X-axis while moving the cursor left or right will control the rotation about the screen Y-axis. Start with the cursor in the corner of the screen and hold down F3, which will control the rotation about the screen Z-axis.

Dynamic Rotation

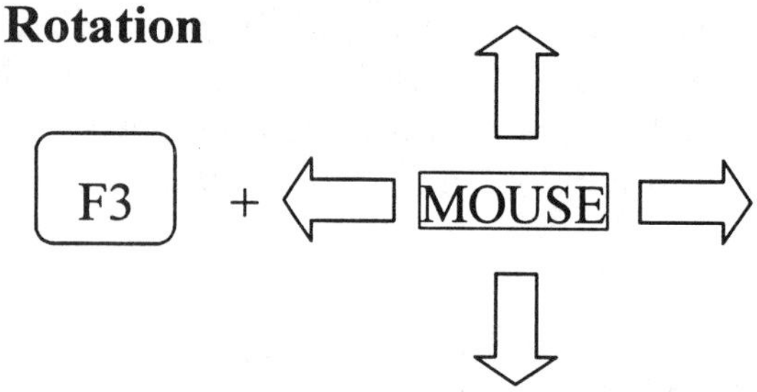

Display Icon Panel

The *Display* icon panel contains various icons to handle different viewing operations. These icons control the screen display, such as the view scale, the view angle, redisplay, and shaded and hidden line displays.

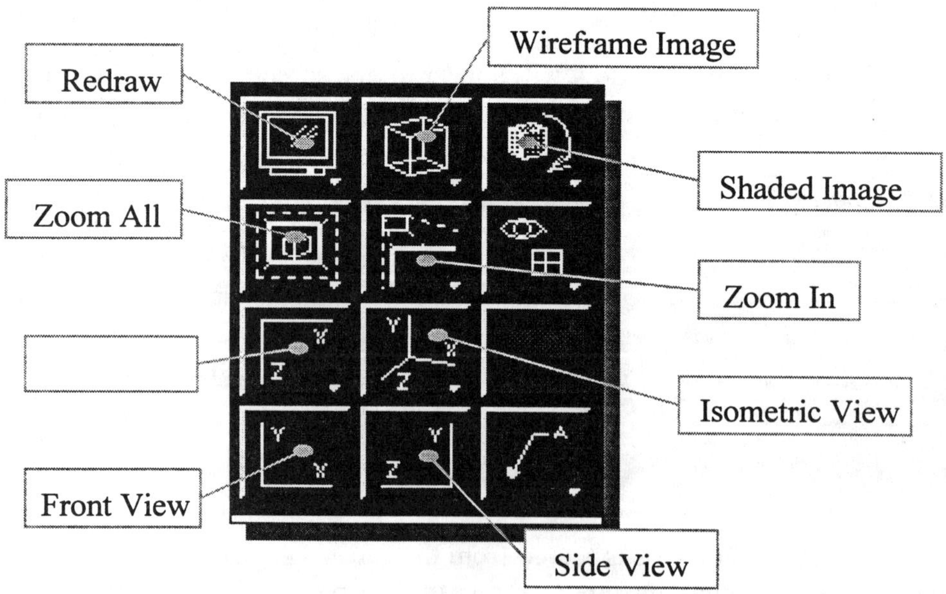

View icons:

Front, *Side*, *Top*, *Bottom*, *Isometric,* and *Perspective*: These six icons are the standard view icons. Selecting any of these icons will change the viewing angle. Try each one as you read its description below

Front View (X-Y Workplane)

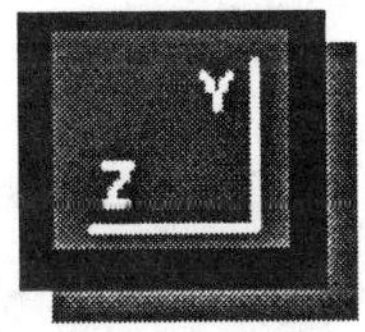

Right Side View

Top View

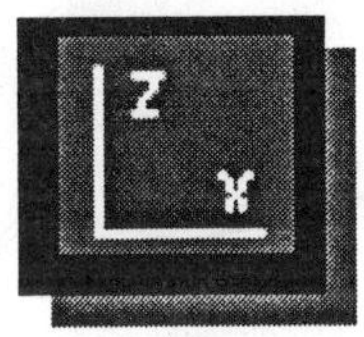

Bottom View

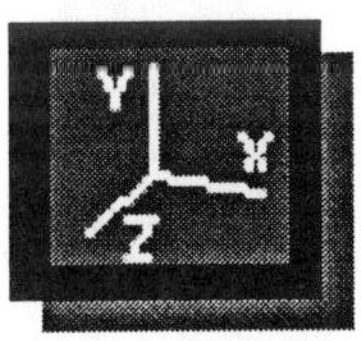

Isometric View

Perspective View

❖ Shaded Solids:

Depending on your display type, you will pick either *Shaded Hardware* or *Shaded Software* to get shaded images of 3-D objects. Shaded Hardware on a workstation with OGL display capability allows real-time dynamic rotation (F3 and the mouse) of the shaded 3-D solids. A workstation with X3D display capability allows the use of the Shaded Software command to get the shaded image without the real-time dynamic rotation capability.

Shaded Hardware

Shaded Software

❖ **Hidden-line Removal:**
This icon generates an image of the 3-D object with all the back lines removed.

Hidden-line Removal

❖ **Wireframe Image:**
This icon allows the display of the 3D objects using the basic wireframe representation scheme.

Wireframe

❖ **Redisplay:**
Use this command to refresh the graphics window.

Redisplay

❖ **Zoom-All:**
Adjust the viewing scale factor so that all objects are displayed.

Zoom-All

❖ **Zoom-In:**
Allows the users to define a rectangular area, by selecting two diagonal corners, which will fill the graphics window.

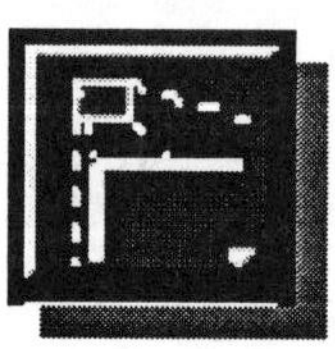
Zoom-In

Workplane – It is an XY CRT, but an XYZ World

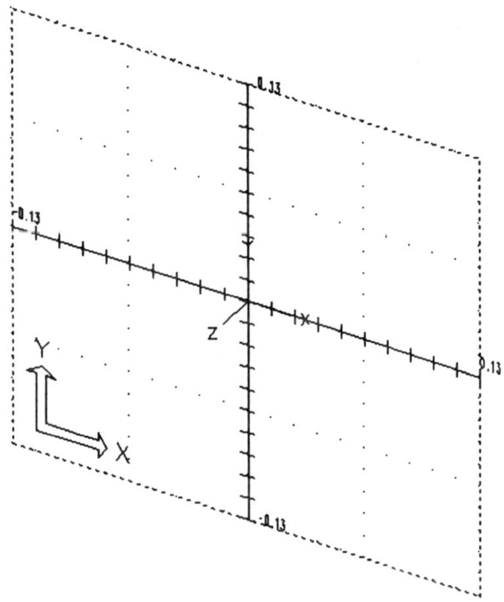

Design modeling software is becoming more powerful and user friendly, yet the system still does only what the user tells it to do. In using a geometric modeler, therefore, we need to have a good understanding of what the inherent limitations are. We should also have a good understanding of what we want to do and what the results to expect based upon what is available.

In most 3-D geometric modelers, 3-D objects are located and defined in what is usually called **world space** or **global space**. Although a number of different coordinate systems can be used to create and manipulate objects in a 3-D modeling system, the objects are typically defined and stored using the world space. The world space is usually a 3-D Cartesian coordinate system that the user cannot change or manipulate.

In most engineering designs, models can be very complex; it would be tedious and confusing if only the world coordinate system were available. Practical 3-D modeling systems allow the user to define **Local Coordinate Systems** or **User Coordinate Systems** relative to the world coordinate system. Once a local system is defined, we can then create geometry in terms of this more convenient system.

Although objects are created and stored in 3-D space coordinates, most of the input and output is done in a 2-D Cartesian system. Typical input devices such as a mouse or digitizers are two-dimensional by nature; the movement of the input device is interpreted by the system in a planar sense. The same limitation is true of common output devices, such as CRT displays and plotters. The modeling software performs a series of three-dimensional to two-dimensional transformations to correctly project 3-D objects onto the 2-D picture plane (monitor).

The I-DEAS ***Workplane*** is a special construction tool that enables the planar nature of the 2-D input devices to be directly mapped into the 3-D coordinate system. The workplane is a local coordinate system that can be aligned to the world coordinate system, an existing face of a part, or a reference plane. By default, the workplane is aligned to the world coordinate system.

The basic design process of creating solid features in the I-DEAS task is a three-step process:

1. Select and/or define the workplane.
2. Sketch and constrain 2-D planar geometry.
3. Create the solid feature.

These steps can be repeated as many times as needed to add additional features to the design. The base feature of the L-Block model was created following this basic design process; we used the default settings where the workplane is aligned to the world coordinate system. We will next add additional features to our design and demonstrate how to manipulate the I-DEAS workplane.

Workplane Appearance

The workplane is a construction tool; it is a coordinate system that can be moved in space. The size of the workplane display is only for our visual reference, since we can sketch on the entire plane, which extends to infinity.

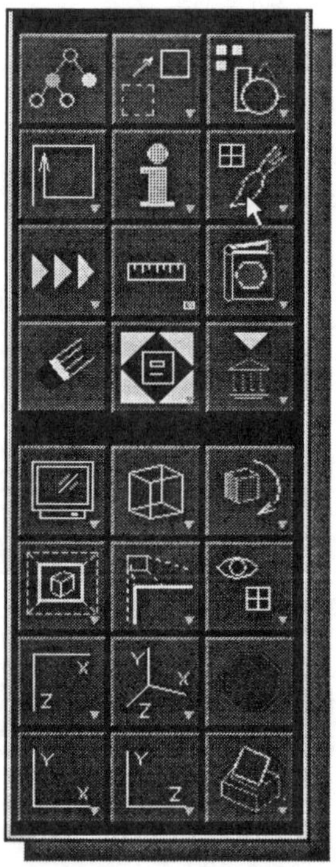

1. Choose **Workplane Appearance** in the icon panel. (The icon is located in the second row of the application icon panel. If the icon is not on top of the stack, press and hold down the left-mouse-button on the displayed icon to display all the choices, then select the *Workplane Appearance* icon.) The *Workplane Attributes* window appears.

2. Toggle **on** the three display switches as shown.

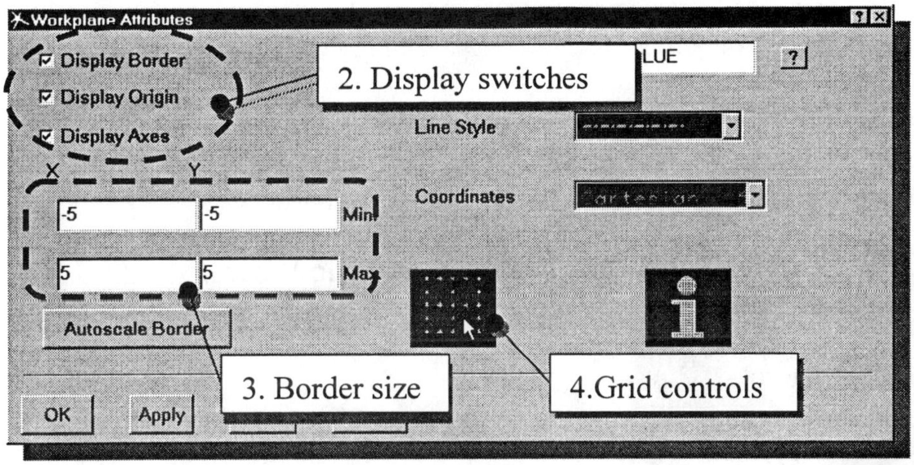

3. Adjust the **Workplane Border Size** by entering the Min. & Max. values as shown.

4. In the *Workplane Attributes* window, click on the **Workplane Grid** button. The *Grid Attributes* window appears.

5. Change the **Grid Size** settings by entering the values as shown.

6. Toggle on the **Display Grid** option if it is not already switched on.

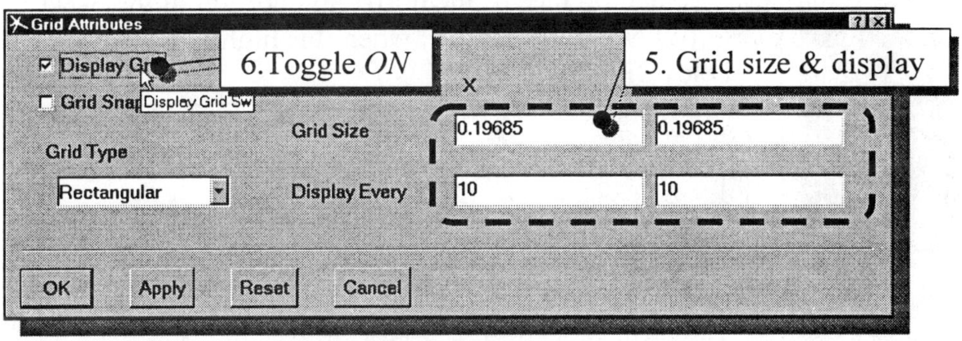

❖ Although the *Grid Snap* option is available, its usage in parametric modeling is not recommended. The *Grid Snap* concept does not conform to the "*shape before size*" philosophy and most real designs rarely have uniformly spaced dimension values.

7. Pick **Apply** to view the effects of the changes.

8. Click on the **OK** button to exit the *Grid Attributes* window.

9. Click on the **OK** button to exit the *Workplane Attributes* window.

10. On your own, use [F3+Mouse] to dynamically rotate the part and observe the workplane is aligned with the surface corresponding to the first sketch drawn.

Step 4: Adding additional features

➢ Sketch In Place

One option to manipulate the workplane is with the *Sketch in Place* command. The *Sketch in Place* command allows the user to sketch on an existing part face. The workplane is reoriented and is attached to the face of the part.

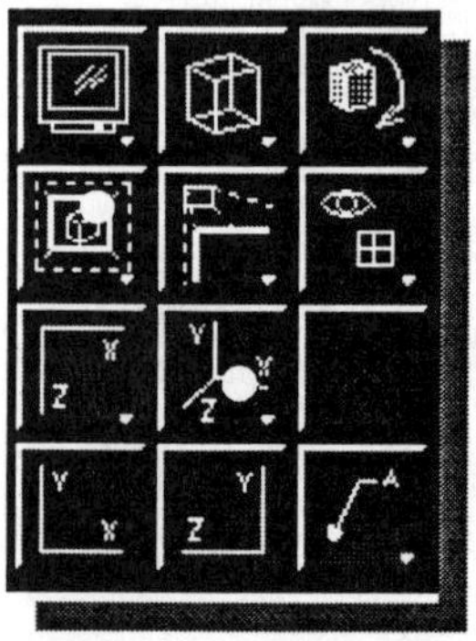

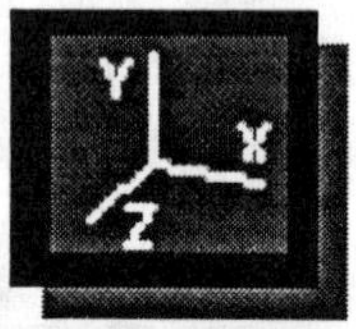

1. Choose **Isometric View** in the display viewing icon panel.

2. Choose **Zoom-All** in the display viewing icon panel.

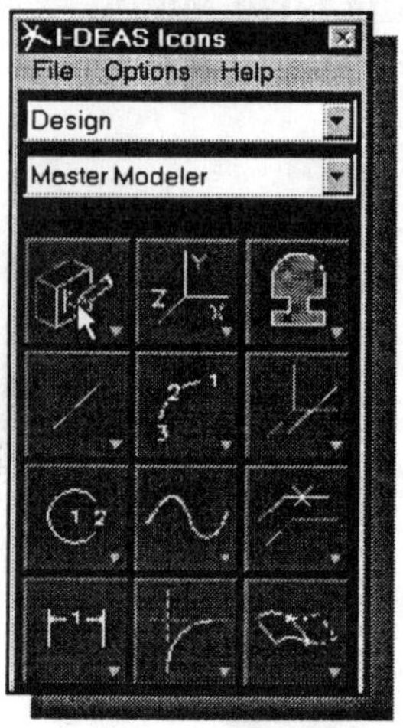

3. Choose **Sketch in Place** in the icon panel. In the prompt window, the message "*Pick plane to sketch on*" is displayed.

4. Pick the top face of the horizontal portion of the 3-D object by left-clicking the surface, when it is highlighted as shown in the below figure.

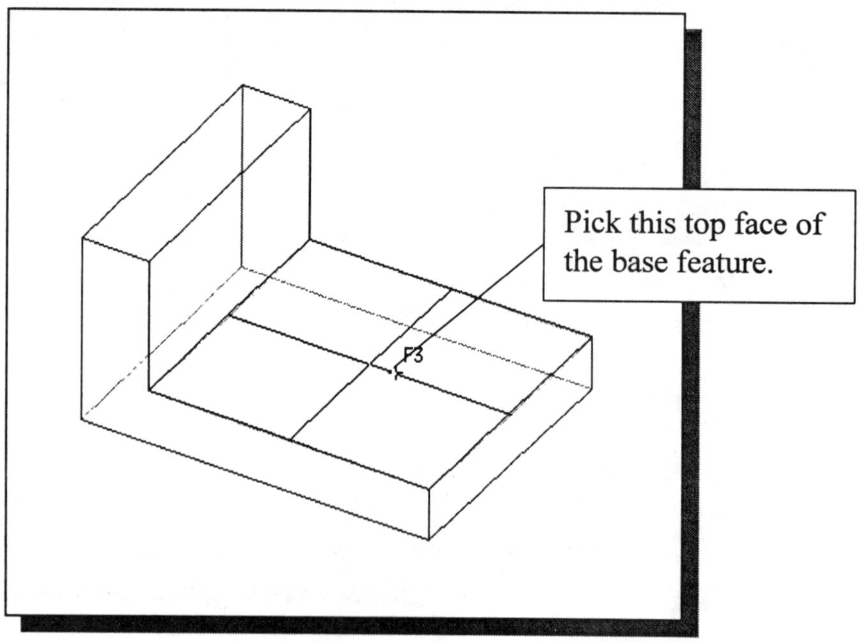

❖ Notice that, at this point, I-DEAS automatically orients the *workplane* to the selected surface. The surface selected is highlighted with a different color to indicate the attachment of the *workplane*.

The *Rectangle* command

Next, we will use the *Rectangle* command to cut out a corner of the 3-D object. The *Rectangle* icon is located at the same location as the *Polylines* icon in the application icon panel. I-DEAS provides three options to create rectangles: *Rectangle by 2 Corners, Rectangle by 3 Corners*, and *Rectangle by Center*. The different icons denote the different methods to create rectangles.

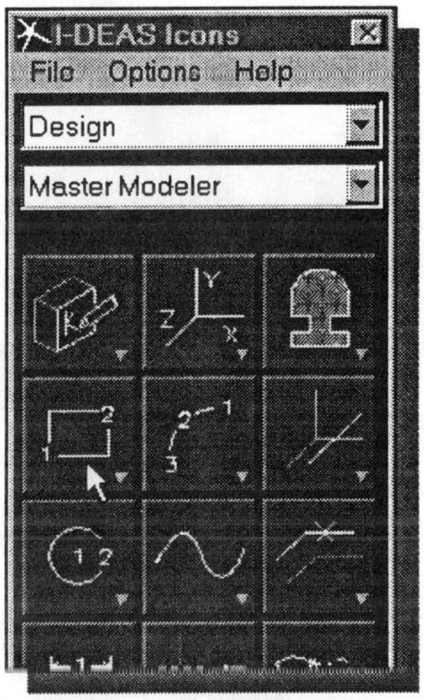

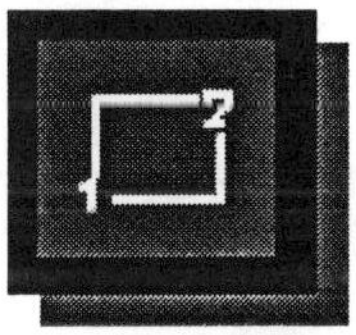

1. Choose **Rectangle by 2 Corners** in the icon panel. This command requires the selection of two locations to identify the two opposite corners of a rectangle. The message "*Locate first corner*" is displayed in the prompt window.

2. Move the graphics cursor near the front corner of the 3-D object. Notice the Dynamic Navigator automatically snaps to the corner and also displays the endpoint symbol. Pick the front corner as shown.

3. The message "*Locate second corner*" is displayed in the prompt window. At this point, move the mouse around to adjust the size of the rectangle. Notice the movement of the mouse is mapped to the workplane. Create a rectangle by clicking at a location toward the inside of the sketching plane; do not align it to the center of the face.

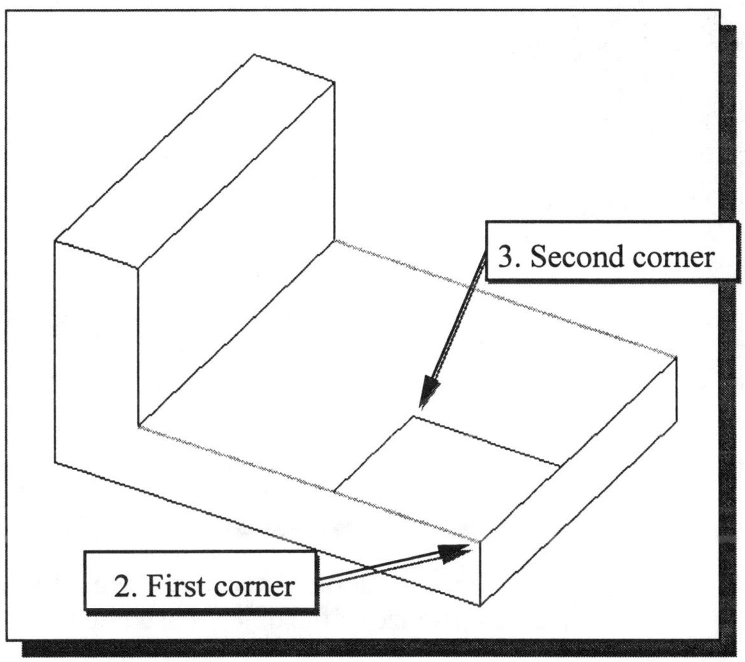

4. Press the **ENTER** key or use the **center-mouse-button** to end the *Rectangle by 2 Corners* command.

Modifying the Size of the Rectangle

1. *Pre-select* the two dimensions of the rectangle by holding down the **SHIFT** key while left clicking the values. The selected dimensions are highlighted.

PRE-SELECT SHIFT + LEFT-mouse-button

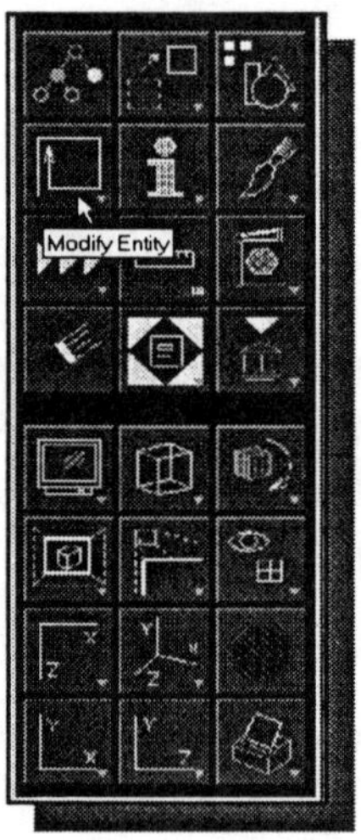

2. Choose **Modify** in the icon panel. The *Dimensions* window appears.

3. In the *Dimensions* window, change the values to the values as shown below.

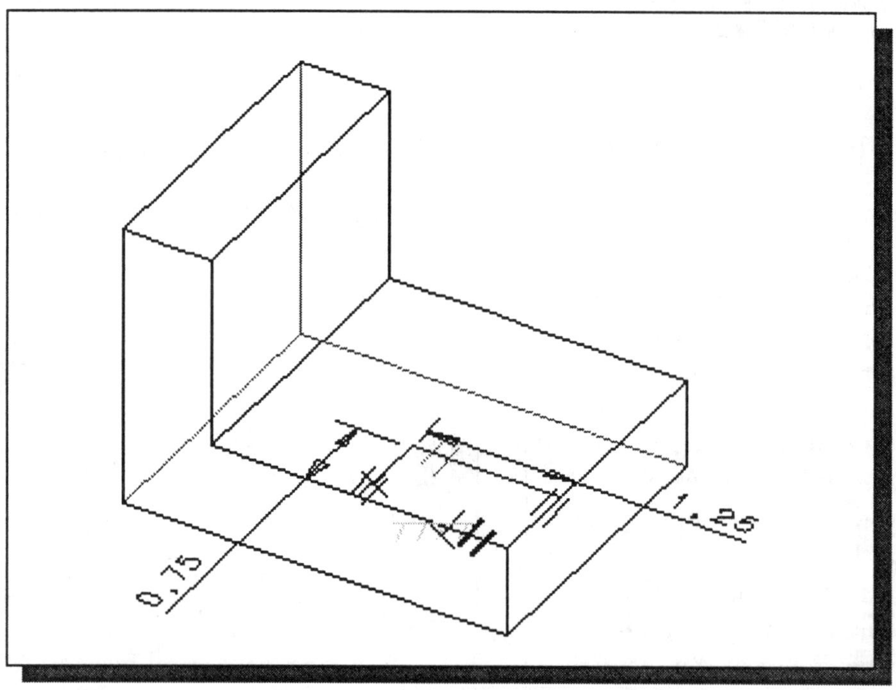

4. Click on the **OK** button to accept the values you have entered and I-DEAS will adjust the size of the object based on the newly entered values.

5. Press the **ENTER** key or the **middle-mouse-button** to end the *Modify* command.

Extrusion – Cutout

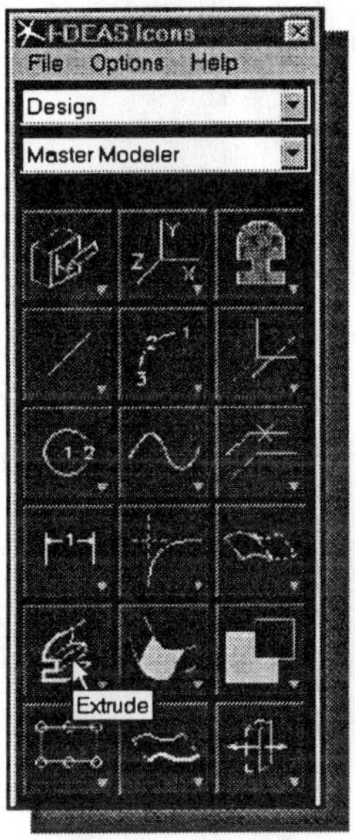

1. Choose **Extrude** in the icon panel. In the prompt window, the message "*Pick curve or section*" is displayed.

2. Pick the rectangle at a location other than a side that coincides with an edge of the L-Shape part.

❖ Attempting to select a line where two entities lie on top of one another (i.e. coincide) causes confusion as indicated by the double line cursor ╬ symbol and the prompt window message "*Pick curve to add or remove (Accept)***". This message indicates I-DEAS needs you to confirm the selected item. If the correct entity is selected, you can continue to select additional entities. To reject an erroneously selected entity, press the [**F8**] key to select a neighboring entity or press the right-mouse-button and highlight *Deselect All* from the popup menu.

3. At the I-DEAS prompt "*Pick curve to add or remove (Done),*" press the **ENTER** key or the **middle-mouse-button** to accept the selection.

4. The *Extrude Section* window appears. Set the *extrude option* to **Cutout**. Note the extrusion direction displayed in the graphics window.

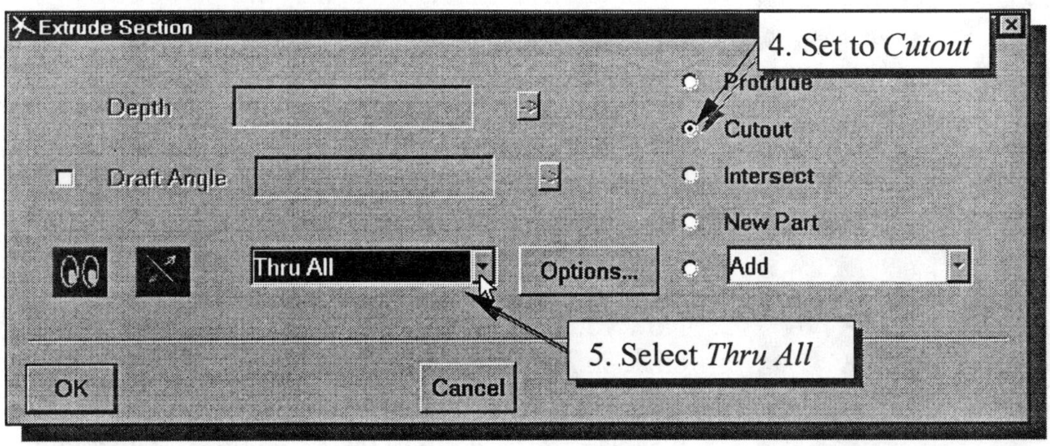

5. Click and hold down the left-mouse-button on the **Depth** menu and select the **Thru All** option. I-DEAS will calculate the distance necessary to cut through the part.

6. Click on the **OK** button to accept the settings. The rectangle is extruded and the front corner of the 3D object is removed.

7. On you own, generate a shaded image of the 3D object.

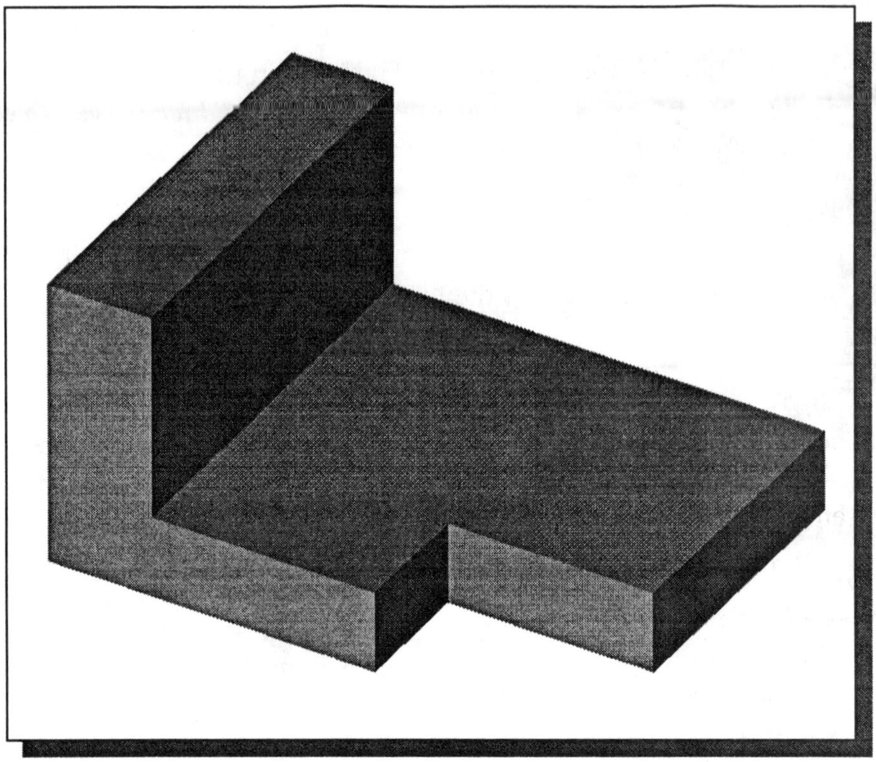

Save the Part and Exit I-DEAS

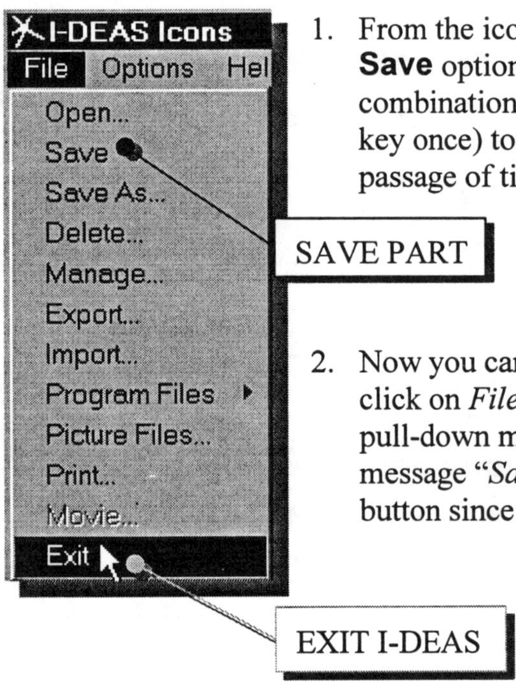

1. From the icon panel, select the **File** pull-down menu. Pick the **Save** option. Notice that you can also use the **Ctrl-S** combination (pressing down the Ctrl key and hitting the "*S*" key once) to save the part. A small watch appears to indicate passage of time as the part is saved.

2. Now you can leave I-DEAS. Use the left-mouse-button to click on *File* in the toolbar menu and select *Exit* from the pull-down menu. A pop-up window will appear with the message "*Save changes before exiting?*" Click on the *NO* button since we have saved the model already.

Questions:

1. What is the first thing we should consider when starting a new model?
2. How does the *I-DEAS Dynamic Navigator* assist us in sketching?
3. How do we reposition and align dimensions?
4. How do you modify more than one dimension at a time?
5. What is the difference in between the *Lines* and *Polylines* commands?
6. How do we change the number of decimal places displayed in dimensions?
7. Identify and describe the following commands:

(a)

(b)

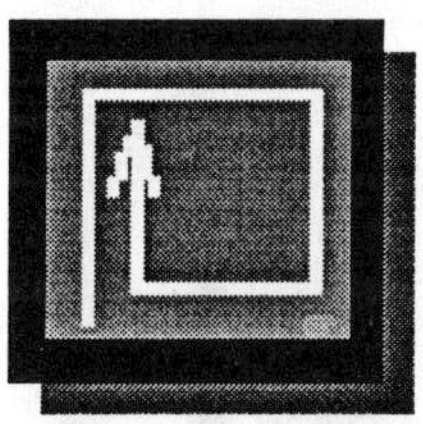

(c)

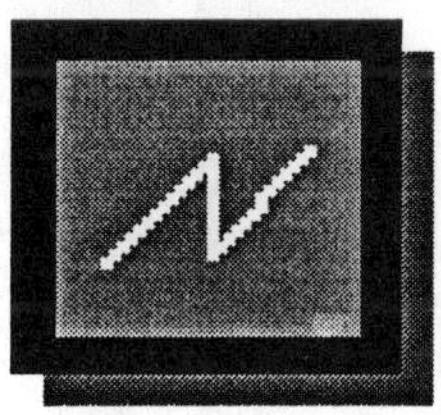

(d)

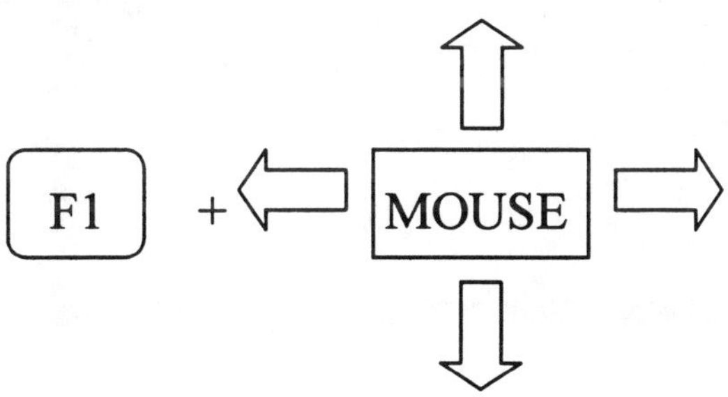

Exercises:

1. Plate Thickness: 0.25

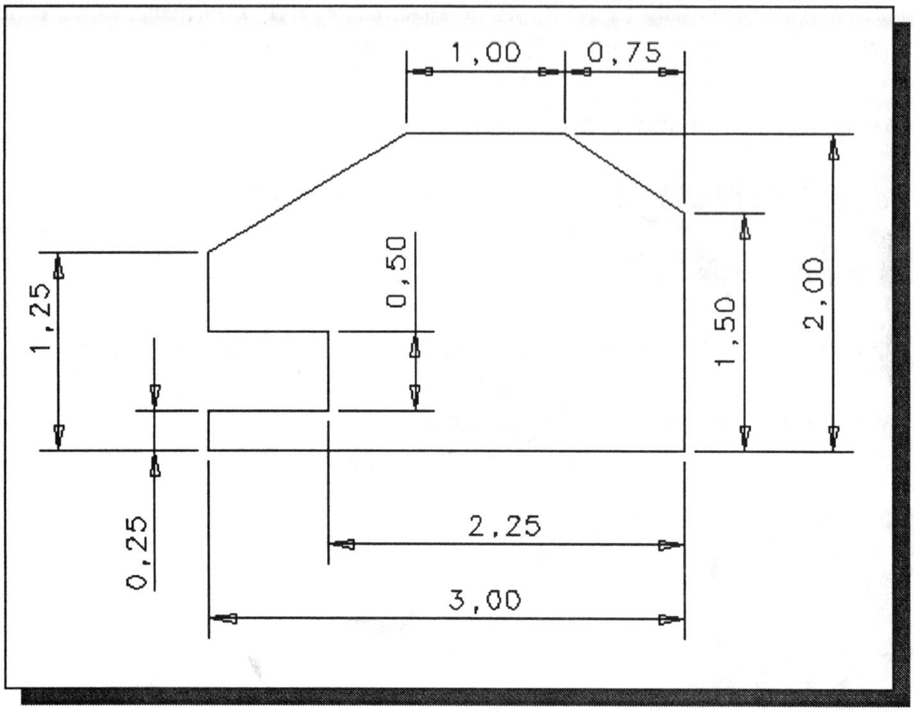

2.

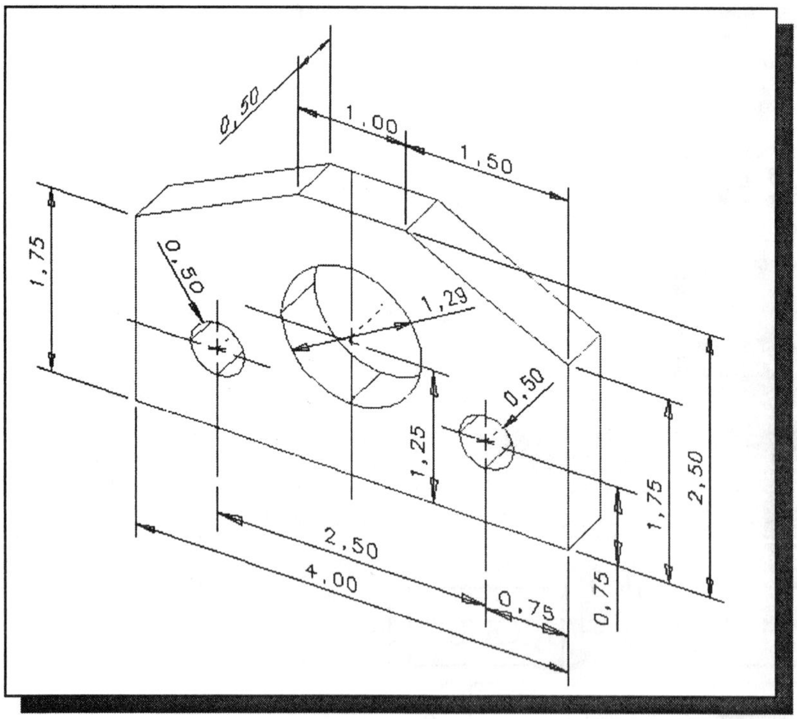

Chapter 3
Constructive Solid Geometry Concept

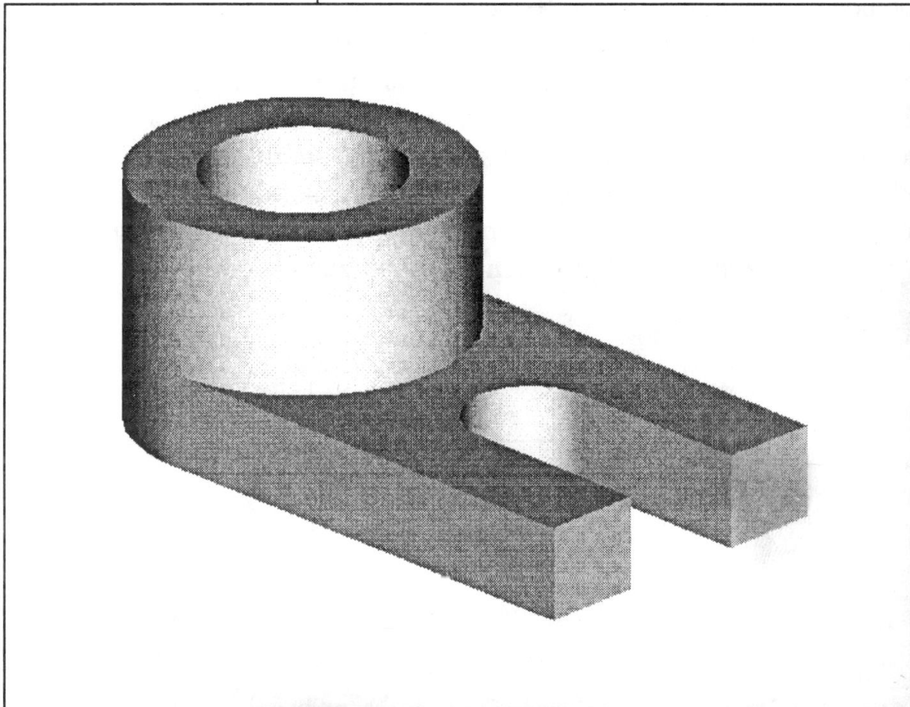

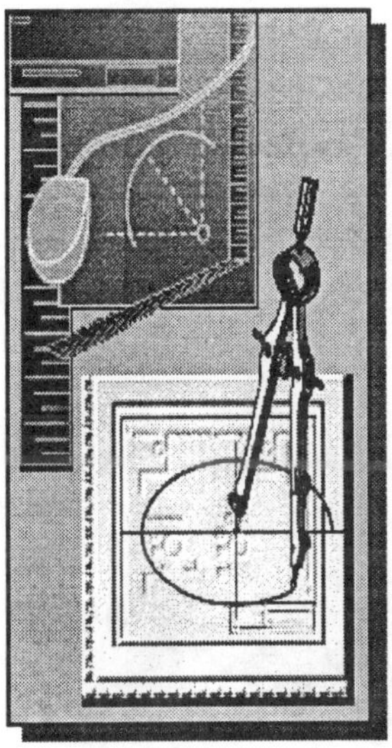

Learning Objectives

When you have completed this lesson, you will be able to:

- ♦ Understand the Basic CSG concepts.
- ♦ Create CSG Binary Trees.
- ♦ Perform the Basic Boolean Operations.
- ♦ Use the Move command.
- ♦ Create Basic Solid Primitives.
- ♦ Use the Catalog Parts.
- ♦ Create Models using Metric Units.

Introduction

In the 1980s, one of the main advancements in **Solid Modeling** was the development of the **Constructive Solid Geometry** (CSG) method. CSG describes the solid model as combinations of basic three-dimensional shapes (**Primitive Solids**). The basic primitive solid set typically includes: Rectangular-prism (Block), Cylinder, Cone, Sphere, and Torus (Tube). Two solid objects can be combined into one object in various ways, and these operations are known as **Boolean operations**. There are three basic Boolean operations: **JOIN (Union)**, **CUT (Difference)**, and **INTERSECT**. The JOIN operation combines the two volumes included in the different solids into a single solid. The CUT operation subtracts the volume of one solid object from the other solid object. The INTERSECT operation keeps only the volume common to both solid objects. The CSG method is also known as the **Machinist's Approach**, as the method is parallel to machine shop practices.

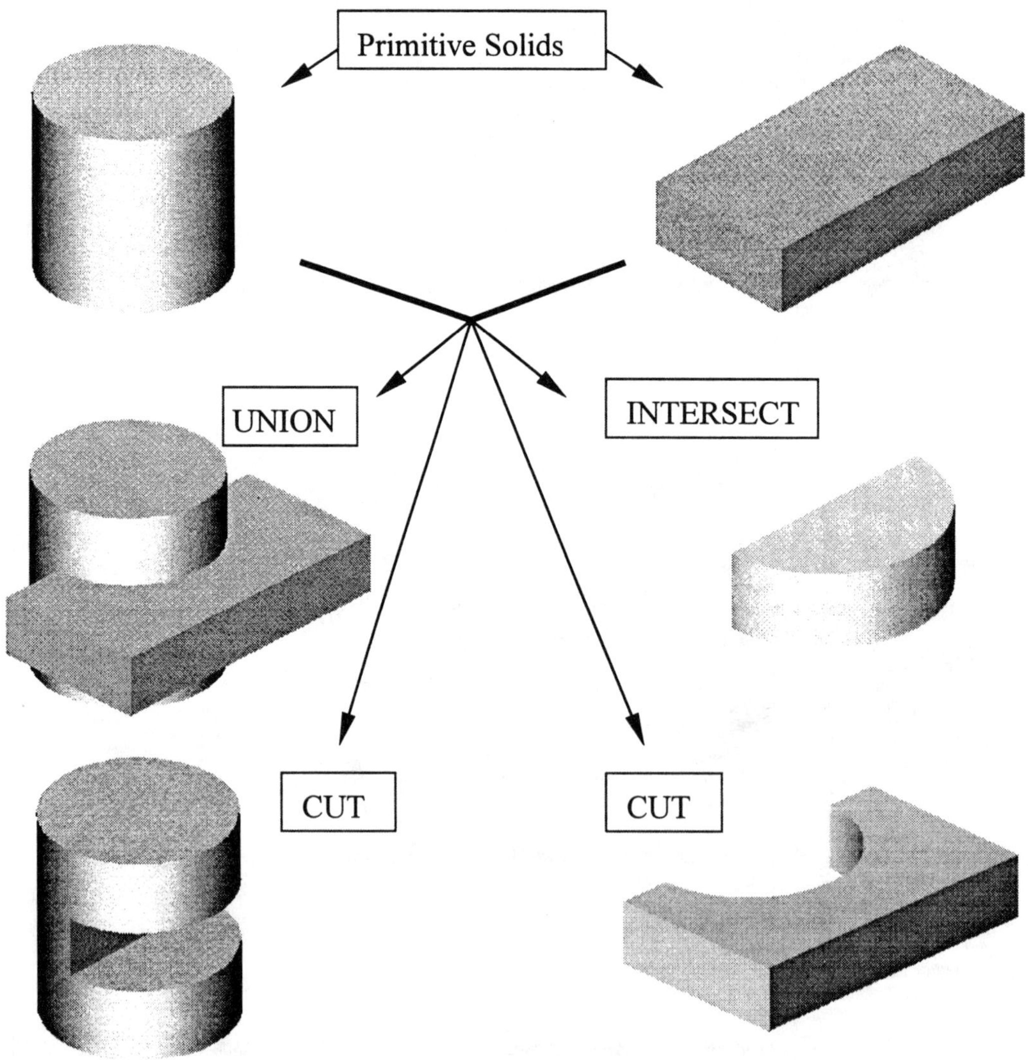

Binary Tree

CSG is also referred to as the method used to store a solid model in the database. The resulting solid can be easily represented as what is called a **binary tree**. In a binary tree, the terminal branches (leaves) are the various primitives that are linked together to make the final solid object (the root). A binary tree is an effective way to keep track of the operations performed, *history,* of the resulting solid. By keeping track of the history, the solid model can be re-built by re-linking through the binary tree. This provides a convenient and intuitive way of modeling that imitates the manufacturing process. We can make modifications at the appropriate links in the binary tree and re-link the rest of the history tree without building a new model.

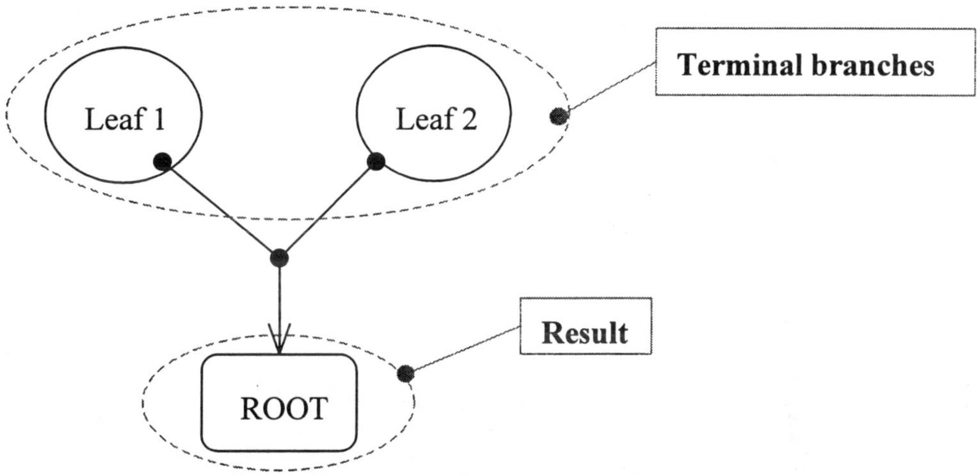

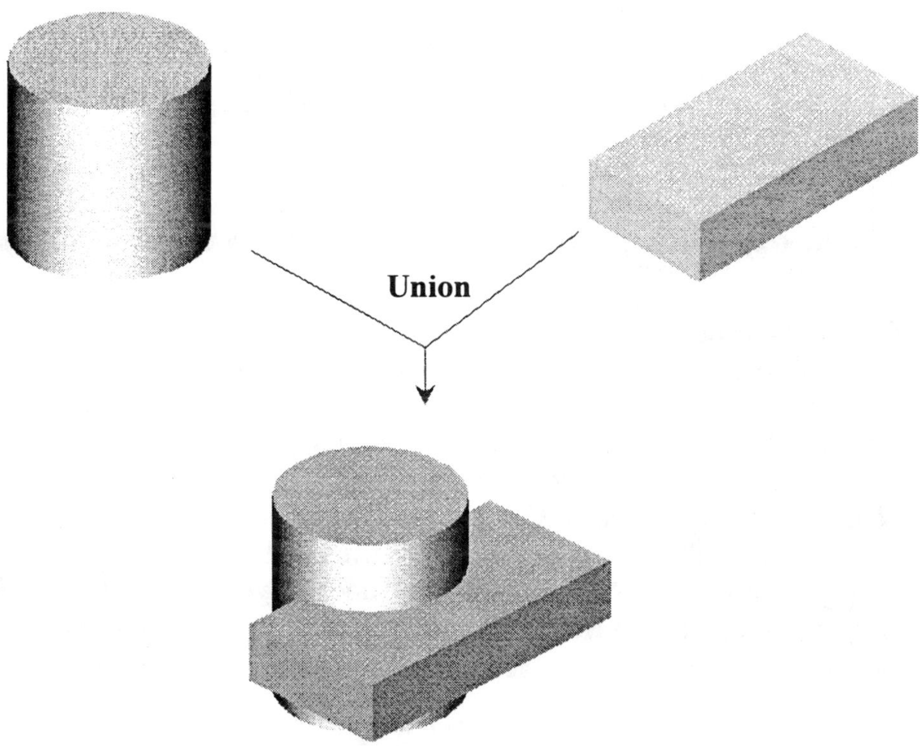

The Locator Design

The CSG concept is one of the important building blocks for feature-based modeling. In *I-DEAS*, the CSG concept can be used as a planning tool to determine the number of features that are needed to construct the model. It is also a good practice to create features that are parallel to the manufacturing process required for the design. With parametric modeling, we are no longer limited to using only the predefined basic solid shapes. In fact, any solid features we create in *I-DEAS* are used as primitive solids; parametric modeling allows us to maintain full control of the design variables that are used to describe the features. In this Chapter, a more in-depth look at the parametric modeling procedure is presented. The equivalent CSG operation for each feature is also illustrated.

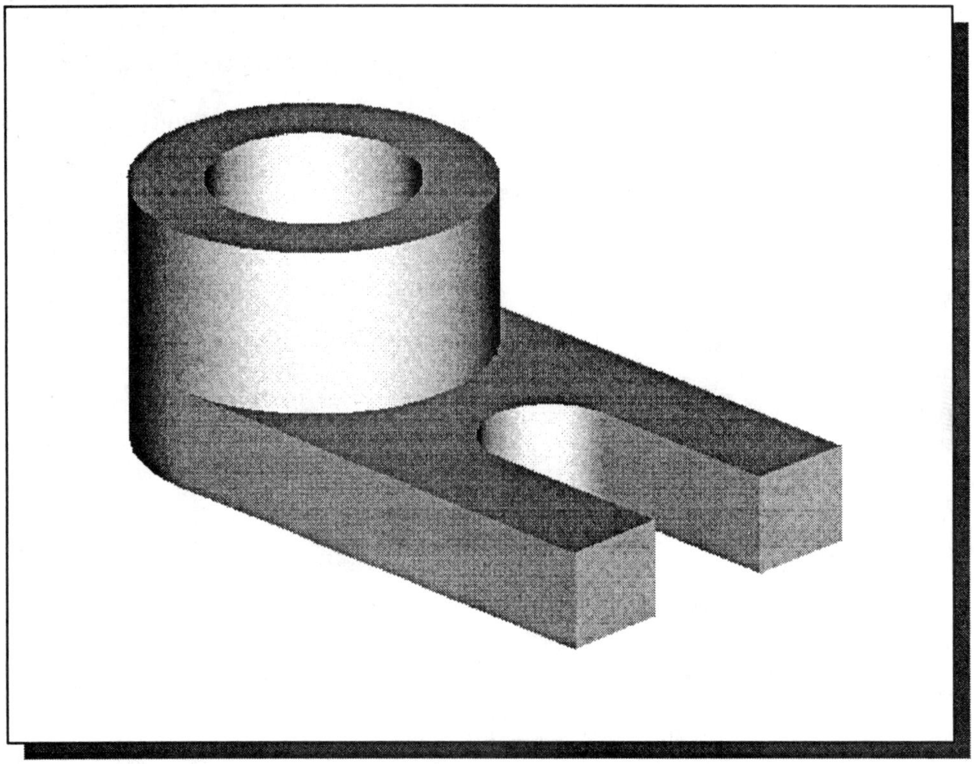

➢ Before going through the tutorial, on your own, make a sketch of a CSG binary tree of the *Locator* design using only two basic types of primitive solids: cylinder and rectangular prism. In your sketch, how many *Boolean operations* will be required to create the model? What is your choice of the first primitive solid to use, and why? Take a few minutes to consider these questions and do the preliminary planning by sketching on a piece of paper. Compare the sketch you make to the CSG binary tree steps shown on page 3-6. Note that there are many different possibilities in combining the basic primitive solids to form the solid model. Even for the simplest design, it is possible to take several different approaches to creating the same solid model.

Starting I-DEAS

1. Select the *I-DEAS* icon or type "*ideas*" at your system prompt to start I-DEAS. The *I-DEAS Start* window will appear on the screen.

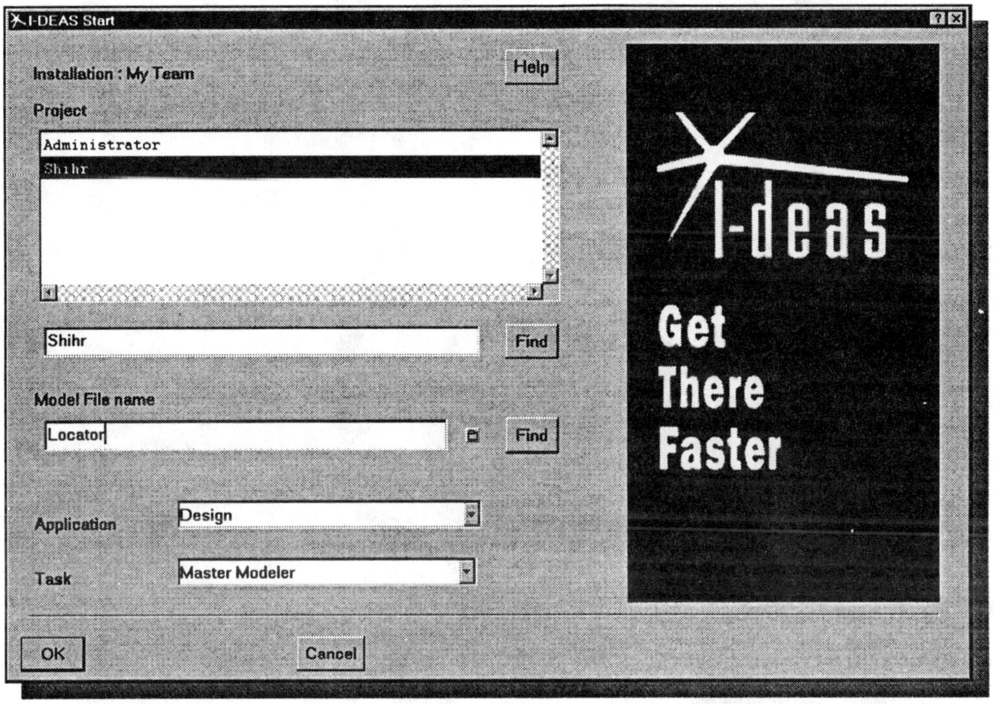

2. Start a new model file by filling in the window items as shown below in the *I-DEAS Start* window:

Project Name: **(Your account Name)**
Model File Name: **Locator**
Application: **Design**
Task: **Master Modeler**
OK

3. After you click **OK**, a *warning window* will appear to tell you that a new model file will be created. Click **OK** to continue.

I-DEAS Warning
! New Model File will be created
OK

❖ Next, I-DEAS will display four windows, the *graphics window*, the *prompt window*, the *list window*, and the *icon panel*. A line of *quick help* text appears at the bottom of the graphics window as you move the mouse cursor over the icons.

The CSG Binary Tree of the Locator Design

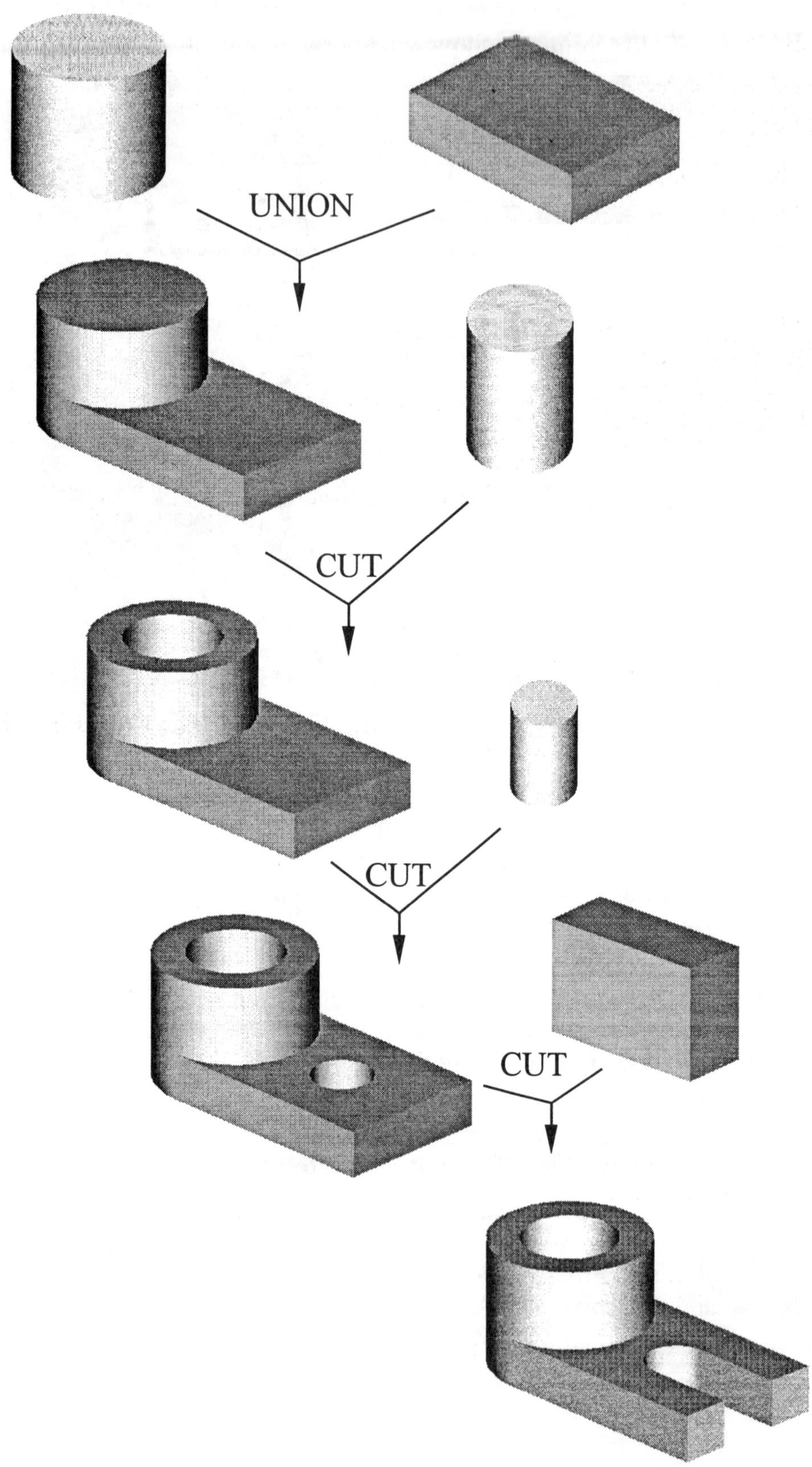

Units Setup

❖ When starting a new model, the first thing we should do is determine the set of units we would like to use. I-DEAS displays the default set of units in the *list window*.

1. Use the left-mouse-button and select the **Options** menu in the icon panel.

1. Use the left-mouse-button and select *Options*.

2. Select **Units**.

2. Select the **Units** option.

3. Inside the *graphics window*, pick **mm (milli newton)** from the pop-up menu. The set of units is stored with the model file when you save.

3. Select **mm (milli newton)**.

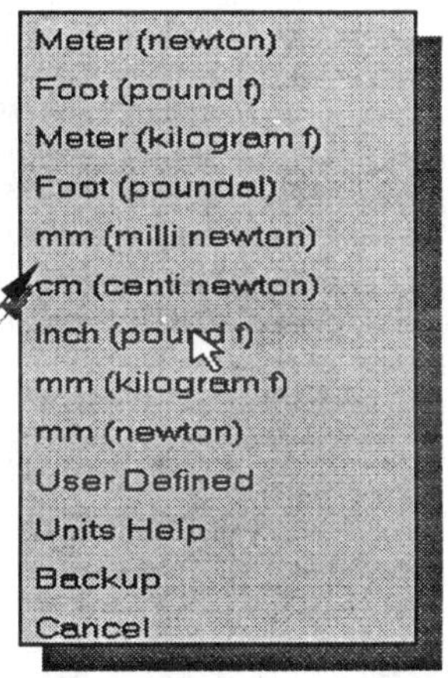

Base Feature

In *parametric modeling*, the first solid feature is called the **base feature,** which usually is the primary shape of the model. Depending upon the design intent, additional features are added to the base feature.

Some of the considerations involved in selecting the base feature:

- **Design Intent** – Determine the functionality of the design; identify the feature that is central to the design.

- **Order of features** – Choose the feature that is the logical base in terms of the order of features in the design.

- **Ease of making modifications** – Select the base feature that is more stable and is less likely to be changed.

We will create a rectangular block as the base feature of the ***Locator*** design.

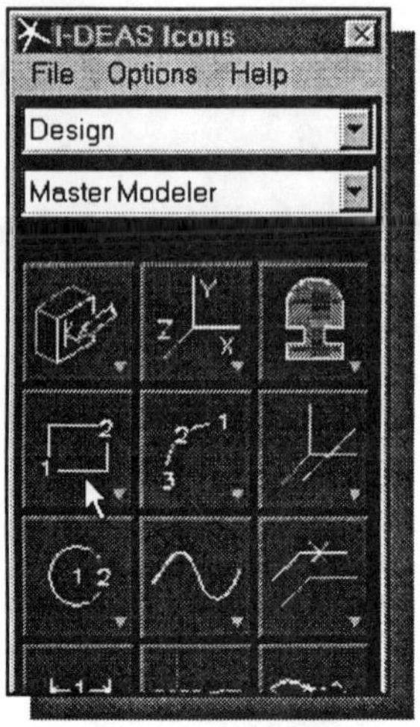

1. Choose **Rectangle by 2 Corners** in the icon panel. This command requires the selection of two locations to identify the two opposite corners of a rectangle. The message "*Locate first corner*" is displayed in the prompt window.

2. Create a rectangle of arbitrary size by selecting two locations on the screen as shown below.

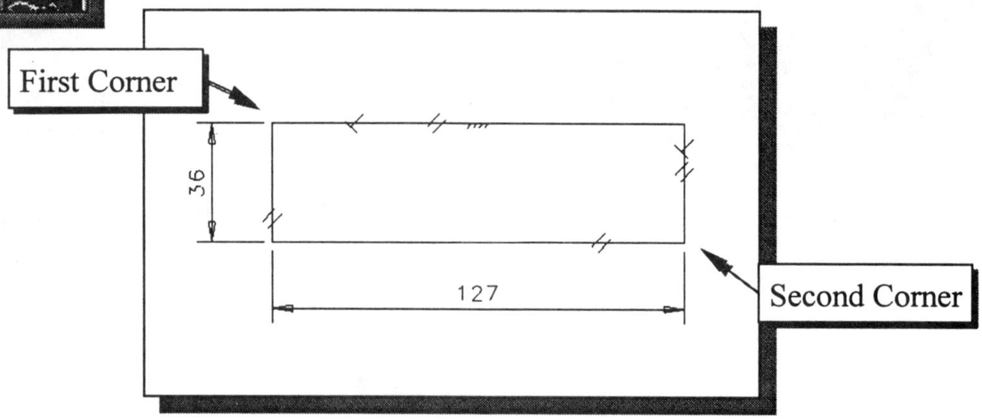

Modifying the Size of the Rectangle

1. *Pre-select* the two dimensions of the rectangle by holding down the **SHIFT** key and left clicking the values. The selected dimension will be highlighted.

PRE-SELECT SHIFT + LEFT-mouse-button

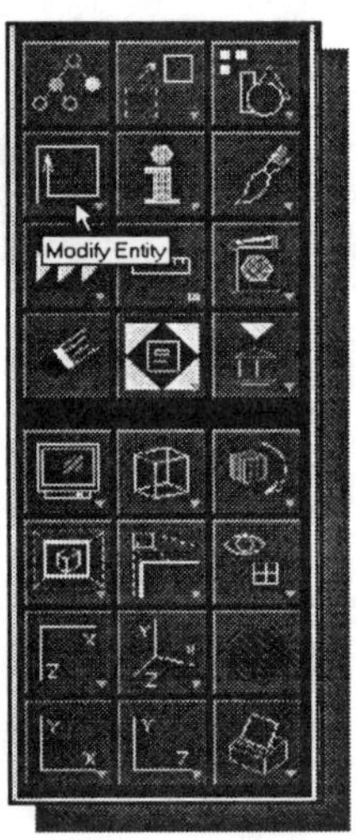

2. Choose **Modify** in the icon panel. The *Dimensions* window appears.

3. In the *Dimensions* window, change the values to the values as shown (15 X 75).

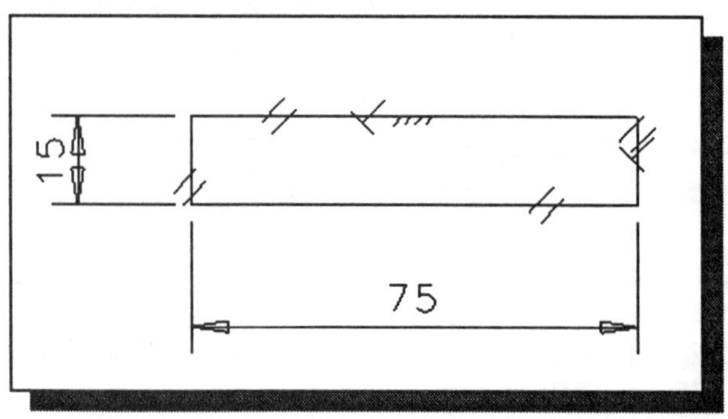

Completing the Base Solid Feature

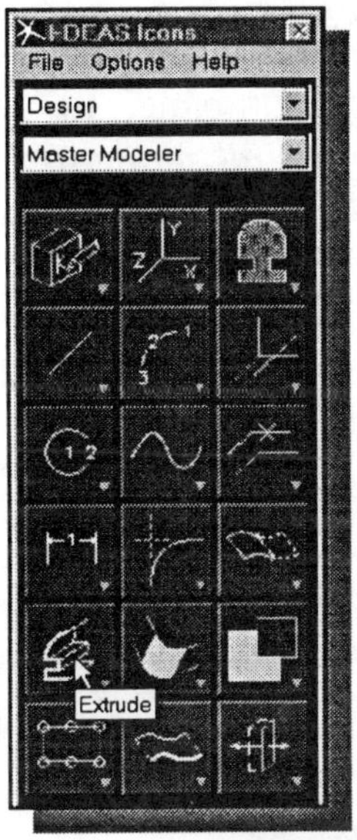

1. Choose **Extrude** in the icon panel. In the prompt window, the message "*Pick curve or section*" is displayed.

2. Pick the rectangle at any location.

3. At the I-DEAS prompt "*Pick curve to add or remove (Done),*" press the **ENTER** key or the **middle-mouse-button** to accept the selection.

4. The *Extrude Section* window will appear on the screen. Enter **50** as the *extrusion distance* and confirm that the *New part* option is switched ***on*** as shown.

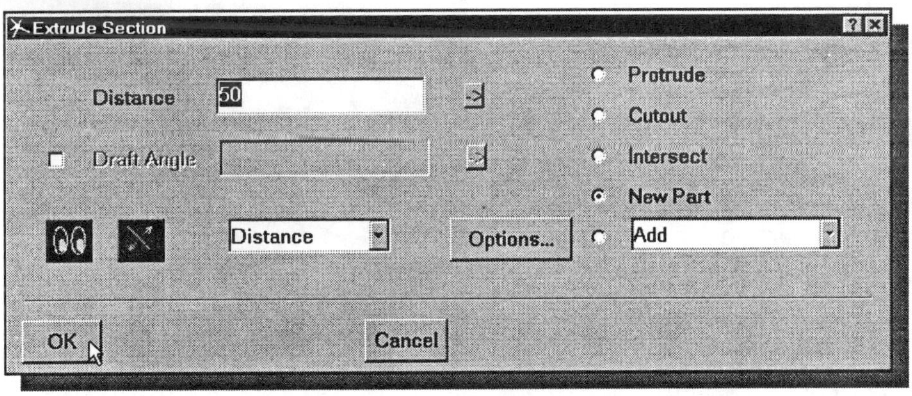

5. Click on the **OK** button to accept the settings and extrude the 2-D section into a 3D solid.

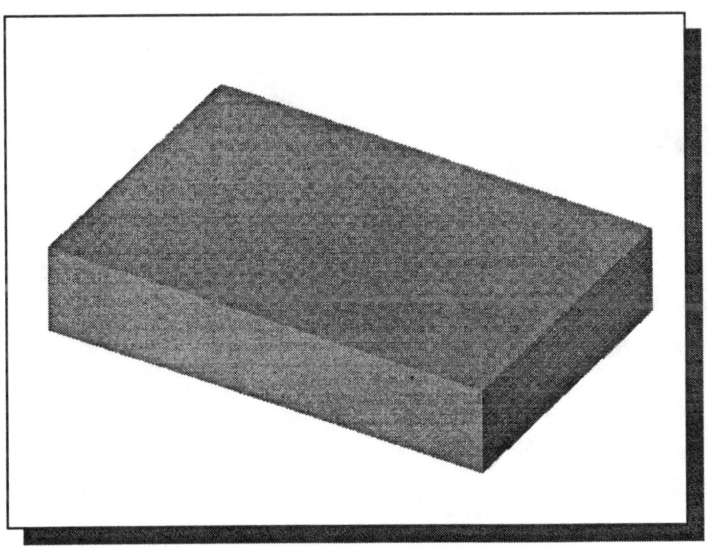

- Notice all of the dimensions disappeared from the screen. All of the dimensional values and geometric constraints are stored in the database by I-DEAS and they can be brought up at any time.

Creating the next solid feature

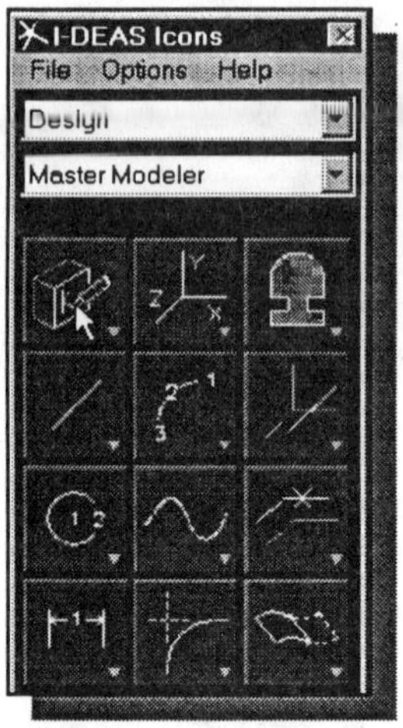

1. Choose **Sketch in Place** in the icon panel. In the prompt window, the message "*Pick plane to sketch on*" is displayed.

2. Use the dynamic rotatation function to display the bottom face of the solid model as shown below.

3. Pick the bottom face of the 3D model when it is highlighted as shown.

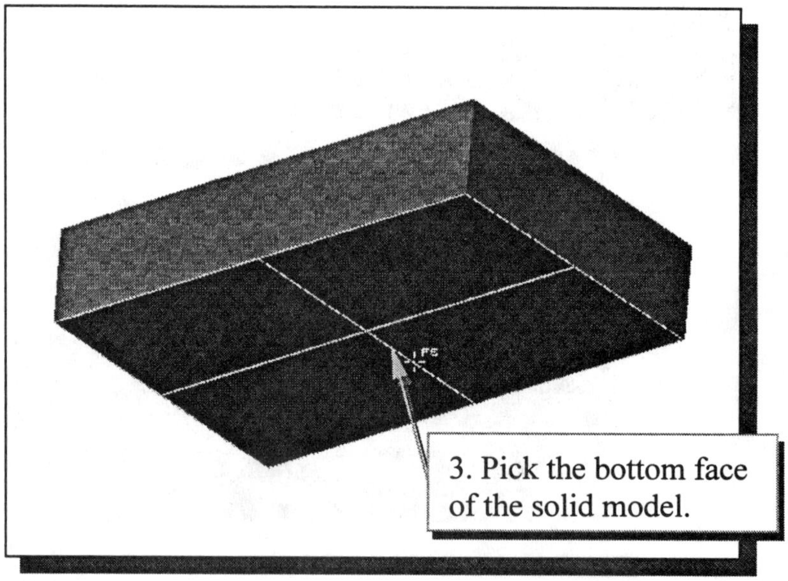

➢ Note that the sketch plane is aligned to the selected face. *I-DEAS* automatically establishes a User-Coordinate-System (UCS) and records its location with respect to the part on which it was created.

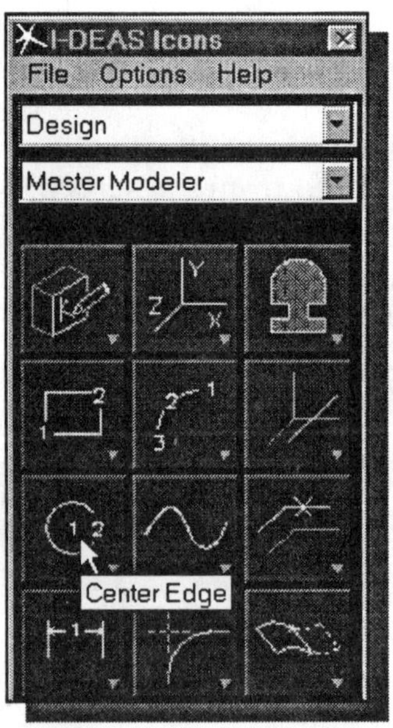

4. Choose *Circle* – **Center Edge** in the icon panel. This command requires the selection of two locations: first the location of the center of the circle and then a location where the circle will pass through.

5. Move the graphics cursor near the midpoint of the shorter edge of the bottom surface. Notice the *Dynamic Navigator* will automatically show alignment to the center of the edge. Click with the **left-mouse-button** to select the position as the center point of the circle.

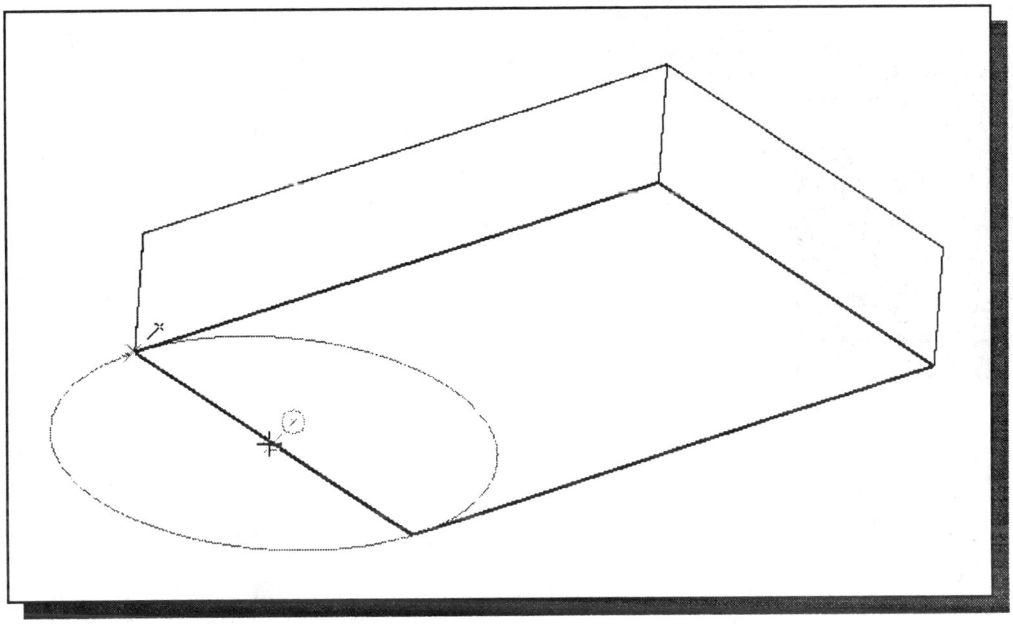

6. Move the graphics cursor near the corner of the bottom surface, click with the **left-mouse-button** when the alignment is displayed as shown. This location is the location where the circle will pass through. Note that the diameter dimension is not necessary since the circle is well defined. If a dimension appears on your screen, delete the circle and create the circle again.

7. Press the **ENTER** key or the **middle-mouse-button** to end the *Circle – Center Edge* command.

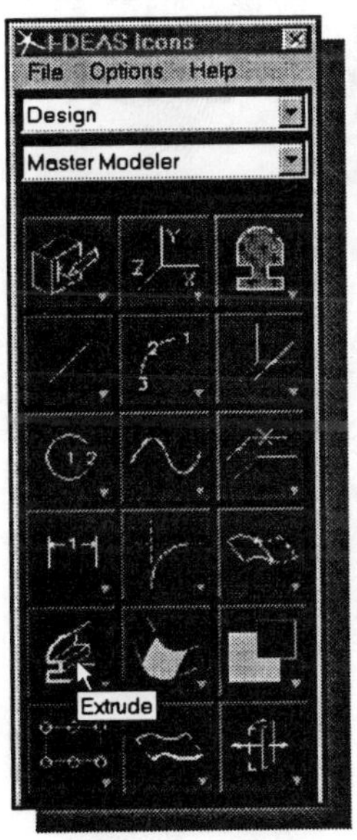

8. Choose **Extrude** in the icon panel. In the prompt window, the message "*Pick curve or section*" is displayed.

9. Pick the circle as the 2D section to be extruded.

10. At the I-DEAS prompt "*Pick curve to add or remove (Done),*" press the **ENTER** key or the **middle-mouse-button** to accept the selection.

11. The *Extrude Section* window will appear on the screen. Enter **40** as the *extrusion distance* and confirm that the *Protrude* option is switched ***on*** as shown.

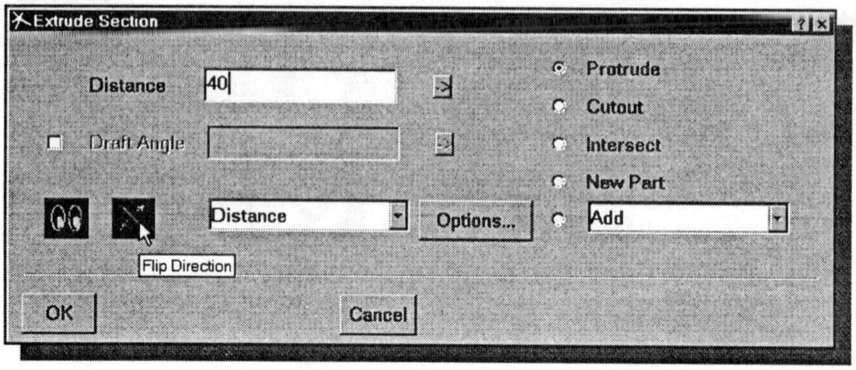

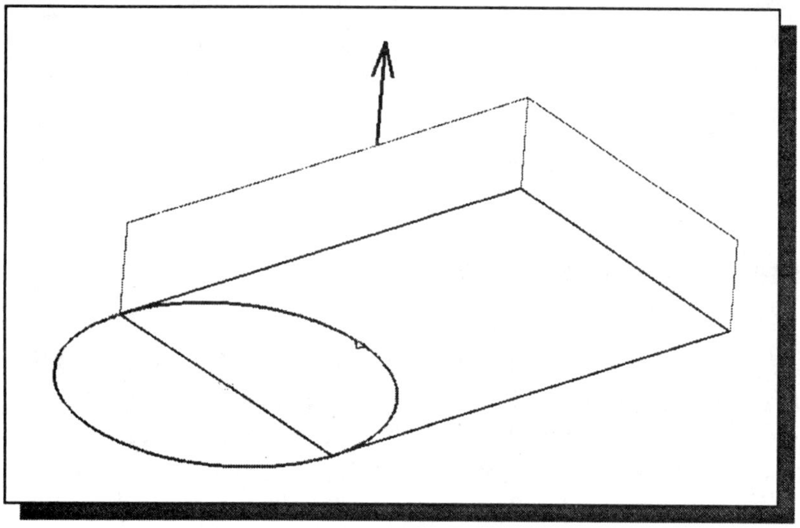

12. Click on the Flip Direction button to reverse the direction of extrusion (upward) as shown below.

13. Click on the **OK** button to proceed with the join operation.

- The two features are joined together into one solid part; the **CSG-Union** operation was performed.

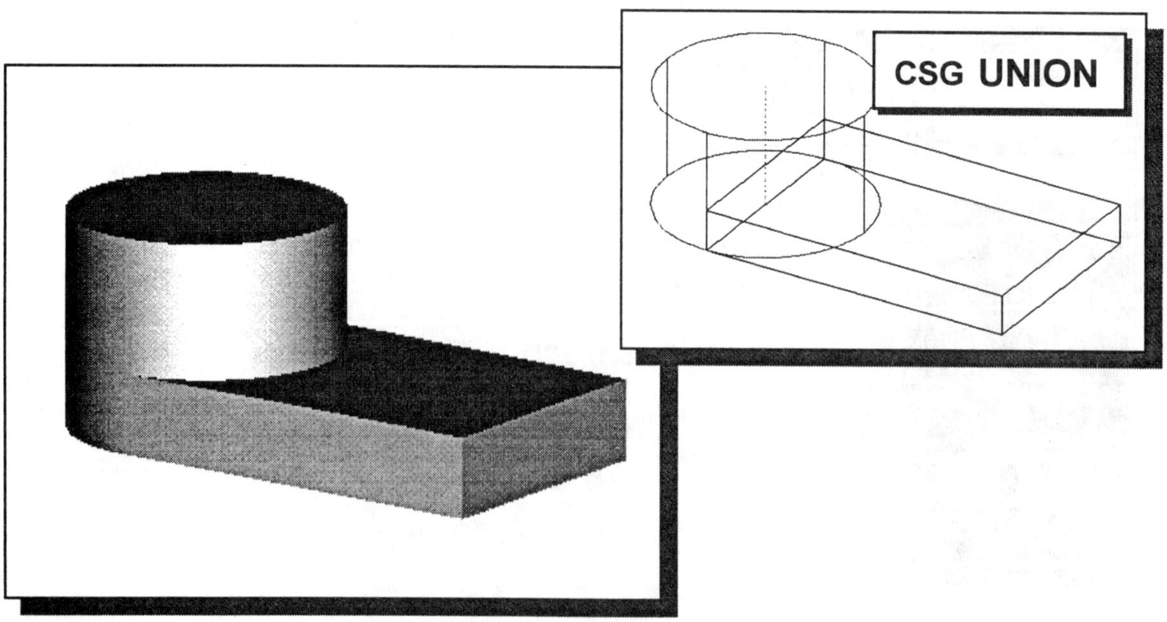

Creating a CUT Feature

- We will create a circular cut as the next solid feature of the design. We will align the sketch plane to the top of the last cylinder feature.

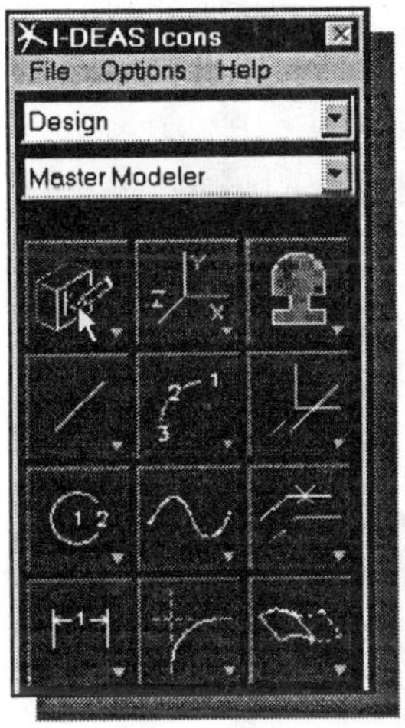

1. Choose **Sketch in Place** in the icon panel. In the prompt window, the message "*Pick plane to sketch on*" is displayed.

2. Pick the top face of the cylinder as shown.

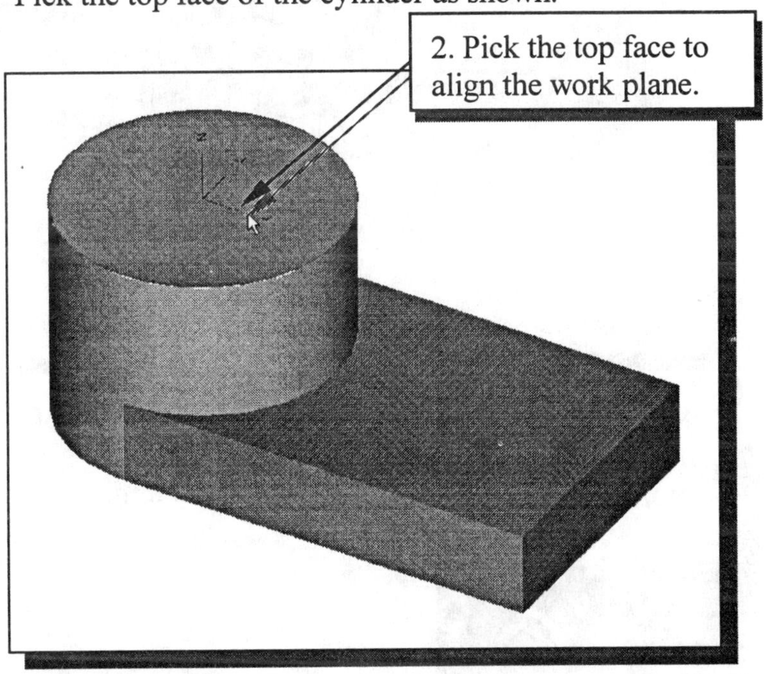

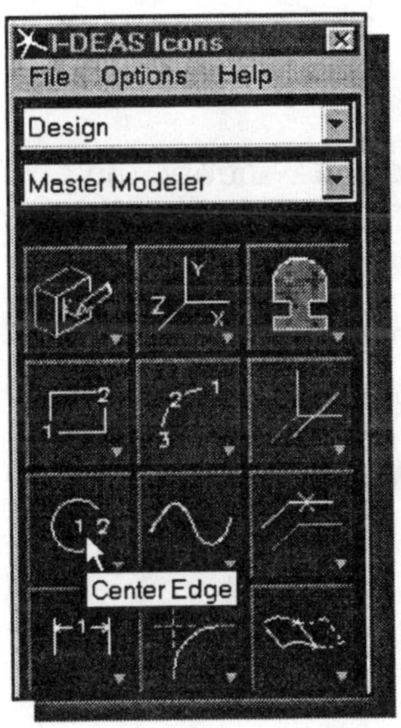

3. Choose *Circle* – **Center Edge** in the icon panel. This command requires the selection of two locations: first the location of the center of the circle and then a location where the circle will pass through.

4. Move the graphics cursor near the center of the cylinder of the 3D solid. Notice the *Dynamic Navigator* will automatically show alignment to the center of the surface. Click with the **left-mouse-button** to select the position as the center point of the circle.

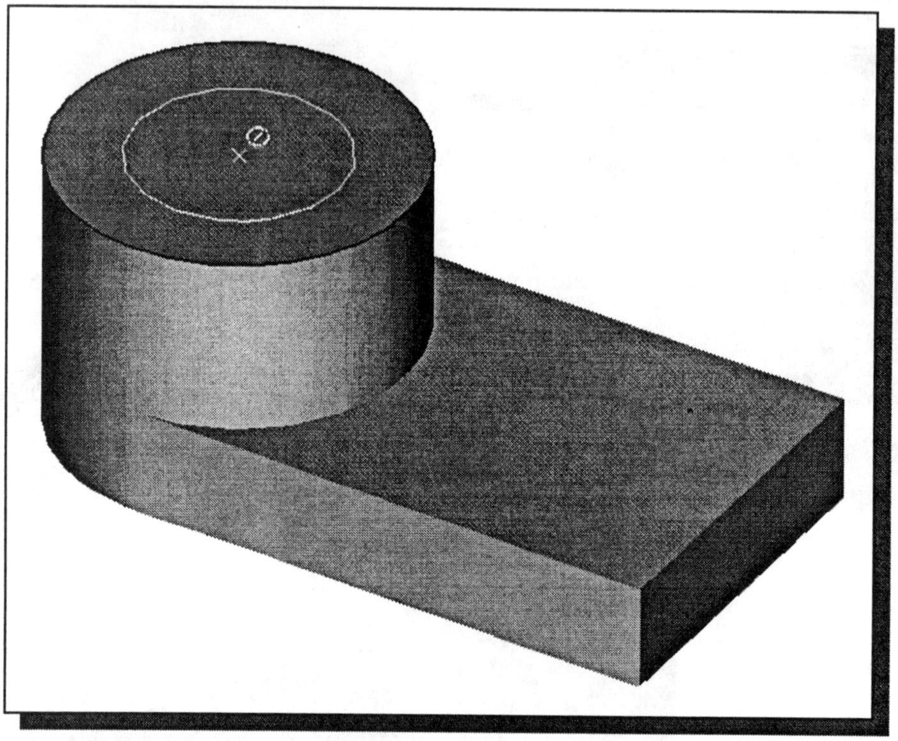

5. Sketch a circle of arbitrary size inside the top face of the cylinder as shown.

6. On your own, modify the dimension to **30** mm.

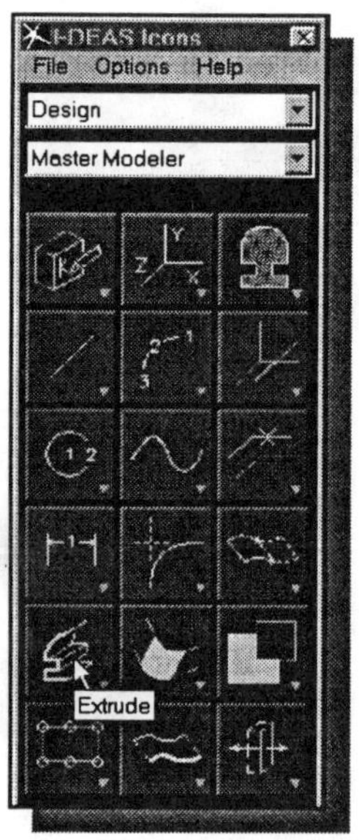

7. Choose **Extrude** in the icon panel. In the prompt window, the message "*Pick curve or section*" is displayed.

8. Pick the circle we just created as the 2D section to be extruded.

9. At the I-DEAS prompt "*Pick curve to add or remove (Done),*" press the **ENTER** key or the **middle-mouse-button** to accept the selection.

10. The *Extrude Section* window appears. Set the *extrude option* to **Cutout**. Note the extrusion direction displayed in the graphics window.

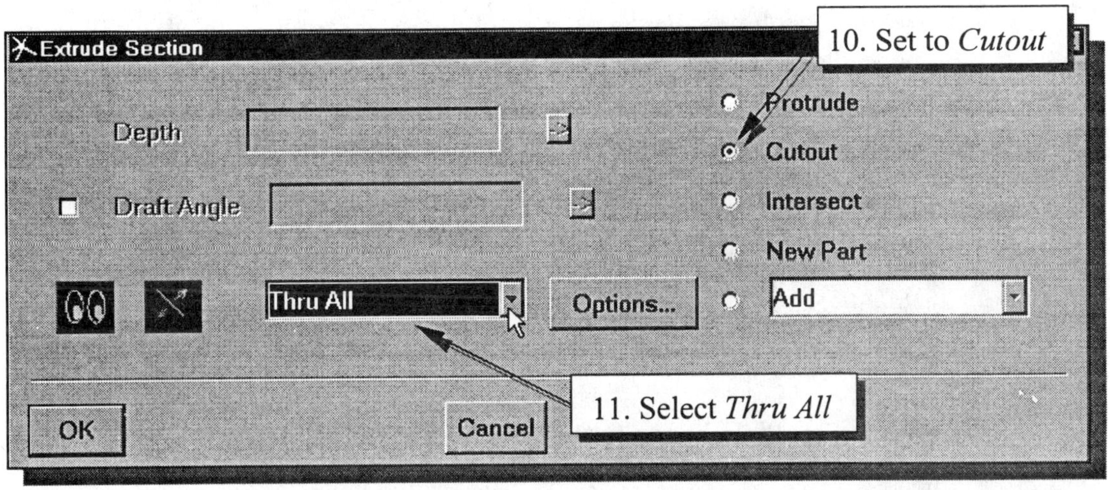

11. Click on and hold down the left-mouse-button on the depth menu and select the **Thru All** option. I-DEAS will calculate the distance necessary to cut through the part.

12. Click on the **OK** button to accept the settings. The circle is extruded into a cylinder and the center of the 3D object is removed.

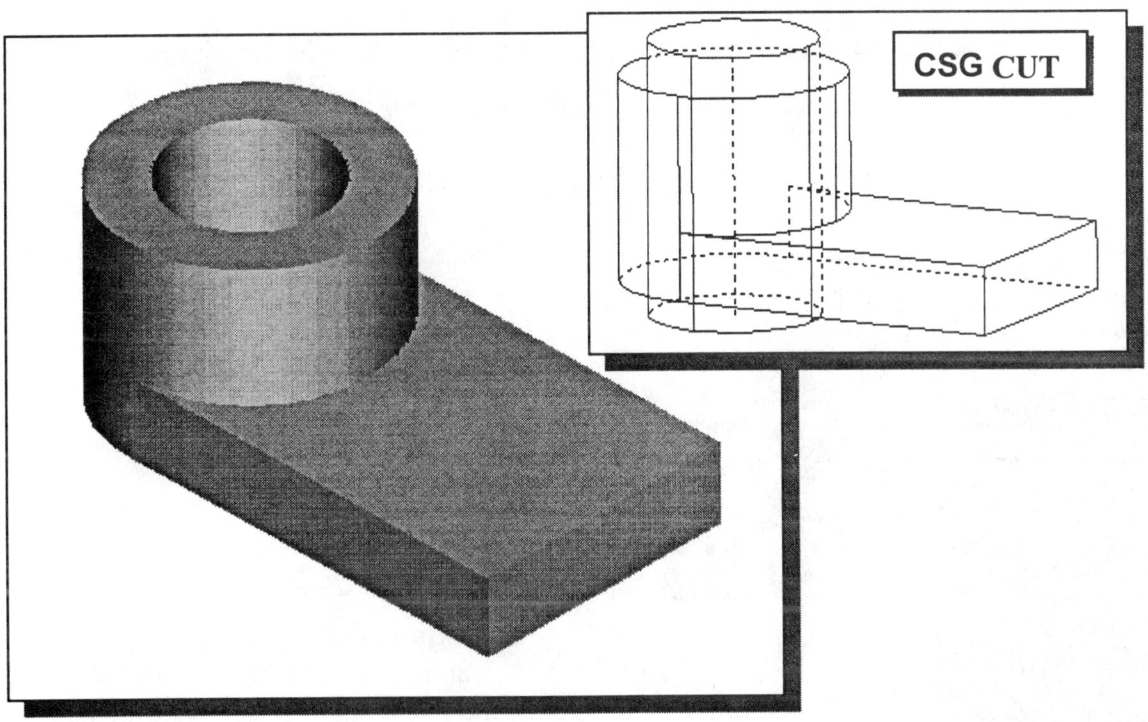

❖ Now is a good time to save the model (Quick key: **[Ctrl]** + [S]). It is a good habit to save your model periodically, just in case something might and probably will go wrong while you are working on the model. You should also save the model after you have completed any major constructions.

The Second Cut Feature

- We will create a circular cut as the next solid feature of the design. We will align the sketch plane to the top of the base feature.

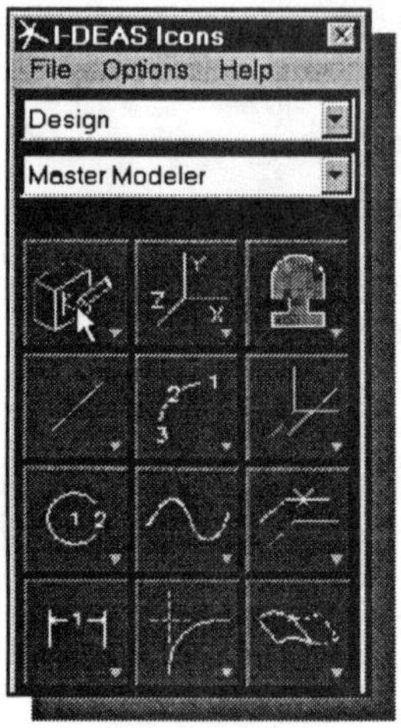

1. Choose **Sketch in Place** in the icon panel. In the prompt window, the message "*Pick plane to sketch on*" is displayed.

2. Pick the top face of the base feature as shown.

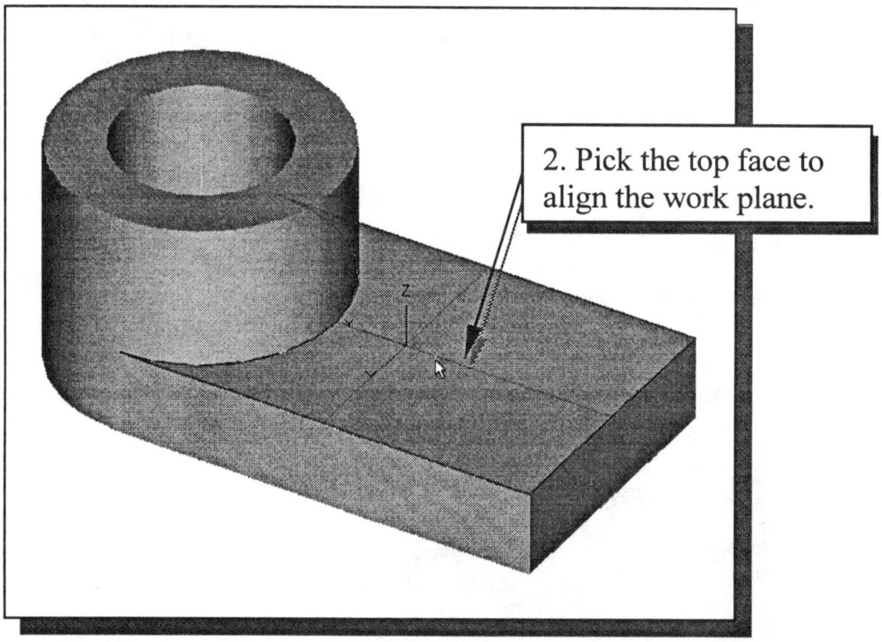

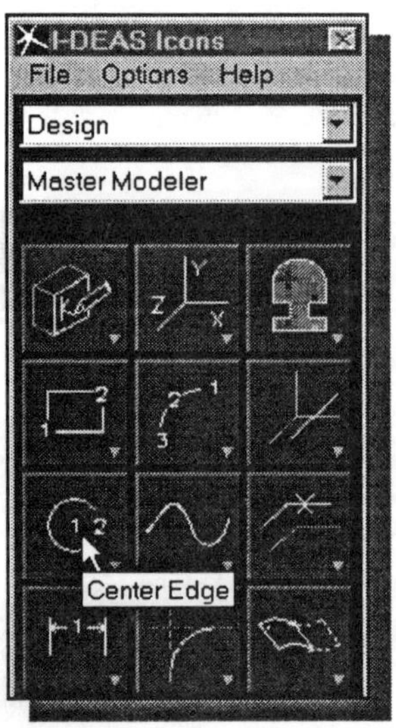

3. Choose *Circle* – **Center Edge** in the icon panel. This command requires the selection of two locations: first the location of the center of the circle and then a location where the circle will pass through.

4. On your own, create a circle (diameter 20 mm) located at 25 mm and 30 mm measured from the front corner of the base feature as shown below.

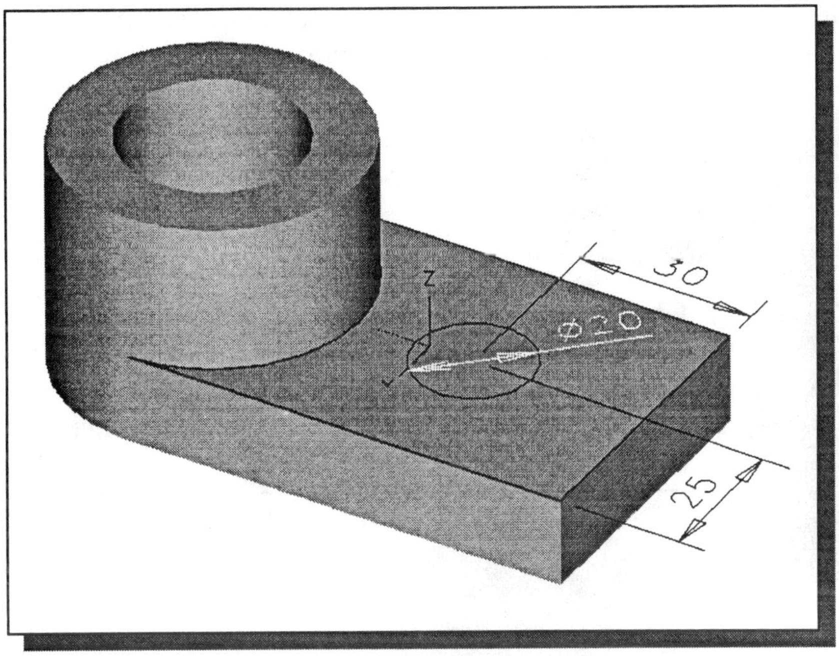

5. On your own, use the ***Extrude*** command and create the cutout through the base of the solid as shown.

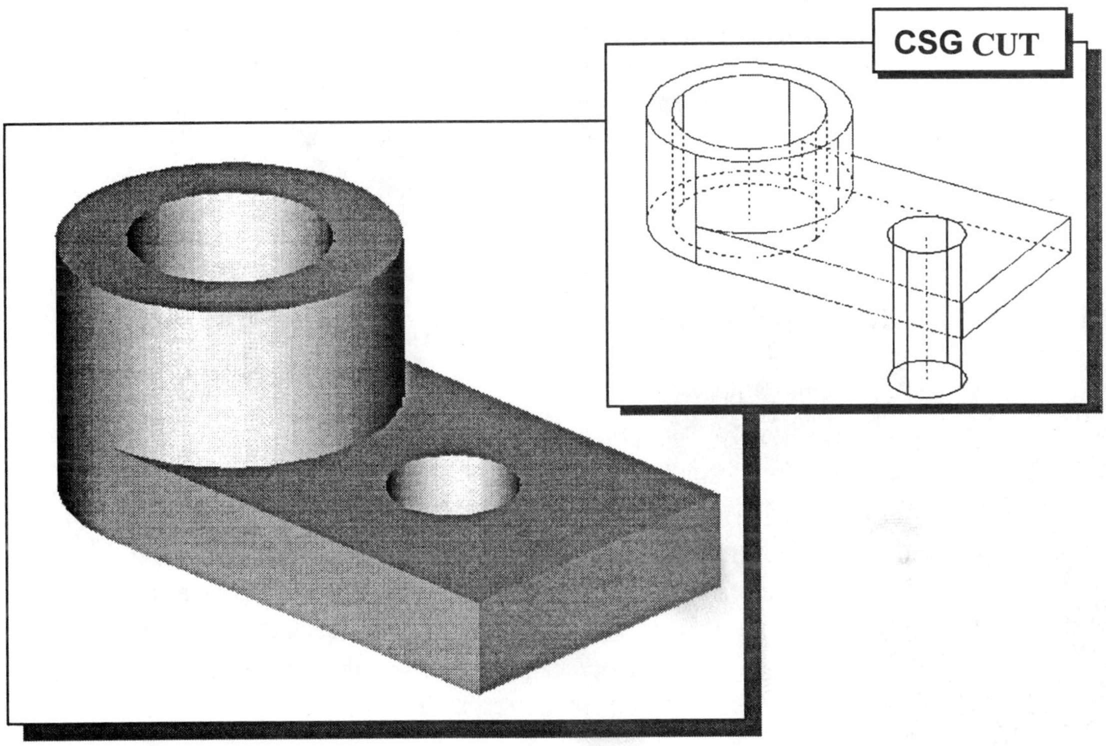

The Third *CUT* Feature

We will create a rectangular cutter as the final solid feature of the part. We will also demonstrate the use of the *Three point Rectangle option.*

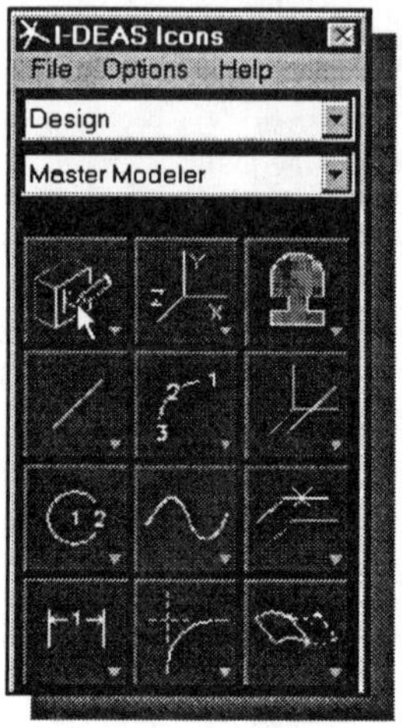

1. Choose **Sketch in Place** in the icon panel. In the prompt window, the message "*Pick plane to sketch on*" is displayed.

2. Pick the top face of the base feature by left-clicking the surface as shown in the below figure.

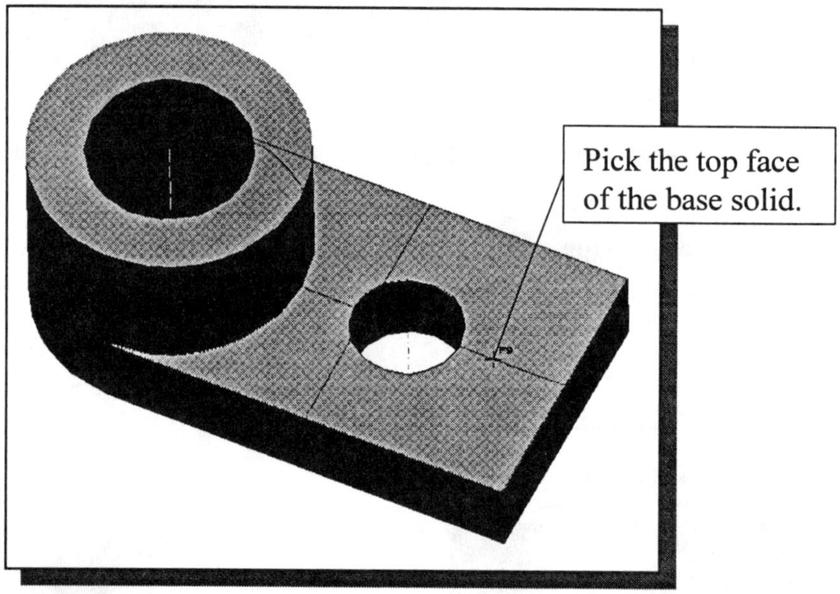

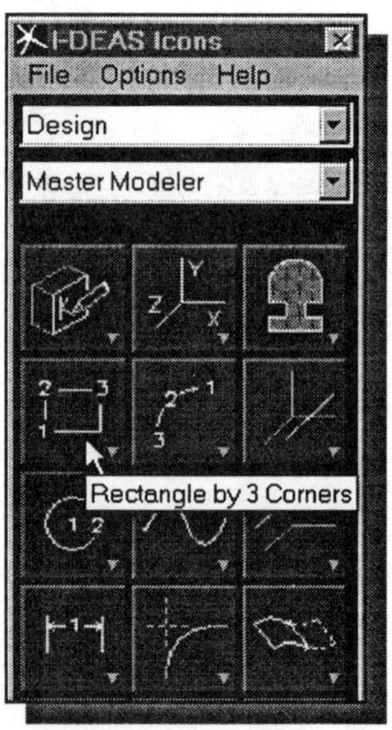

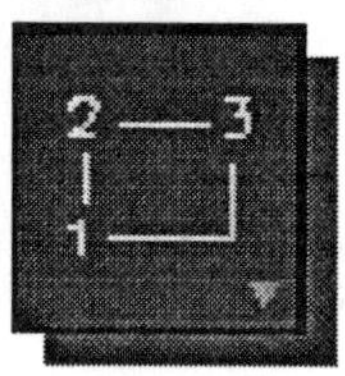

3. Choose **Rectangle by 3 Corners** in the icon panel. This command requires the selection of three locations to identify three specific alignments of a rectangle. The message "*Locate first corner*" is displayed in the prompt window.

4. Create a rectangle by selecting the three corners as shown. The first and third points are aligned to the circular cut feature.

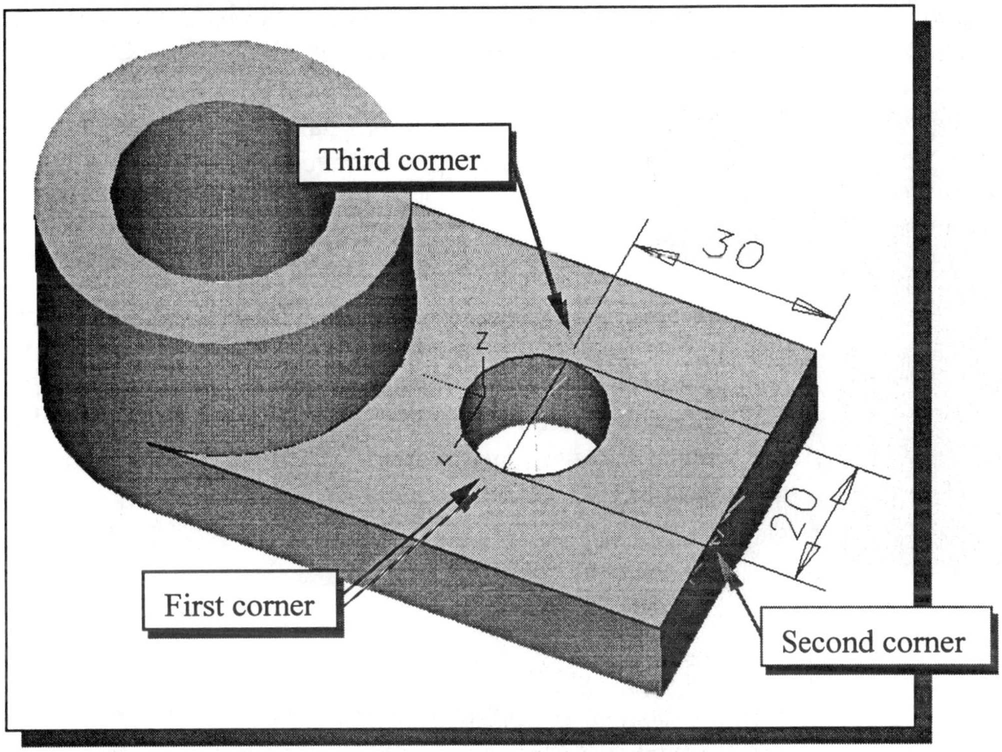

6. On your own, complete the *cut feature* using the *Thru All* option.

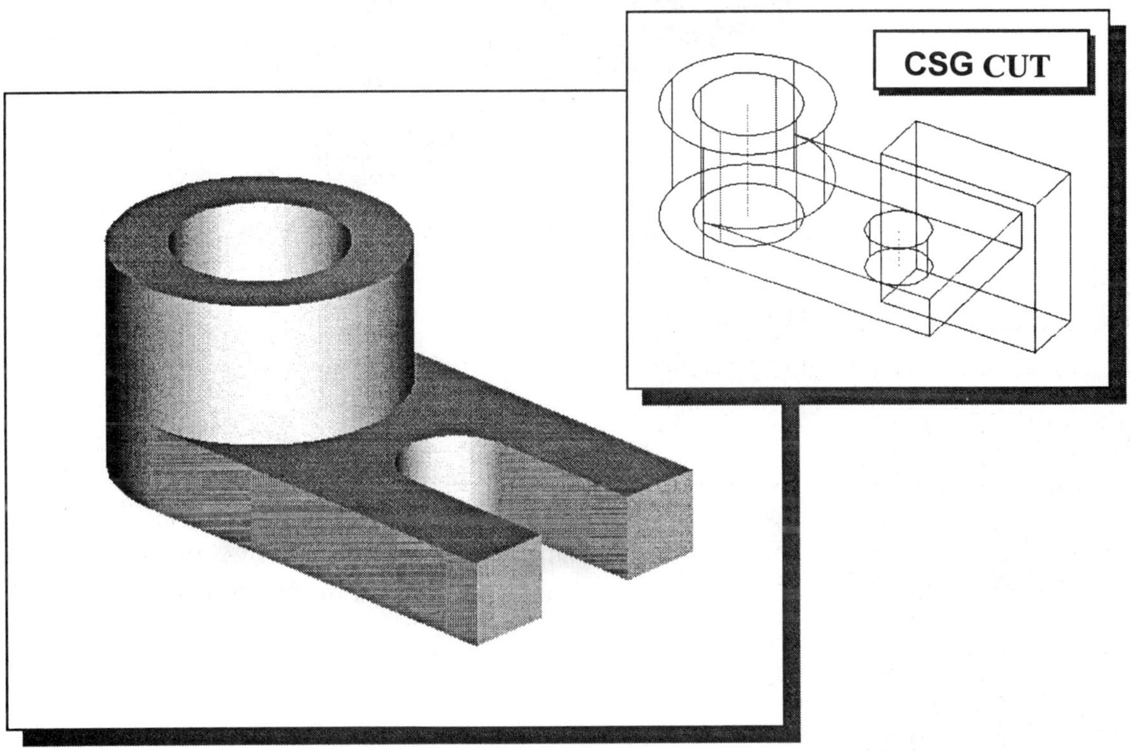

Save the Part and Exit I-DEAS

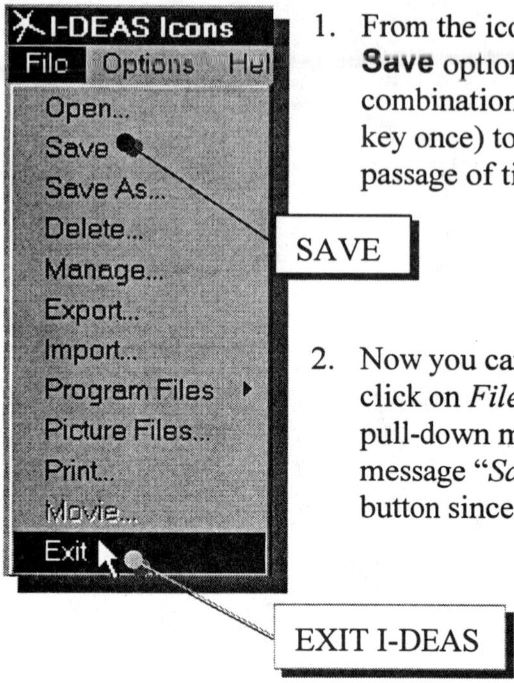

1. From the icon panel, select the **File** pull-down menu. Pick the **Save** option. Notice that you can also use the **Ctrl-S** combination (pressing down the Ctrl key and hitting the "*S*" key once) to save the part. A small watch appears to indicate passage of time as the part is saved.

2. Now you can leave I-DEAS. Use the left-mouse-button to click on *File* in the toolbar menu and select *Exit* from the pull-down menu. A pop-up window will appear with the message "*Save changes before exiting?*" Click on the *NO* button since we have saved the model already.

➢ The CSG concept described in this Chapter is the underlying mainstream method that is used in almost all of the available solid modelers today. The solid modeling software performs the **Boolean operations** either implicitly or explicitly. One should always consider the CSG approach in creating solid models; the simplicity of the CSG approach also makes it extremely powerful.

Questions:

1. List and describe the three basic *Boolean operations* commonly used in computer geometric modeling software?

2. What is a *Primitive Solid*?

3. What does *CSG* stand for?

4. Which Boolean operation keeps only the volume common to the two solid objects?

5. What are the considerations in choosing the base feature of a solid model?

6. Using the CSG concepts, create *Binary Tree* sketches showing the steps you plan to use to create the two models shown on the next page:

Ex. 1)

Ex. 2)

Exercises: Create the following designs using the CSG approach.
Note: All Units are in inches.

1. (First feature: Create a circular plate Ø16.0x1.0)

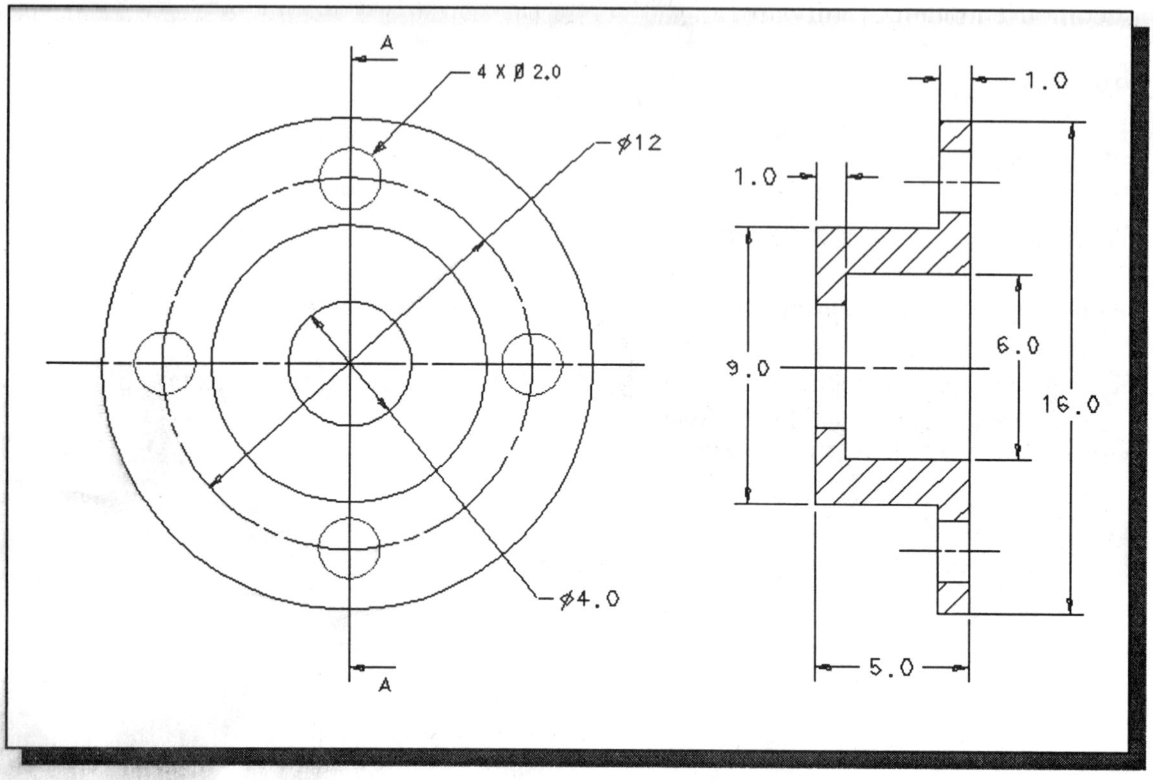

2. (First feature: Create a rectangular block 4.5x0.75x3.0)

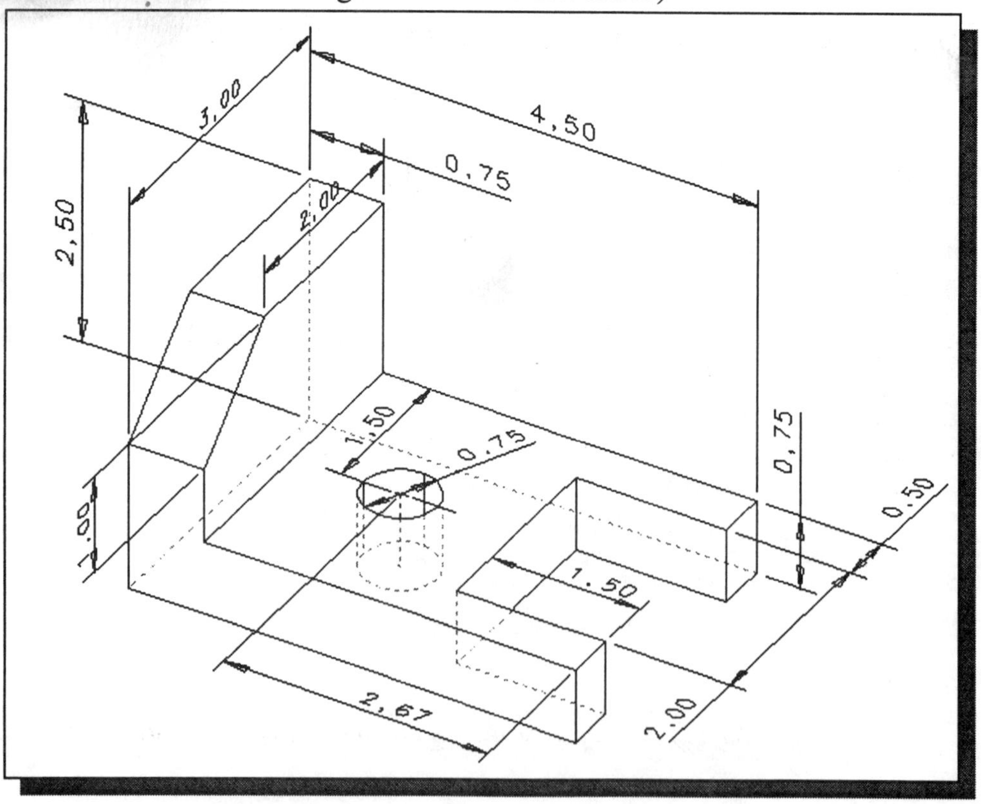

Chapter 4
Feature Relations – History Tree

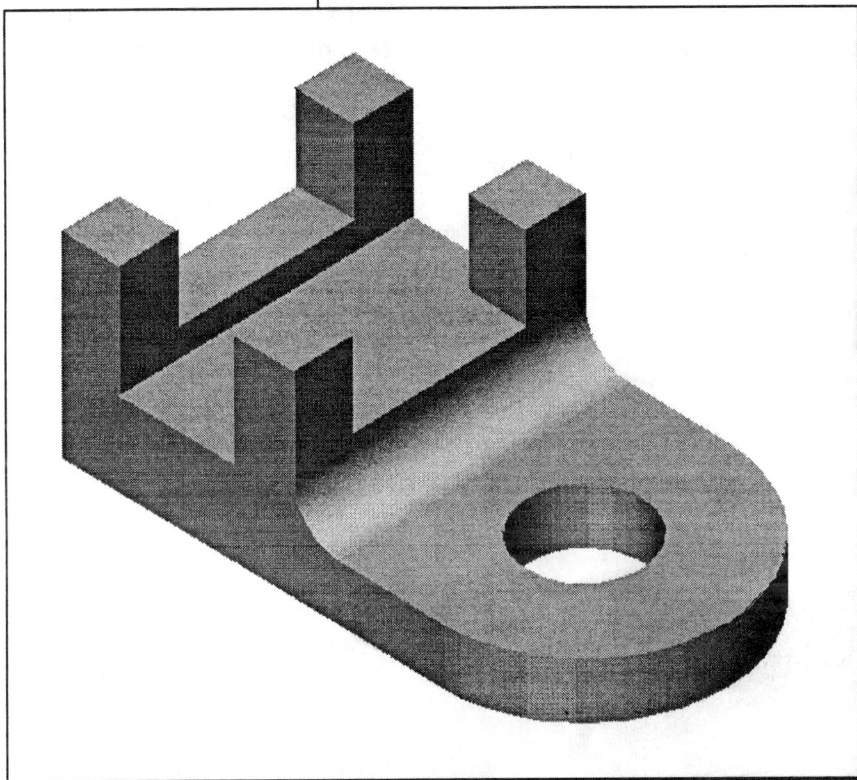

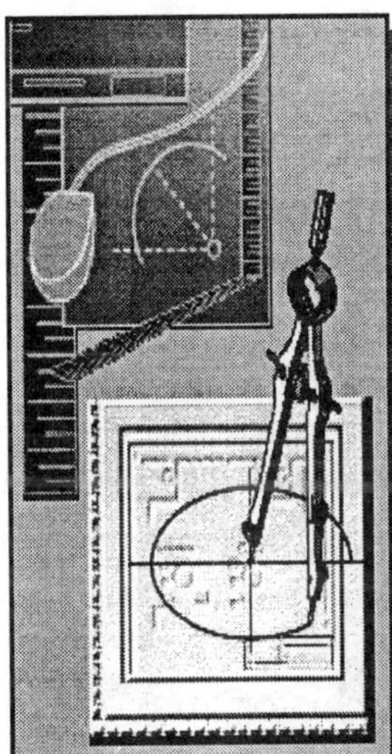

Learning Objectives

When you have completed this lesson, you will be able to:

- ♦ Understand Feature Relations.
- ♦ Use the History Tree Access Command.
- ♦ Modify and Update Dimensions.
- ♦ Perform History-Based Part Modifications.
- ♦ Use the Extrude options.
- ♦ Perform Basic Design Changes.

Introduction

In *I-DEAS*, the **design intents** are embedded into features in the **history tree**. The structure of the model history tree resembles that of a **CSG binary tree**. A CSG binary tree contains only *Boolean relations*, while the ***I-DEAS*** **history tree** contains all features, including *Boolean relations*. A history tree is a sequential record of the features used to create the part. This history tree contains the construction steps, plus the rules defining the design intent of each construction operation.

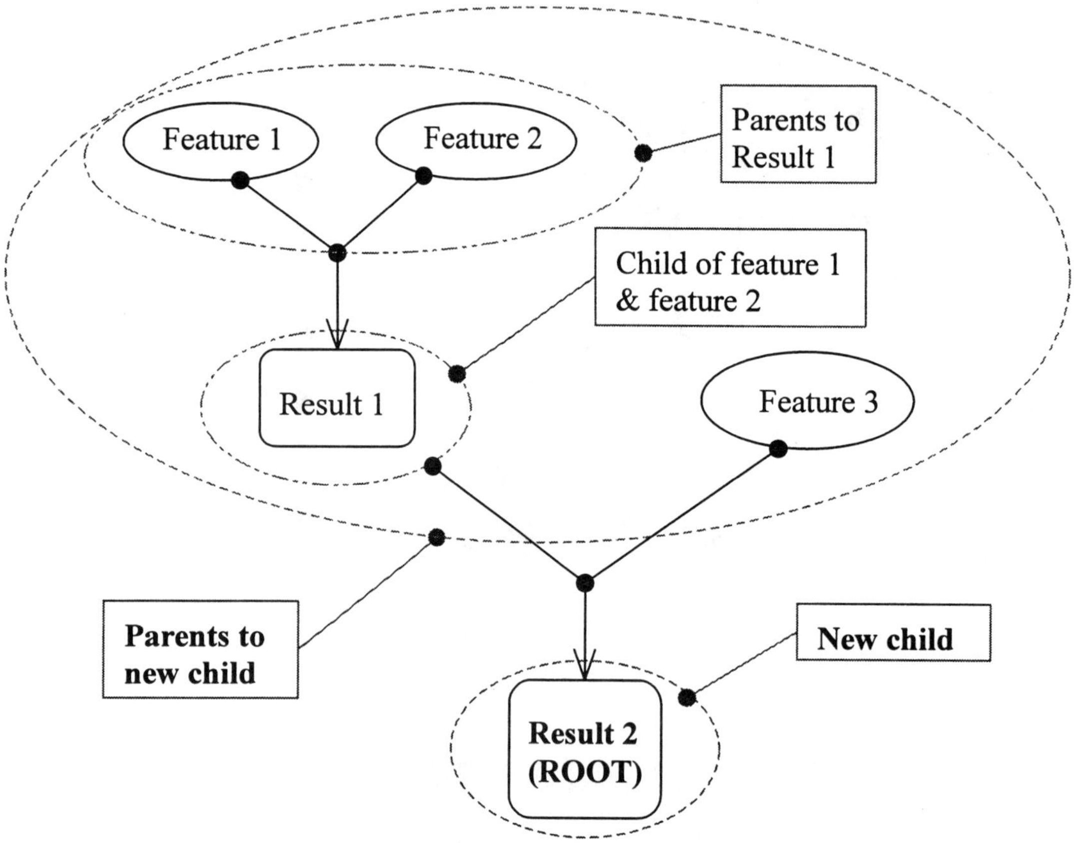

In a model history tree, each time a new modeling event is created, previously defined features can be used to define information such as size, location and orientation. The referenced features become **PARENT** features to the new feature, and the new feature is called the **CHILD** feature. The parent/child relationships determine how a model reacts when the features in the model change, thus capturing design intent. It is crucial to keep track of these parent/child relations. Any modification to a parent feature can change one or more of its children. It is therefore important to think about your modeling strategy before you start creating anything. It is also important to plan ahead for possible design changes that might occur and set up the parent/child relations accordingly. Part modification can be done by accessing the specific feature in the model history tree. Once the modification is completed, the model is updated by re-linking the rest of the history tree without building the model from scratch.

In *I-DEAS*, the model history tree gives information about modeling order as well as information about the feature. Part modifications can be accomplished very quickly by accessing the features in the history tree. It is therefore important to understand and utilize the feature history tree to modify designs. *I-DEAS* remembers the history of a part, including all the rules that were used to create it, so that changes can be made to any operation that was performed to create the part. In *I-DEAS*, to modify a feature, we access it by selecting the feature in the graphics window or in the **part history tree.** The model history tree is a major difference of **FEATURE-BASED CAD SOFTWARE**, such as *I-DEAS*, from previous generation CAD systems.

The Saddle Bracket Design

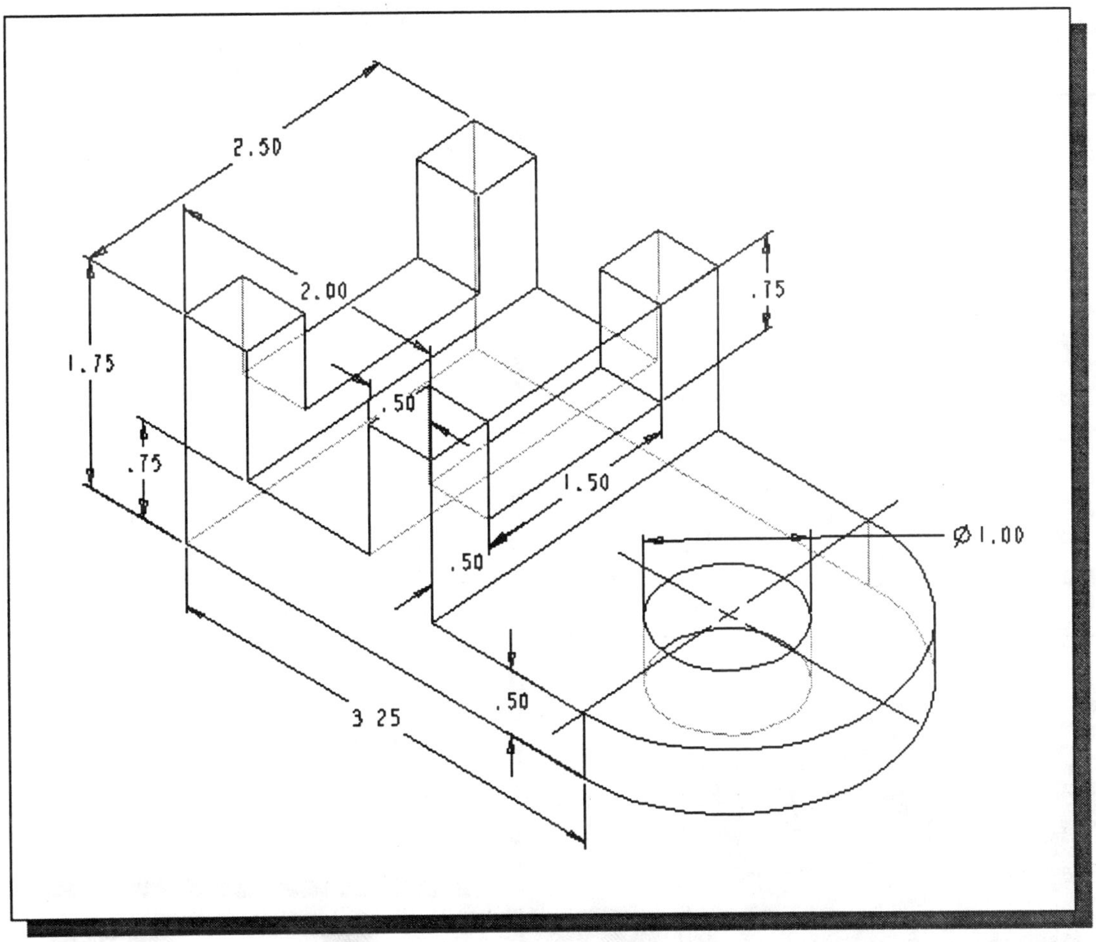

❖ Based on your knowledge of I-DEAS Master Modeler so far, how many features would you use to create the design? Which feature would you choose as the **BASE FEATURE**, the first feature, of the model? What is your choice for arranging the order of the features? Would you organize the features differently if additional features, such as fillets or chamfers, may be added in the design? Take a few minutes to consider these questions and do preliminary planning by sketching on a piece of paper. You are also encouraged to create the model on your own prior to following through the tutorial.

Modeling Strategy

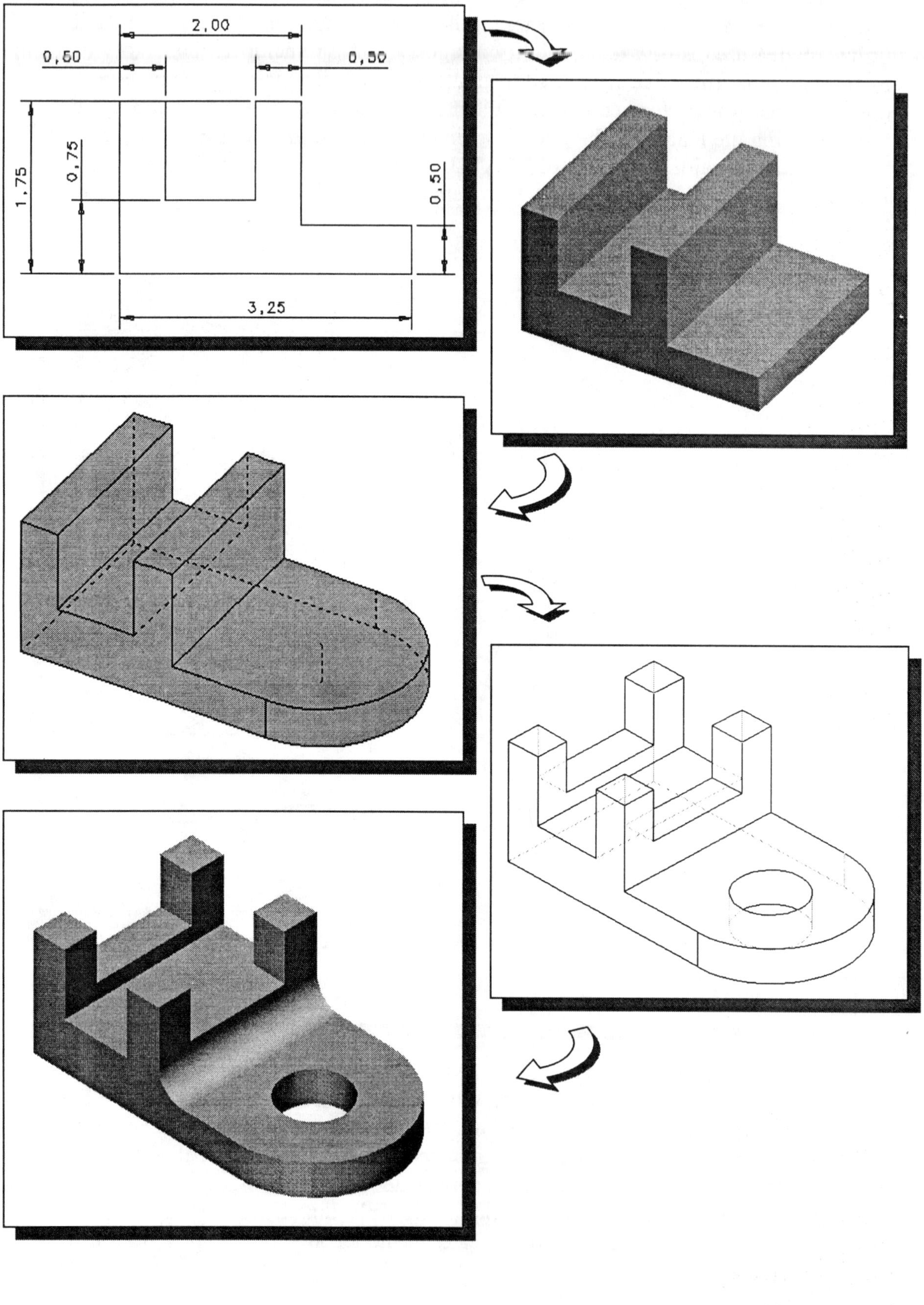

Starting I-DEAS

1. Select the *I-DEAS* icon or type "*ideas*" at your system prompt to start I-DEAS. The *I-DEAS Start* window will appear on the screen.

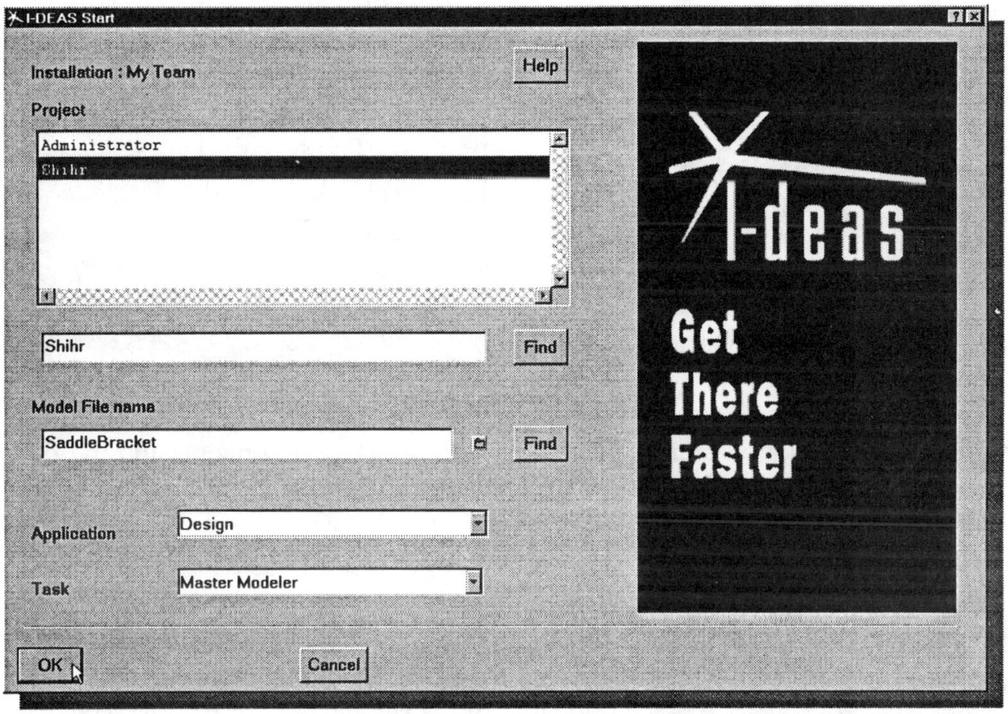

2. Start a new model file by filling in the items as shown below in the *I-DEAS Start* window:

Project Name: **(Your account Name)** Model File Name: **SaddleBracket** Application: **Design** Task: **Master Modeler** **OK**

3. After you click on the **OK** icon, a *warning window* will appear to tell you that a new model file will be created. Click **OK** to continue.

I-DEAS Warning
! New Model File will be created **OK**

❖ Next, I-DEAS will display four windows, the *graphics window*, the *prompt window*, the *list window*, and the *icon panel*. A line of *quick help* text appears at the bottom of the graphics window as you move the mouse cursor over the icons.

4. Use the left-mouse-button and select the **Options** menu in the icon panel.

5. Select the **Units** option.

6. Inside the graphics window, pick **Inch (pound f)** from the pop-up menu. The set of units is stored with the model file when you save.

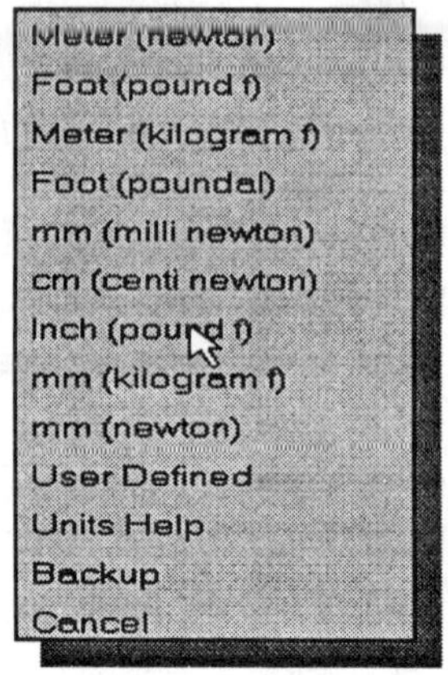

Base Feature

We will create the model by creating four solid features (CSG concept) and the first solid feature, the **base feature**, will be the bottom section of the model. Keep in mind that this selection is not necessarily the best selection and other choices are also feasible. We will first do a 2-D sketch to establish the base feature.

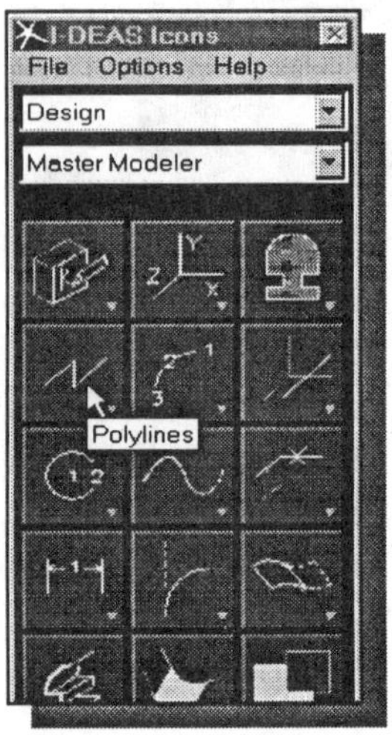

1. Pick **Polylines** in the icon panel. (The icon is located in the second row of the task specific icon panel.)

2. Start at the lower left corner and make a rough sketch as shown below. Create the sketch by following the design philosophy of "shape before size."

3. On your own, use the **Delete** and **Dimension** commands to create and place the dimensions as shown. Do not be overly concerned with the dimensional values; we will adjust the values in the next section.

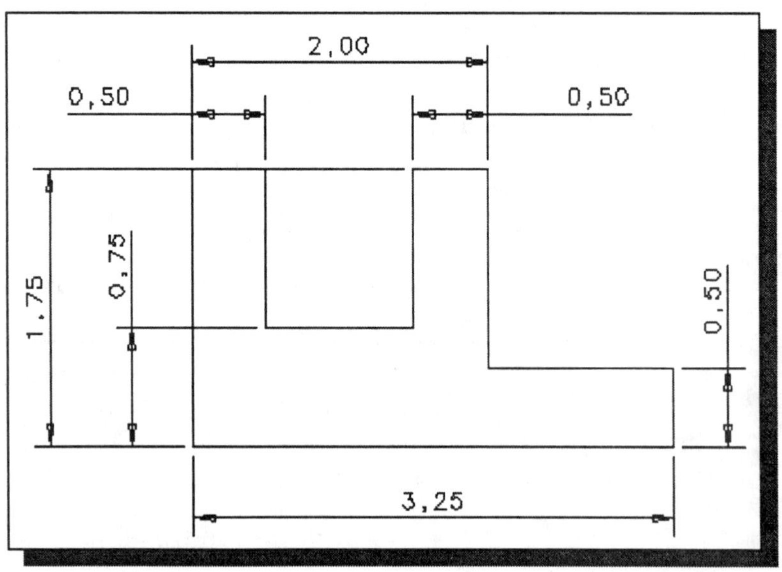

Modifying Dimensional Values

We will use the *Modify* command to adjust the dimensional values to the desired values.

1. Pre-select all the dimensions by holding down the **SHIFT** key and left-clicking on all of the displayed dimensional values. The selected items will be highlighted.

PRE-SELECT SHIFT + LEFT-mouse-button

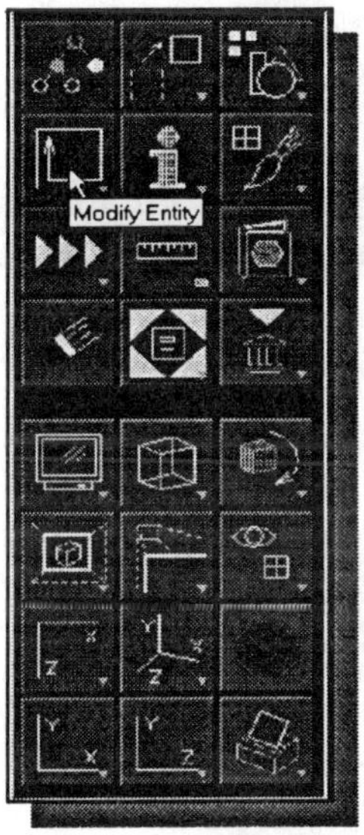

2. Choose **Modify** in the icon panel. The *Dimensions* window appears.

3. In the *Dimensions* window, change the values to the desired values by clicking and typing in the appropriate boxes. (Do not press the ENTER key.) Select from the list and enter the dimensional value in *the input box*.

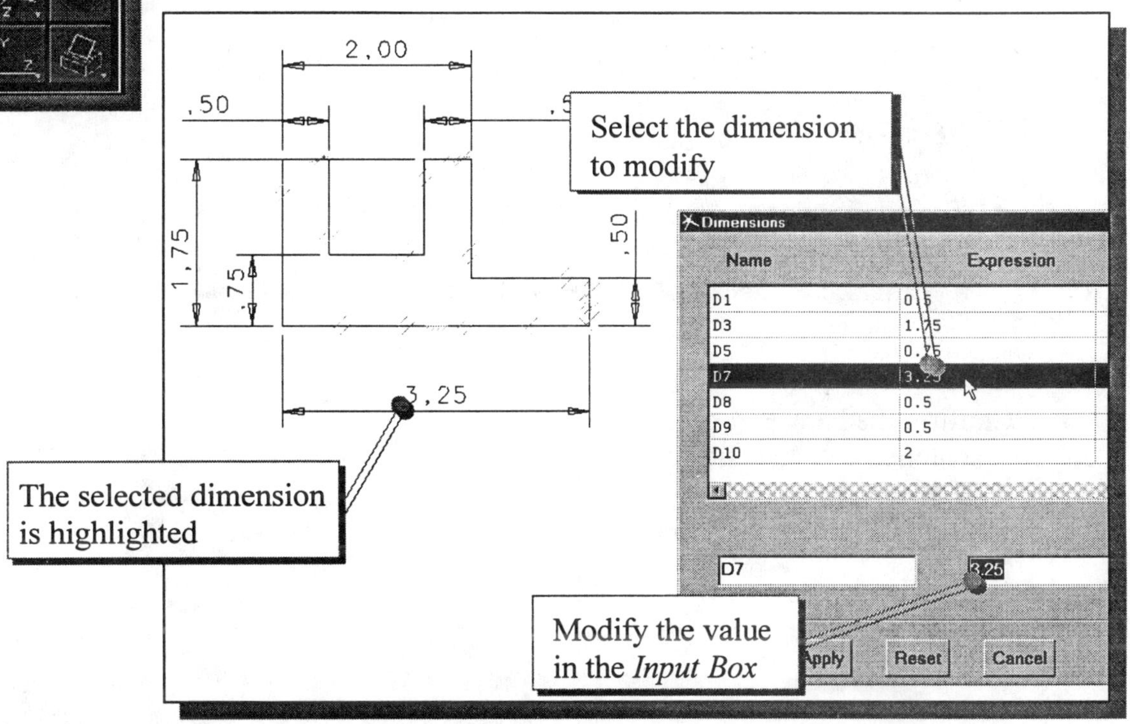

4. Click the **OK** icon to accept the values you have entered and I-DEAS will adjust the size of the object based on the new values.

5. Press the **ENTER** key or the **middle-mouse-button** to end the *Modify* command.

Extrusion

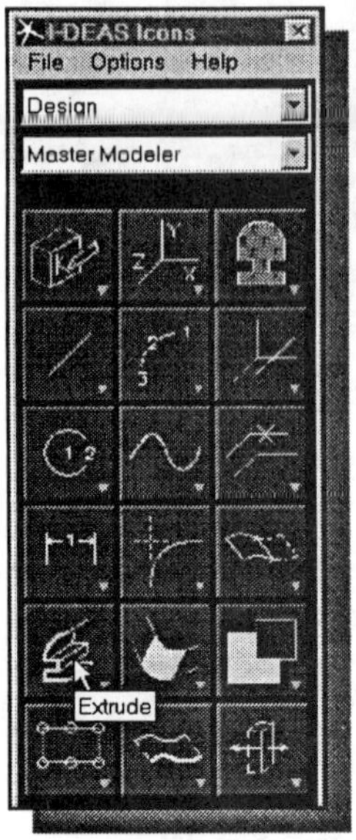

1. Choose **Extrude** in the icon panel. In the prompt window, the message "*Pick curve or section*" is displayed.

2. Pick any edge of the 2-D shape. By default, the *Extrude* command will automatically select all segments of the shape that forms a closed region.

3. Notice the I-DEAS prompt "*Pick curve to add or remove (Done).*" We can select more entities or deselect any entity that has been selected. Picking the same geometric entity will toggle the selected entity "on" or "off" with each left-mouse-button click. Press the **ENTER** key or the **middle-mouse-button** to accept the selected entities.

4. The *Extrude Section* window will appear on the screen. Enter **2.5** as the extrusion distance as shown below.

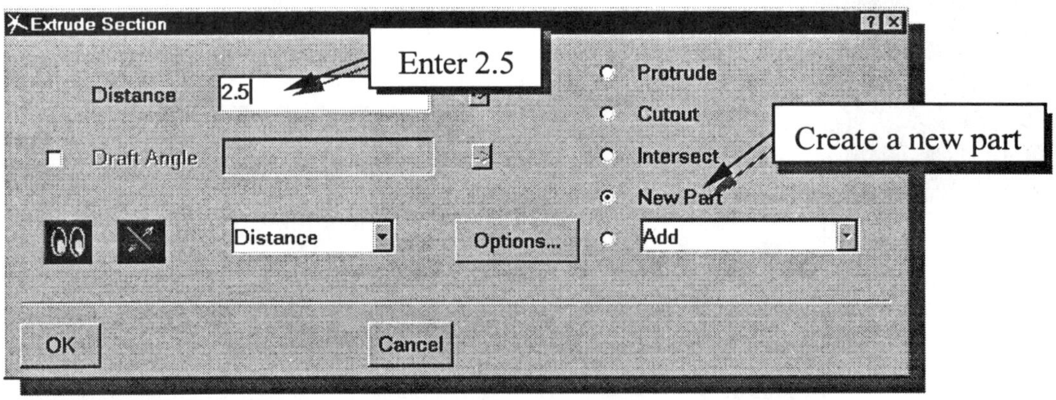

5. Confirm the New Part option is switched **ON** and click on the **OK** icon to accept the settings and create the solid feature.

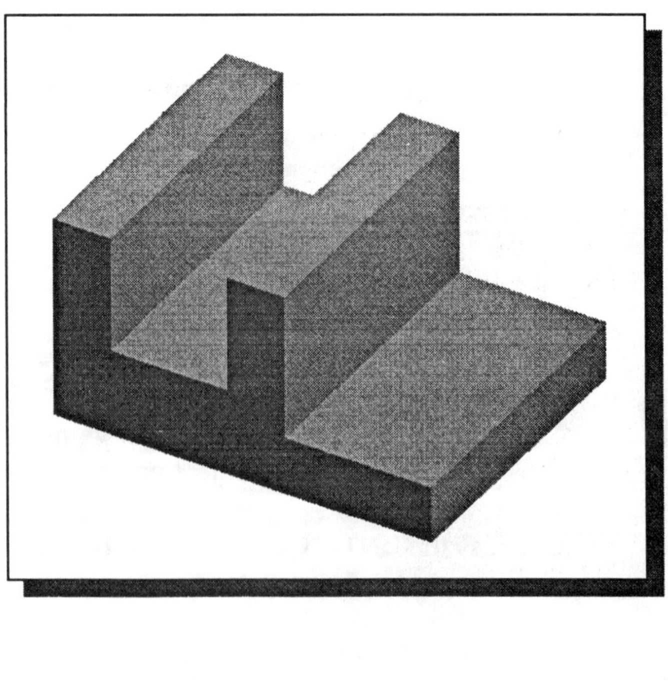

Add Additional Features

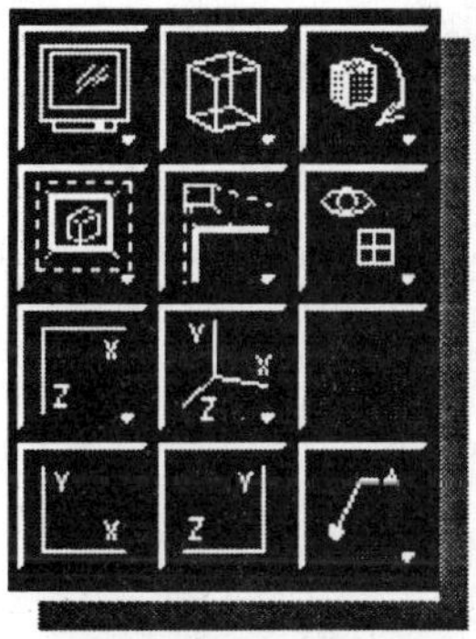
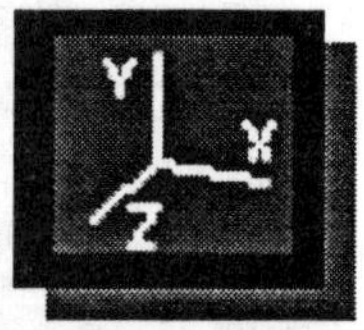

1. Choose **Isometric View** in the display viewing icon panel.

2. Choose **Zoom-All** in the display viewing icon panel.

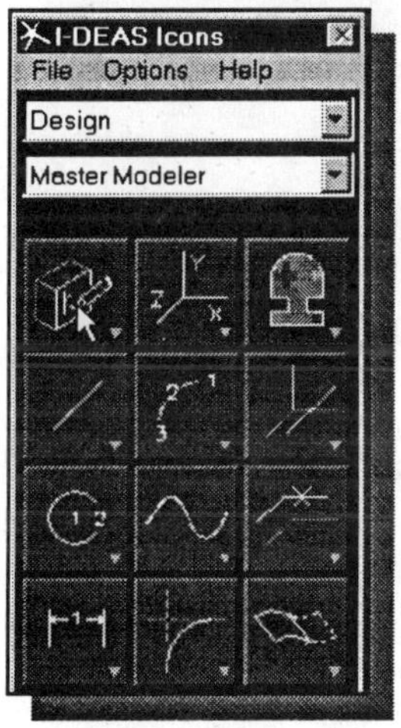

3. Choose **Sketch in Place** in the task specific icon panel. In the prompt window, the message "*Pick plane to sketch on*" is displayed.

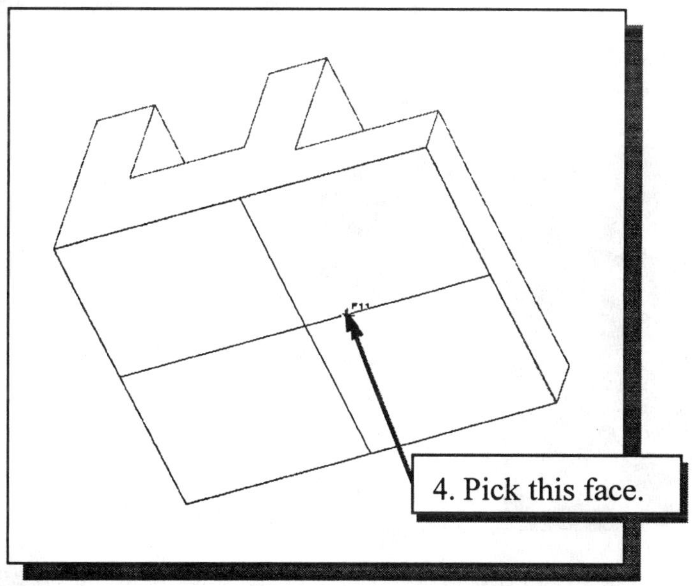

4. Pick the bottom horizontal surface of the 3-D model as shown.

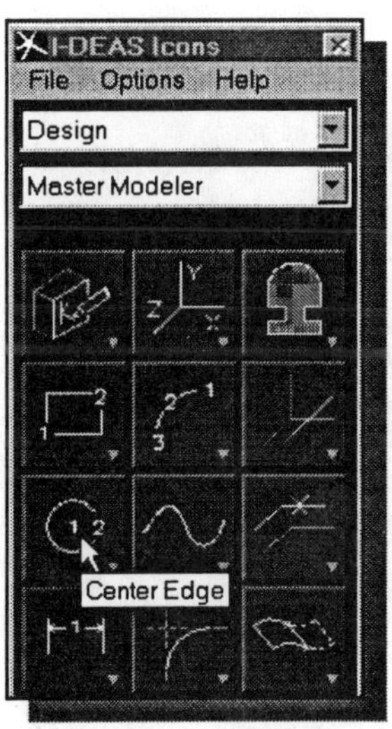

5. Choose *Circle* – **Center Edge** in the icon panel. This command requires the selection of two locations: first the location of the center of the circle and then a location where the circle will pass through.

6. Pick the midpoint of the right-edge of the bottom-surface when the alignment symbol is displayed as shown.

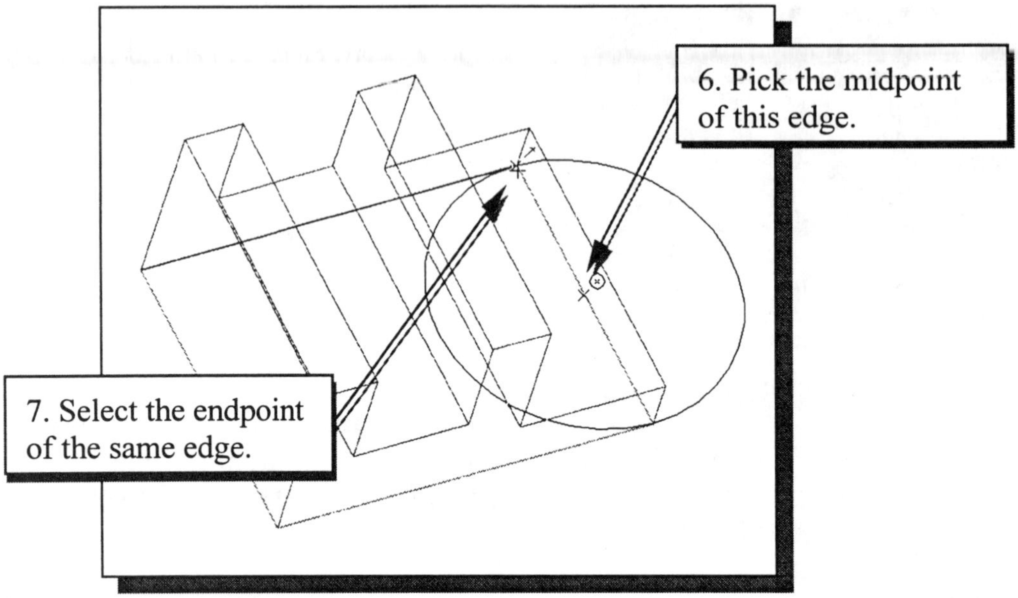

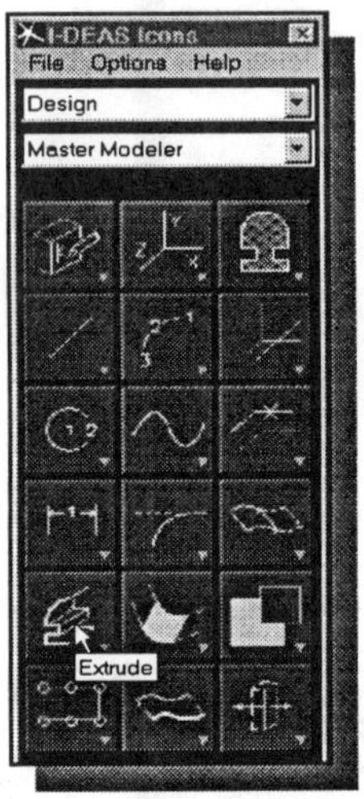

7. Pick the front endpoint of the same edge to create a circle.

8. Choose **Extrude** in the icon panel. In the prompt window, the message "*Pick curve or section*" is displayed.

9. Pick the circle we just created.

10. Press the **ENTER** key to accept the selected entity.

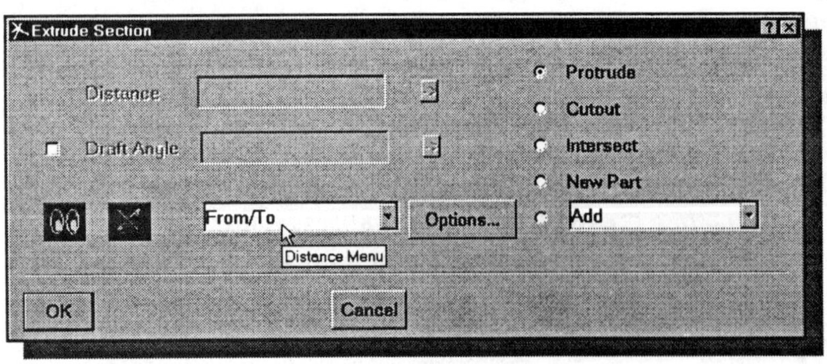

11. The *Extrude Section* window will appear on the screen. Select **From/To** in the *distance menu* as shown in the figure.

❖ The **From/To** option allows us to select the starting and ending references to calculate the extrusion distance.

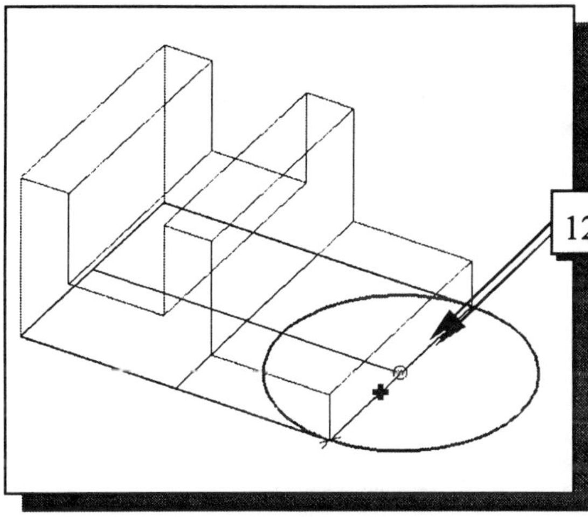

12. Select the bottom edge of the base feature as the starting reference as shown.

❖ Notice the bottom surface is highlighted and the graphics cursor changed shape indicating other selections are also feasible.

13. In the *prompt window*, the message "*Pick entity to extrude from (Accept)* **" is displayed. Press the **ENTER** key or the **middle-mouse-button** to accept the selection.

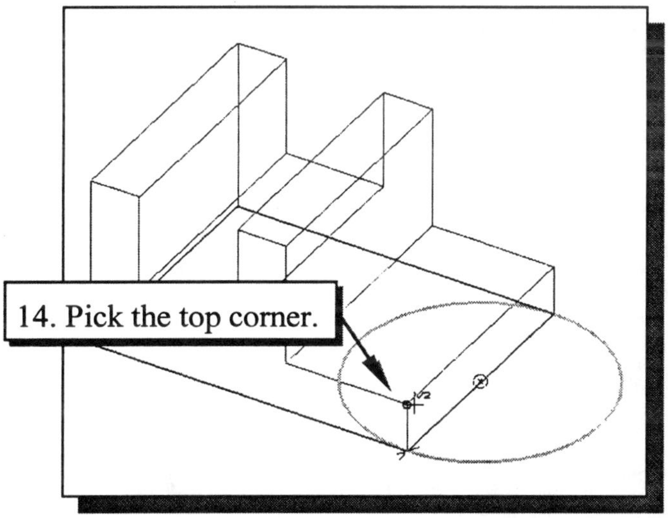

14. Select the top corner of the base feature as the ending reference to calculate the extrusion distance. (Note the **Vxx** symbol identifying the vertex.)

❖ Notice the selection was completed once we selected the top corner of the base feature.

15. Click on the **OK** button to create the solid feature.

❖ Now is a good time to save the model (Quick key: [**Ctrl**] + [**S**]). It is a good habit to save your model periodically, just in case something might go wrong while you are working on the model. You should also save the model after you have completed any major constructions.

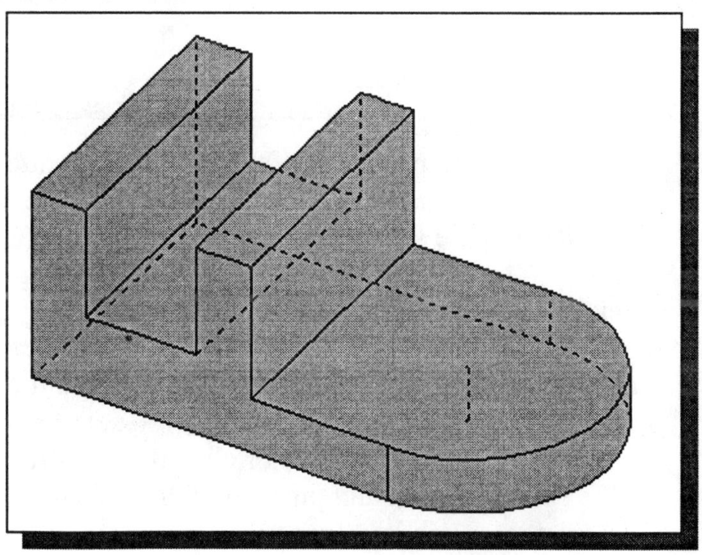

Examining the History Tree

1. Choose **Wireframe** in the icon panel. (The icon is located in the first row of the display icon panel.) Note that many of the history access options are only visible in wireframe display mode.

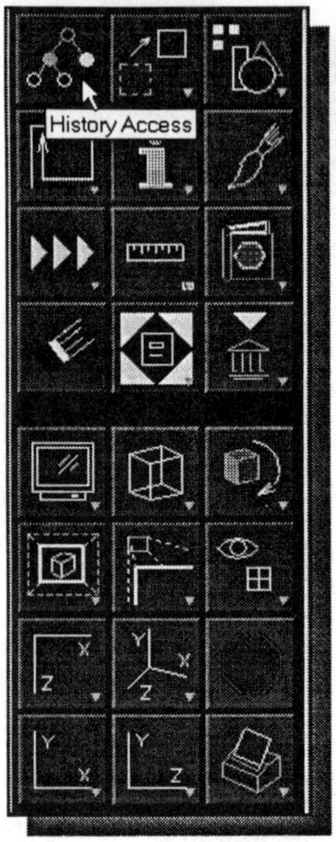

2. Choose **History Access** in the icon panel. (The icon is located in the first row of the application icon panel.)

3. In the *prompt window*, the message "*Pick part, feature or reference geometry*" is displayed. Select any edge of the solid model and notice a white bounding box around the part indicating the model is selected.

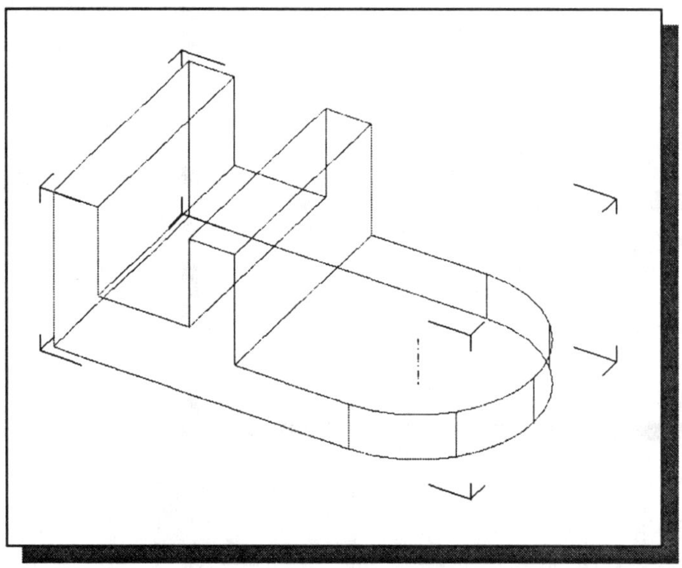

❖ In I-DEAS, multiple clicks of the left-mouse-button are used to access the part's **History Tree hierarchy**. The first click picks the Part (a white bounding box around the part), and the second click picks the Feature (a yellow bounding box around the feature). You can also pre-select prior to selecting the *History Access* icon. The first click picks Edge or Face (selection is highlighted), the second click picks the whole Part (a white bounding box around the part), and the third click picks the Feature (a yellow bounding box around the feature). Pick the part.

4. Press the **ENTER** key or click the **middle-mouse-button** to accept the selected item and proceed with the *History Access* command. The *History Access* window appears.

History Access Window

The *History Access* window contains:

- General part and feature information, such as names and characteristics.
- Status, such as suppressed and problem features.
- History, or how the part was created.

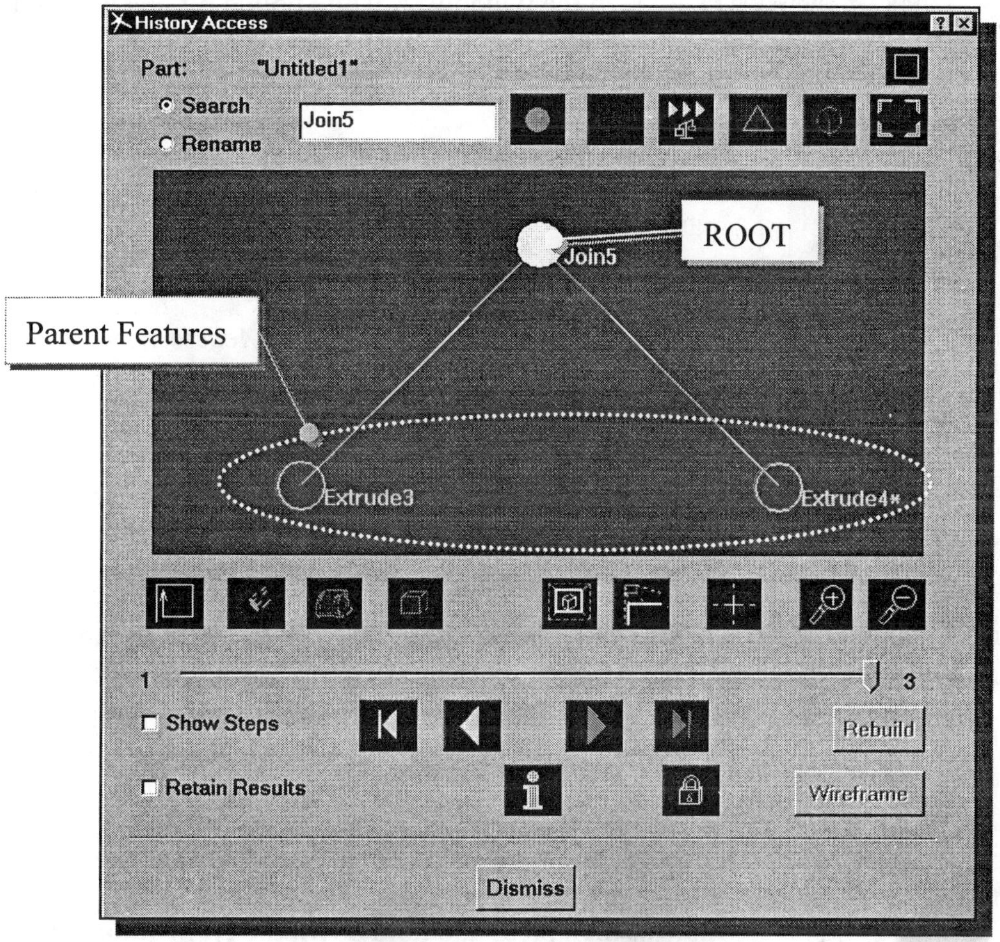

The top portion of the *History Access* window contains basic part and feature information. We can change the name of the selected feature by toggling on the *Rename* option and typing in the *Feature name* box.

The center of the *History Access* window is a graphical display of the History Tree of the selected part. Use the left-mouse-button (single click) to select different nodes, or press and drag the left-mouse-button to dynamically pan the History Tree display. The History Tree display also provides useful diagnostic information about the status of the model. The lines connecting nodes are normally green. Red and yellow lines denote errors and warnings on the step. A dashed-line indicates a suppressed feature. The History Tree can also be used to display one feature at a time to make sure that every feature is correctly dimensioned and constrained.

Currently, our model contains three nodes: two leaves and a root. The two leaves contain the geometry definitions and parameters of the two parent features: the extruded polyline sketch and the extruded circle.

1. Click on either node of the parent features and notice the selected feature is highlighted in the graphics window.

2. Click on the **ROOT** node in the window. A white bounding box around the part and the feature name (*Join5*) signify the part is the result of a *Boolean* operation that joins the two parent features (extruded shape and cylinder).

3. Switch on the **Show Steps** option. This option allows us to display the individual steps performed in creating the part.

4. Click on the **Fast Backward** button in the *History Access* window. The graphics window now displays only the "extruded shape" and the "cylinder block" has disappeared.

5. Click on the **Single Step Forward** button in the window. The 2D circle of the second feature appears on the screen. We have literally "gone back in time" to recreate the exact steps performed in creating the part.

6. Click on the **Single Step Forward** button again. The circle is extruded and the complete model reappears on the screen.

7. Click on the **Dismiss** button to exit the *History Access* window.

❖ If the part or any of its features is still highlighted (a white or yellow bounding box), move the cursor inside the graphics window, then press and hold down the **right-mouse-button** to select the **Deselect All** option.

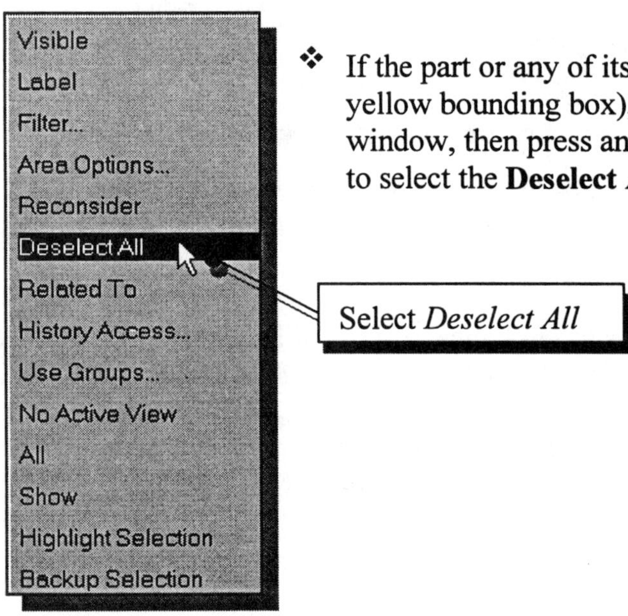

Rectangular CUT feature

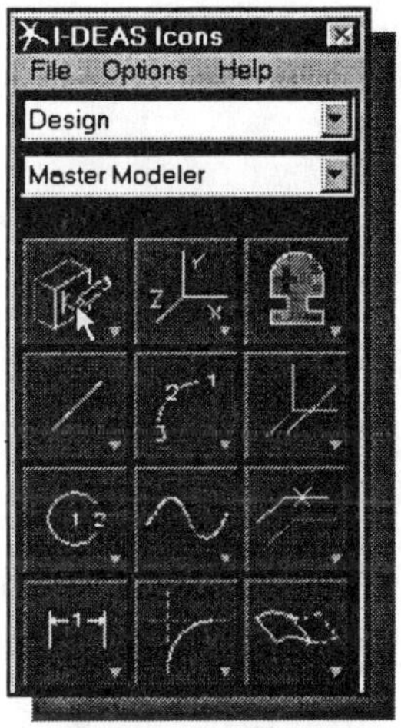

1. Choose **Sketch in Place** in the icon panel. In the prompt window, the message "*Pick plane to sketch on*" is displayed.

2. Pick the vertical face of the 3-D model as shown.

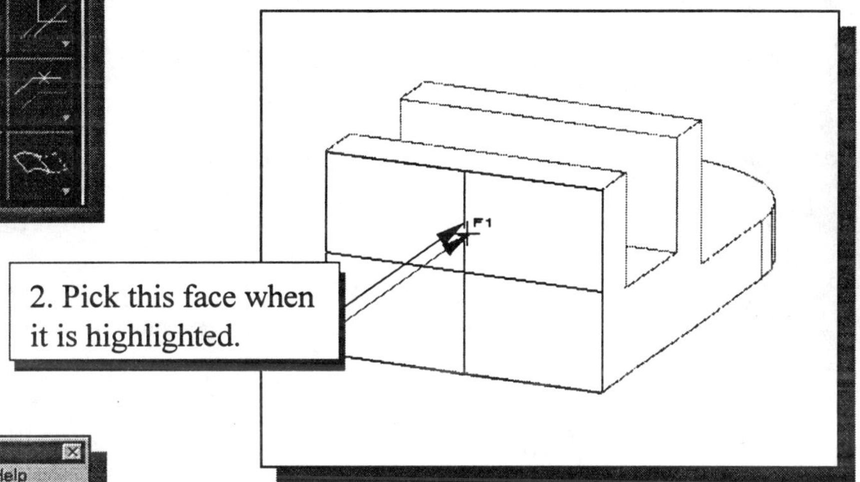

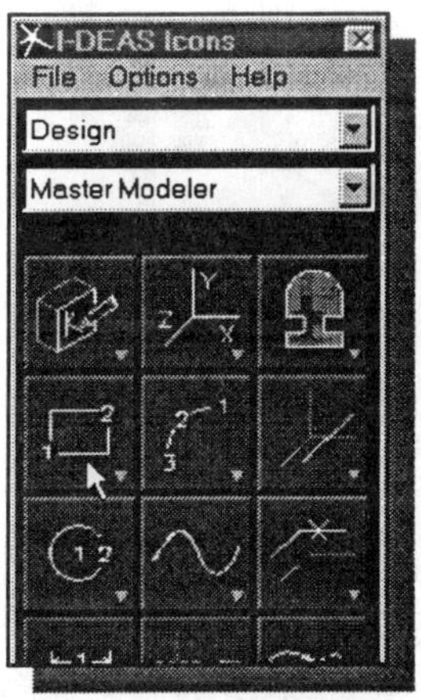

3. Choose **Rectangle by 2 Corners** in the icon panel. If the icon is not on top of the stack, press and hold down the left-mouse-button on the displayed icon to display all the choices. The message "*Locate first corner*" is displayed in the prompt window.

4. Pick the first corner along the top edge of the vertical face.

5. Move the cursor to the vicinity of the second corner and click the left-mouse-button to complete a rectangle of arbitrary size as shown.

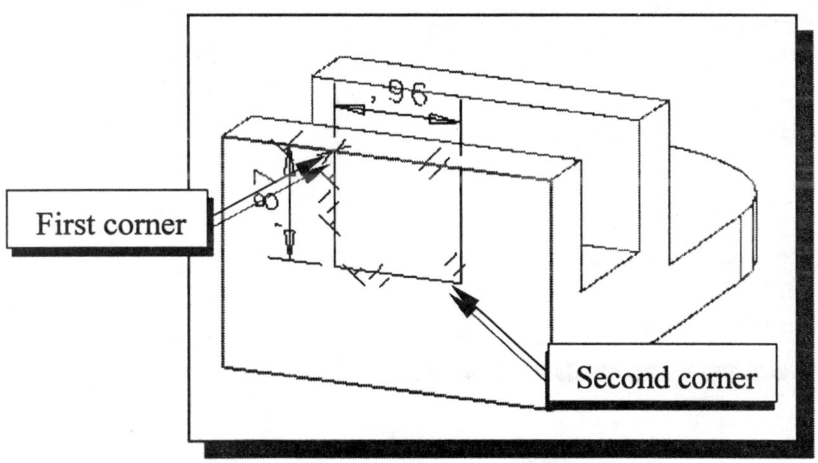

Adding a Location Dimension

The dynamic navigator automatically added size dimensions of the sketched rectangle; we will add a location dimension to position the rectangle.

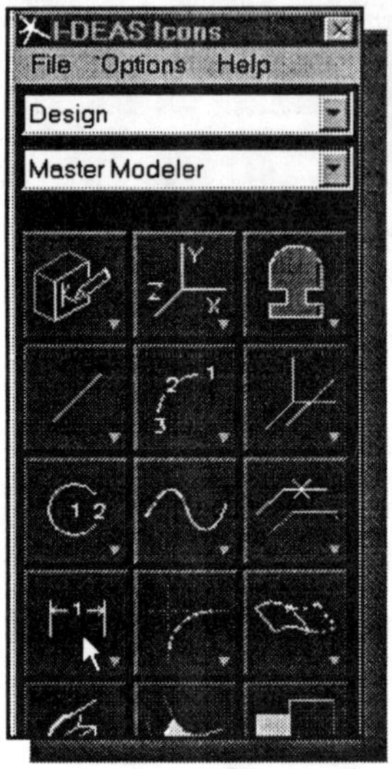

1. Choose **Dimension** in the icon panel. The message "*Pick the first entity to dimension*" is displayed in the prompt window.

2. Pick the top corner of the 2-D rectangle as shown. (Note the displayed corner symbol, CCXX.)

3. Pick the vertical edge of the solid object as shown.

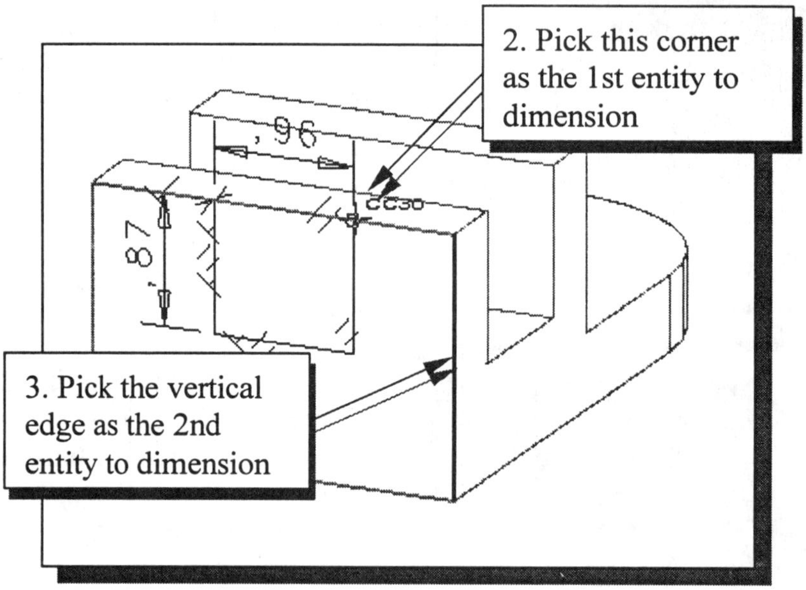

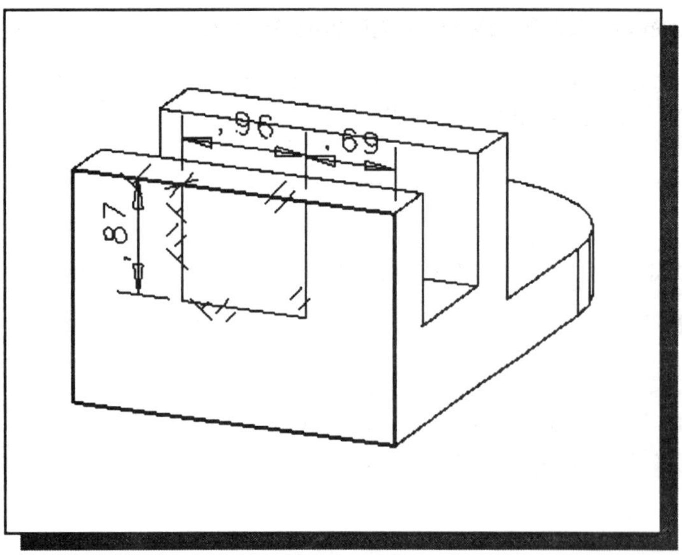

4. Position the dimension text above the par and press the left-mouse-button.

5. Press the **ENTER** key or click the **middle-mouse-button** to end the *Dimension* command.

Modify Dimensions

1. Pre-select all the dimensions by holding down the **SHIFT** key and left-clicking on all of the dimensional values. The selected items will be highlighted.

PRE-SELECT SHIFT + LEFT-mouse-button

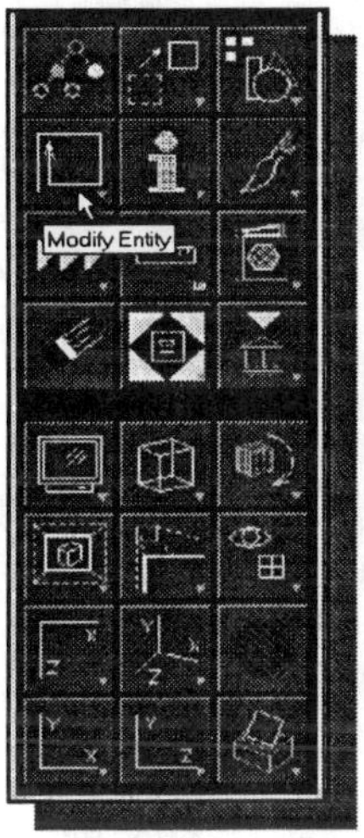

2. Choose **Modify** in the icon panel. The *Dimensions* window appears.

3. In the *Dimensions* window, change the values to the values shown in the below figure. (Do not press the **ENTER** key after each input). Select from the list and enter the dimensional value in the input box.

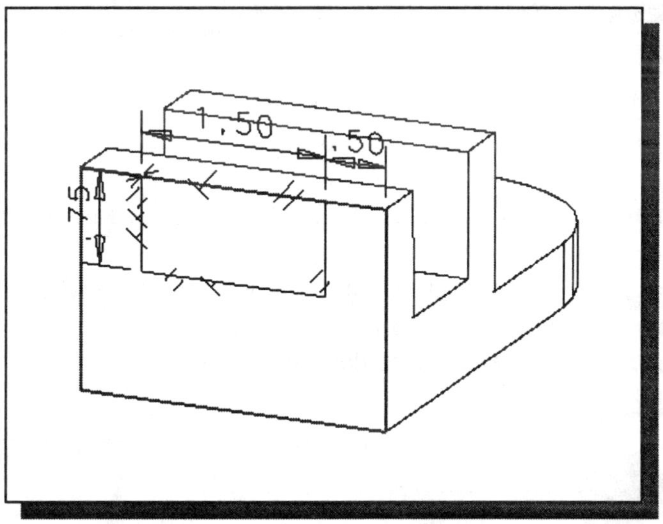

4. Click on the **OK** button to accept the values you have entered. I-DEAS will adjust the size of the object based on the new values.

Extrude - *Until Next* option

In I-DEAS Master Modeler, several options are available with the *Extrude* command. We will demonstrate the use of the *Until Next* option.

1. Choose **Extrude** in the icon panel. In the prompt window, the message "*Pick curve or section*" is displayed.

2. Pick the rectangle we just created. The selected rectangle is highlighted.

3. Press the **ENTER** key or the **middle-mouse-button** to accept the selected entity.

4. The *Extrude Section* window appears. Set the *extrude option* to **Cutout**.

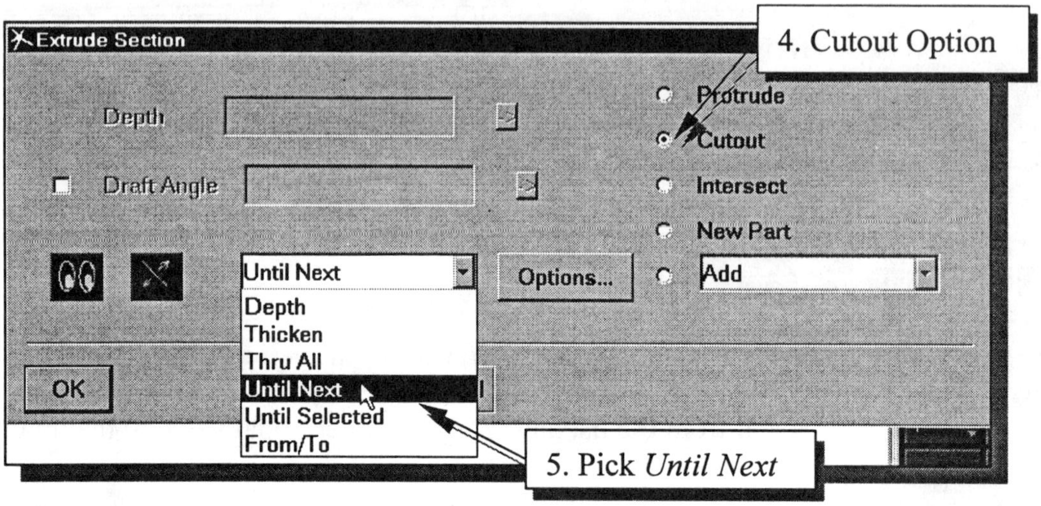

5. Select the **Until Next** option. I-DEAS will calculate the distance necessary to cut to the next surface of the part.

6. Click on the **OK** button to accept the settings and perform the cut.

7. Use the dynamic rotation function and the **Shaded** option to dynamically rotate and view the 3-D model. Reset the display to *wireframe* and *Isometric View* before continuing to the next section.

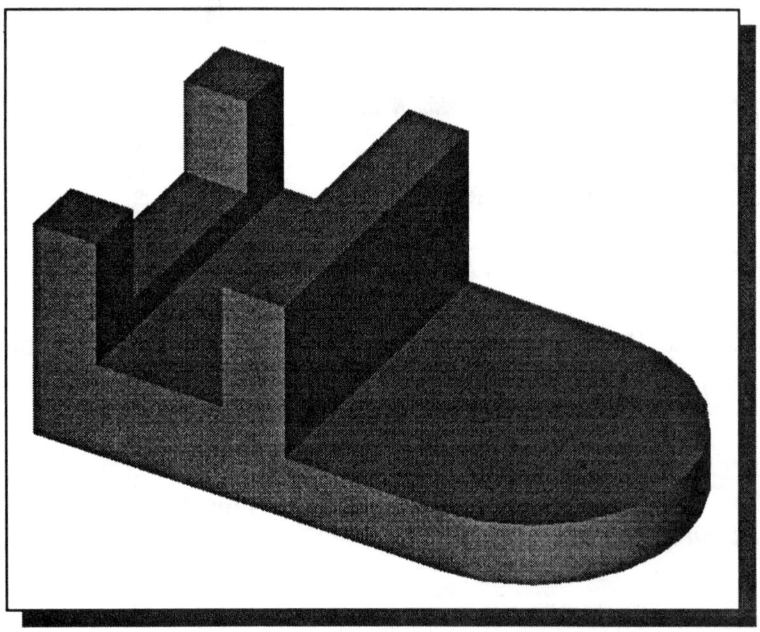

❖ Now is a good time to save the model (Quick key: [**Ctrl**] + [**S**]). It is a good habit to save your model periodically, just in case something might go wrong while you are working it. You should also save the model after you have completed any major constructions.

Create the next CUT Feature

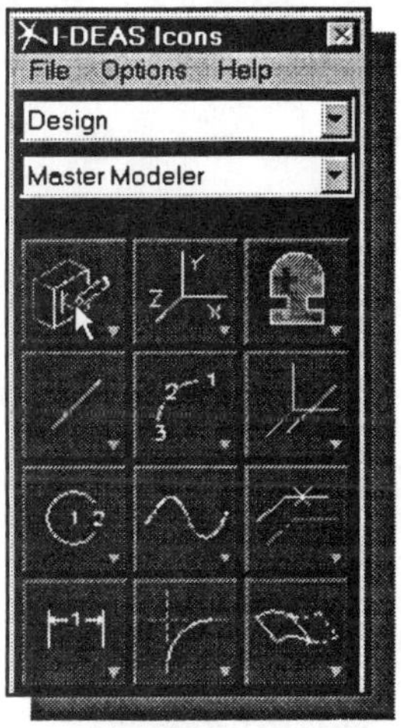

1. Choose **Sketch in Place** in the icon panel. In the prompt window, the message "*Pick plane to sketch on*" is displayed.

2. Pick the bottom surface of the 3-D object as shown.

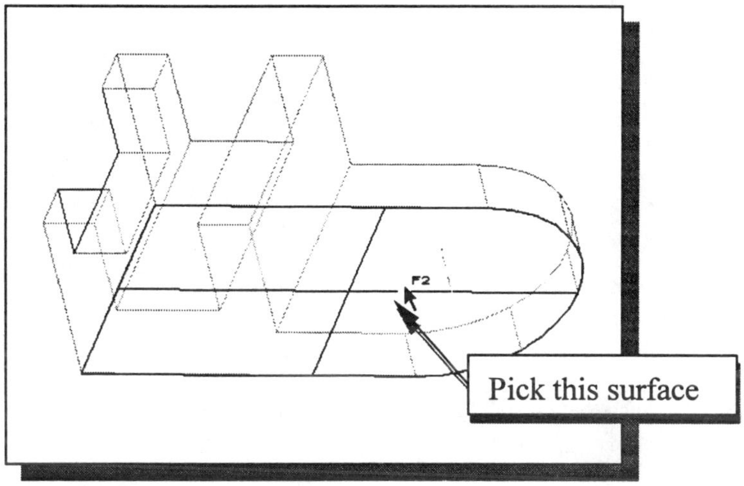

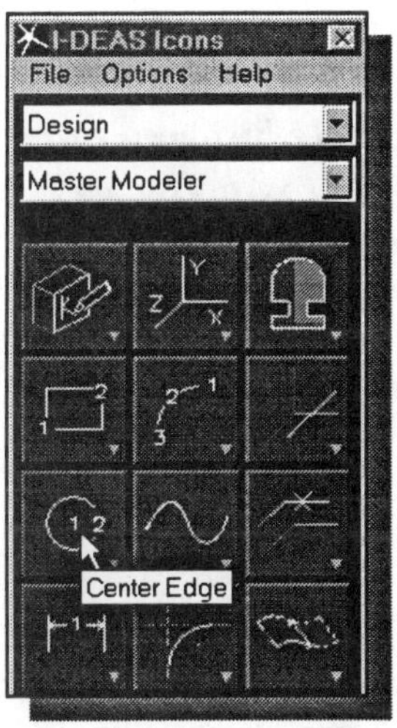

3. Choose *Circle* – **Center Edge** in the icon panel.

4. Pick the center of the arc on the highlighted workplane. Before completing the sketch of the circle, proceed to next step.

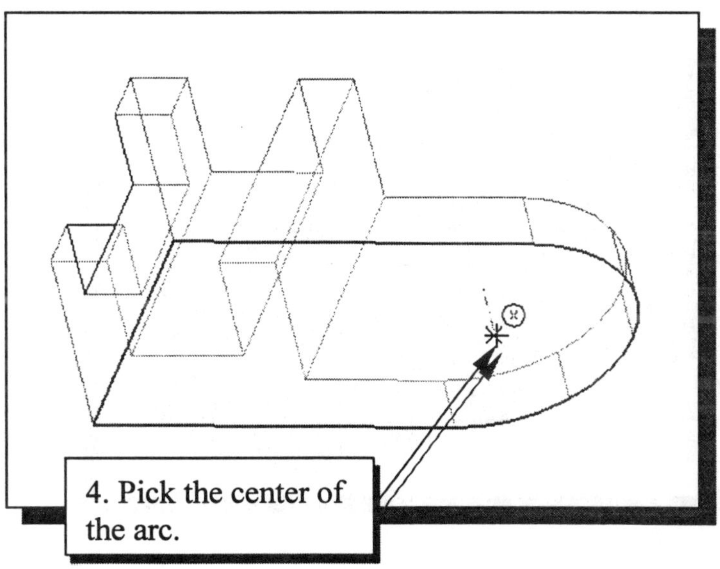

5. Move the cursor inside the graphics window, press and hold down the right-mouse-button. Pick **Options...** in the Option menu. The *Circle by Center and Edge Options* window appears.

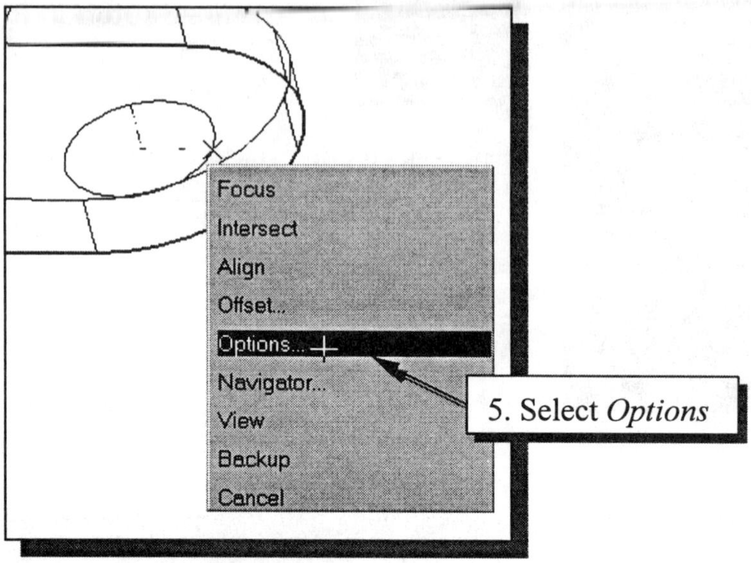

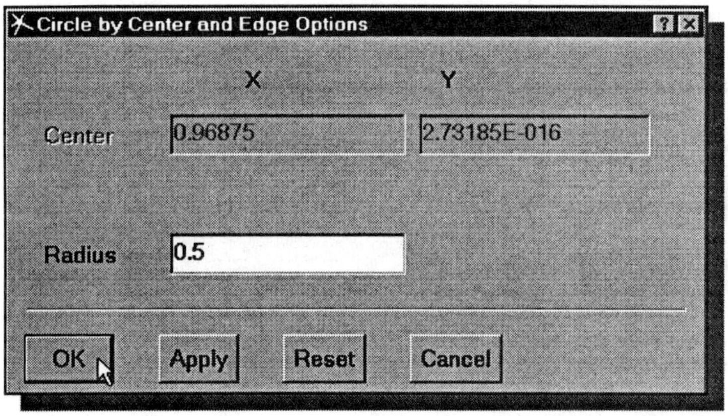

6. Enter the radius of **0.5** in the *Radius* box.

7. Click on the **OK** button to exit the *Circle by Center and Edge Options* window and create the circle.

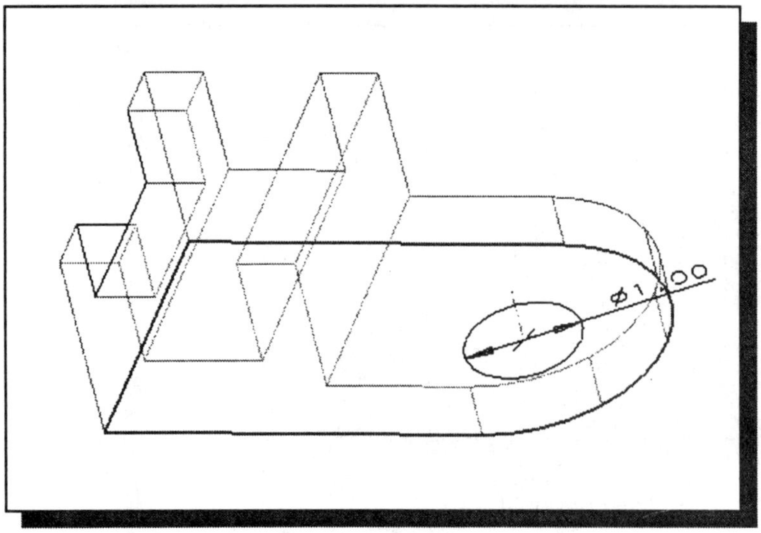

8. Press the **ENTER** key or click the **middle-mouse-button** to exit the *Circle By Center and Edge* command.

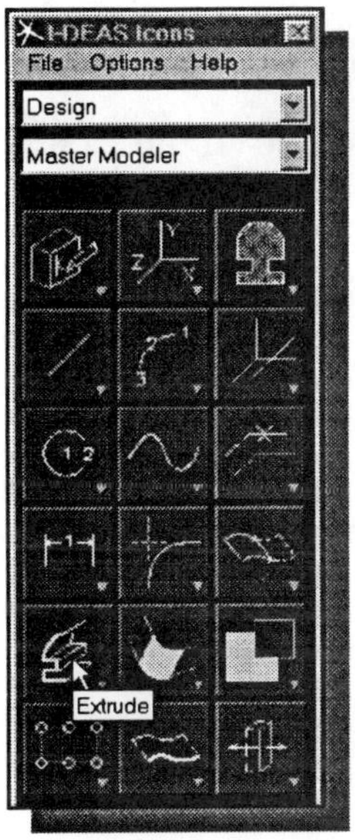

9. Choose **Extrude** in the icon panel. In the prompt window, the message "*Pick curve or section*" is displayed.

10. Select the circle we just created.

11. Press the **ENTER** key or the **middle-mouse-button** to accept the selected entity.

12. In the *Extrude Section* window, select the **Cutout** option.

13. In the Depth menu select the **Thru All** option.

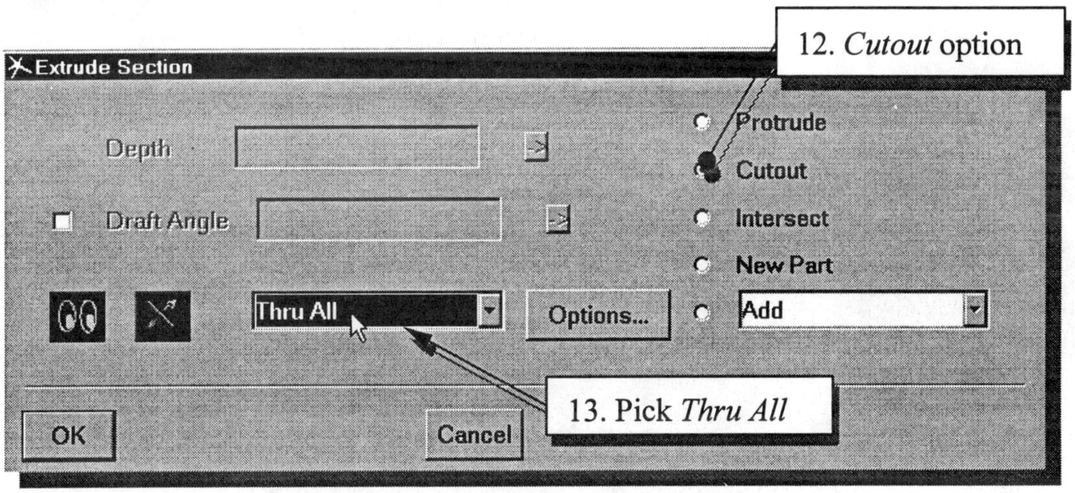

14. Click on the **OK** button to proceed with the cutout.

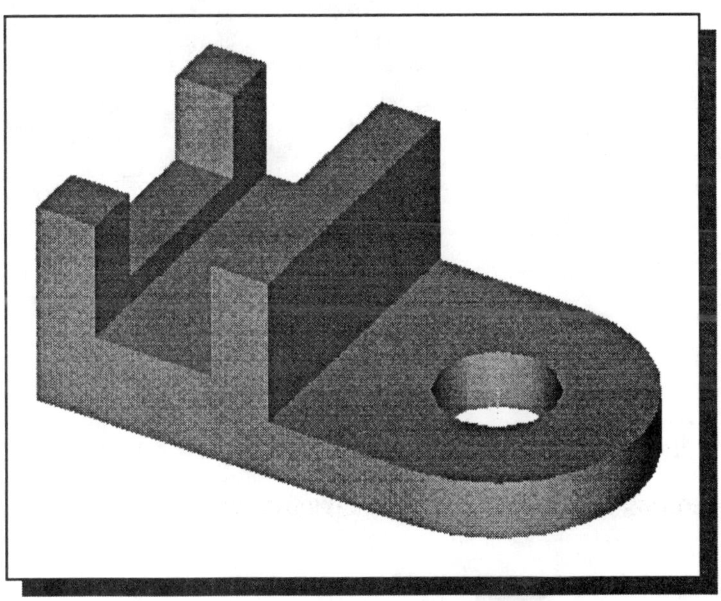

Examining the History Tree

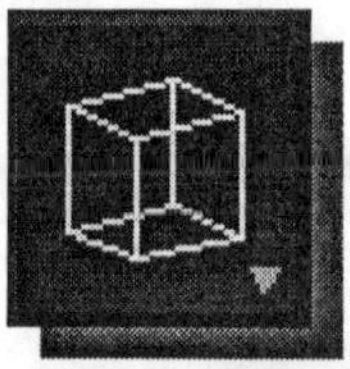

1. Choose **Wireframe** in the icon panel. (The icon is located in the first row of the display icon panel.)

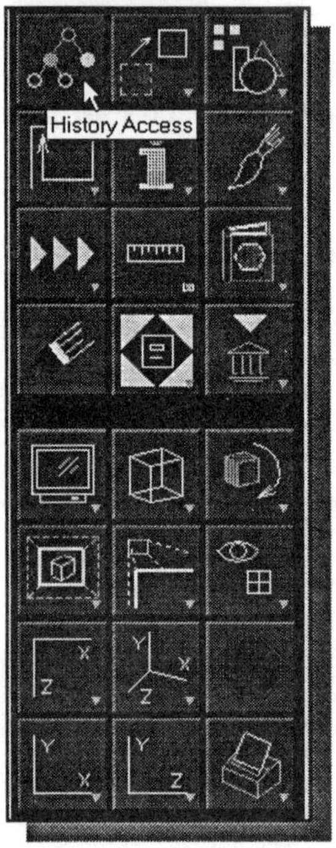

2. Choose **History Access** in the icon panel. (The icon is located in the first row of the application icon panel.)

3. Pick any edges of the 3-D model.

4. Press the **ENTER** key or the **middle-mouse-button** to accept the selection.

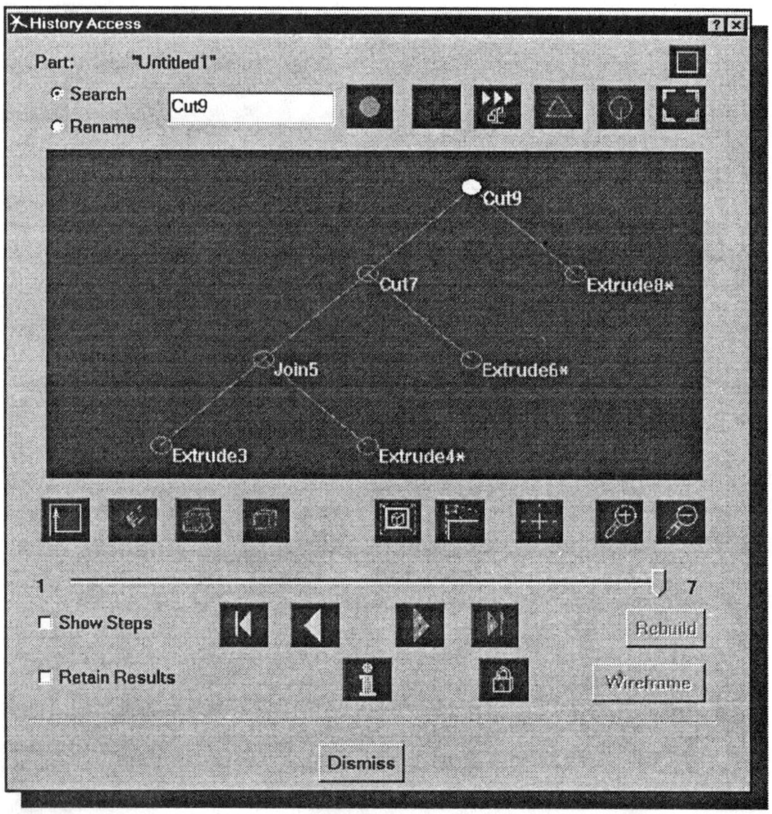

❖ Note that the history has grown with the added *Extruded* features and *Cut* features.

History-based Part Modifications

The I-DEAS Master Modeler uses the *history-based part modifications* approach, which enables us to make modifications to the appropriate features in the history tree and re-link the rest of the history tree. We can think of it as going back in time to modify some aspects of the modeling steps used to create the solid model. We can modify any feature that we have created. We can change feature dimensions; we can flip the direction of an extrusion or change an extrusion from *cutout* to *protrude*; we can also insert, delete, and reorder features.

1. Turn on the **Show Steps** option.

2. Click the **Single Step Backward** button. The corresponding feature, which is the circular extrusion, is highlighted in the graphics window.

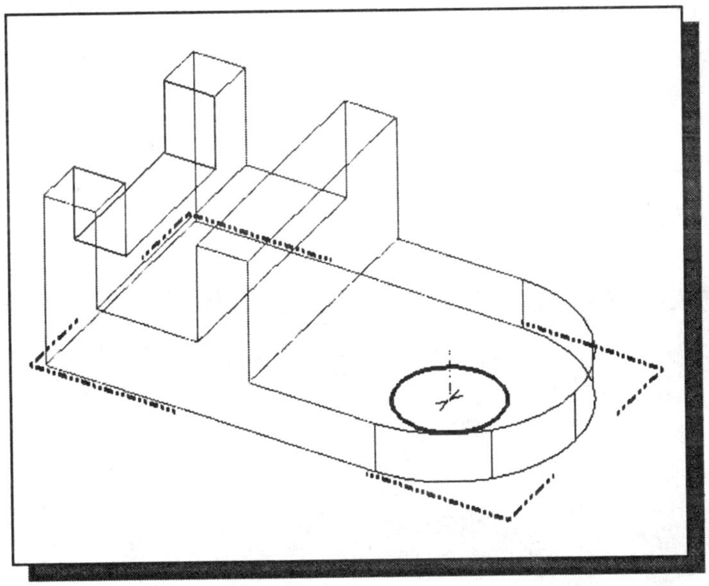

3. On your own, reposition the *History Access* window and reposition the model on the screen for better viewing of the features.

4. Click the **Single Step Backward** button again. The circular cutout disappears and a white bounding box around the rectangular cutout is displayed.

5. Click the **Single Step Backward** button again. The sketched 2-D rectangle is highlighted in the graphics window.

6. Click on the **Modify** icon in the *History-Access* window.

7. Pick **Feature Parameters** in the pop-up menu. This selection opens the *Extrude Section* window. We will modify the depth of the cutout to cut through the entire model.

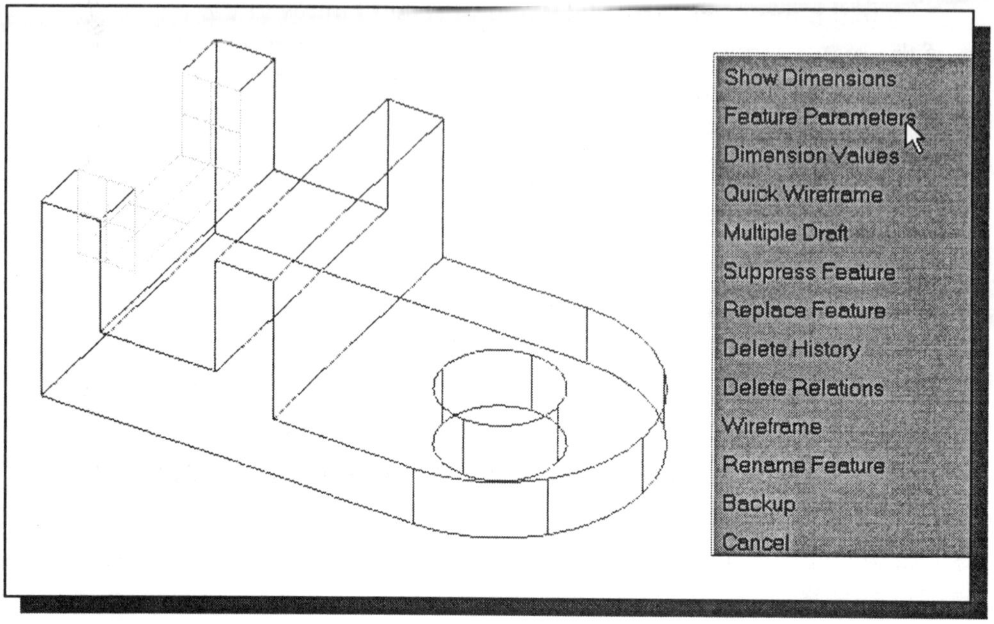

8. In the *Extrude Section* window, click and hold on the *Until Next* button. From the list select the **Thru All** option.

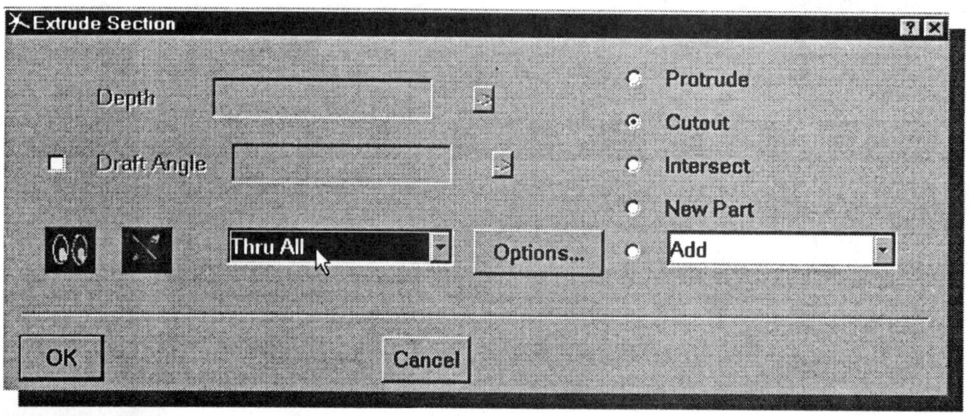

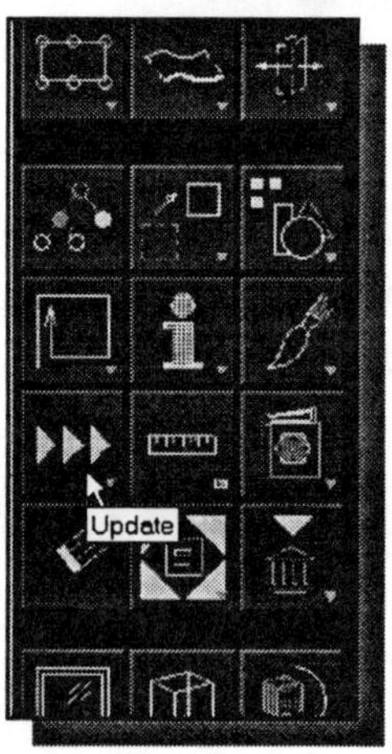

9. Click on the **OK** button to accept the settings and exit the *Extrude Section* window.

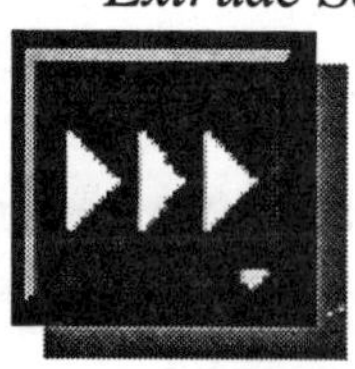

8. Pick **Update** in the icon panel. (The icon is in the third row of the *application specific icon panel*.) I-DEAS will rebuild the model by re-linking through the *Model History Tree*. The model should appear as shown on the next page.

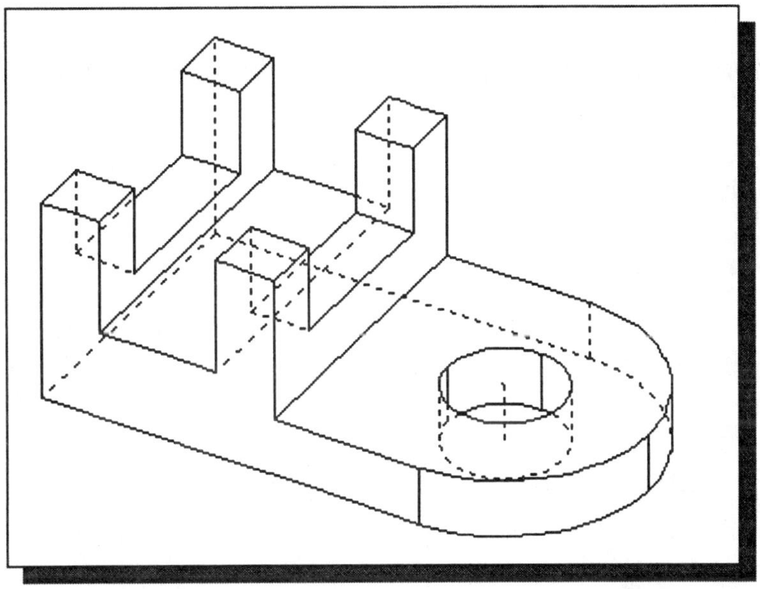

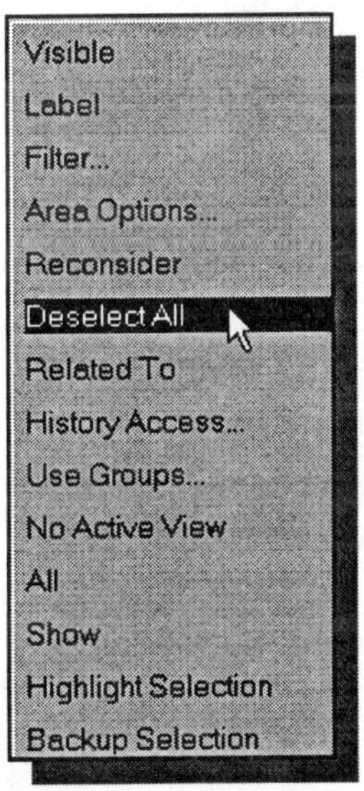

9. The rectangular cut feature is still highlighted (a yellow bounding box). Move the cursor inside the graphics window, then press and hold down the right-mouse-button to select the **Deselect All** option.

❖ Now is a good time to save the model (Quick key: [**Ctrl**] + [**S**]). It is a good habit to save your model periodically, just in case something might go wrong while you are working it. You should also save the model after you have completed any major constructions.

A Design Change

Engineering designs usually will go through many revisions and changes. I-DEAS provides an assortment of tools to handle design changes quickly and effectively. We will demonstrate some of the tools available by changing the base feature of the design.

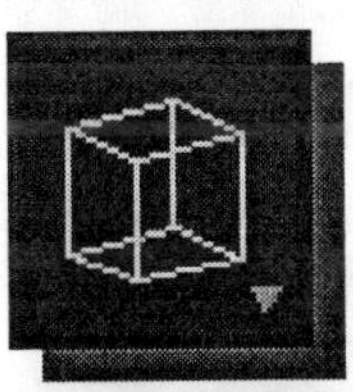

1. Choose **Wireframe** in the icon panel. (The icon is located in the first row of the display icon panel.)

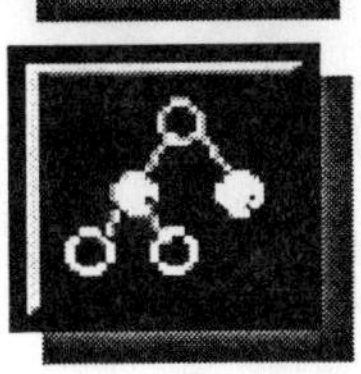

2. Choose **History Access** in the icon panel.

3. Pick any edge of the part.

4. Press the **ENTER** key or the **middle-mouse-button** to accept the selection.

5. Turn on the **Show Steps** option.

6. Click on the **Fast Backward** button in the *History Access* window. The graphics window now displays only the first "extruded shape."

7. Pick **Modify** in the *History Access* window.

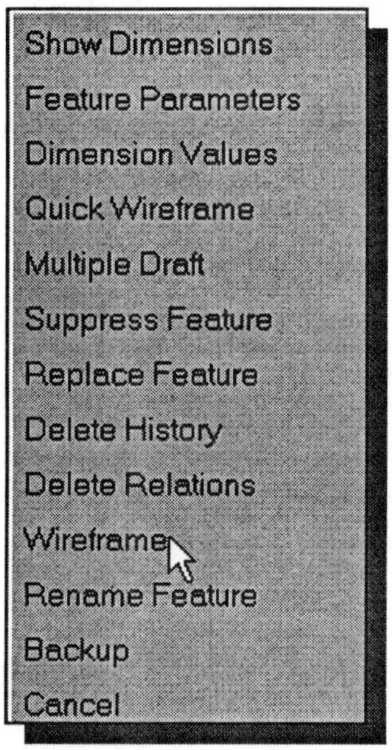

8. Pick **Wireframe** in the *Option* menu.

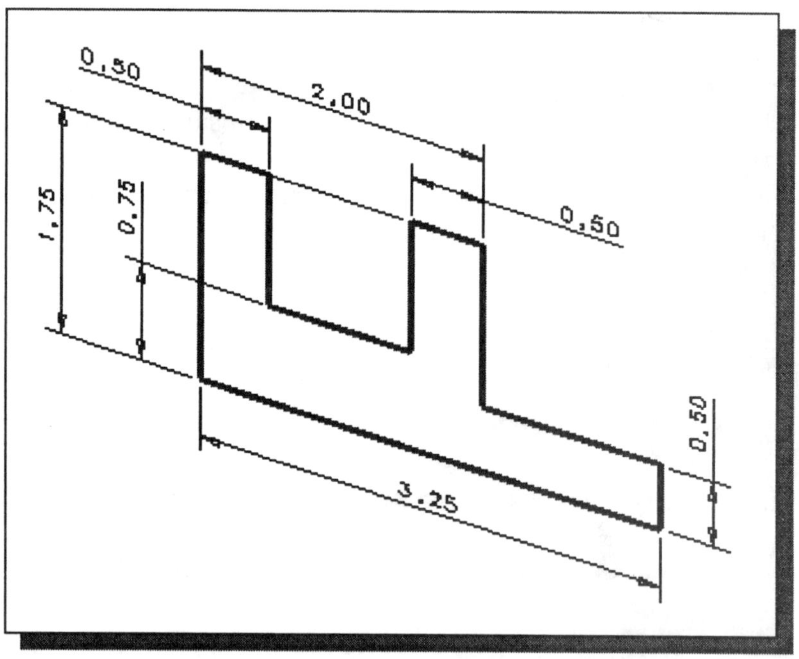

❖ The original 2-D sketch of the base feature is displayed in the graphics window. We have literally gone back in time and any modifications we make to the original sketch will be reflected in the final model. We will change one of the dimensional values and add a fillet at one of the corners. (Instructions for making the changes are included on the following pages.)

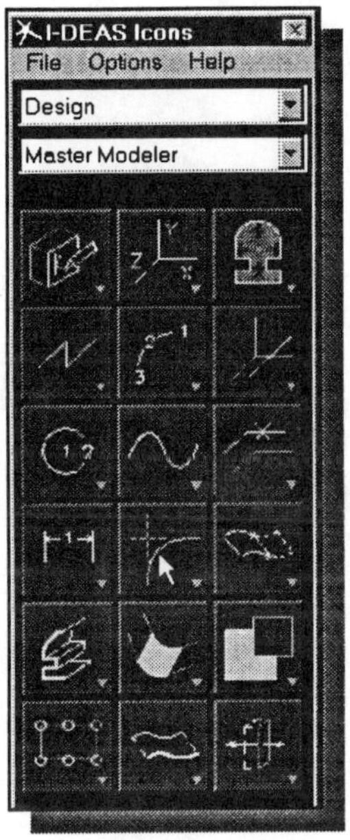

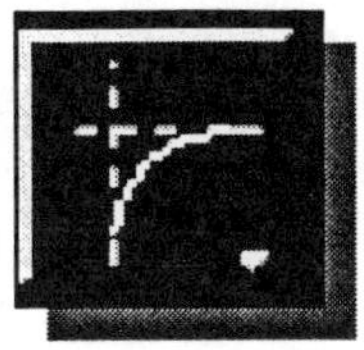

9. Choose two-dimensional **Fillet** in the icon panel. The message "*Pick section, curve or corner to fillet*" is displayed in the prompt window.

10. Pick the corner as shown in the figure (note the displayed **CCXX** symbol.) The *Fillet* window opens and a fillet appears on the part.

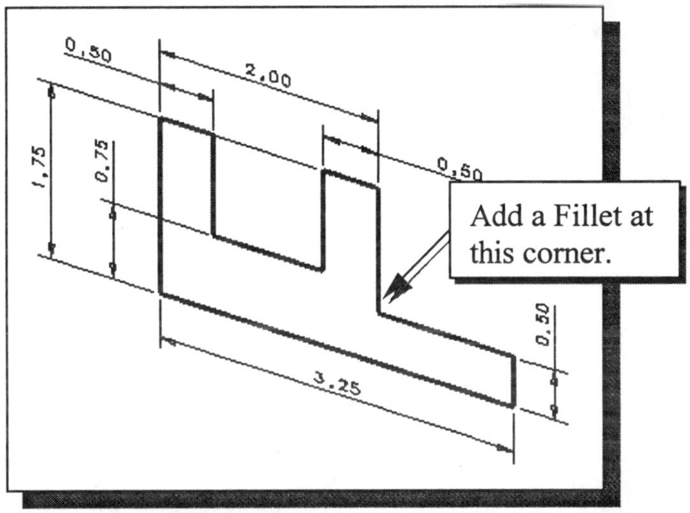

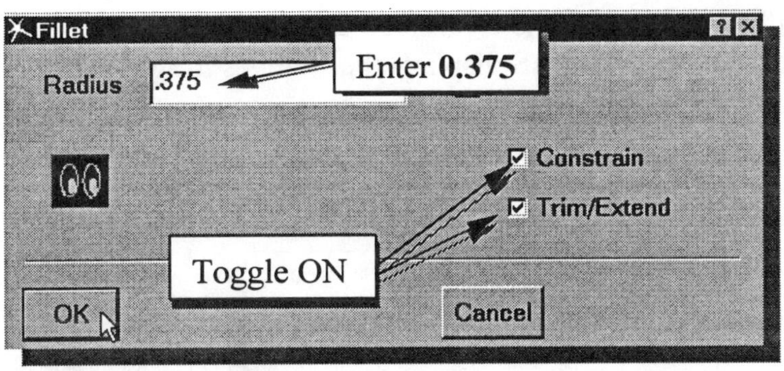

11. In the *Fillet* window, enter **0.375** as the radius. Also confirm the *Constrain* and *Trim/Extend* options are turned on.

12. Click on the **OK** button to create the fillet.

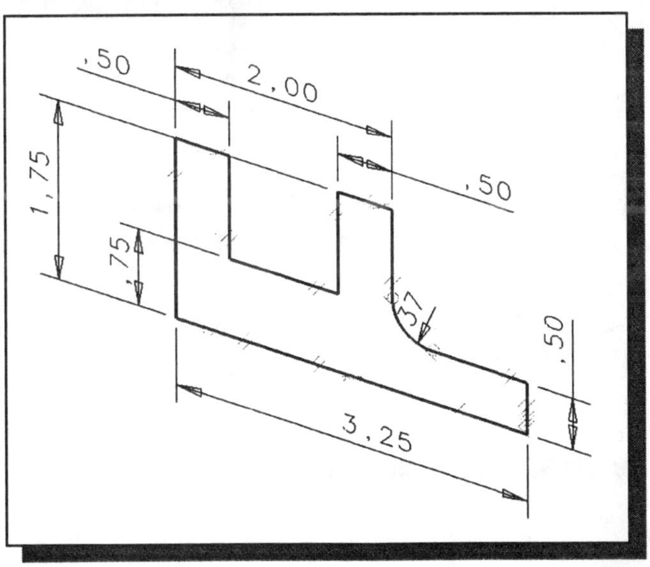

13. Press the **ENTER** key or click the **middle-mouse-button** to end the *Fillet* command.

14. Pick **Modify** in the application specific icon panel.

15. Select the overall height dimension and modify it to **2.0** in the usual manner.

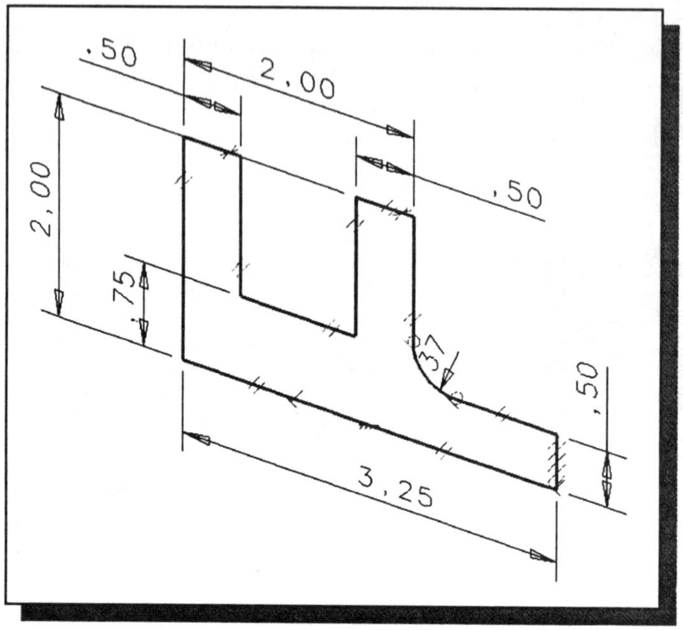

16. Pick **Update** in the icon panel. (The icon is in the third row of the application specific icon panel.) The "extrusion feature" of the 2-D sketch will be updated first. I-DEAS displays the changes in two separate windows.

17. The *updated feature* is displayed in the graphics window; the original model is also displayed.

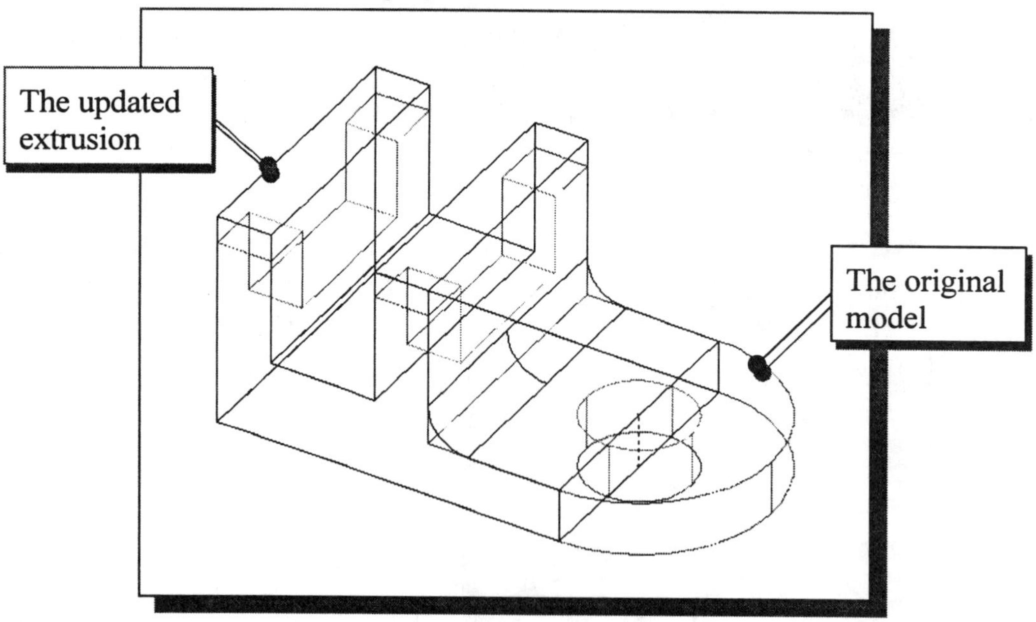

18. Pick **Update** again. The system will now rebuild the part, by re-linking the features in the *History Tree*, with the updated extrusion feature.

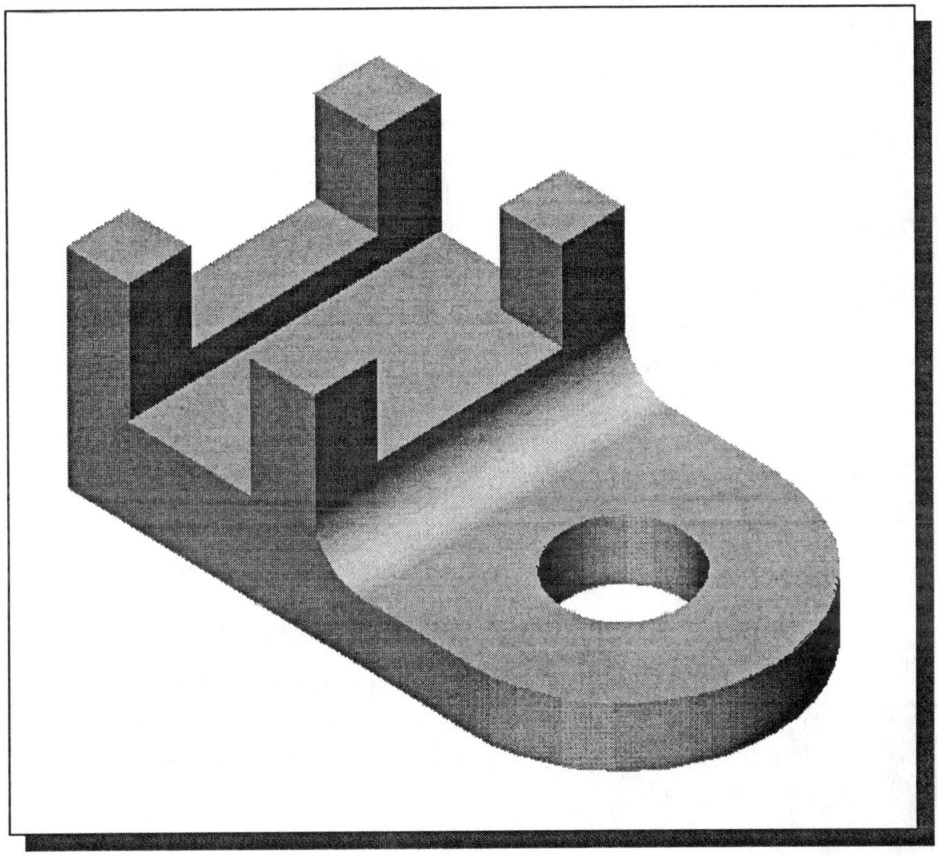

❖ In a typical design process, the initial design will undergo many analyses, testing and reviews. The *history-based part modification* approach is an extremely powerful and flexible method that allows us to quickly update the design. With this in mind, PLANNING AHEAD will help the organization and thus makes parametric modeling very flexible and powerful.

Questions:

1. What is the difference between the I-DEAS *History Tree* and a CSG *Binary Tree*?
2. When extruding, what is the difference between *Distance* and *Until Next*?
3. What is the I-DEAS *history-based part modifications* approach?
4. What determines how a model reacts when the features in the model change?
5. In *I-DEAS*, how do we access the *Model History Tree*?
6. How do you select the *Deselect All* option?
7. Identify the following commands:

(a)

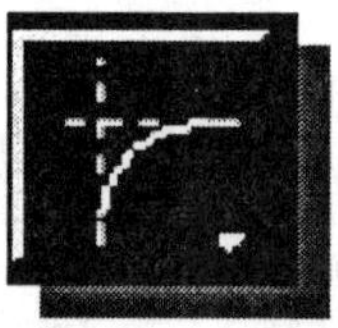

(b)

(c)

(d)

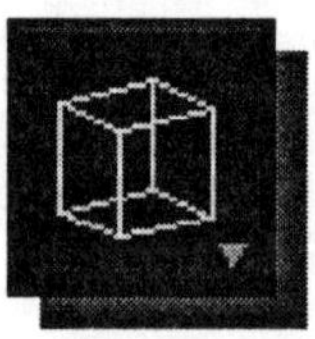

Exercises:

1.

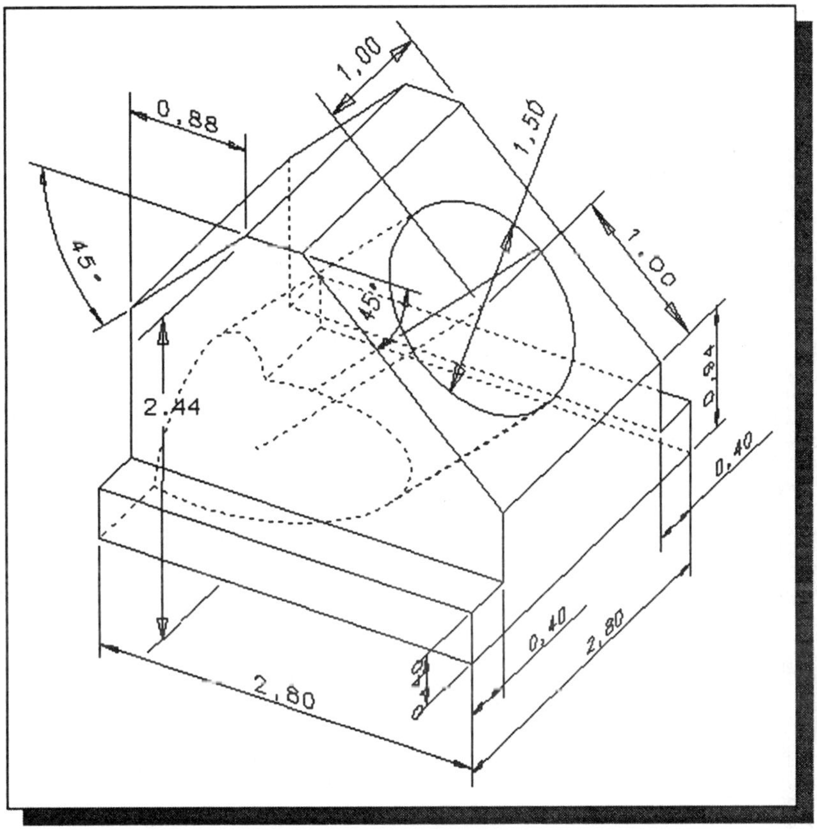

2.

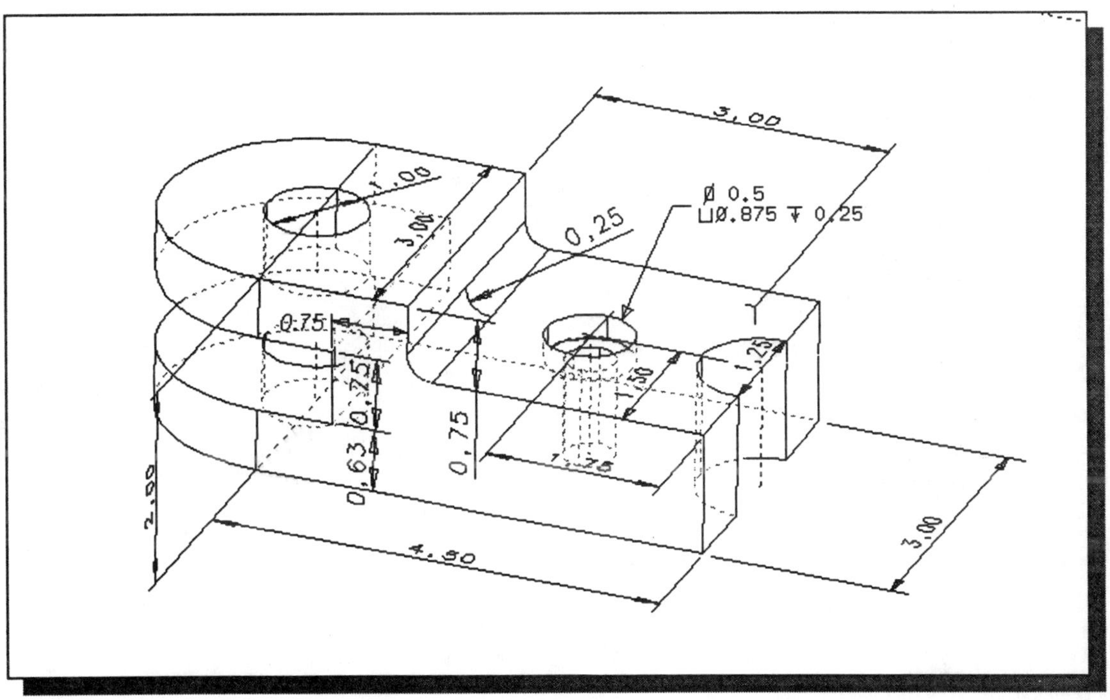

Notes:

Chapter 5
Parametric Constraints Fundamentals

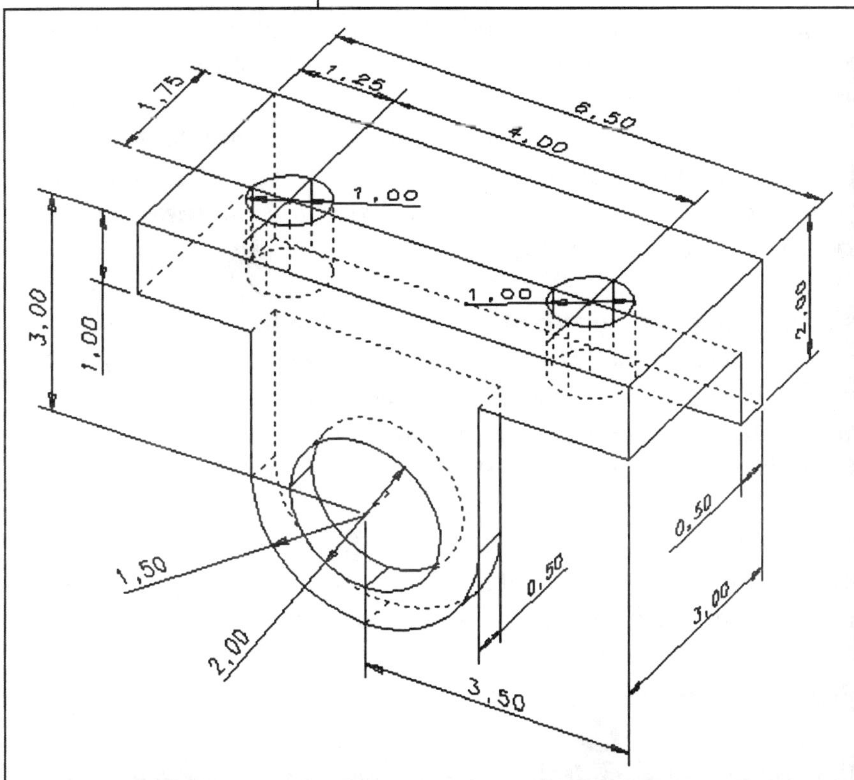

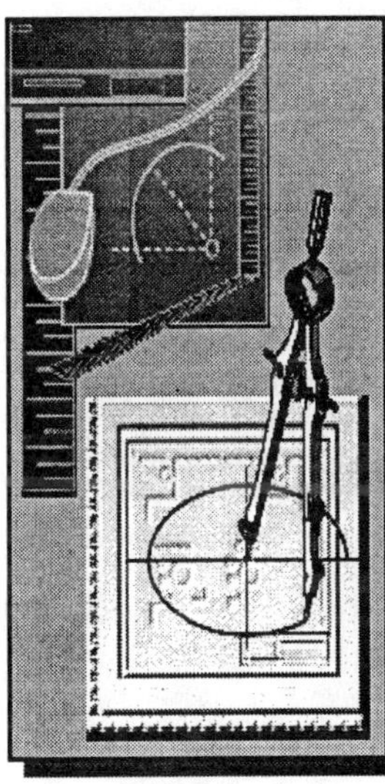

Learning Objectives

When you have completed this lesson, you will be able to:

- **Understand Constraint Color Codes.**
- **Create Parametric Relations.**
- **Use Dimensional Variables.**
- **Add and Delete Geometric Constraints.**
- **Use the Match Option.**
- **Identify Derived Dimensions.**
- **Control the Dynamic Navigator.**
- **Create Fully Constrained Geometry.**

CONSTRAINTS and RELATIONS

A primary and essential difference between parametric modeling and previous generation computer modeling is that parametric modeling captures the *design intent*. In the previous Chapters, we have implemented the design philosophy of "*shape before size*" by creating rough sketches and then adjusting the sketched geometry using the ***Modify*** and ***Dimension*** commands. In performing geometric constructions, dimensional values are necessary to describe the **SIZE** and **LOCATION** of constructed geometric entities. Besides using dimensions to define the geometry, we can also apply geometric rules to control geometric entities. More importantly, *I-DEAS* can capture design intent through the use of **geometric constraints, dimensional constraints**, and **parametric relations.** In *I-DEAS*, there are two types of constraints: **geometric constraints** and **dimensional constraints**. For part modeling in *I-DEAS*, constraints can be applied to 2-D *wireframes* and 2-D *sections*. **Wireframe** refers to the basic geometry entities such as lines, arcs, etc. **Section** refers to the basic shape that can be extruded into a solid or a surface. **Geometric constraints** are **geometric restrictions** that can be applied to geometric entities; for example, *horizontal*, *parallel*, *perpendicular*, and *tangent* are commonly used *geometric constraints* in *parametric modeling*. **Dimensional constraints** are used to describe the SIZE and LOCATION of individual geometric shapes. In *I-DEAS*, **parametric relations** are user-defined mathematical equations composed of dimensional variables and/or *design variables*. In parametric modeling, features are made of geometric entities with both relations and constraints describing individual design intent. In this Chapter, we will discuss the fundamentals of parametric relations and geometric constraints.

Create a Simple Plate Design

- In parametric modeling, dimensions are design parameters that are used to control the size and location of geometric features. Dimensions are more than just values; they can also be used as feature control variables. This concept is illustrated by the following example.

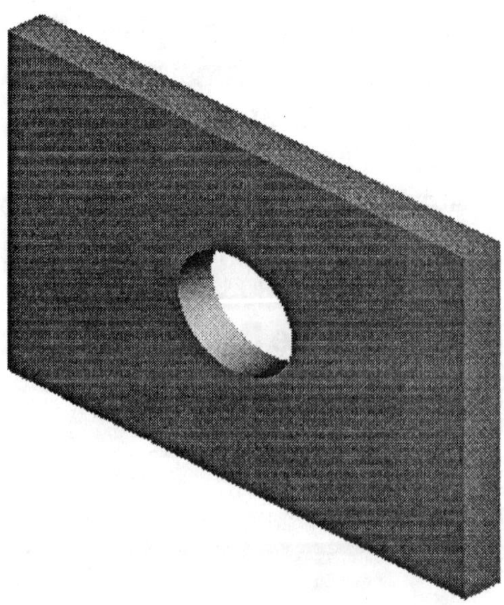

Starting I-DEAS

1. Login to the computer and bring up I-DEAS Master Series. Start a new model file by filling in the items as shown below in the *I-DEAS Start* window:

   Project Name: **(Your account Name)**
   Model File Name: **Plate**
   Application: **Design**
   Task: **Master Modeler**
   OK

2. In the *warning window*, click on the **OK** button to create a new model file.

3. Select **Units** under the *Options* toolbar in the icon panel, and select **Inch (pound-f)** from the menu.

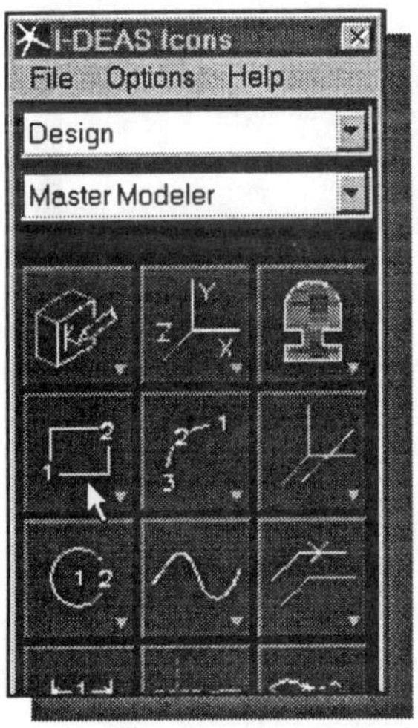

4. Choose **Rectangle by 2 Corners** in the icon panel. The message "*Locate first corner*" is displayed in the prompt window.

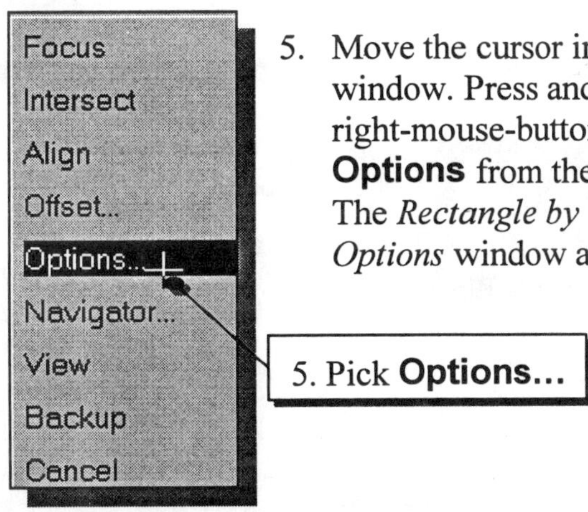

5. Move the cursor inside the graphics window. Press and hold down the right-mouse-button to select **Options** from the Option menu. The *Rectangle by Two Points Options* window appears.

6. Enter **(0,0)** and **(5,3)** for the first and second corners of the rectangle. Use the [**Tab**] key, or the **left-mouse-button** to move the cursor from field to field.

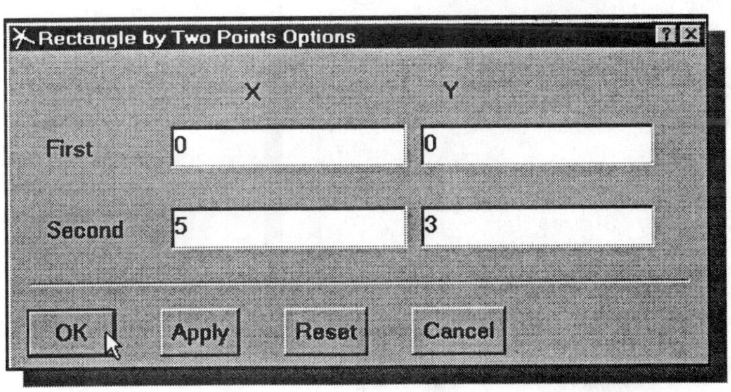

7. Click on the **OK** button to create the rectangle.

❖ I-DEAS automatically creates the height and width dimensions of the rectangle.

8. Choose **Zoom-All** in the display viewing icon panel.

9. Choose *Circle* – **Center Edge** in the icon panel.

10. Create a circle of arbitrary size inside the rectangle as shown.

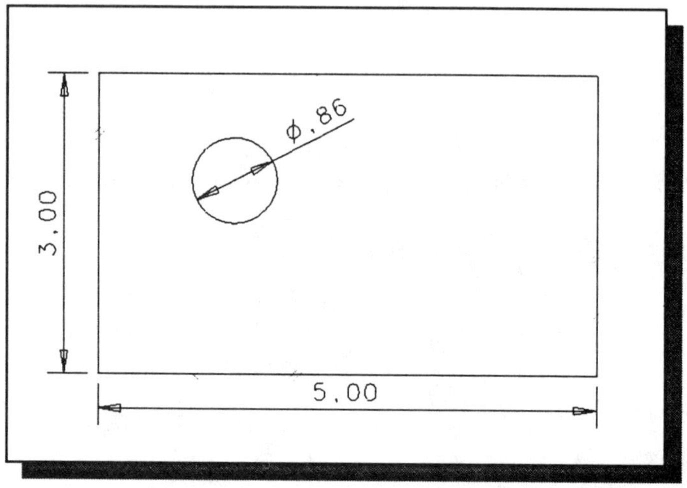

11. Press the **ENTER** key or the **middle-mouse-button** to end the *Circle* command.

❖ Note that I-DEAS created the size dimension of the circle. We will next add the location dimensions to control the location of the circle.

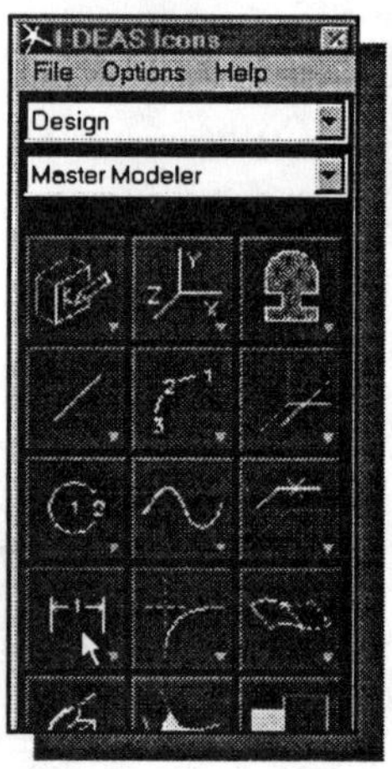

12. Choose **Dimension** in the icon panel.

13. We will start with the horizontal location dimension. Pick the center of the circle.

14. Select the left-vertical edge of the rectangle.

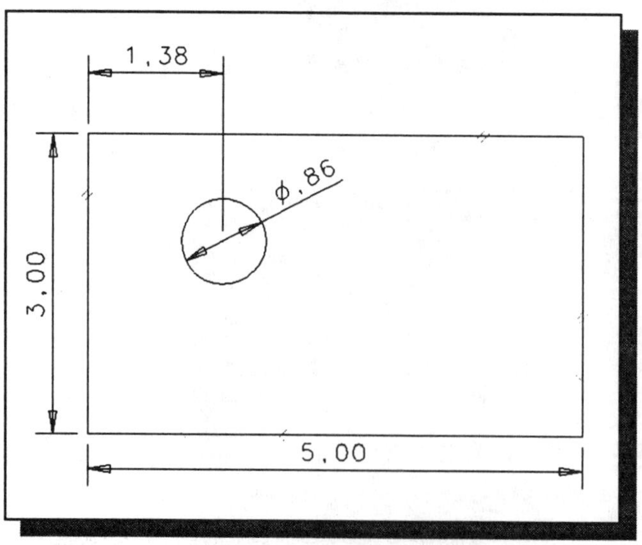

15. Place the text above the top of the rectangle as shown.

16. Next, we will add the vertical location dimension of the circle. Pick the center of the circle.

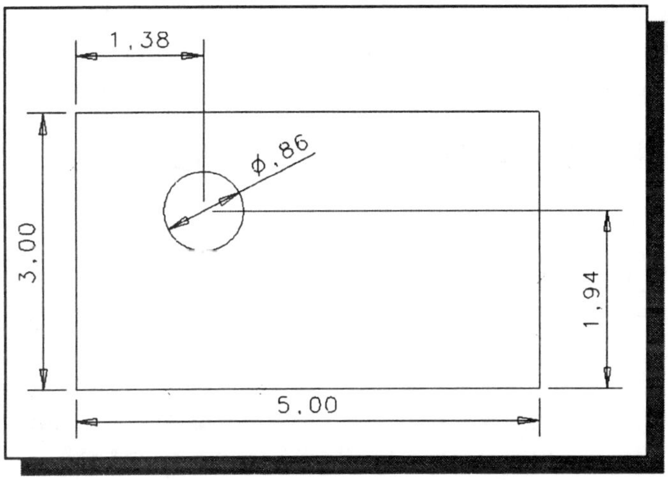

17. Pick the bottom edge of the rectangle.
18. Place the text to the right of the rectangle as shown.
19. Press the **ENTER** key or click the center-mouse-button to exit the *Dimension* command.

Modifying Dimensional Values

❖ The five dimensions on the screen describe the size and/or location of the plate design. We can adjust the location of the circle simply by modifying the two location dimensions. In this example, we will adjust the two location dimensions of the circle so that the circle is located at the center of the plate.

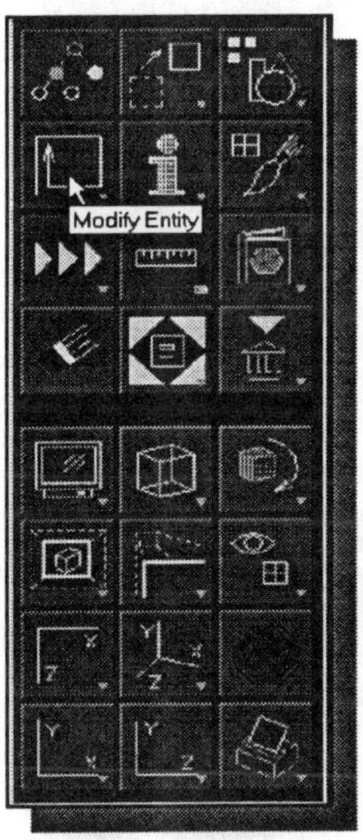

1. Choose *Modify* in the icon panel.

2. On your own, adjust the two location dimensions and the diameter of the circle so that the design is as shown in the below figure.

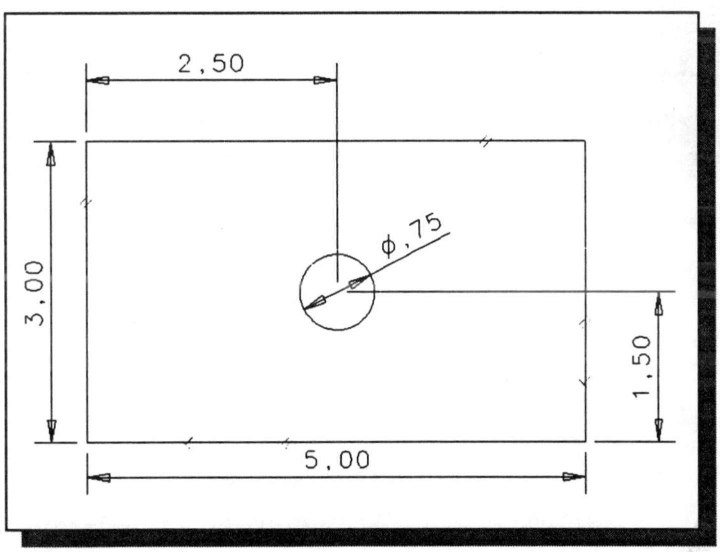

Dimensional Values and Dimensional Variables

Let us look at our current design, which represents a plate with a hole. The established dimensional values describe the size and/or location of the plate and the hole. As illustrated in the previous section, we can adjust the location of the hole by modifying the location dimensions. If a modification is required to change the size of the plate, the location of the hole will remain the same as described by the two dimensional values. This is okay if that is the design intent. On the other hand, the *design intent* may require (1) keeping the hole at the center of the plate at all times and (2) maintaining the size of the hole to be one-fourth of the height of the plate. In I-DEAS, we can establish a set of parametric relations using the dimensional variables to capture the design intent described above in statements (1) and (2).

Initially in I-DEAS Master Modeler, dimensional values are used to identify the size and location of geometric entities. The dimension-text generated by the *Navigator* or the *Dimension* command also reflects the actual location or size of the entity. Each dimension is also assigned a name that allows the dimension to be used as a control variable. By moving the mouse near a dimension in the graphics window, the dimensional variable name is displayed. The default format is "Dxx," where the "xx" is a number that I-DEAS increments automatically each time a new dimension is added. These dimensional variables can be used in user-defined equations to capture the design intent.

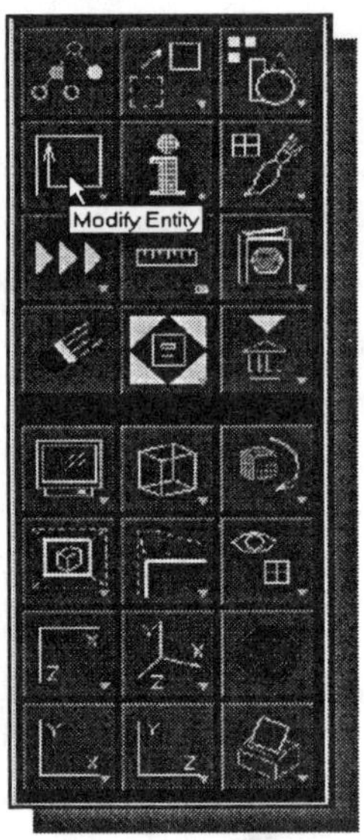

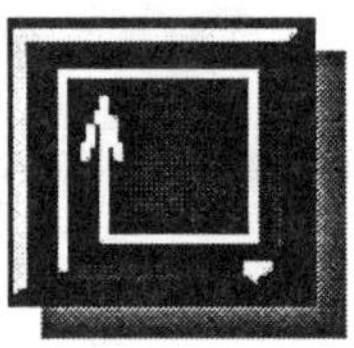

1. Choose **Modify** in the icon panel.

2. Pick the horizontal location dimension of the center of the circle (**2.5**). The *Modify Dimension* window appears.

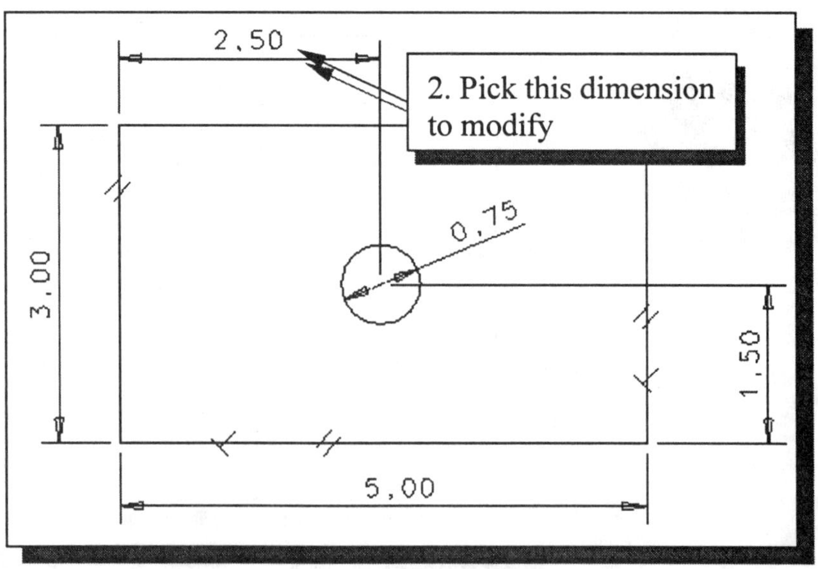

3. Click on the **Right Arrow** icon next to the dimensional value to display options. Select the **Match** option. In the prompt window, the message "*Pick a dimension*" is displayed. Note that the dimension variable name for this dimension is **D4**.

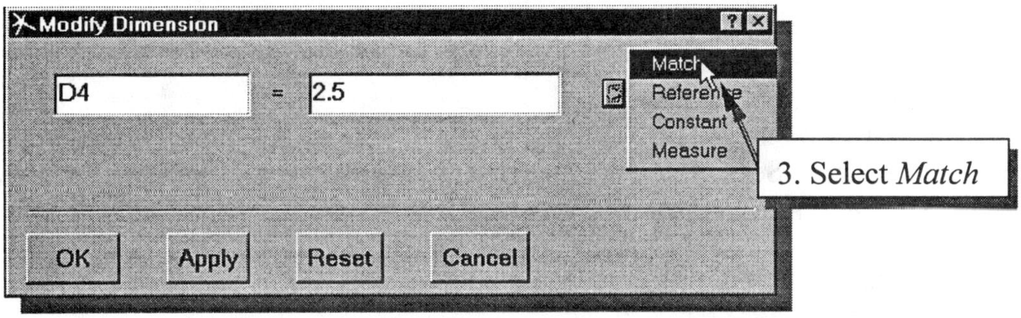

4. Select the width dimension of the rectangle (**5.0**). The *Modify Dimension* window reappears. Note that the 5.0-inch dimension variable name, as displayed in the *Modify dimension* window, is designated as **D2**.

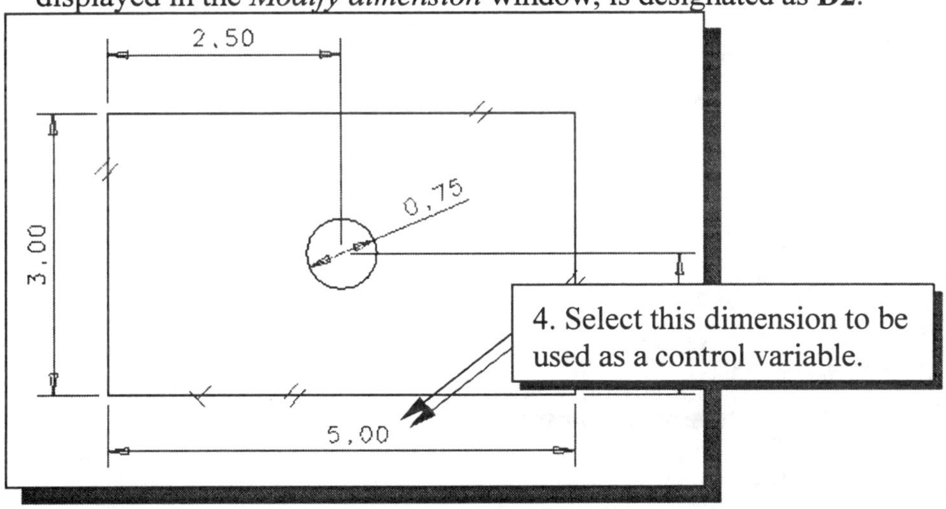

5. In the *Dimension Value* box, type "**/2**" ("*divided by 2*") to the end of the selected control dimensional variable name. This step establishes the parametric relation such that the hole will be located at the center of the plate whenever the horizontal width of the plate is changed.

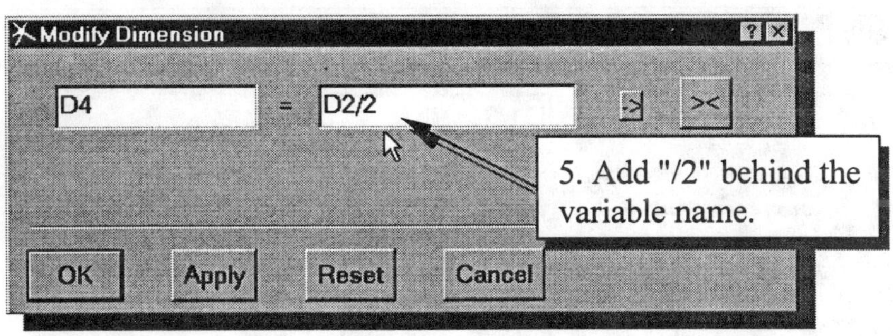

6. Click on the **OK** icon to apply the modification. Note that the dimension <2.5> now appears in pointed parentheses, which means it is a derived dimension.

Additional Parametric Relations

We will repeat the above steps and create two more parametric relations.

1. Select the vertical location dimension of the center of the circle (**1.5**). The *Modify Dimension* window appears.

2. Click on the **Right Arrow** icon next to the dimensional value to display options. Select the **Match** option. In the prompt window, the message "*Pick a dimension*" is displayed.

3. Pick the vertical dimension of the rectangle (**3.0**). The *Modify Dimension* window appears.

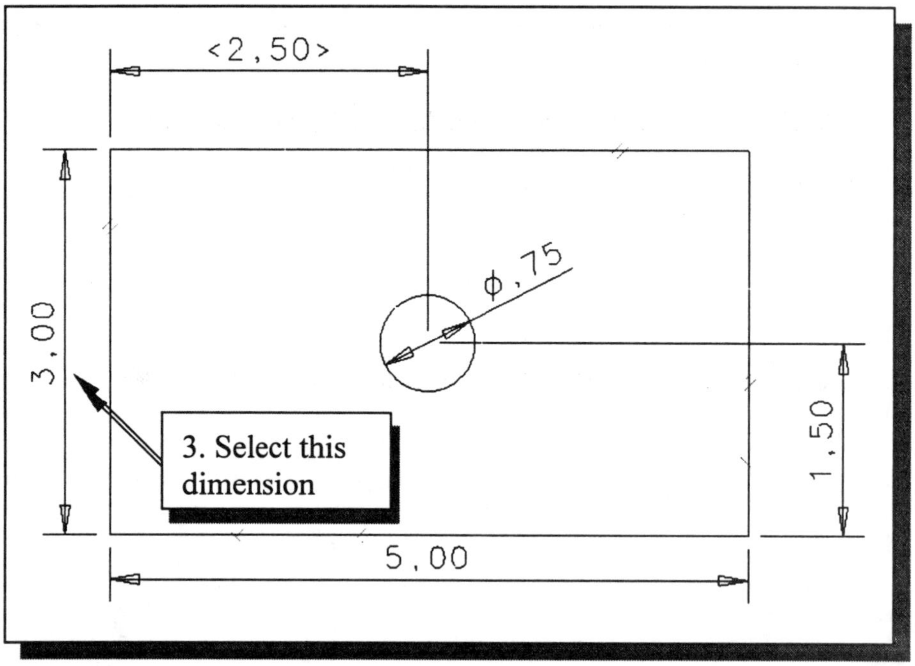

4. In the *Dimension Values* box, type "**/2**" ("*divided by 2*") to the end of the selected control dimensional variable name.

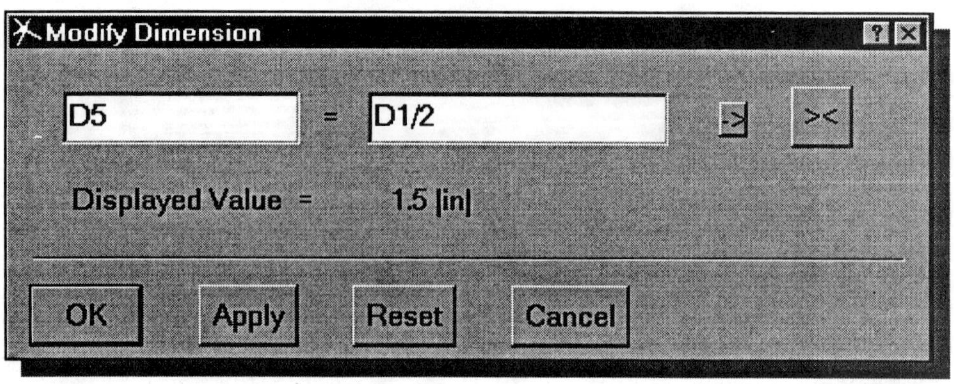

5. Click on the **OK** icon to proceed. Again notice that the <1.50> dimension appears between pointed parenthesis.

❖ We next proceed to establish a parametric relationship between the hole diameter and the vertical height dimension such that the hole diameter equals one-quarter of the height dimension.

6. Pick the diameter dimension of the circle (**0.75**). The *Modify Dimension* window appears.

7. Click on the **Right Arrow** icon next to the dimensional value to display options. Select the **Match** option. In the prompt window, the message "*Pick a dimension*" is displayed.

8. Select the vertical dimension of the rectangle (**3.0**). The *Modify Dimension* window reappears.

9. In the *Dimension Values* box, add "**/4**" ("*divided by 4*") to the end of the dimensional variable name shown.

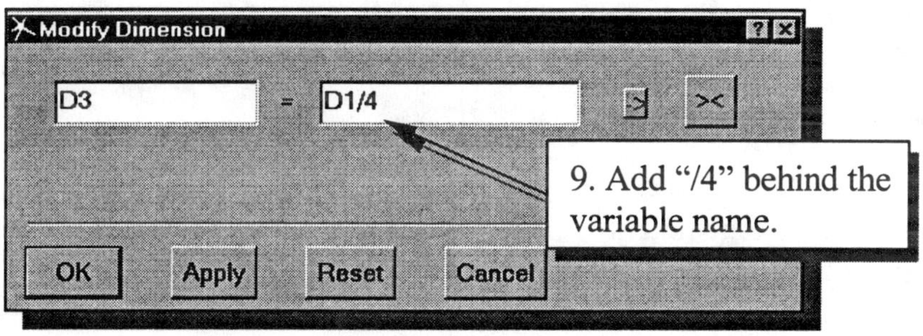

10. Click on the **OK** icon to proceed.

11. Press the **ENTER** key or click the **middle-mouse-button** to exit the *Modify Dimension* command.

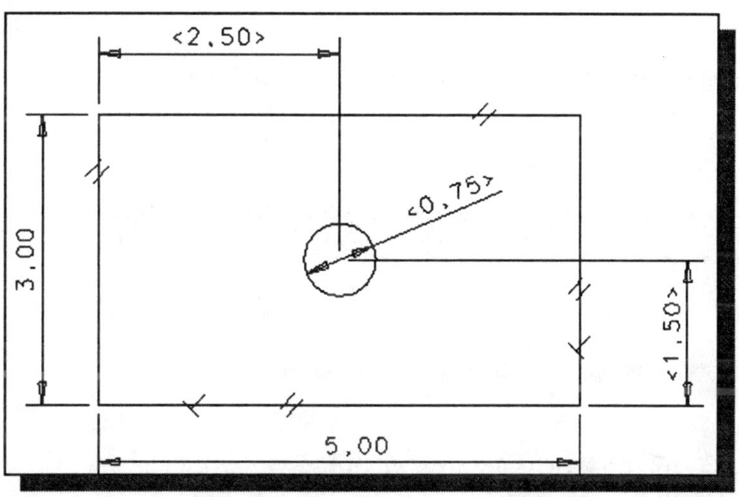

❖ Notice, at this point, the dimension values displayed are the same values as before except the dimensional values we modified now are in pointed parentheses. (In Version 5 of I-DEAS Master Series, a box appears around the text.) The parentheses signify the values are derived from user written mathematical expressions.

Adjusting the Control Dimensions

To demonstrate the effects of the parametric relations we have entered, let's modify the size of the rectangle to 3 X 2 inches.

1. Choose **Modify** in the icon panel. The *Dimensions* window appears.

2. On your own, modify the width of the rectangle to **3** inches.

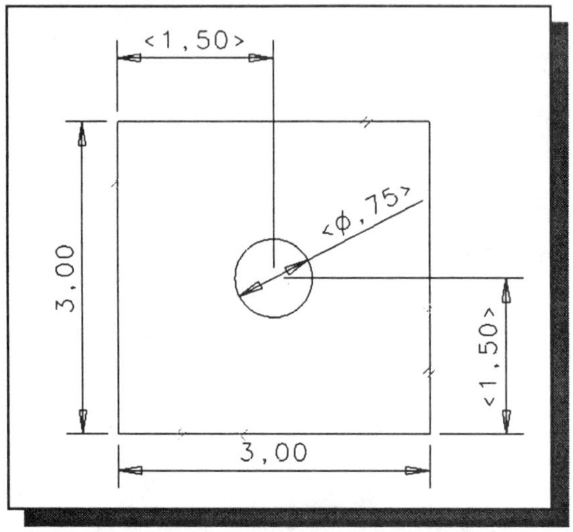

3. On your own, modify the height of the rectangle to **2** inches.

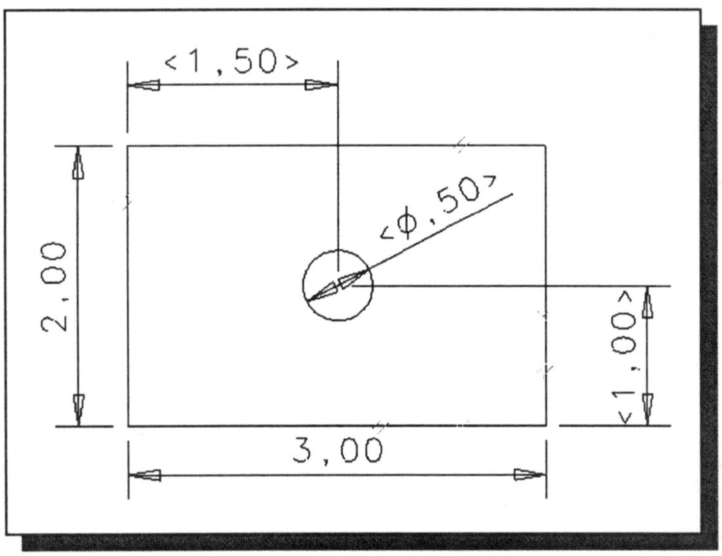

❖ The size of the rectangle is adjusted as new values are entered. The parametric relations are also applied and maintained. The design intent, previously expressed by statement (1) and (2) at the beginning of this section, is now embedded into the model.

➢ On your own, use the **extrude** command and create a 3-D solid model using a plate-thickness of **0.25** (Select both the rectangle and the circle to extrude.) Experiment with modifying the parametric relations and dimensions through the *History Tree Access* option. Save the model file before proceeding to the next section.

Opening a New Model File

1. From the icon panel, select the **File** pull-down menu and pick **Open**. You can also use **Ctrl-O** to open a new model file.

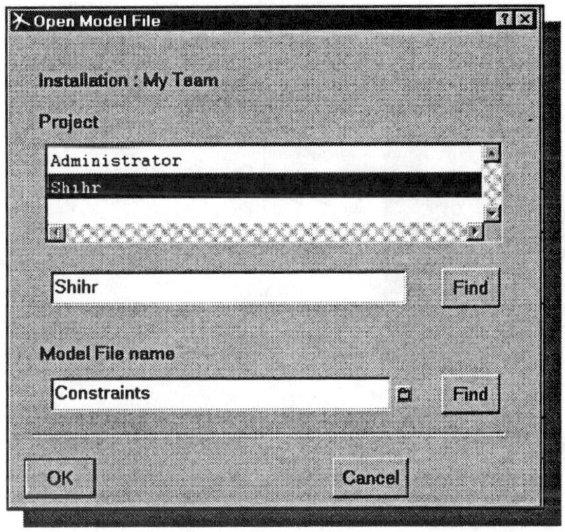

2. Enter **Constraints** as the new model file name as shown.

3. Click on the **OK** button to proceed.

❖ Note that I-DEAS will search for the file in the default drive; since this is a new model file the warning window will appear on the screen.

4. In the *warning window*, click on the **OK** button to create a new model file.

5. Select **Units** under the *Options* toolbar in the icon panel, and select **Inch (pound-f)** from the menu.

Fully Constrained Geometry

In *I-DEAS*, as we create 2D sketches, geometric constraints such as *horizontal* and *parallel* are automatically added to the sketched geometry. In most cases, additional constraints and dimensions are needed to fully describe the sketched geometry beyond the geometric constraints added by the system. Although we can use *I-DEAS* to build partially constrained or totally unconstrained solid models, the models may behave unpredictably as changes are made. In most cases, it is important to consider the design intent and to add proper constraints to geometric entities. In the following sections, a simple triangle is used to illustrate the different tools that are available in *I-DEAS* to create/modify geometric and dimensional constraints.

Automatic Application of Constraints – The Dynamic Navigator

In I-DEAS Master Modeler, as we create wireframe entities such as lines and circles on a workplane, we can use the Dynamic Navigator to automatically add dimensions and/or geometric constraints. The Dynamic Navigator is active during sketching operations, which means the Dynamic Navigator is available when we are using any of the following Sketching tools icon stacks:

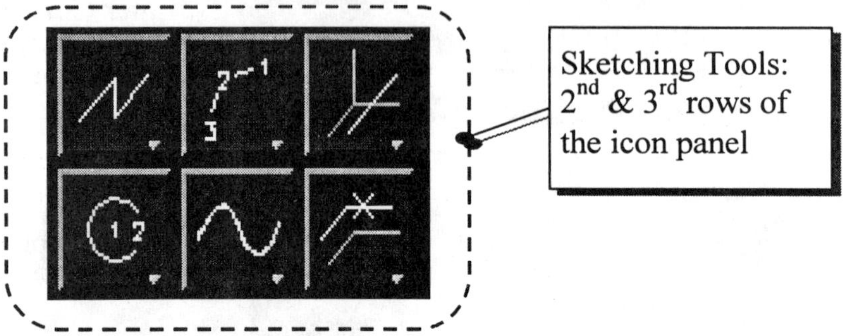

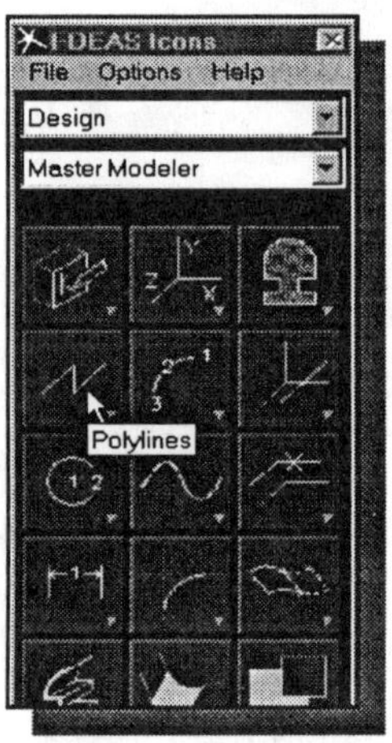

1. Choose **Polylines** in the icon panel. In the prompt window, the message "*Locate start*" is displayed.

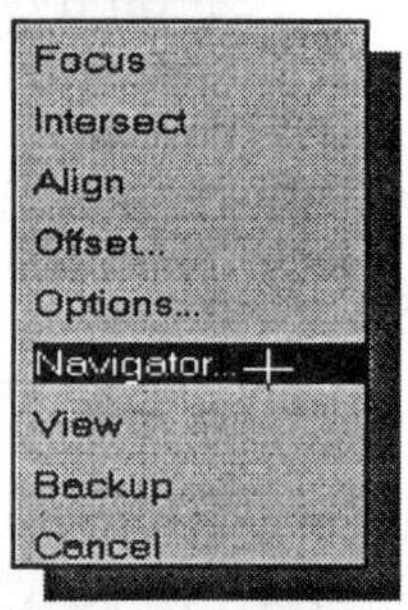

2. Move the cursor inside the graphics window. Press and hold down the right-mouse-button to display the popup menu. From the popup menu select the **Navigator...** option. The *Navigator Controls* window appears.

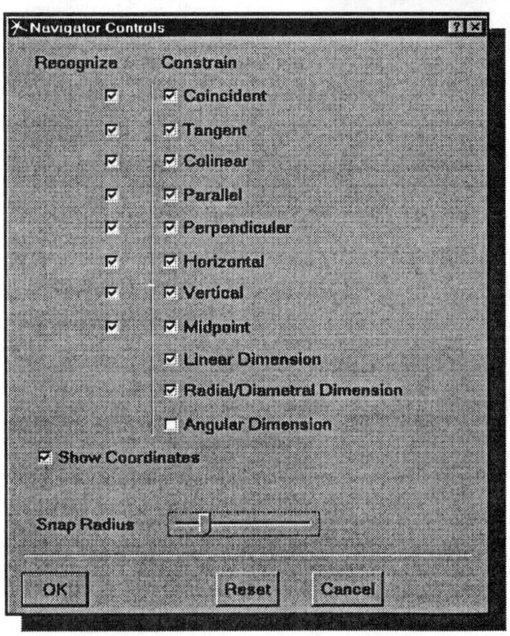

❖ In the *Navigator Controls* window, the first column is a set of boxes that can be used to control what the *Dynamic Navigator* will recognize. The second column of boxes controls whether the *Dynamic Navigator* will add the recognized geometric constraints and/or dimensional constraints on the geometry being created. The *Dynamic Navigator* will not add the constraint if it is not recognizable. Therefore, if we switch "**off**" the *Recognize* option, the *Constrain* option is also switched **off**. Alternatively, we can temporarily disable the *Dynamic Navigator*, while constructing wireframe geometry, by holding down the **CONTROL** key (**Ctrl** key).

3. Click on the **OK** icon to accept the default settings and exit the *Navigator Controls* window. No changes were made.

4. Use the left-mouse-button and select any position in the graphics window. Move the mouse around and notice the *Horizontal Ground* symbol or the *Vertical Ground* symbol appears when the rubber band line is horizontal or vertical.

➢ **The Dynamic Navigator will add the *Horizontal Ground* or the *Vertical Ground* to the first horizontal or vertical line sketched in the graphics window. The constrained line is then used as a fixed-reference in subsequent parametric modeling. Additional constraints are added relative to this reference entity.**

5. Press the **ENTER** key or click the **middle-mouse-button** once to restart the *Polylines* command. The message "*Locate start*" is displayed in the prompt window.

6. Move the cursor inside the graphics window. Press and hold down the right-mouse-button to select the **Navigator...** option. The *Navigator Controls* window appears.

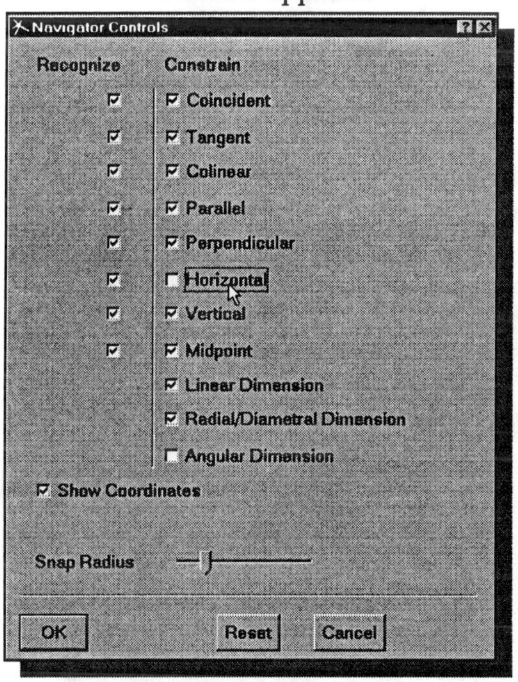

7. Use the left-mouse-button and switch **off** the *Constrain* box for **Horizontal.** The *Dynamic Navigator* will still recognize when a line is horizontal but will not add the constraint.

8. Click on the **OK** icon to exit the *Navigator Controls* window.

9. Use the left-mouse-button and select any position inside the graphics window. Move the cursor around and notice the *Horizontal Ground* symbol is displayed in white, which means the constraint will not be added to the geometry. The *Vertical Ground* symbol appears in a color other than white, which means the constraint will be added to the geometry.

10. Create an inclined line by picking a starting location and moving up toward the right side as shown on the next page.

11. We will next create a vertical line. Move the graphics-cursor directly below the last point and aligned to the starting point of the polyline. Notice the *Vertical* constraint is automatically added to the line.

12. Complete the triangle by moving the graphics cursor near the starting point, then left-click. The *Perpendicular* constraint is automatically added to both lines.

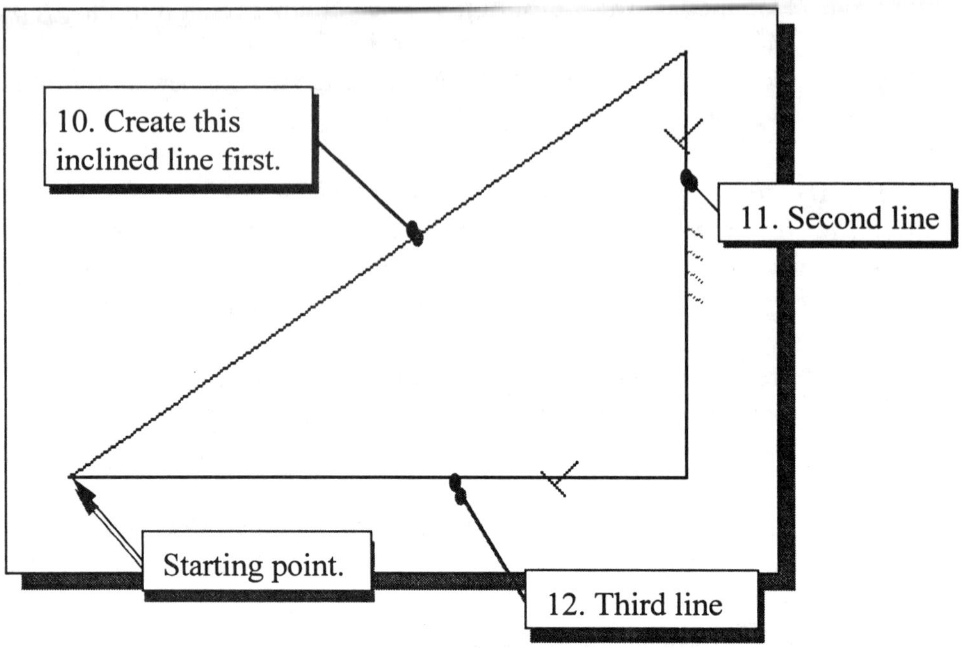

Constrain and Dimension Options

Although we can use I-DEAS Master Modeler to build partially constrained or totally unconstrained solid models, the models may behave unpredictably as changes are made. It is crucial to consider the design intent and add proper constraints to geometric entities.

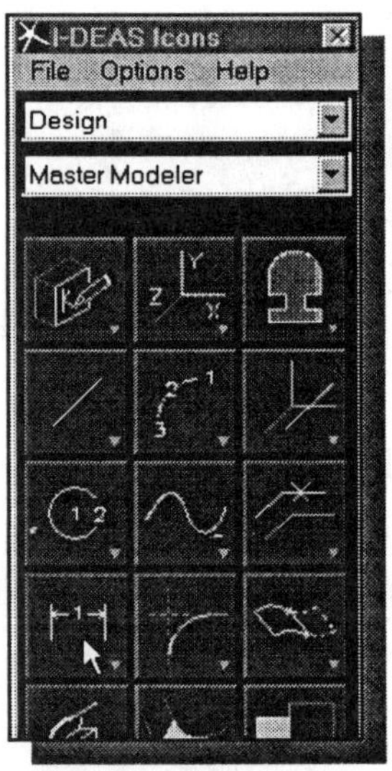

1. Press and hold down on the *Dimension* icon to display the other icons in the stack. Select the **Constrain & Dimension...** option.

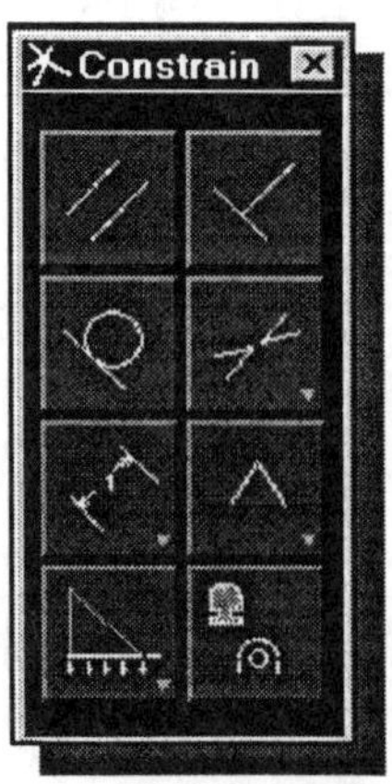

The *Constrain* window appears on the screen.

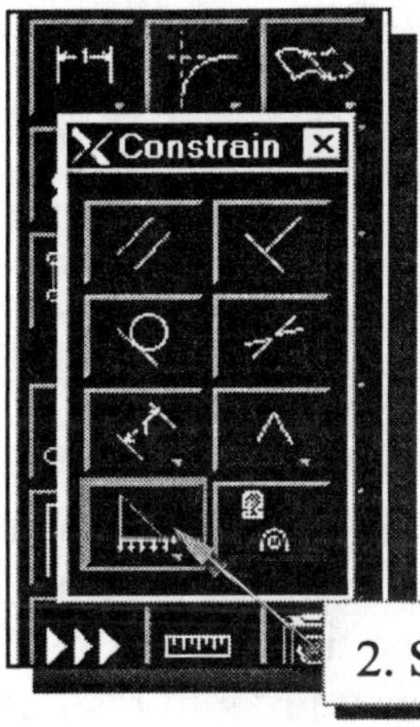

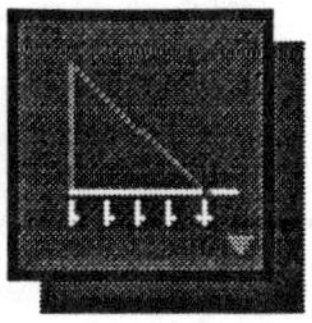

2. Choose **Show Free** in the *Constrain* window. In the prompt window, the message "*Pick entity*" is displayed. Notice the blue vertical line, which indicates the line is fully constrained. The horizontal line and inclined line are displayed in other colors, which indicate that they are not fully constrained.

❖ **The Dynamic Navigator constraint color-codes:**

- **Blue indicates fully constrained geometry.**
- **Green indicates unconstrained geometry.**
- **Other colors indicate partially constrained geometry.**
- **Arrows indicate the direction of movement.**

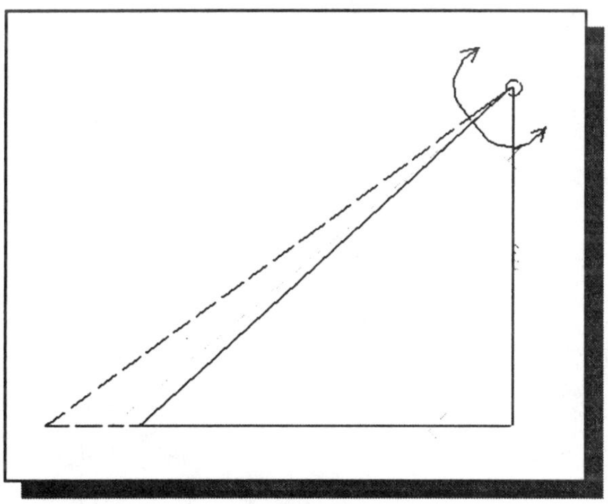

3. Pick the inclined line.

4. Press the **ENTER** key or click the **middle-mouse-button** to accept the selection and an animation will show the direction the entity is free to move.

❖ The inclined line is free to rotate about the top corner, the length of the line can vary as the line is rotated.

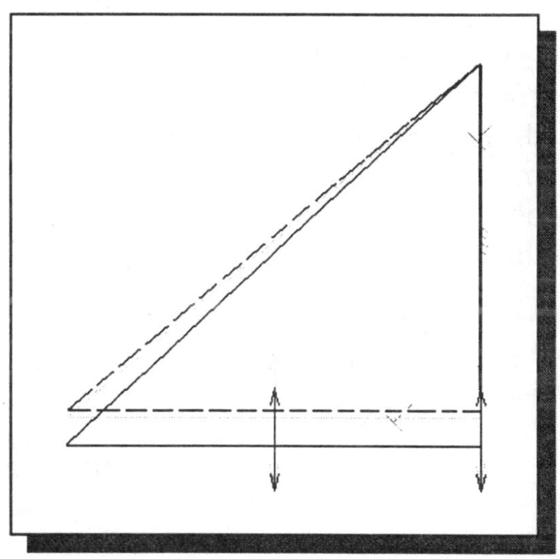

5. Pick the horizontal line.

6. Press the **ENTER** key or click the **middle-mouse-button** and observe the direction the entity is free to move.

❖ The horizontal is free to move up and down but is constrained to remain perpendicular to the vertical side. The length of the inclined line can vary as the horizontal line is moved upward or downward.

7. Click on the **[X]** icon, or choose from menu, to close the *Constrain* window.

❖ Geometric constraints can also be used to control the direction in which changes can occur. For example, in the current design we can add a horizontal dimension to control the length of the horizontal line. If the length of the line is then modified to a greater value, I-DEAS will lengthen the line toward the left side. This is due to the fact that the *Vertical Ground* constraint will restrict any horizontal movement of the horizontal line toward the right side

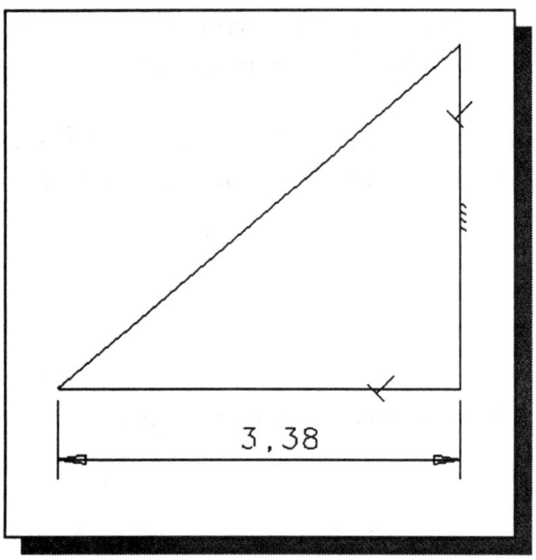

➤ On your own, create the horizontal dimension as shown and modify the dimension value to observe the effects of the existing constraints.

❖ Is the geometry fully constrained after we added the length dimension? How many more constraints are needed to fully constrain the triangle?

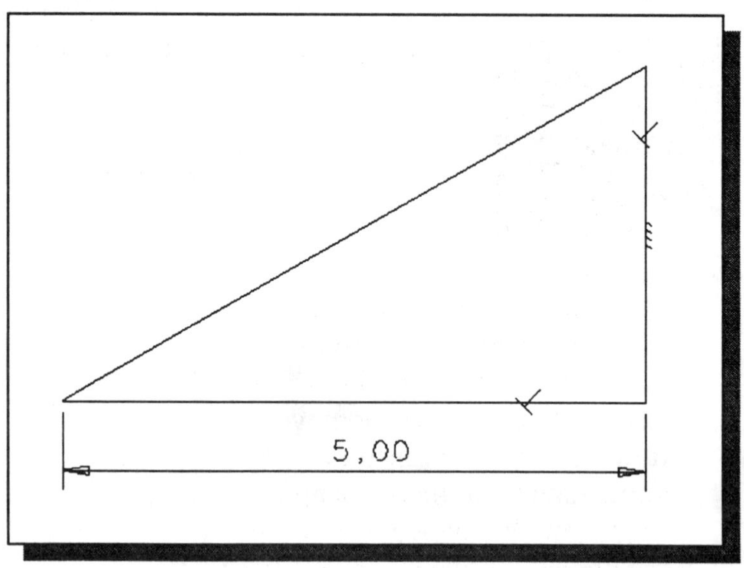

Deleting Geometric Constraints

Geometric constraints are control variables. They are also entities that can be removed using the *Delete* command.

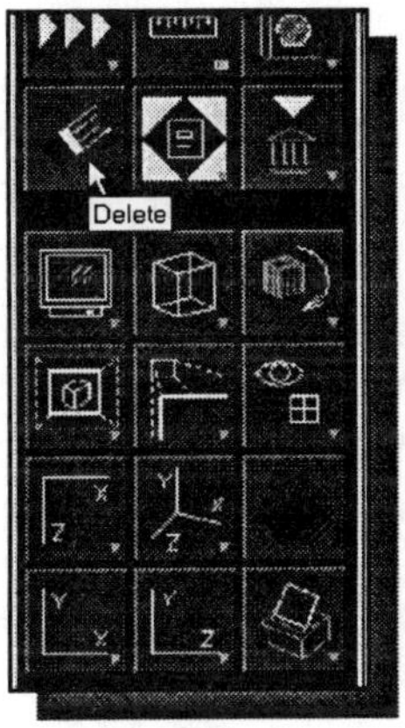

1. Choose **Delete** in the icon panel.

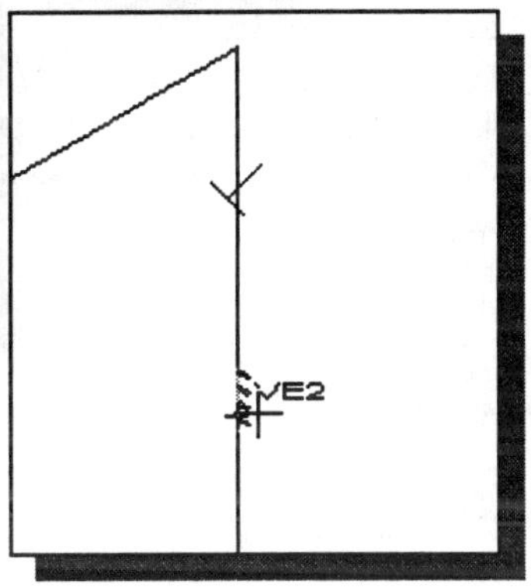

2. Pick the **Vertical Ground** constraint. Notice the variable name “VEx” signifying the entity is a *Vertical* constraint. (Use the dynamic-zoom function, **[F2]**+**[Mouse]**, to help in selecting the constraint.)

3. Select **Yes** or press the **ENTER** key to confirm deletion of one constraint.

Adding Dimensional Constraints

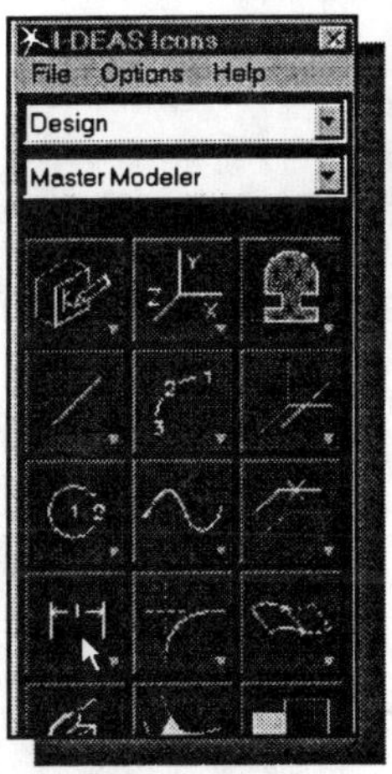

1. Choose **Dimension** in the icon panel.

2. Add the horizontal and vertical dimensions as shown. (Note that the values may appear differently on your screen; we are using the dimensions to illustrate constraining the sketched geometry.)

❖ On your own, use the **Show Free** command to observe the directions the triangle can freely move. The two dimensions and the perpendicular constraint are sufficient to define the triangle shape, but the triangle is free to move in all directions since there isn't any *Ground* constraint.

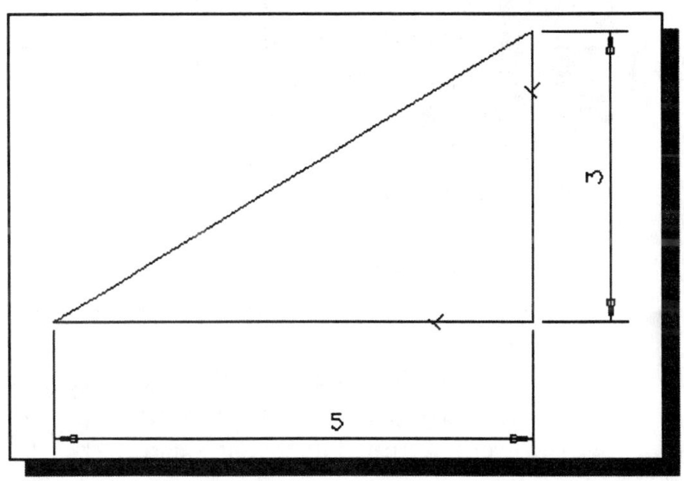

Adding Geometric Constraints Manually

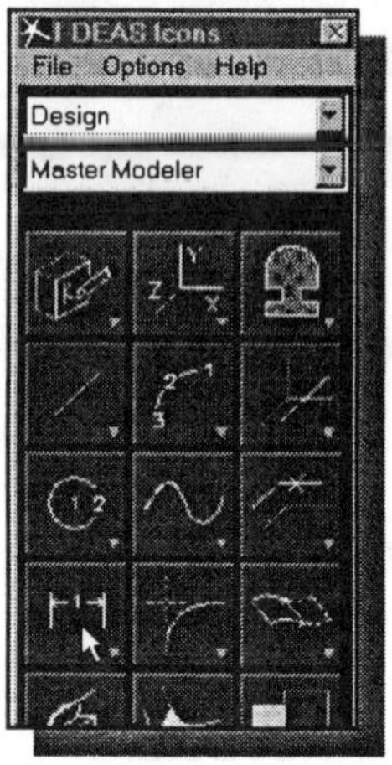

1. Press and hold down the left-mouse-button on the ***Dimension*** icon to display the other icons in the stack. Slide the cursor downward to select the **Constrain & Dimension...** option. The *Constrain Options* window appears.

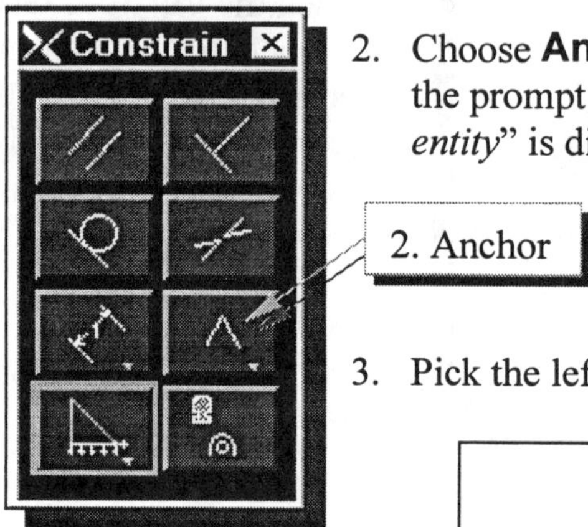

2. Choose **Anchor** in the pop-up window. In the prompt window, the message "*Pick entity*" is displayed.

3. Pick the left corner of the triangle.

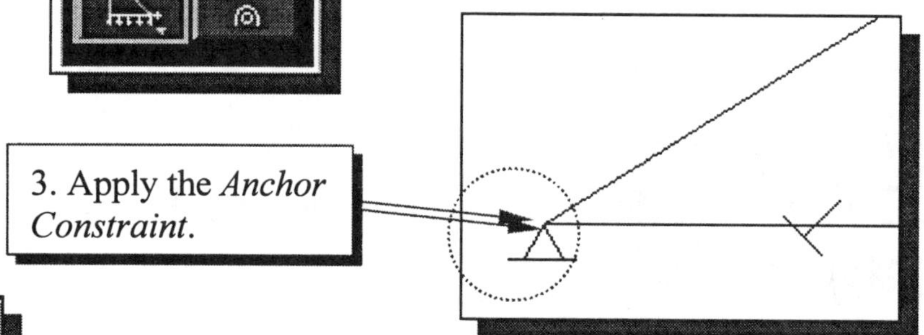

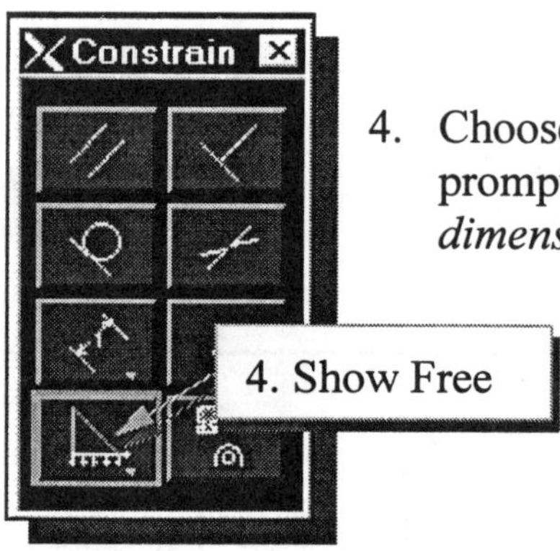

4. Choose **Show Free** in the *Constrain* pop-up window. In the prompt window, the message "*Pick point, curve, section or dimension*" is displayed.

5. Pick the horizontal line.

6. Press the **ENTER** key or **the middle-mouse-button** to accept the selection and observe the direction the triangle is free to move. The left corner is stationary because of the *Anchor* constraint. The triangle can only pivot about this fixed point.

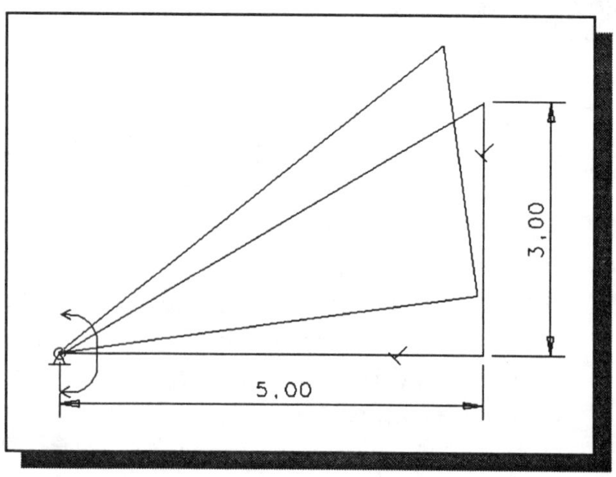

7. Press and hold down on the ***Anchor*** icon to display the other choices. Slide the cursor downward and select the **Horizontal Ground** option. In the prompt window, the message "Pick a point or curve" is displayed.

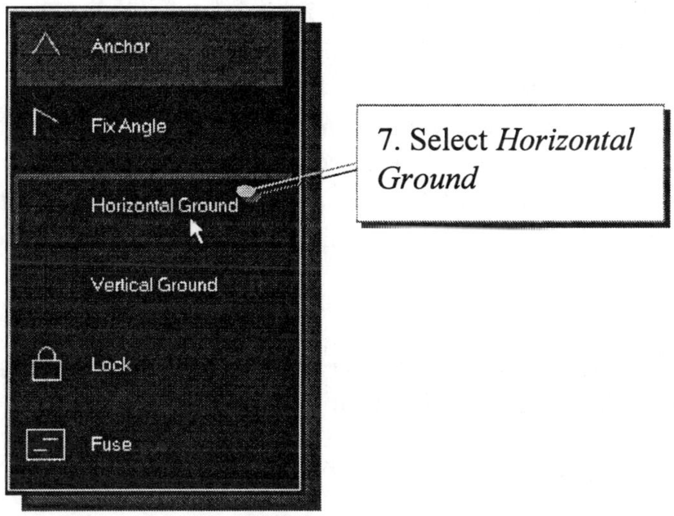

8. Pick the horizontal line to place the horizontal ground constraint.

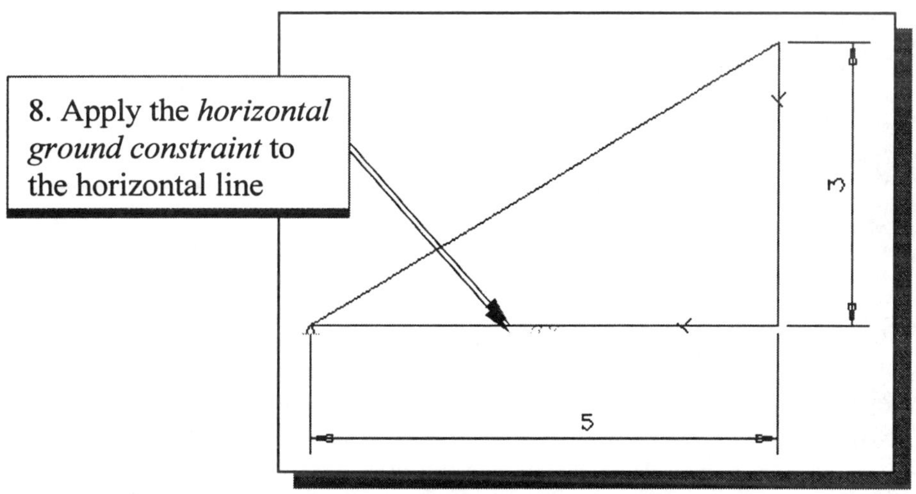

9. Choose **Show Free** and examine the color codes of the triangle. The entire triangle appears blue, indicating that it is fully constrained.

- The applied horizontal ground constraint, the horizontal dimension, and the anchor constraint at the lower-left corner, completely define the size and location of the bottom edge of the triangle. The perpendicular constraint and the height dimension also fully describe the location of the top corner of the triangle. The combination of **Dimensional constraints** and **Geometric constraints** are used to form **geometric restrictions** to the SIZE and LOCATION of individual geometric entities. Note that many combinations exist to obtain the same fully constrained geometry. For example, we can remove the height dimension and add an angle dimension between the inclined line and the horizontal line.

Over-constraining and Reference Dimensions

- We can use I-DEAS to build partially constrained or totally unconstrained solid models. In most cases, these types of models may behave unpredictably as changes are made. I-DEAS will not let us over-constrain a sketch; additional dimensions can still be added to the sketch, but they will be used for reference only. These additional dimensions are called **reference dimensions**. *Reference dimensions* do not constrain the sketch; they only reflect the values of the dimensioned geometry. They are enclosed in parentheses to distinguish them from normal (parametric) dimensions. A *reference dimension* can be converted to a normal dimension only if another dimension or geometric constraint is removed.

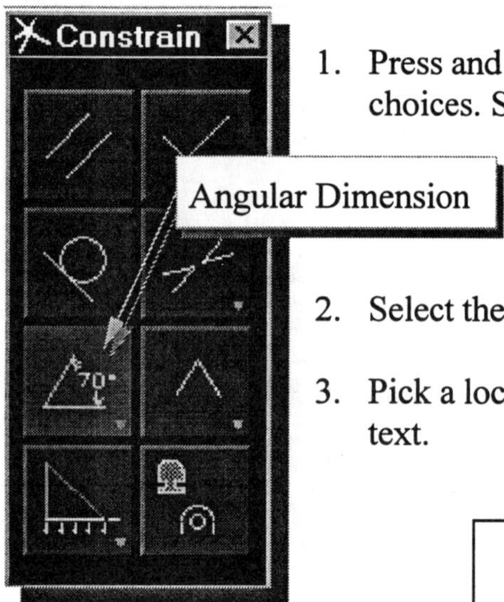

1. Press and hold down on the ***Dimension*** icon to display the other choices. Select the **Angular Dimension** option.
2. Select the horizontal line and the inclined line.
3. Pick a location that is inside the triangle to place the dimension text.

❖ In I-DEAS, reference dimensions are displayed in parentheses, which means it cannot be modified.

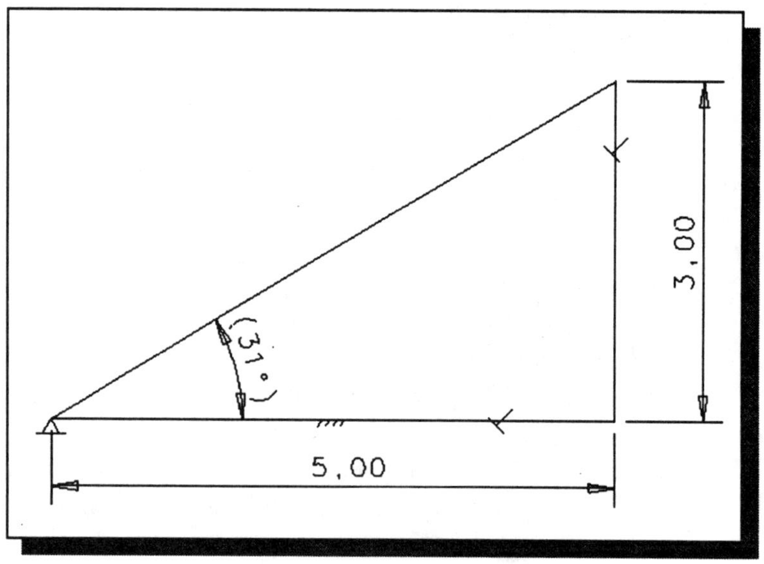

4. Press the **ENTER** key or **the middle-mouse-button** to end the angular dimension command.

➢ On your own, modify the height dimension to **4** and observe the changes to the 2D sketch and the reference dimension.

Adding Additional Geometry and Constraints

1. Choose *Circle* – **Center Edge** in the icon panel.

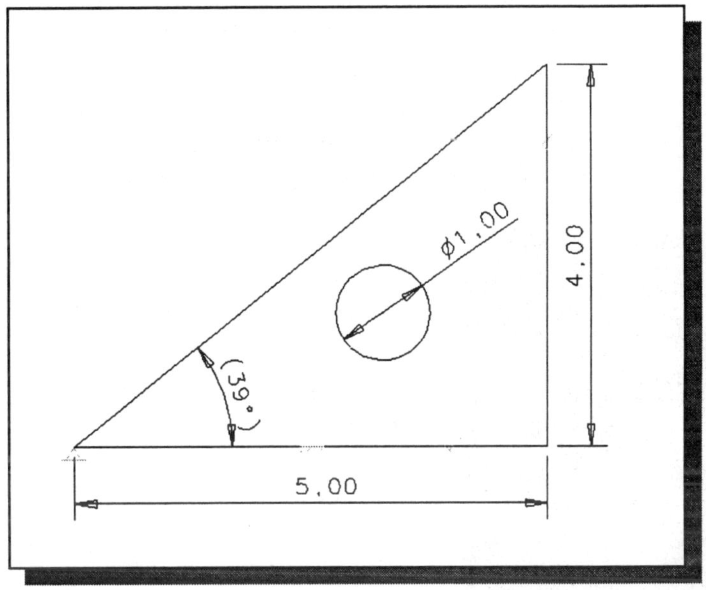

2. Create a circle of arbitrary size inside the rectangle as shown.

3. Press the **ENTER** key or the **middle-mouse-button** to end the *Circle* command.

➢ Note that I-DEAS automatically creates the size dimension of the circle. On your own, modify the diameter to **1.00** inch.

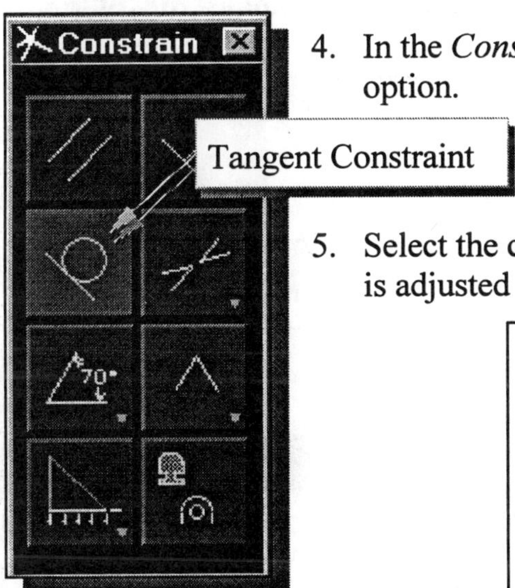

4. In the *Constrain* window, select the **Tangent constraint** option.

5. Select the circle and the inclined line. The location of the circle is adjusted as shown.

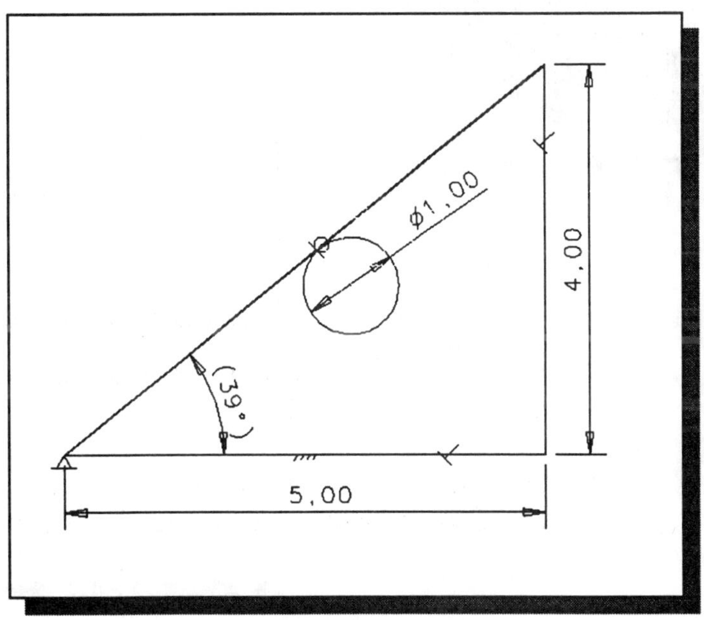

- How many more constraints or dimensions will be necessary to fully constrain the circle? Which constraints or dimensions would you suggest to fully constrain the geometry?

6. On your own, **delete** the diameter dimension.

7. Apply another **Tangent constraint** between the circle and the vertical line.

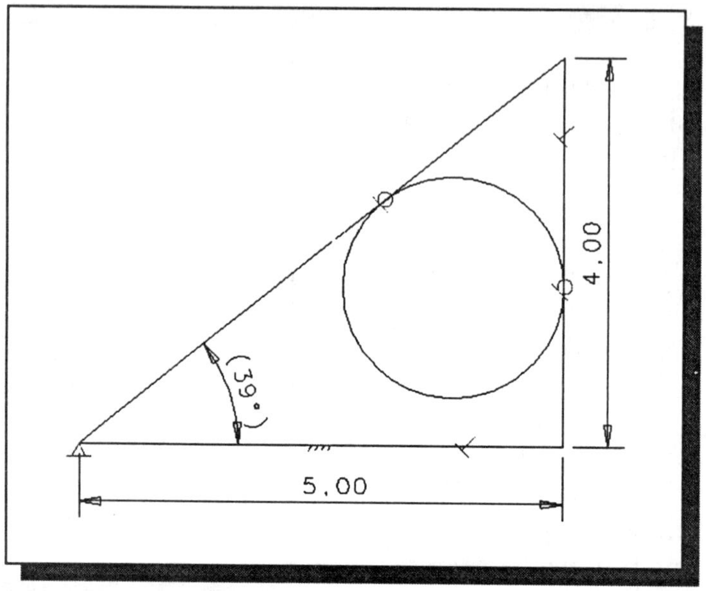

❖ The size of the circle is adjusted to maintain the two tangent constraints applied. Is the circle fully constrained?

8. On your own, delete the **Tangent constraint** we just applied.

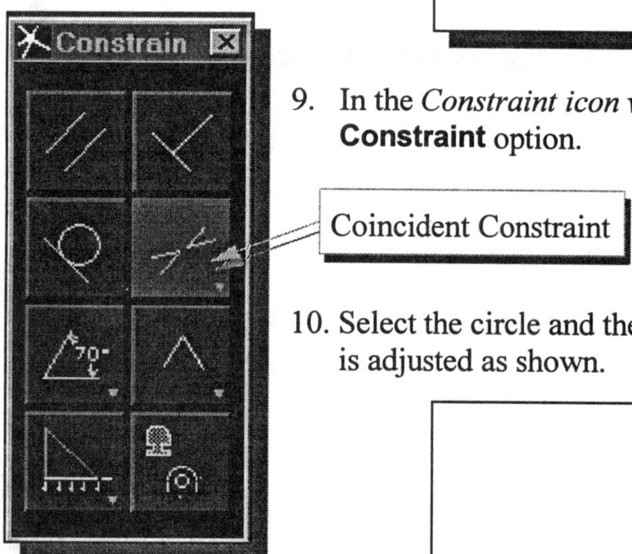

9. In the *Constraint icon window,* select the **Coincident/Collinear Constraint** option.

10. Select the circle and the vertical line. The location of the circle is adjusted as shown.

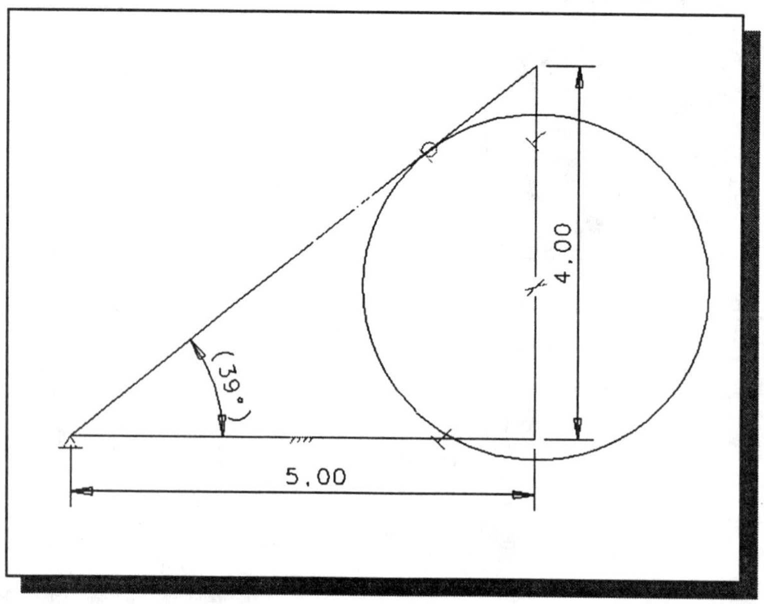

❖ On your own, use **Show Free** and examine the color codes of the sketched geometry.

- The above examples illustrate that application of different constraints affects the geometry differently. Applying proper constraints allows us to create very intelligent CAD models that can be modified/revised fairly easily. The design intents are embedded in the CAD model's database. On your own, experiment with applying different constraints to establish different geometry as shown in the below figures. Reminder: **Reset** the constraint-options in the *Navigator Control* window before exiting I-DEAS.

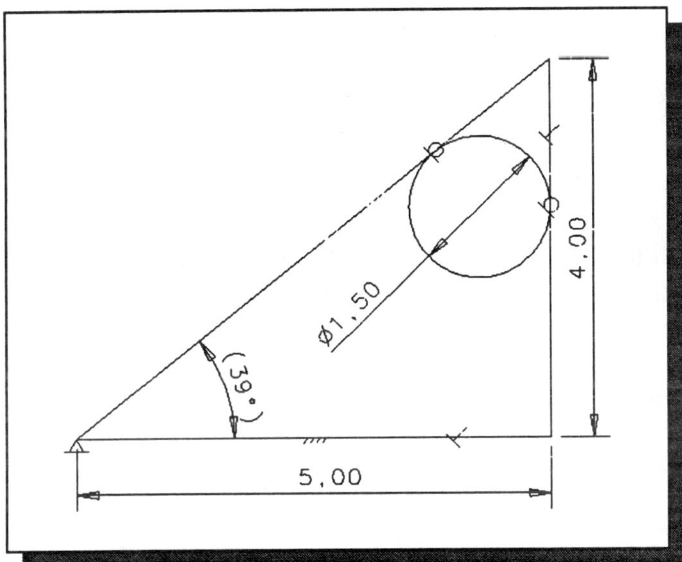

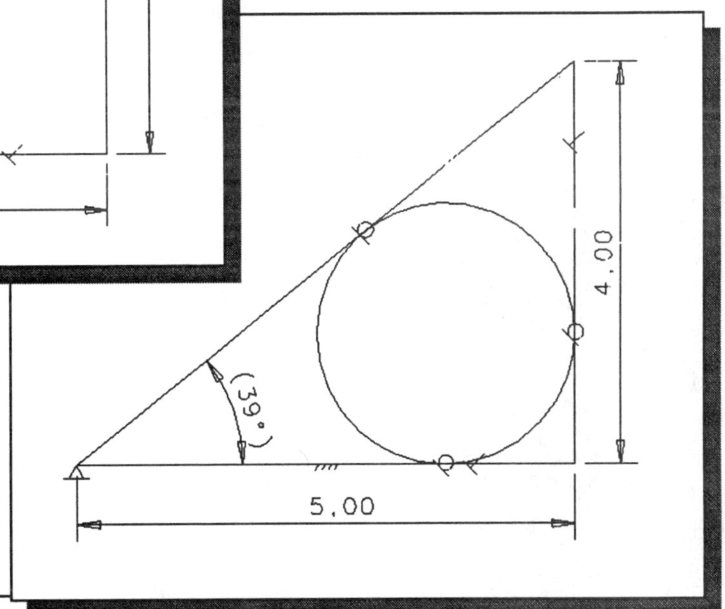

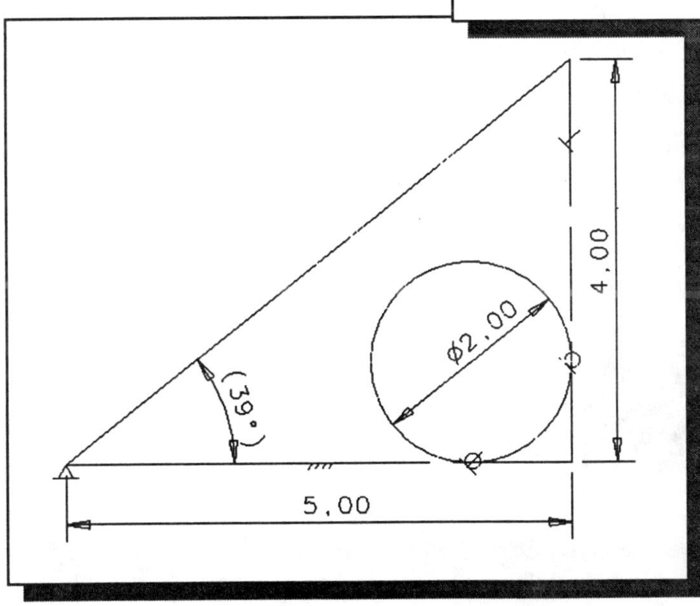

Questions:

1. What is the difference between *Dimensional Constraint* and *Geometric Constraint*?

2. Which color is used in I-DEAS to identify fully constrained geometry?

3. How do we access the *Navigator Controls* window?

4. Describe the *Match* option located in the *Modify Dimension* window.

5. List and describe the different constraint color codes.

6. List and describe three geometric constraints used in the chapter.

7. Does I-DEAS allow us to build partially constrained or totally unconstrained solid models? What are the advantages and disadvantages of building these types of models?

8. Identify and describe the following commands.

(a)

(b)

(c)

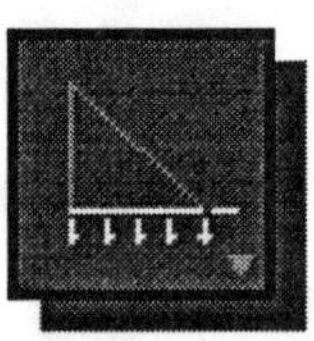

(d)

Exercises:

(Create and establish three parametric relations for each of the following designs.)

1.

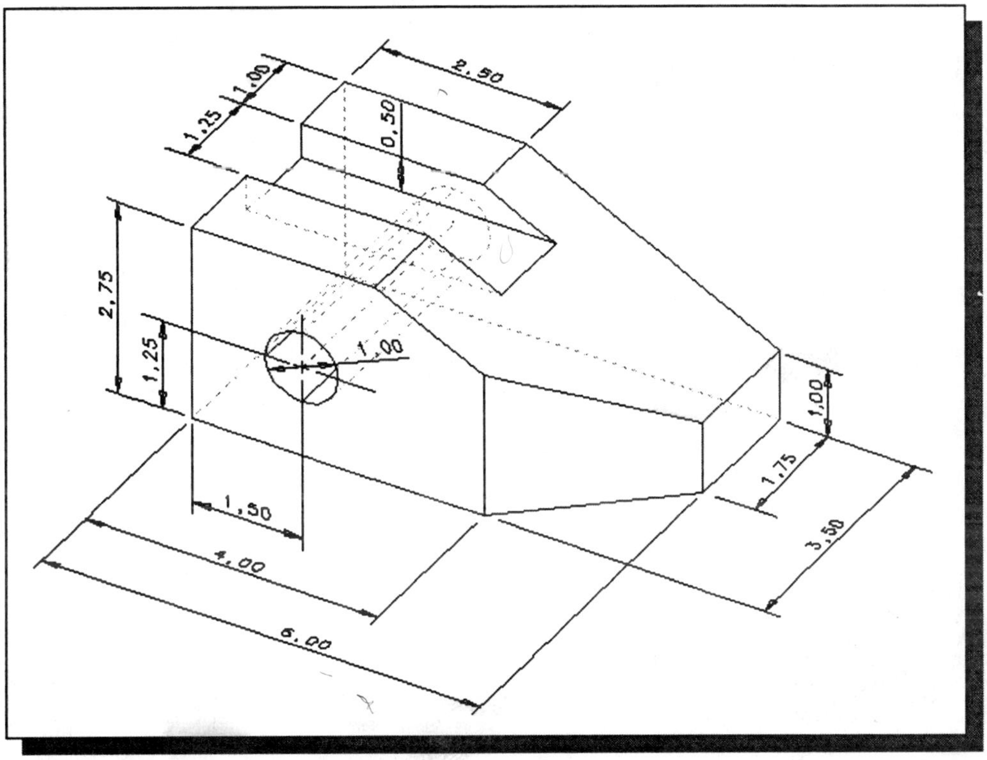

2.

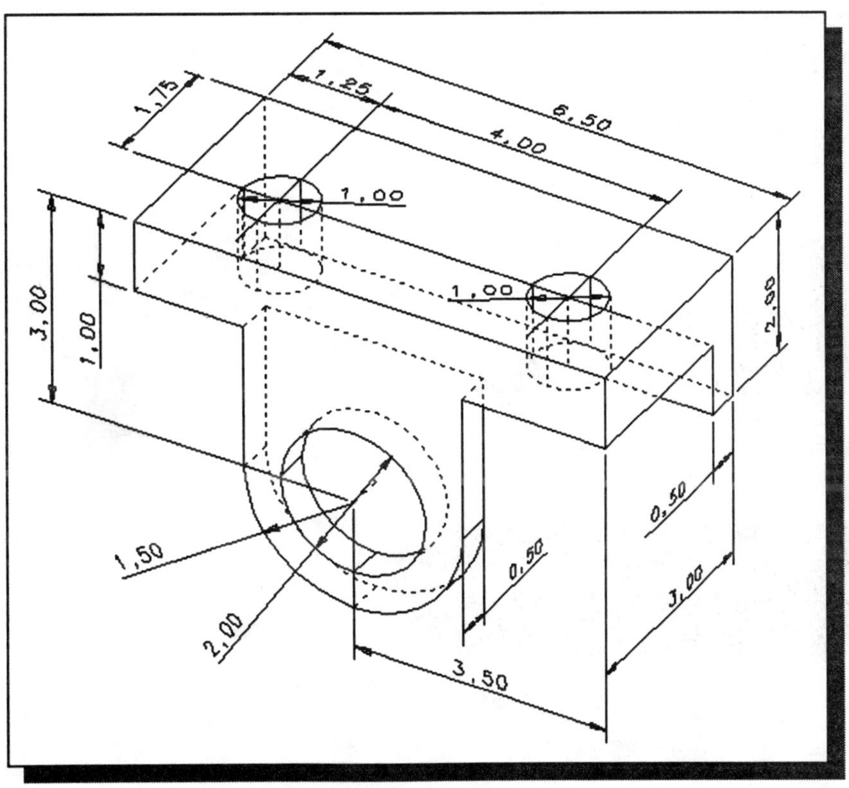

Notes:

Chapter 6
Geometric Construction Tools

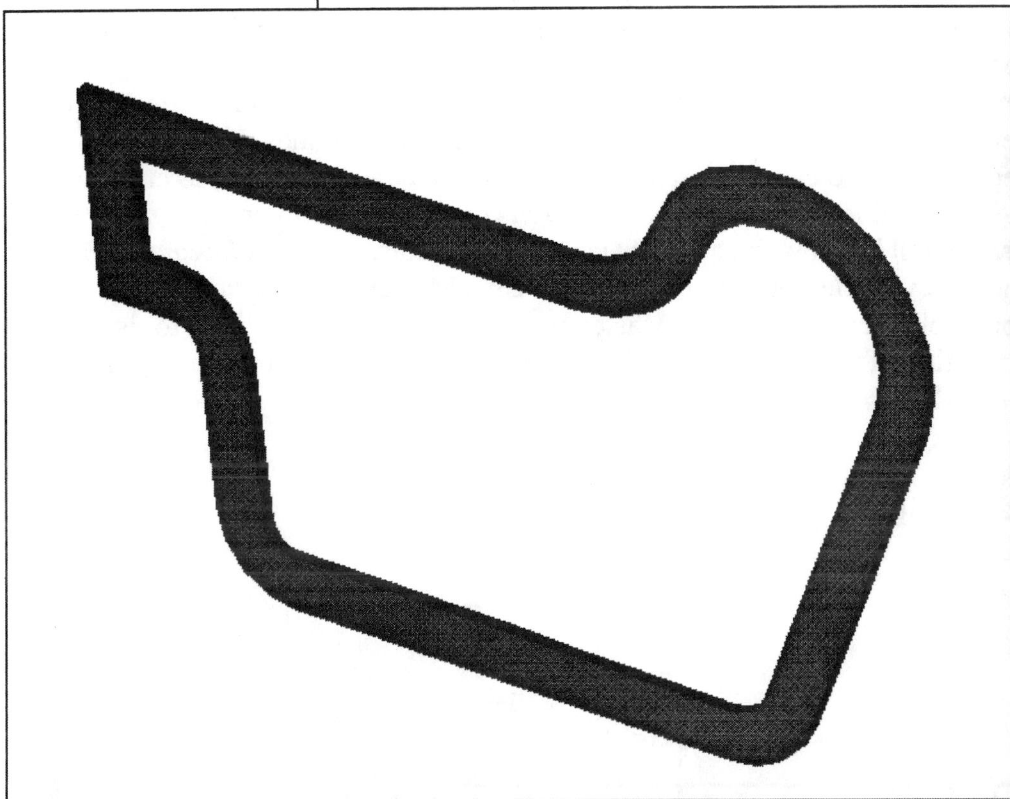

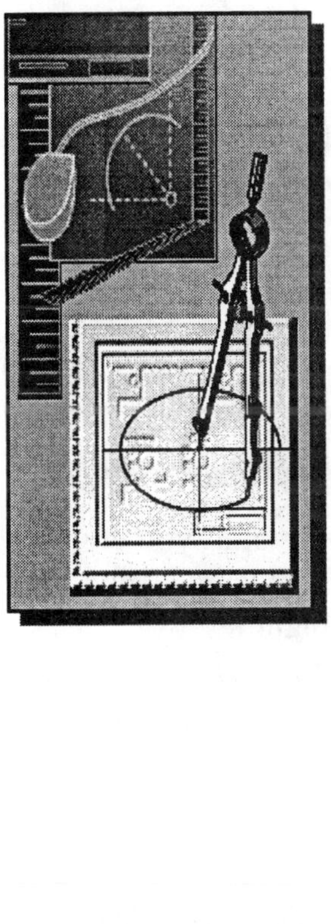

Learning Objectives

When you have completed this lesson, you will be able to:

- ♦ Use the Trim/Extend command.
- ♦ Use the Offset command.
- ♦ Understand the Haystack Geometry Approach.
- ♦ Use the 2-D Fillet command.
- ♦ Duplicate wireframe geometry using the Move command.
- ♦ Use the Selection Filter.
- ♦ Apply Geometric Constraints Manually.

Introduction

The main characteristics of solid modeling are the accuracy and completeness of the geometric database of three-dimensional objects. However, working in three dimensional space using input and output devices that are largely two-dimensional in nature is potentially tedious and confusing. I-DEAS Master Modeler provides an assortment of two-dimensional construction tools to make the creation of wireframe geometry easier and more efficient. The I-DEAS Master Modeler includes two types of wireframe geometry: **Curves** and **Sections. Curves** are basic geometric entities such as lines, arcs, etc. A **section** is a group of curves used to define a boundary. The boundary can be closed or open and can contain holes. Sections are commonly used to create extruded and revolved features. An *invalid section* consists of self-intersecting curves. In this Chapter, we will begin with basic 2-D construction tools, such as *trim and extend*, then introduce the very flexible and powerful I-DEAS Master Modeler *haystack geometry* approach to create *sections*. Mastering the geometric construction tools along with the application of proper constraints and parametric relations is the true essence of *parametric modeling.*

The Gasket Design

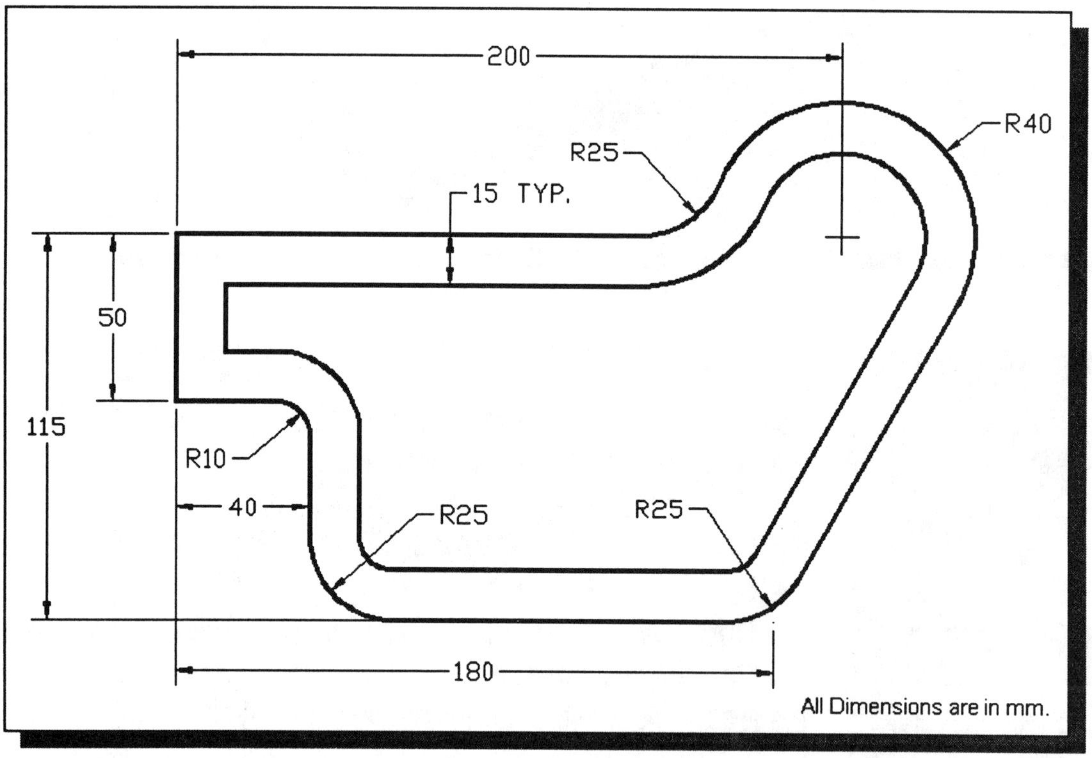

❖ Based on your knowledge of I-DEAS Master Modeler so far, how would you create this design? What are the more difficult geometries involved in the design? Take a few minutes to consider a modeling strategy and do preliminary planning by sketching on a piece of paper. You are also encouraged to create the design on your own prior to following through the tutorial.

Modeling Strategy

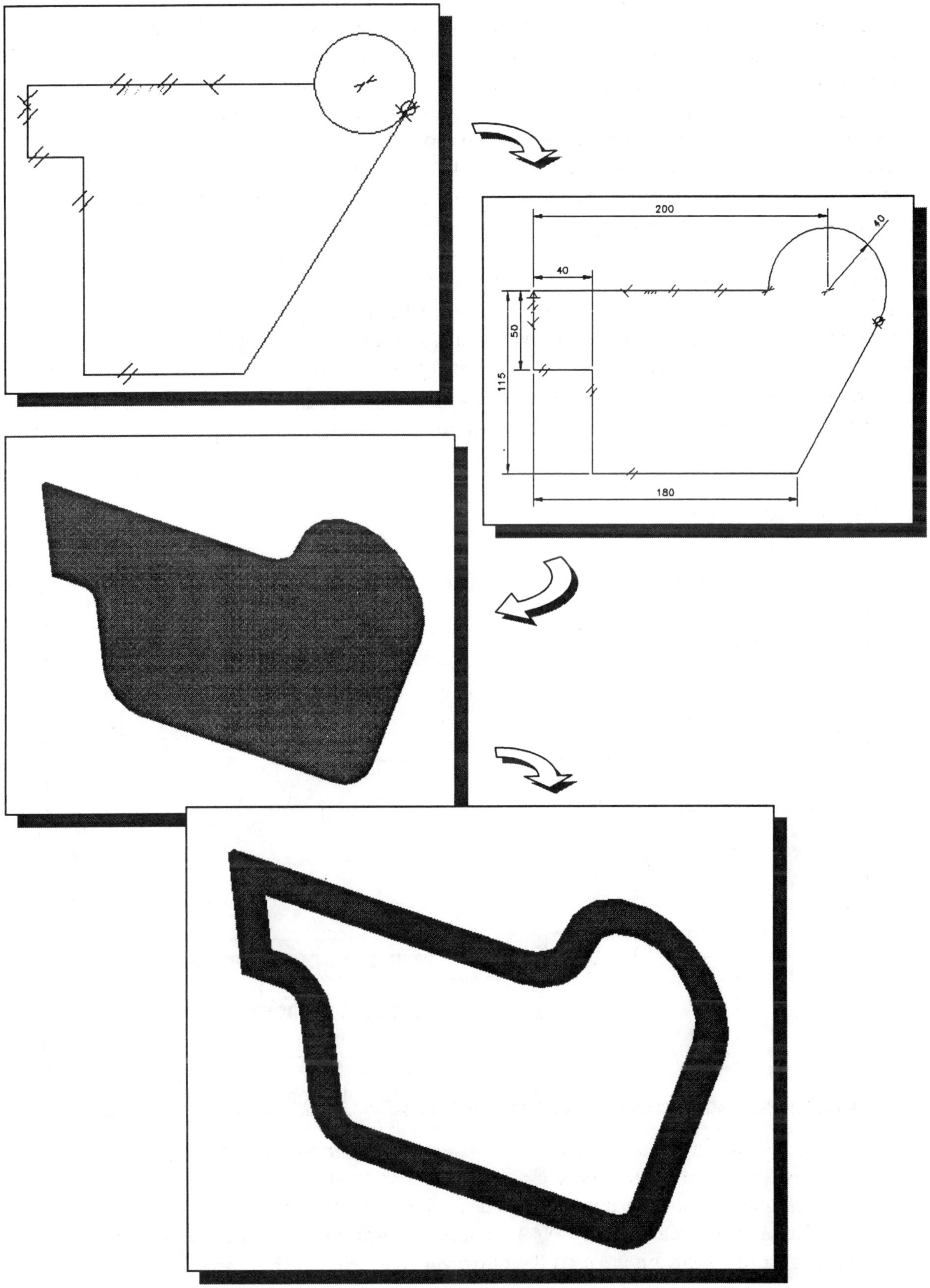

Starting I-DEAS

1. Login to the computer and bring up I-DEAS Master Series. Start a new model file by filling in the items as shown below in the *I-DEAS Start* window:

Project Name: **(Your account Name)**
Model File Name: **Gasket**
Application: **Design**
Task: **Master Modeler**
OK

2. After you click **OK**, a *warning window* will appear to tell you that a new model file will be created. Click **OK** to continue.

3. We will create the design using the default units: millimeter and milli-newton (**mm_(milli_newton)**). Confirm the settings by examining the units settings displayed in the I-DEAS *list window*.

2-D Sketching

We will create the model using different 2-D construction tools. We will first concentrate on the outline of the design.

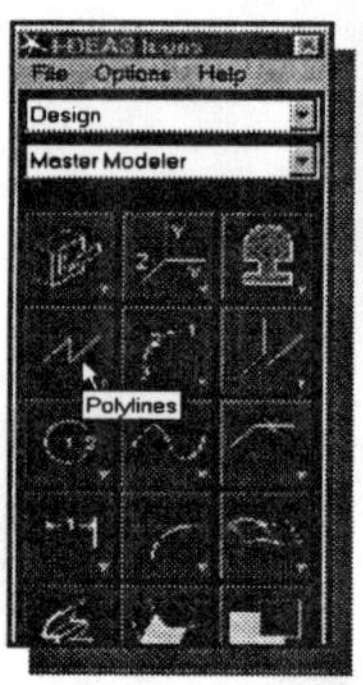

1. Choose **Polylines** in the icon panel. The message "*Locate start*" is displayed in the prompt window.

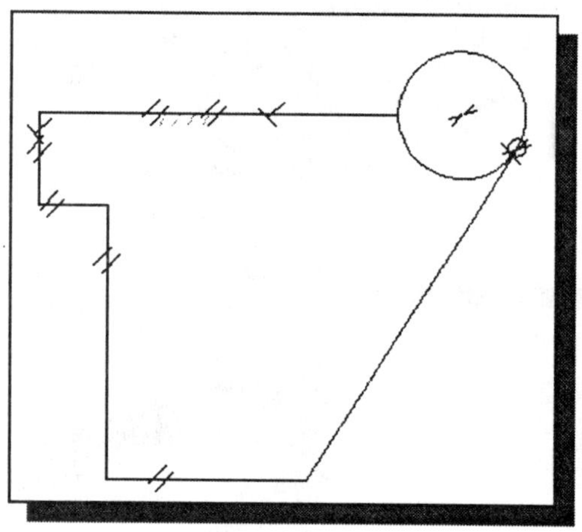

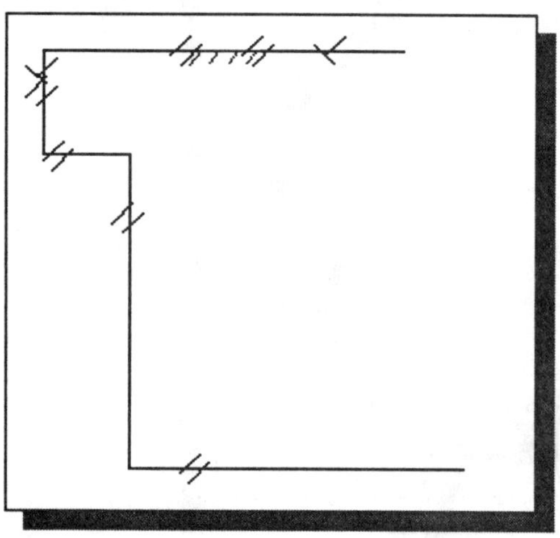

2. Create a sketch as shown. Start the sketch from the top-right corner. The line segments are all parallel and/or perpendicular to each other. We will intentionally make the line segments of arbitrary length, as it is quite common during design stage that not all of the values are determined.

3. Press the **ENTER** key or the **middle-mouse-button** twice to end the *Polylines* command.

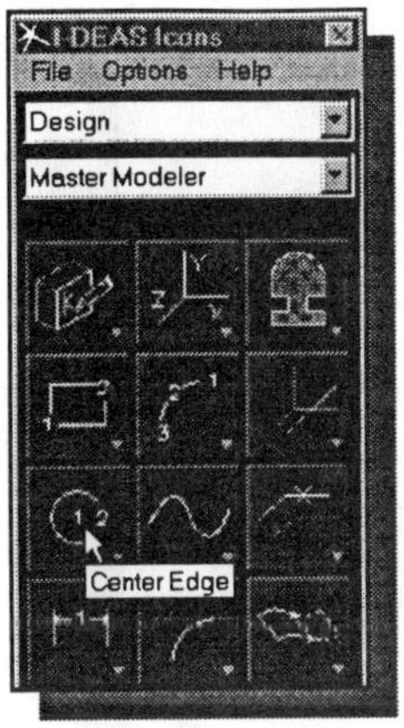

4. Choose *Circle* – **Center Edge** in the icon panel. The message "*Locate center*" is displayed in the prompt window.

5. Pick the center point to the right of the top horizontal line. Use the Dynamic Navigator to align the center point of the circle to the horizontal line.

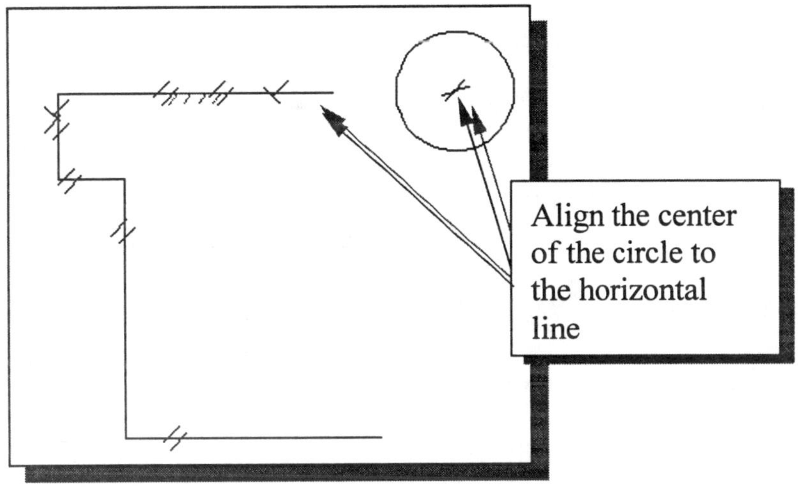

6. We will intentionally leave a gap in between the line and the circle. Move the cursor toward the left and create a circle of arbitrary size by clicking once with the left-mouse-button.

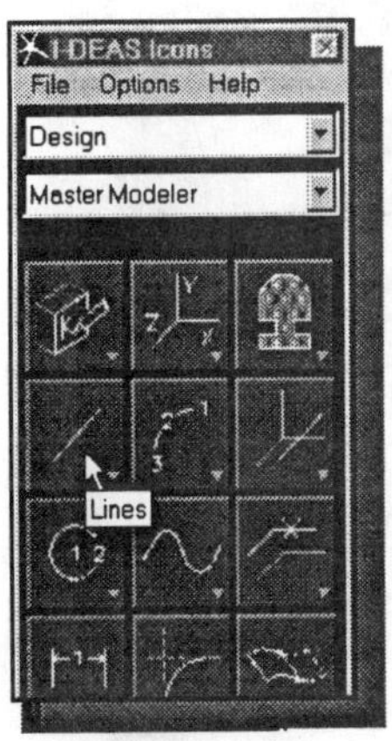

7. Choose **Lines** in the icon panel. (The icon is located at the same icon stack as the *Polylines* icon.) The message "*Locate start*" is displayed in the prompt window.

8. Move the cursor near the upper portion of the circle and pick a location on the circle when the *Tangency* symbol is displayed.

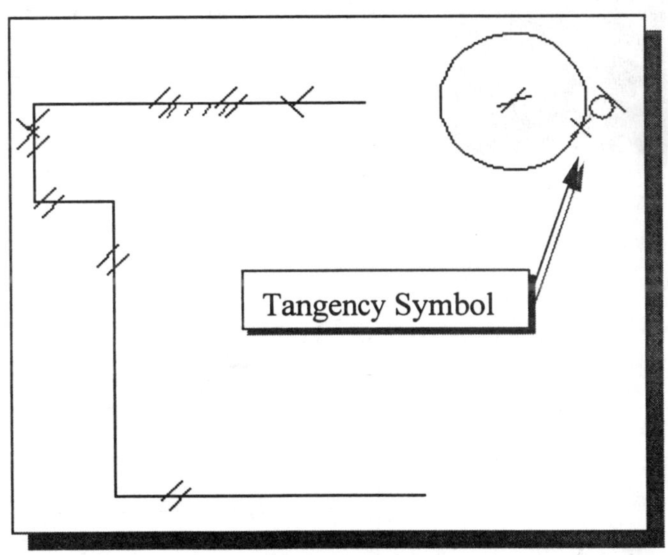

9. For the other end of this line, use the *Dynamic Navigator* to select a point on the lower horizontal line that is at about one-third from the right endpoint. Note the different constraint symbols displayed.

10. Press the **ENTER** key or the **middle-mouse-button** to end the *Lines* command.

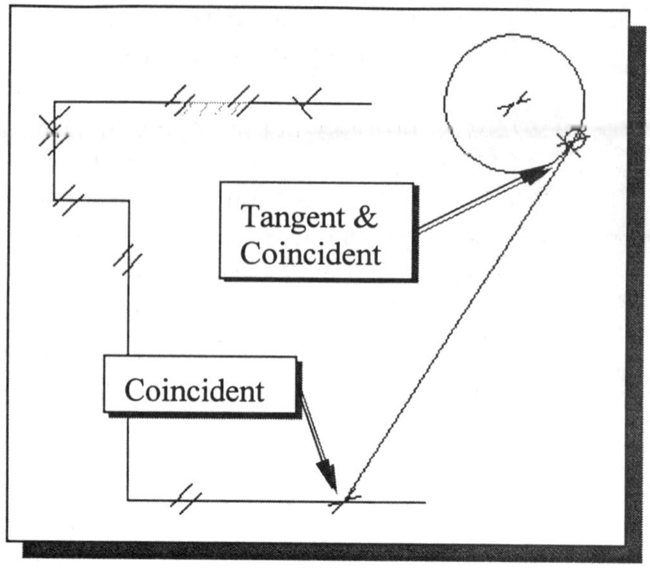

Using the *Trim/Extend* Command

The ***Trim/Extend*** command can be used to shorten/lengthen an object so that it ends precisely at a boundary. As a general rule, the way we pick the curve determines which side of the curve will be modified.

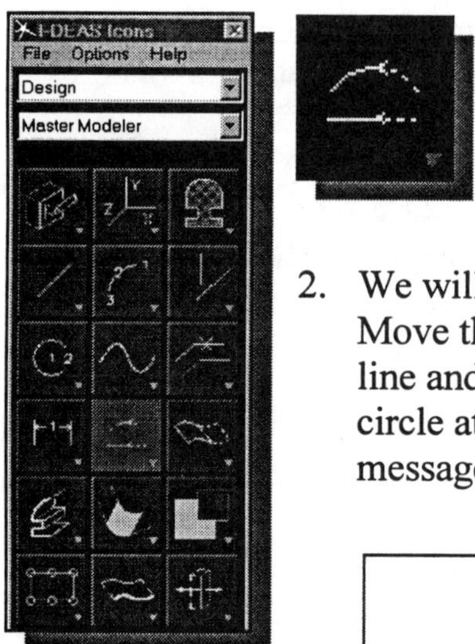

1. Choose **Trim/Extend** in the icon panel. The icon is located in the fourth row of the task specific icon panel. The message "*Pick curve to trim*" is displayed in the prompt window.

2. We will first trim the bottom horizontal line to the inclined line. Move the cursor near the right endpoint of the bottom horizontal line and pick the line. I-DEAS Master Modeler will place a small circle at the endpoint indicating the side to be modified. The message "*Pick curve to trim to*" is displayed in the prompt window.

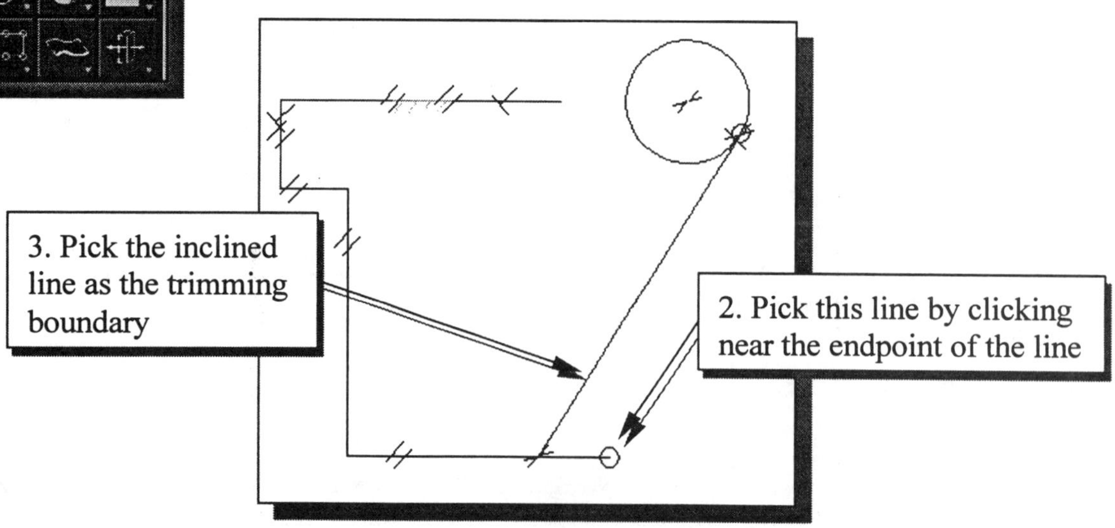

3. Pick the inclined line as the trimming boundary. The horizontal line is trimmed precisely to the inclined line.

4. We will next extend the top horizontal line to the circle. I-DEAS Master Modeler uses the same command for trim or extend. The **trim** operation is performed if the endpoint goes past the selected boundary and the **extend** operation is performed if the curve needs to be lengthened to reach the selected boundary. Move the cursor near the right endpoint of the top horizontal line and select the line. I-DEAS Master Modeler will place a small circle at the endpoint indicating the side to be modified. The message "*Pick curve to trim to*" is displayed in the prompt window.

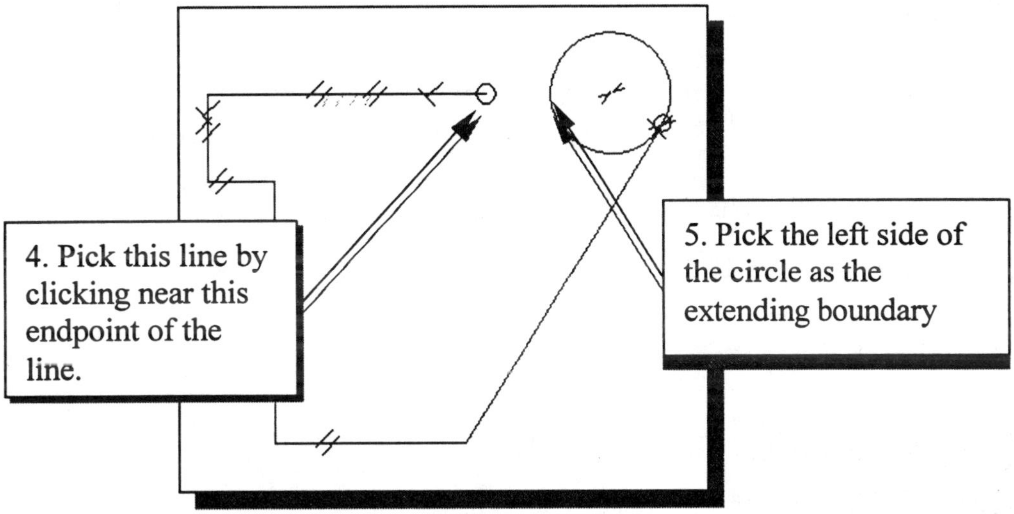

5. Pick the left side of the circle as the extending boundary. The top horizontal line is extended precisely to the circle as shown below. Because a line could intersect at two locations with a circle, the way we select the boundary determines how the line is extended.

6. Press the **ENTER** key or the **middle-mouse-button** to end the *Trim/Extend* command.

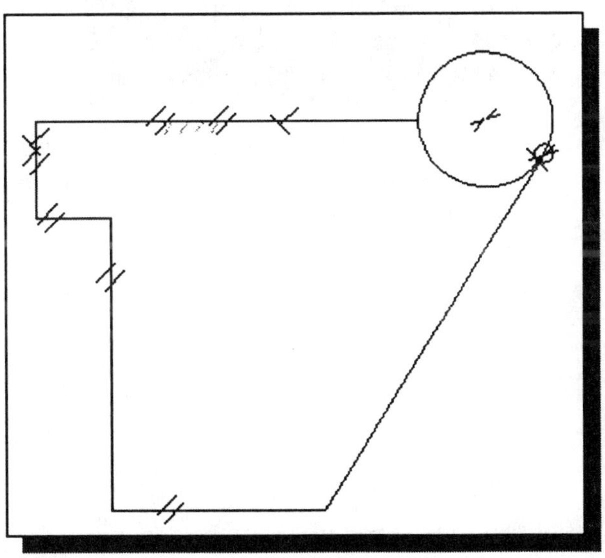

Adding Additional Constraints

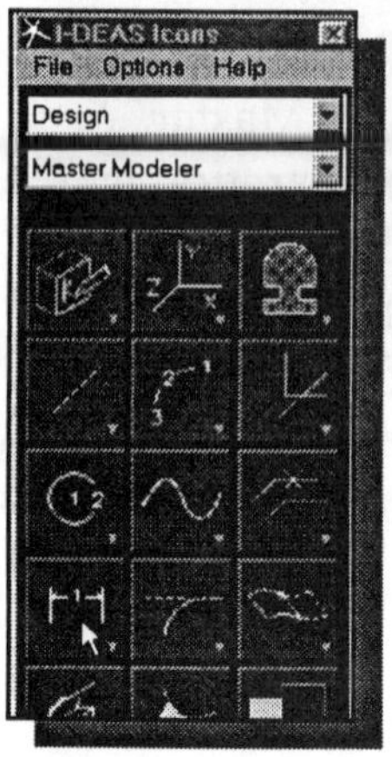

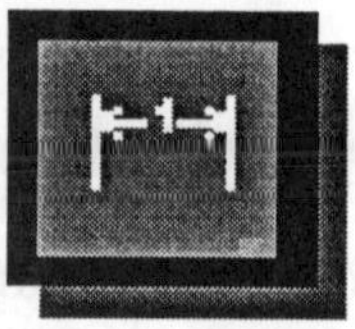

1. Choose **Dimension** in the icon panel. Add the horizontal location dimension, from the top-left vertical edge to the center of the circle as shown.

❖ Do not be overly concerned with the dimensional values, we are still working on creating a rough sketch and the dimensional values will be adjusted in the next section.

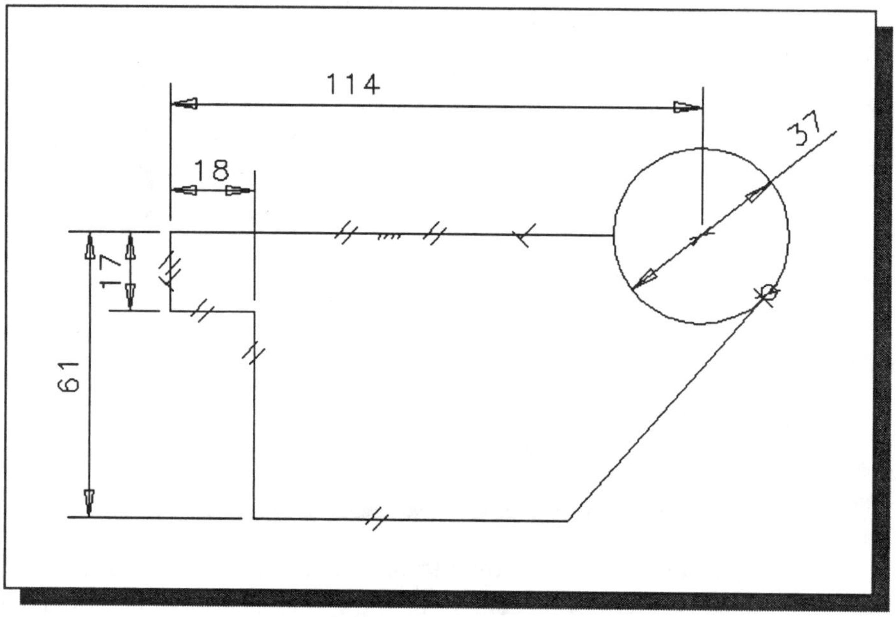

2. On your own, reposition the dimensions so that the sketch appears as shown in the above figure.

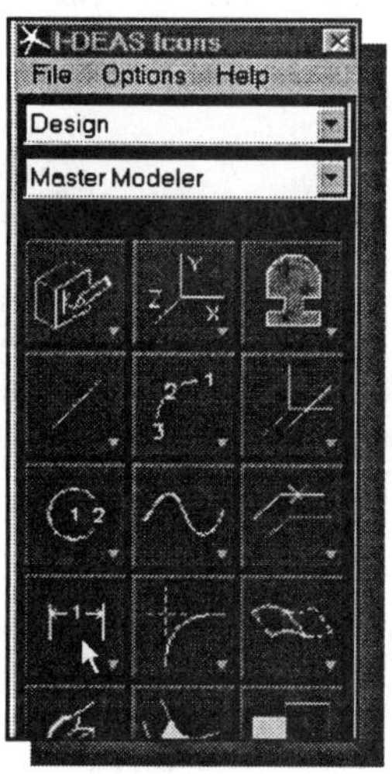

3. Press and hold down on the ***Dimension*** icon to display the other choices. Slide the cursor downward to select the **Constrain & Dimension...** option. The *Constrain* menu appears.

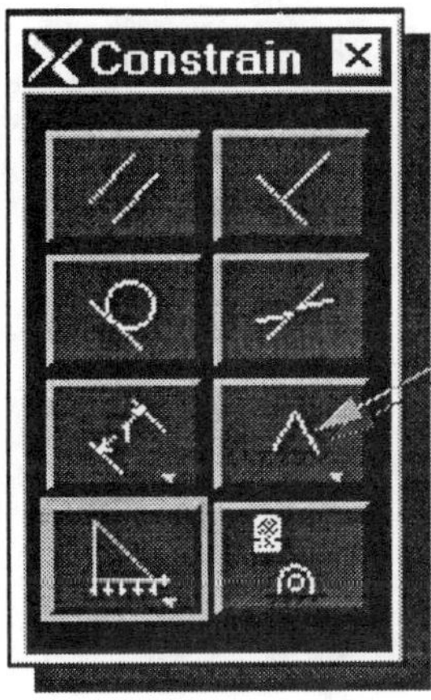

4. We will restrict horizontal movement of the sketch by placing an *anchor constraint*. Choose **Anchor** in the pop-up menu. In the prompt window, the message "*Pick a point or curve*" is displayed.

5. Pick the top-left corner of the sketch to apply the *anchor constraint*.

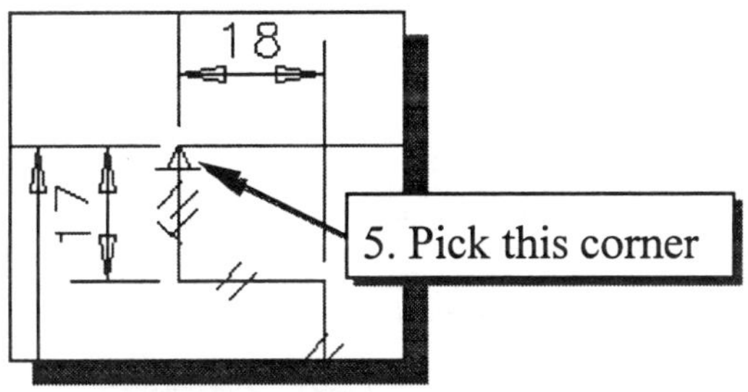

➢ We will also add a *coincident constraint* to assure coincidence between the top horizontal line and the circle.

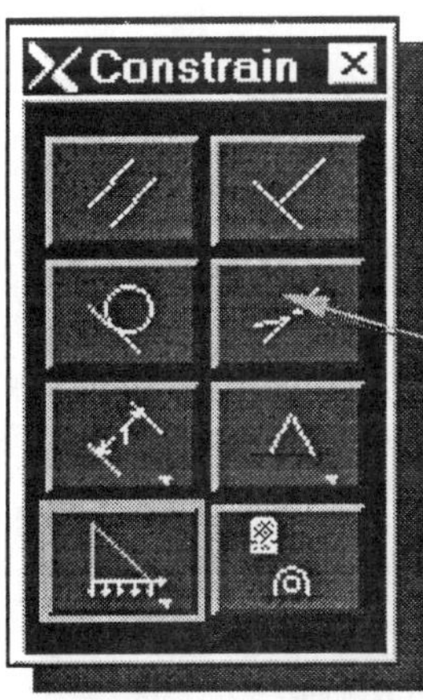

6. Choose **Coincident** in the pop-up menu. In the prompt window, the message "*Pick the first entity to constrain*" is displayed.

7. Pick the right endpoint of the top horizontal line.

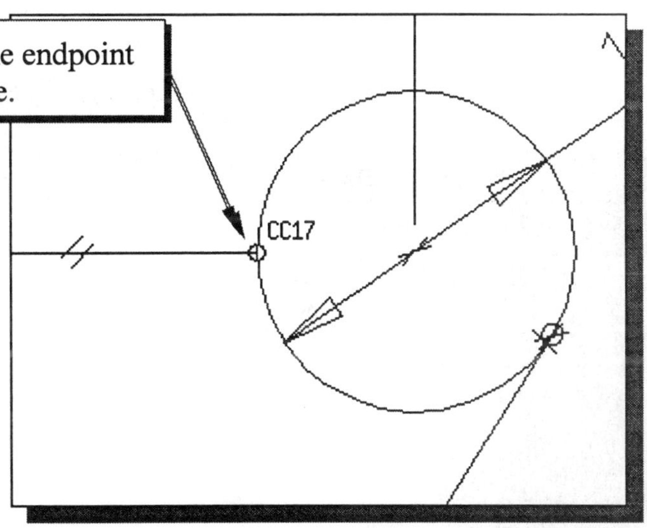

8. In the *prompt window*, the message "*Pick the second entity to constrain*" is displayed. Pick the circle. The coincident constraint will restrict the length of the horizontal line to be always trimmed/extended to the circle.

9. On your own, use the **Show Free** command to examine the constraint conditions of the sketched shape.

10. On your own, add the bottom dimension so that the sketched shape is fully constrained as shown.

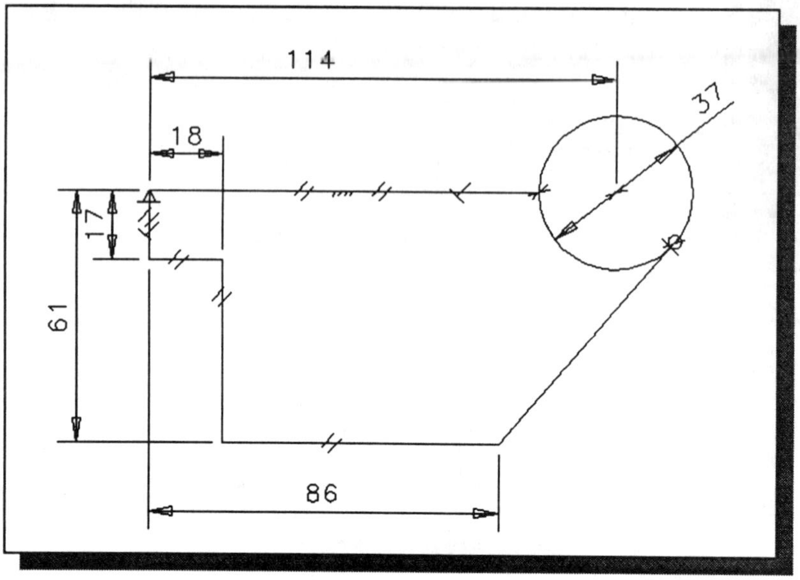

11. Click on the **[X]** button to close the *Constrain* window.

11. Close the window

Modifying Dimensional Values

Next we will modify the dimensional values to the desired values.

1. Pre-select all the dimensions by holding down the SHIFT key and left clicking on all of the dimensional values. The selected items will be highlighted.

PRE-SELECT SHIFT + LEFT-mouse-button

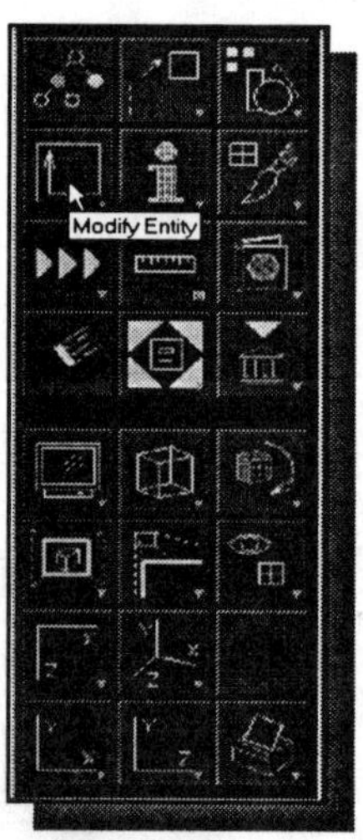

2. Choose **Modify** in the icon panel. The *Modify Dimensions* window appears.

3. In the *Modify Dimensions* window, change the values to the desired values as shown below.

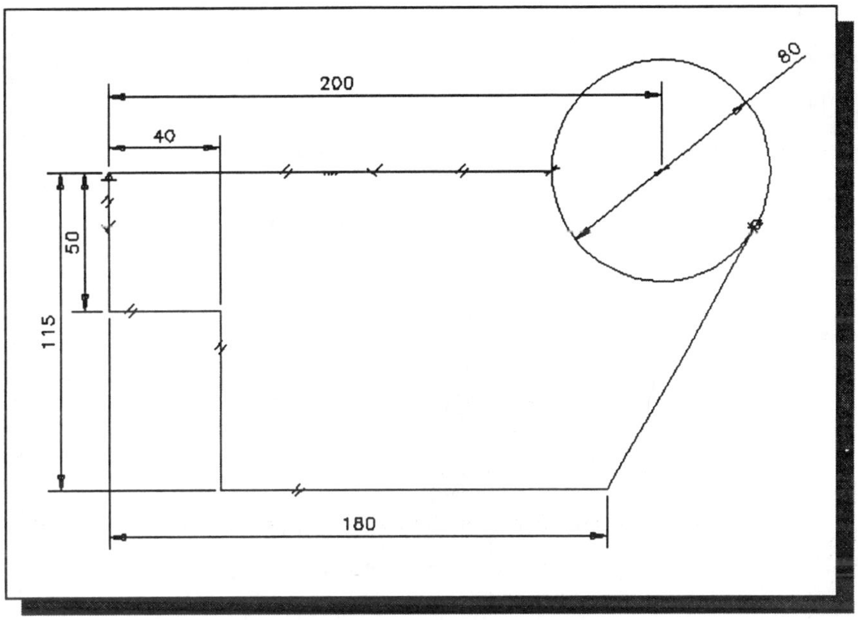

➢ Note that by applying proper constraints to the sketched wireframe geometry, a ***variational constraint network*** is created that assures the geometry shape behaves predictably as changes are made.

Making a Copy of the Sketch using the Move Command

To demonstrate two methods of editing the wireframe geometry, we will create a copy of the 2-D sketch using the *Move* command.

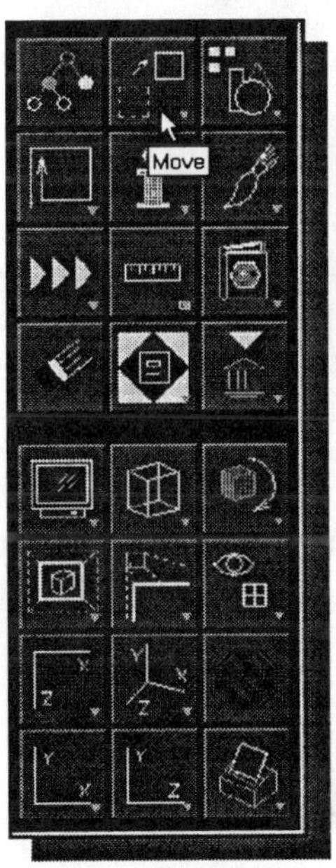

1. Choose **Move** in the icon panel. The message "*Pick entity to move*" is displayed in the prompt window.

❖ As the design becomes more complex, it maybe harder to select the desired entities. We will demonstrate using the *filter* option to aid the selection of the sketched geometry.

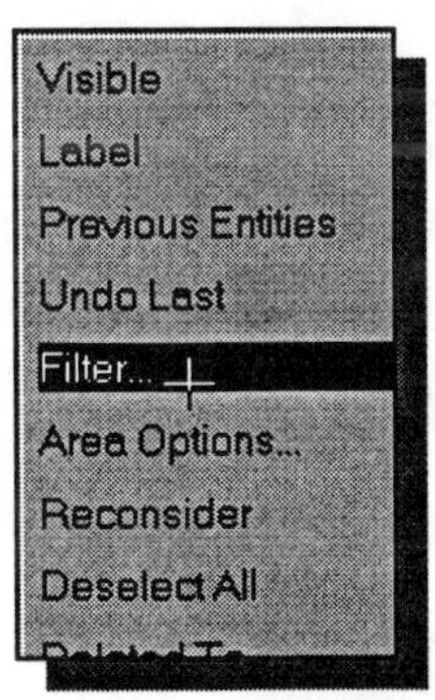

2. Move the cursor inside the graphics window. Press and hold down the right-mouse-button to display the *Option* menu.

3. Pick the **Filter...** option. This will bring up the *Selection Filter* window, which is used to control the types of entities that are selectable.

4. By default, all entities are selectable. Therefore, no items are listed under the *Non-Pickable* box. Click on the ***Select All*** button that is below the *Pickable* box. Notice that all items in the box are highlighted, this signifies all entries are selected.

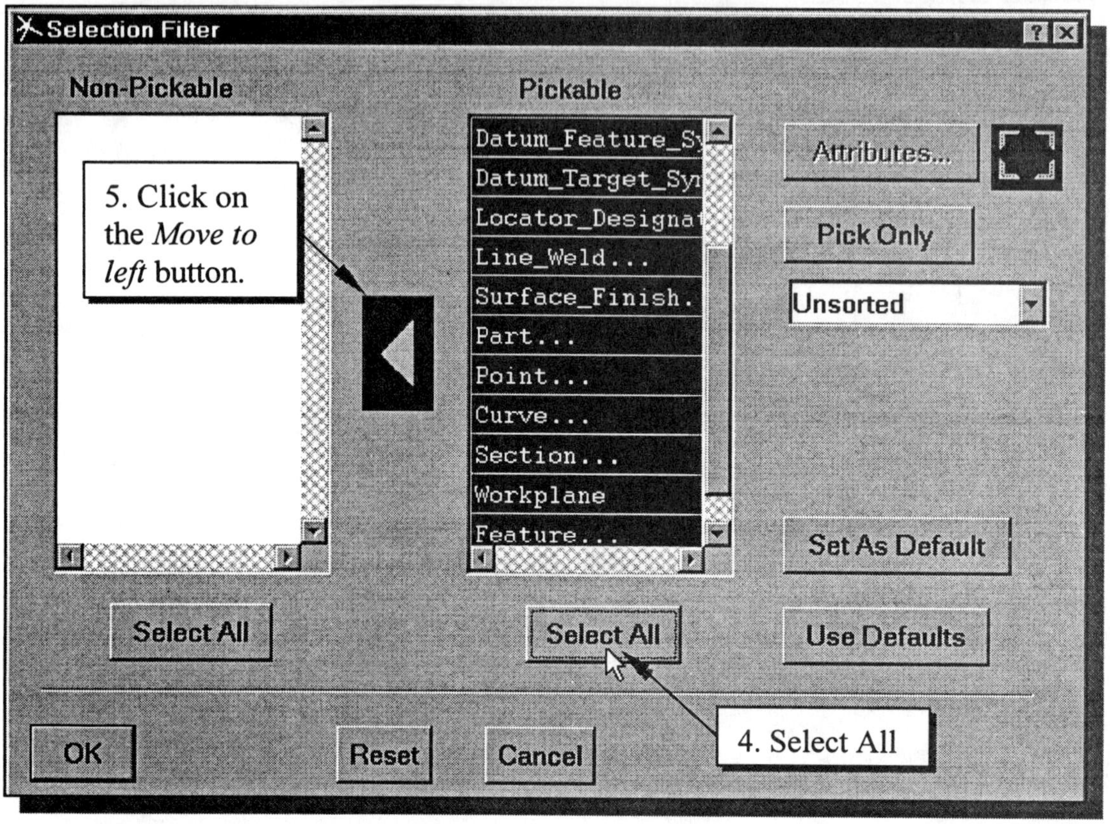

5. Click on the **solid triangle** button located in between the *Non-pickable* and *Pickable* boxes, this is the *Move to left* button. This will move all the highlighted entries from one box to the other, which will make all entities non-pickable.

6. In the *Non-Pickable* list box, use the scroll bar to scroll downward and pick **Curve** from the list.

7. Click on the **solid triangle** button in between the *Non-pickable* and *Pickable* boxes, the *Move to right* button. This will make *Curve* the only *pickable* type of entity.

8. Click on the **OK** button to exit the *Selection Filter* window. Now, only *curves* are pickable items.

9. Move the cursor inside the graphics window. Press and hold down the **right-mouse-button** to display the *Option* menu.

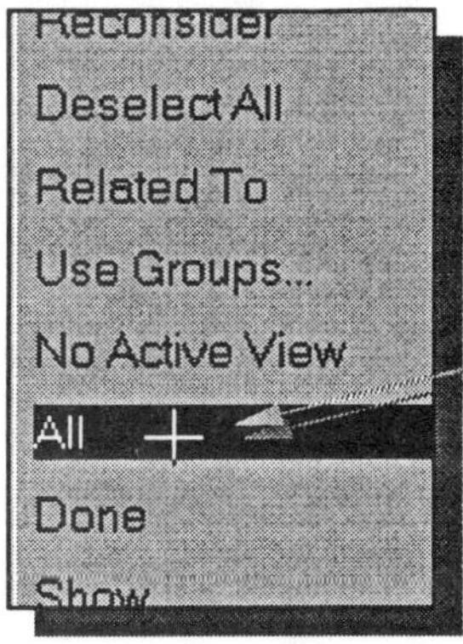

10. Select the **All** option. This option causes all the *Curves* to be selected, which includes all the lines and the circle created thus far. All curves change color to indicate they have been picked.

11. Press the **ENTER** key or the middle-mouse-button to accept the selected entities.

12. Select the **Copy Switch** option in the pop-up menu.

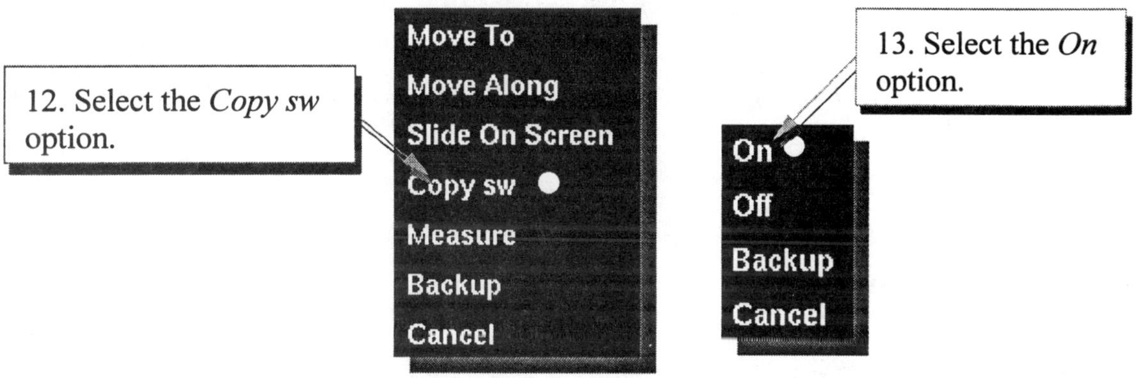

13. Select the **ON** option in the pop-up menu.

14. In the prompt window, the message "*Enter translation x,y,z (0.0,0.0,0.0)*" is displayed. We will place the copy toward the right side of the original sketch. Type: **300,0,0** in the prompt window and press the **ENTER** key to proceed with the *Move* command.

15. The message "*Enter number of copies (1)*" is displayed in the prompt window. Press the **ENTER** key to accept the default value and proceed to create the copy.

16. Click on the **Zoom-All** icon to view both images on the screen.

❖ I-DEAS has created a copy of the original sketch, including all the geometric constraints. In I-DEAS Master Modeler, the *Copy Switch* is a convenient way to duplicate *wireframe entities* (such as lines, arcs, and circles).

First Construction Method – Trim/Extend

We will next demonstrate two different methods to complete the 2-D sketch. The first method is to use the *Trim/Extend* command and manually adjust the shape of the geometry. We will apply the command on the copy that we just created.

1. Use the *Dynamic Viewing* command to pan to the right.

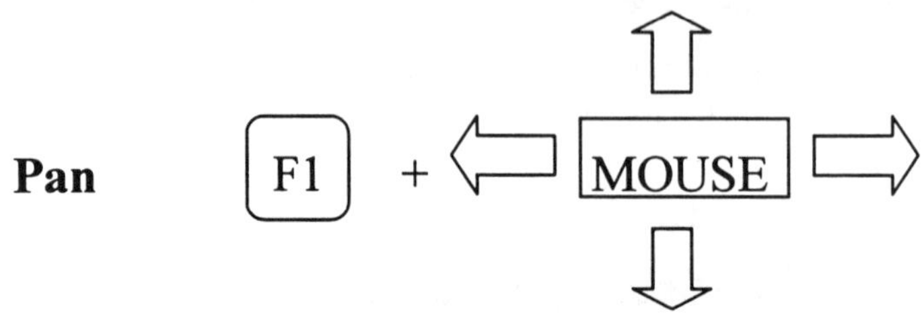

2. Use the *Dynamic Viewing* command to zoom in/out and adjust the viewing of the display.

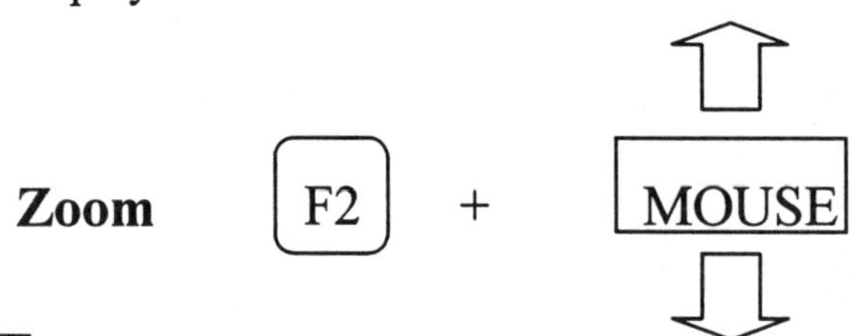

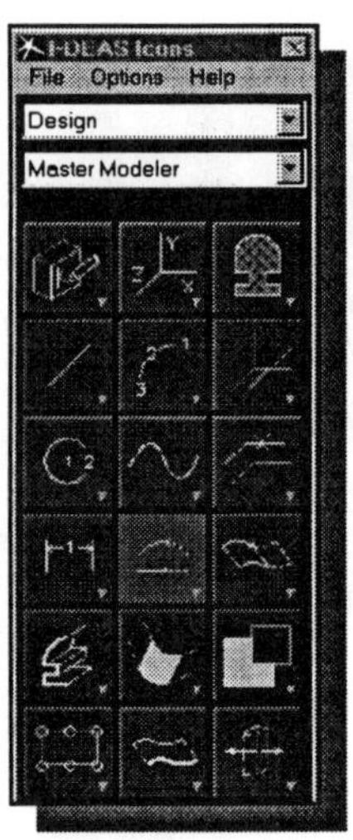

3. Choose **Trim/Extend** in the icon panel. The message "*Pick curve to trim*" is displayed in the prompt window.

4. Pick the lower portion of the circle. A circle is treated as a wireframe entity that begins and ends at the same location. The message "*Pick curve to trim to*" is displayed in the prompt window.

5. Pick the inclined line as the boundary. An arc will replace the circle as shown. By trimming this way, we are controlling the direction of the trim to avoid any ambiguity.

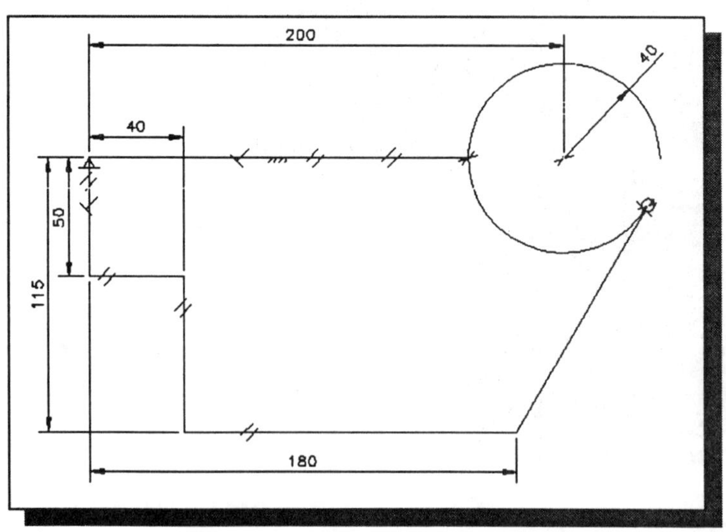

6. We will continue to trim/extend the arc to keep only the upper portion of the arc. Pick the lower end of the arc.

7. Pick the top horizontal line. The bottom of the arc is removed.

8. Pick the right-hand end of the arc.

9. Pick the inclined line to extend the arc.

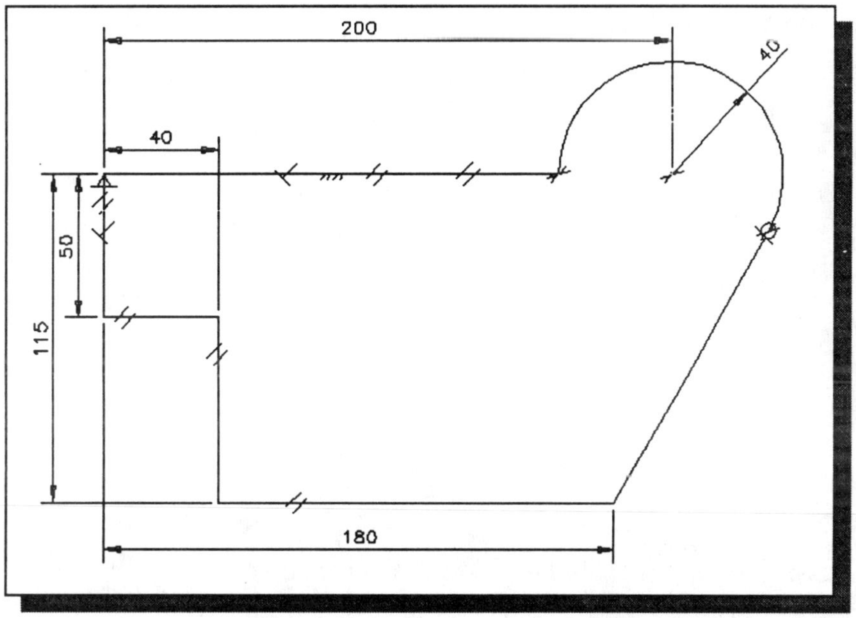

❖ The completed shape took quite a few steps using the *Trim/Extend* command. However, we will next investigate an alternate approach that uses "*Haystack Geometry.*" The "*Haystack Geometry*" approach can be used to automatically select neighboring entities to form a closed region called a ***section.***

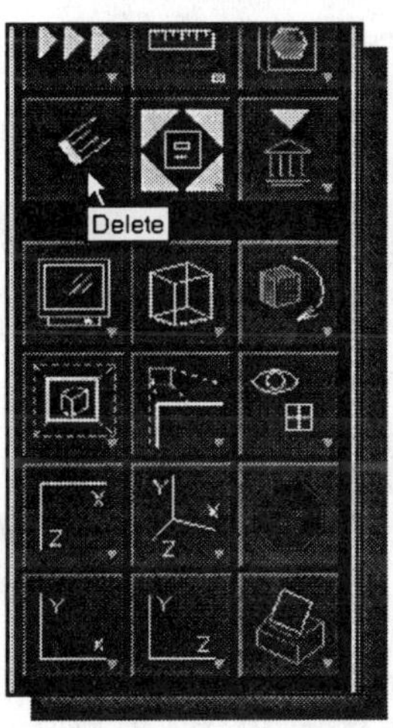

➢ On your own, use the *Filter* option and delete the copy we have created and modified in this section. For the rest of the tutorial, we will concentrate on the original sketch.

Creating 2-D Fillets

Before demonstrating the "*Haystack Geometry*" approach, we will add additional construction geometry to the sketch shape.

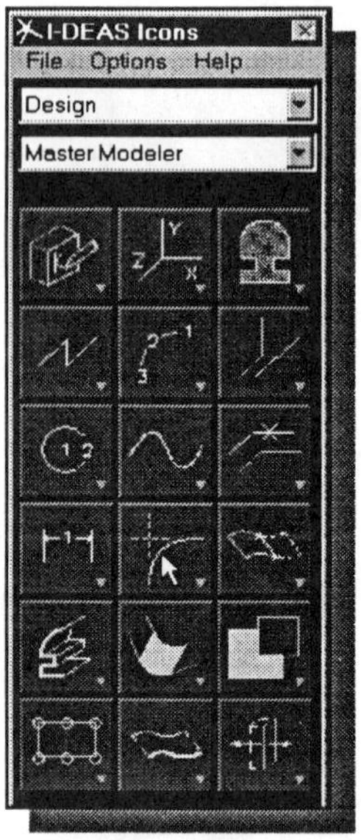

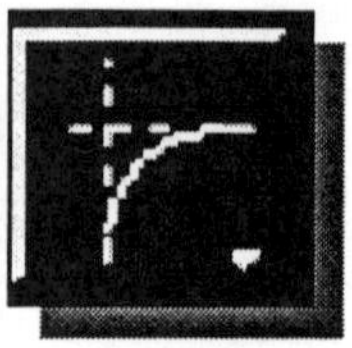

1. Choose **2-D Fillet** in the icon panel. (The icon is located in the fourth row of the task specific icon panel. The icon is located in the same icon stack as the *Trim/Extend* icon.)

❖ Note that there are two fillet commands available in I-DEAS *Master Modeler*; this is the *2-D Fillet* icon.

2. The message "*Pick section, curve or corner to fillet*" is displayed in the prompt window. Select the circle.

3. Select the top horizontal line. The *Fillet* window appears.

4. In the *Radius* box, enter the value of **25**.

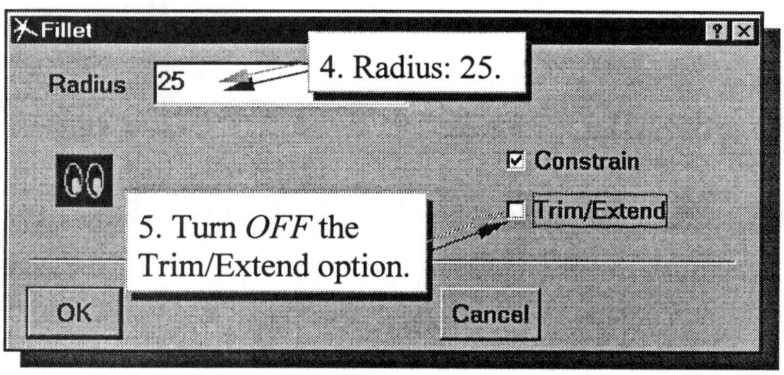

5. Confirm that the *Constrain* option is switched ***ON*** and turn ***OFF*** the *Trim/Extend* option. We will keep all the construction geometry to demonstrate the effects of using the "*Haystack Geometry*" approach.

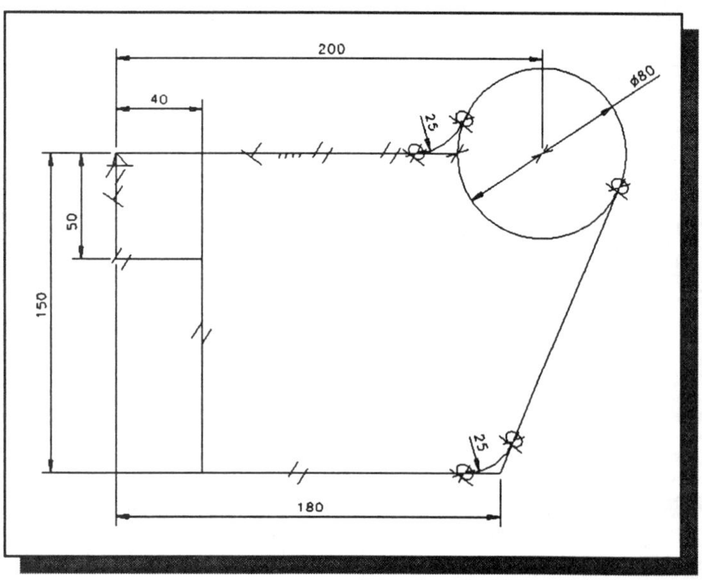

6. Select the **OK** icon to create the fillet. Your 2-D sketch should appear as shown.

7. Create another fillet at the lower-right corner as shown.

8. Examine all the construction geometry involved to create an outline of the design.

9. Press the **ENTER** key or the **middle-mouse-button** to end the *Fillet* command.

Second Construction Method – Haystack Geometry

In *I-DEAS*, **sections** are closed regions that are defined from sketches. Sections are used as cross sections to create solid features. For example, ***Extrude***, ***Revolve***, ***Sweep***, and ***Loft*** operations all require the definition of at least a single section. The sketches used to define a section can contain additional geometry since the additional geometry entities are consumed when the feature is created. To create a section we can create single or multiple closed regions, or we can select existing solid edges to form closed regions. A section cannot contain self-intersecting geometry; regions selected in a single operation form a single section. As a general rule, we should dimension and constrain sections to prevent them from unpredictable size and shape changes. *I-DEAS* does allow us to create under-constrained or non-constrained sections; the dimensions and/or constraints can be added/edited later.

Haystacking is a grouping mechanism that allows us to select only the wireframe entities that we wish to include in the section. *Haystacking* is a tool that helps maintain design intents by reducing the amount of trimming necessary to build a section.

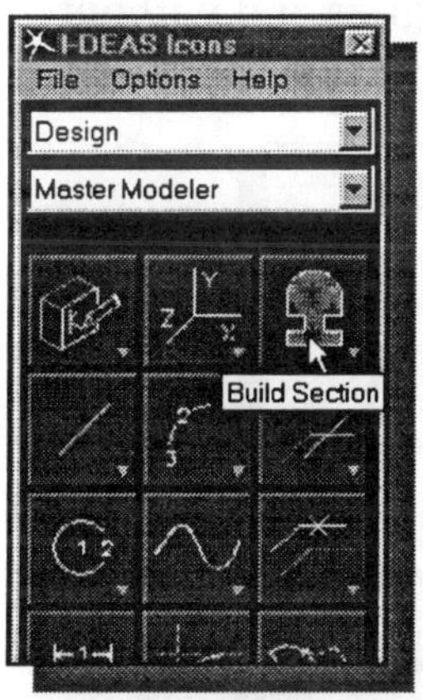

1. Select the **Build Section** icon. The message "*Pick curve or section*" is displayed in the prompt window.

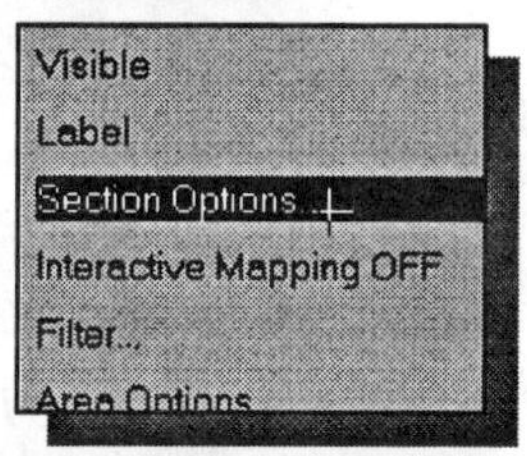

2. Move the cursor inside the graphics window. Press and hold down the right-mouse-button to select the **Section Options...** option. The *Section Options* window appears.

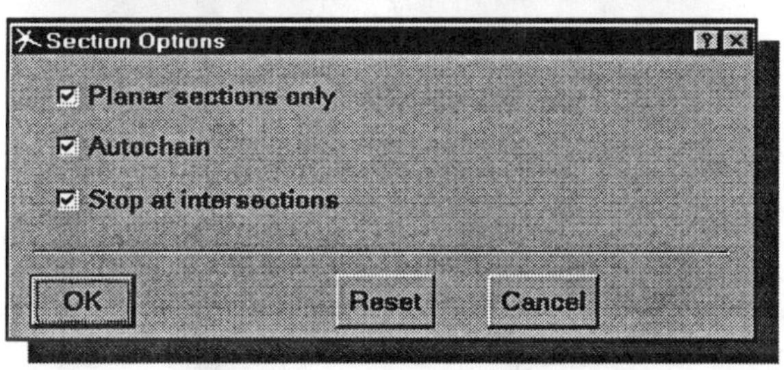

3. Switch **on** the ***Stop at intersections*** option so that all options in the section options window are turned on as shown.

- "*Planar Sections*" is redundant at this point because we have only a two-dimensional sketch. However, for a three-dimensional model it would restrict selections to entities in a single plane.

- "*Autochaining*" automatically links successive entities together either when they intersect at only one point or after a new segment is selected.

- "*Stop at intersections*" causes the section outline to proceed only to the next intersection where it awaits selection of the next segment before proceeding to build the section.

4. Pick the inclined line. The selected line-segment is highlighted and I-DEAS expects us to select additional entities that will form a closed region. The message "*Pick curve to continue*" is displayed in the prompt window.

5. Select the upper portion of the circle.

6. Select the fillet-arc tangent to the circle and the line. All connected line-segments are selected automatically with the autochaining option switched *on.*

7. Select the fillet-arc at the lower-right corner. This will complete the selections, which form a closed region. A new **SECTION** is created; notice the different color and line-weight shown.

8. The message "*Pick curve to add or remove (Done)*" is displayed in the prompt window. Press the **ENTER** key or the **middle-mouse-button** to end the *Build Section* command.

❖ The section is created without modifying any wireframe entities and without deleting previous constraints and dimensions.

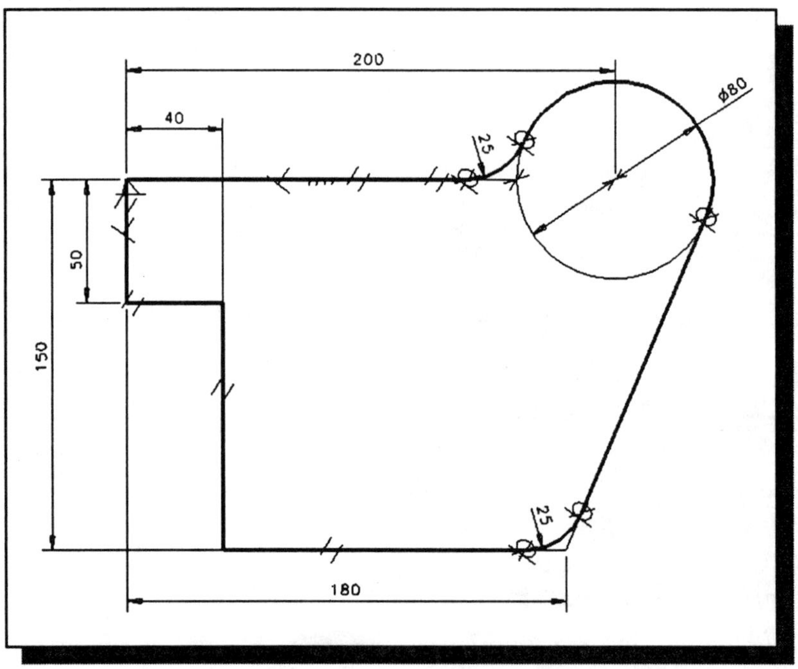

➢ The *Haystacking* approach eliminates the need to trim the wireframe geometry manually and a section is created automatically. This approach encourages engineering content over drafting technique, which is one of the key features of I-DEAS over other solid modeling software.

➢ Now is a good time to save your design (Use the Quick key: **[Ctrl]** + **[S]**). It is a good habit to save your design periodically, just in case something might and probably will go wrong while you are working on the computer. You should also save the design after you have completed any major constructions.

Creating Additional 2-D Fillets on the Section

The ***2-D Fillet*** command can also be used to modify **SECTION** geometry.

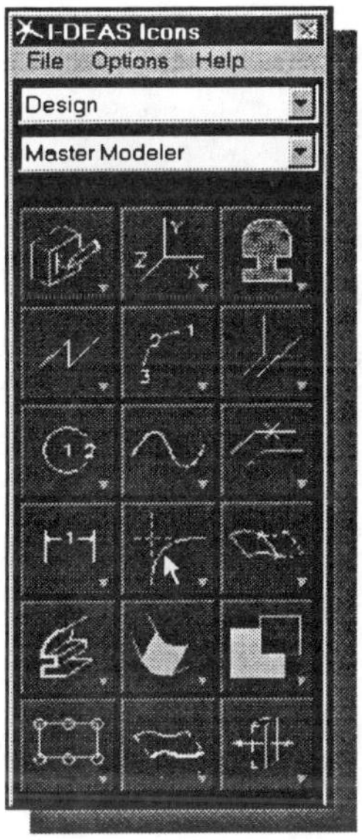

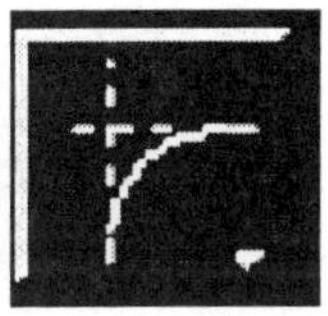

1. Choose **2-D Fillet** in the icon panel. (The icon is located in the fourth row of the task specific icon panel.) The message "*Pick section, curve or corner to fillet*" is displayed in the prompt window.

2. Pick the lower left corner of the section. (Watch the different variable names displayed as the cursor is moved along the section, and select **CCx** for the corner.) The *Fillet* window appears.

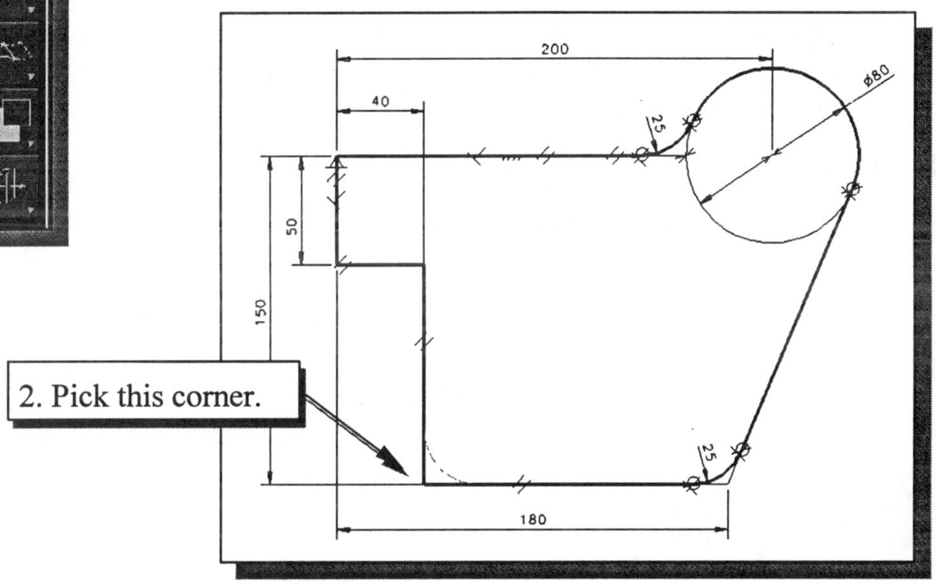

3. In the *Radius* box, enter the value of **25**.

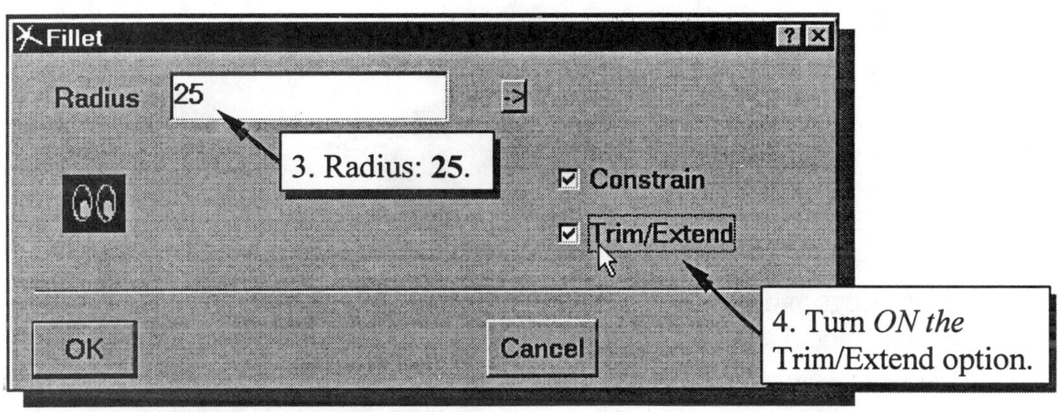

4. Turn **ON** the *Trim/Extend* option and confirm the *Constrain* option is also switched *ON*.

5. Click on the **OK** icon to create the fillet.

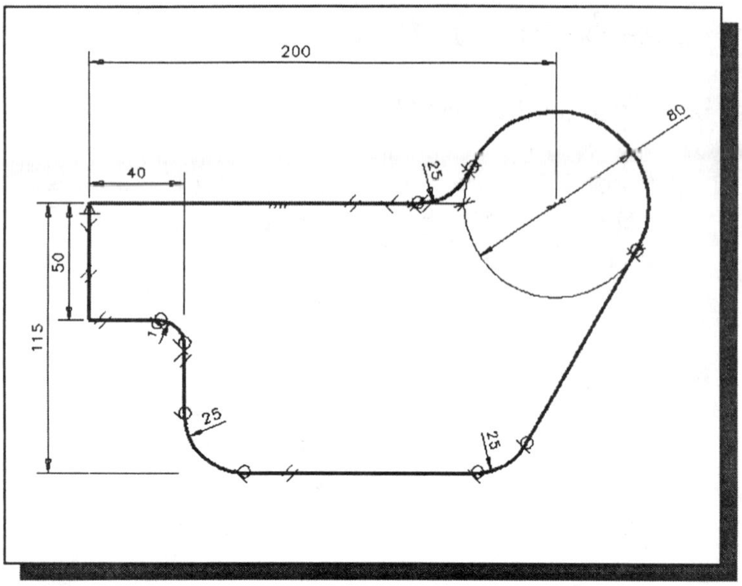

6. On your own, add a *radius 10* fillet on the inside corner. The section should appear as shown.

Extrusion

We will next create the 3-D model using the *Extrude* command.

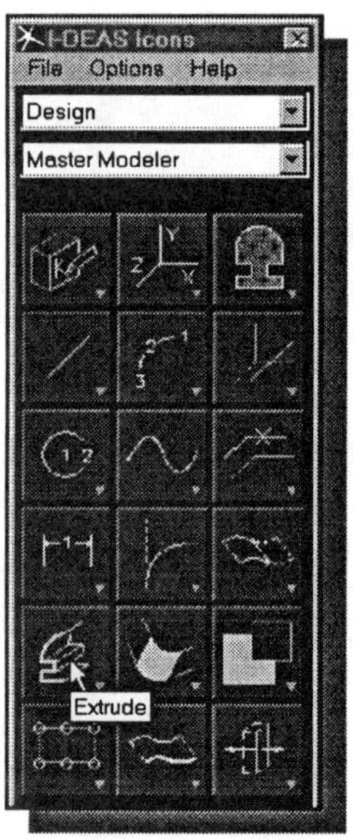

1. Using the **Extrude** command, select the sketched section, accept the selection, and fill in the items as shown below at the *Extrude Section* window:

New Part
Distance: **5**
OK

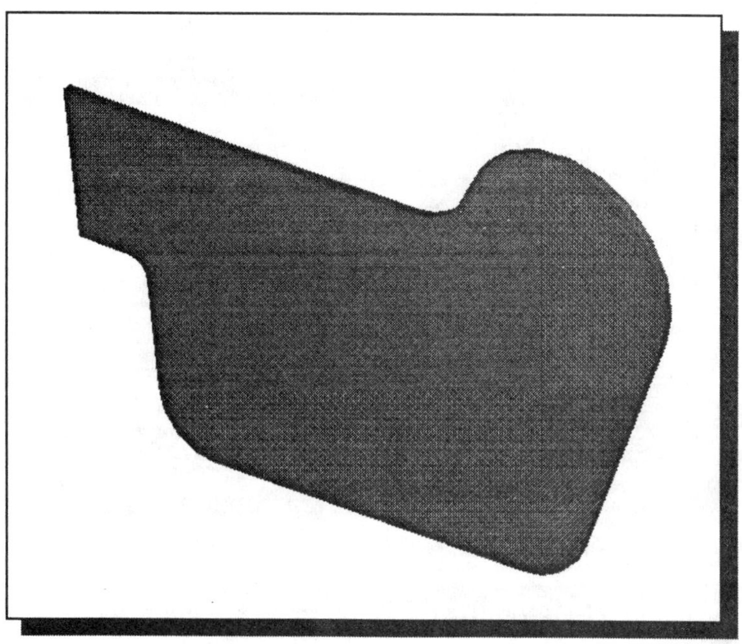

2. Click the **OK** button to accept the settings and create the 3-D model.

➢ Now is another good time to save your design (Use the Quick key: [**Ctrl**] + [**S**]).

Create an OFFSET Feature

To complete the design, we will create a cutout feature by using the *OFFSET* command. First we will set up the sketching plane to align with the front face of the 3-D model.

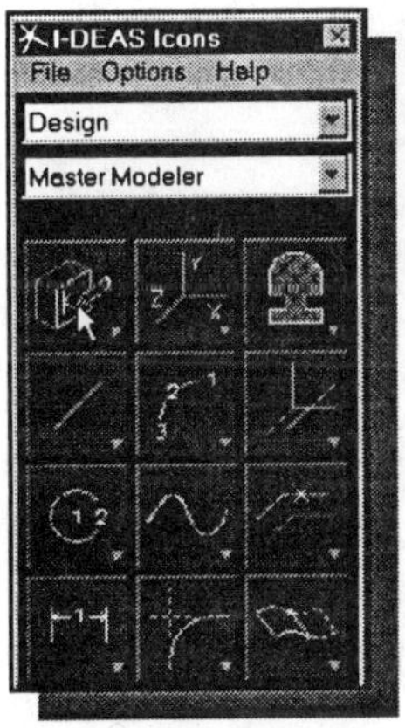

1. Choose **Sketch in Place** in the icon panel. In the prompt window, the message "*Pick plane or surface*" is displayed.

2. Select the front face of the 3-D model. (If necessary, switch to the Isometric display to help in selecting the front surface.)

➢ To simplify the creation of the offset geometry, we will first create a *reference section.*

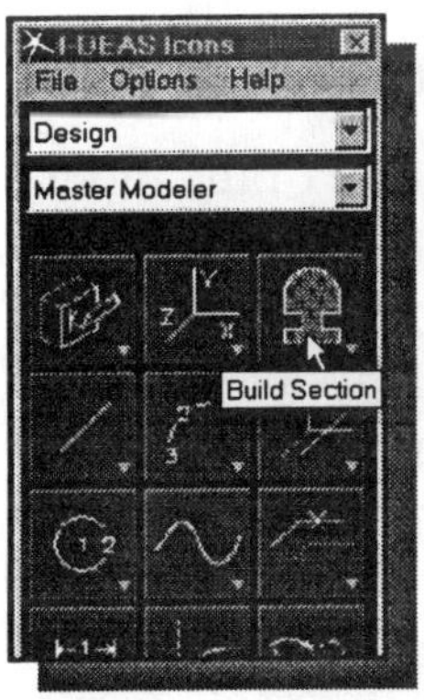

3. Select the **Build Section** icon. The message "*Pick curve or section*" is displayed in the prompt window.

4. Select any edge of the front face of the 3-D model. I-DEAS will automatically select all of the connecting geometry to form a closed region.

5. Press the **ENTER** key or the **middle-mouse-button** to end the *Build Section* command.

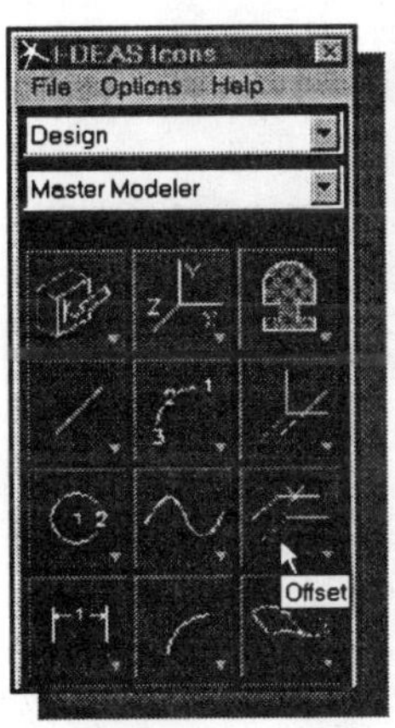

6. Choose **Offset** in the icon panel. The message "*Pick section or curve to offset*" is displayed in the prompt window.

7. Select the reference section we just created.

8. Press the **ENTER** key or the **middle-mouse-button** to accept the selection. The *Offset* window appears.

9. In the *Distance* box, type in the value of **15**.

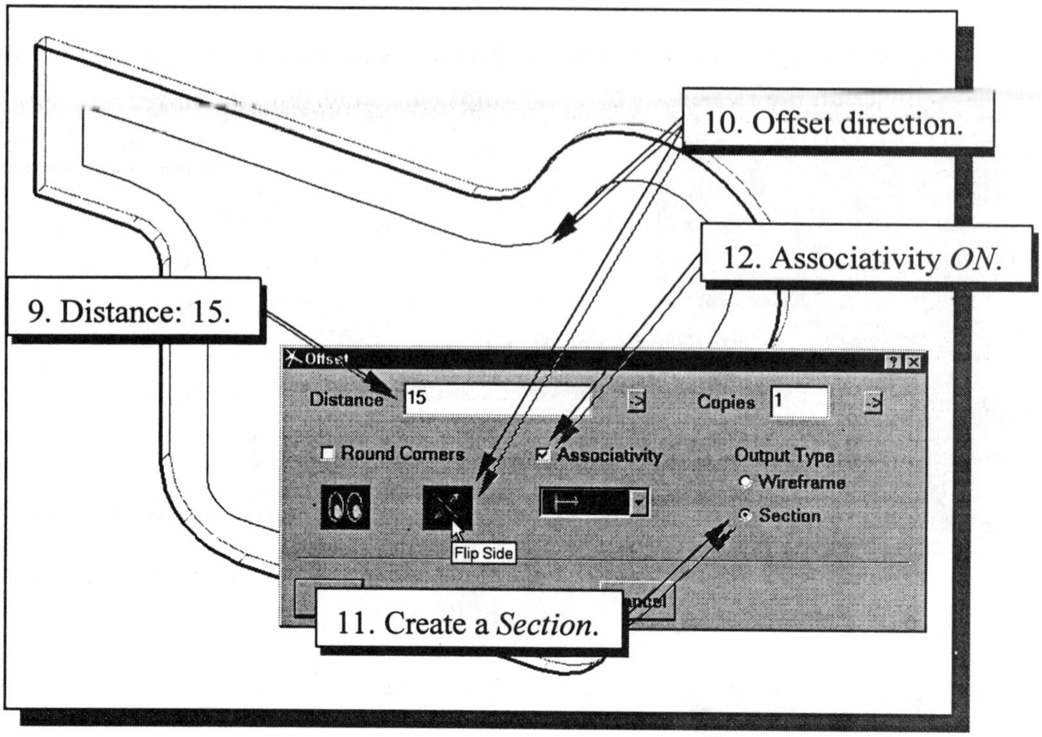

10. Click on the **Arrows** icon to set the offset direction to the inside of the model.

11. Click **ON** the **Section** switch to create a new section as the offset geometry.

12. Confirm the ***Associativity*** switch is turned **ON** and **one** copy of geometry will be created.

13. Confirm the ***Round Corners*** switch is turned **OFF** and click on the **OK** icon to create the *offset geometry.*

14. Press the **ENTER** key or the **middle-mouse-button** to end the *Offset* command.

Completing the CUTOUT

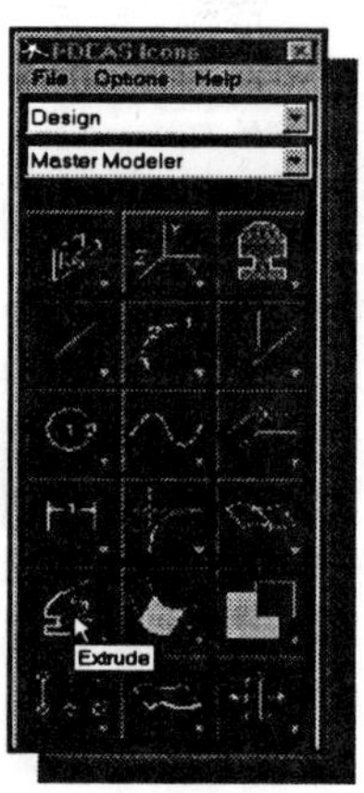

1. Choose **Extrude** in the icon panel. In the prompt window, the message "*Pick curve or section*" is displayed.

2. Pick the offset section we just created. The selected section is highlighted.

3. Press the **ENTER** key to accept the selected entity.

4. The *Extrude Section* window appears. Set the extrude option to **Cutout**.

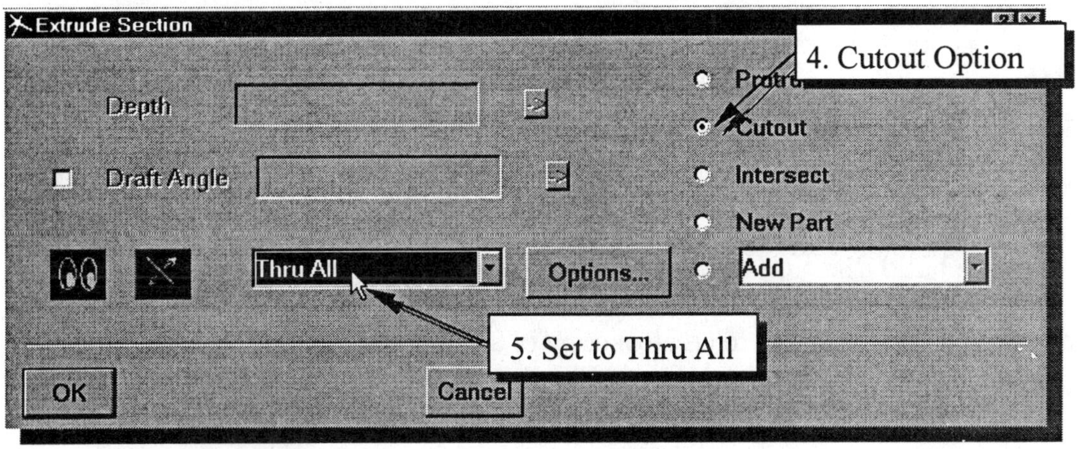

5. Press and hold down the left-mouse-button on the *Depth* menu and select the **Thru All** option

6. Click on the **OK** icon to accept the settings and complete the model.

➢ With the *Associativity switch* turned **ON**, the offset geometry will be automatically updated with the original geometry. On your own, adjust the overall height of the design to **150** millimeters and confirm that the offset geometry is adjusted accordingly.

Questions:

1. What are the two types of wireframe geometry available in I-DEAS Master Modeler?
2. What is the main advantage of using the *Haystack Geometry* approach?
3. In I-DEAS, can we quickly select only the sketched curves? How?
4. How do we create a *Section* in I-DEAS?
5. Can we build a section that consists of self-intersecting curves?
6. Describe the procedure to create a copy of a sketched 2-D wireframe geometry?
7. Identify and briefly describe the following commands:

(a)

(b)

(c)

(d)

Exercises: All units are in inches.

1.

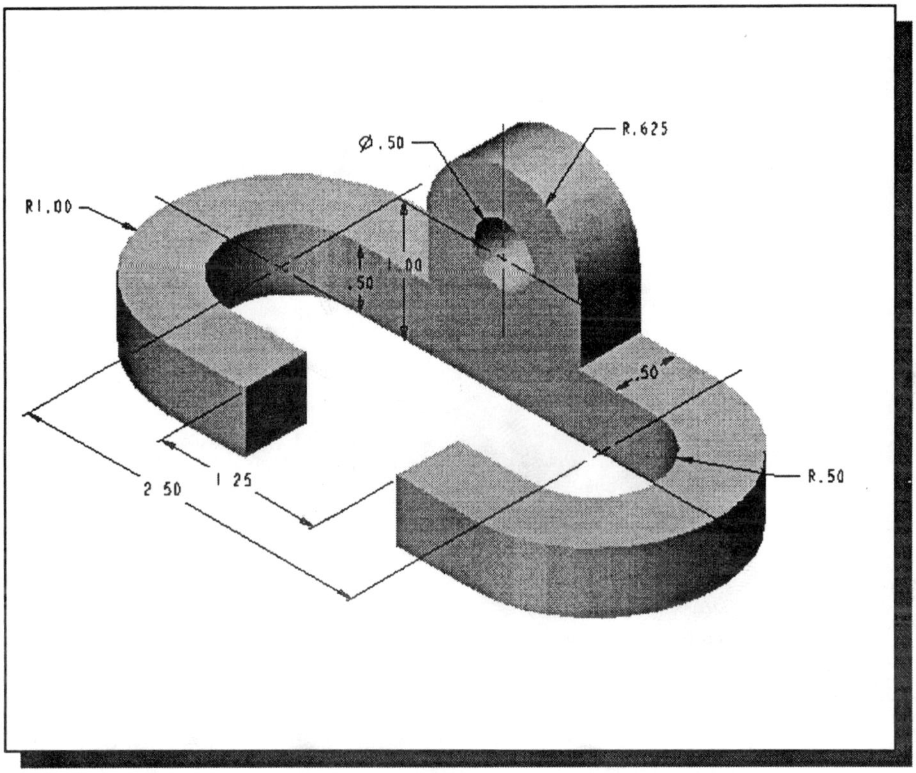

2. Plate Thickness: 0.25 (Use the *Haystack Geometry* approach)

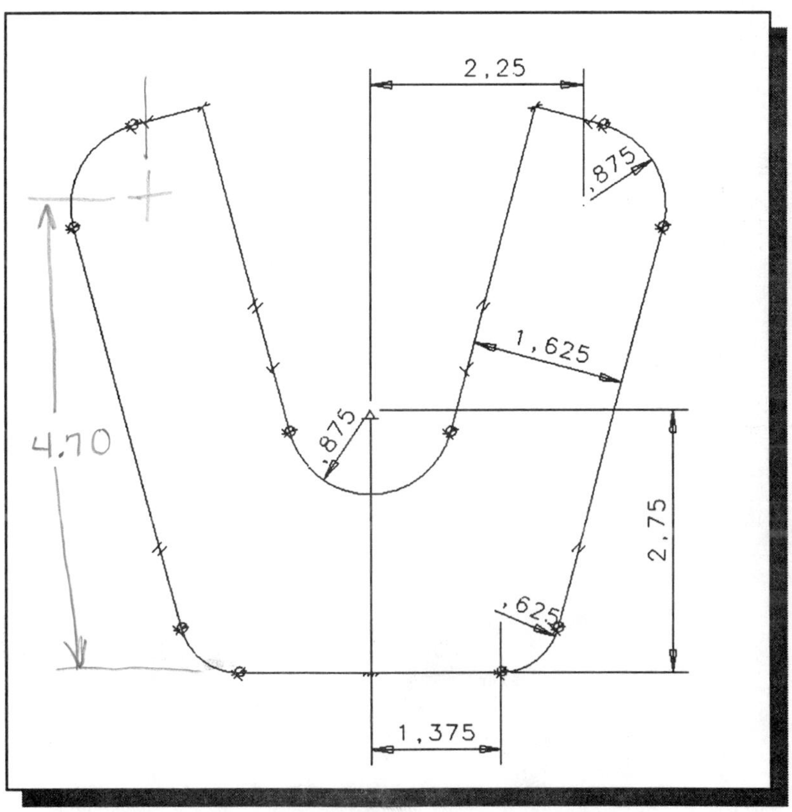

Notes:

Chapter 7
The BORN Technique and Reference Geometry

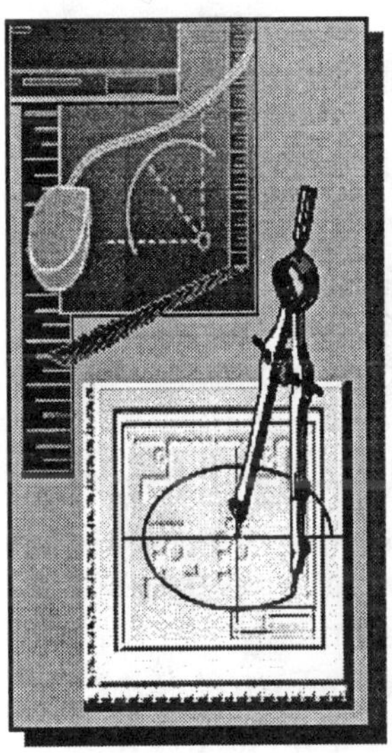

Learning Objectives

When you have completed this lesson, you will be able to:

- ♦ Understand the BORN technique.
- ♦ Use the FOCUS option.
- ♦ Create Reference Geometry.
- ♦ Create Revolved cutouts.
- ♦ Create Coordinate Systems.
- ♦ Understand the importance of Feature interactions.

The BORN Technique

In the previous Chapters, we have chosen the base feature to be an extruded solid object. All subsequent features, therefore, are children of the base feature. The base feature is the center of all features and is considered as the key-feature of the design. This approach to creating solid models places more emphasis on the selection of the base feature. In most cases, this approach can be used to create adequate and proper solid models.

A more advanced technique of creating solid models is what is known as the "Base Orphan Reference Node" (**BORN**) technique. The basic concept of the BORN technique is to create a Cartesian coordinate system as the first feature prior to creating any solid features. With the Cartesian coordinate system established, we then have three mutually perpendicular datum planes (the XY, YZ, and ZX planes) available for use as sketching planes. The three datum planes can also be used as references for dimensions and geometric constructions. Using this technique, the first node in the history tree is called an "orphan," meaning that it has no history to be replayed. The technique of creating the reference geometry in this "base node" has been called the "Base Orphan Reference Node" (BORN) technique.

I-DEAS Master Modeler allows us to create multiple parts in a single CAD file. Using the BORN technique, we will first establish and identify the individual part by creating an associated coordinate system. We can then do things like add offset coordinate systems and reference geometry. All subsequent solid features can then use the coordinate system and/or reference geometry as their sketching planes. The base solid feature is still important, but the base solid feature is no longer the ONLY choice for selecting the sketching plane for subsequent solid features. This approach provides us with more options while we are creating parametric solid models. More importantly, this approach provides greater flexibility for part modifications and design changes.

Reference Geometry

Feature-based Parametric Modeling is a cumulative process. The relationships that we define between features determine how a feature reacts when other features are changed. Because of this interaction, certain features must, by necessity, precede others. A new feature can use previously defined features to define information such as size, shape, location and orientation. I-DEAS Master Modeler provides several tools to automate this process. This Chapter demonstrates the use of reference geometry and the BORN technique. Reference geometry can be thought of as user-definable datum, which is updated with the part geometry. We can create reference planes, lines, or points that do not already exist. Reference geometry can be used to align features or to orient parts in an assembly. Reference geometry can also be used to identify original geometry that disappeared following some construction actions. This Chapter also demonstrates the use of the *Focus* option to help geometry construction; the *Focus* option allows us to create reference geometry using existing geometry. The established feature interactions in the CAD database assures capturing of the design intent.

The Guide Block Design

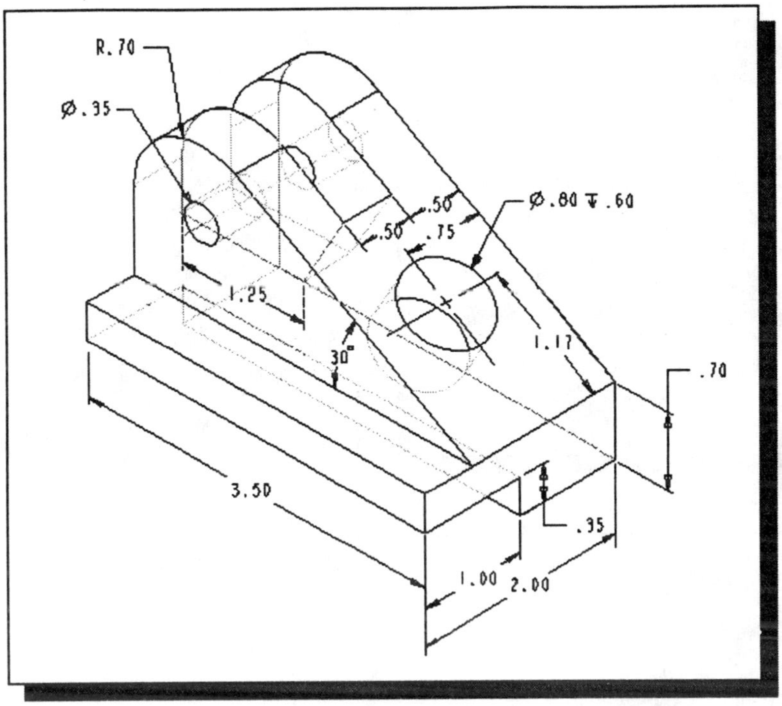

❖ Based on your knowledge of I-DEAS Master Modeler so far, how many features would you use to create the design? Which feature would you choose as the **BASE FEATURE** of the model? What is your choice in arranging the order of the features? What are the more difficult features involved in the design? Would you organize the features differently if the **BORN** technique were to be used to create the design? Take a few minutes to consider these questions and do preliminary planning by sketching on a piece of paper. You are also encouraged to create the model on your own prior to following through the tutorial.

Starting I-DEAS

1. Login to the computer and bring up I-DEAS Master Series. Start a new model file by filling in the items as shown below in the *I-DEAS Start* window:

   Project Name: **(Your account Name)**
   Model File Name: **Guide_Block**
   Application: **Design**
   Task: **Master Modeler**
   OK

2. After you click on the **OK** button, a *warning window* will appear to tell you that a new model file will be created. Click **OK** to continue.

3. On your own, set the units to **Inch (pound f)**.

Modeling Strategy

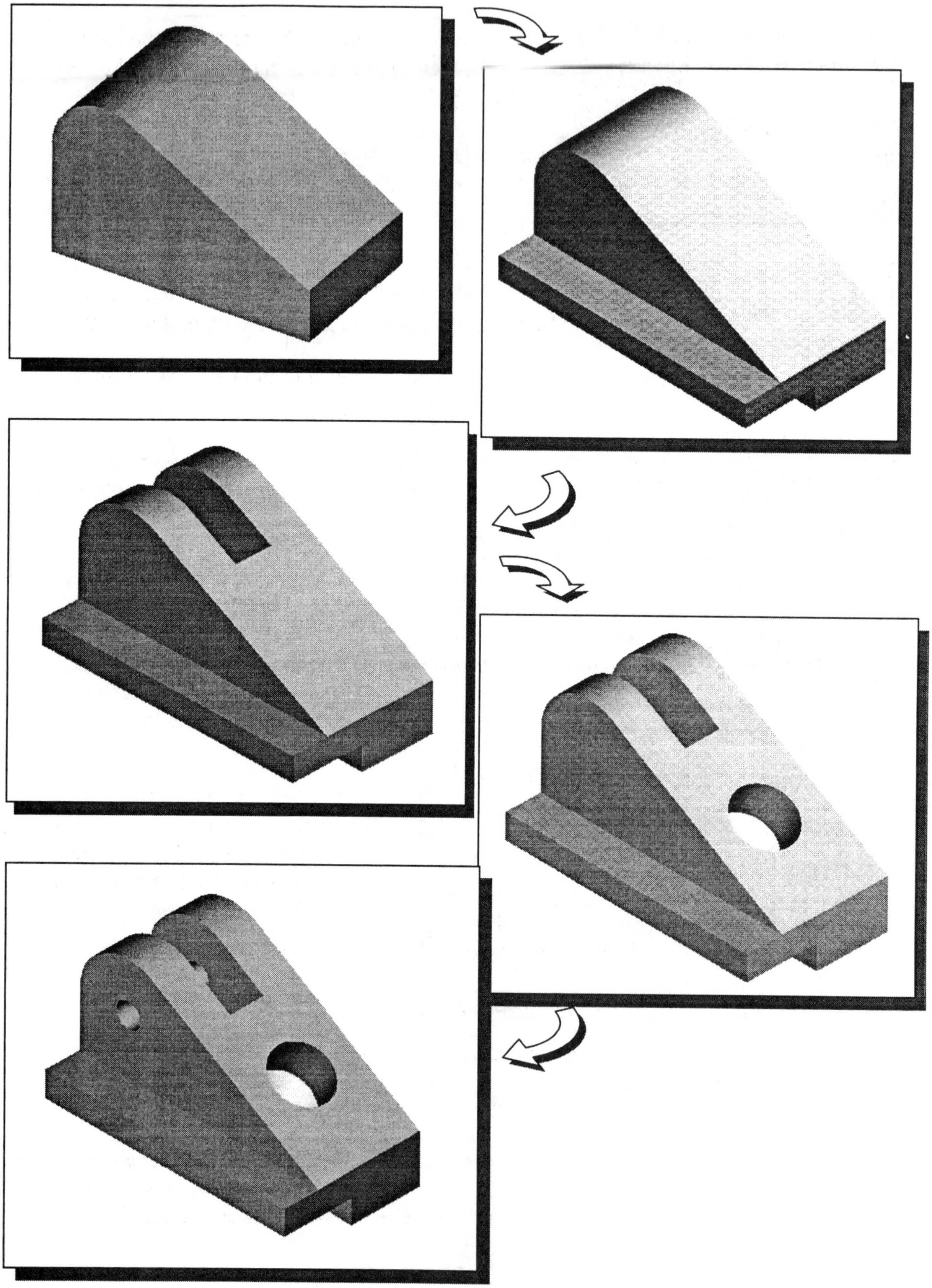

Applying the BORN Technique

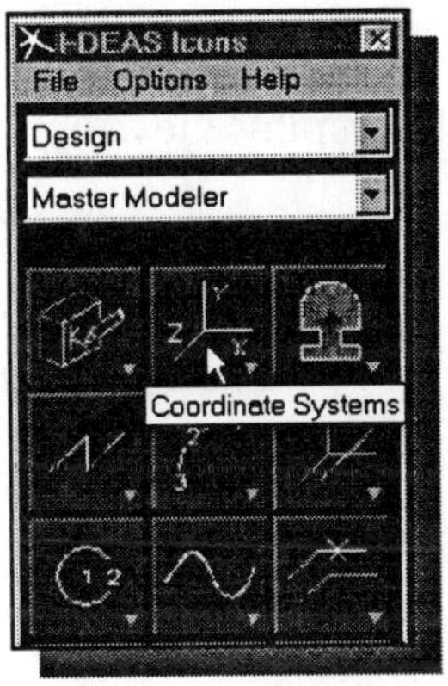

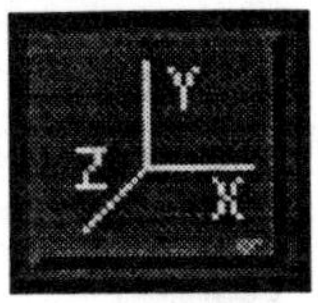

1. Choose **Coordinate Systems** in the icon panel. (The icon is located in the first row of the task icon panel.)

2. In the prompt window, the message "*Pick entity for coordinate system to reference*" is displayed. Select the **workplane** by left-clicking once on any of the edges.

3. In the prompt window, the message "*Select coordinate system component to define (Done)*" is displayed. Press the **ENTER** key or the **middle-mouse-button** to accept the default settings.

❖ By default, the user coordinate system is aligned to the world coordinate system.

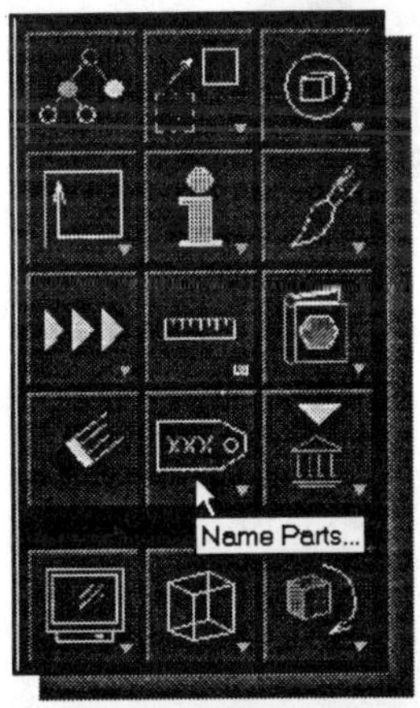

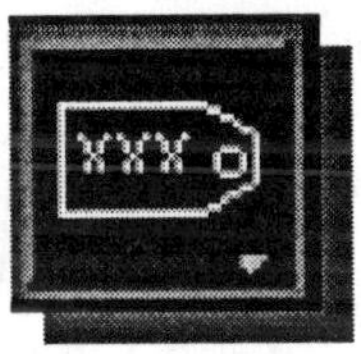

4. Choose **Name Parts...** in the icon panel. (The icon is located in the last row of the application specific icon panel.)

5. The message "*Pick part to name*" is displayed in the prompt window. Pick any edge of the coordinate system we just created. The *Name* window appears.

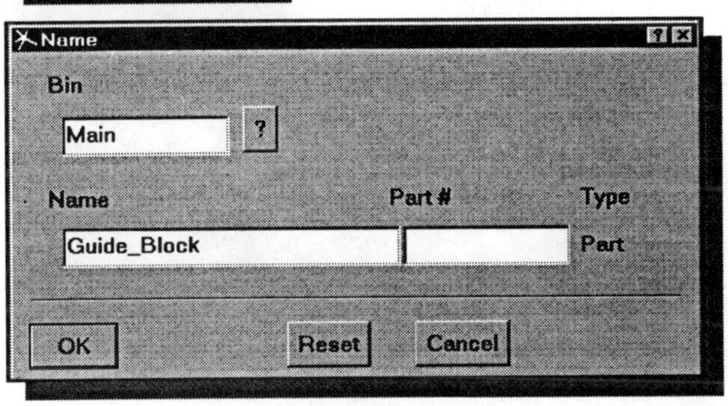

6. In the *Name* window, we can assign or change the name, number, and bin of a part. Each field on the window is limited to 80 characters. In the *Name* box, type in "**Guide_Block**."

7. Click on the **OK** icon to proceed.

8. The message "*Pick part to name (Done)*" is displayed in the prompt window. Press the **ENTER** key or the **middle-mouse-button** to end the *Name Parts* command.

❖ By creating the coordinate system and naming it as a part, we have established the coordinate system as the first feature of the part. We can now proceed to create solid features referencing the three mutually perpendicular datum planes.

Creating the Base Feature

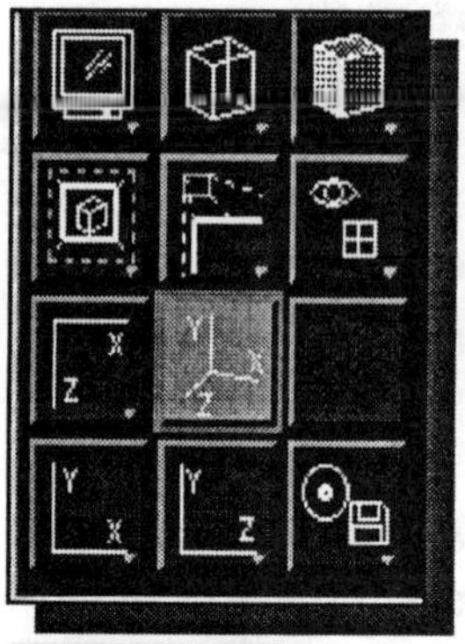

1. Choose **Isometric View** in the display viewing icon panel.

2. Choose **Zoom-All** in the display viewing icon panel.

3. Choose **Sketch in Place** in the icon panel.

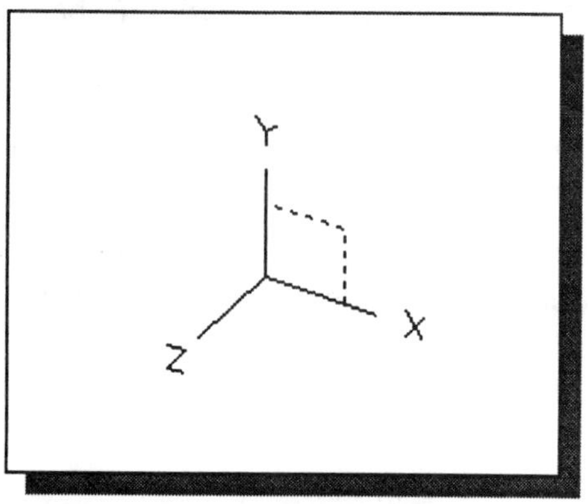

4. In the prompt window, the message "*Pick plane to sketch on*" is displayed. Pick one of the edges of the **XY plane** of the coordinate system. Note that even though the workplane is at the same orientation of the XY-plane of the coordinate system, selecting the XY-plane assures the sketch is attached to the established part, Guide_Block.

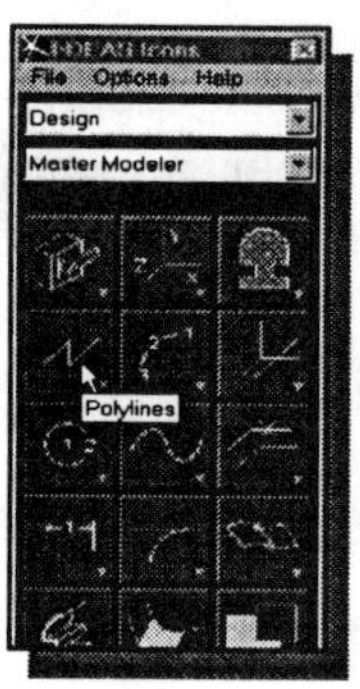

5. Select the **Polylines** command in the icon panel.

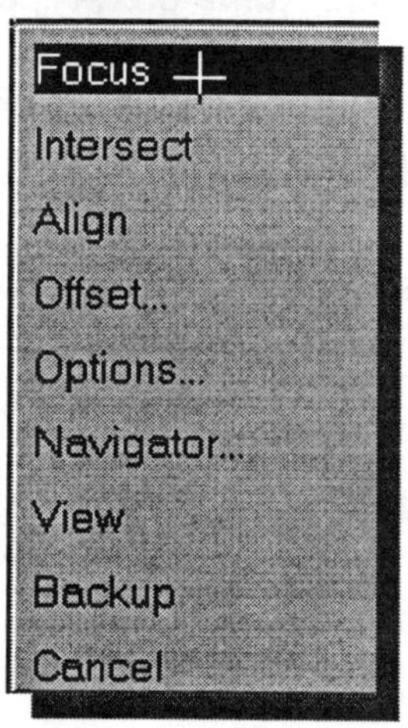

6. Move the cursor inside the graphics window. Press and hold down the right-mouse-button to display the option menu. Select the **Focus** option. The message "*Pick entity*" is displayed in the prompt window.

❖ The *Focus* option allows us to create reference geometry using existing geometry and/or coordinate systems.

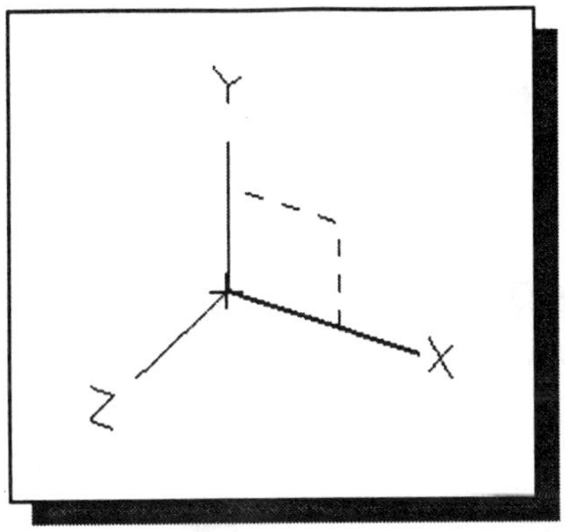

7. Select the origin of the coordinate system to create a reference point.

8. The displayed graphics cursor indicates several choices are feasible for the selection. Press the **ENTER** key or the **middle-mouse-button** to accept the selection.

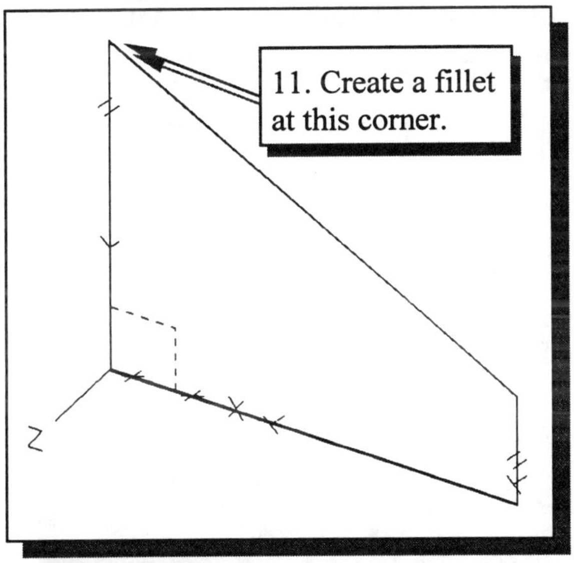

9. Create a sketch as shown. (Do not be overly concerned with the actual size of the sketch. We will modify the dimensions later.)

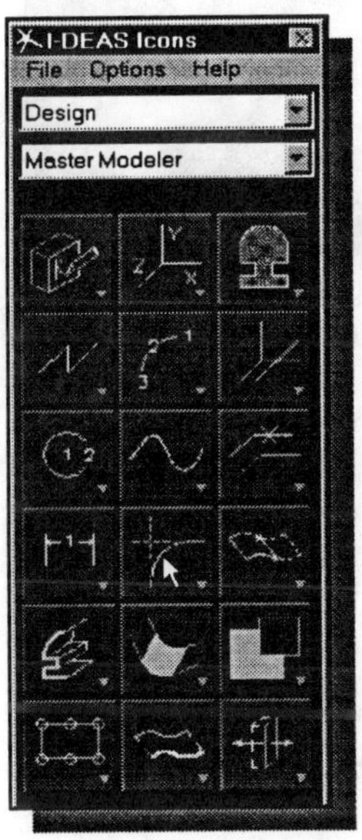

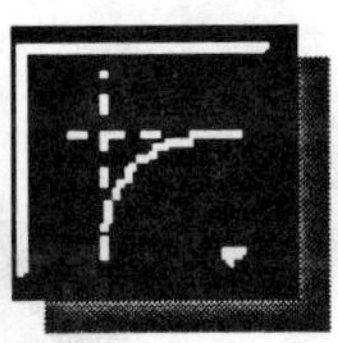

10. Choose **2-D Fillet** in the icon panel. There are two fillet commands available in I-DEAS Master Modeler. Select the *2-D fillet* icon. The message *"Pick section, curve or corner to fillet"* is displayed in the prompt window.

11. Pick the top corner as shown in the above figure.

12. In the *Fillet* window, confirm the *Constrain* and *Trim/Extend* options are switched ***on***. Click on the **OK** icon to create the fillet.

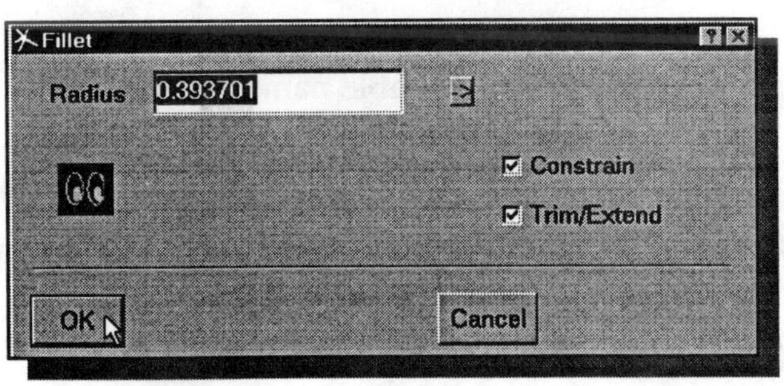

13. Press the **ENTER** key or the middle-mouse-button to end the *Fillet* command.

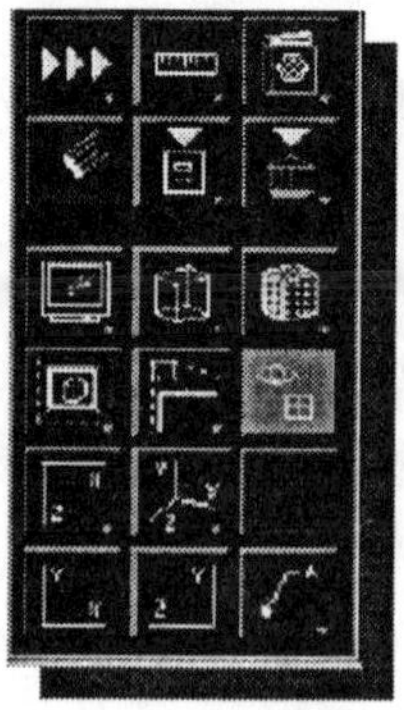

14. Choose **View Workplane** in the icon panel.

➤ On your own, use the **Dimension** and **Delete** commands to create the four key dimensions as shown in the figure. Do not be overly concerned with the dimension values; we will modify the dimensions next.

15. Pre-select all the dimensions by holding down the **SHIFT** key and left-clicking on all of the dimensional values. The selected items will be highlighted.

PRE-SELECT SHIFT + LEFT-mouse-button

16. Choose **Modify** in the icon panel. We will use dimensional variables to control the shape's size. Modify the variable names and expressions as shown in the below figure.

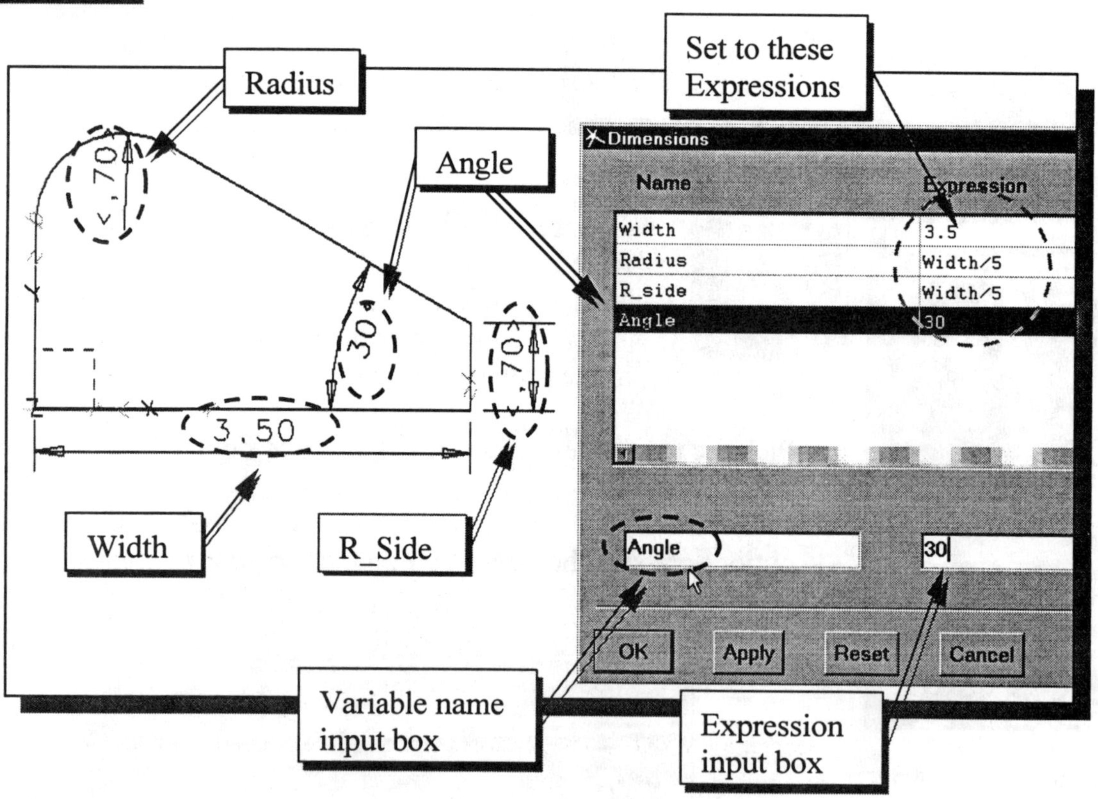

17. Click on the **OK** button to proceed with the modifications.

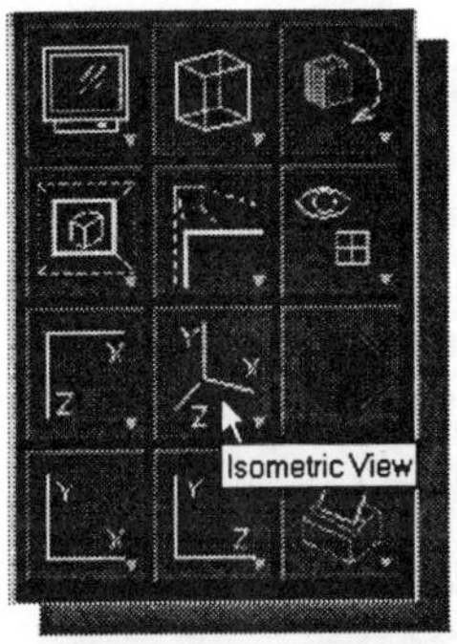

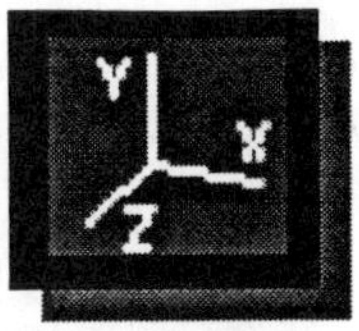

18. Choose **Isometric View** in the display viewing icon panel.

19. Choose **Zoom-All** in the display viewing icon panel.

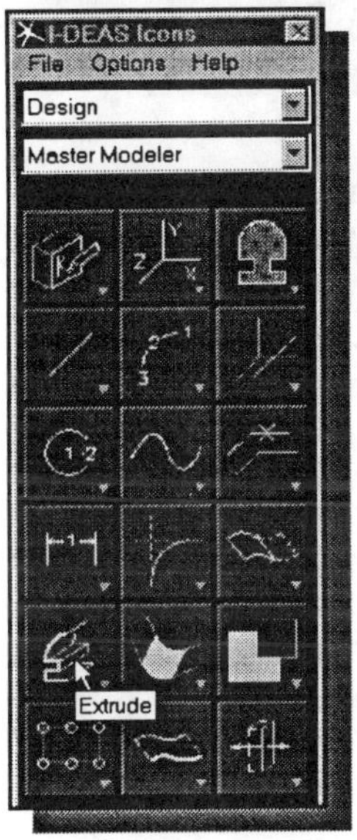

20. Click on the **Extrude** command icon.

21. Select any edges of the sketched section.

22. Press the **ENTER** key or the **middle-mouse-button** to accept the selected objects.

23. In the *Extrude Section* window, set the extrusion distance to **2.0** and confirm the ***Protrude*** option is switched ***on***. Note that since the coordinate system is associated with the part "*Guide_block*," we want to use the *Protrude* option to add to the existing part.

24. Click on the **OK** button to create the solid feature.

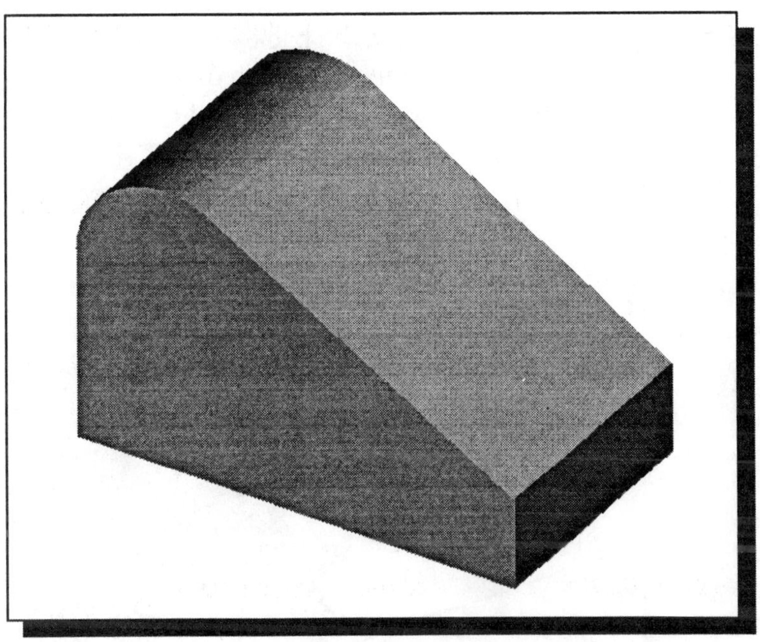

❖ Now is a good time to save the model (Quick key: [Ctrl] + [S]). It is a good habit to save your model periodically, just in case something might and probably will go wrong while you are working on the model. You should also save the model after you have completed any major constructions.

Create a Reference Plane

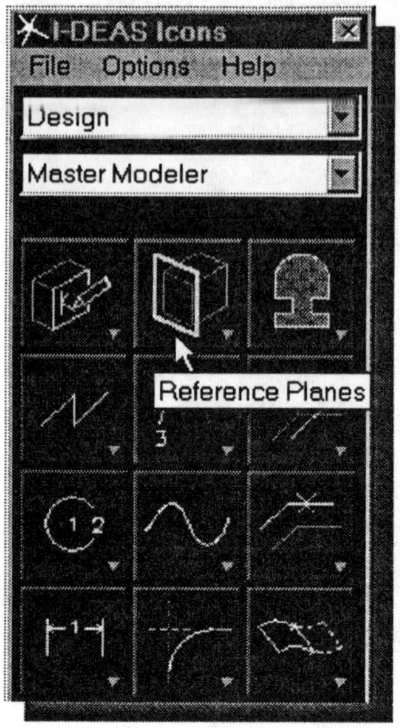

1. Choose **Reference Planes** in the icon panel. The message "*Pick plane*" is displayed in the prompt window.

❖ The icon is located in the first row of the task specific icon panel. The icon is located in the same stack as the *Coordinate Systems* icon. Press and hold down the left-mouse-button on the icon stack to display other choices.

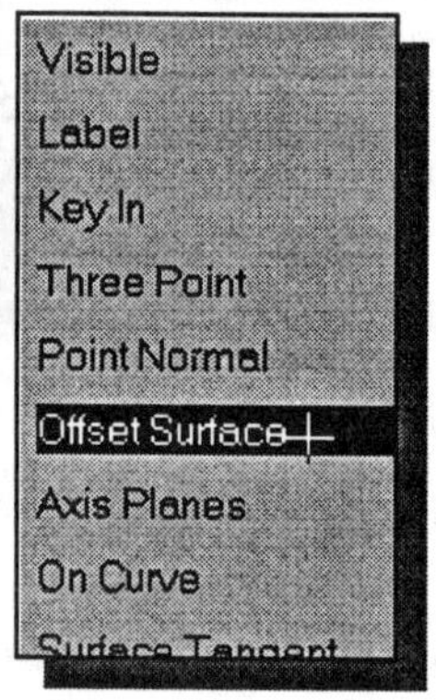

2. Move the cursor inside the graphics window. Press and hold down the right-mouse-button, and select **Offset Surface**. The message "*Pick plane to offset*" is displayed in the prompt window.

3. Pick one of the edges of the **XY-plane** of the coordinate system. A dashed rectangle aligned to the XY-plane will appear on the screen.

❖ Note that we could also select the back surface of the 3-D model to establish the reference plane. The main advantage of selecting the XY-plane is so that the created reference plane is not dependent on the existing solid feature.

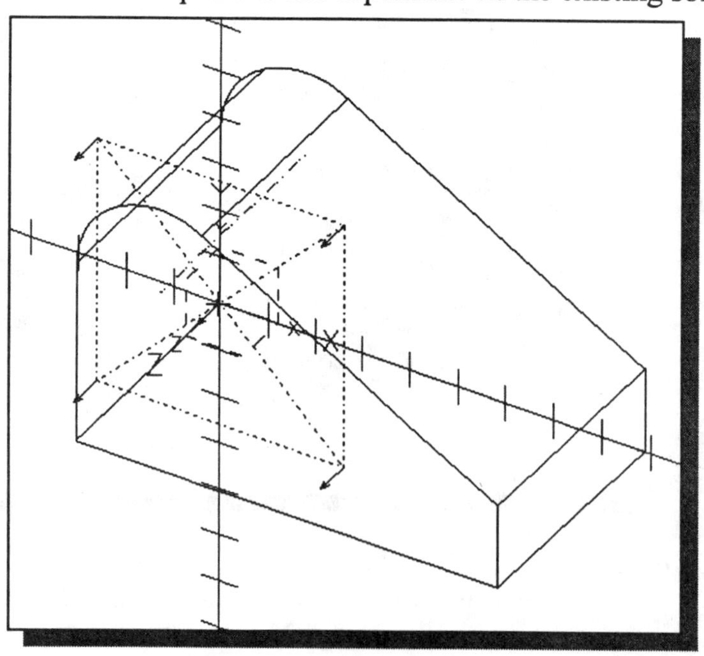

4. At the "*Enter offset distance (0.0)*" prompt, enter the value of **1.50**. I-DEAS automatically assigns the variable name "**Surfaceoffset**" to this dimension. The value indicates the location of a new reference plane relative to the displayed direction.

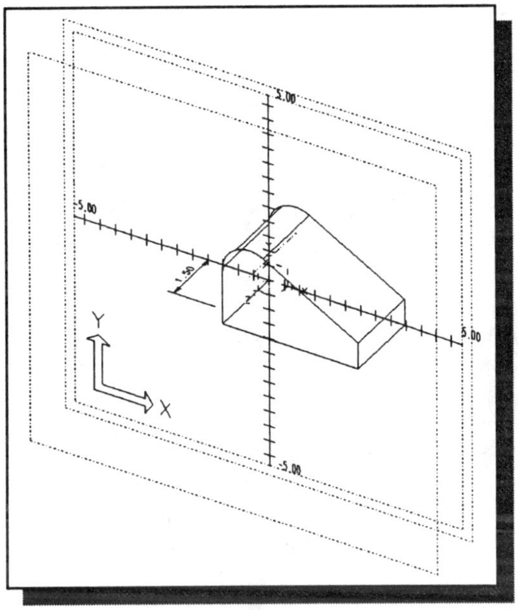

5. Press the **ENTER** key or the **middle-mouse-button** to exit the *Reference Planes* command.

6. Click the **Zoom-All** icon to view the established reference plane.

❖ A dimension of 1.50 and two dashed rectangles appear in the graphics window representing two reference planes. The first reference plane is aligned to the XY-plane of the coordinate system; the second reference plane is 1.5 units away from the first reference plane. (To place the reference plane in a location opposite to the direction displayed, enter a negative value.)

Creating a 2-D Sketch on the Reference Plane

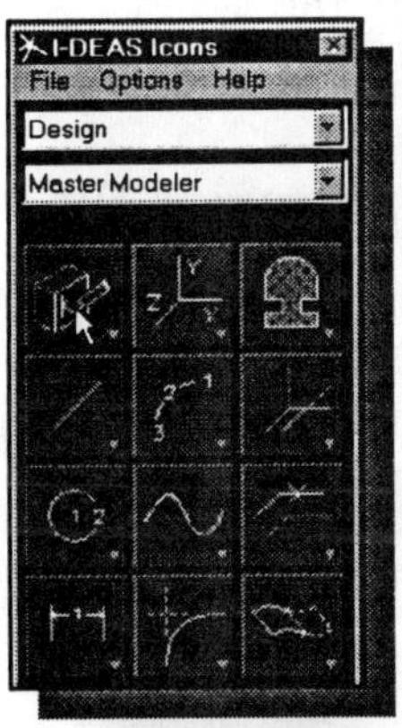

1. Choose **Sketch in Place** in the icon panel. In the prompt window, the message "*Pick plane to sketch on*" is displayed.

2. Pick any edge of the forward most reference plane (RF2 symbol) we just created. Note this is the reference plane that is 1.5 inches away from the back face of the model.

3. Choose **Rectangle by 2 Corners** in the icon panel. The message "*Locate first corner*" is displayed in the prompt window.

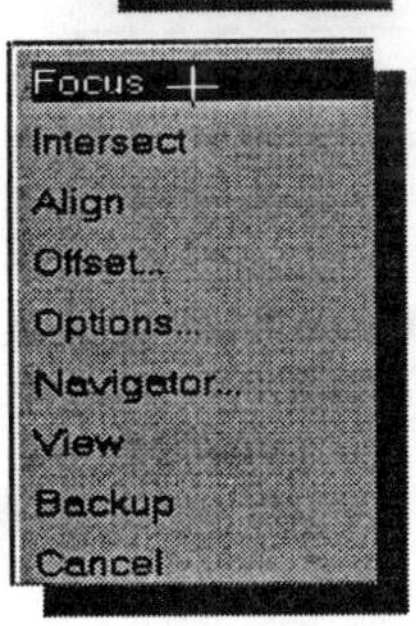

4. Move the cursor inside the graphics window. Press and hold down the right-mouse-button to display the option menu. Choose **Focus** in the option menu. The message "*Pick entity*" is displayed in the prompt window.

5. Pick the back inclined line of the 3-D model. A new line is projected onto the reference plane. You can think of this line as an additional *alignment constraint*. The *Focus* option enables us to make sure the *sketched object* is aligned with entities that are not on the same plane.

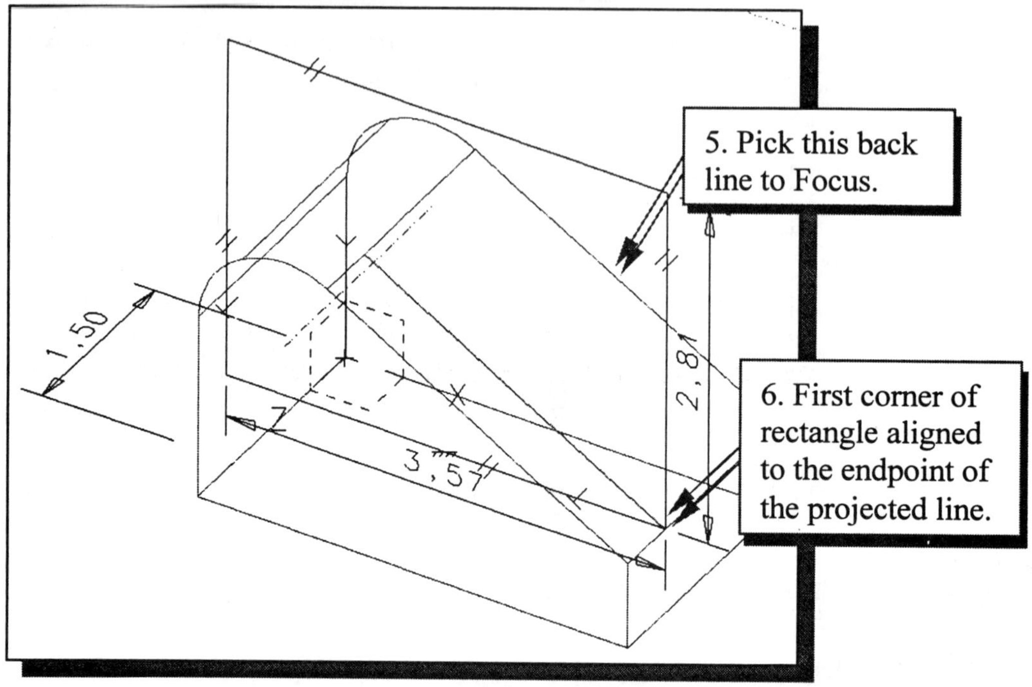

6. In response to the prompt that reads "Locate first corner", select the lower endpoint of the newly created *Focus Line*.

7. Move the cursor up and to the left and create a rectangle of arbitrary size. We will adjust the size of the rectangle by adding parametric relations.

8. Press the **ENTER** key or the **middle-mouse-button** to exit the *Rectangle* command.

Modifying Dimensions

1. Pre-select all dimensions on the rectangle by holding down the **SHIFT** key and left- clicking on all of the dimensional values. The selected items will be highlighted.

PRE-SELECT SHIFT + LEFT-mouse-button

2. Choose **Modify** in the icon panel. We will use dimensional variables to control the shape's size.

3. On your own, use the **MATCH** option and set the width of the rectangle equal to the overall width of the 3-D model. Also set the height of the rectangle equal to one-half of the overall width of the 3-D model.

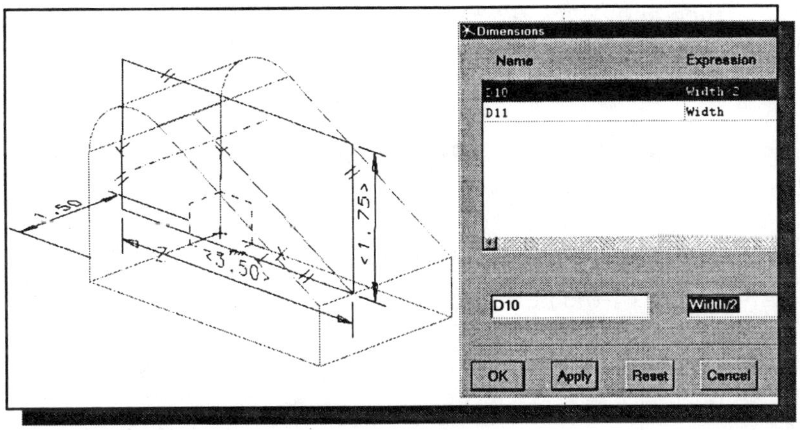

4. Click on the **OK** button to apply the changes.

5. Press the **ENTER** key or the **middle-mouse-button** to exit the *Modify* command.

6. Select the **Front view** icon and verify width and alignment of the rectangle.

7. Select the **Isometric view** icon and return to *Isometric view*.

Making the First Cutout

1. Choose **Extrude** in the icon panel. In the prompt window, the message "*Pick curve or section*" is displayed.

2. Pick the rectangle we just created.

3. Press the **ENTER** key or the **middle-mouse-button** to accept the selected entity.

4. In the *Extrude Section* window, select **Cutout**.

5. If necessary, click on the **Flip Direction** button to flip the direction of the cutout toward the front of the solid object.

6. Press and hold down the left-mouse-button on the **Depth** icon and select the **Until Next** option.

7. Click the **OK** icon to create the *cutout*.

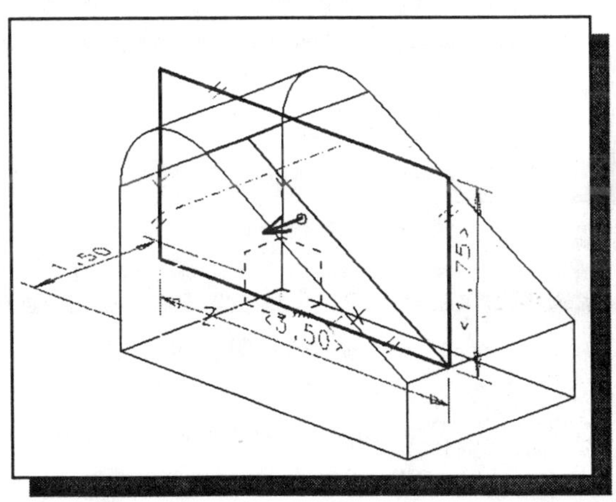

Second Cutout – Without Creating a New Reference Plane

1. Choose **Sketch in Place** in the icon panel. In the prompt window, the message "*Pick plane to sketch on*" is displayed.

2. Pick the right-hand side vertical face of the 3-D model.

3. Choose **Rectangle by 2 Corners** in the icon panel. The message "*Locate first corner*" is displayed in the prompt window.

4. Snap to and pick the lower front corner of the 3-D model as the first corner of the new rectangle.

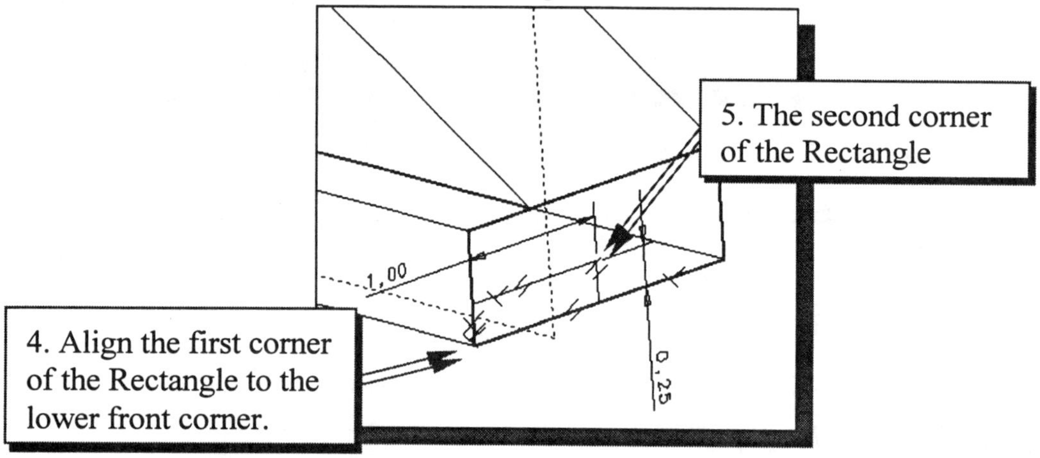

5. Move the cursor to the right and make a rectangle. We will control the size of the rectangle by adding parametric relations. We will next establish equations to control the dimension of the rectangle.

6. Press the **ENTER** key or the **middle-mouse-button** to end the current command.

7. To pre-select the two dimensions, hold down the **SHIFT** key and left-click on all of the dimensional values. The selected items will be highlighted.

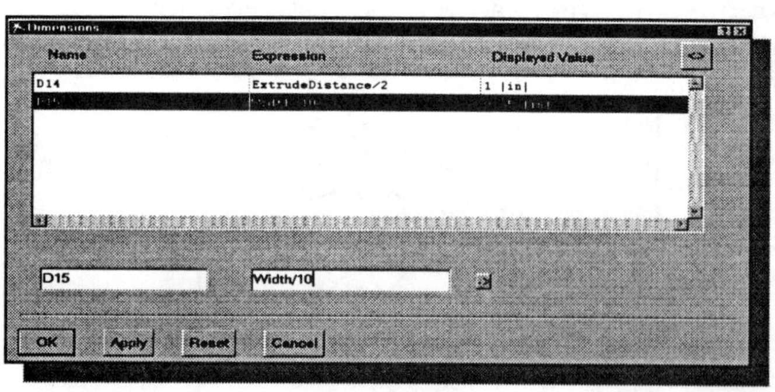

8. Use the **Modify** icon and adjust the dimensional constraints of the rectangle as shown. Height of rectangle = **Width/10**, Width of rectangle = **ExtrudeDistance/2**. What are the values associated with the two variable names? How can we find out these values?

9. Click on the **OK** icon to apply the modifications.

10. Press the **ENTER** key or the **middle-mouse-button** to end the *Modify* command.

Making the Second Cutout

1. Choose **Extrude** in the icon panel. In the prompt window, the message "*Pick curve or section*" is displayed.

2. Pick the rectangle we just created.

3. Press the **ENTER** key to accept the selected entity.

4. In the *Extrude Section* window, select **Cutout**.

5. Press and hold down the left-mouse-button on the **Depth** icon and select the **Thru All** option.

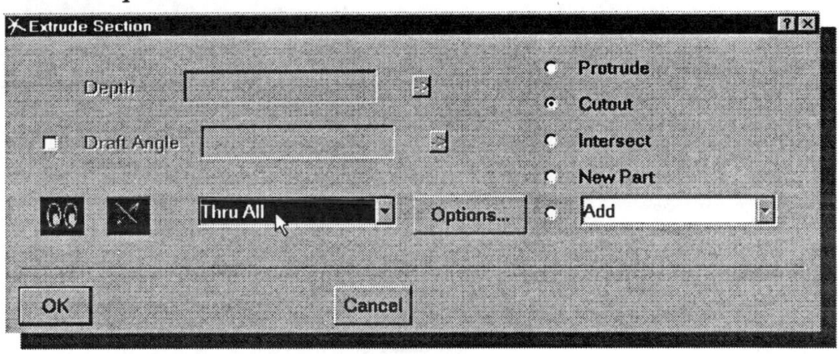

6. Click on the **OK** icon to create the cutout.

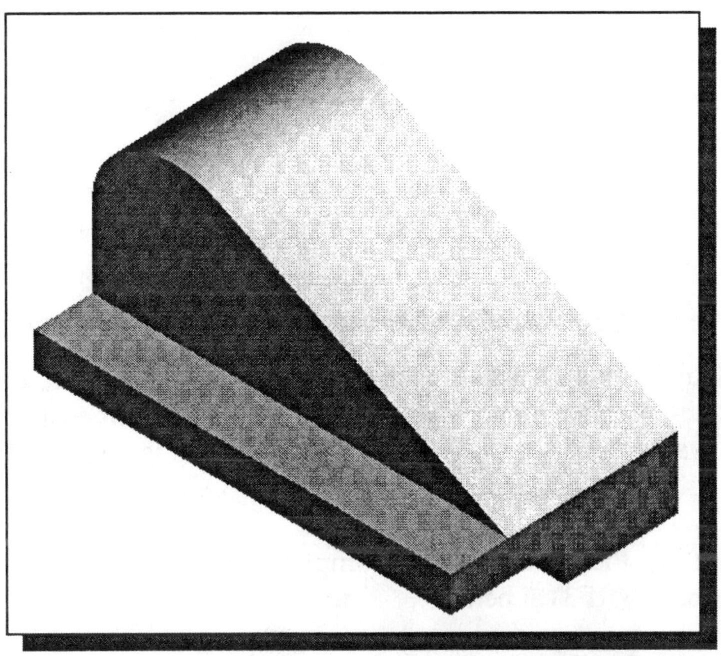

❖ As can be seen, we could have made an additional reference plane for the second cutout, or not have created the reference plane for the first cutout. I-DEAS Master Modeler provides many tools for different design considerations. You are encouraged to experiment with other options to accomplish the same tasks.

Third Cutout – Using A New Reference Plane

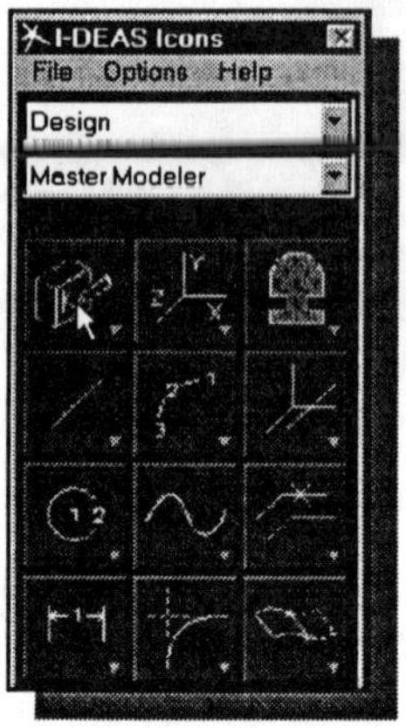

1. Choose **Reference Planes** in the icon panel. (The icon is located in the first row of the task specific icon panel.) The message "*Pick plane*" is displayed in the prompt window.

2. Move the cursor inside the graphics window. Press and hold down the right-mouse-button and select **Offset Surface**. The message "*Pick plane to offset*" is displayed in the prompt window.

3. Select the back face of the 3-D object as shown. Note that I-DEAS will display a rectangle with arrows pointing away from the 3-D object. This indicates the default direction for the offset.

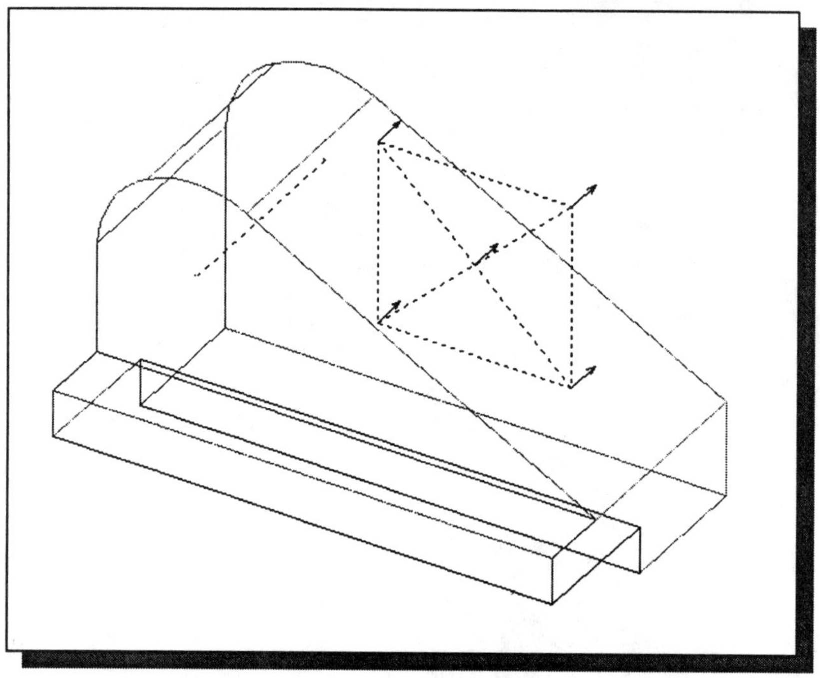

4. In the prompt window, type in "**- 0.75**". I-DEAS automatically assigns the variable name "Surfaceoffset_1" to this dimension. The negative value indicates the new reference plane is to be placed in the opposite direction of the displayed direction.

5. Press the ENTER key to complate this selection. A new reference plane (RF3) appears.

❖ I-DEAS Master Modeler automatically assigns a name to this reference plane. Move the graphics cursor over any edge of the reference plane to see the name assigned (**RFx**, where RF stands for Reference). Note that we could also select the XY-plane of the coordinate system to create the new reference planes. The main consideration is the established *parent/child relationship*.

6. Modify the location dimension of the new reference plane **SurfaceOffset_1** to **SurfaceOffset/2**.

7. Click on the **Update** icon to update the modification.

8. Choose **Sketch in Place** in the icon panel. In the prompt window, the message "*Pick plane to sketch on*" is displayed.

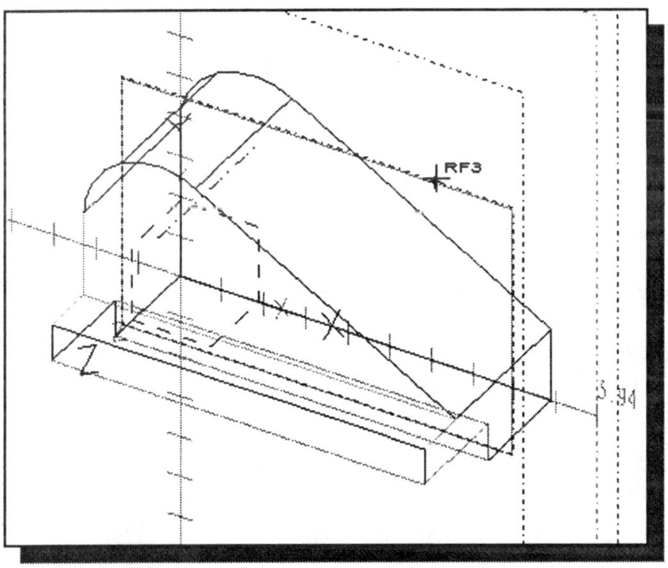

9. Pick the reference plane (RF3) we just created. This reference plane is the last reference plane we created.

10. Choose **Polylines** in the icon panel. The message "*Locate start*" is displayed in the prompt window.

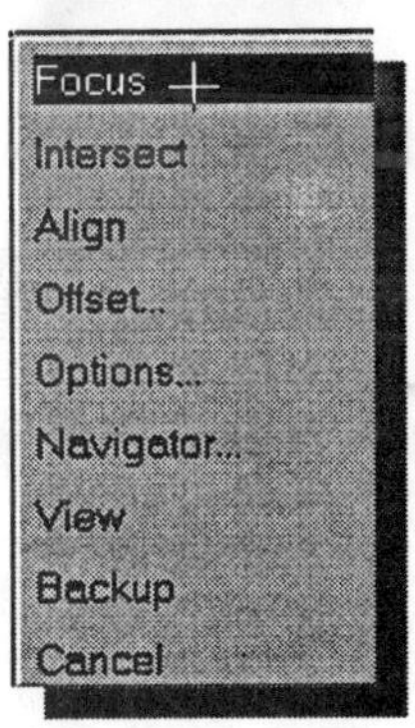

11. Move the cursor inside the graphics window. Press and hold down the right-mouse-button to display the option menu. Select the **Focus** option.

12. The message "*Pick entity*" is displayed in the prompt window. Pick the back inclined line of the 3-D model as shown in the figure. A focus line is projected onto the sketching plane.

13. Using the Dynamic Navigator, pick a location along and at about one-third from the top endpoint of the FOCUS line (*Point 1* as shown).

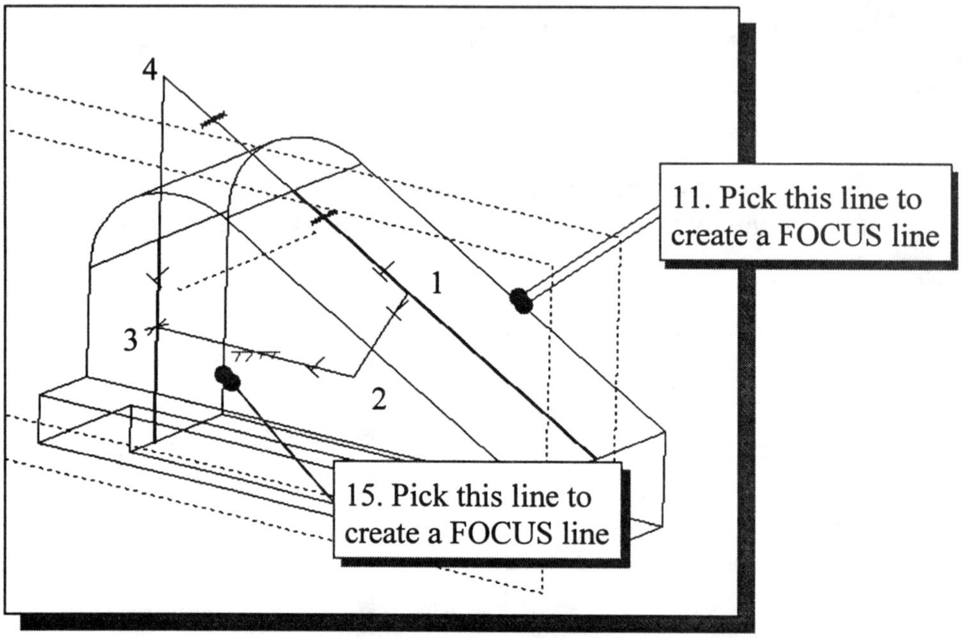

14. Move the cursor downward and use the Dynamic Navigator to create a line perpendicular to the FOCUS line (*Point 2* as shown).

15. With the cursor still inside the graphics window, press and hold down the right-mouse-button to display the *Option* menu. Select the **Focus** option. The message "*Pick entity*" is displayed in the prompt window.

16. Pick the back left vertical edge of the 3-D model. A focus line is projected onto the work plane.

17. Move the cursor downward and use the Dynamic Navigator to create a horizontal line perpendicular to the FOCUS line (*Point 3* as shown).

18. Move the cursor upward along the inclined FOCUS line and pick the point when both focus lines are highlighted. This signifies the alignment of the point to both lines. Use the Dynamic Viewing functions to assist in locating this point (*Point 4* as shown).

19. Complete the polygon by picking the starting point of the polygon (*Point 1* as shown).

20. Press the **ENTER** key or the **middle-mouse-button** to end the *Polylines* command.

Parametric Relations

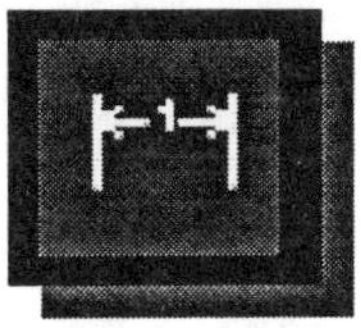

1. Use the *Dimension* command and create the two dimensions as shown. Using the *Focus* option assures the proper constraints of the sketched 2-D shape and no additional dimensions are required. We will modify the dimensions by adding parametric relations.

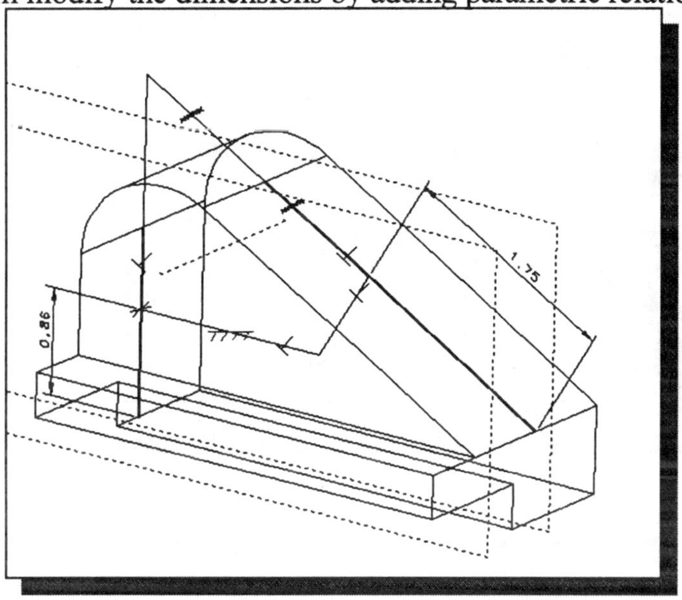

2. Use the **Modify** command and modify the dimensions as shown below.

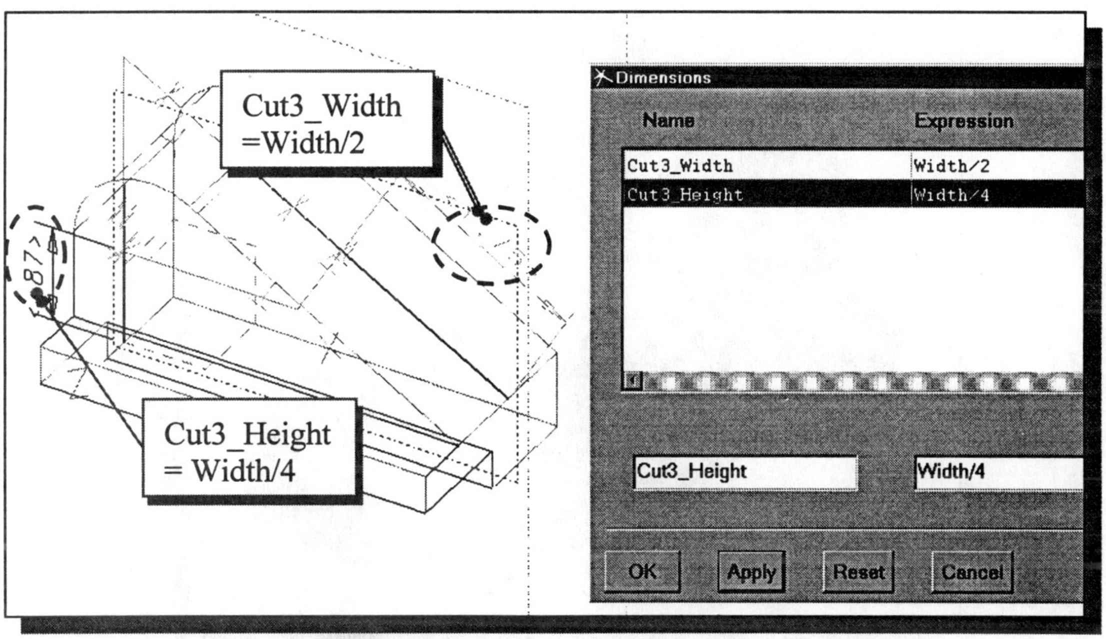

3. Click on the **OK** button to apply the changes.

4. Press the **ENTER** key or the **middle-mouse-button** to exit the *Modify* command.

Making the Third Cutout

1. Choose **Extrude** in the icon panel. In the prompt window, the message "*Pick curve or section*" is displayed.

2. Pick the polygon we just created.

3. Press the **ENTER** key or the **middle-mouse-button** to accept the selected entity.

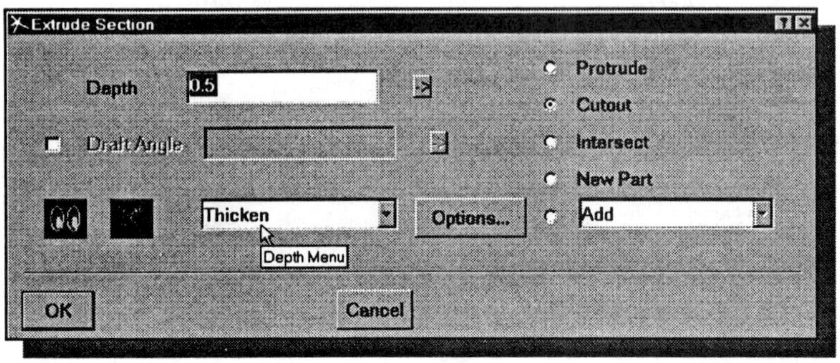

4. In the *Extrude Section* window, select **Cutout**.

5. Enter the value of **0.5** in the *Distance* box.

6. Select the **Thicken** option in the Depth menu.

❖ The *Thicken* option will create a solid extrusion on both sides of the sketching plane. The *Distance* entered with the *Thicken* option is the total extrusion distance.

7. Click on the **OK** button to create the *cutout*.

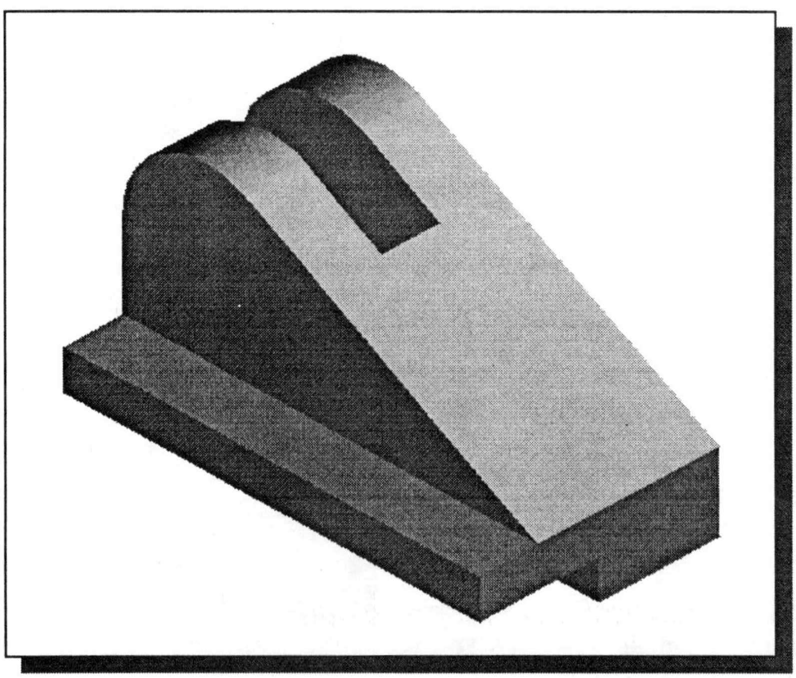

❖ Now is a good time to save the model (Quick key: **[Ctrl]** + **[S]**). It is a good habit to save your model periodically, just in case something might go wrong while you are working on the model. You should also save the model after you have completed any major constructions.

Creating a Drill-Hole Using the REVOLVE Command

2-D sketch on the reference plane

1. Choose **Sketch in Place** in the icon panel. In the prompt window, the message "*Pick plane to sketch on*" is displayed.

2. Pick the same reference plane (RF3) we used as sketching plane for the last feature. Note that each time a solid feature is created, the workplane is realigned to the world coordinate system.

3. Choose **Polylines** in the icon panel. The message "*Locate start*" is displayed in the prompt window.

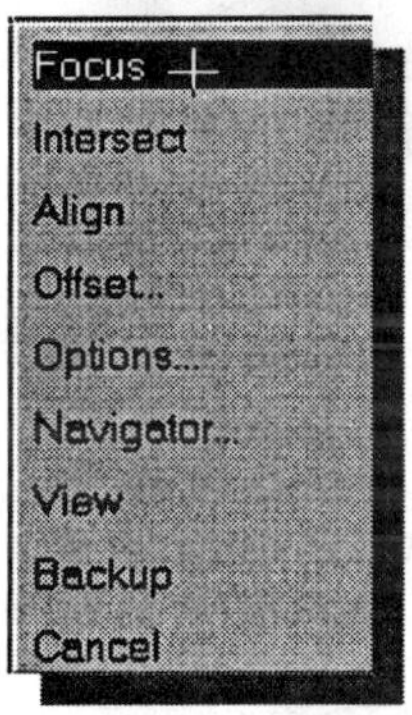

4. Move the cursor inside the graphics window. Press and hold down the right-mouse-button to display the option menu. Select the **Focus** option. The message "*Pick entity*" is displayed in the prompt window.

5. Pick the back inclined line of the 3-D model. A *focus line* is projected onto the reference plane.

6. Using the Dynamic Navigator, pick a location along and at about one-third from the right side endpoint of the FOCUS line (*Point 1* as shown).

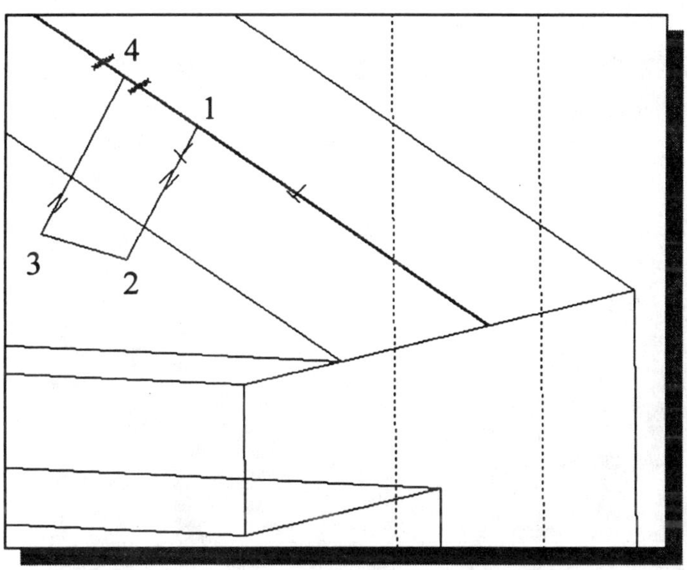

7. Move the cursor downward and use the Dynamic Navigator to create a line perpendicular to the FOCUS line (*Point 2* as shown).

8. Move the cursor toward the left and pick a location as shown (*Point 3* as shown).

9. Move the cursor upward and pick a location along the FOCUS line when the parallel symbol appears (*Point 4* as shown).

10. Complete the polygon by picking the starting point of the polygon (*Point 1* as shown).

Parametric Relations

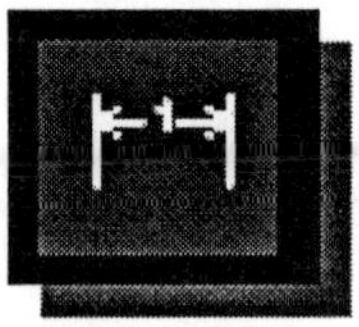

1. Use the *Dimension* command to create the key dimensions as shown. We will modify the dimensions by adding parametric relations.

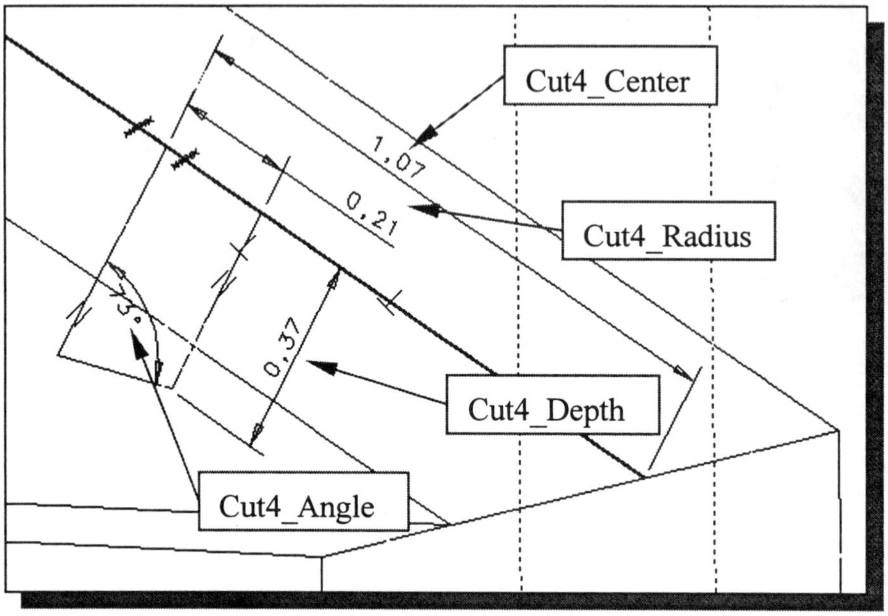

2. Pre-select all the dimensions by holding down the **SHIFT** key and left-clicking on all of the dimensional values. The selected items will be highlighted.

3. Use the **Modify** command and modify the dimensions as shown.

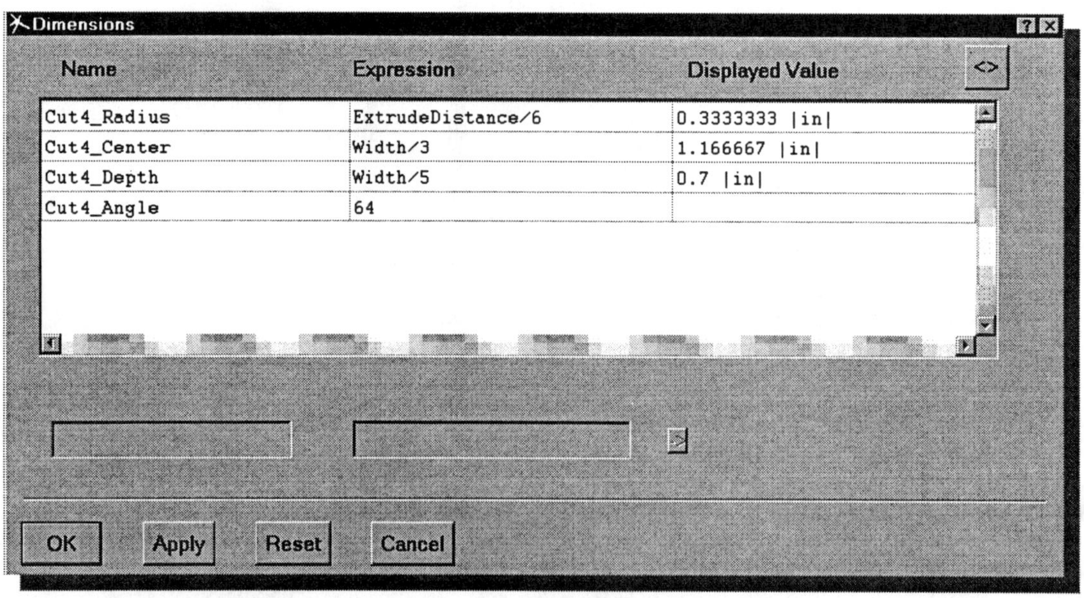

4. Click on the **OK** button to apply the changes.

5. Press the **ENTER** key or the **middle-mouse-button** to exit the *Modify* command.

Making a Revolved Cutout

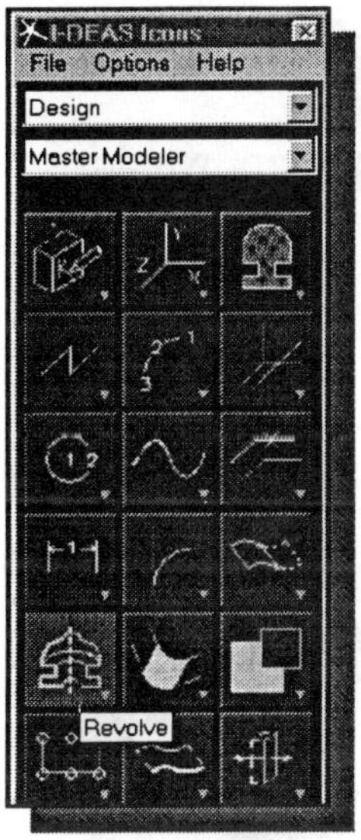

1. Choose **Revolve** in the icon panel. This icon is located in the same icon stack as the *Extrude* icon. In the prompt window, the message "*Pick curve or section*" is displayed.

2. Pick the polygon we just created. Watch the prompt, you may need to pick the top-edge to complete the selection.

3. Press the **ENTER** key or the **middle-mouse-button** to accept the selected entity.

4. At the "*Pick axis to revolve about*" prompt, pick the left edge of the polygon as shown.

5. In the *Revolve Section* window, enter the item selections as shown.

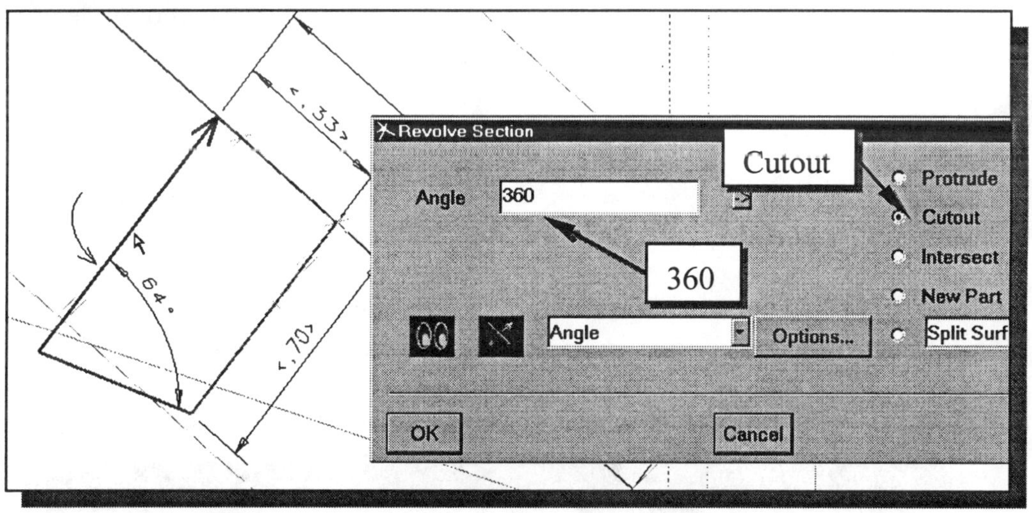

6. Click on the **OK** button to create the cutout.

❖ Now is a good time to save the model (Quick key: [**Ctrl**] + [**S**]). It is a good habit to save your model periodically, just in case something might go wrong while you are working on the model. You should also save the model after you have completed any major constructions.

Drill Through Hole

2-D sketch on the reference plane

1. Choose **Sketch in Place** in the icon panel. In the prompt window, the message ***"Pick plane to sketch on"*** is displayed.

2. Pick the reference plane we created for the first cutout.

3. Choose *Circle* – **Center-edge** in the icon panel. The message "*Locate center*" is displayed in the prompt window.

4. Move the cursor inside the graphics window. Press and hold down the right-mouse-button to display the option menu. Select the **Focus** option. The message "*Pick entity*" is displayed in the prompt window.

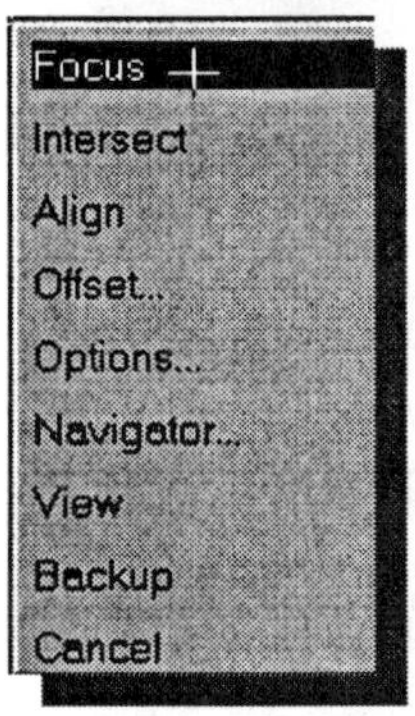

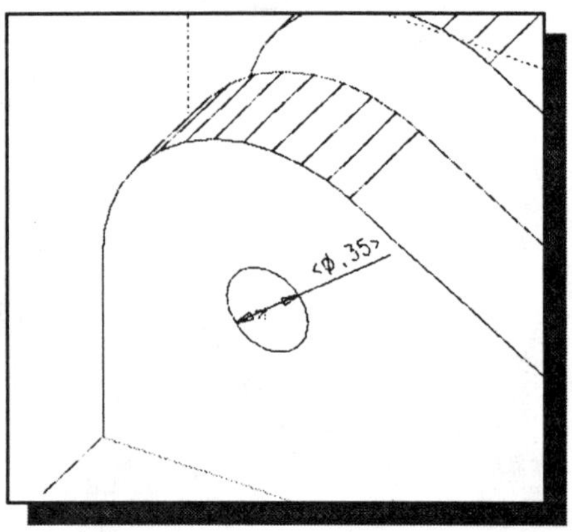

5. Pick one of the endpoints of the axis of the arc. A reference point is projected onto the reference plane.

6. Pick the reference point as the center of the new circle.

7. Pick another location to create a circle of arbitrary size.

8. Use the **Modify** command and modify the diameter as shown.

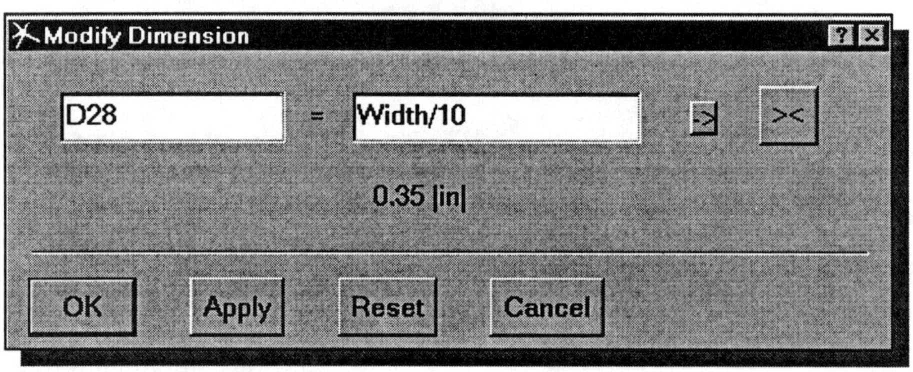

9. Choose **Extrude** in the icon panel.

10. Pick the circle just created.

11. Press the **ENTER** key or the **middle-mouse-button** to accept the selection.

12. In the *Extrude Section* window, select **Cutout**.

13. Press and hold down the left-mouse-button on the **Depth** icon and select the **Thru All** option.

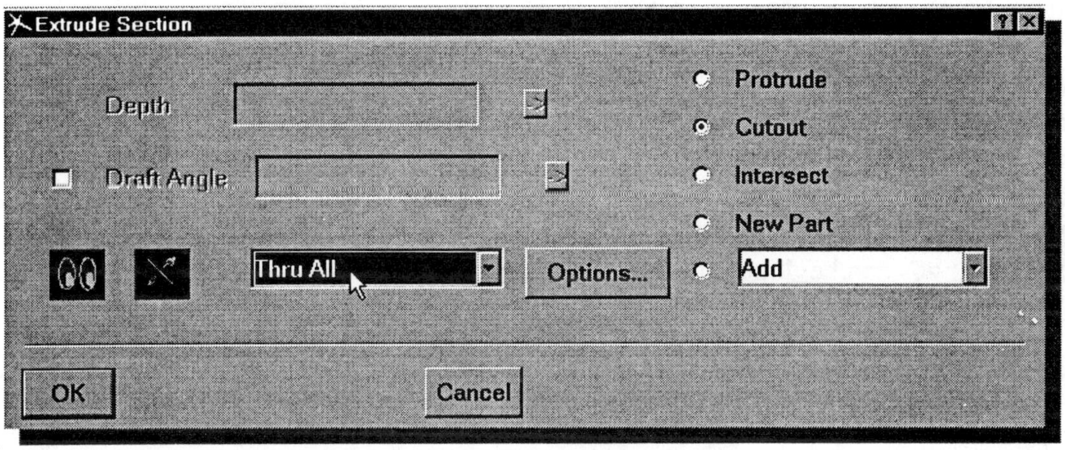

14. Click on the **OK** button to perform the *cutout*.

A Design Change

In a typical design process, the initial design will undergo many analyses, testing, and reviews. The *history-based part modifications* approach is an extremely powerful tool that enables us to quickly update the design. At the same time, it is quite clear that PLANNING AHEAD is very important in doing parametric modeling.

The model we constructed contains four controlling dimensions: the overall width, the extrude-distance of the base, the angle of the incline surface and the drill angle. Use the *History Access*, *Show Dimensions* and *Modify* commands to adjust the overall width of the part to **4.5** inches and the extrude-distance to **1.75**. With parametric modeling, design changes can be done quickly while maintaining the design intent.

Questions:

1. Describe the advantages of using the *BORN* technique.

2. What are the advantages of using *Reference Geometry*?

3. Describe the differences between *Extrude* and *Revolve*.

4. Describe the *Offset Surface* option under *Reference Plane*.

5. Why use *Parametric relations*?

6. What is the result of the parametric expression *Width*3/4+.25*?

7. Which command do we use to make sure the *sketched object* is aligned with existing geometric entities that are not on the same plane?

8. Identify and describe the following commands:

(a)

(b)

(c)

(d)

Exercises:

1.

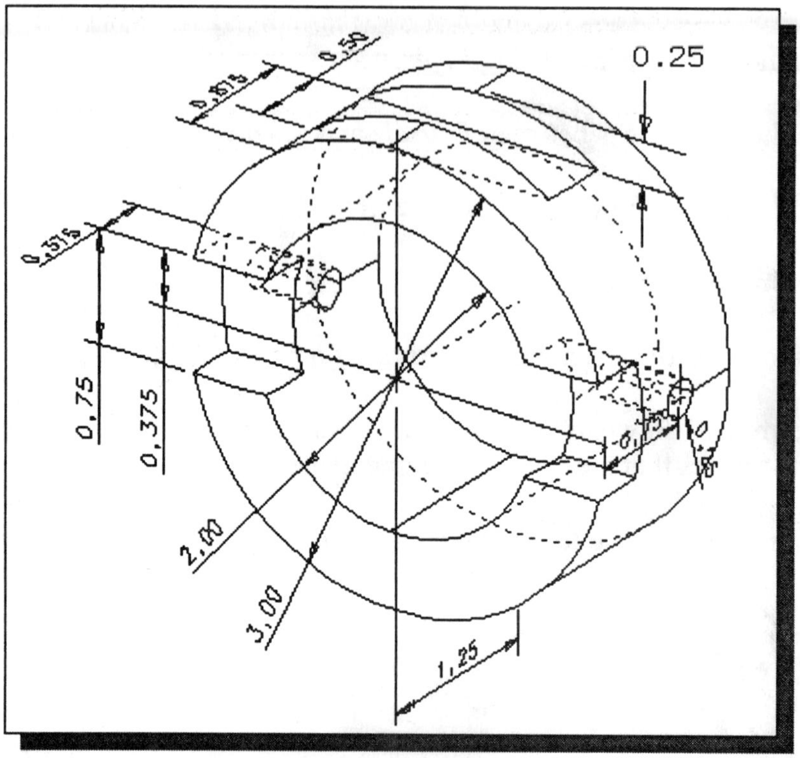

2.

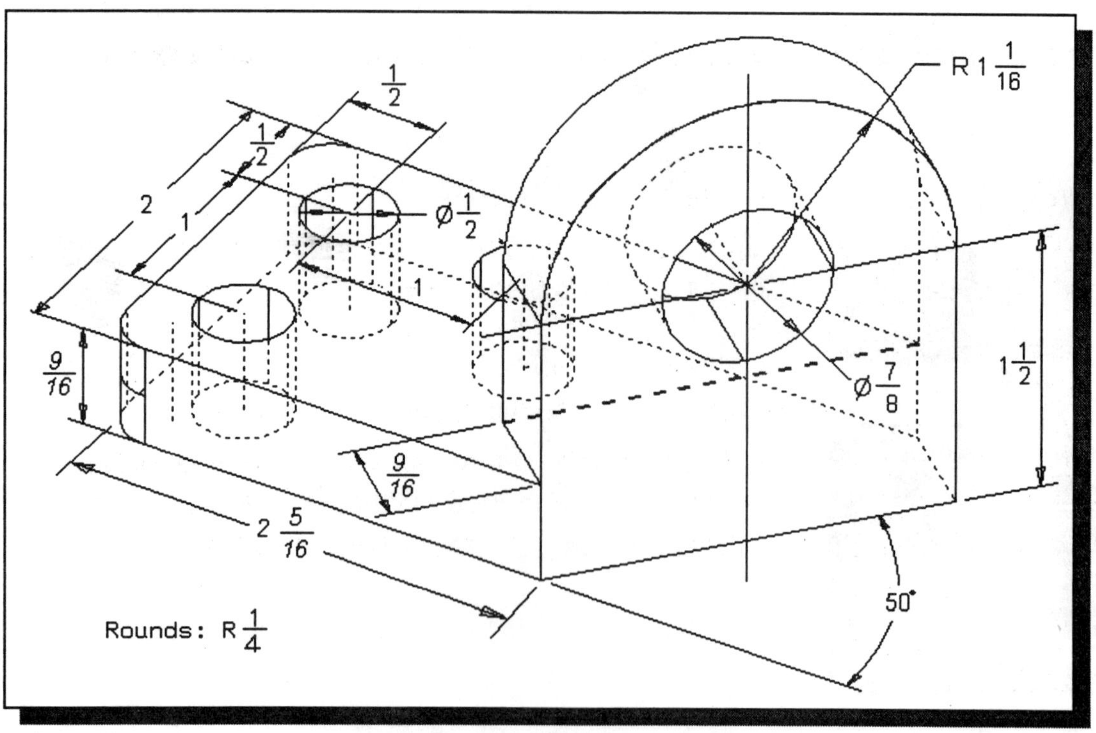

Chapter 8
3-D Annotation and Associated Drawings

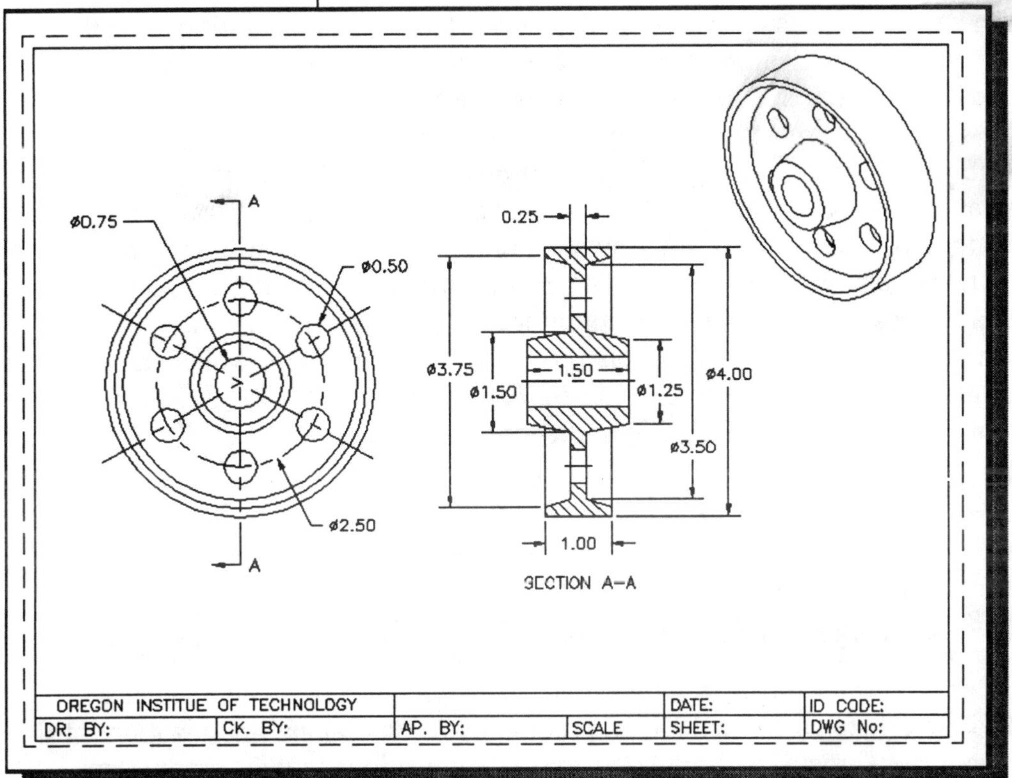

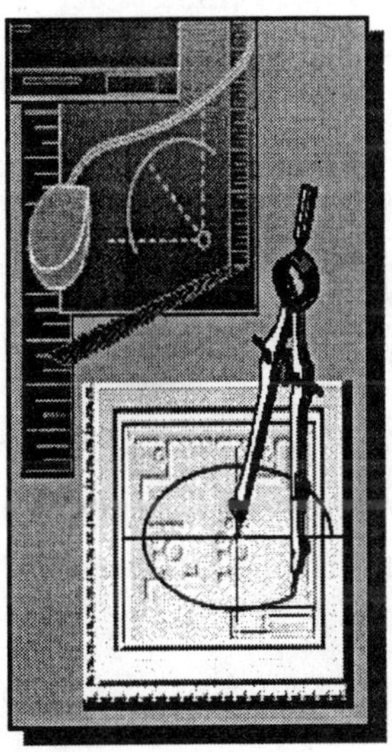

Learning Objectives

When you have completed this lesson, you will be able to:

- **Open Existing Model Files.**
- **Use the Print/Plot command.**
- **Create 3-D Annotation.**
- **Understand the Associative Functionality.**
- **Use the Master Drafting Application to create Drawing Layouts.**
- **Arrange and Manage 2-D Views in Master Drafting.**
- **Create Notes, Dimensions in Master Drafting**

3D Annotation and Drawings from Parts

I-DEAS provides users with the ability to access the powerful digital product information for communication and in support of operations such as inspection, manufacturing, or purchasing. With software/hardware improvements, it is now feasible to use the solid modeling software to document and communicate all production and manufacturing information in a three-dimensional (3D) environment. In *I-DEAS 8*, exciting and unique tools are now available for documenting and communicating product designs. We can apply 3D-based annotation, in conjunction with engineering drawing conventions, directly to the solid model or assembly. This new solids-based documentation approach provides the ability to create, manage, and deliver process-specific information without the need for paper-based documentation. With this new set of tools, the mental translation of 3D models to two-dimensional (2D) drawings for communicating information and then back to 3D models for manufacturing is replaced with a representative 3D prototype that provides all necessary information to communicate and manufacture the product. This approach means faster and more precise product communication, which can greatly improve the product development process. In *I-DEAS 8*, the standard 2D drawing documentation symbols are also available in the 3D-based annotation mode.

With the capabilities of parametric solid modeling software, the importance of two-dimensional drawings is decreasing. Drafting is now considered one of the downstream applications of using solid modeling. In many production facilities, solid models are being used to generate machine tool paths for *computer numerical control* (CNC) machine tools. Solid models can also used in *rapid prototyping* to create 3D physical models out of plastic resins, powdered metal, etc. Ideally, the solid model database should be used directly to generate the final product. However, many organizations still require the use of two-dimensional drawings for the applications in their production facilities. In I-DEAS, model views can be used to automatically create 2D views in I-DEAS Master Drafting. Using the solid model as the starting point for a design, solid modeling tools can easily create all the necessary two-dimensional views. In this sense, solid modeling tools are making the process of creating two-dimensional drawings more efficient and effective.

I-DEAS provides **associative functionality** in the different I-DEAS applications. This functionality allows us to change the design at any level, and the system reflects it at all levels automatically. For example, a solid model can be modified in the Master Modeler and the system automatically reflects all changes in the associated drawing views as well as the associated 3D annotation.

In this chapter, we will use the Saddle Bracket model created in chapter 4 to demonstrate the procedure of adding 3D annotation directly on the solid models and the procedure of creating an associated multi-view drawing of the model.

Changing the Color of the 3-D Model

1. Login to the computer and bring up I-DEAS 8. Open the Saddle Bracket model by filling in the items as shown below in the *I-DEAS Start* window:

Project Name: **(Your account Name)** Model File Name: **SaddleBracket** Application: **Design** Task: **Master Modeler** OK

2. I-DEAS will now search for and load the existing model file into memory.

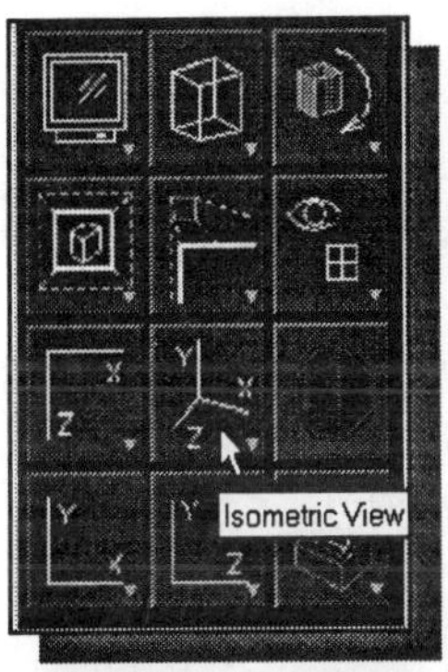

3. Choose **Isometric View** in the display viewing icon panel.

4. Choose **Zoom-All** in the display viewing icon panel.

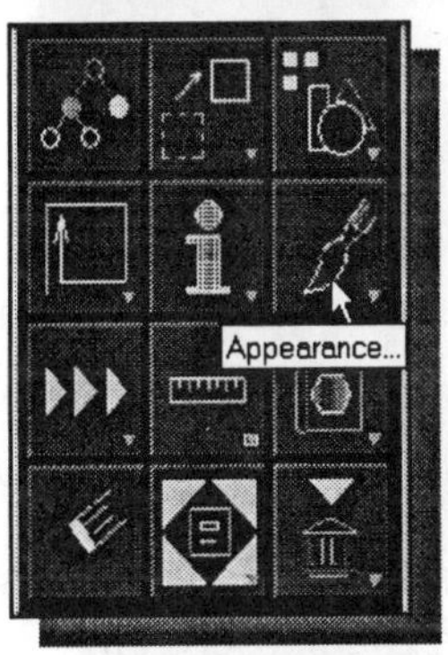

5. Pick **Shaded Software** or **Shaded Hardware** icon to view the solid model.

6. Choose **Appearance** in the icon panel. (The icon is located in the second row of the application specific icon panel.) The message "*Pick entity to modify*" is displayed in the prompt window.

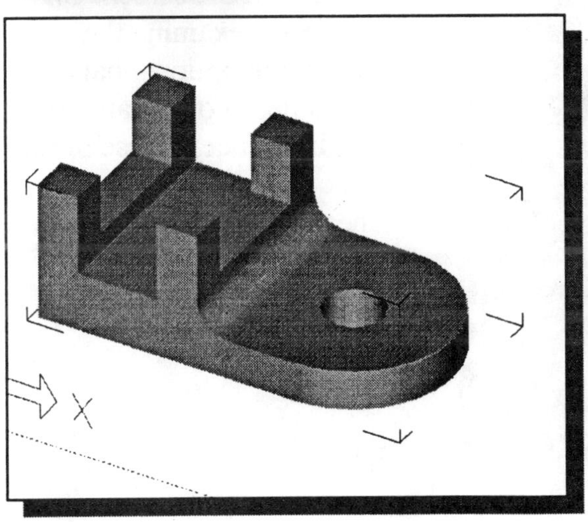

7. Pick the solid model by clicking the same edge twice. A white box bounding the entire model appears.

8. Press the **ENTER** key or the **middle-mouse-button** to continue.

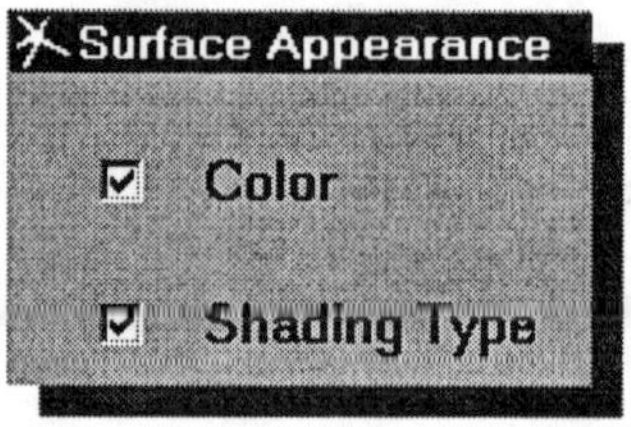

9. In the *Surface Appearance* window, switch **ON** the *Color* option.

10. Click on the [**?**] button, the **Color Of Object** icon, to display a color list.

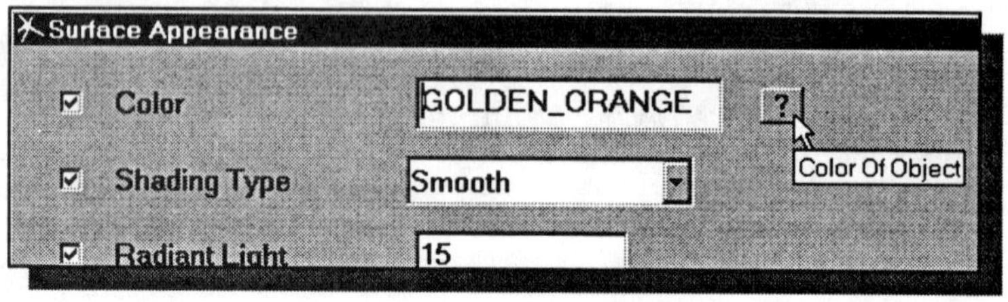

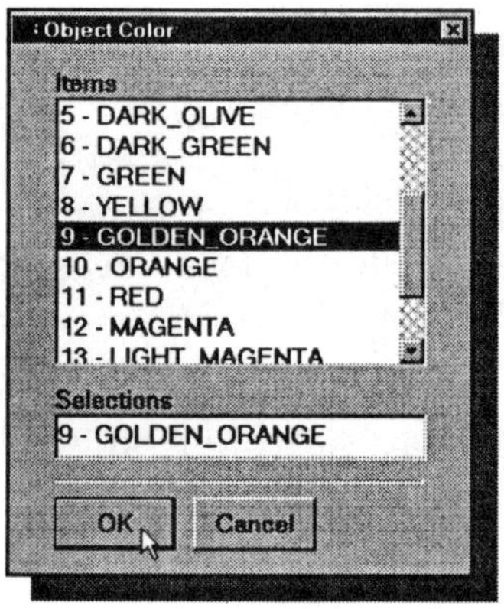

11. Set the color to **Golden_Orange**.

12. Click on the **OK** button to accept the settings and close the *Object Color* window.

13. Click on the **OK** button to close the *Surface Appearance* window and adjust the color of the 3D model.

3D Annotation – Linear Dimension

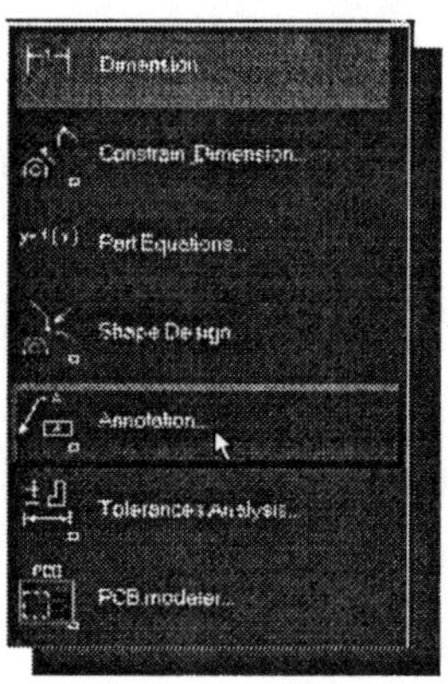

1. Press and hold the left-mouse-button on the **Dimension** icon in the icon panel and select the ***Annotation*** options.

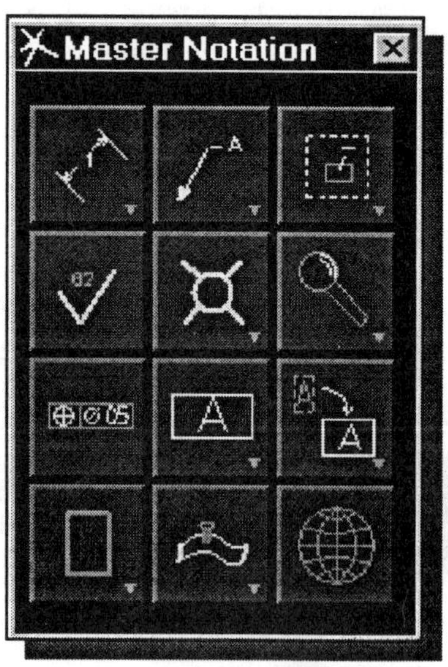

❖ The *Master Notation* window appears on the screen. On your own, examine the annotation options that are available. In our example, we will introduce the use of the basic dimension options: linear, diameter, radius.

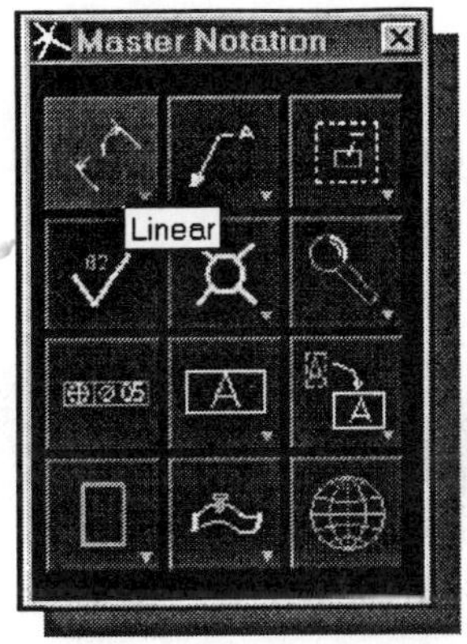

2. In the *Master Notation* window, click on the **Linear dimension** icon with the left-mouse-button.

❖ The **linear dimension** option allows us to create a linear dimension (straight-line distance) between different types of geometric entities.

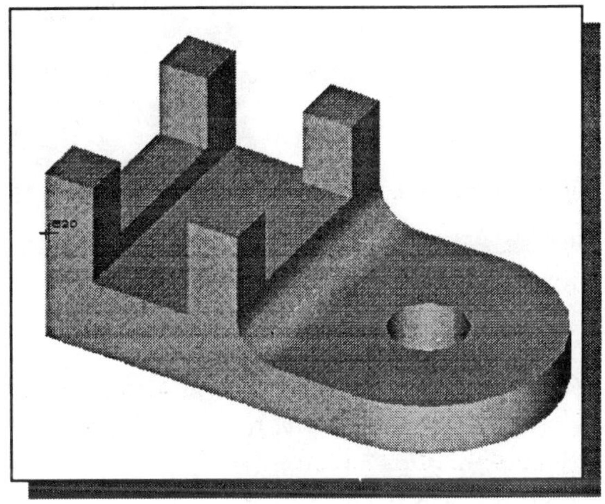

3. In the prompt window, the message "*Pick a vertex, linear edge, or planar face*" is displayed. Pick the left-edge of the front face of the base feature as shown in the figure. (Notice the **Exx** symbol identifying the highlighted entity is an edge.)

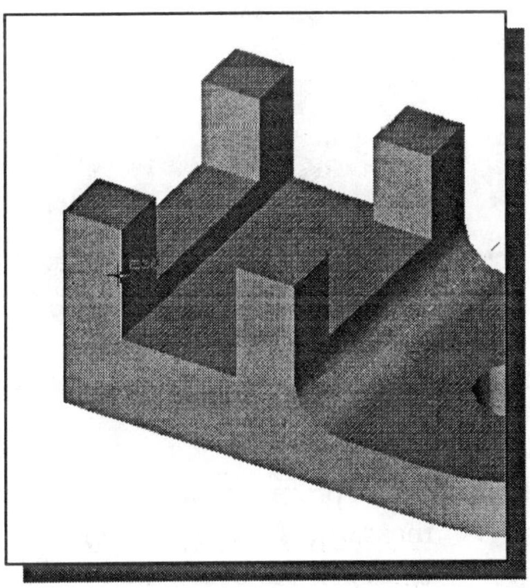

4. In the prompt window, the message "*Pick a vertex or a linear edge*" is displayed. Pick the second left-edge of the front face of the base feature as shown in the figure. (Notice the **Exx** symbol identifying the highlighted entity is an edge.)

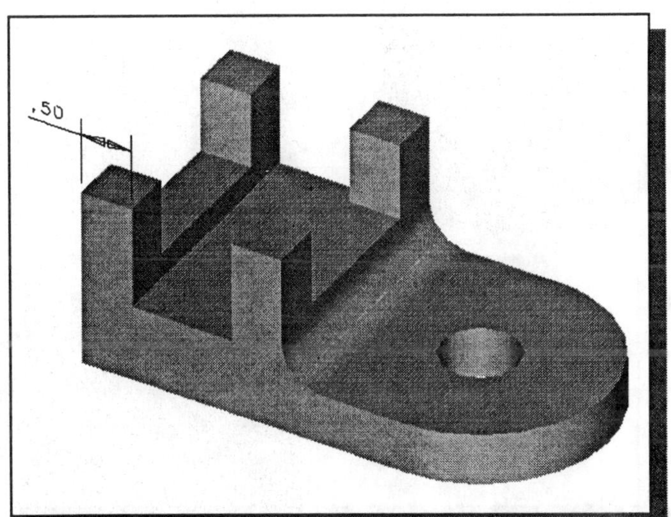

5. In the prompt window, the message "*Pick text position*" is displayed. Place the dimension text above the model as shown in the figure.

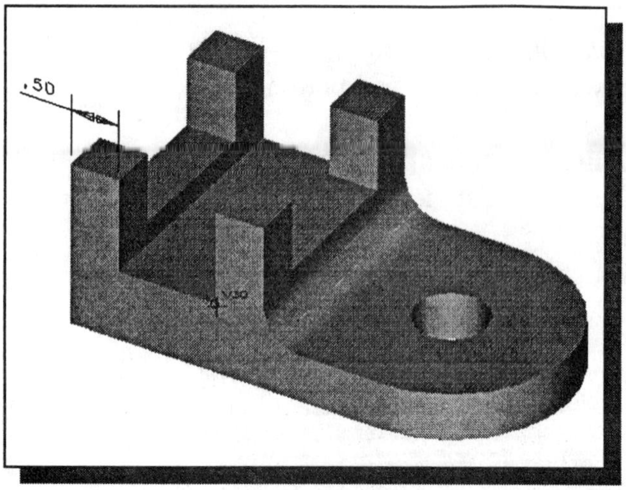

6. In the prompt window, the message "*Pick a vertex, linear edge, or planar face*" is displayed. Pick the right inside corner of the u-shape of the base feature as shown in the figure. (Notice the **Vxx** symbol identifying the highlighted entity is a vertex.)

7. In the prompt window, the message "*Pick a vertex or a linear edge*" is displayed. Pick the bottom-edge of the front face of the base feature as shown in the figure. (Notice the **Exx** symbol identifying the highlighted entity is an edge.)

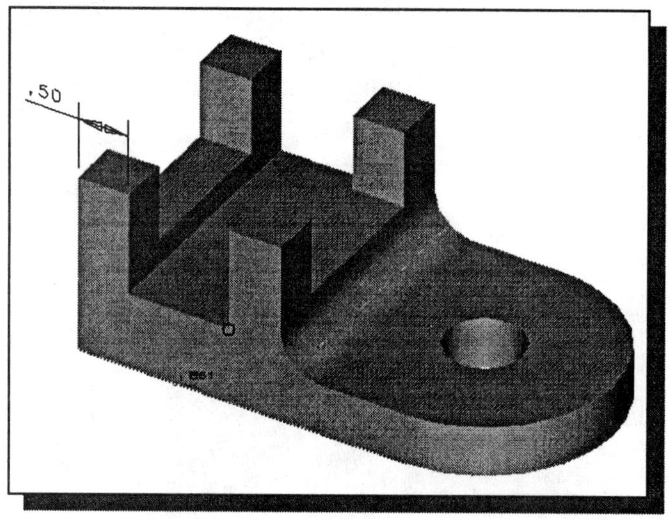

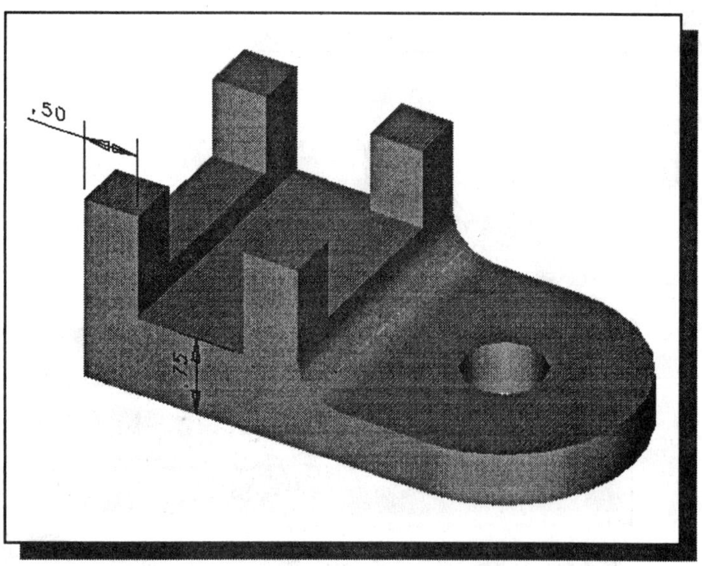

8. In the prompt window, the message "*Pick text position*" is displayed. Place the dimension text below the model as shown in the figure.

❖ The linear dimension option is used to create a straight-line distance. Selecting two parallel lines, or a point and a line, on the same plane will create a linear dimension describing the perpendicular distance in between.

9. On your own, repeat the above steps and create the linear dimensions as shown in the figure.

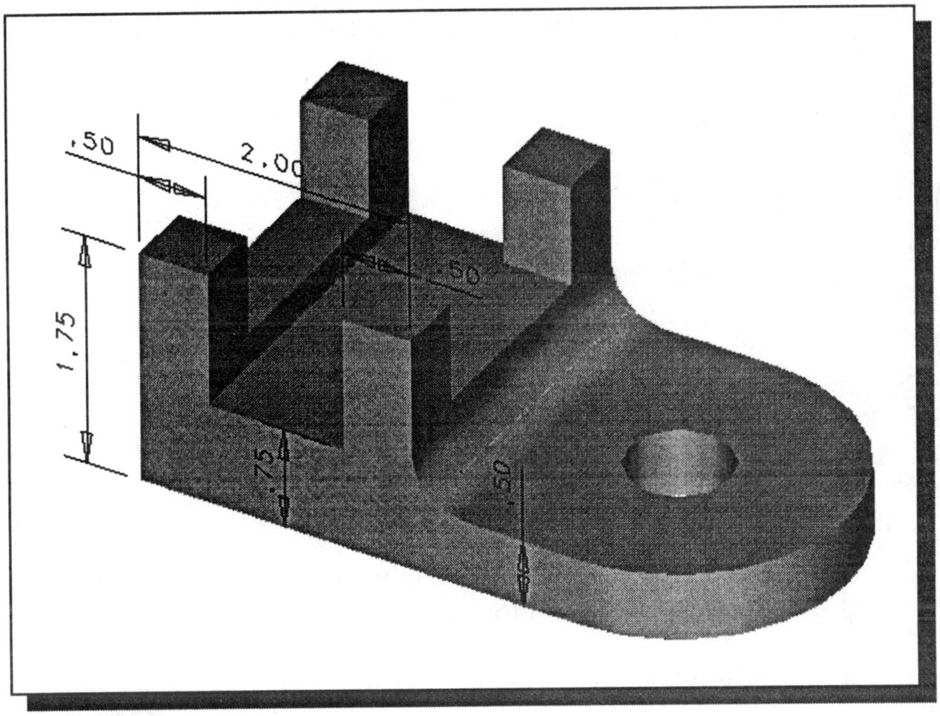

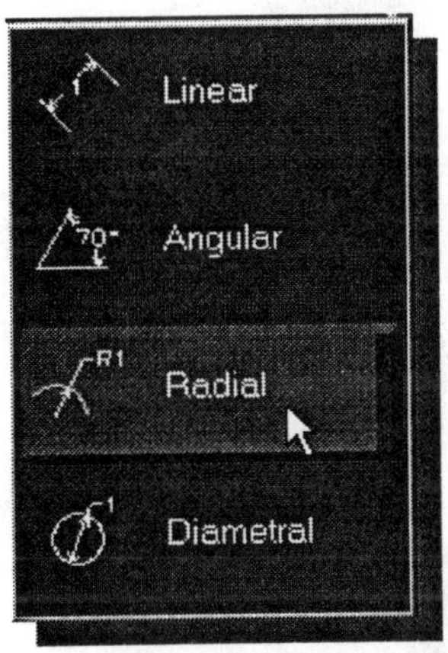

10. In the *Master Notation* window, press and hold down the left-mouse-button on the **Linear dimension** icon to display additional options. Select the **Radial dimension** option with the left-mouse-button.

11. Select the arc in the front face of the base feature as shown.

12. Place the dimension text above the arc as shown.

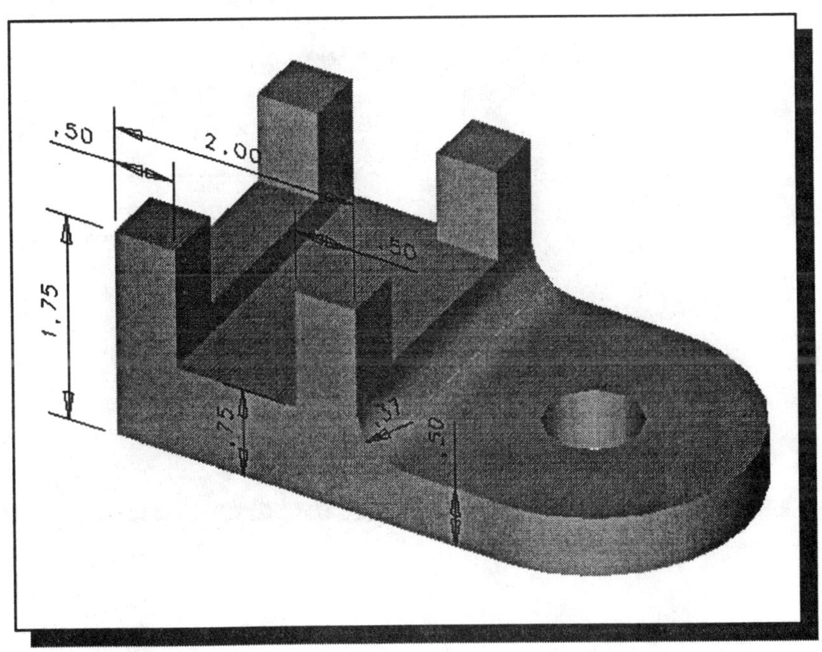

❖ We have completed the annotation for the 2D sketch of the base feature.

Changing the Appearance of Dimensions

We can adjust the appearance of dimensions by using the ***Appearance*** command.

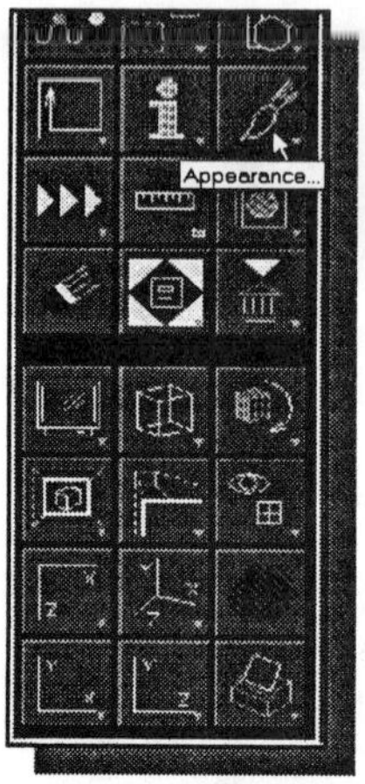

1. Choose **Appearance** in the icon panel. (The icon is located in the second row of the application icon panel. If the icon is not on top of the stack, press and hold down the left-mouse-button on the displayed icon, then select the **Appearance** icon.) The message "*Pick entity to modify*" is displayed in the prompt window.

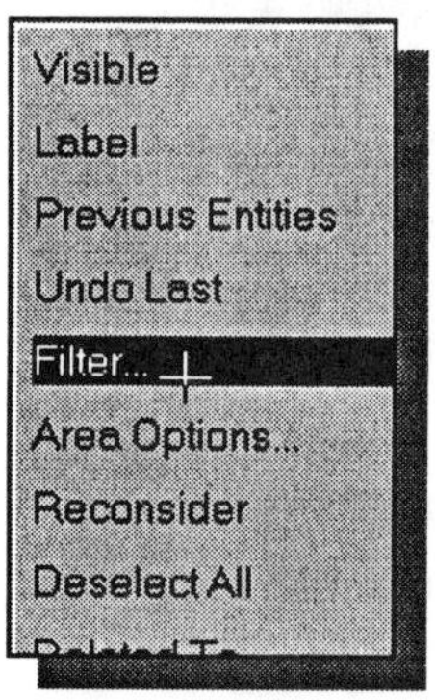

2. Move the cursor inside the graphics window. Press and hold down the right-mouse-button to display the option menu.

3. Pick the **Filter...** option. This will bring up the *Selection Filter* window, which is used to control the types of entities that are selectable.

4. By default, all entities are selectable. Select **Dimension** in the *Pickable* box.

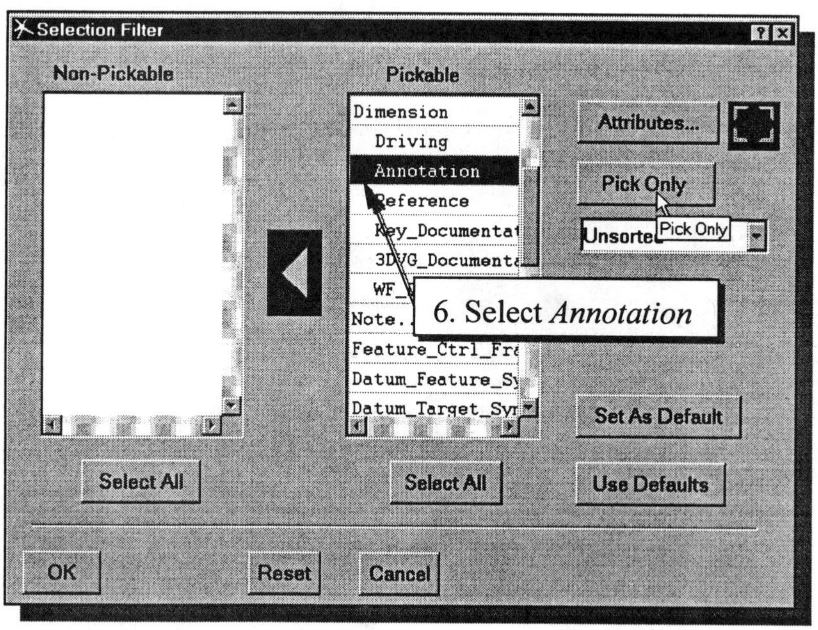

5. Double-click with the left-mouse-button to display the different types of dimensions.

6. Select **Annotation** in the *Pickable* box.

7. Click on the **Pick Only** button, located to the right of the *Pickable* box, which will set *Annotation Dimension* as the only selectable entity type.

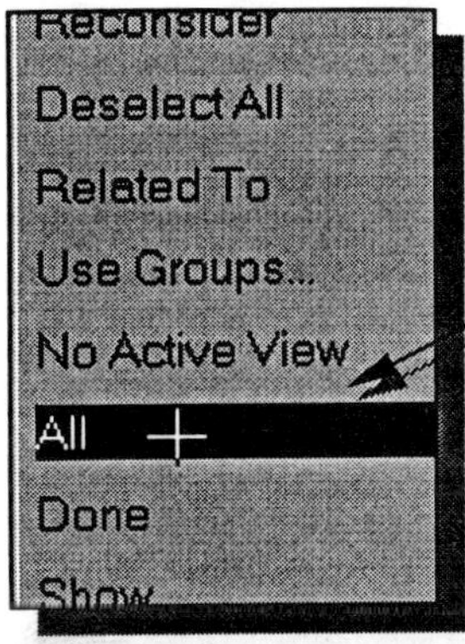

8. Move the cursor inside the graphics window. Press and hold down the **right-mouse-button** to display the option menu.

9. Select all displayed dimensions.

9. Select the **All** option. We have selected all of the displayed *Annotation Dimensions*.

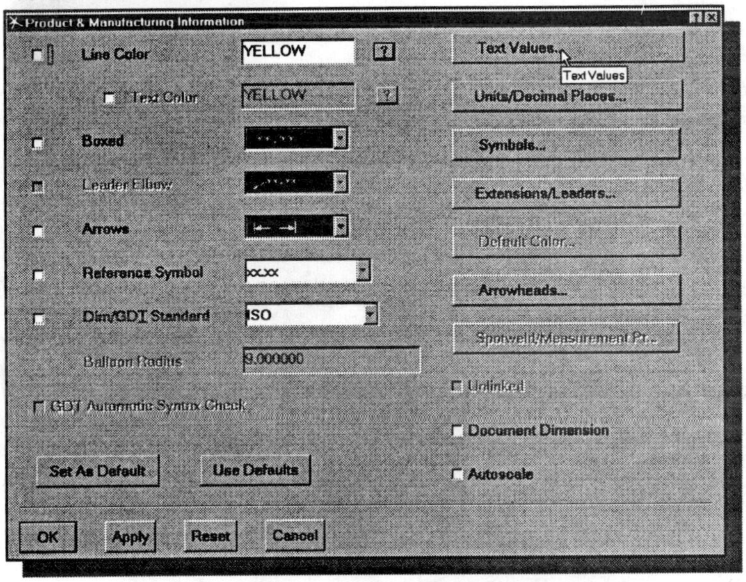

10. Press the **ENTER** key or the **middle-mouse-button** to accept the selected entities.

11. In the *Product & Manufacturing Information* window, click on the **Text Values** button. The *Text Values* window appears.

12. Enter **.125** as the new *dimension height*.

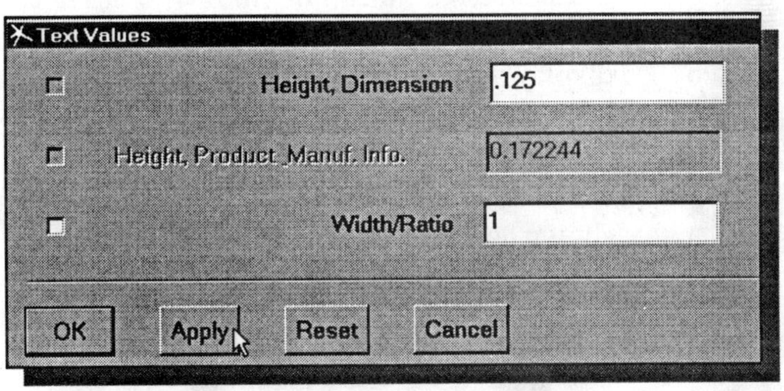

13. Click on the **Apply** button to make the modification.

14. Click on the **OK** button to accept the modification.

15. Click on the **OK** button to exit the *Product & Manufacturing Information* window.

16. Press the **ENTER** key or the **middle-mouse-button** to end the *Appearance* command.

Adding Additional 3D Annotation

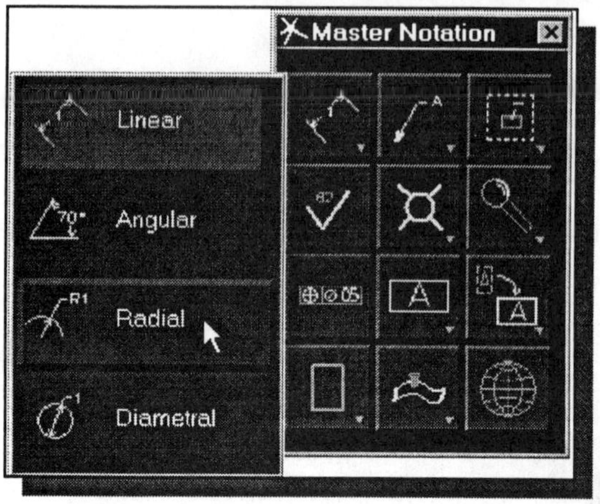

1. In the *Master Notation* window, press and hold down the left-mouse-button on the **Linear dimension** icon to display additional options. Select the **Radial dimension** option with the left-mouse-button.

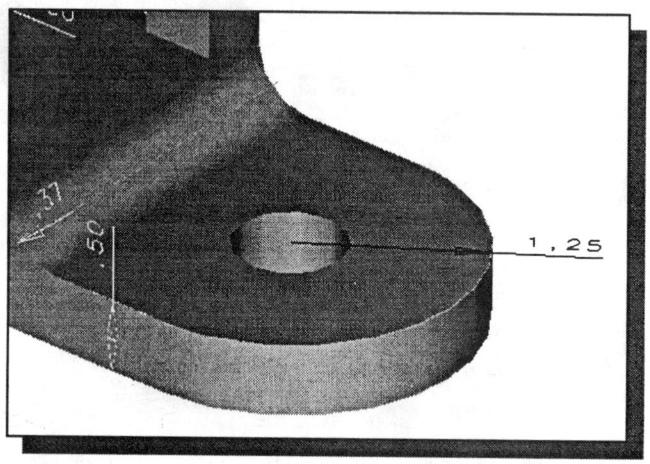

2. Select the arc in the top-horizontal face of the model as shown.

3. Place the dimension text toward the right side of the model as shown.

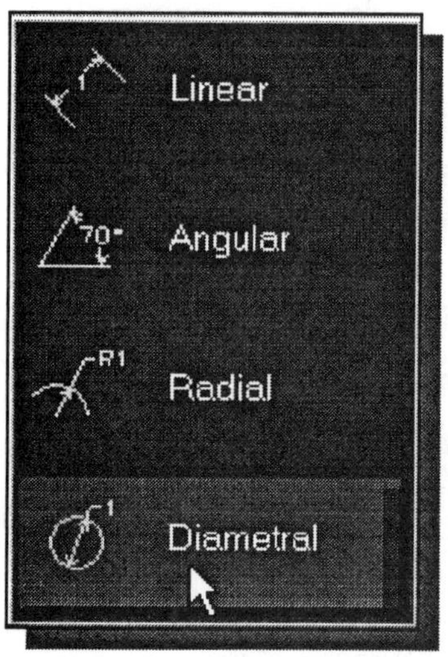

4. In the *Master Notation* window, press and hold down the left-mouse-button on the **Radial dimension** icon to display additional options. Select the **Diametral dimension** option with the left-mouse-button.

5. On your own, create the dimension for the hole feature as shown.

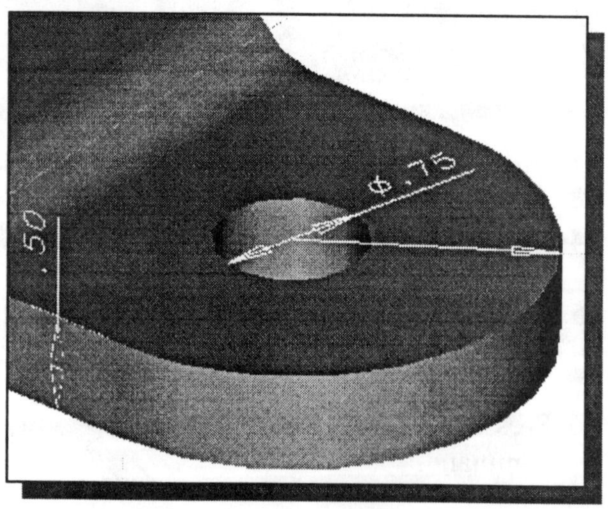

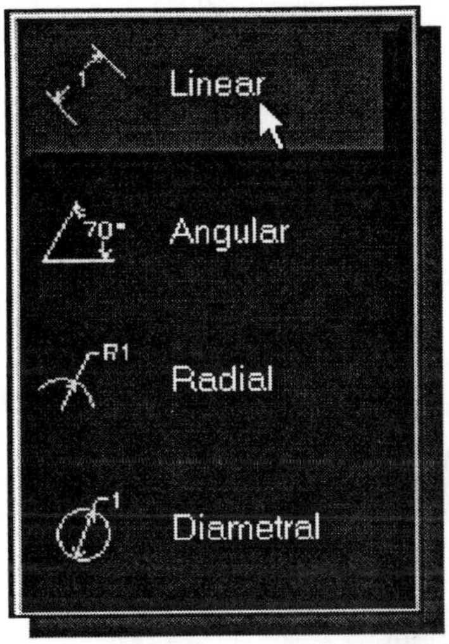

6. In the *Master Notation window*, press and hold down the left-mouse-button on the **Diametral dimension** icon to display additional options. Select the **Linear dimension** option with the left-mouse-button.

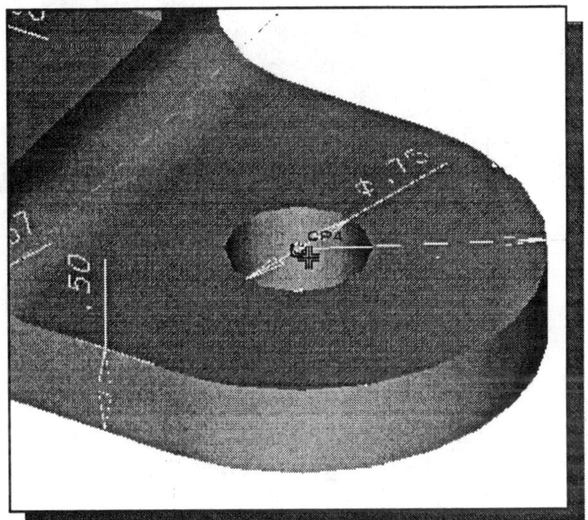

7. Select the center of the hole feature in the top-horizontal face of the model as shown. (Notice the **Cxx** symbol identifying the center point.)

8. Press the **ENTER** key or the **middle-mouse-button** to accept the selection.

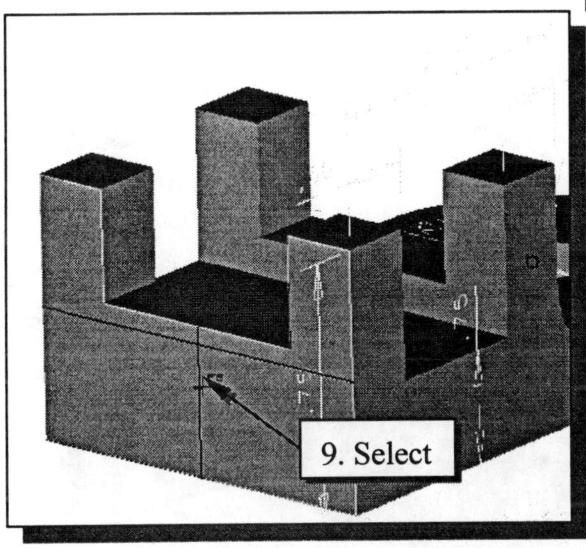

9. On your own, rotate the solid model and select the vertical plane as shown.

10. Select the bottom arc to define the placement plane as shown.

11. Place the dimension text toward the front of the model.

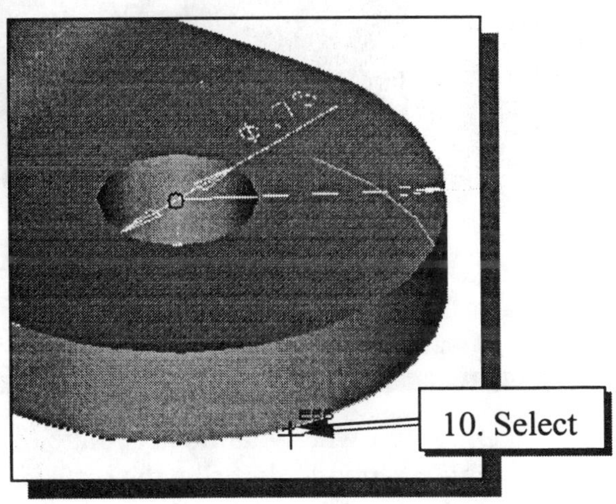

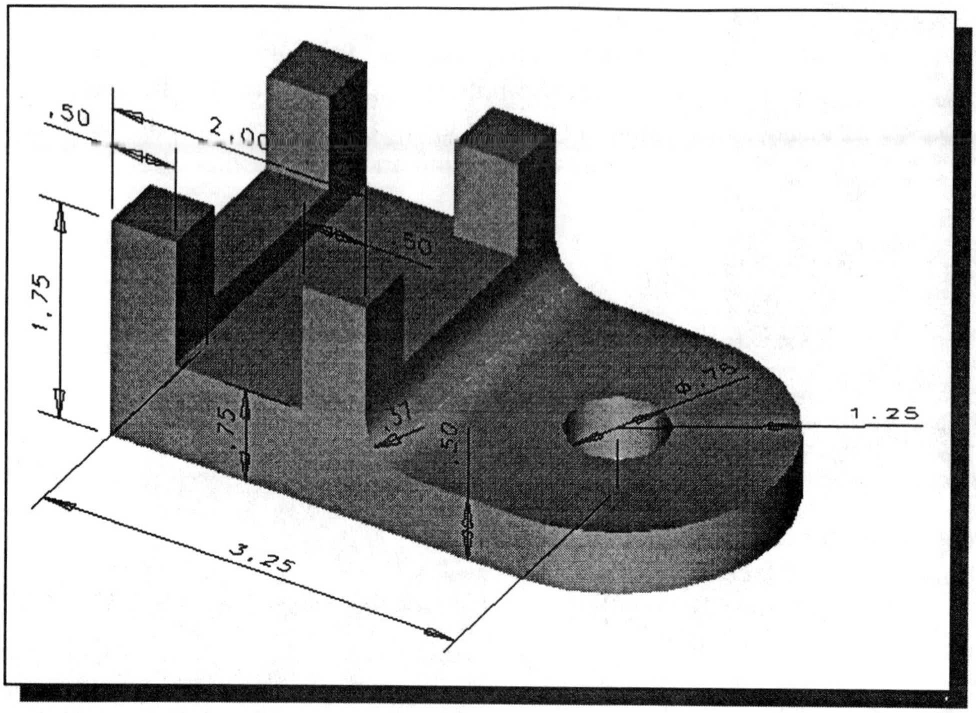

12. On your own, add the annotation for the center-cut feature on the vertical surface as shown below.

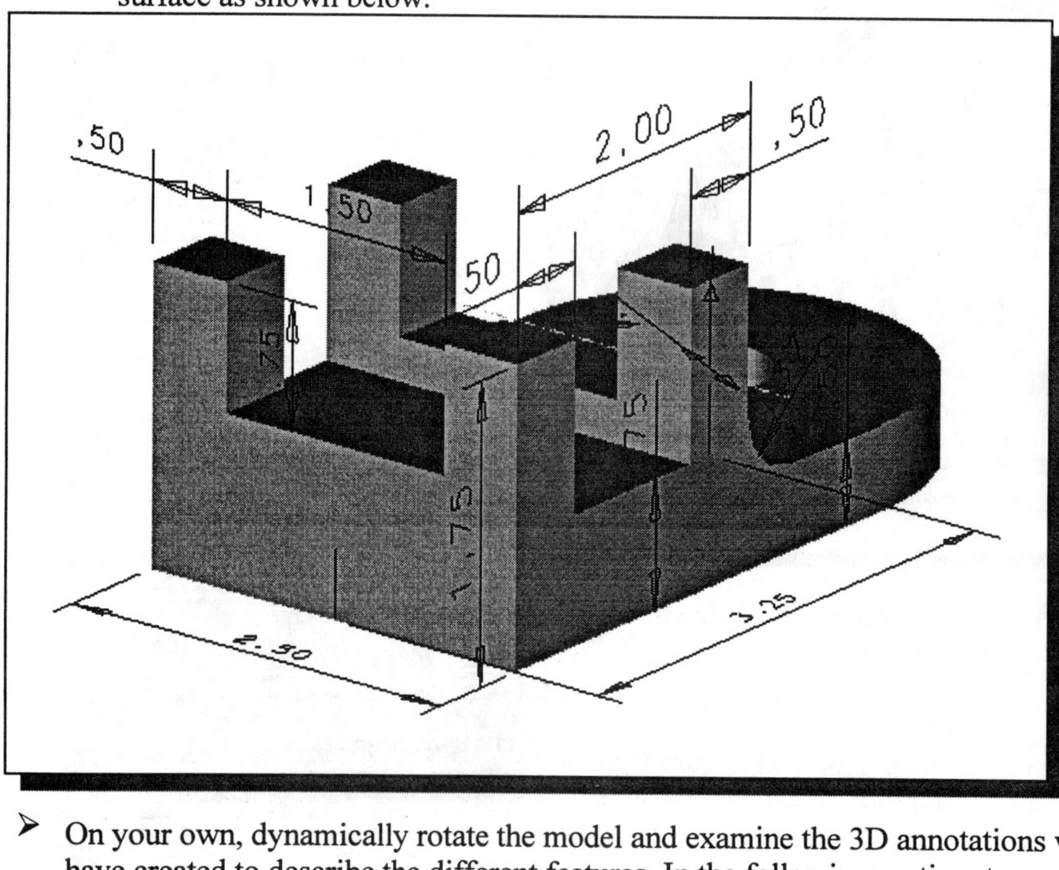

➢ On your own, dynamically rotate the model and examine the 3D annotations we have created to describe the different features. In the following section, two methods of displaying the 3D annotation dimensions are illustrated.

First Method - Model Views

❖ **Model Views** are views defined by users; these views can be used to communicate design and production information among design teams and manufacturing groups.

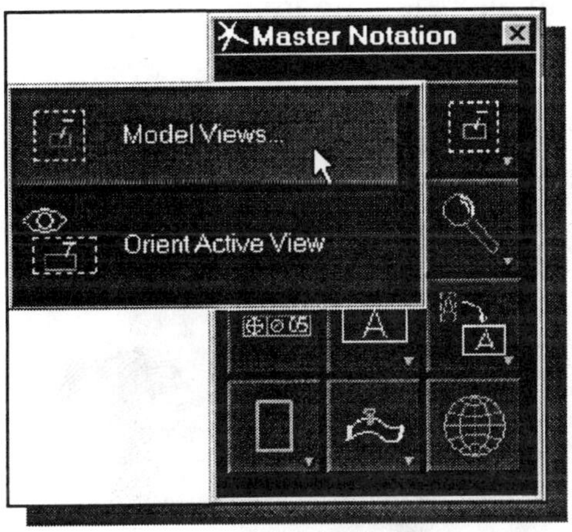

1. In the *Master Notation* window, press and hold down the left-mouse-button on the top-right icon to display all options. Select the **Model Views** option with the left-mousc-button.

❖ Currently, the only item listed is the "No Active view" option, which indicates there are no user-defined model views

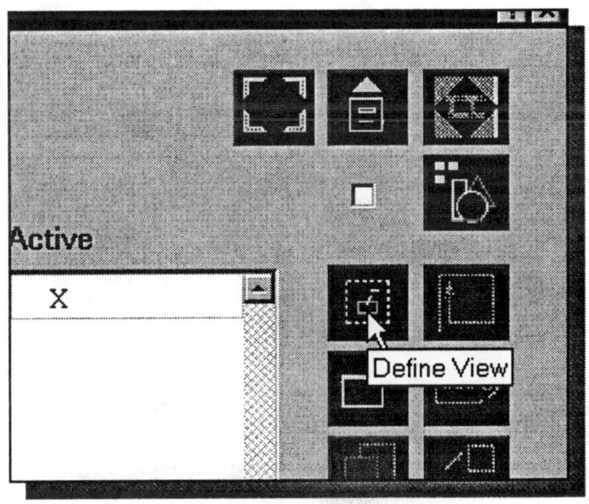

2. In the *Views* window, click on the **Define View** button as shown.

❖ The **Define View** option allows us to use standard views or define new viewing directions. In this example, we will use the standard views provided by the system.

3. In the *Define* window, select **Front** in the *View Type* list.

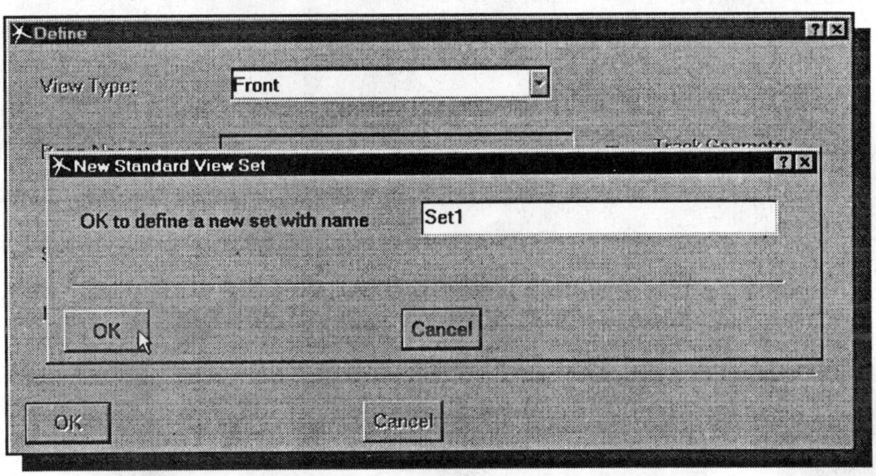

4. In the *New Standard View Set* window, click on the **OK** button to accept the default set name **Set1**.

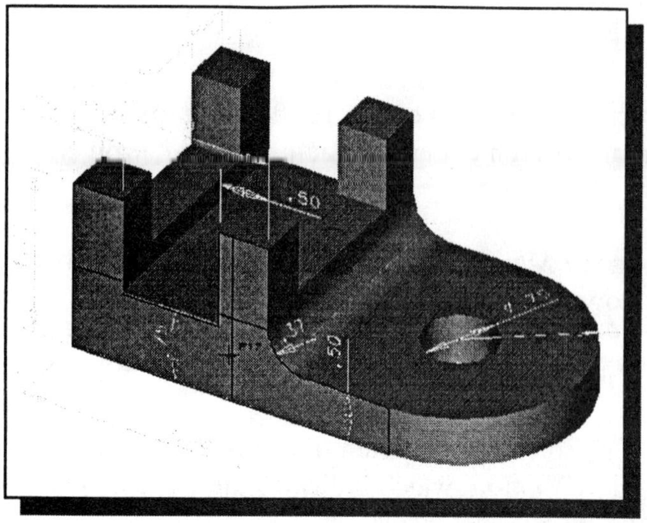

5. In the prompt window, the message *"Select plane to define Front view or MB3 for other options."* is displayed. Select the front face of the model as shown in the below figure.

6. Confirm the viewing direction is pointing toward the front side of the model. Select **Yes** in the popup menu.

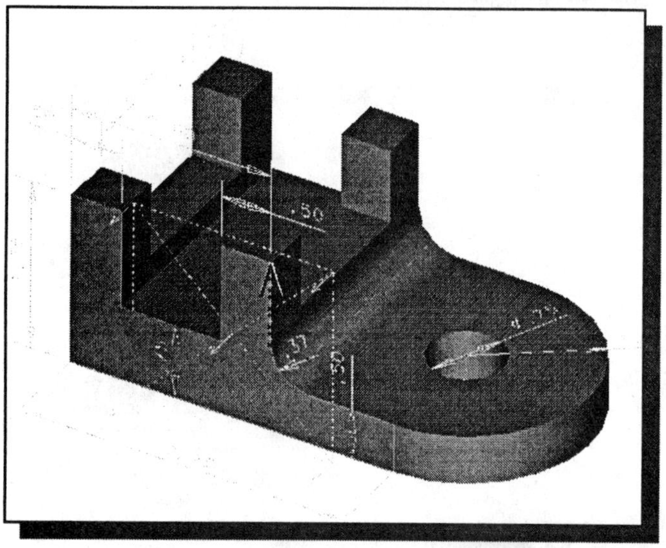

7. Select one of the vertical edges to define the ***up vector***, the orientation of the view.

8. Confirm the arrow is pointing upward as shown. Select **Yes** in the popup menu.

9. Click on the **OK** button to accept the settings and exit the *Define View* window.

10. In the *Views* window, a new view is added to the list. Since this is the first view we defined, it is set as a **base view**. Additional views can be derived from this view.

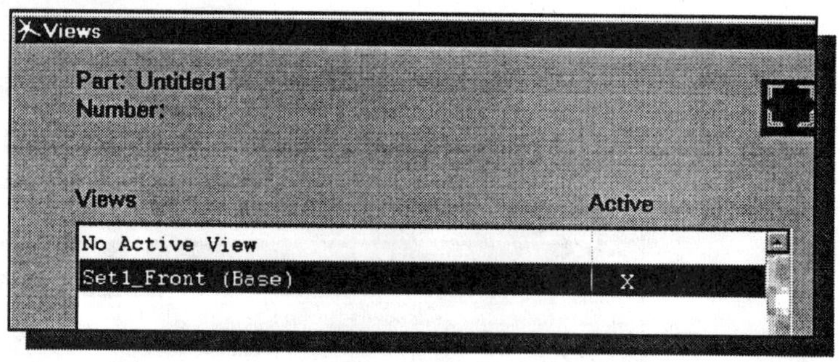

11. On your own, define three additional views: **Top, Right**, and **Isometric** by selecting them from the *View Type* list.

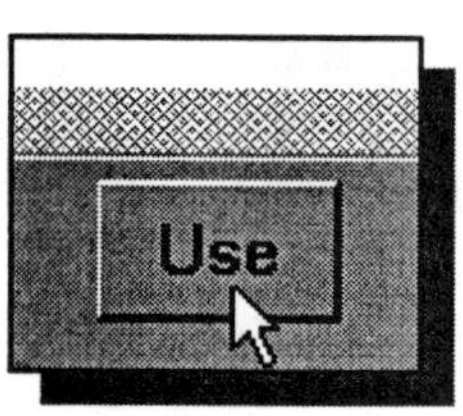

➤ By selecting the different views in the *View Type* list, followed by clicking the **Use** button, we can quickly switch to different views to look at the applied 3D annotation. Note that we can only have one active view at a time. Click on the **Dismiss** button to exit the *Views* window before proceeding to the next section.

Display Filters

The display of the applied 3D annotation dimensions can be switched on or off by using the *Display Filters* option.

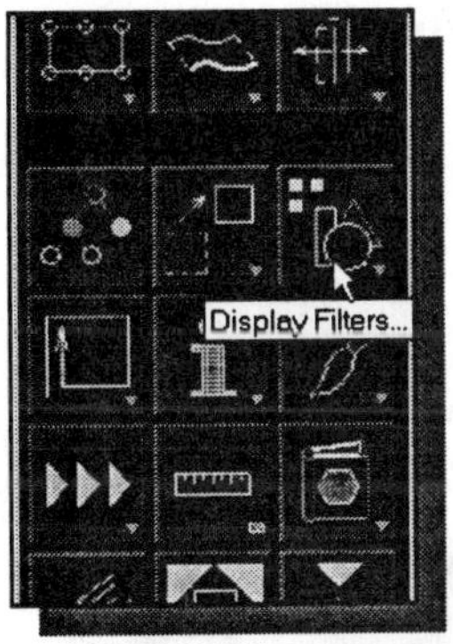

1. Choose **Display Filters...** in the icon panel. (The icon is located in the first row of the application specific icon panel.)

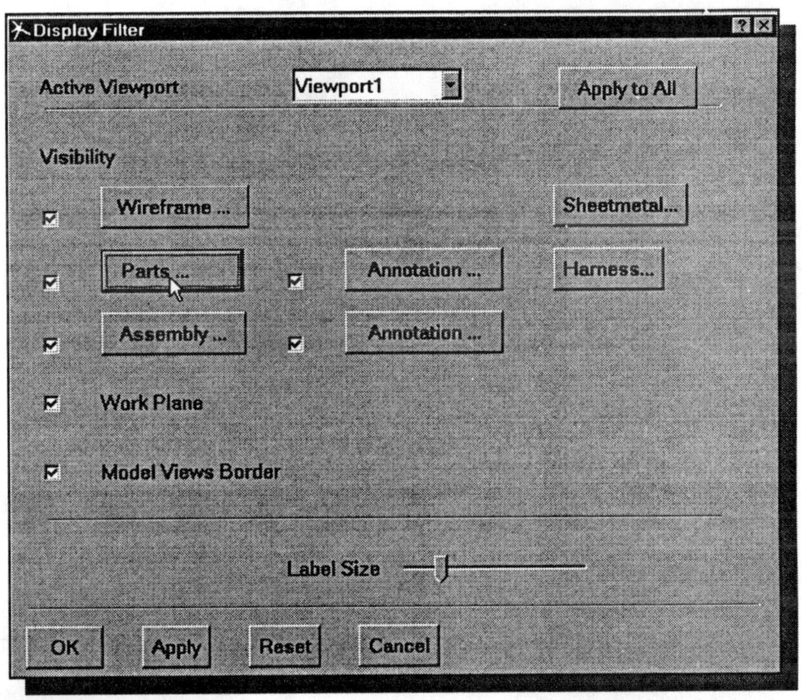

❖ In *I-DEAS*, the *Display Filters* options are used to control the display of created models and work planes. Any objects related to the models, including dimensions, can be switched on or off at any time.

2. In the *Display Filter* window, click on the **Parts...** button as shown in the figure.

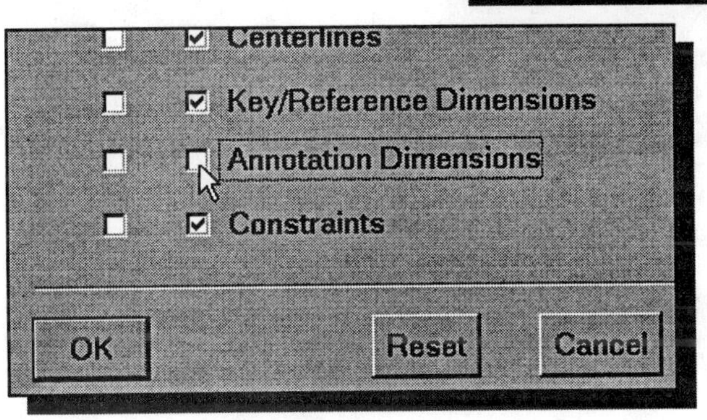

3. In the *Part Display Filter* window, turn off the display of the *Annotation Dimensions* by clicking at the visibility box in front of the item as shown in the figure.

4. Click on the **OK** button to accept the settings and exit the *Part Display Filter* window.

5. Click on the **OK** button to accept the settings and exit the *Display Filter* window.

❖ The model is displayed with all 3D annotation dimensions switched off.

Second Method - Multiple Viewports

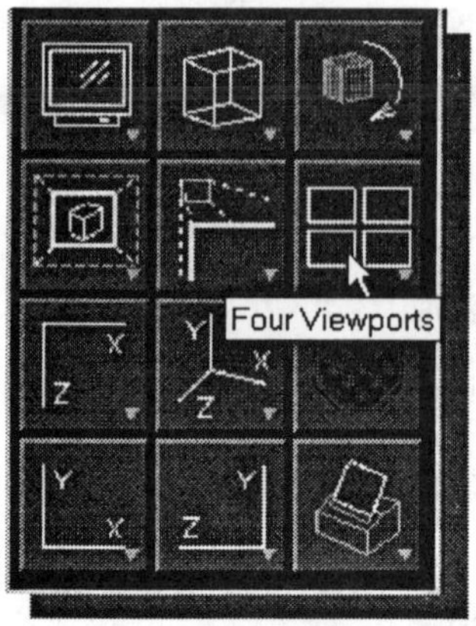

1. Choose **Four Viewports** in the display icon panel. (The icon is located in the second row of the display icon panel.)

❖ Four equal-size viewports appear on the screen, all showing the same view of the model. Note that the multiple viewports option does not change the database of the model; we have only one model.

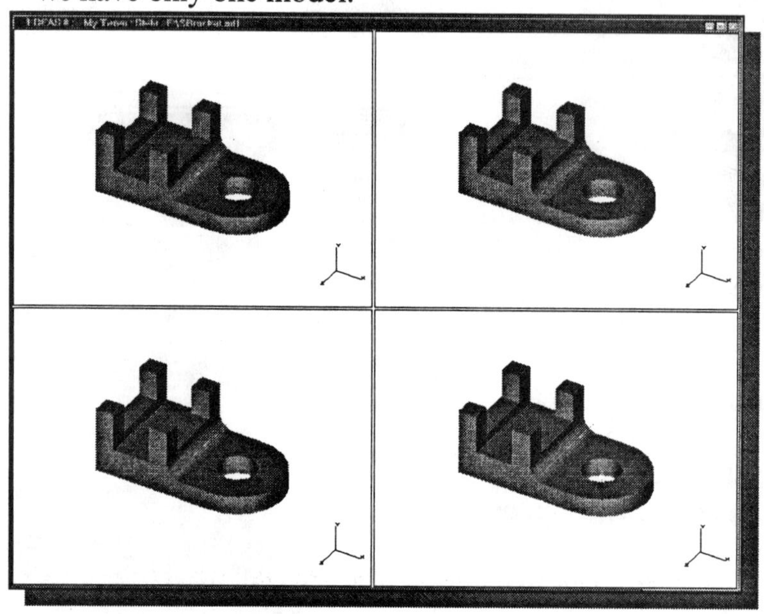

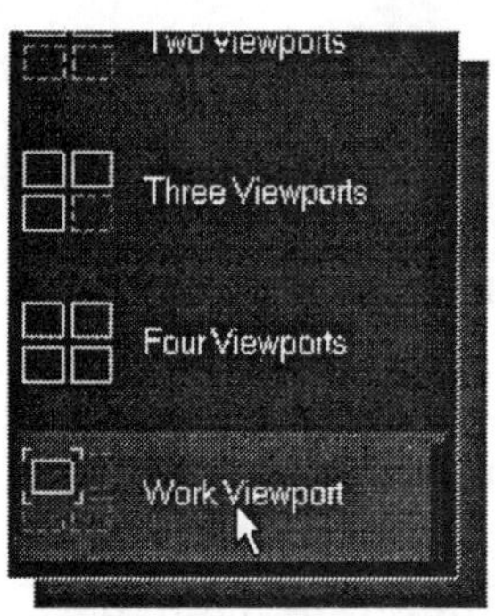

2. Choose **Work Viewport** in the display icon panel. (The icon is located at the same stack of icons as the **Four Viewports** icon.)

❖ The **Work Viewport** option allows us to select a viewport as the default *work viewport*, in which we can control the display using the display options.

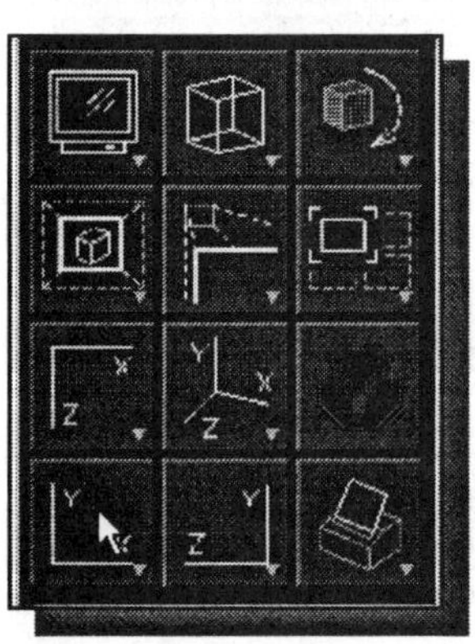

3. Click inside the lower left viewport to set it as the *work viewport*.

4. Click on the **Front View** icon in the display icon panel to switch the display to front view as shown.

5. On your own, repeat the above steps and adjust the display of the four viewports as shown.

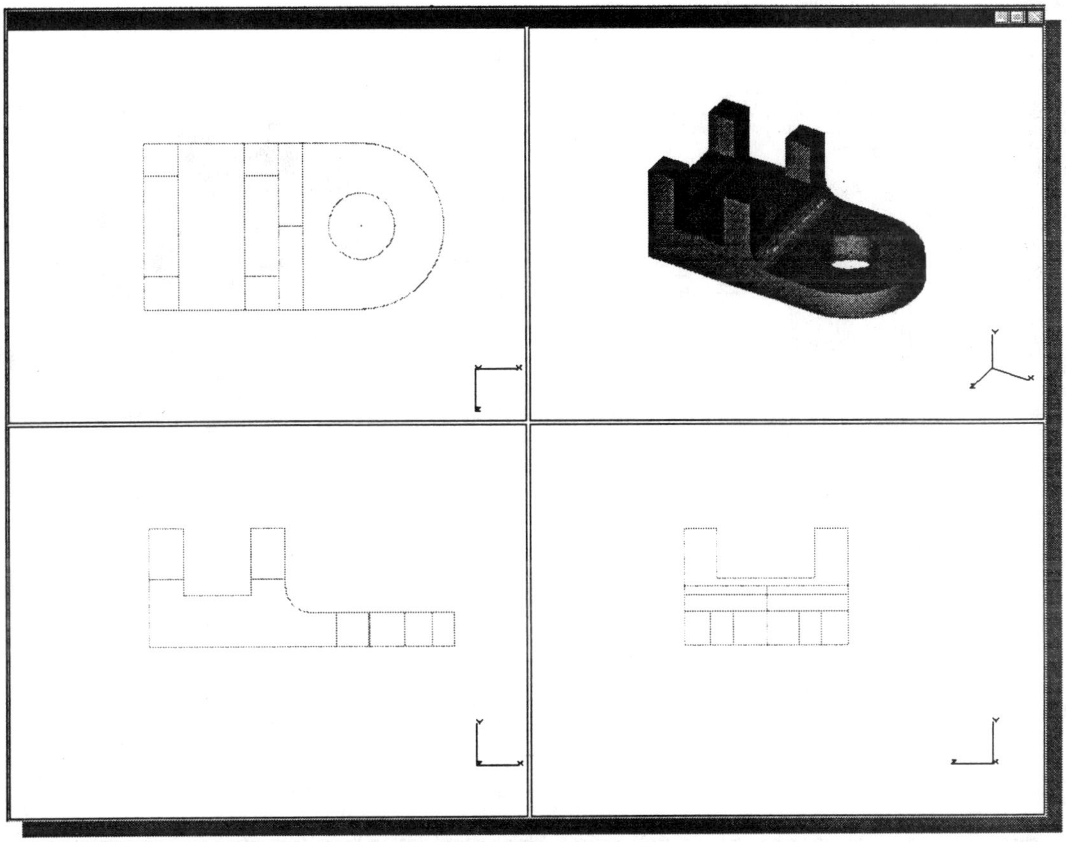

❖ Note that the *Dynamic Viewing* options are available in all viewports, simply by moving the cursor inside the viewport prior to performing the *Dynamic Viewing* options.

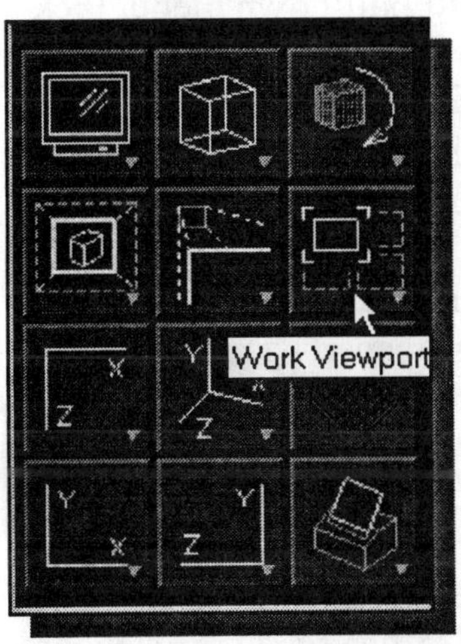

6. Choose **Work Viewport** in the display icon panel. (The icon is located at the same stack of icons as the **Four Viewports** icon.)

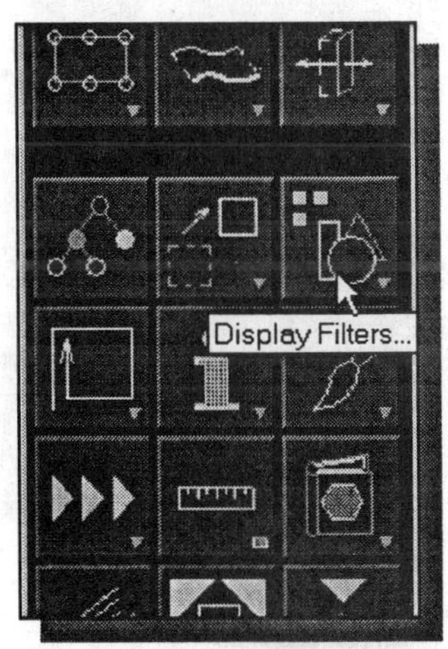

6. Choose **Display Filters...** in the icon panel. (The icon is located in the first row of the application specific icon panel.)

7. On your own, switch on the display of the annotation dimensions in the viewport. Note that the **Display Filters** options only affect the work viewport.

8. On your own, repeat the above steps and display the annotation dimensions in the top-left viewport and the lower-right viewport.

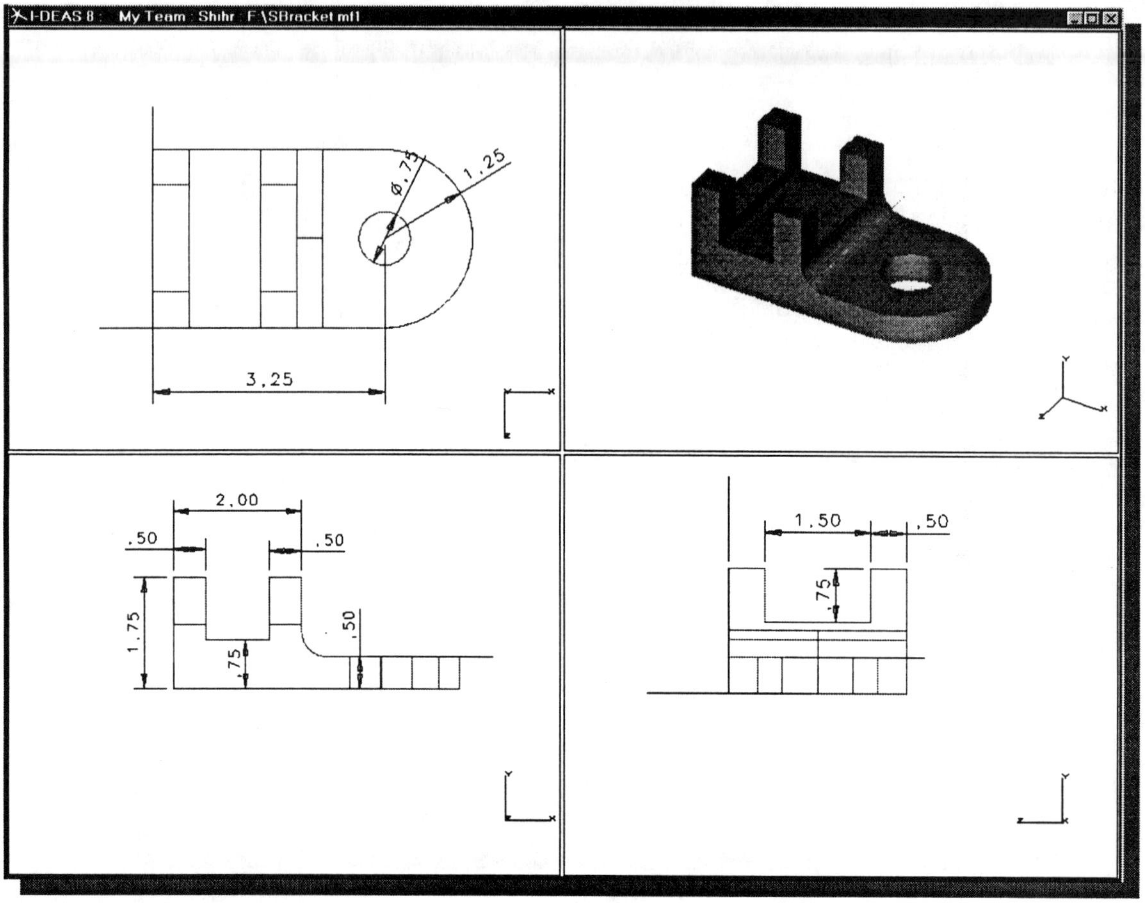

9. From the icon panel, select the **File** pull-down menu. Pick the **Save** option. Notice that you can also use the **Ctrl-S** combination (pressing down the Ctrl key and hitting the "*S*" key once) to save the part. A small watch appears to indicate passage of time as the part is saved.

❖ The viewports information is retained and stored in the model file. When the model file is opened again, the four viewports will be restored with the current settings. The 3D annotation combined with the *Model Views* or the *Multiple viewports* allow design information to be communicated in 3D format without using any 2D drafting processes; the parametric model is also available for updating and modifications. In this sense, *I-DEAS* has set a new standard in design annotation and documentation.

Naming the Part

❖ In the following sections, we will next illustrate the procedure to generate a 2D drawing from the 3D model. Prior to switching to the *I-DEAS Master Drafting* application, we will first assign a name to the part so that the database can be transferred between applications.

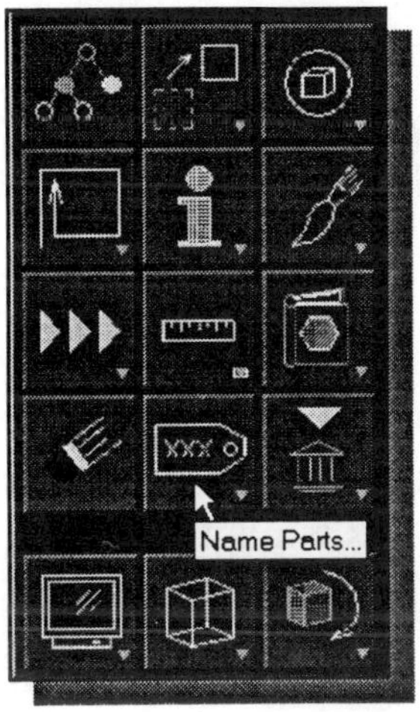

1. Choose **Name Parts...** in the icon panel. (The icon is located in the last row of the application specific icon panel.)

2. The message "*Pick part to name*" is displayed in the prompt window. Pick any edges of the solid model. The *Name* window appears.

3. In the *Name* window, we can assign or change the name, number, and bin of a part. Each field on the window is limited to 80 characters. In the *Name* box, type in "**Saddle_Bracket**."

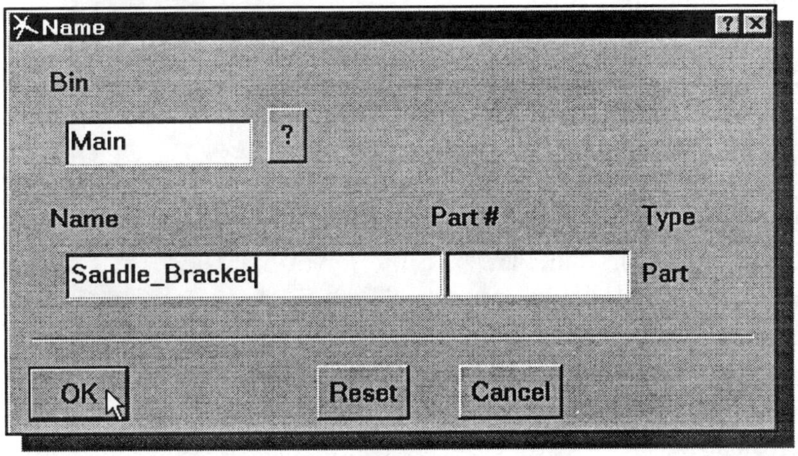

4. Click on the **OK** icon to proceed.

5. The message "*Pick part to name (Done)*" is displayed in the prompt window. Press the **ENTER** key or the **middle-mouse-button** to end the *Name Parts* command.

The I-DEAS Master Drafting Application

❖ The main function of the *Master Drafting* application is to allow users to generate 2D views from 3D models. When we create a drawing layout in the *Master Drafting* application, *I-DEAS* automatically projects the 3D model onto a 2D planes using the user-defined layout settings; all operations in the *Master Drafting* application are 2D in nature.

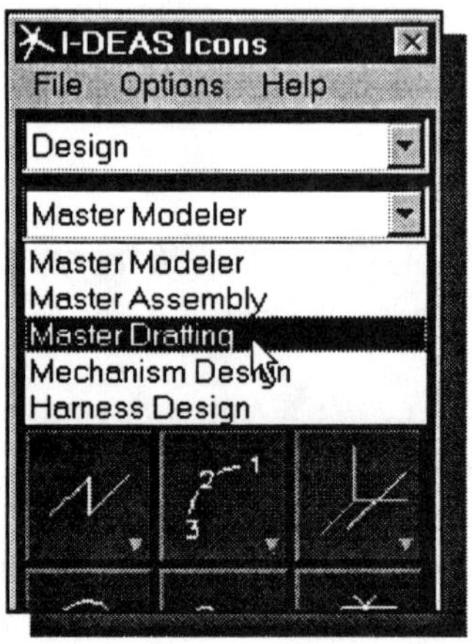

1. Click with the **left-mouse-button** in the *Task* toolbar area to display other options and select the **Master Drafting** task.

❖ The screen arrangement of the *Master Drafting* application remains the same as that of the *Master Modeler*, but you will see a different set of icons in the icon panels, and the solid model is removed from the graphics window. The *Master Drafting* icon panel consists of three groups of tools.

♦ The first group in the icon panel consists of 2D view-related commands, dimensions-related commands, and 2D geometric construction tools. The first rows of the icon panel are 2D view-related commands, such as creating new views or moving views. The second, third and fourth rows of the icon panel are used to add additional dimensions and notes. The last two rows are 2D geometric construction tools, such as adding centerlines, or adding circles.

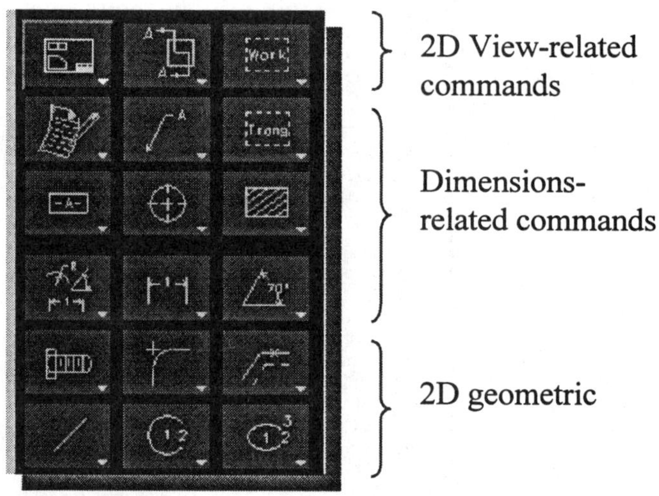

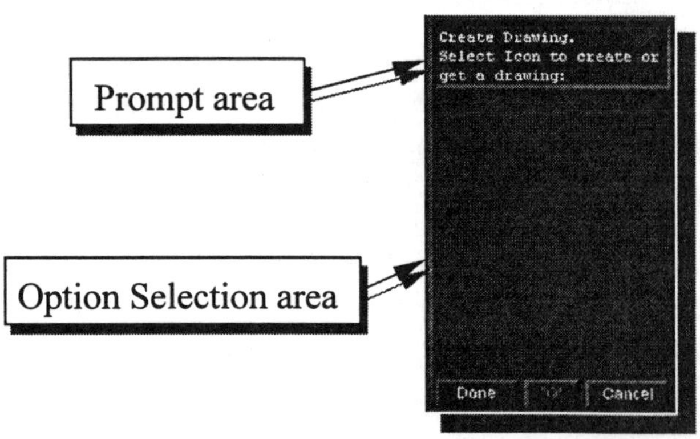

♦ The center portion of the icon panel is the option selection area and the prompt area. Most of the user option selections and inputs are done in this portion of the icon panel.

- The bottom section of the icon panel contains *General Utilities*, such as the *Modify* commands, *Zoom* commands and *Redisplay* commands.

General Utilities

2. Choose **Create Drawing** in the icon panel. (The icon is located in the first row of the icon panel.)

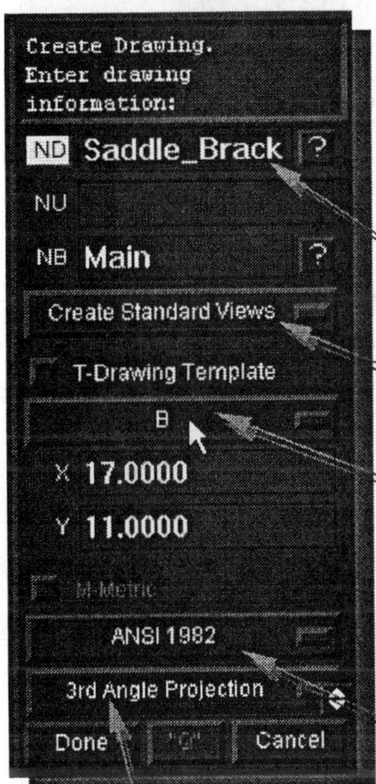

3. In the prompt window, the message "*Create Drawing. Enter drawing information:*" is displayed. Confirm the name of the **Saddle_Bracket** model is displayed below the prompt area as shown.

4. Choose the **Create Standard Views** option.

5. Select the **B size** paper for the drawing layout.

6. Noticed the *ANSI standard* and the *3rd Angle Projection* settings. Click on the **Done** button to accept the settings and proceed with the next option selections.

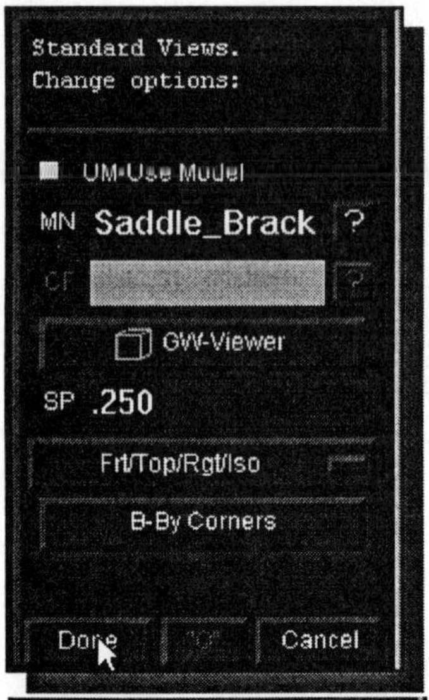

7. In the prompt area, the message "*Standard Views. Change options:*" is displayed. Confirm the settings are as shown:

   - **Use Model** option is switched ***on***.
   - Front/Top/Right/Isometric (**Frt/Top/Rgt/Iso**) layout.
   - Spacing in between views (**SP**): **0.25** inches.

8. Click on the **Done** button to accept the settings and proceed with the creation of the drawing layout.

❖ *I-DEAS* will now display the layout of the four selected drawing views.

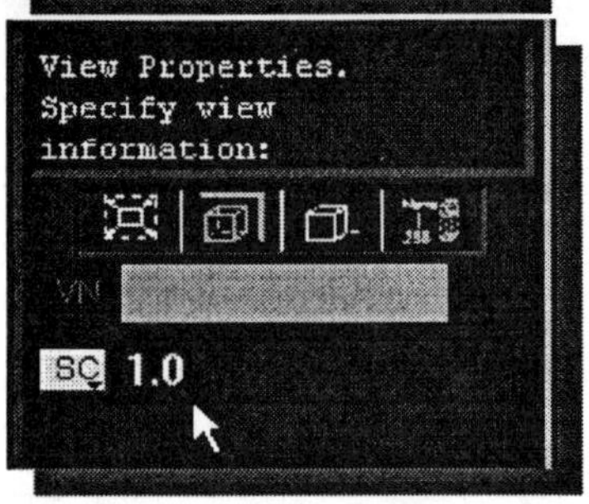

9. In the prompt area, the message "*View Properties. Specify view information:*" is displayed. Adjust the Scale factor of the views to 1.0 as shown in the figure.

10. Click on the **Done** button to accept the settings and proceed with the creation of the drawing views.

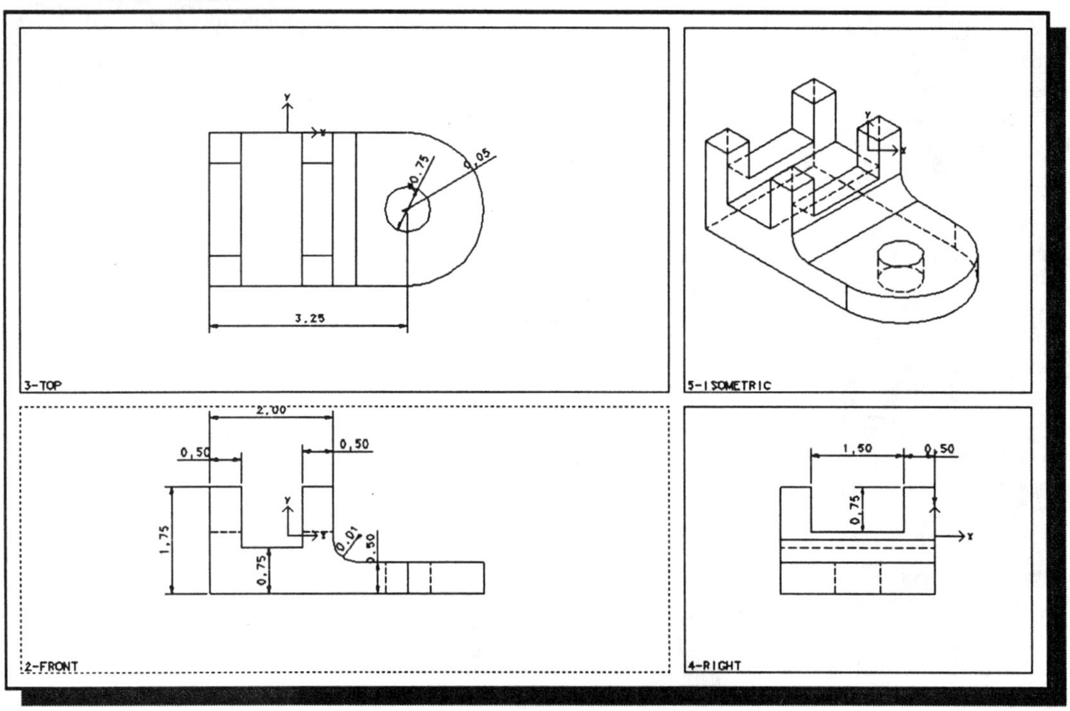

❖ The *Master Drafting* application generates 2D views by projecting the 3D model to two-dimensional (2D) planes defined by the view layout. In general, I-DEAS does a fairly good job in creating the projected 2D views.

Repositioning the Work View

1. Inside the graphics window, the dashed view border identifies the ***work view***. On your own, change the *work view* by clicking inside the displayed views with the left-mouse-button. Set the **front view** as the *work view* before proceeding to the next step.

1. Choose **View Origin** in the icon panel. The icon is located in the first row of the icon panel. Press and hold the left-mouse-button on the displayed icon location and choose the icon from the displayed list.

2. The message "*Move View Origin. Locate Move Start:*" is displayed in the prompt area. Move the cursor near the displayed coordinate system in the front view. Note the displayed alignment as shown below. Left-mouse-click once to choose the origin as the *Move Start* location.

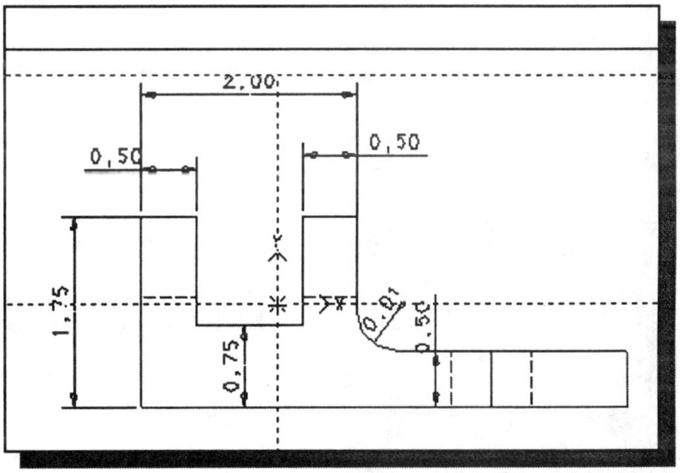

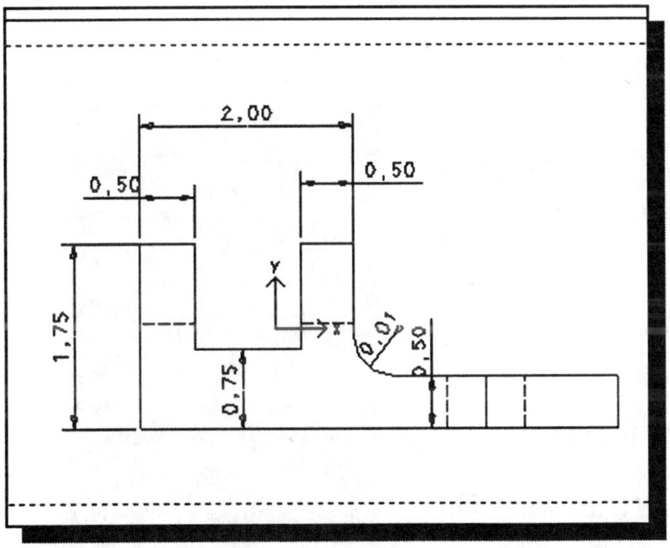

3. Move the cursor downward and select a location below the last point. Notice a vertical alignment symbol appears in the top view when the views are aligned.

4. On your own, repeat the above steps and align the views so that all dimensions are visible and views are aligned as shown below.

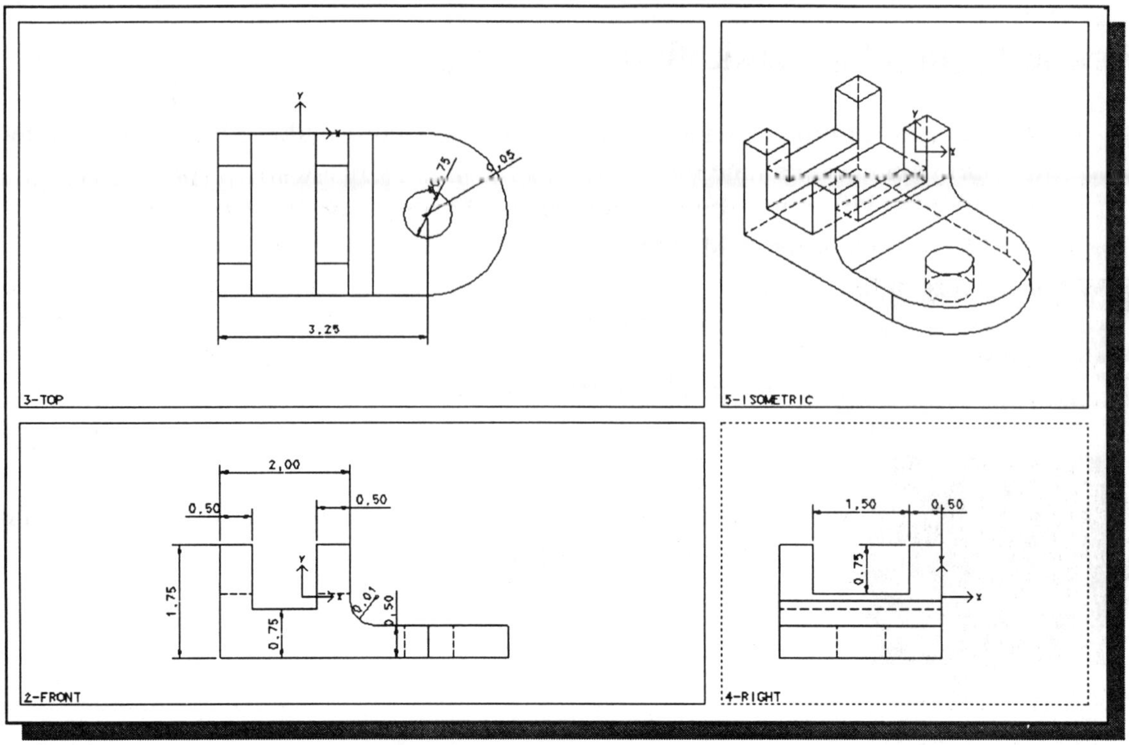

Hiding View Borders and View Names

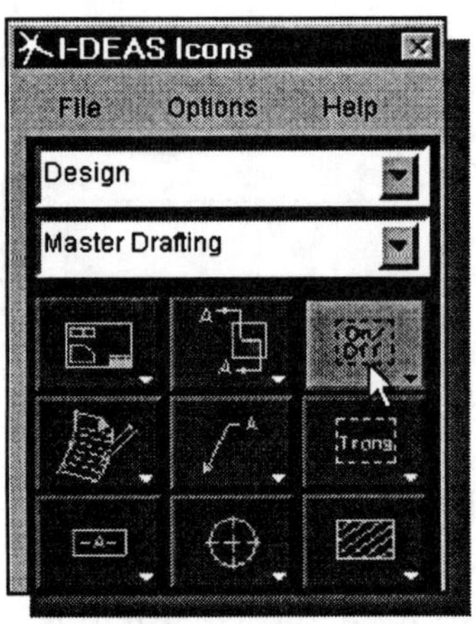

1. Choose **View Visibility** in the icon panel. The icon is located in the first row of the icon panel. Press and hold the left-mouse-button on the displayed icon location and choose the icon in the displayed list.

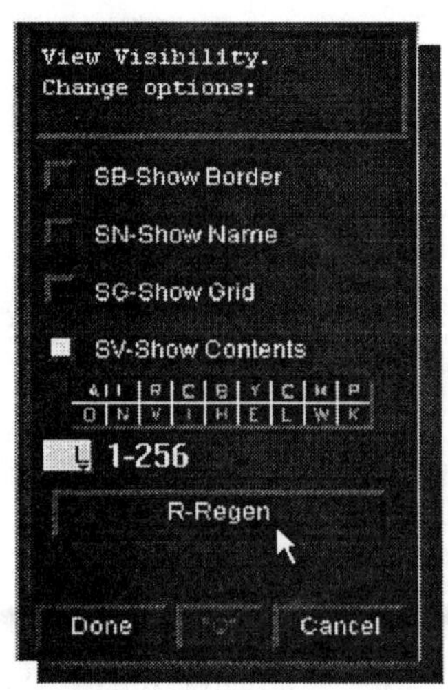

2. The message "*View Visibility. Change Options:*" is displayed in the prompt area. Toggle *Off* the *Show Border* and *Show Name* options.

3. Click on the **Regen** button to apply the changes to the *work view*.

4. Click on the **Done** button to accept the changes.

5. On your own, repeat the above steps and switch *Off* the display of all view borders and view names.

Hiding Dimensions and Projected Entities

The annotation dimensions are automatically displayed in the drawing layout. Typically, most of the displayed linear dimensions are projected and aligned correctly in the *Master Drafting* application. The orientation of 3D annotation dimensions for curves (radii and diameters) are more likely to appear incorrectly in the 2D drawings, as they were positioned freely in the 3D space. We can use the *Hide* command to temporarily remove those dimensions. We can also *Hide* any dimensions, or any geometric entities, from the views where they are not needed for the production drawings. Hiding entities does not delete them. They can be redisplayed with the *Show* command.

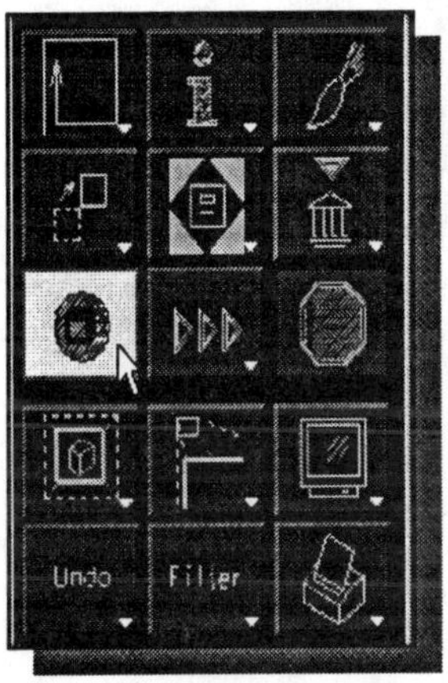

1. Choose **Hide** in the icon panel. (The icon is located in the third row of the general utility icon panel.)

2. The message "*Hide. Select entities:*" is displayed in the prompt area. Select all of the dimensions, which are not aligned and/or oriented correctly, by clicking on the dimensions. Note that we can select in all views; the first click will activate the view and the second click will select the object inside the view.

3. On your own, hide all of the unwanted dimensions displayed in the views.

4. Click on the **Done** button to accept the selections and temporarily remove the selected objects from the screen.

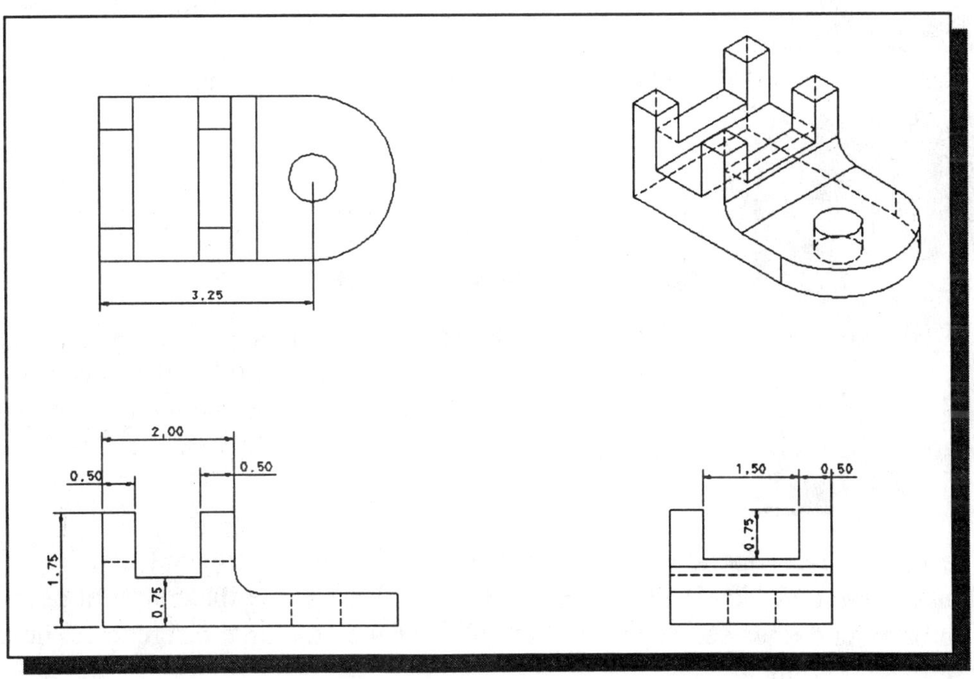

Adding Centerlines

1. Set *Line Type* to **Centerline**. Three icons are located in the center of the icon panel: the first icon is the *Color Setting* icon, the second icon is *Line Width*, and the third icon is the *Line Type* icon.

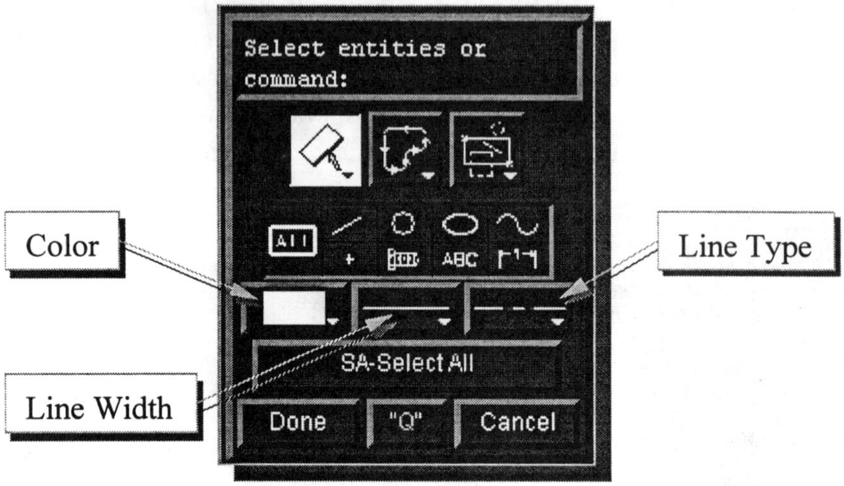

2. Choose **Circle Center** in the upper section of the icon panel. Selecting the icon by pressing and holding the left-mouse-button on the displayed icon location and choosing the icon from the displayed list.

3. Click inside the top view to set the view as the work view.

4. Pick the small circle to place the center marks.

5. Click on the **Done** button to end the *Circle Center* command.

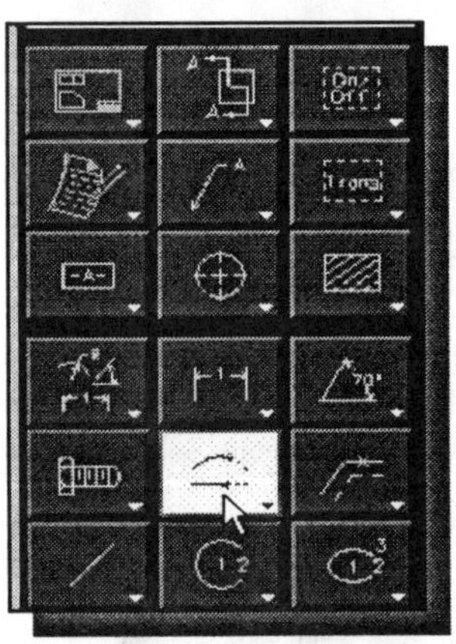

6. Choose **Trim/Extend** in the upper section of the icon panel. Select the icon by pressing and holding the left-mouse-button on the displayed icon location and choosing the icon from the displayed list.

❖ The *Trim/Extend* operation of the *Master Drafting* application is the same as the *Trim/Extend* command in the *Master Modeler*. First select the endpoint of an object to trim or extend, then select an existing entity or location on the screen as the trim/extend boundary.

7. On your own, adjust the center mark as shown in the figure.

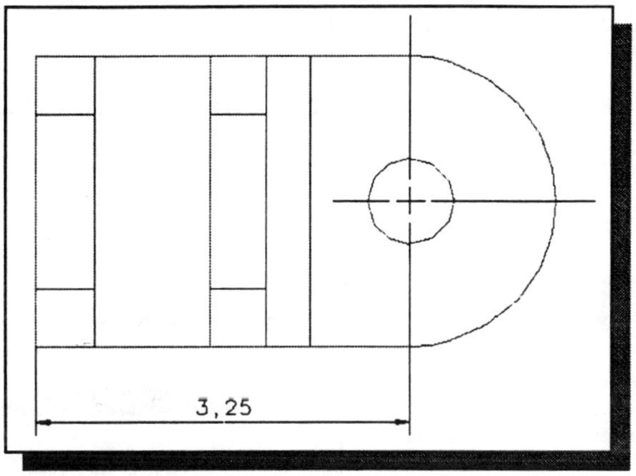

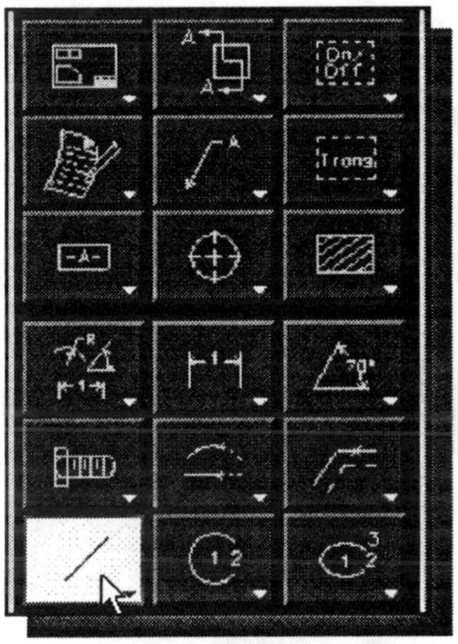

8. Choose **Lines**. The icon is located in the last row in the upper section of the icon panel.

9. Create a horizontal centerline aligned to the left endpoint of the center mark as shown in the figure.

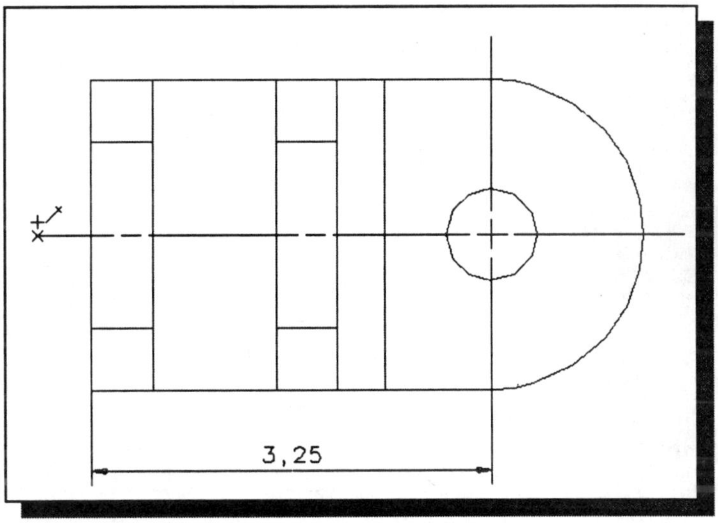

10. On your own, repeat the above steps and create the additional centerlines needed for the 2D drawing.

Adding Additional Reference Dimensions

In the *Master Drafting* application, we can also add additional dimensions and annotations in the drawing layout. The dimensions and annotations added are treated as *reference dimensions*. *Reference dimensions* exist only in *Master Drafting mode* and they are updated with any part changes made in the *Master Modeler*.

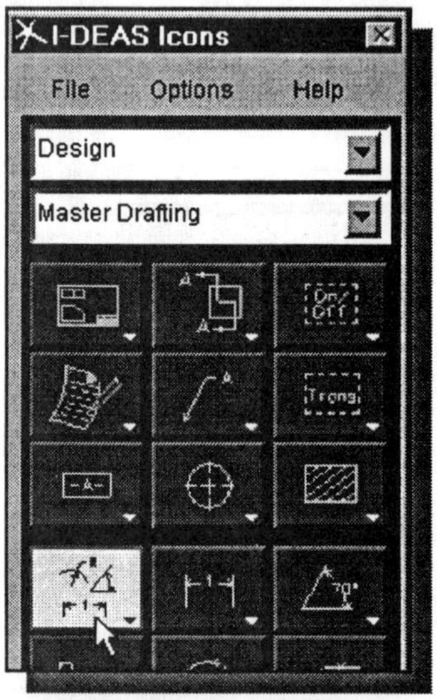

1. Choose **Dynamic Dimension** in the icon panel. (The icon is located in the fourth row of the icon panel.)

❖ This command is similar to the general dimension command in the *Master Modeler*; the way we choose entities determines the type of dimensions to be created.

2. The message "*Dynamic dimension. Select entity*" is displayed in the prompt window. Pick the small circle in the top view.

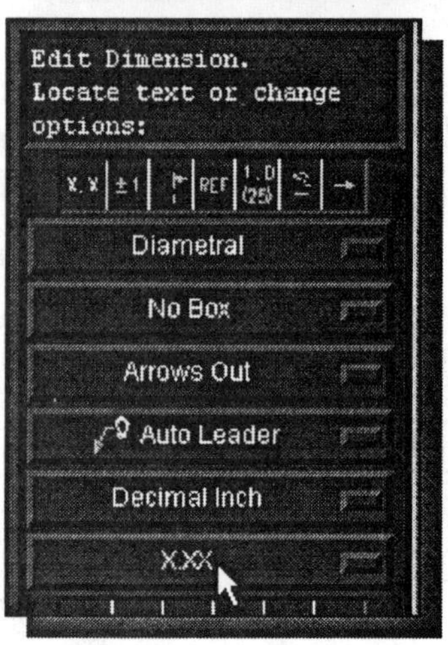

3. Place the text toward the right side of the view.
4. In the option menu area, set the arrow option to **Arrows out** and the number of digits displayed after the decimal point to **two** as shown in the figure.
5. Click on the **Done** button to accept the settings and crate the dimension.

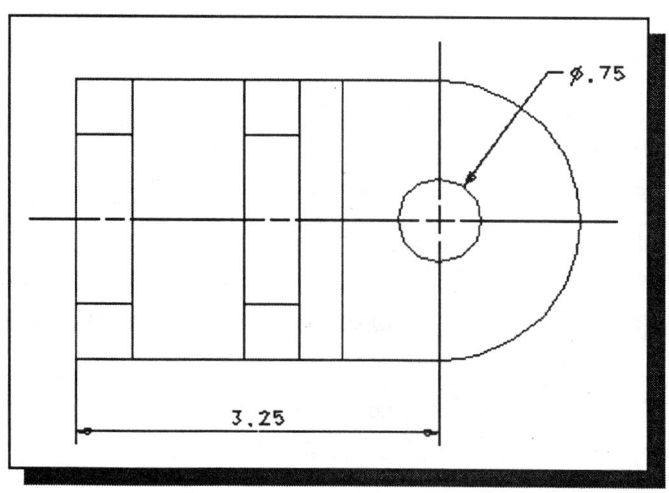

6. On your own, repeat the above steps and create the dimensions necessary in the 2D views.

Changing the Displayed Hidden Line Style

1. Inside the graphics window, Set the **Isometric view** as the *work view* by clicking on the isometric view. Note that since the view border is switched off, it is harder to identify the current work view.

2. Choose **View Properties** in the icon panel. The icon is located in the first row of the icon panel. Select the icon by pressing and holding the left-mouse-button on the displayed icon location and choosing the icon from the displayed list.

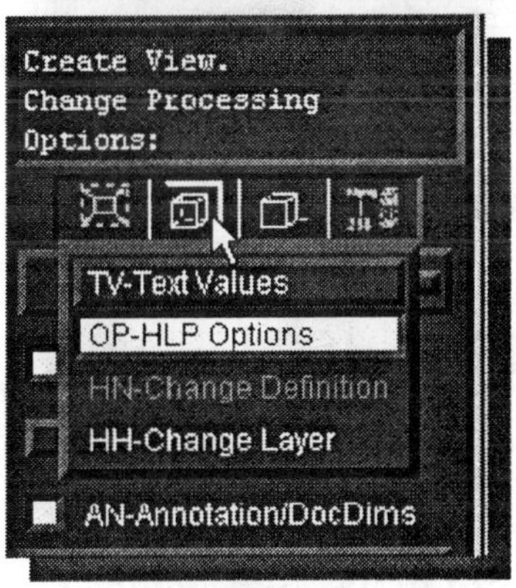

3. Press and hold the left-mouse-button on top of any of the icon inside the menu option area to display the option list as shown.

4. Select the **HLP Options** as shown.

5. In the option menu area, change the hidden line option to **Hidden Removed** as shown.

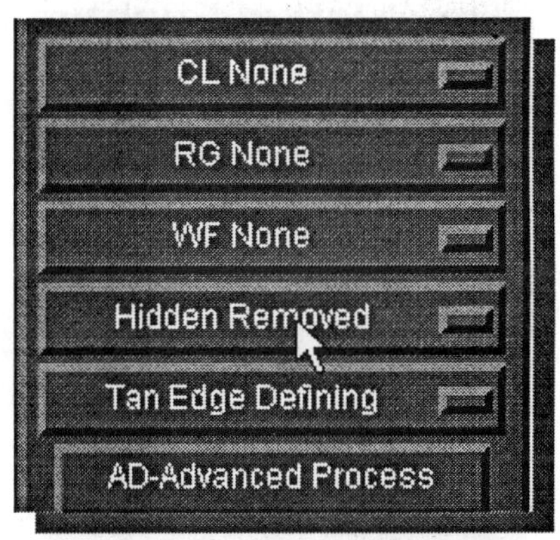

6. Click on the **Done** button to accept the settings.

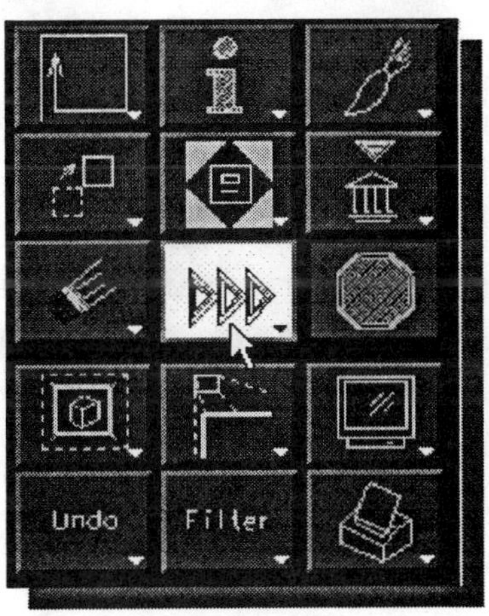

7. Choose **Complete Update** in the icon panel as shown.

8. Click on the **Done** button to accept the settings and regenerate the Isometric view.

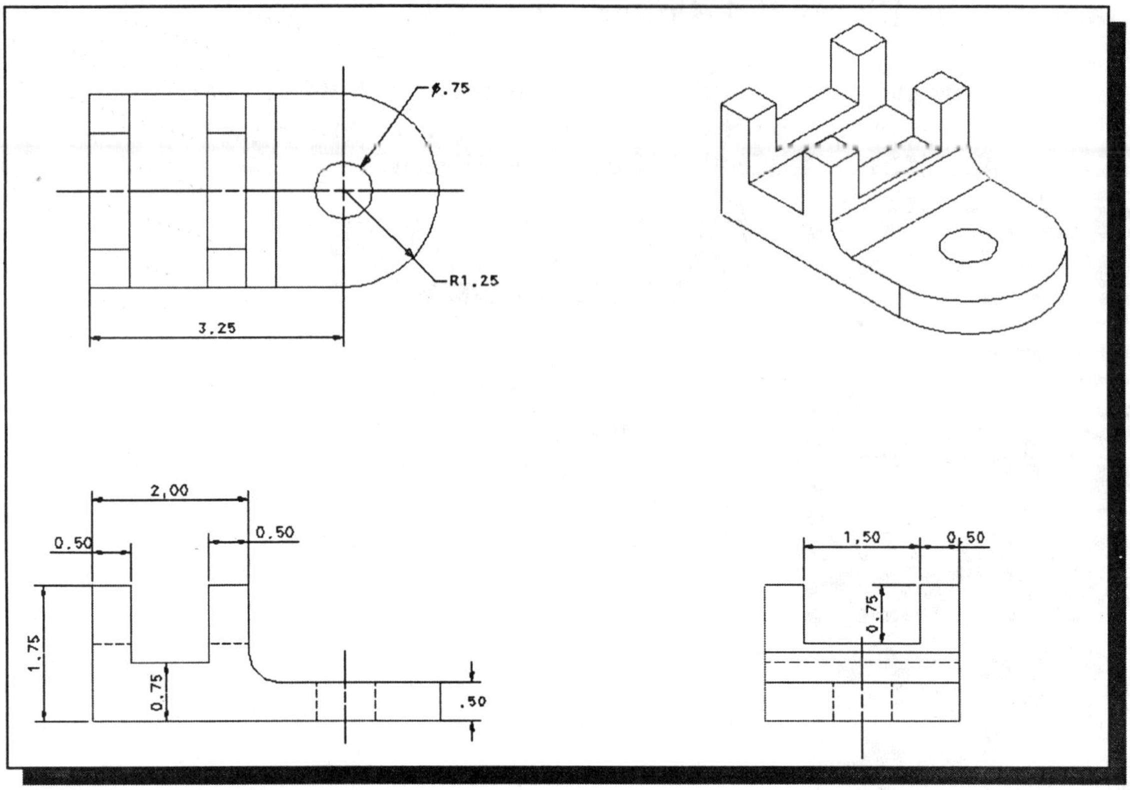

Associative Functionality - Modifying the Solid Model

1. Click with the **left-mouse-button** in the *Task* toolbar area to display other options and select the ***Master Modeler*** task.

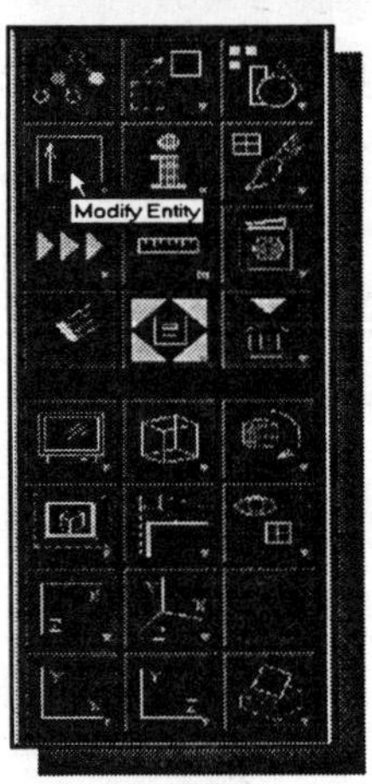

2. Choose **Modify** in the icon panel. (The icon is located in the second row of the application icon panel.)

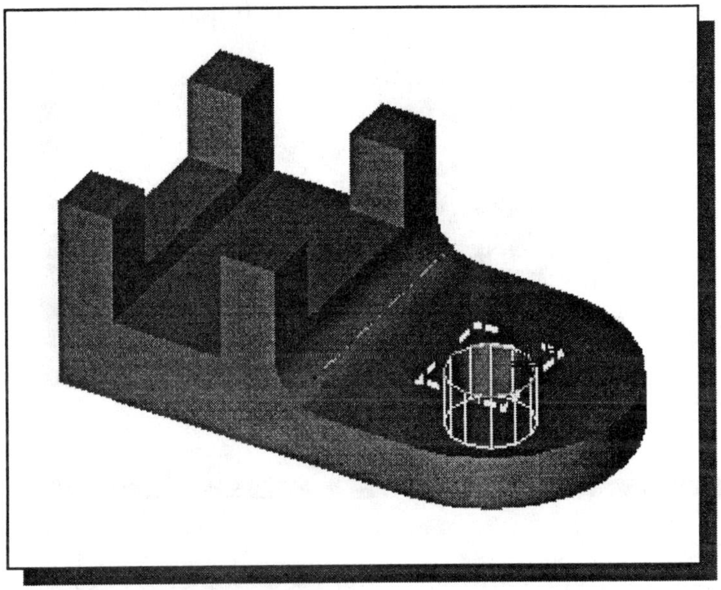

3. The message "*Pick entity to modify*" is displayed in the prompt window. Select the small cutout hole, by clicking on the top circle twice, in the isometric view.

4. Press the **ENTER** key or the right-mouse-button to accept the selection.

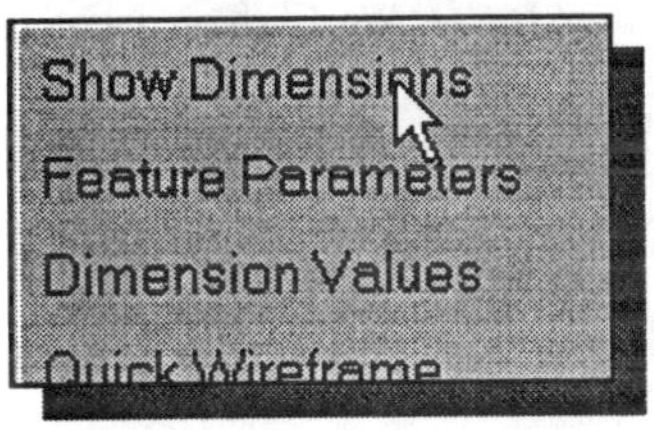

5. Choose **Show dimensions** in the popup menu.

6. Click on the diameter of the circle to modify.

7. In the *Modify Dimensions* window, change the dimension value to **1.0**.

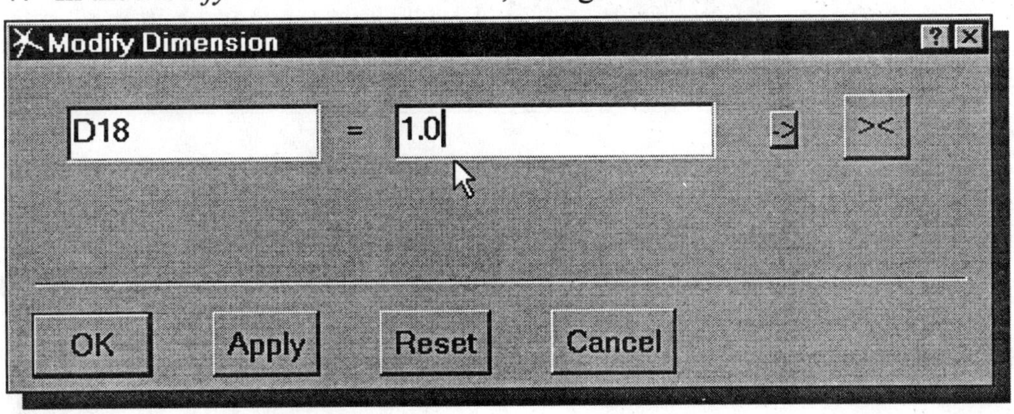

8. Click on the **OK** button to exit the *Modify Dimensions* window.

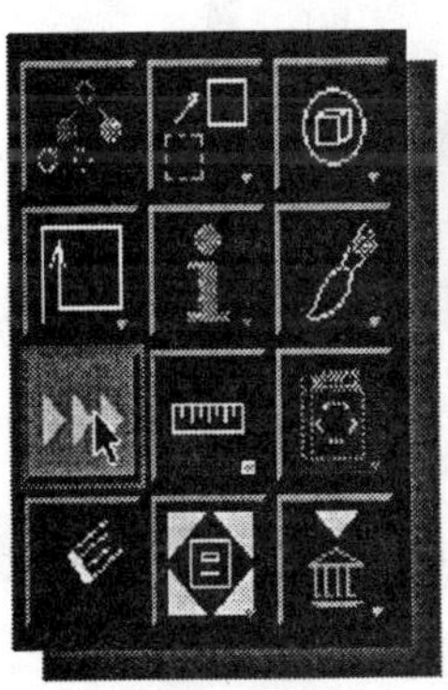

9. Click on the **Update** icon to proceed with the modification.

❖ *I-DEAS* will now update the model and the 3D annotation dimensions are also updated.

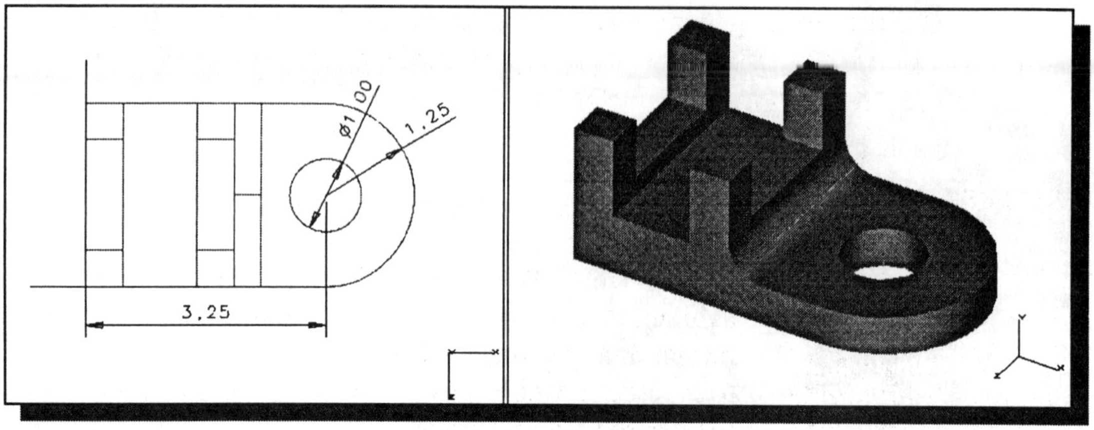

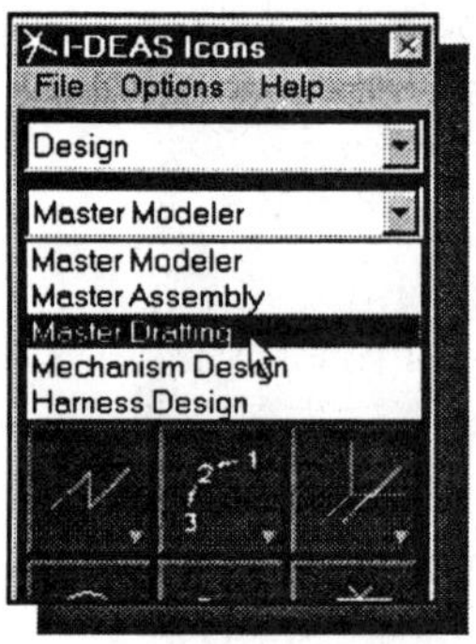

10. Click with the **left-mouse-button** in the *Task* toolbar area to display other options and select the ***Master Drafting*** task.

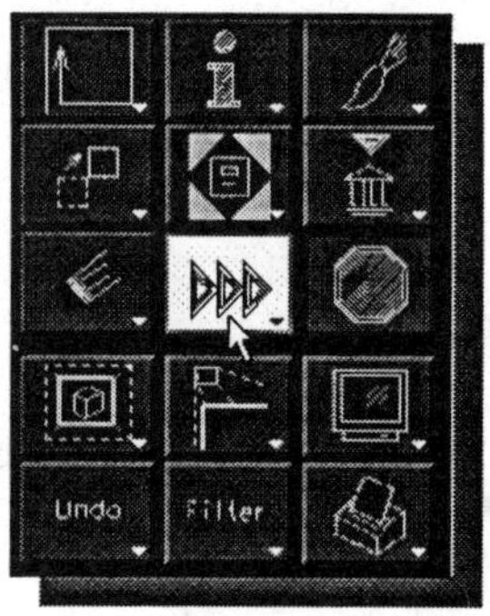

11. Choose **Complete Update** in the icon panel as shown.

12. Click on the **Done** button to regenerate the 2D views.

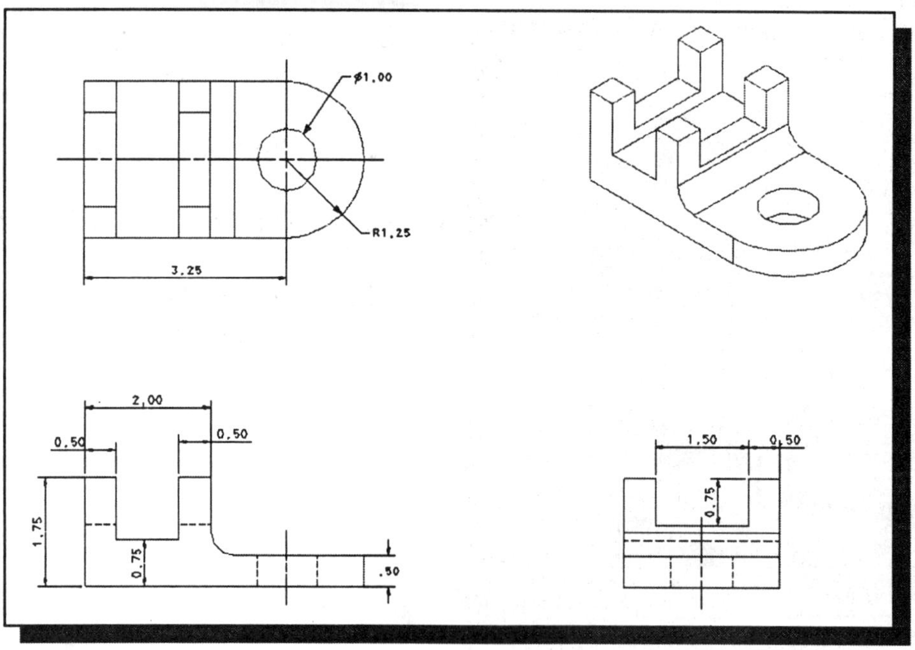

❖ I-DEAS' *Associative Functionality* allows us to change the design at any time, and the system reflects the change at all levels automatically.

Printing the 2D Drawing

➢ We will illustrate the general procedure to create an A-size print with a laser-jet printer. Consult with your instructor or technical support personnel to find out the type of printer available for your systems.

1. Select **Print** under the *File* toolbar in the icon panel.

2. In the *I-DEAS Print* window, choose the printer that is available on your system. Note that you can also create bitmap images, such as BMP, TIFF, JPEG, or CGM format, to be used in web pages and word-processors by choosing the desired output format.

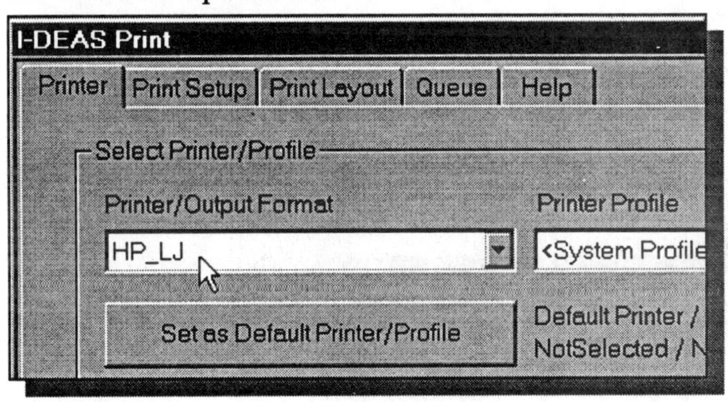

3. In the *I-DEAS Print* window, click on the **Print Setup** tab.

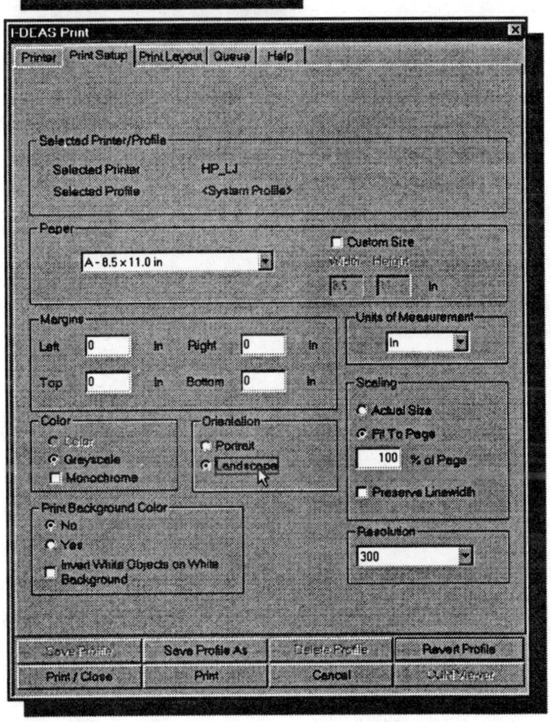

4. Choose the proper paper size, **A-8.5 X11 in** for a laser-jet printer.

5. Set the *Print Orientation* to **Landscape**.

6. Set the *Scaling* option to **Fit to Page**.

7. Click on the **Print/Close** button to create the hard copy and exit the *Print* utility.

Questions:

1. What does I-DEAS' *3D annotation* allow us to do?

2. Which command do you use to move a view in *Master Drafting*?

3. Which command do you use to reposition 2D views in *Master Drafting*?

4. Can *extra Dimensions* be added to the solid model in I-DEAS?

5. What are the main differences between *3D annotation* and *Master Drafting*?

6. Identify and describe the following commands:

(a)

(b)

(c)

(d)

(e)

Exercises: Create the designs, associated 3D annotation and 2D drawings.

1.

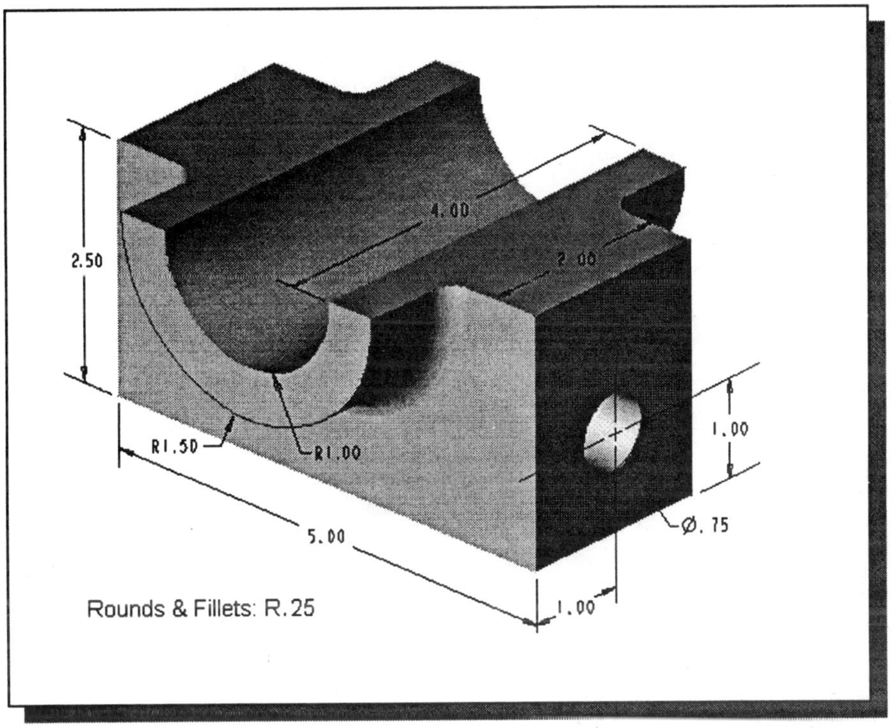

2.

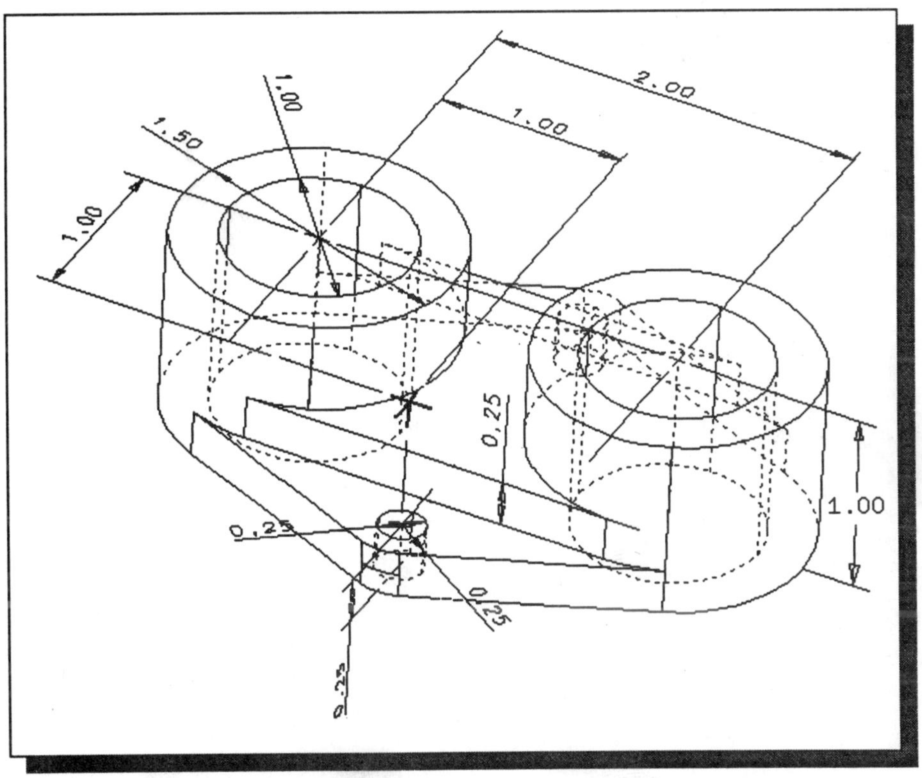

NOTES:

Chapter 9
Symmetrical Features in Designs

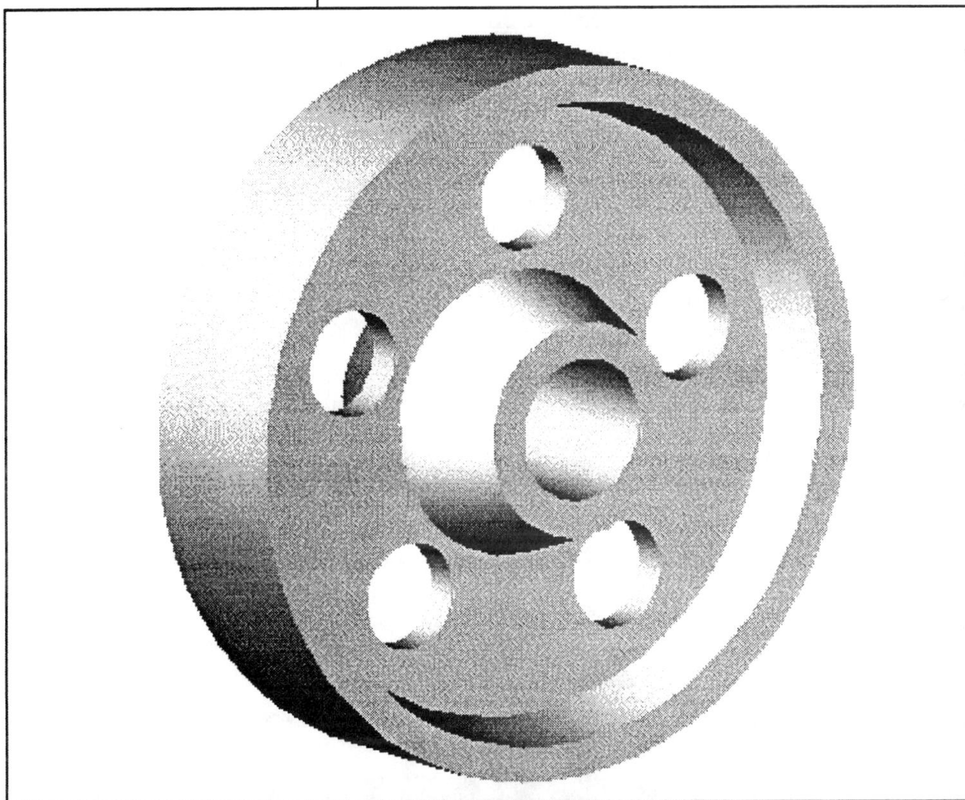

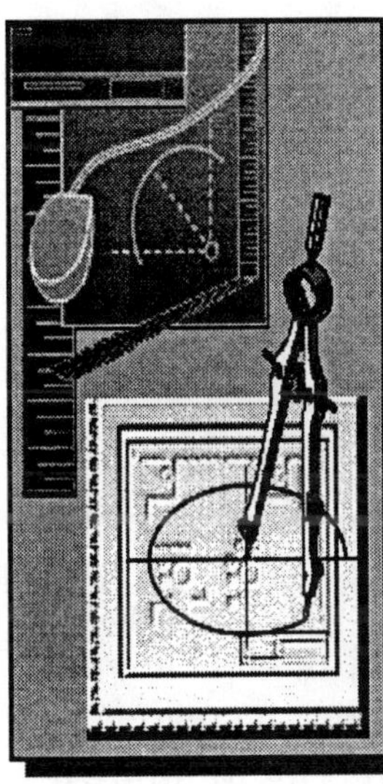

Learning Objectives

When you have completed this lesson, you will be able to:

- ♦ Create Revolved solid parts.
- ♦ Create Drawings From Solids.
- ♦ Understand the I-DEAS Associative Functionality.
- ♦ Create Circular Patterns.
- ♦ Arrange and Manage 2-D Views in Master Drafting.
- ♦ Create Symmetrical Features in Designs.

Introduction

In parametric modeling, it is important to identify and determine the features that exist in the design. *Feature-based parametric modeling* enables us to build complex designs by working on smaller and simpler units. This approach simplifies the modeling process and allows us to concentrate on the characteristics of the design. Symmetry is an important characteristic that is often seen in designs. Symmetrical features can be created easily by using the assortments of tools that are available in feature-based modeling systems, such as *I-DEAS*.

The modeling technique of extruding two-dimensional sketches along a straight line to form three-dimensional features, as illustrated in the previous chapters, is an effective way to construct solid models. For designs that involve cylindrical shapes, shapes that are symmetrical about an axis, revolving two-dimensional sketches about an axis can form the needed three-dimensional features. In solid modeling, this type of feature is called a **Revolved Feature**.

In *I-DEAS*, besides using the *Revolve* command to create revolved features, several options are also available to handle symmetrical features. For example, we can create multiple identical copies of symmetrical features with the ***Feature Array*** command, or create mirror images of models using the ***Mirror Feature*** command. In this Chapter, the construction and modeling techniques of these more advanced features are illustrated.

A Symmetrical Design: PULLEY

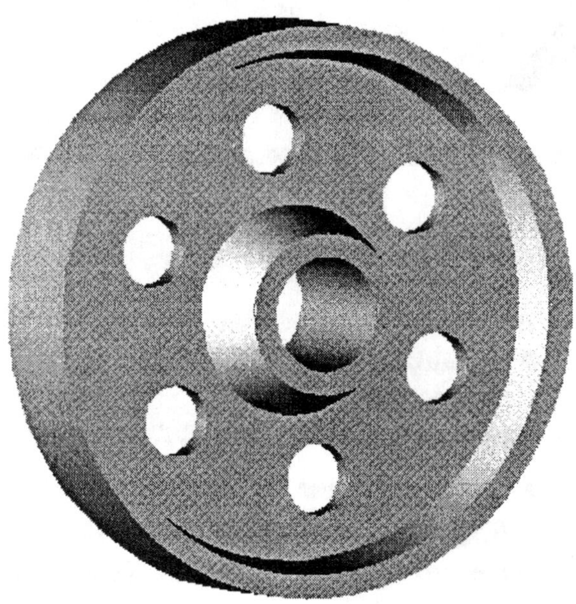

❖ Based on your knowledge of *I-DEAS*, how many features would you use to create the design? Which feature would you choose as the **base feature** of the model? Identify the symmetrical features in the design and consider other possibilities in creating the design. You are encouraged to create a similar model on your own prior to following through the tutorial.

Modeling Strategy - A Symmetrical Design

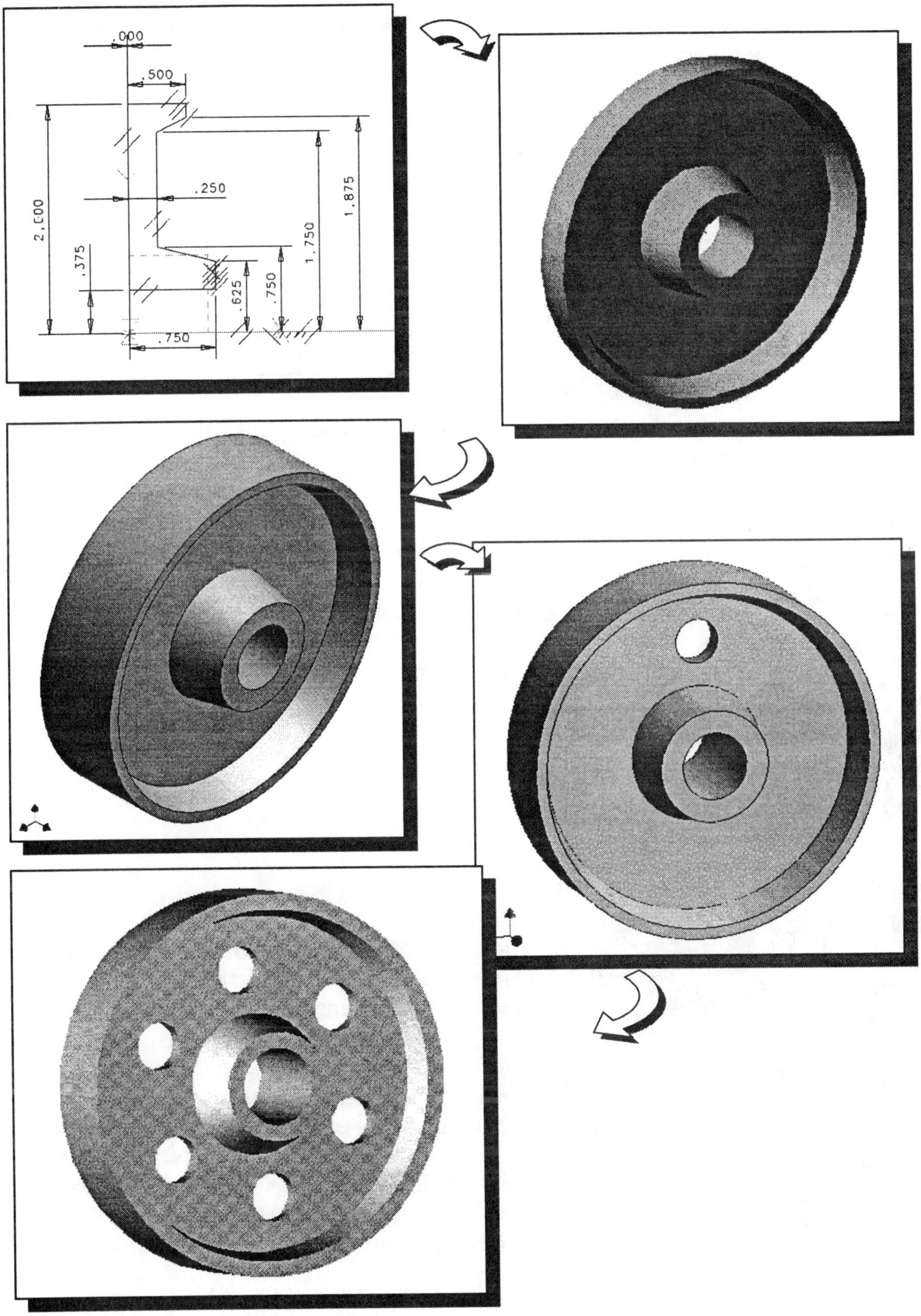

Starting I-DEAS

1. Login to the computer and bring up I-DEAS Master Series. Start a new model file by filling in the items as shown below in the *I-DEAS Start* window:

> Project Name: **(Your account Name)**
> Model File Name: **Pulley**
> Application: **Design**
> Task: **Master Modeler**
> OK

2. After you click on the **OK** button, a *warning window* will appear to tell you that a new model file will be created. Click **OK** to continue.

> I-DEAS Warning
> **! New Model File will be created**
> OK

3. Select the **Options** menu in the icon panel.

4. Select the **Units** option in the pull-down menu.

5. Set the unit to **Inch (pound f)** by selecting from the pop-up menu.

Applying the BORN Technique

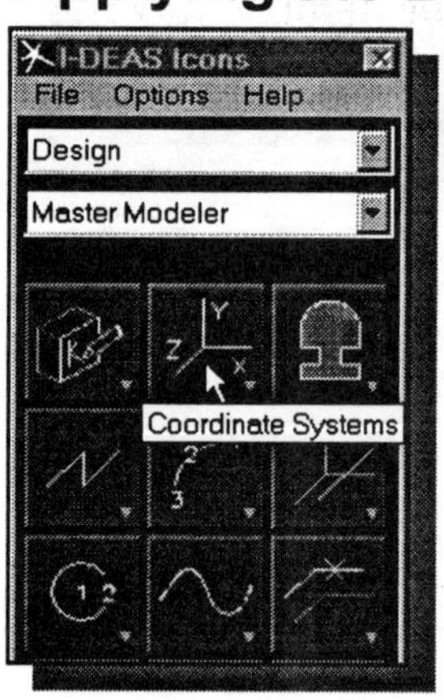

1. Choose **Coordinate Systems** in the icon panel. (The icon is located in the first row of the application icon panel.)

2. In the prompt window, the message "*Pick entity for coordinate system to reference*" is displayed. Select the **workplane** by left-clicking once on any of the edges.

3. In the prompt window, the message "*Select coordinate system component to define (Done)*" is displayed. Press the **ENTER** key or the **middle-mouse-button** to accept the default settings.

❖ By default, the user coordinate system is aligned to the world coordinate system.

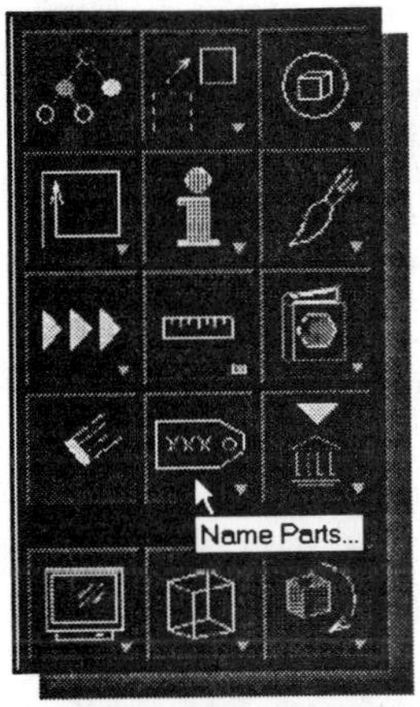

4. Choose **Name Parts...** in the icon panel. (The icon is located in the last row of the application specific icon panel.)

5. The message "*Pick part to name*" is displayed in the prompt window. Pick any edge of the coordinate system we just created. The *Name* window appears.

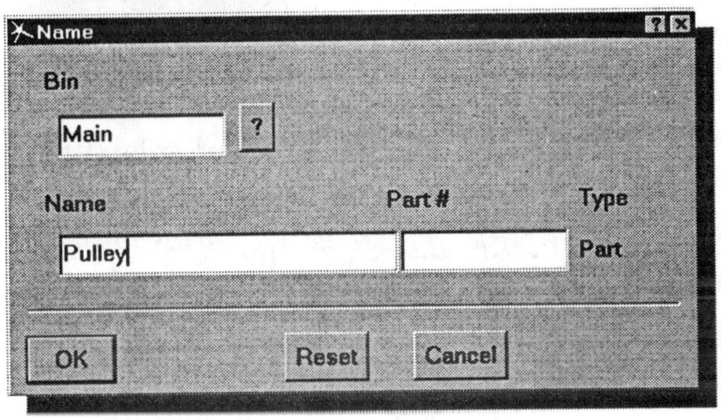

6. In the *Name* window, we can assign or change the name, number, and bin of a part. Each field on the window is limited to 80 characters. In the *Name* box, type in "**Pulley**" as the part name.

7. Click on the **OK** icon to proceed.

8. The message "*Pick part to name (Done)*" is displayed in the prompt window. Press the **ENTER** key or the **middle-mouse-button** to end the *Name Parts* command.

Creating the Base Feature

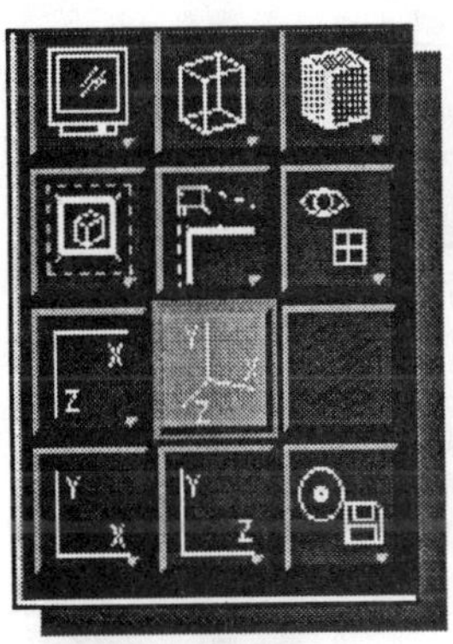

1. Choose **Isometric View** in the display viewing icon panel.

2. Choose **Zoom-All** in the display viewing icon panel.

3. Choose **Sketch in Place** in the icon panel.

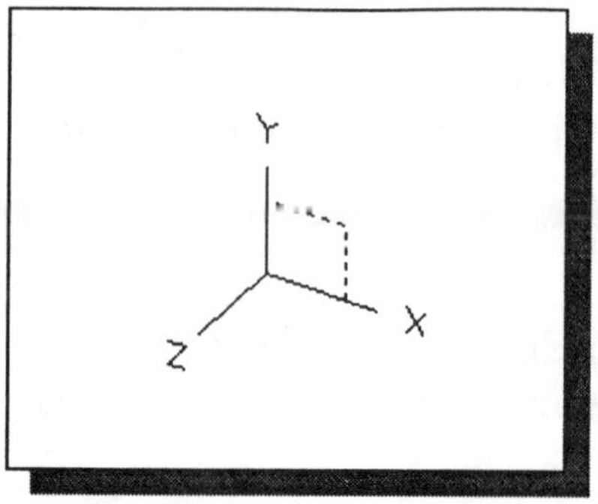

4. In the prompt window, the message "*Pick plane to sketch on*" is displayed. Pick one of the edges of the **XY plane** of the coordinate system. Note that even though the workplane is at the same orientation of the XY-plane of the coordinate system, selecting the XY-plane assures the sketch is attached to the base node, the established coordinate system.

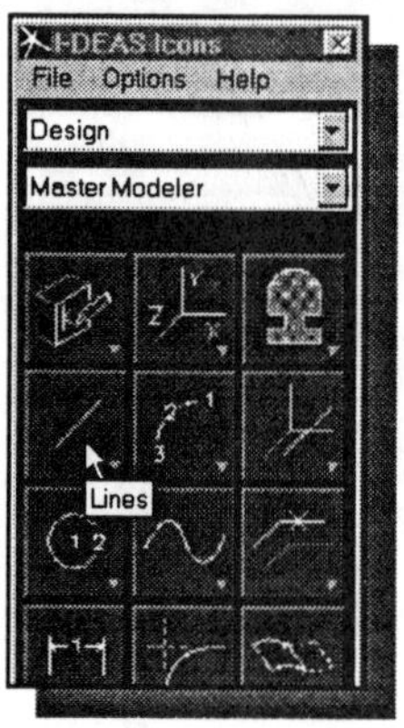

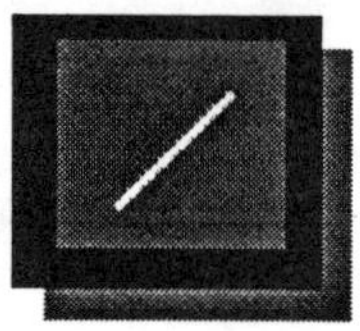

5. Select the **Lines** command in the icon panel.

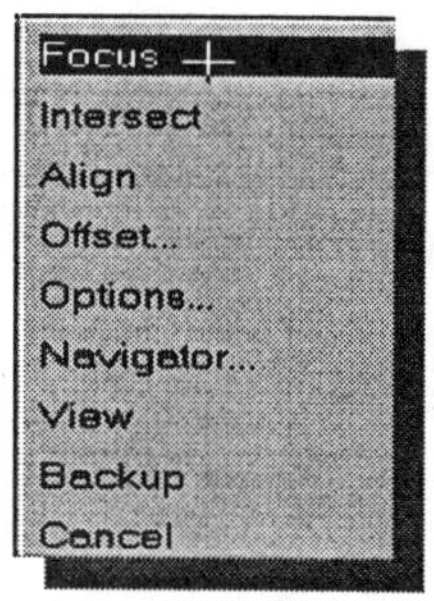

6. Move the cursor inside the graphics window. Press and hold down the right-mouse-button to display the option menu. Select the **Focus** option. The message "*Pick entity*" is displayed in the prompt window.

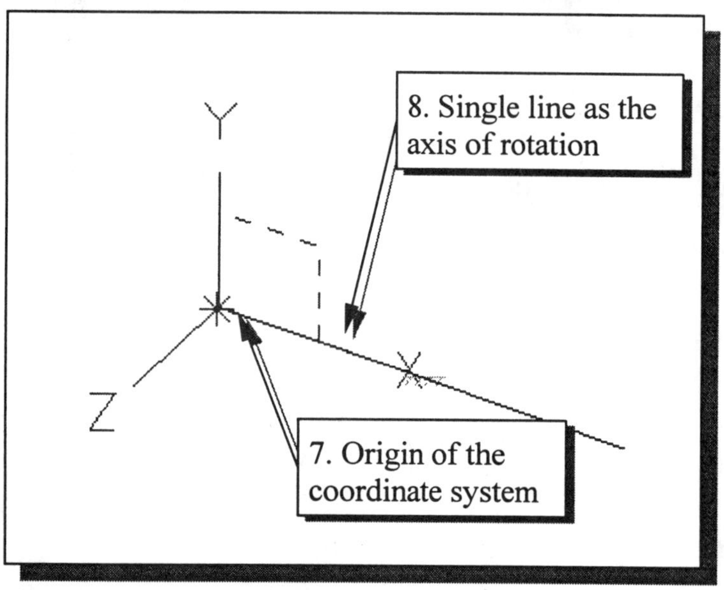

7. Select the **origin** of the coordinate system to create a reference point.

8. Select the reference point we just created and create a line along the X-axis as shown.

❖ For the **Revolve** operation, we need to define a 2-D sketch and an axis of rotation. The axis of rotation could be any line-segment, including reference geometry.

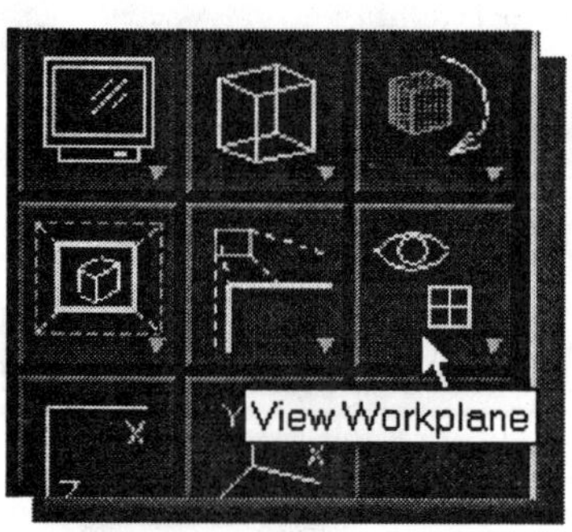

9. Choose **View Workplane** in the *display icon panel* to align the current *workplane* to the screen.

❖ For the **Revolve** operation, we need to define a 2-D sketch and an axis of rotation. The 2-D sketch needs to be a valid *section* (no self-intersecting edges), and the axis selected cannot cause the resultant model to intersect with itself. The axis of rotation can be one of the edges, but the axis cannot go through the middle of the *section.*

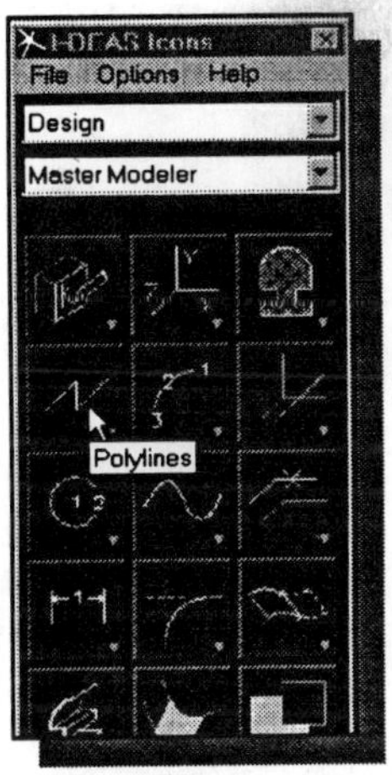

10. Pick **Polylines** in the icon panel. (The icon is located in the second row of the *task specific icon panel.*)

11. Create a closed-region sketch with the left vertical edge aligned to the origin of the coordinate system as shown below. (Note that the pulley design is symmetrical about a horizontal axis as well as a vertical axis, which allows us to simplify the 2D sketch as shown below.)

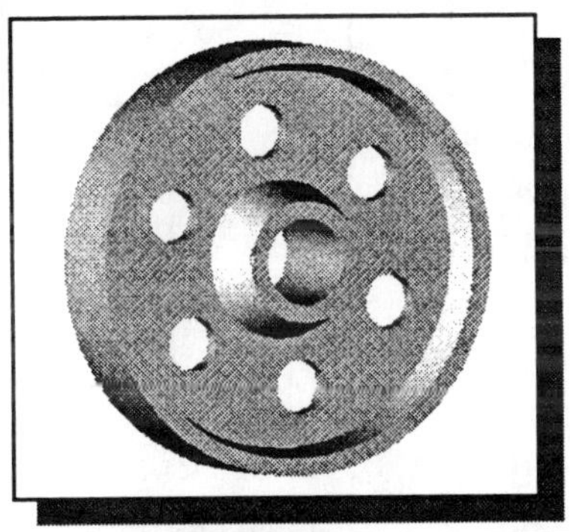

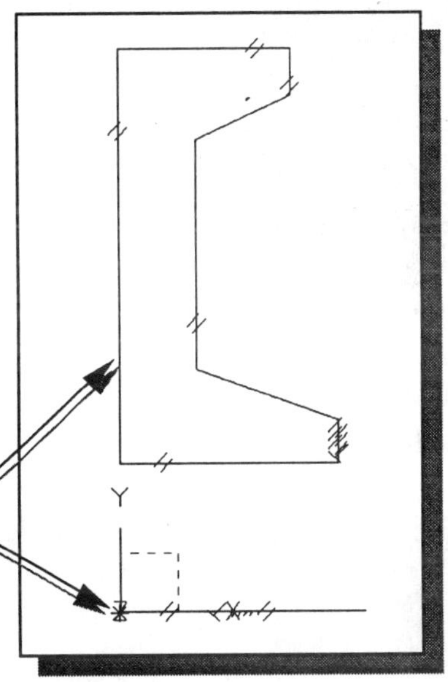

Align the left edge of the sketch to the origin of the coordinate system

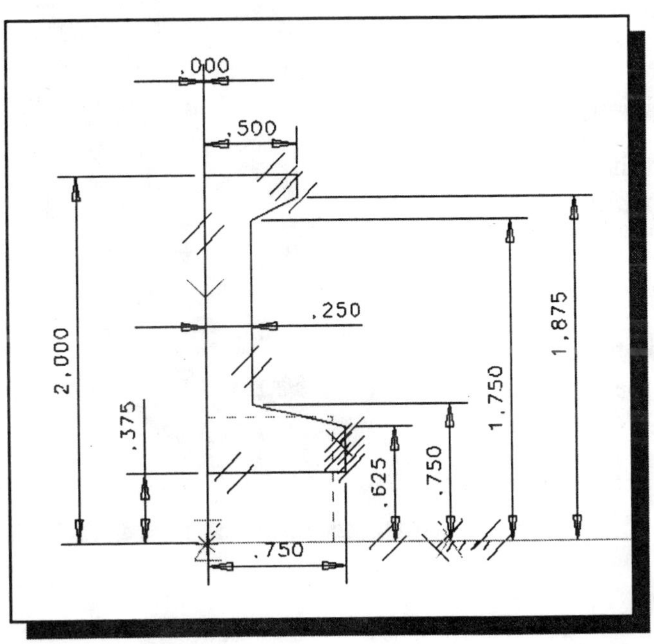

12. On your own, create and modify the dimensions as shown below.

13. On your own, use the *Show Free* command to confirm the 2D sketch is fully constrained.

Creating a Revolved Feature

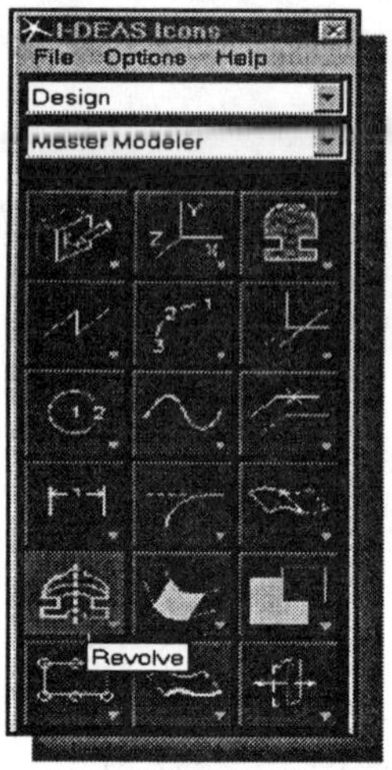

1. Choose **Revolve** in the icon panel. (The icon is located in the fifth row of the task specific icon panel. The icon is located in the same icon stack as the *Extrude* icon.)

2. In the prompt window, the message "*Pick curve or section*" is displayed. Pick the polygon we just created.

3. The message "*Pick curve to add or remove (Done)*" is displayed in the prompt window. Press the **ENTER** key or the **middle-mouse-button** to continue.

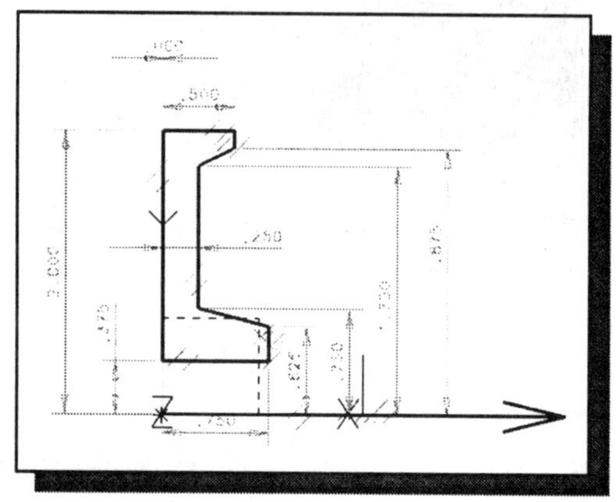

4. The message *"Pick axis to revolve about*" is displayed in the prompt window. Pick the single line we created as the axis of rotation.

5. In the *Revolve Section* window, confirm the settings are set to **360 degrees, Angle**, and **Protrude**.

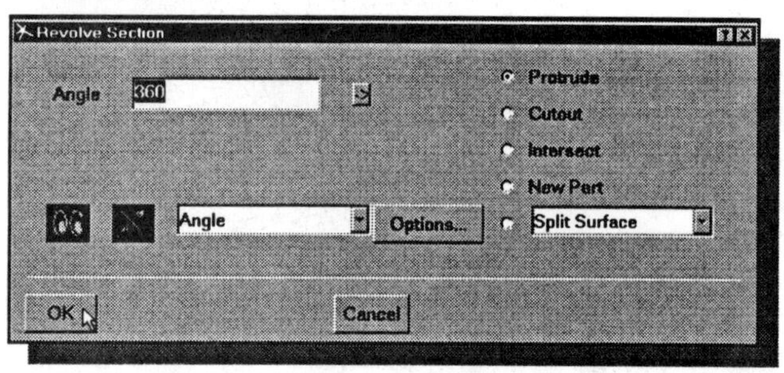

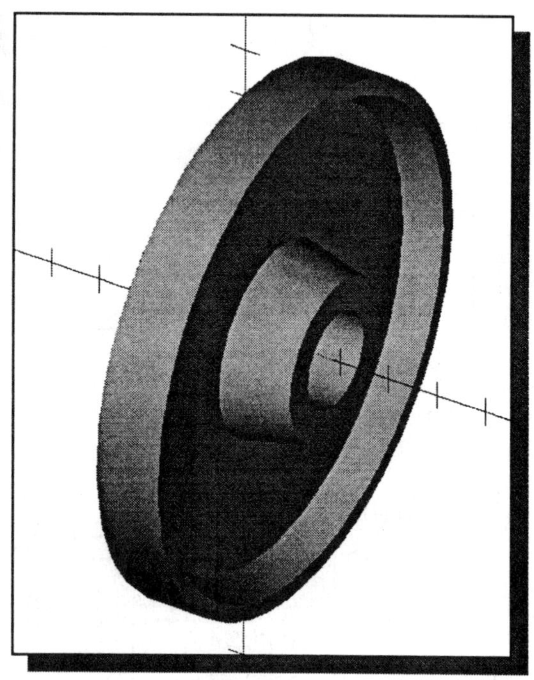

6. Click on the **OK** button to accept the settings and create the *Revolved feature*.

➢ Use the *dynamic rotation function* to dynamically rotate and examine the constructed 3-D model.

Mirroring Features

- In *I-DEAS*, features can be mirrored to create and maintain complex symmetrical features. We can mirror a feature about a workplane or a specified surface. We can create a mirrored feature while maintaining the original parametric definitions, which can be quite useful in creating symmetrical features. For example, we can create one quadrant of a feature, then mirror it twice to create a solid with four identical quadrants.

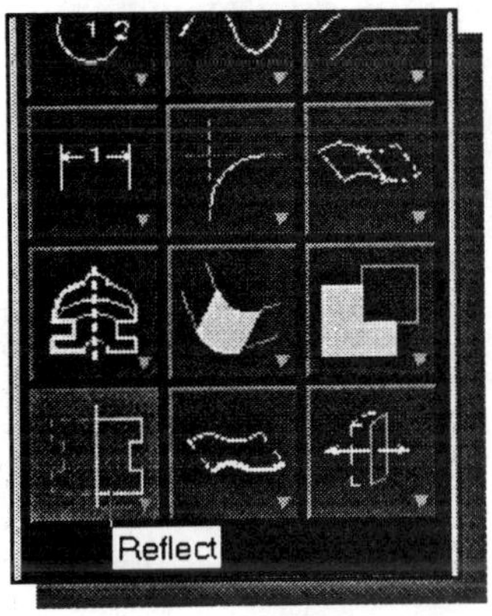

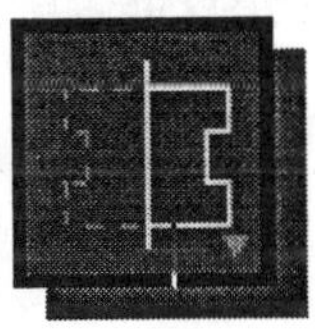

1. Select the ***Reflect*** command in the icon panel. (The icon is located in the last row of the application specific icon panel.)

2. In the prompt window, the message "*Pick part or section to Reflect*" is displayed. *I-DEAS* expects us to select features to be mirrored. Select any edge of the 3D base feature.

3. Press the **ENTER** key or the **middle-mouse-button** to accept the selection.

4. In the prompt window, the message "*Pick plane from part for relational Reflect*" is displayed. *I-DEAS* expects us to select a reference plane to create the mirrored feature. Select the face of the base feature as shown.

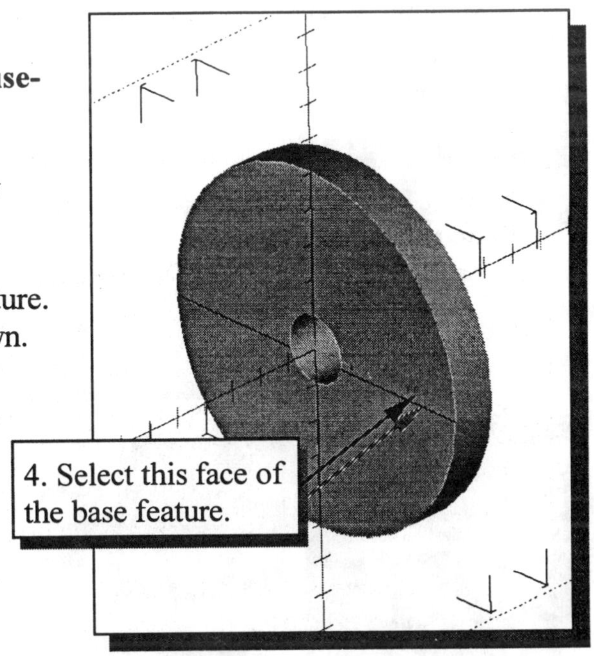

5. Select **Keep Both** in the popup menu and create the mirrored feature.

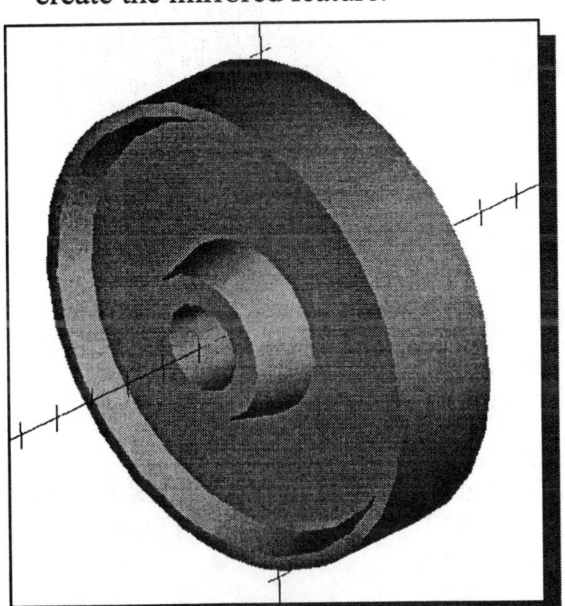

➢ Use the *Dynamic Rotation* function and the *Shaded, Wireframe* options to dynamically rotate and examine the created 3-D model.

Creating an Extruded Feature as a Pattern Leader

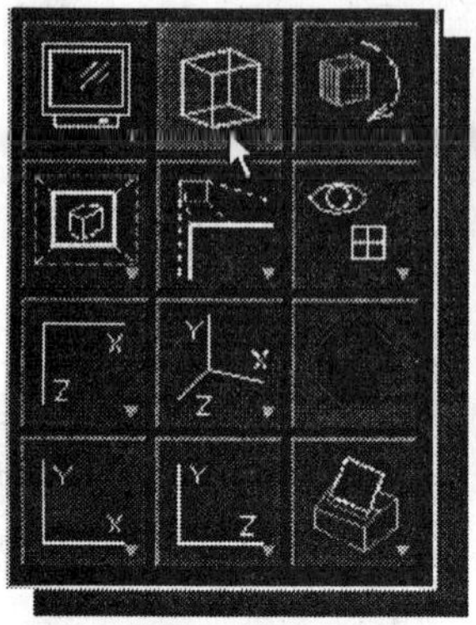

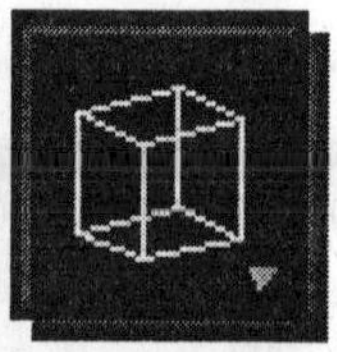

1. Choose **Wireframe** in the *display viewing icon panel.*

2. Choose **Isometric View** in the *display viewing icon panel.*

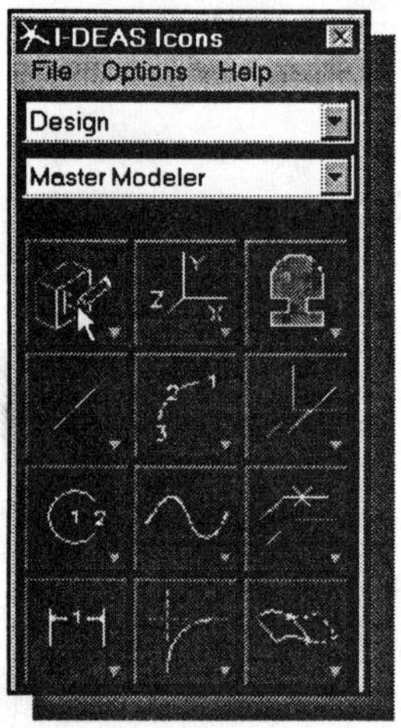

3. Choose **Sketch in Place** in the *icon panel.*

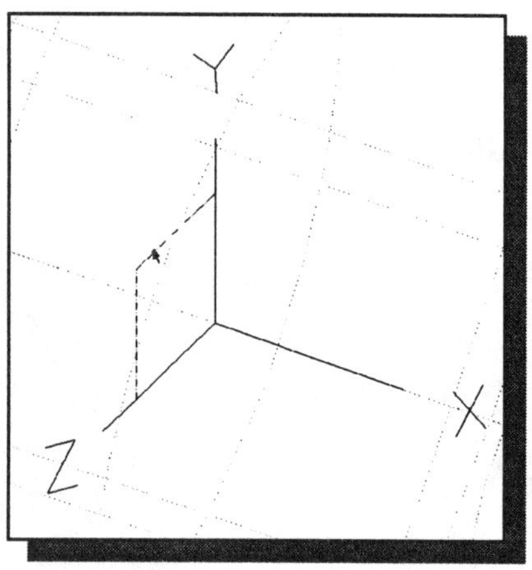

4. In the *prompt window*, the message "*Pick plane to sketch on*" is displayed. Pick one of the edges of the **YZ plane** of the coordinate system as shown in the figure. Use the *Dynamic Zoom* function to assist the selection of the workplane.

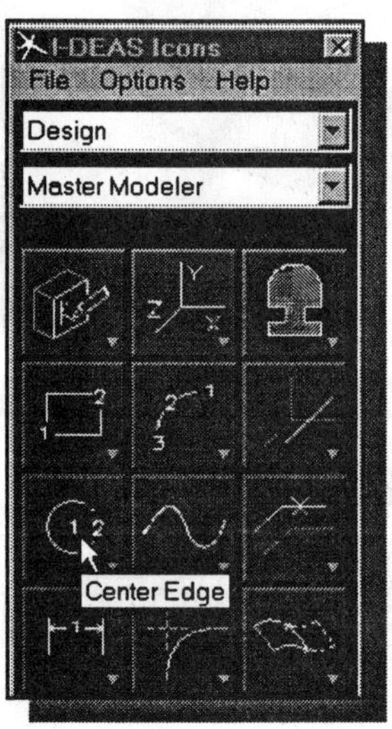

5. Choose *Circle* – **Center Edge** in the icon panel. The message "*Locate center*" is displayed in the *prompt window*.

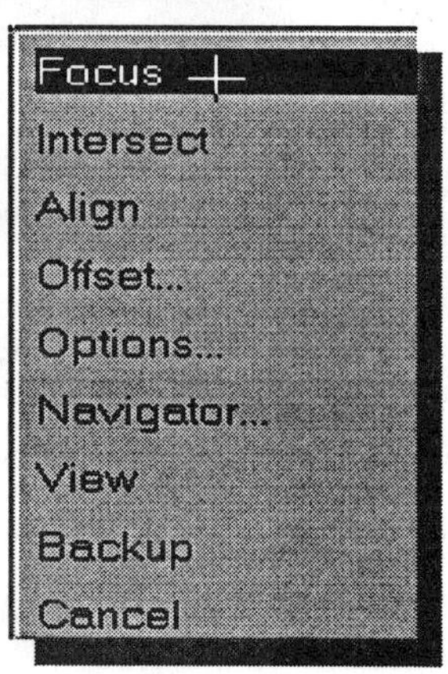

6. Move the cursor inside the graphics window. Press and hold down the right-mouse-button to display the option menu. Select the **Focus** option. The message "*Pick entity*" is displayed in the prompt window.

7. Select the **origin** of the coordinate system to create a reference point.

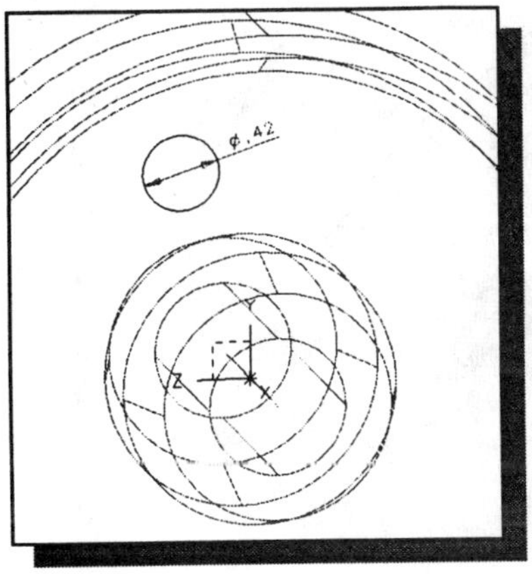

8. Create a circle above and **NOT aligned to** the Y-axis of the coordinate systems as shown in the figure. We will add dimensions to constrain the location of the circle.

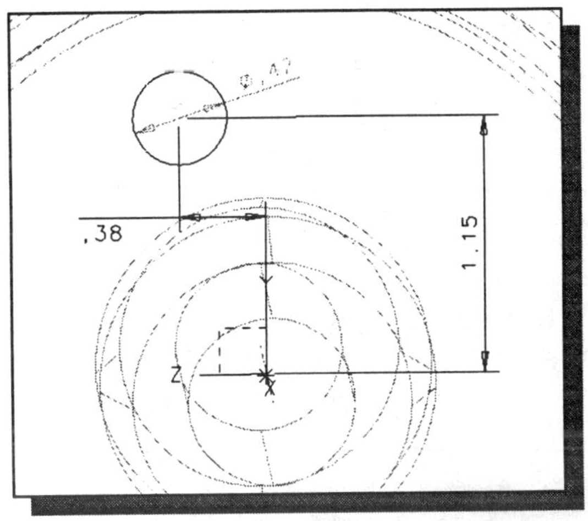

9. On your own, create two dimensions to constrain the location of the circle. (Hint: use the popup menu to create horizontal/vertical components of the default linear dimension.) Note that the values on your screen might appear differently than the values shown here.

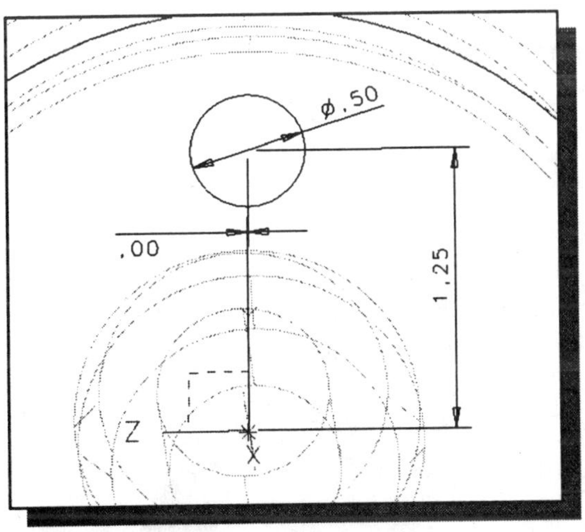

10. On your own, modify the diameter of the circle to **0.5** and the location dimensions to **1.25** and **0.0** as shown.

➢ On your own, confirm the circle is fully constrained.

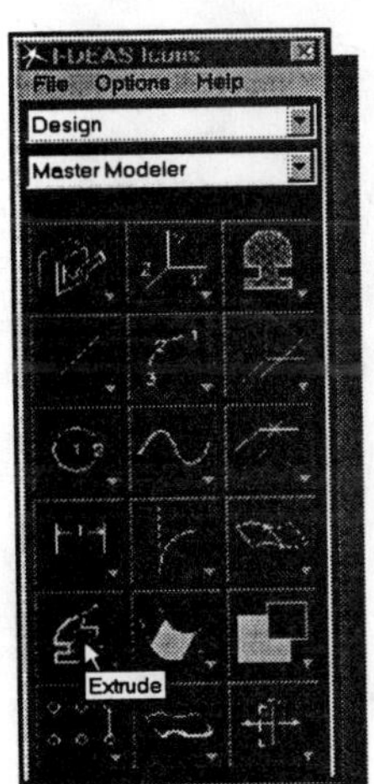

11. Choose **Extrude** in the icon panel.

12. In the *prompt window*, the message "*Pick curve or section*" is displayed. Pick the circle as the 2D section to be extruded.

13. At the I-DEAS prompt "*Pick curve to add or remove (Done),*" press the **ENTER** key or the **middle-mouse-button** to accept the selection.

14. In the *Extrude Section* window, enter **1.0** as the *Extrusion Depth.*

15. Set the *extrusion type* to **Cutout**.

16. Choose **Thicken** as the *Depth option.*

17. Click on the **OK** button to proceed with the **Cut** operation.

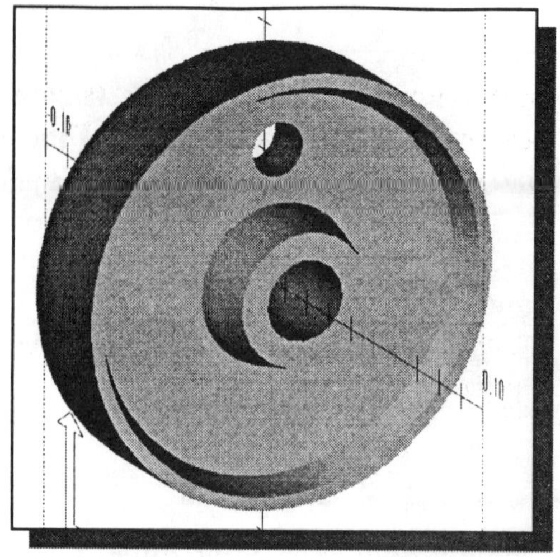

Circular Pattern

❖ In *I-DEAS*, existing features can be easily duplicated. The ***Circular Pattern*** command allows us to create a polar array of features. The patterned features are parametrically linked to the original feature; any modifications to the original feature are also reflected in the arrayed features.

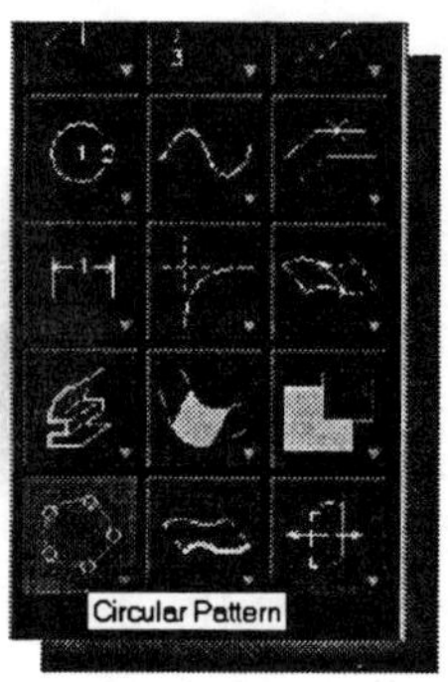

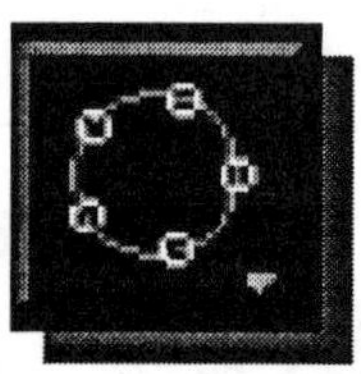

1. Choose **Circular Pattern** in the icon panel. (The icon is located in the last row of the task specific icon panel.)

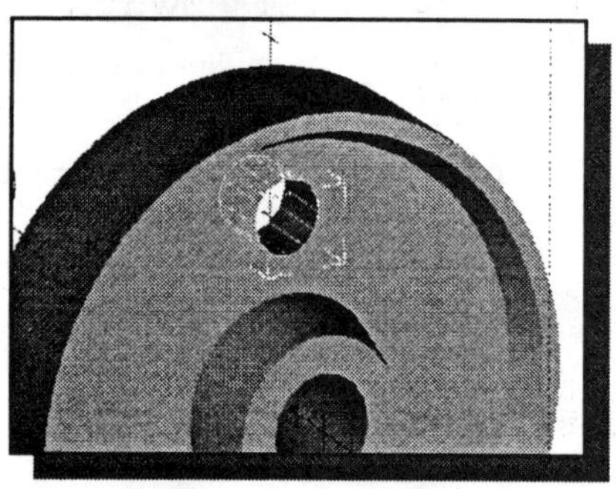

2. The message "*Pick part or feature to make a pattern of*" is displayed in the prompt window. Select the cut feature by clicking twice on the cylindrical surface of the feature. Note the yellow bounding box identifying the selected feature.

3. Press the **ENTER** key or the **middle-mouse-button** to accept the selection.

❖ Next, *I-DEAS* expects us to identify a plane to create the pattern. We will switch to the wireframe display mode to select the YZ-plane of the part coordinate system.

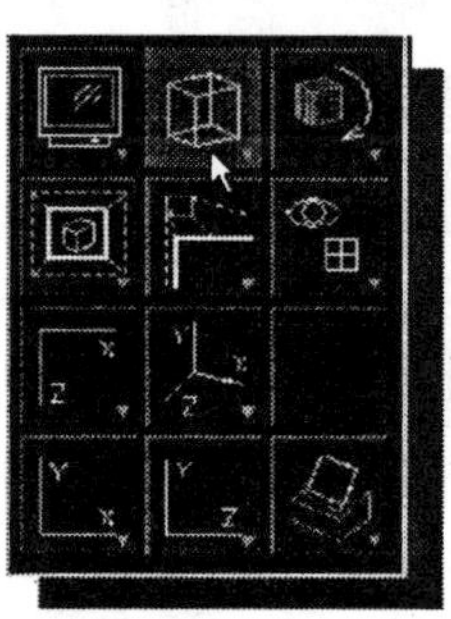

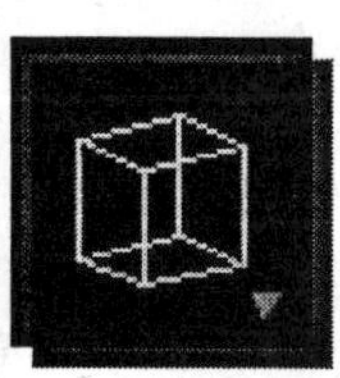

4. Choose **Wireframe** in the display viewing icon panel.

5. In the prompt window, the message "*Pick patterning plane*" is displayed. Pick the **YZ-plane** of the part coordinate system as shown.

6. In the prompt window, the message "*Pick a center point for circular pattern*" is displayed. Select the origin of the part coordinate system as shown in the figure.

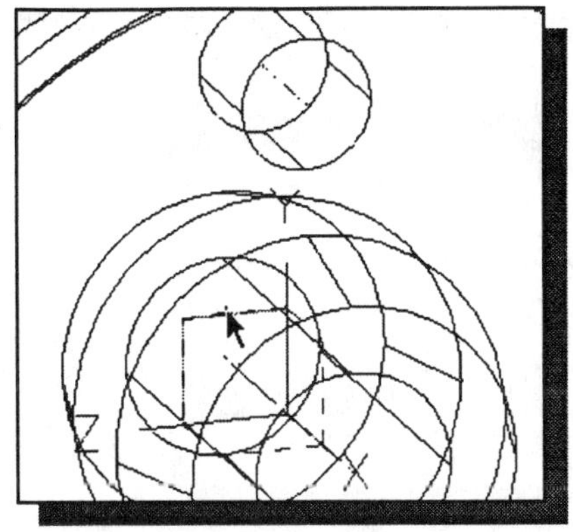

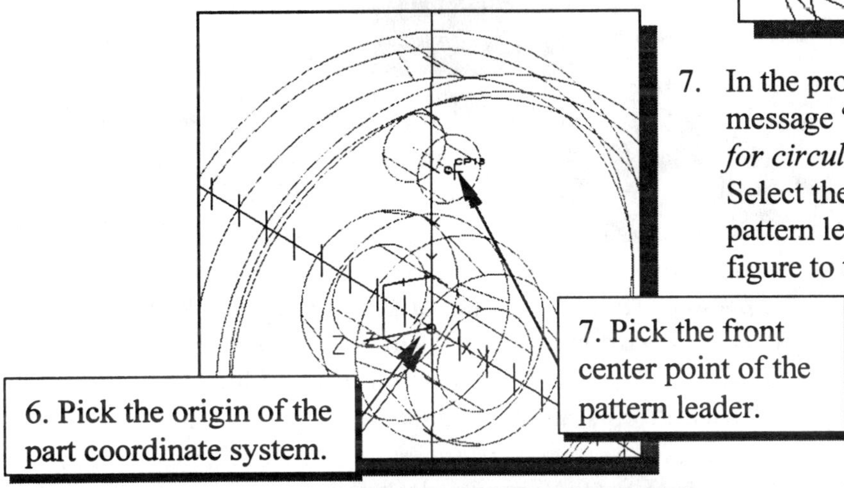

7. In the prompt window, the message "*Pick a radius end point for circular pattern*" is displayed. Select the front center point of the pattern leader as shown in the figure to the left.

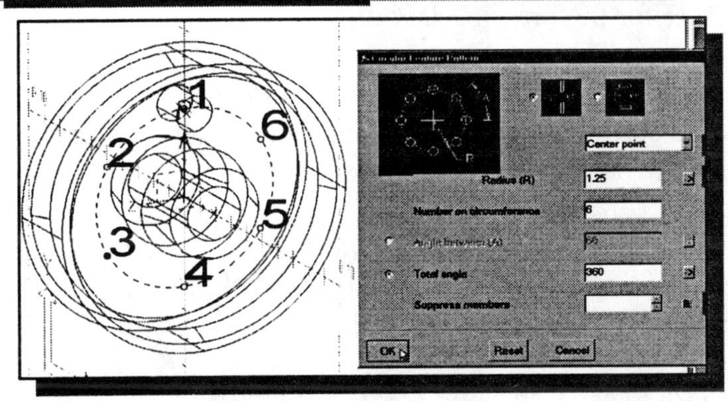

8. In the *Circular Pattern* window, change the *Number on Circumference* value to **6** and the *Total Angle* to **360**.

9. Click on the **OK** button to create the circular pattern consisting of six cut holes.

➢ The *Circular Pattern* is created as a *single feature*, which can easily be modified through the *History Tree*. Imagine the time and effort involved if we were to create six separate holes of the same design.

Creating a Template Title Block

1. Click with the **left-mouse-button** in the *Task* toolbar area to display other options and select the **Master Drafting** task.

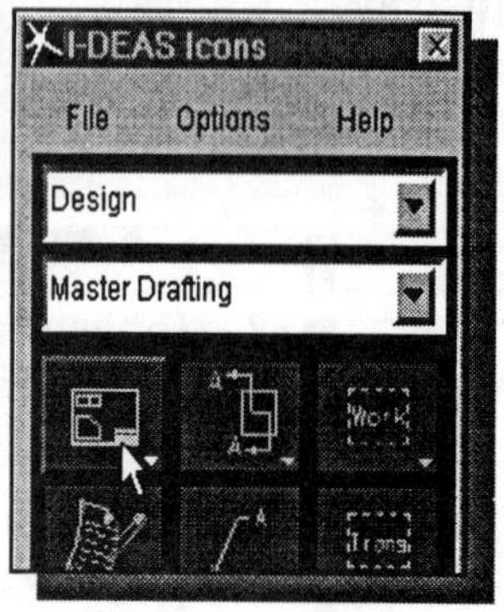

2. Choose **Create Drawing** in the icon panel. (The icon is located in the first row of the icon panel.)

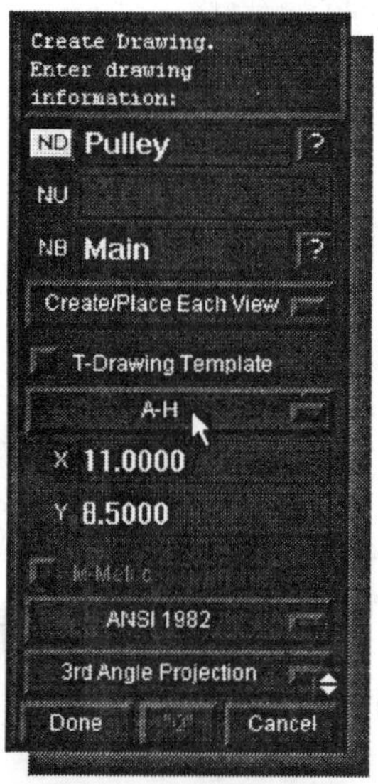

3. In the *prompt window*, the message "*Create Drawing. Enter drawing information:*" is displayed. Confirm the settings are set as follows: **Create/Place Each View** and the **Drawing Template** option is turned off.

4. Select the **A-H** for the drawing layout.

5. Notice the *ANSI standard* and the *3rd Angle Projection* settings. Click on the **Done** button to accept the settings and proceed with the next option selections.

6. In the prompt area, the message "*Create View. Locate border first corner:*" is displayed. Click on the **Cancel** button to exit the *Create View* command.

7. Set *Line Width* to **Medium** and *Color* to **Green** in the option selection area as shown.

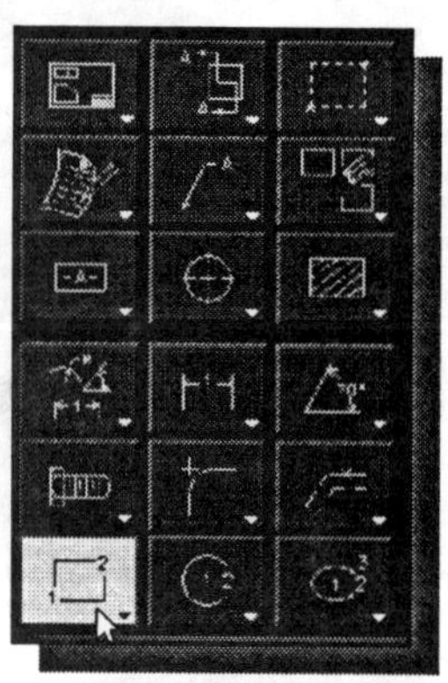

8. Choose **Rectangle by 2 Corners** in the icon panel. This command requires the selection of two locations to identify the two opposite corners of a rectangle.

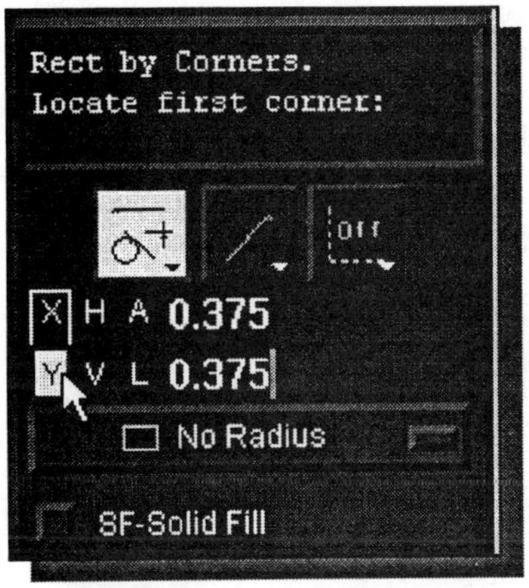

9. The message "*Locate first corner*" is displayed in the prompt window. Click on the **[X-Y]** column and enter **0.375** as the X and Y coordinates of the first corner of the rectangle.

10. Confirm the settings are as shown in the figure at left and click on the **Done** button to accept the settings.

❖ Three keyboard-input options are available in identifying locations in the Master Drafting application. The **[X-Y]** option allows us to enter values for the X/Y coordinates relative to the origin. The **[H-V]** option allows us to enter horizontal/vertical values relative to the last point selected on the screen. The **[A-V]** option allows us to input values in polar coordinates format.

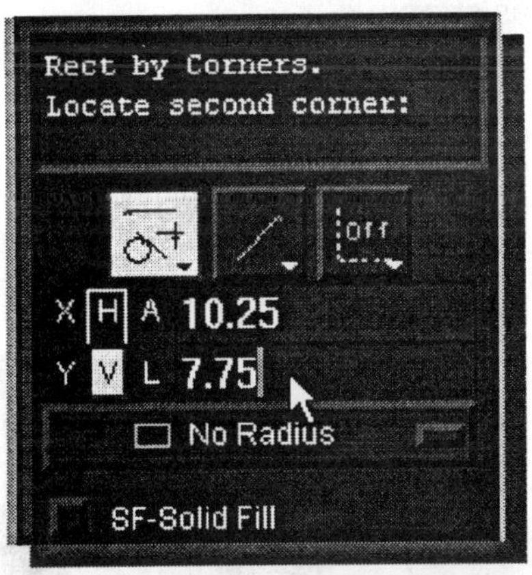

11. The message "*Locate Second corner*" is displayed in the prompt window. Note that *I-DEAS* automatically switched the input to the [H-V] option. Enter **10.25** and **7.75** as the width and height of the rectangle.

12. Click on the **Done** button to accept the settings and create the rectangle.

13. Click on the **Done** button to end the *Rectangle* command.

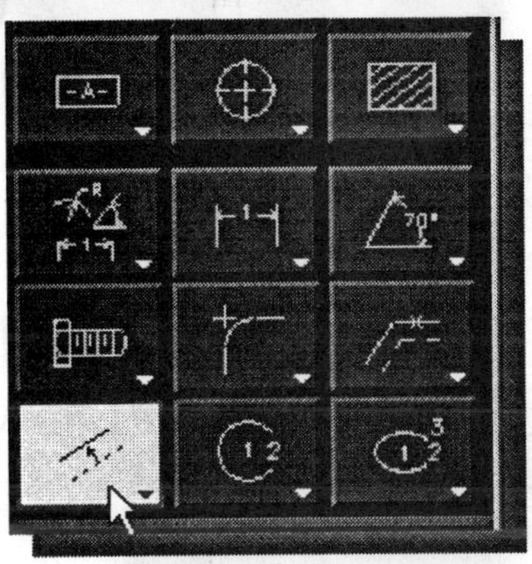

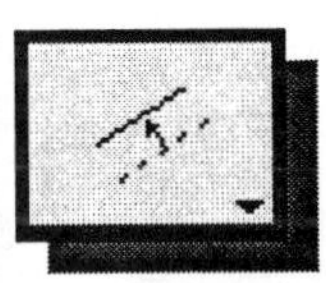

14. Choose **Parallel Line** in the icon panel. This command allows us to create a parallel line referencing existing entities on the screen.

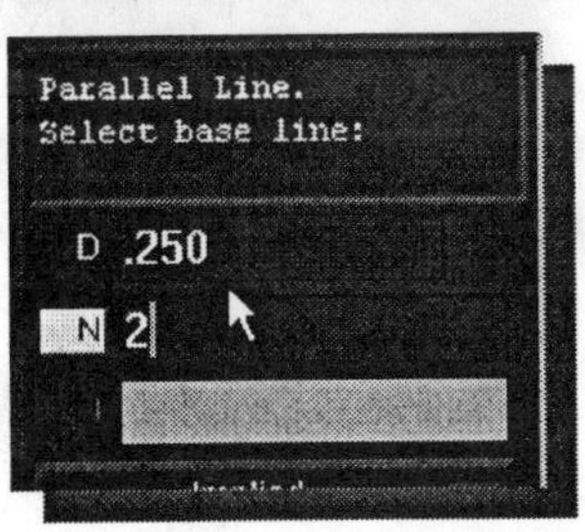

15. We will first create lines parallel to the bottom edge of the created rectangle. Enter **0.25** as the parallel distance and **2** as the number of lines to create.

16. Select the bottom edge of the rectangle inside the graphics window.

17. Click above the selected line to create two parallel lines.

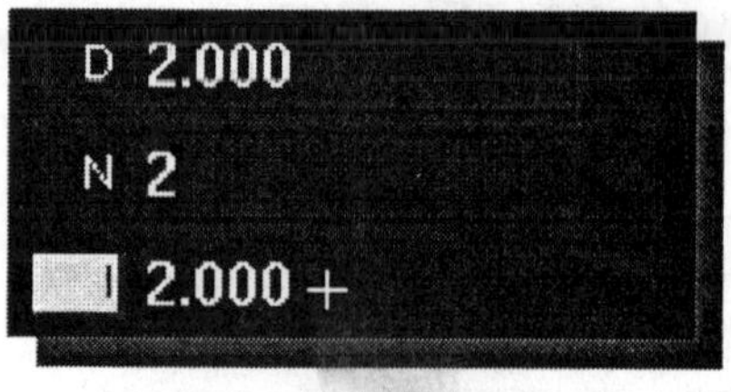

18. In the *option selection* menu, enter the settings as shown.

19. Select the left edge of the rectangle.

20. Pick a location inside the rectangle to create two parallel lines.

21. Choose **Trim/Extend** in the upper section of the icon panel.

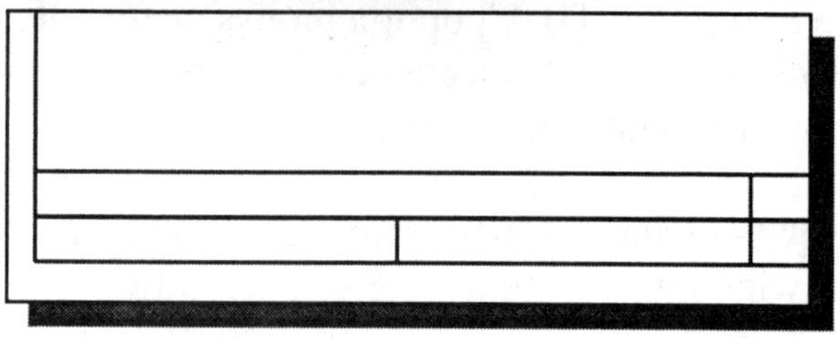

22. Trim the two lines so that they appeared as shown.

23. Repeat the above steps and create the additional lines as shown below.

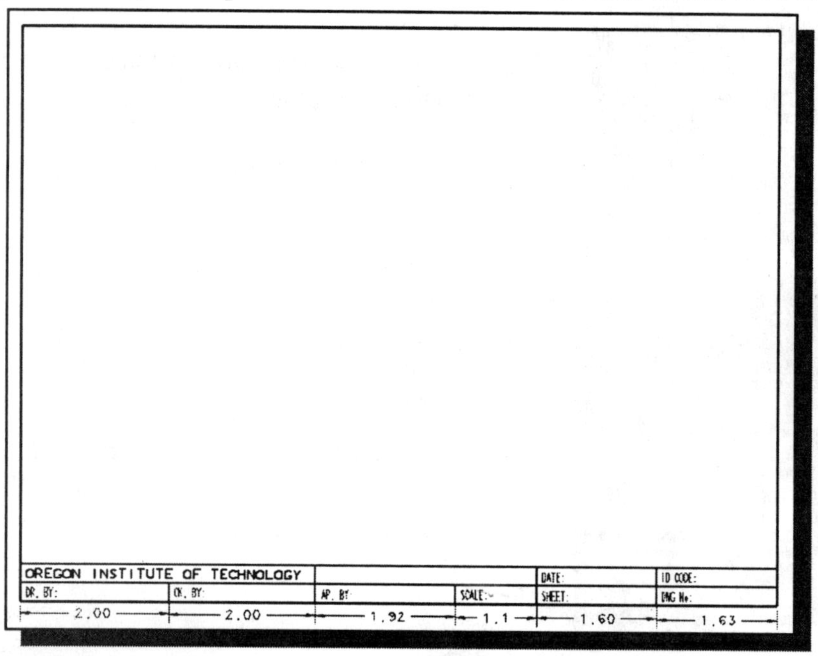

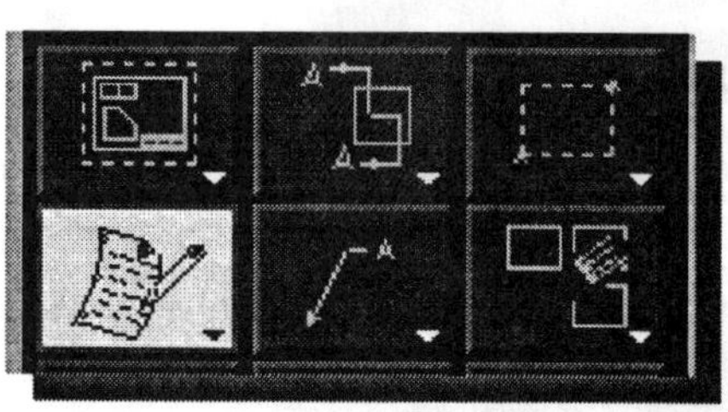

24. Choose **Note** in the icon panel and complete the title block as shown in the above figure. (Hint: use a *WR* (width ratio) of *0.5* and *1.0* to adjust the spacing of letters.)

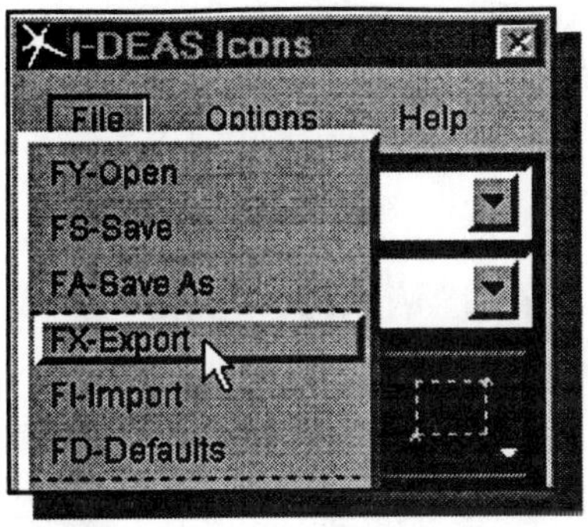

25. Select **Export** in the *File* pull down menu. To select the command, press and hold the left-mouse-button on top of the **File** icon to display the option list as shown.

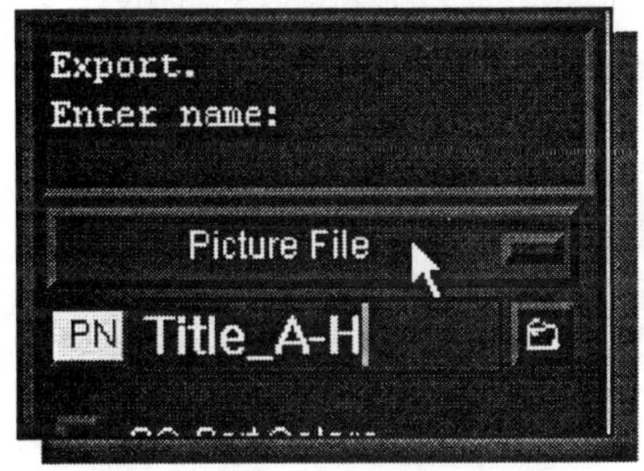

26. Select **Picture File** as the file format to export.

27. Enter **Title_A-H** as the filename.

28. Click on **Done** to save the file.

❖ We have created a template title block file that can be brought into any *I-DEAS* drawing by using the [*File=>Import*] option. Note that you can also export the title block using other formats, such as the CGM format or the DXF format.

Adding 2D Views

1. Choose **Create View** in the icon panel. (The icon is located in the first row of the icon panel.)

2. In the prompt area, the message "*Create View. Locate border first corner:*" is displayed. Click and drag with the left-mouse-button to identify the size of the view as shown.

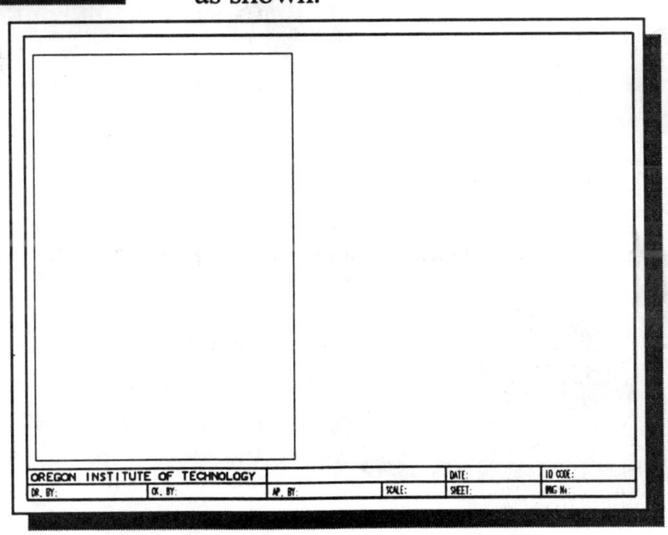

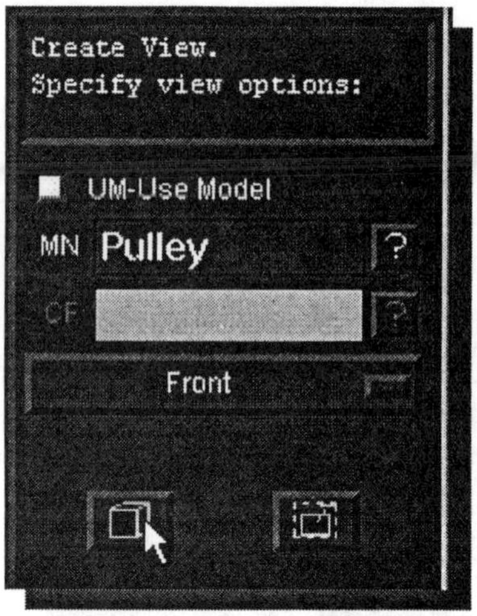

3. In the *option selection area*, confirm the *Use Model* option is turned **on** and the *Model name* is set to **Pulley** as shown.

4. Click on the **Display 3D Model Window** icon.

❖ Besides using the standard views, as illustrated in the previous chapter, we can also define the views on-the-fly.

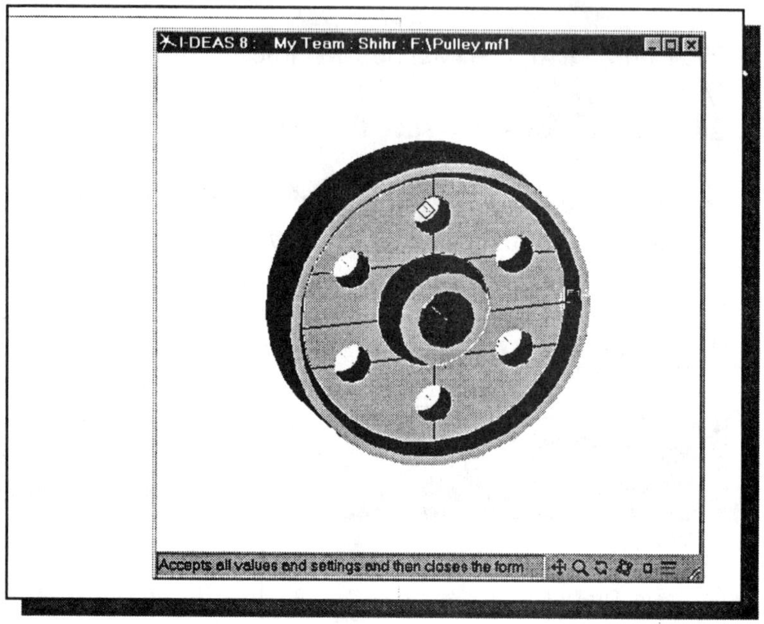

5. Inside the *3D Model* window, select the inside circular face as shown. (Note that the Dynamic Viewing Functions are available in this popup window.)

6. Confirm the viewing direction is pointing forward and click **Yes** in the popup menu.

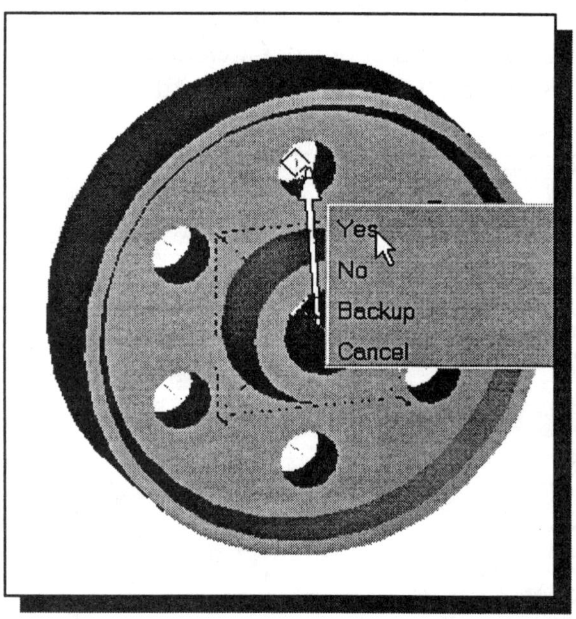

7. In the *prompt area*, the message "*Pick Up-Vector*" is displayed. *I-DEAS* expects us to identify the upward direction to orient the 2D view. Select any center near the center of the model.

8. Select the center point of the pattern leader.

9. An arrow appears on the screen. Click **Yes** in the *popup window* to accept the settings.

10. In the *prompt area*, click **Yes** to accept the view orientation settings.

11. In the *option selection area*, click **Done** to accept the view orientation settings.

12. In the *option selection area*, enter **0.75** as the scale factor for the front view.

13. In the *option selection area*, click **Done** to create the view.

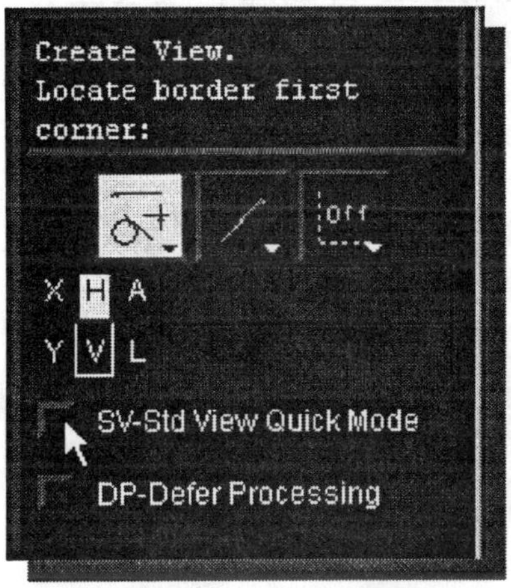

14. In the *option selection* area, switch **off** the *SV-Std View Quick Mode* option as shown.

15. Create a rectangle near the upper right corner of the title block. (Refer to the figure below for the approximate size of the rectangle.)

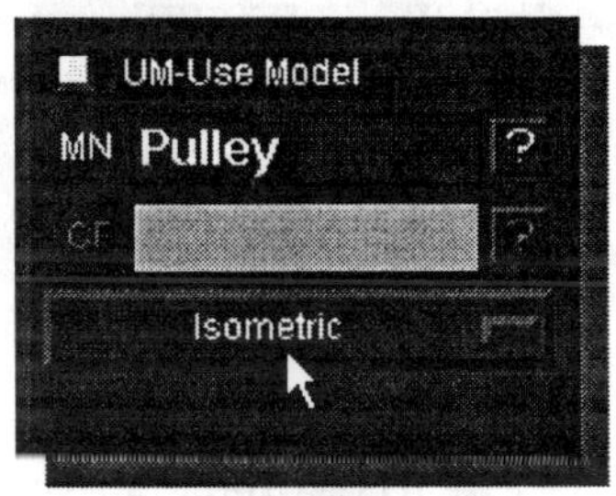

16. Choose **Isometric** in the option selection area as shown.

17. In the *option selection area*, click **Done** to accept the view orientation settings.

18. In the *option selection area*, enter **0.5** as the scale factor for the isometric view.

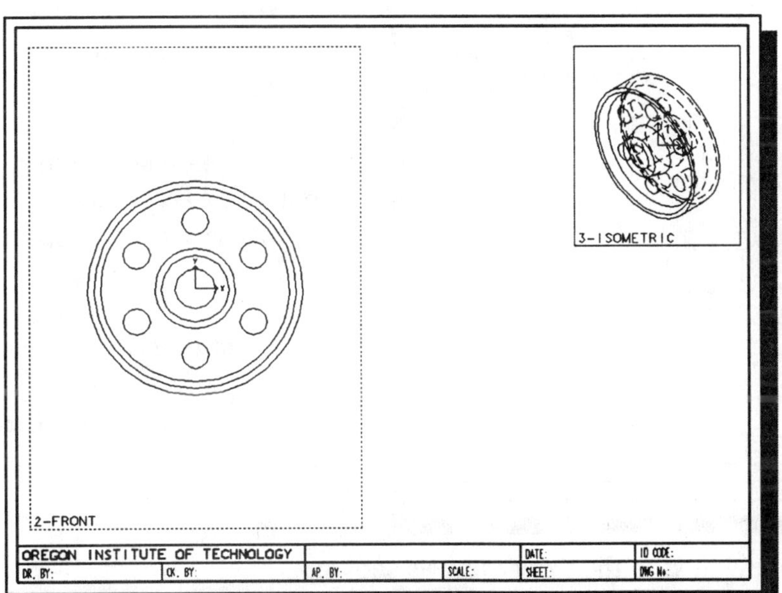

19. In the option selection area, click **Done** to create the view.

20. In the option selection area, click **Cancel** to end the *Create View* command.

Adding a Section View

1. Choose **Section View** in the icon panel. (The icon is located in the first row of the task specific icon panel.)

2. The message "*Section view. Select Parent view*" is displayed in the prompt area. Pick the **Front** view inside the *graphics window*.

3. The message "*Cut Plane. Locate point or select option to define line*" is displayed in the prompt area. Click on the **NV-Vertical** icon as shown.

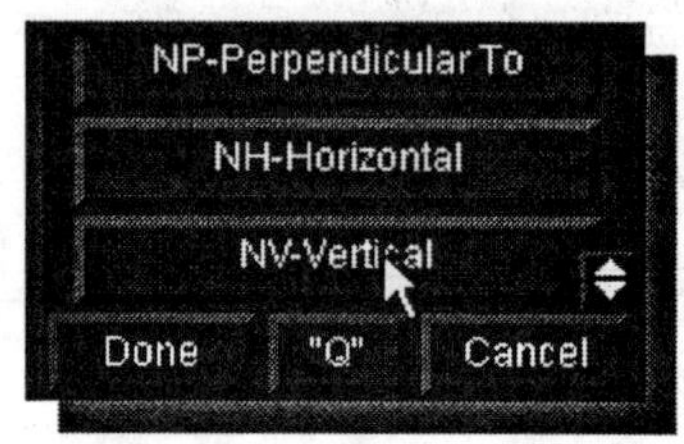

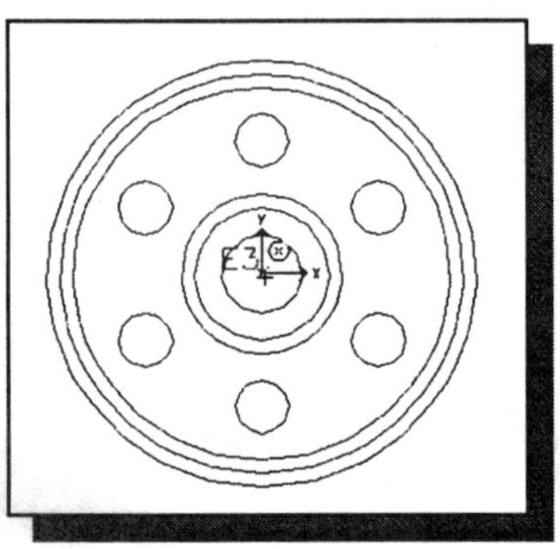

4. Select the center of the front view as shown.

5. Select location that is above the front view and a location below to define a cutting plane line.

6. In the *option selection* area, click **Done** to accept the selections.

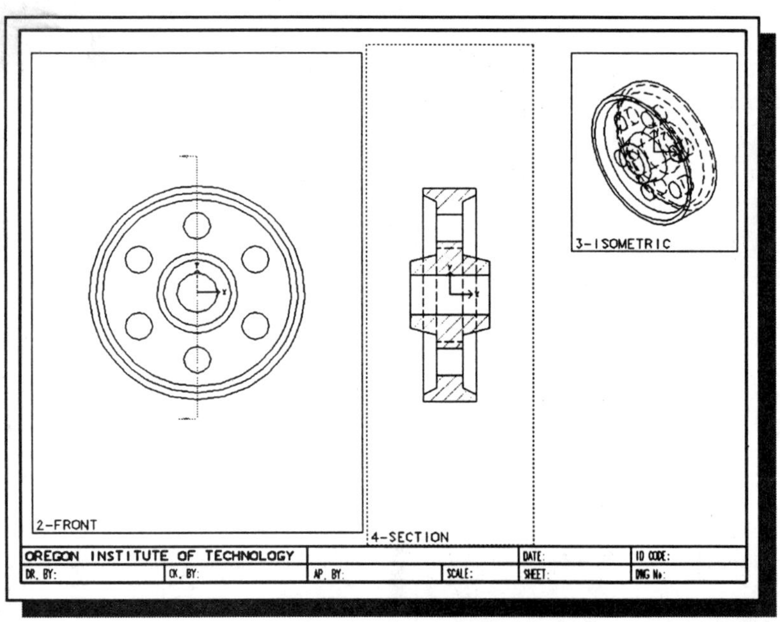

7. Click on the left side of the front view to define the viewing direction of the section view.

8. In the option selection area, click **Done** to accept the settings for the cutting plane line.

9. In the option selection area, click **Done** to accept the settings for the scale factor of the view.

10. Place the section view next to the front view as shown.

11. In the option selection area, click **Cancel** to end the *Section View* command.

Resizing the Views and Completing the Drawing

1. Inside the *graphics window*, set the **Front view** as the *work view* by clicking on the front view.

2. Choose **View Border** in the icon panel. (The icon is located in the first row of the task specific icon panel.)

3. Resize the view border by creating a rectangle defining the view border of the Front view.

4. Repeat the above steps and resize the other views.

5. On your own, complete the drawing by adding the necessary dimensions and centerlines; also create a printout of the completed 2D drawing.

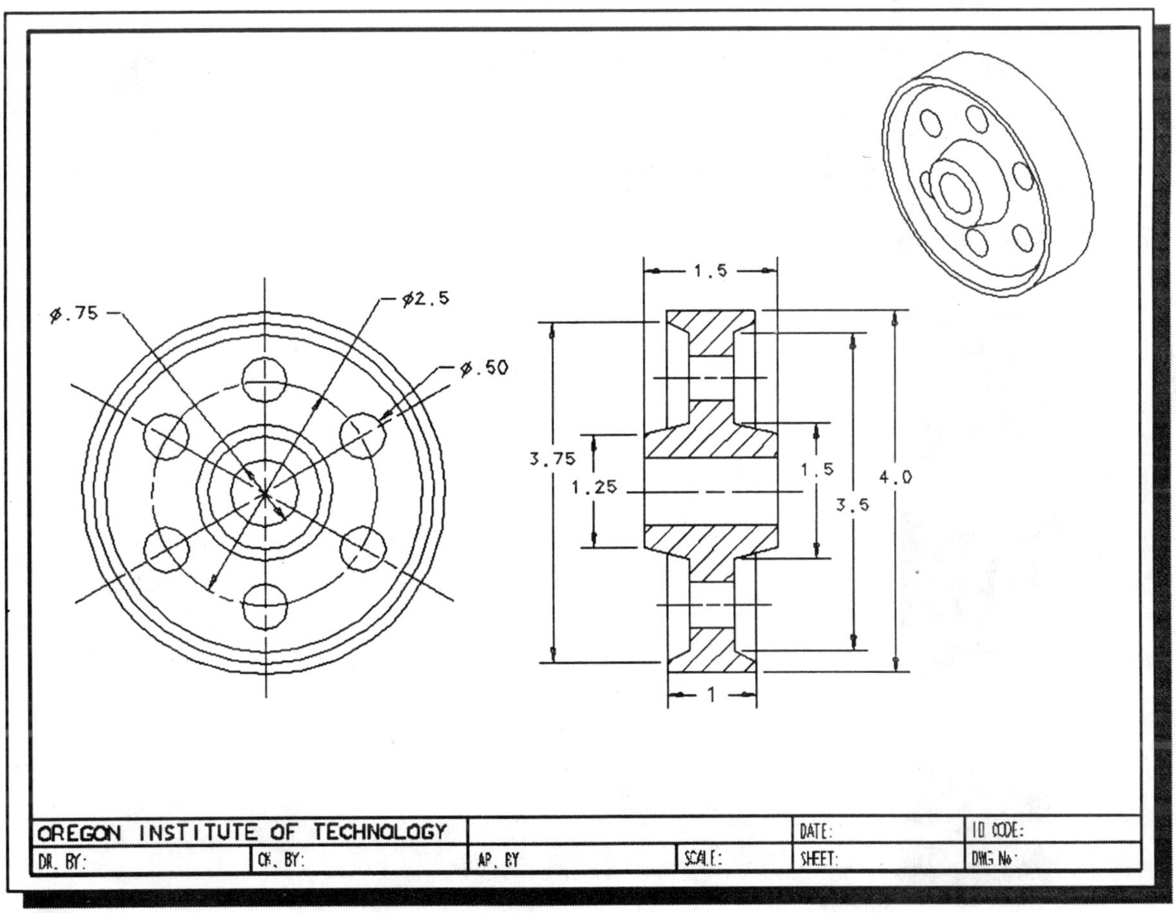

Questions:

1. List the different symmetrical features created in the *Pulley* design.
2. What are the advantages of using *Drawing Template*?
3. Describe the steps required in using the *Mirror Feature* command.
4. Why is it important to identify symmetrical features in designs?
5. When and why should we use the *Pattern* option?
6. Which command do you use to resize a view in the *Master Drafting application*?
7. Identify and describe the following commands:

(a)

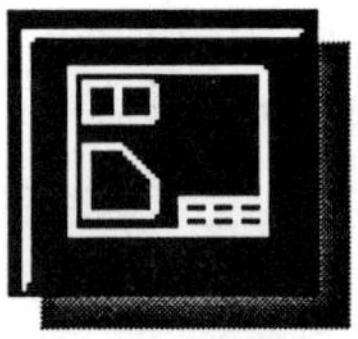

(b)

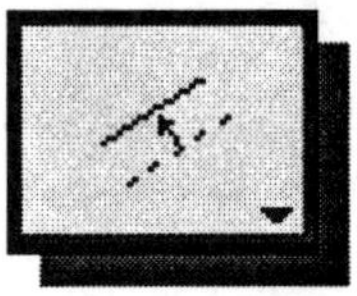

(c)

(d)

(e)

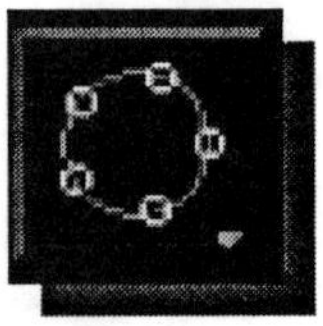

Exercises: (Construct the Solid Models and use the Master Drafting application to generate 2D drawings from the 3D Models.)

1.

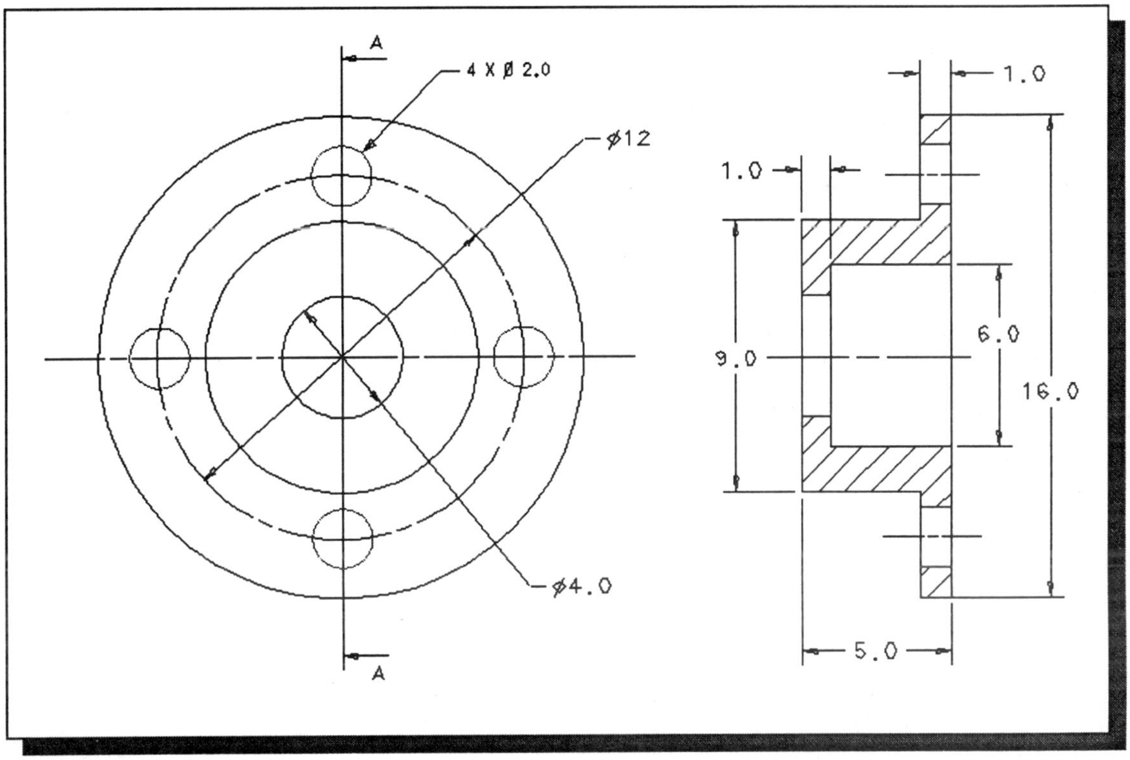

2.

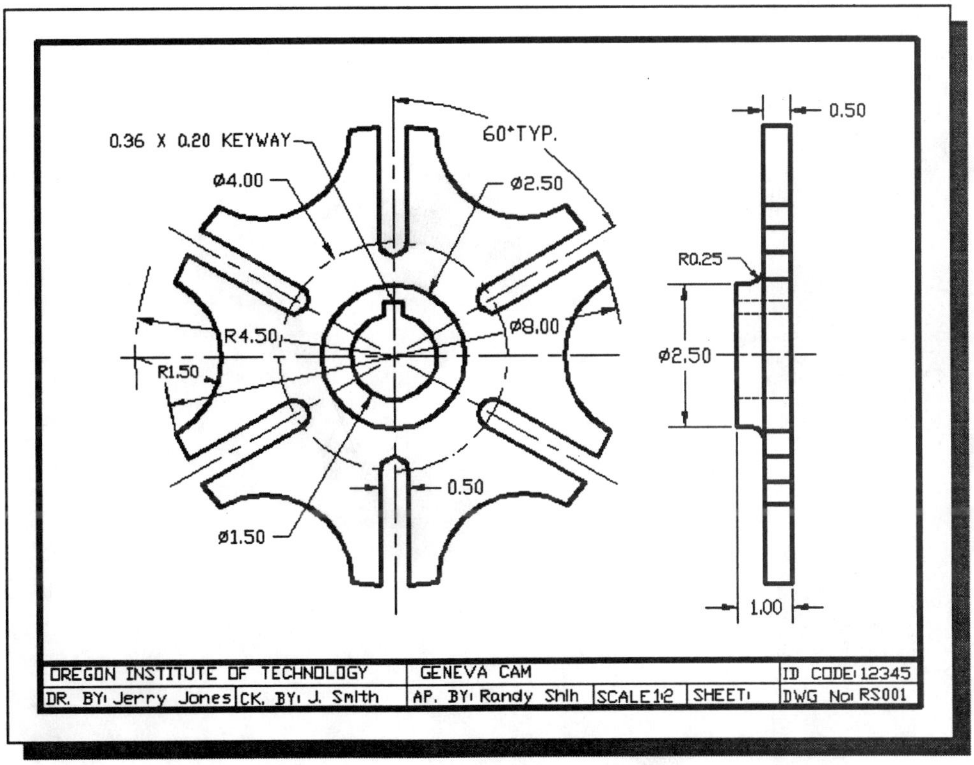

NOTES:

Chapter 10
Three-Dimensional Construction Tools

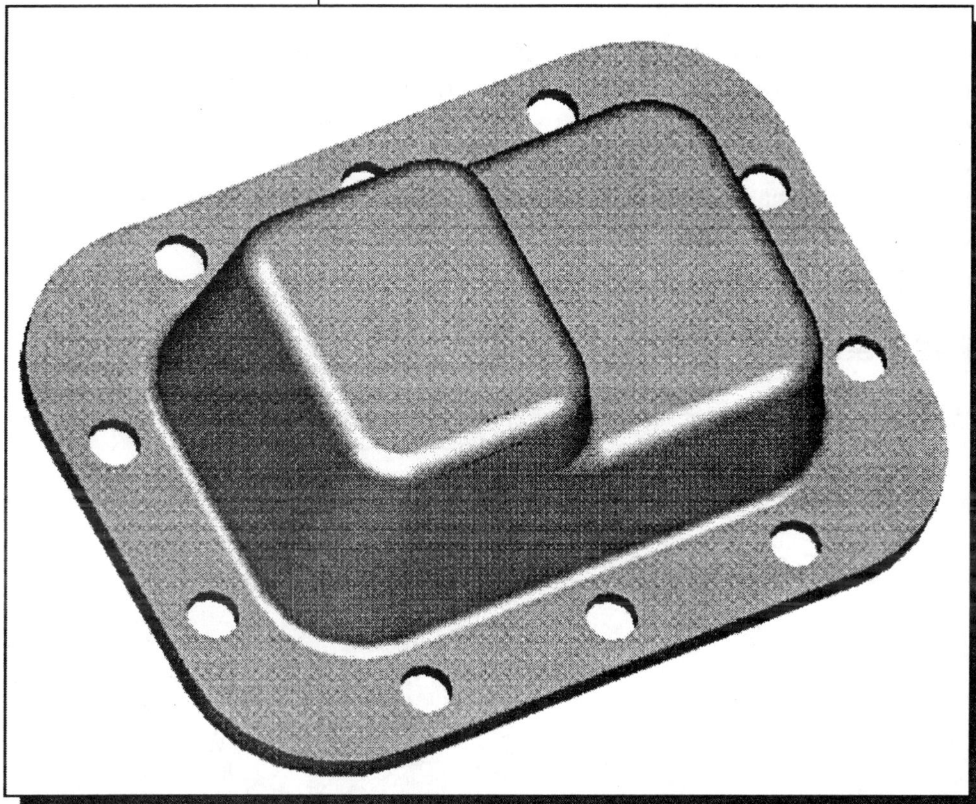

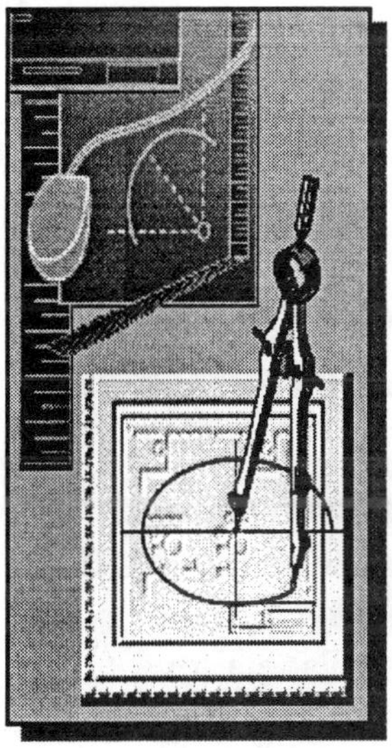

Learning Objectives

When you have completed this lesson, you will be able to:

- ◆ Create Draft Angle Features.
- ◆ Use the 3-D Rounds & Fillets command.
- ◆ Create Rectangular Patterns.
- ◆ Use the Shell command.
- ◆ Change the Model color.
- ◆ Use the Extract Section command.
- ◆ Get and Put Away Parts.

Introduction

I-DEAS Master Modeler provides an assortment of three-dimensional construction tools to make the creation of solid models easier and more efficient. In this chapter, we will examine the procedures to create the *Draft Angle* feature, the *Shell* feature and also for creating three-dimensional *Rounds* and *Fillets* along edges of a solid model. These features are common characteristics of molded parts. The three-dimensional *Fillets* and the *Shell* commands will usually create complex three-dimensional spatial curves and surfaces. These commands are more sensitive to the associated geometric entities. For this reason, the *3-D fillets* and the *shell* features are created last, after all associated solid features are created. In this chapter, we will also examine the different methods to reference to existing surfaces.

A Thin-walled Design: OIL SINK

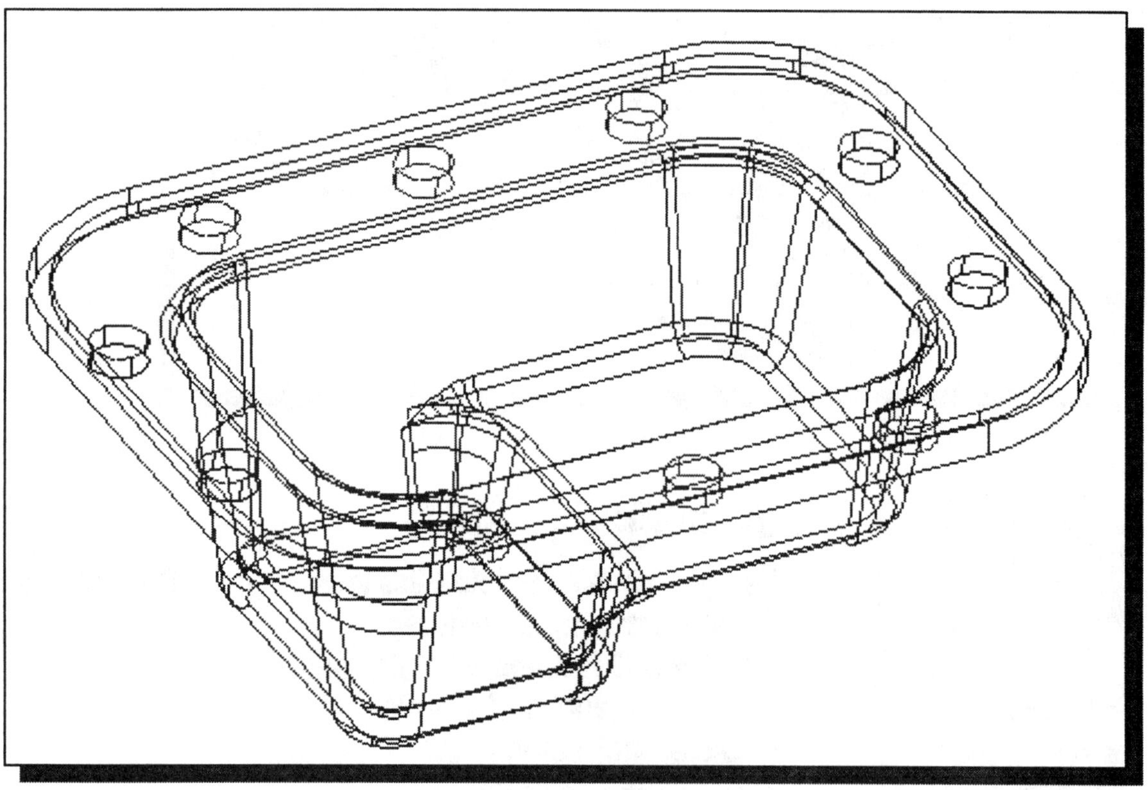

❖ Based on your knowledge of I-DEAS Master Modeler so far, how many features would you use to create the design? Which feature would you choose as the **BASE FEATURE** of the model? What are the more difficult features involved in the design? What is your choice in arranging the order of the features? Take a few minutes to consider these questions and do preliminary planning by sketching on a piece of paper. You are also encouraged to create the design on your own prior to following through the tutorial.

Modeling Strategy

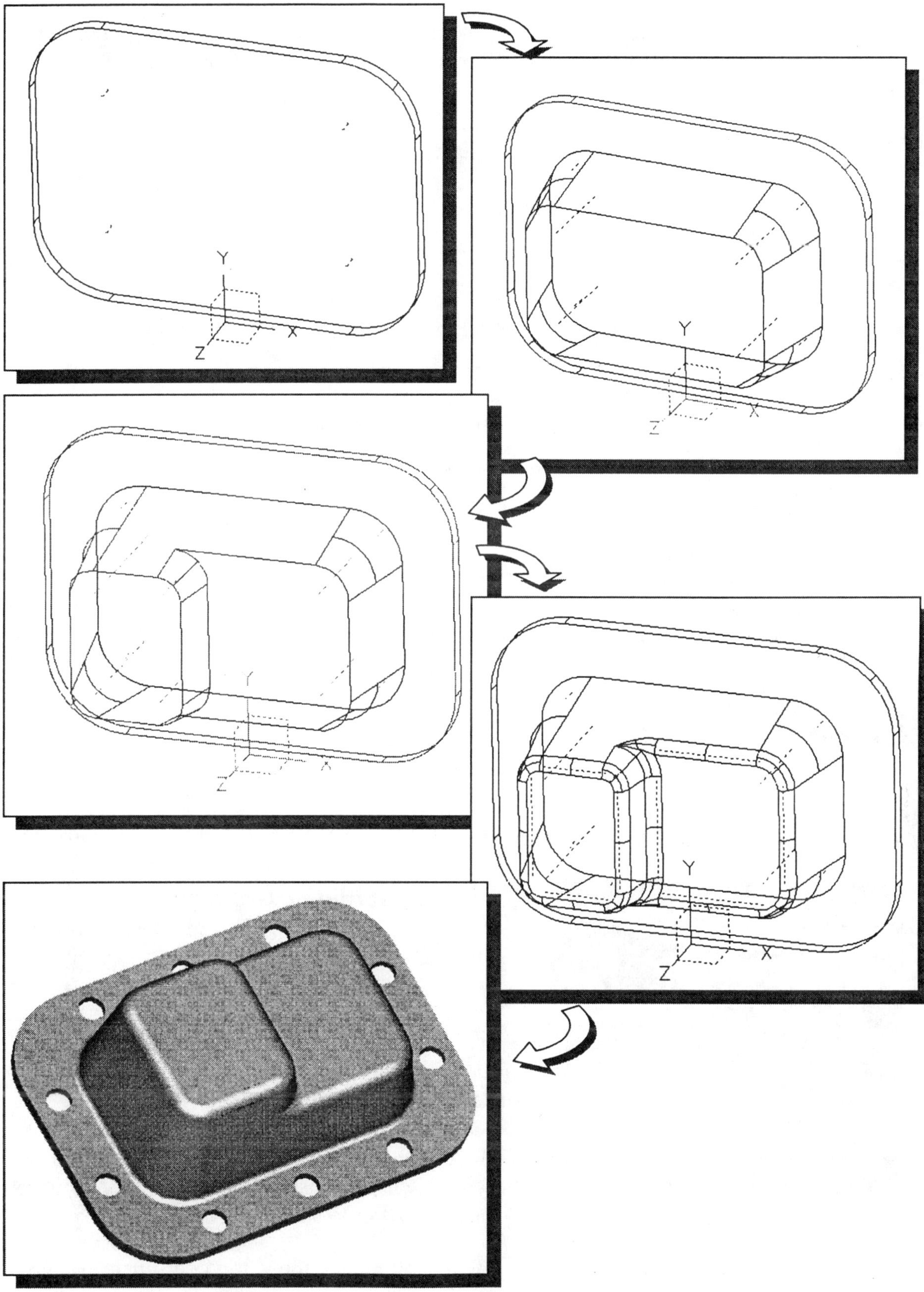

Starting I-DEAS

1. Login to the computer and bring up I-DEAS. Start a new model file by filling in the items as shown below in the *I-DEAS Start* window:

Project Name: **(Your account Name)**
Model File Name: **Oil_sink**
Application: **Design**
Task: **Master Modeler**
OK

2. After you click on the **OK** button, a *warning window* will appear to tell you that a new model file will be created. Click **OK** to continue.

I-DEAS Warning
! New Model File will be created
OK

3. Select the **Options** menu in the icon panel.

4. Select the **Units** option in the pull-down menu.

5. Set the unit to **Inch (pound f)** by selecting from the pop-up menu.

Applying the BORN Technique

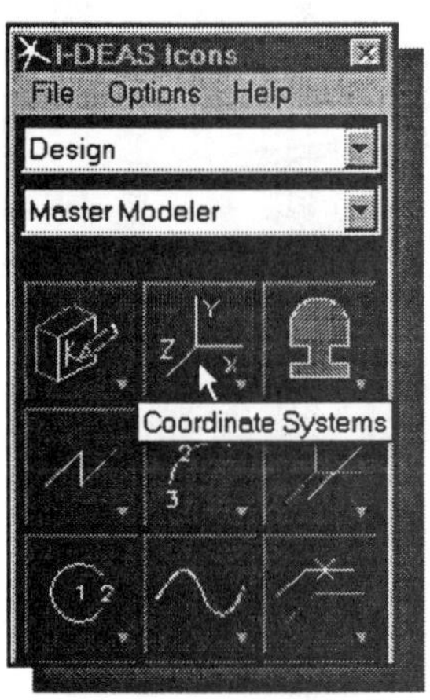

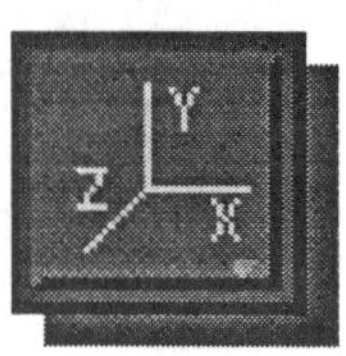

1. Choose **Coordinate Systems** in the icon panel. (The icon is located in the first row of the task icon panel.)

2. In the prompt window, the message "*Pick entity for coordinate system to reference*" is displayed. Select the **workplane** by left-clicking once on any of the edges.

3. In the prompt window, the message "*Select coordinate system component to define (Done)*" is displayed. Press the **ENTER** key or the **middle-mouse-button** to accept the default settings.

❖ By default, the user coordinate system is aligned to the world coordinate system.

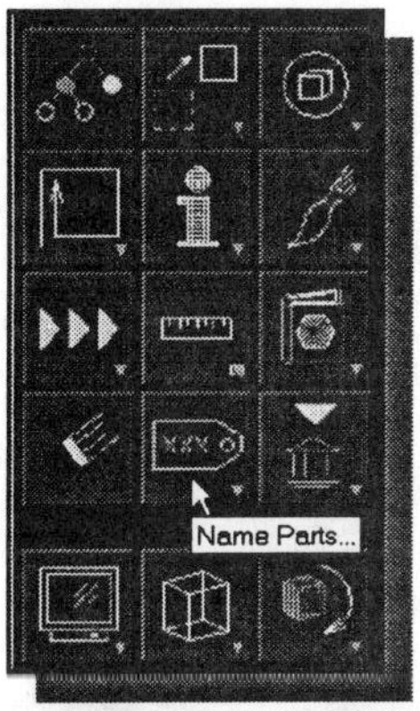

4. Choose **Name Parts...** in the icon panel. (The icon is located in the last row of the application specific icon panel.)

5. The message "*Pick part to name*" is displayed in the prompt window. Pick any edges of the coordinate system we just created. The *Name* window appears.

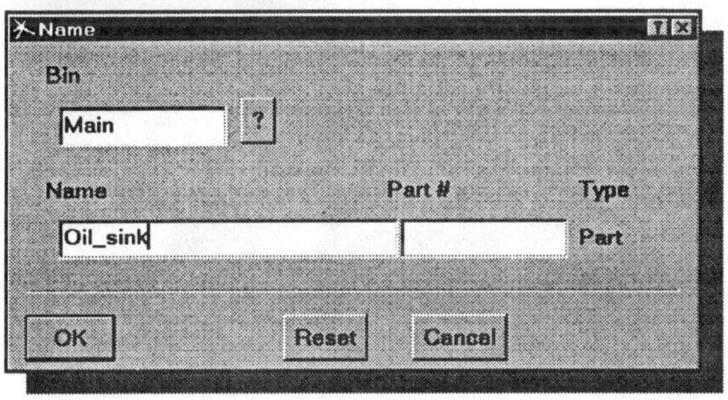

6. In the *Name* window, we can assign or change the name, number, and bin of a part. In the *Name* box, type in "**Oil_Sink**" as the part name

7. Click on the **OK** icon to proceed.

8. The message "*Pick part to name (Done)*" is displayed in the prompt window. Press the **ENTER** key or the **middle-mouse-button** to end the *Name Parts* command.

The Base Feature

1. Create a sketch on the XY-Plane of the part coordinate system, add and modify dimensions as shown. (Hint: Start with the *Sketch In Place* command, then use the *Rectangle* and the *2-D Fillets* commands.)

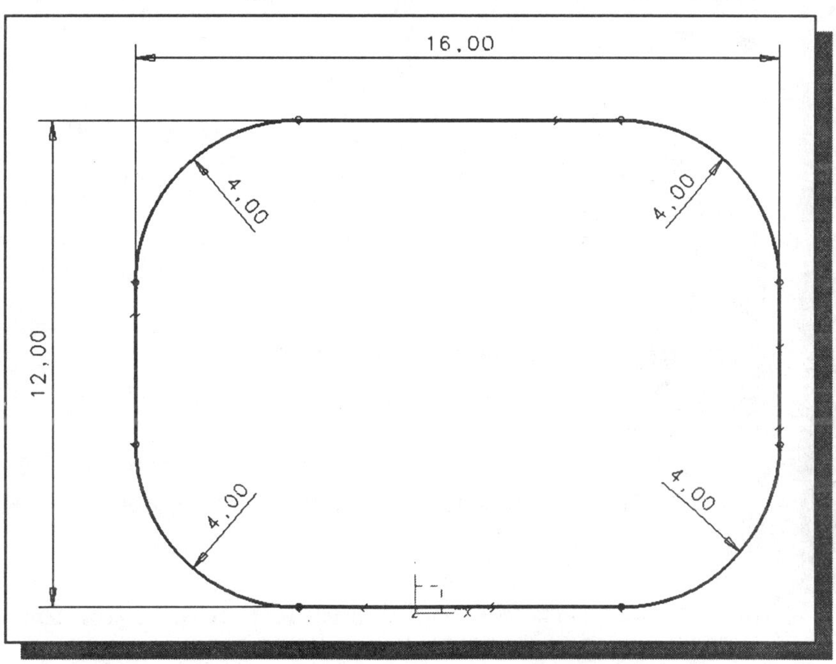

2. Choose **Extrude** in the icon panel. Use the *Protrude* option and create a solid feature that is **0.625** inches thick in the positive Z-direction.

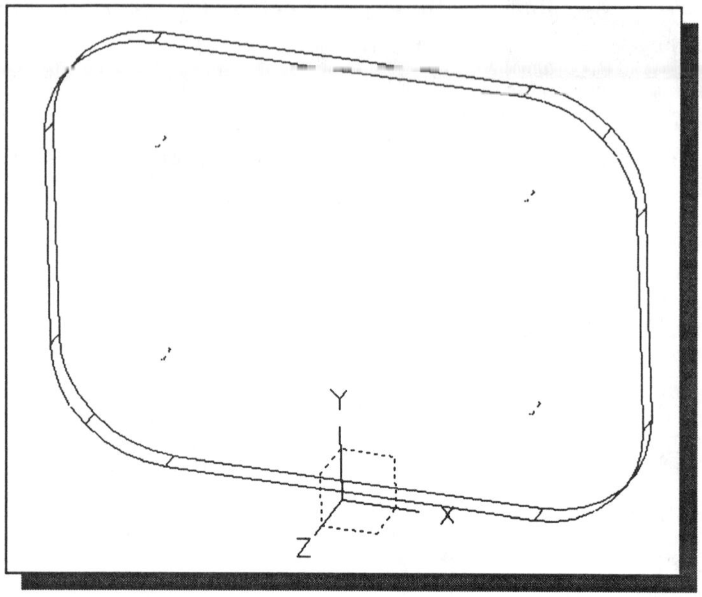

Create an OFFSET Feature

In I-DEAS, several options are available to create geometry from existing solid features. The *FOCUS* option demonstrated in previous chapters is one option available to assure the alignment of entities. We will now use the *Build Section* command to construct reference geometries from the existing surfaces.

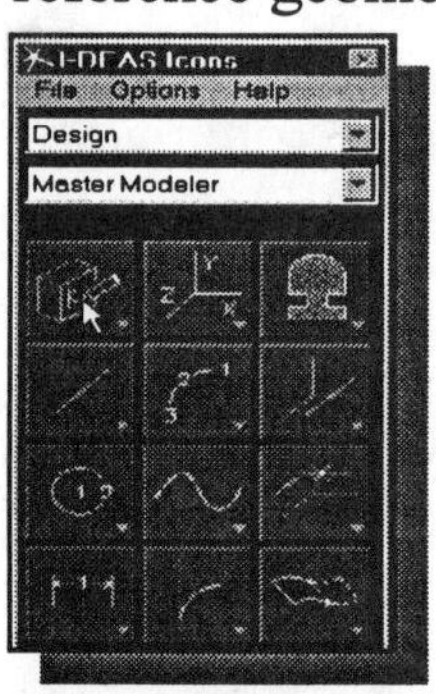

1. Choose **Sketch in Place** in the icon panel. In the prompt window, the message "*Pick plane or surface*" is displayed.

2. Select the front face of the 3-D model. (If necessary, switch to the Isometric display to help select the front surface.)

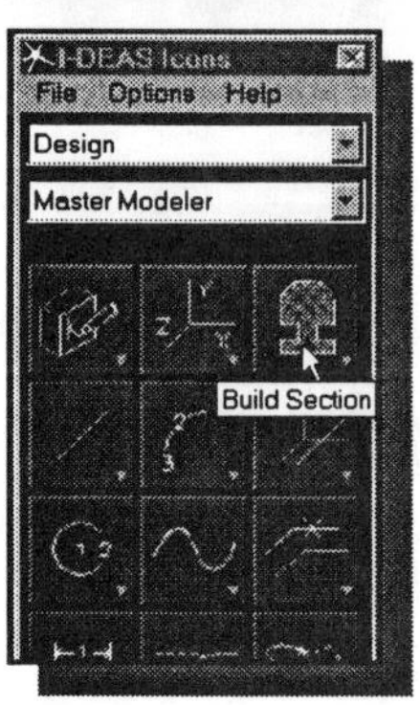

3. Select the **Build Section** icon. The message "*Pick curve or section*" is displayed in the prompt window.

4. Select any edge of the front face of the 3-D model. I-DEAS will automatically select all of the connecting geometry to form a closed region.

5. Press the **ENTER** key or the **middle-mouse-button** to end the *Build Section* command.

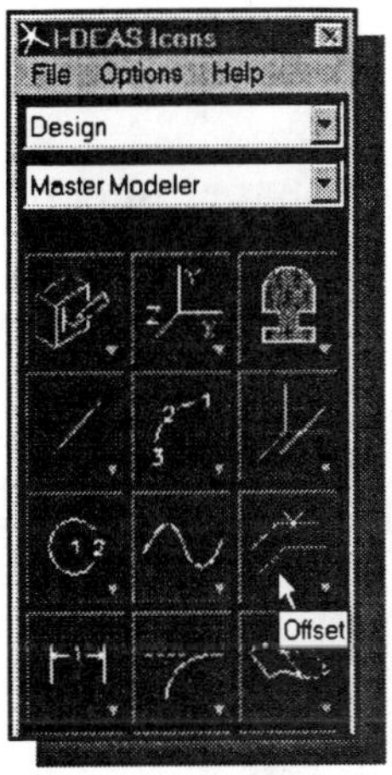

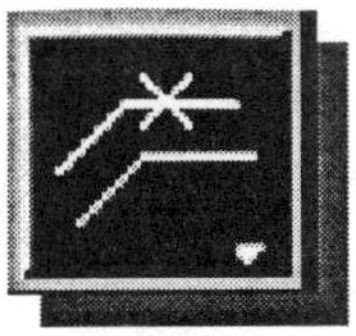

6. Choose **Offset** in the icon panel. The message "*Pick section or curve to offset*" is displayed in the prompt window.

7. Select the reference section we just created.

8. Press the **ENTER** key or the **middle-mouse-button** to accept the selection. The *Offset* window appears on the screen.

9. In the *Distance* input box, type in the offset distance of **2**.

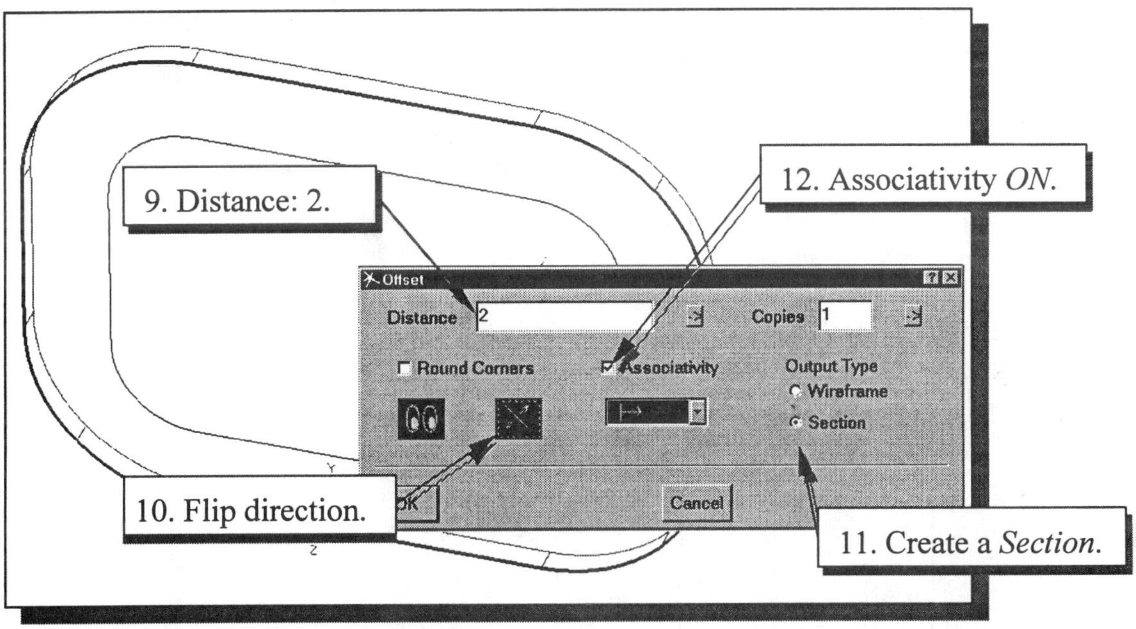

10. Click on the **Arrows** icon to change the offset direction to the inside of the model.

11. Click on the **Section** switch to create a new section as the offset geometry.

12. Confirm the ***Associativity*** switch is turned **ON** and **one** copy of geometry will be created.

13. Confirm the ***Round Corners*** switch is turned **OFF** and click on the **OK** icon to create the *Offset* geometry.

14. Press the **ENTER** key or the **middle-mouse-button** to end the *Offset* command.

Extrude using the Draft Angle Option

1. Choose the **Extrude** command. Select the last sketched shape. Accept the selection.

2. Enter an extrusion *Distance* of **4.0**.

3. In the *Extrude Section* window, switch **ON** the *Draft Angle* option and enter a draft angle of ***-15*** degrees.

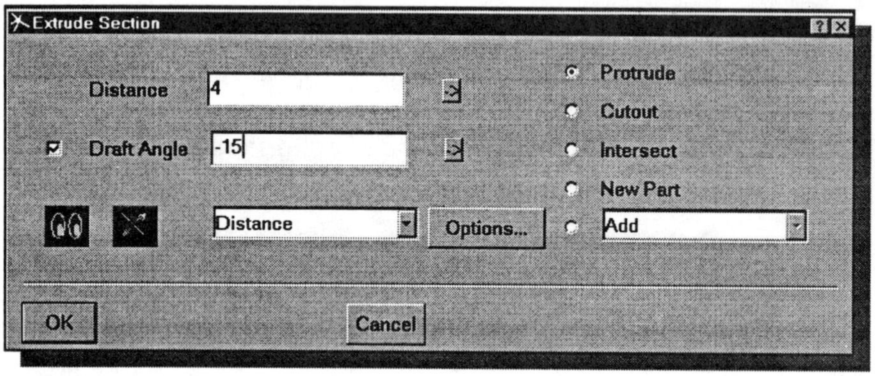

4. If necessary, click on the **Arrowheads** icon so that the extrusion is in the positive Z-direction.

5. Confirm the *Protrude* option is switched ***ON*** and click on the **OK** icon to create the protrusion.

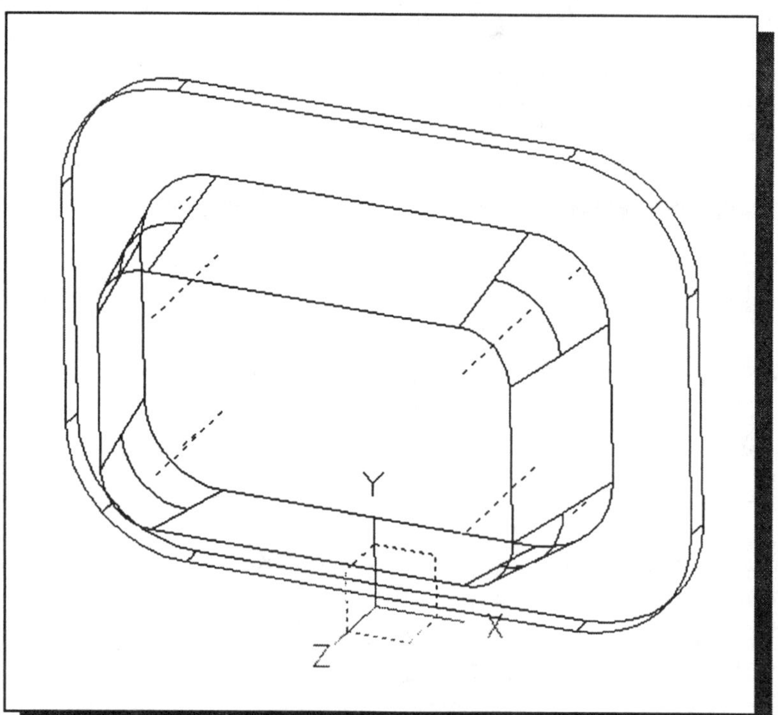

Extract Section

In I-DEAS, the *Extract Section* command allows us to extract surfaces or curves (both section and wireframe entities) from existing surfaces. No implied association exists between the extracted geometry and the original surfaces. This command is typically used to generate derived curves and surfaces from an existing part; the extracted 2D geometry can then be used to create new parts.

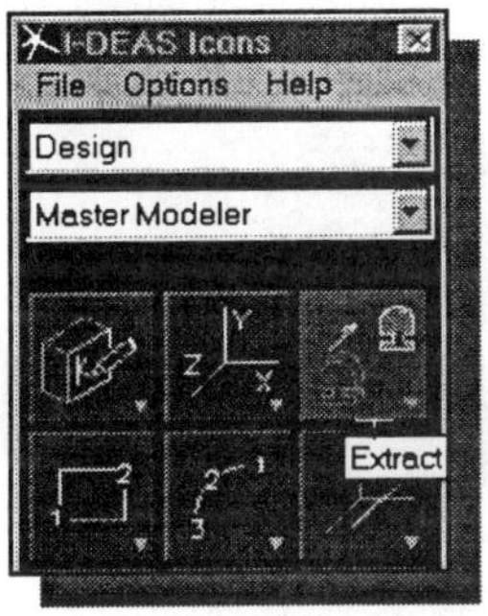

1. Choose **Extract** *section* in the icon panel. The icon is located in the first row of the task icon panel. (The icon is located in the same stack as the *Build Section* icon.)

2. In the prompt window, the message "*Pick entity to extract*" is displayed. Pick the front surface of the solid object as shown.

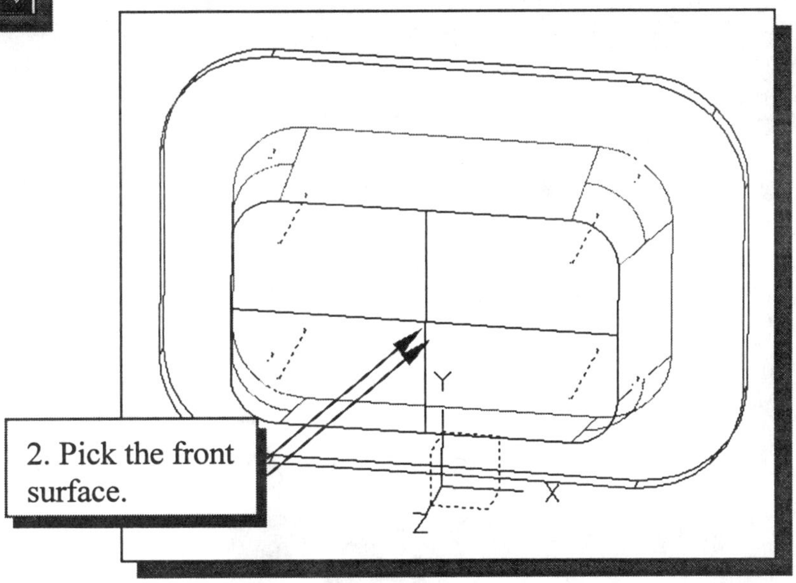

3. In the prompt window, the message "*Pick entity to extract (Done)*" is displayed. Press the **ENTER** key to accept the selection.

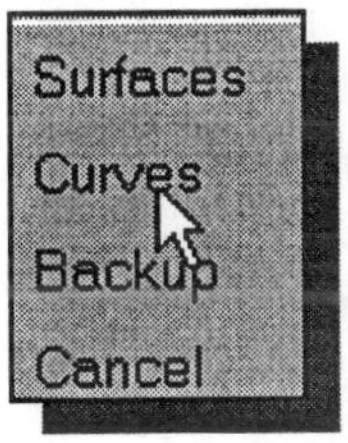

4. In the prompt window, the message "*Select extract option (Surfaces)*" is displayed. Pick **Curves** in the pop-up menu.

5. In the prompt window, the message "*OK to extract 8 curves (Yes)*" is displayed. Pick **Yes** in the pop-up menu.

❖ Note that, at this point, there exist three sets of geometry; all aligned at the front face of the solid object: (1) The front surface of the solid object; (2) The extracted 2-D section; and (3) The extracted 2-D wireframe.

Put Away the Solid Object

To simplify selection of the extracted geometry and avoid any mistakes on the solid object, we will first *PUT AWAY* the solid object and then edit the extracted geometry.

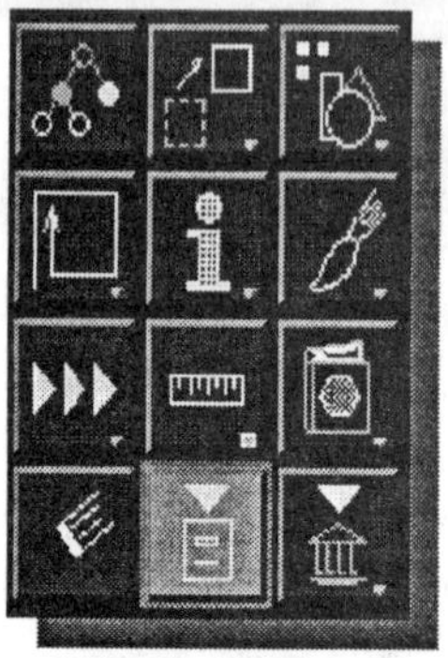

1. Choose **Put Away** in the icon panel. The icon is located in the fourth row of the application icon panel. (The icon is located in the same stack as the *Name Part* icon.)

2. In the prompt window, the message "*Pick part to put away*" is displayed. Pick any edge of the 3-D solid part. The part is now put into the *I-DEAS BIN* and disappears from the screen.

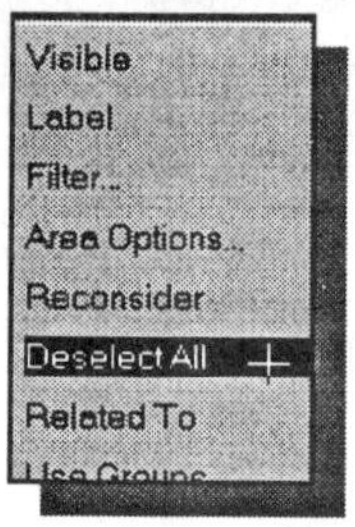

3. In the prompt window, the message "*Pick part to put away (Done)*" is displayed. Press the **ENTER** key or the **middle-mouse-button** to end the current command.

4. Inside the graphics window, press and hold down the **right-mouse-button** to display the *Option* menu and select **Deselect All** to release any pre-selected entities.

Modify the Extracted Geometry

1. Choose **Sketch in Place** in the icon panel. In the prompt window, the message "*Pick plane to sketch on*" is displayed.

2. Pick any edges of the extracted wireframe in the graphics window.

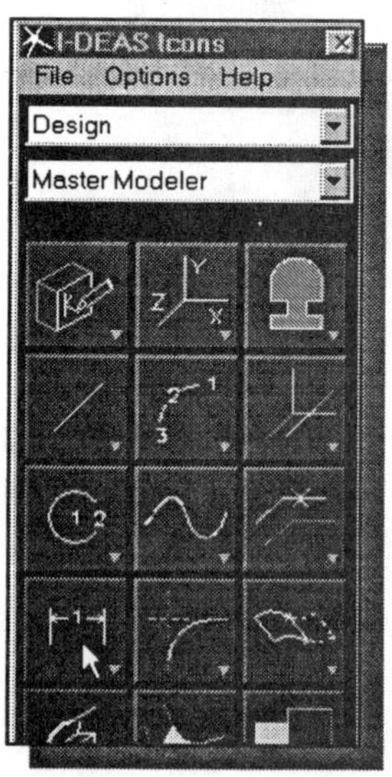

3. Press and hold down on the *Dimension* icon to display the other choices. Select the **Constrain & Dimension...** option.

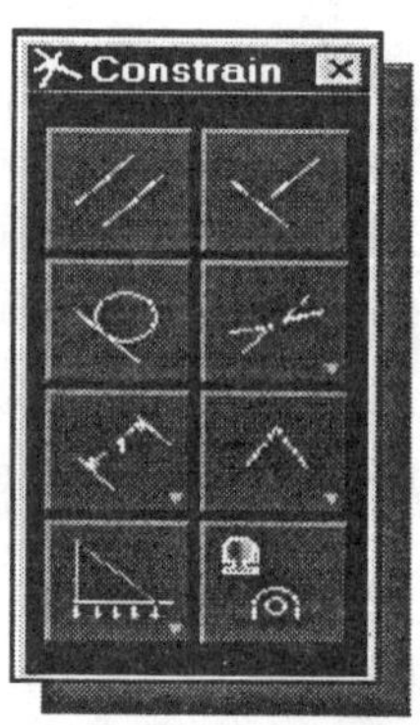

The *Constrain* window appears on the screen.

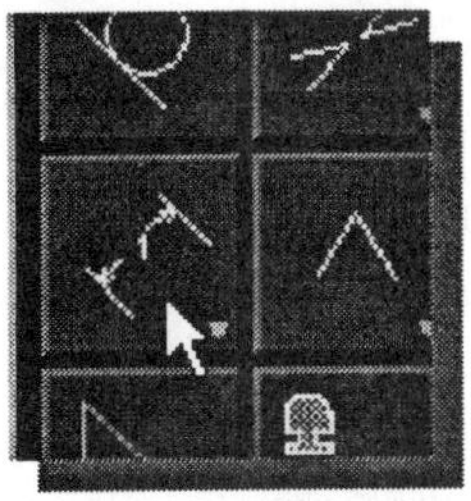

4. Choose **Linear dimension** in the *Constrain* window. The message "*Pick the first entity to dimension*" is displayed in the prompt window.

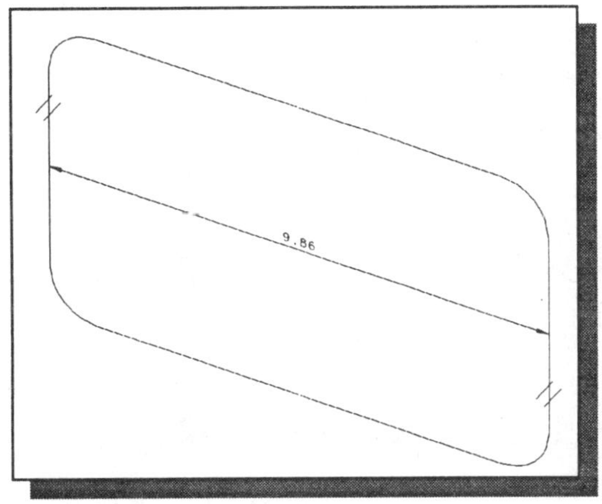

5. Pick the two vertical lines and create a horizontal dimension as shown in the figure.

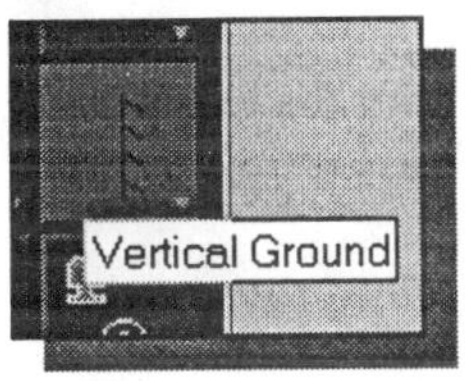

6. Choose **Vertical Ground** in the *Constrain* window. The message "*Pick a point or a curve*" is displayed in the prompt window.

7. Select the left vertical edge of the extracted geometry. Adding this constraint assures the modification of the width dimension behaves more predictably.

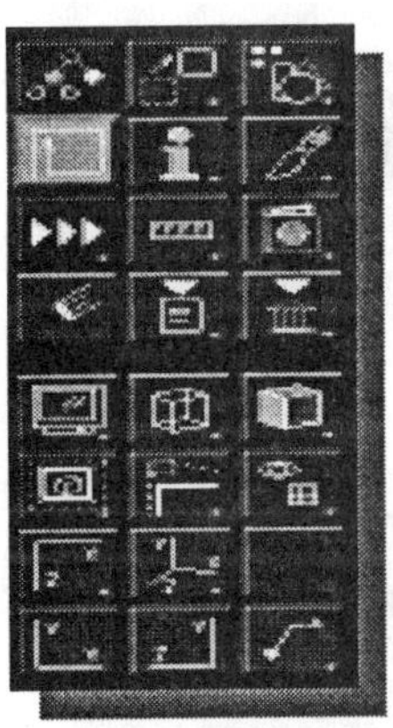

8. Choose **Modify** in the icon panel. (The icon is located in the second row of the application icon panel.)

9. The message "*Pick entity to modify*" is displayed in the prompt window. Pick the dimension we just created.

10. In the *Modify Dimension* window, click inside the value input box and add "**/2**" to the end of the displayed dimension value.

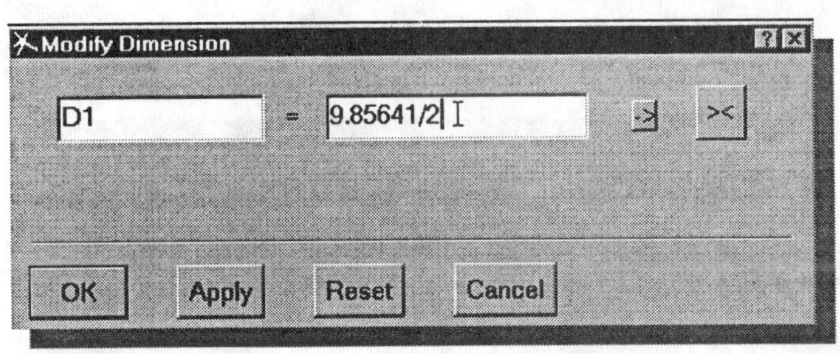

11. Click on the **OK** button to accept the settings and adjust the size of the geometry.

12. Press the **ENTER** key or the **middle-mouse-button** to end the *Modify* command.

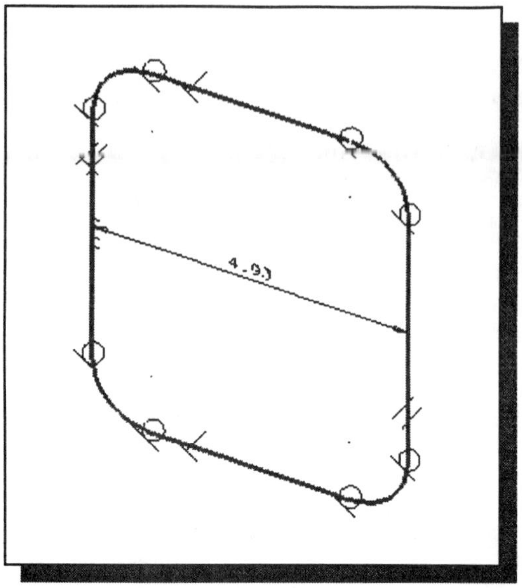

13. On your own, apply additional constraints to the extracted geometry as shown. Note that I-DEAS automatically switches to wireframe geometry as the constraints are applied. (Hint: Apply the *Tangent*, *Parallel* and *Perpendicular* constraints by selecting corresponding entities.)

❖ At this point, the extracted geometry is not associated with the solid model. Additional constraints can be applied after the section is attached to the solid part.

Retrieve the Solid Object from the BIN

We will next retrieve the *Oil_Sink* part from the BIN.

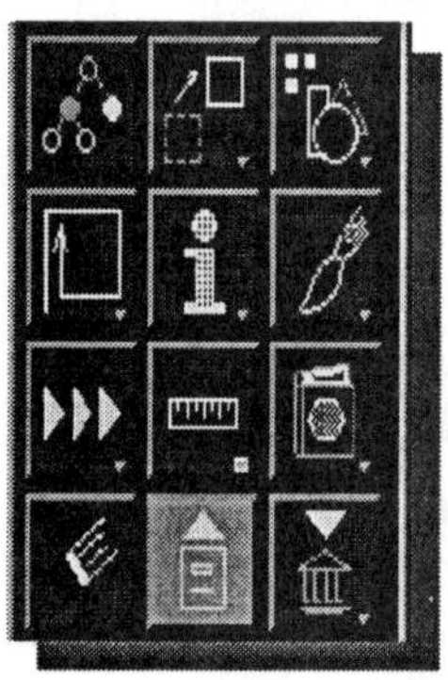

1. Choose **Get** in the icon panel. The icon is located in the fourth row of the application icon panel. (The icon is located in the same stack as the *Name Parts* icon.) The *Get* window appears.

2. Pick the **Oil_sink** part in the *Main Bin* part list.

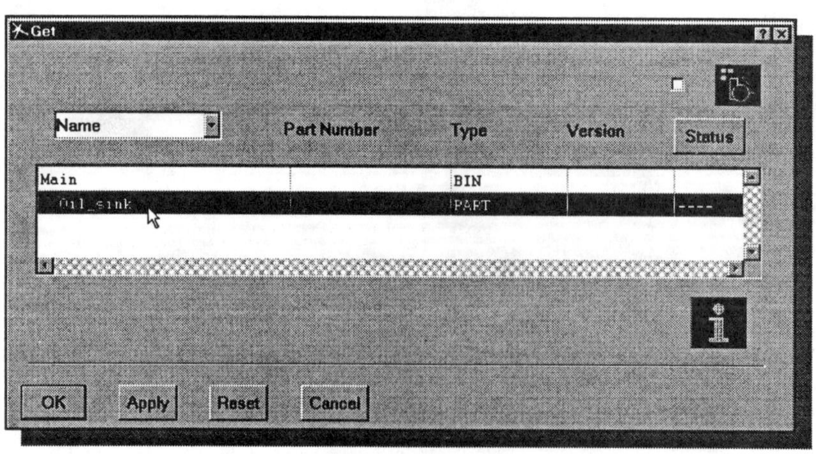

3. Click on the **OK** button to place the part back on the workbench.

Create the Next Extrusion

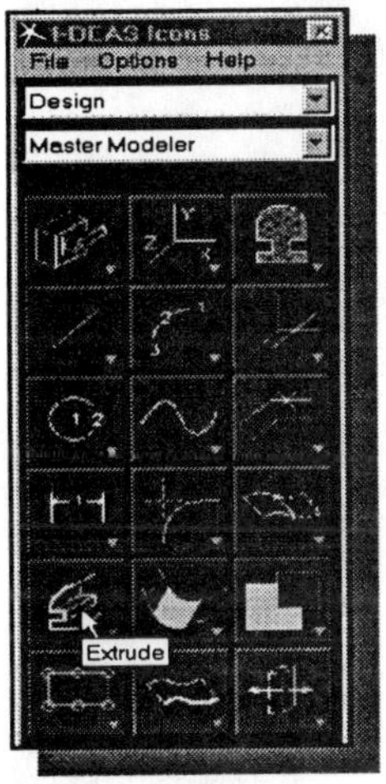

1. Choose **Extrude** in the icon panel.

2. Select any edge of the modified section.

3. Press the **ENTER** key or click the **middle-mouse-button** once to accept the selection.

4. In the *Extrude Section* window, enter **2** as the extrusion distance.

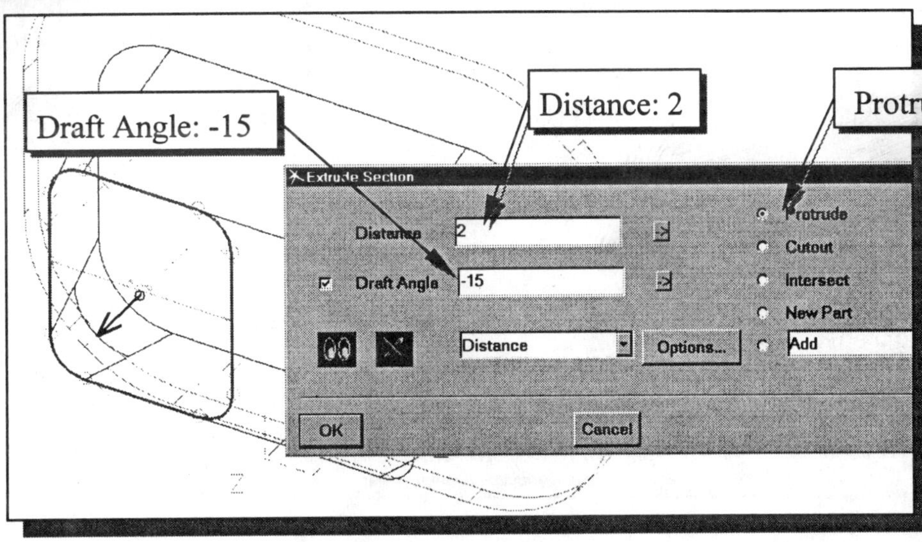

5. Set the *Draft Angle* to **-15** degrees.

6. Set the *Feature* option to **Protrude**.

7. Click on the **OK** icon to accept the settings.

8. The message "Pick the part to be protruded to" appears in the prompt window. Pick any edge of the original solid model to attach the protrusion.

❖ Now is a good time to save the model (Quick key: [Ctrl] + [S]).

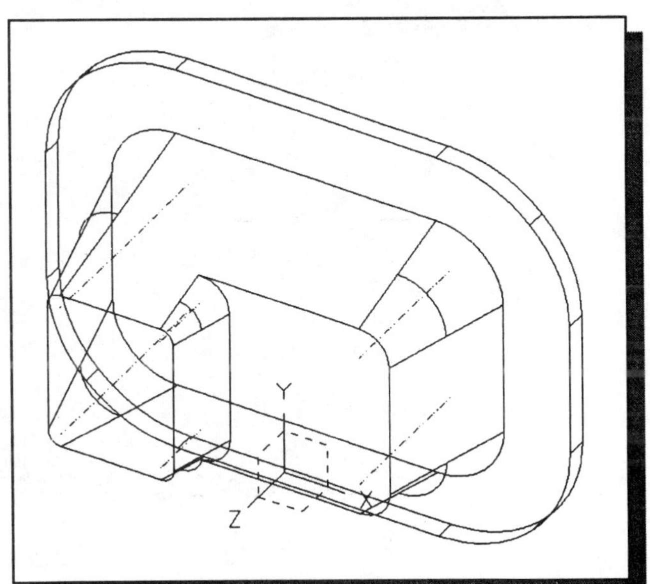

Creating 3-D Rounds and Fillets

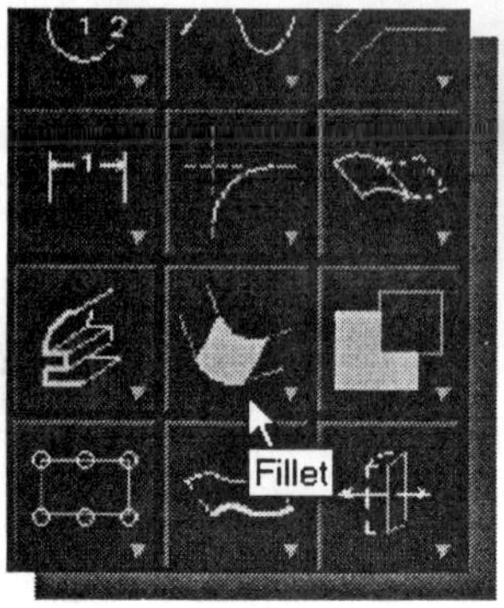

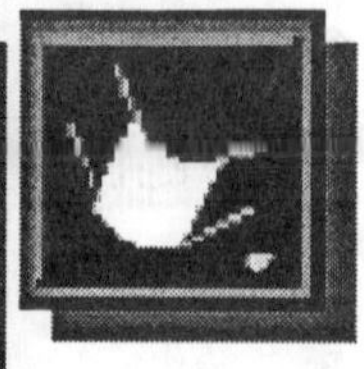

1. Select the **3-Dimensional Fillets** icon. (The icon is located in the fifth row of the task specific icon panel.) The message "*Pick edges, vertices or surface to fillet/round*" is displayed in the prompt window.

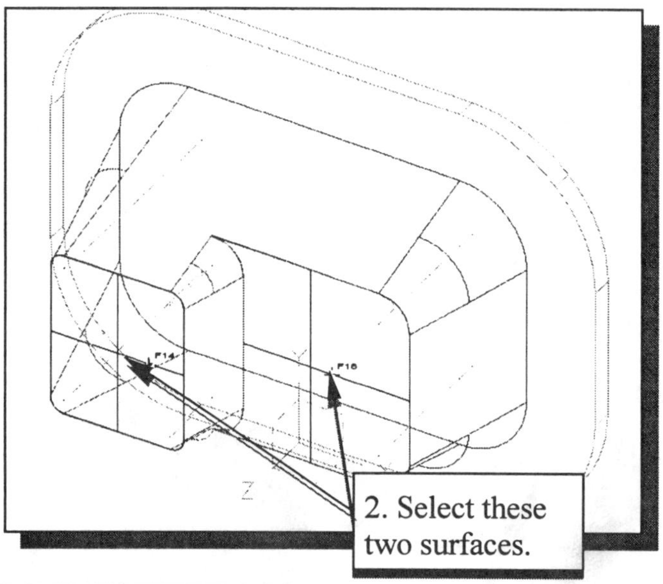

2. Pick the two vertical surfaces as shown. (Use the **SHIFT** key to select.)

3. Press the **ENTER** key or the **middle-mouse-button** to accept the selection.

4. In the prompt window, enter the value of **1.0** as the radius of the round. A preview of the new radius for the round is displayed.

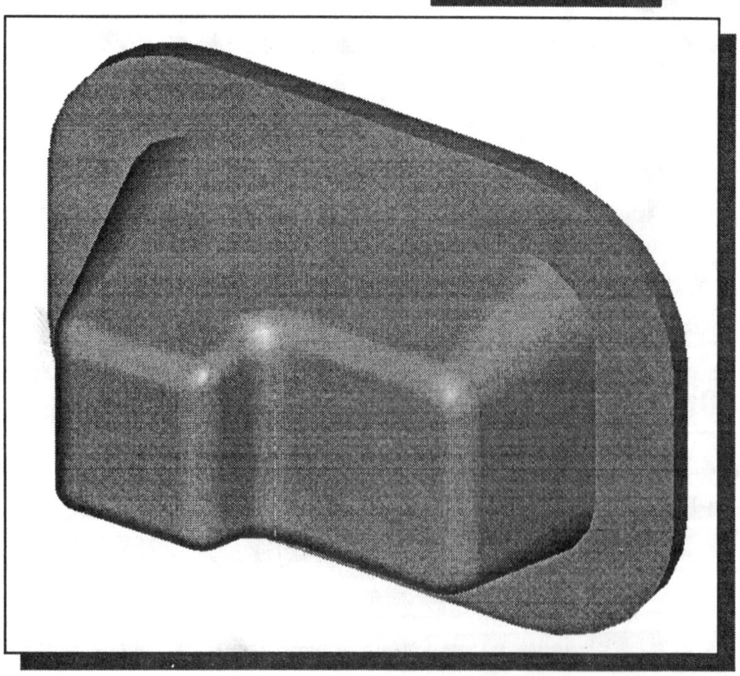

5. Press the **ENTER** key or the **middle-mouse-button** to create the rounded edges.

Creating 3-D Fillets - Edge Chain option

1. Select the **3-Dimensional Fillets** icon. (The icon is located in the fifth row of the task specific icon panel.)

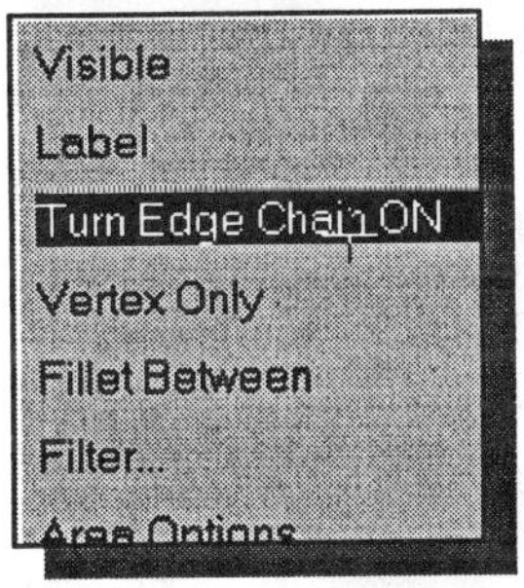

2. Move the cursor inside the graphics window. Press and hold down the right-mouse-button to display the option menu. Select the **Turn Edge Chain ON** option. (Do not select anything if you see *Edge Chaining OFF* in the list.) With this option, the system will automatically select neighboring edges of the selected object.

3. The message "*Pick edges, vertices or surface to fillet/round*" is displayed in the prompt window. Pick the edge as shown and notice the connected edges are also selected.

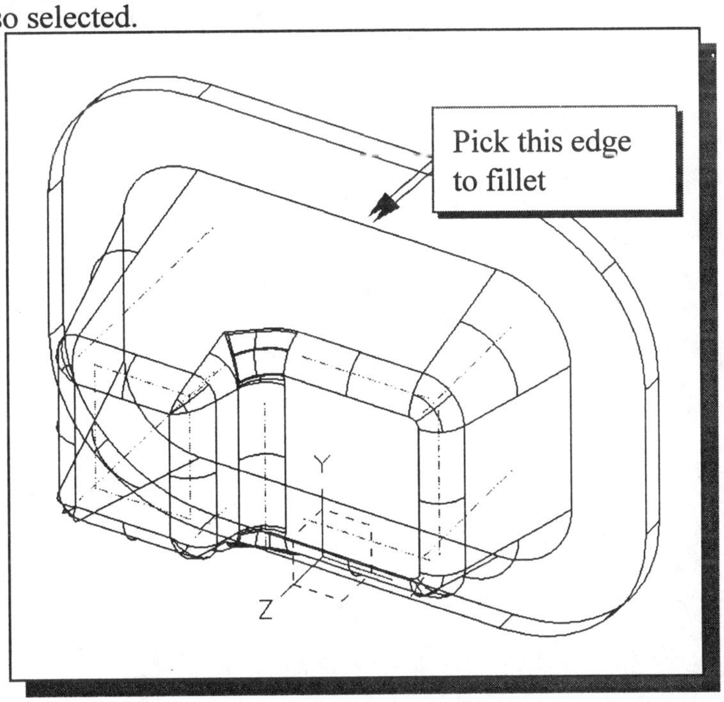

4. Press the **ENTER** key or the **middle-mouse-button** to accept the selection.

5. In the prompt window, enter the value of **0.50** for the radius of the round. A preview of the new radius for the round is displayed.

6. Press the **ENTER** key or the **middle-mouse-button** to create the rounded edges.

7. Press the **ENTER** key or the **middle-mouse-button** to end the *Fillet* command.

The Shell Feature

The *Shell* feature creates new faces by offsetting existing ones inside or outside of their original positions.

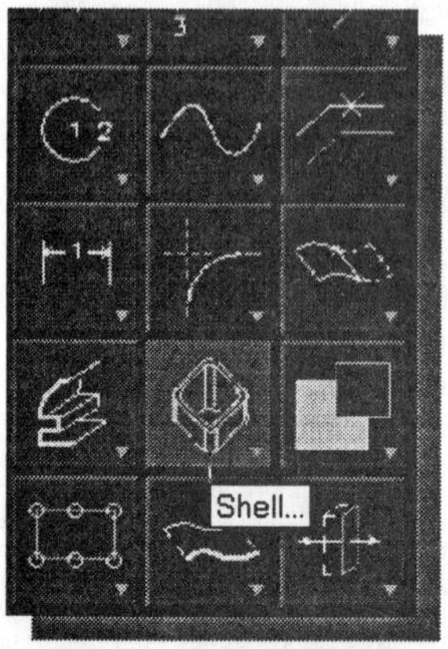

1. Choose **Shell** in the icon panel. (The icon is located in the fifth row of the task specific icon panel. The icon is located at the same icon stack as the *3-D Fillets* command.)

2. The message "*Pick part or volume to shell*" is displayed in the prompt window. Pick the front surface of the 3-D solid.

3. Press the **ENTER** key or the **middle-mouse-button** to continue. The *Shell* window appears.

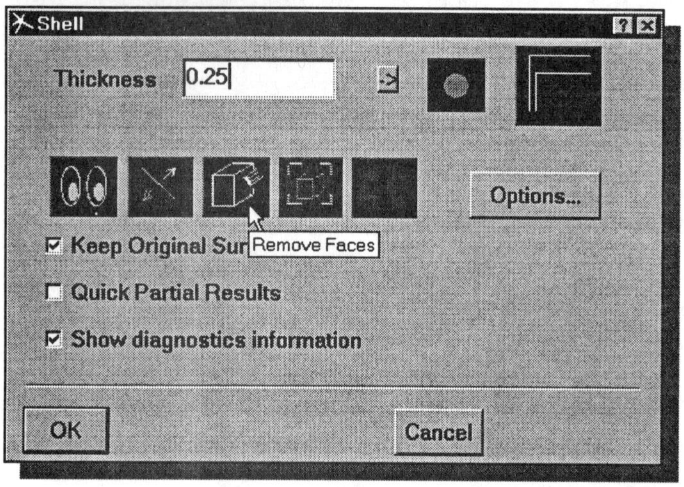

4. In the *Shell* window, set the thickness to **0.25.**

5. In the *Shell* window, click on the **Remove Faces** icon.

6. Dynamically rotate the 3-D model and pick the backside of the oil sink, the surface aligned to the world coordinate system. (I-DEAS will remove this surface before creating the shell feature.)

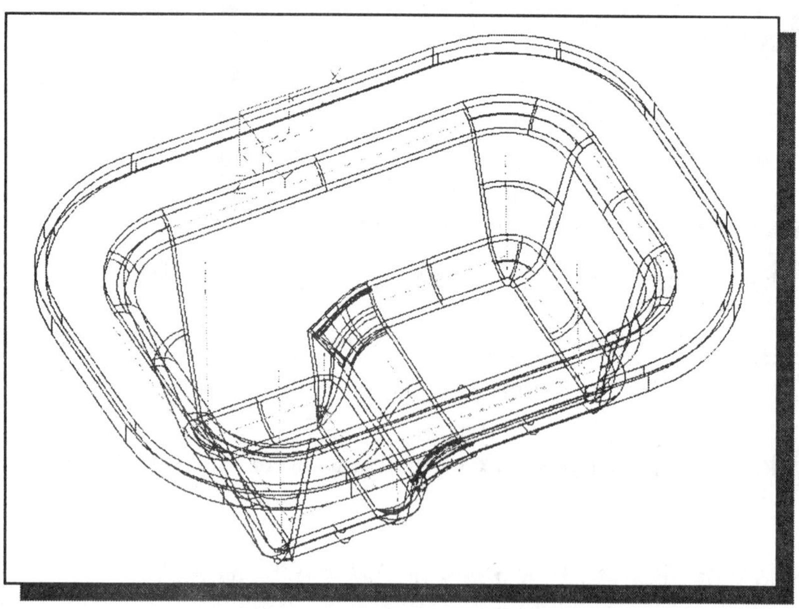

7. Press the **ENTER** key or the **middle-mouse-button** to continue. The *Shell* window reappears.

8. Click on the **OK** button to continue with the *Shell* command.

❖ Now is a good time to save the model (Quick key: [Ctrl] + [S]).

Changing the Color of the 3-D Model

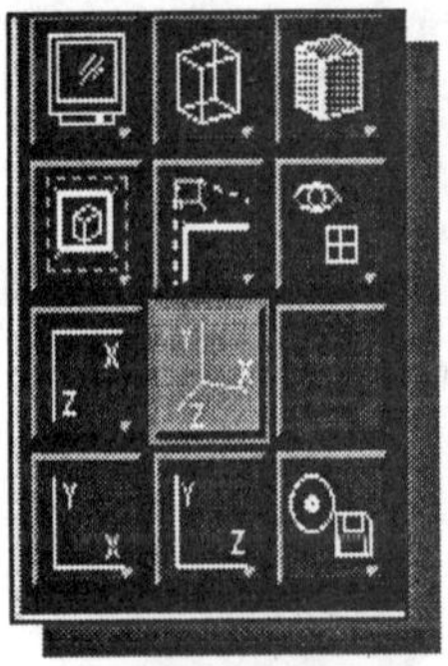

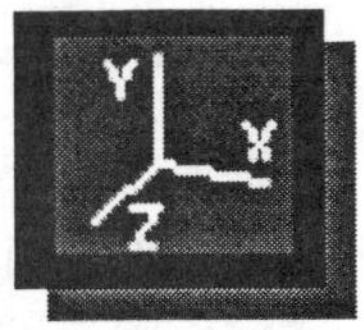

1. Choose **Isometric View** in the display viewing icon panel.

2. Choose **Zoom-All** in the display viewing icon panel.

3. Pick **Shaded Software** or **Shaded Hardware** to view the thin-walled model.

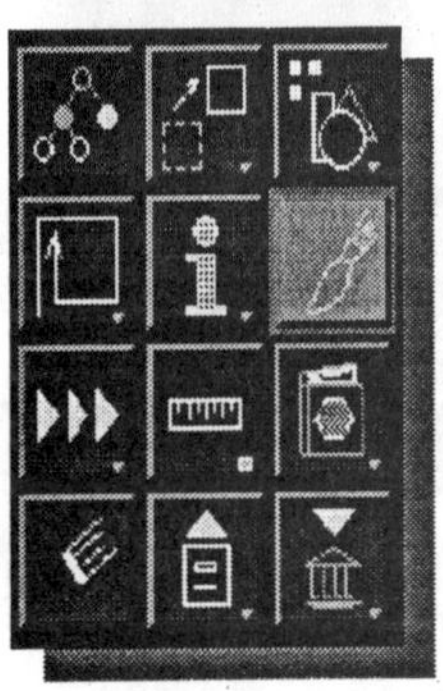

4. Choose **Appearance** in the icon panel. (The icon is located in the second row of the application specific icon panel.) The message "*Pick entity to modify*" is displayed in the prompt window.

5. Pick the entire model by clicking the same edge twice. A white box bounding the entire model appears.

6. Press the **ENTER** key or the **middle-mouse-button** to accept the selection.

7. In the *Surface Appearance* window, switch **ON** the *Color* option then click on the [?] button to display a color list. Set the color to **Golden_Orange**.

8. Click on the **OK** button to accept the settings and close the *Object Color* window.

9. Click on the **OK** button to close the *Surface Appearance* window and change the color of the 3-D model.

Creating a Rectangular Pattern

1. Choose **Sketch in Place** in the icon panel. In the prompt window, the message "*Pick plane to sketch on*" is displayed.

2. Pick the front surface of the base feature in the graphics window.

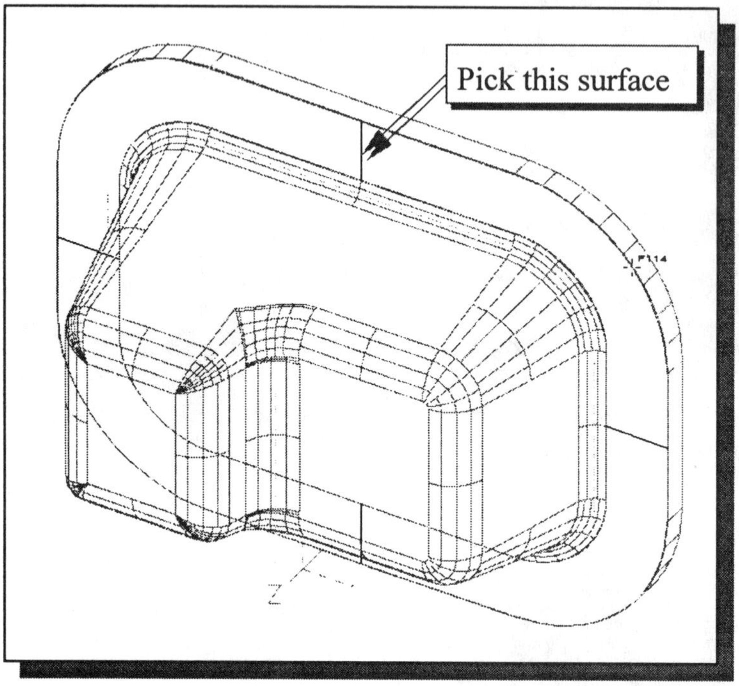

3. Choose *Circle* – **Center Edge** in the icon panel. The message "*Locate center*" is displayed in the prompt window.

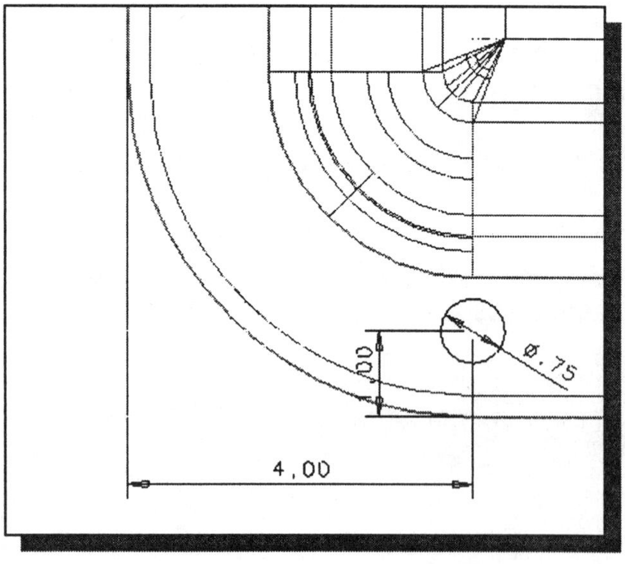

4. Create a circle with a diameter of **0.75** inch at 4.0 inches and 1.0 inch from the bottom and left edge of the base feature as shown.

5. On your own, use the **Extrude** command to create a cut feature through the base feature.

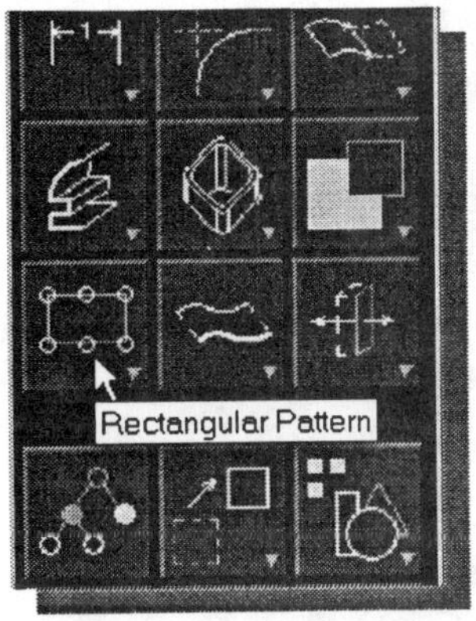

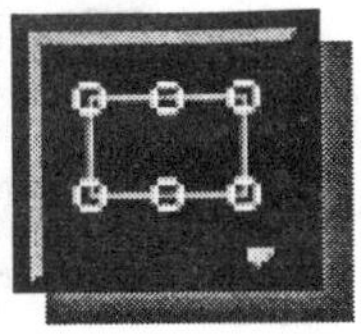

6. Choose **Rectangular Pattern** in the icon panel. (The icon is located in the last row of the task specific icon panel.)

7. Pick the circular hole we just created by clicking twice on the circular geometry. A yellow bounding box appears to indicate the cylinder is selected.

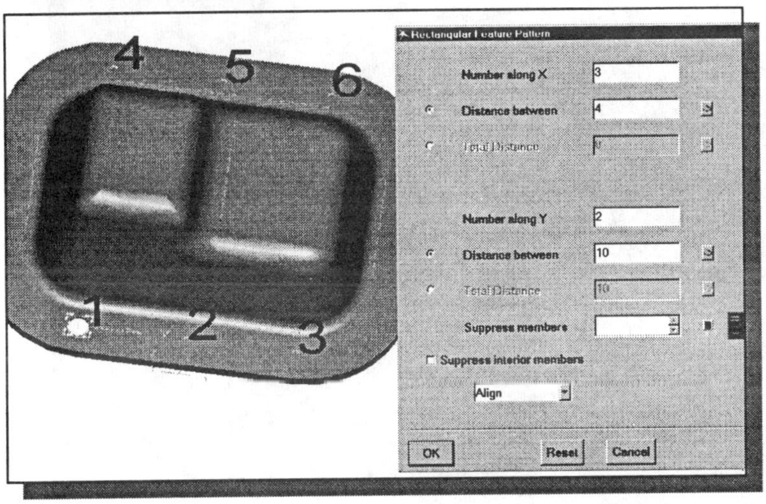

8. Pick the front face of the base feature as the patterning plane.

9. Inside the *Rectangular Feature Pattern* window, enter **3** as the *Number* of copies along the X-axis and **4** as the *Distance Between* the copies.

10. Enter **2** as the *Number along Y* and **10** as the *Distance Between* the pattern copies.

11. Click on the **OK** icon to create the pattern.

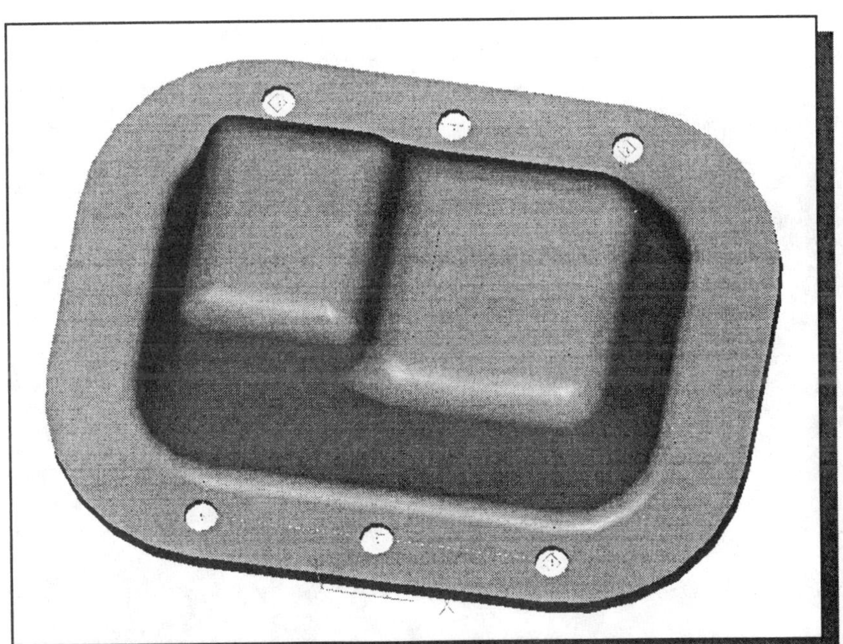

Creating Another Rectangular Pattern

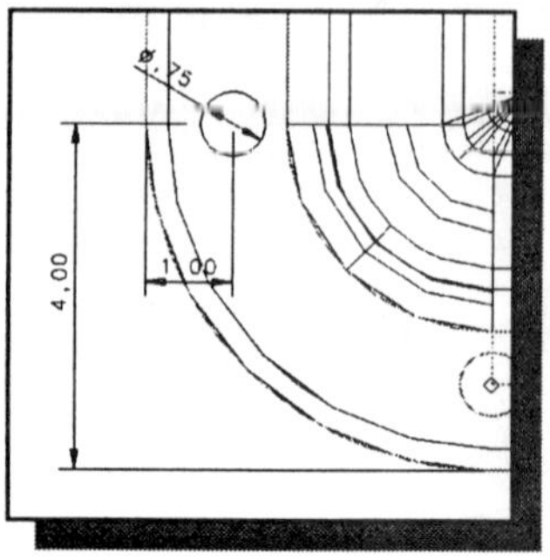

1. On your own, repeat the above steps and create a cut feature as shown (circular hole; diameter 0.75; located at 4.0 inches away from the bottom edge of the base feature and 1.0 inch away from the left edge of the base feature).

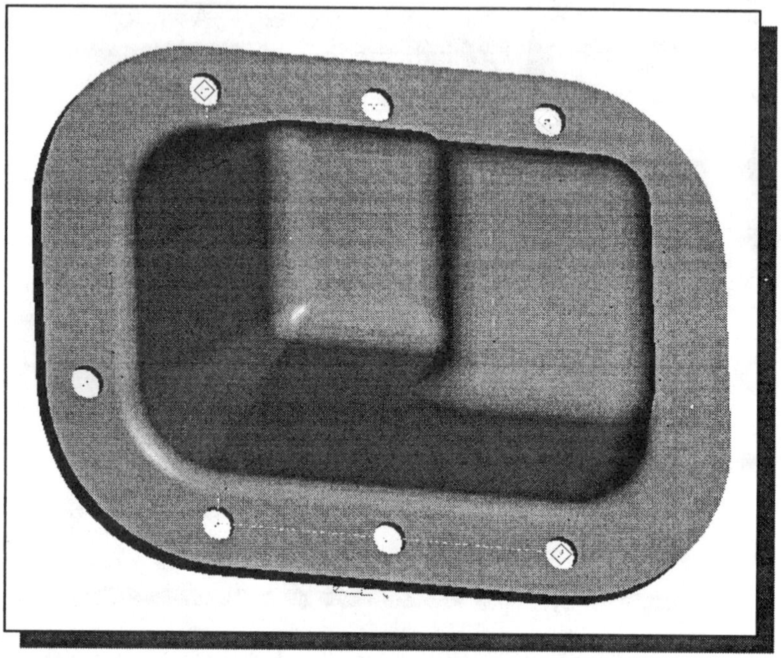

12. Create a rectangular pattern as shown. Enter **2** as the *Number along X* and **14** as the *Distance between* the pattern columns. Enter **2** as the *Number along Y* and **4** as the *Distance between* the pattern rows as shown in the below figure.

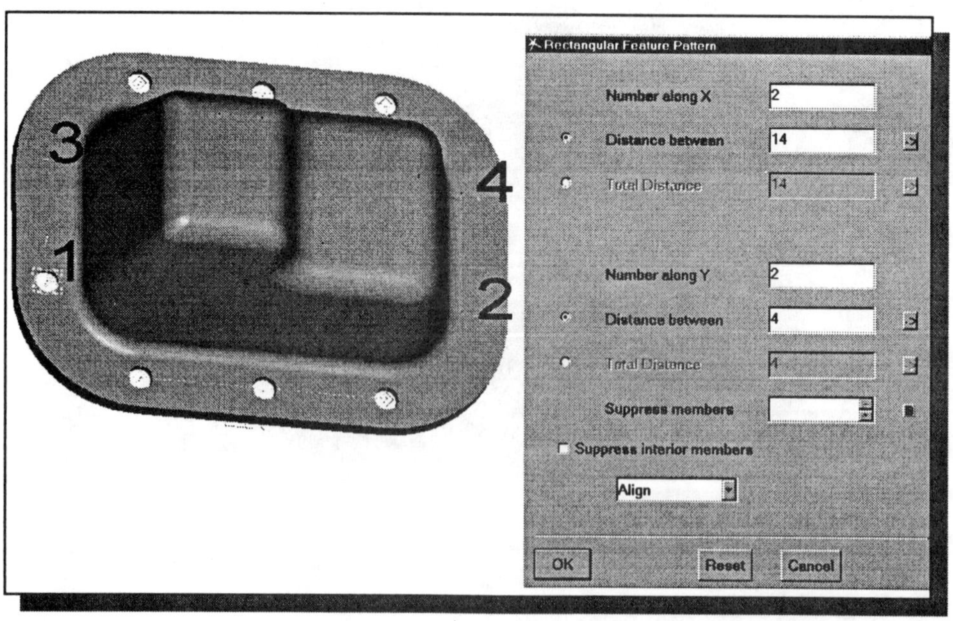

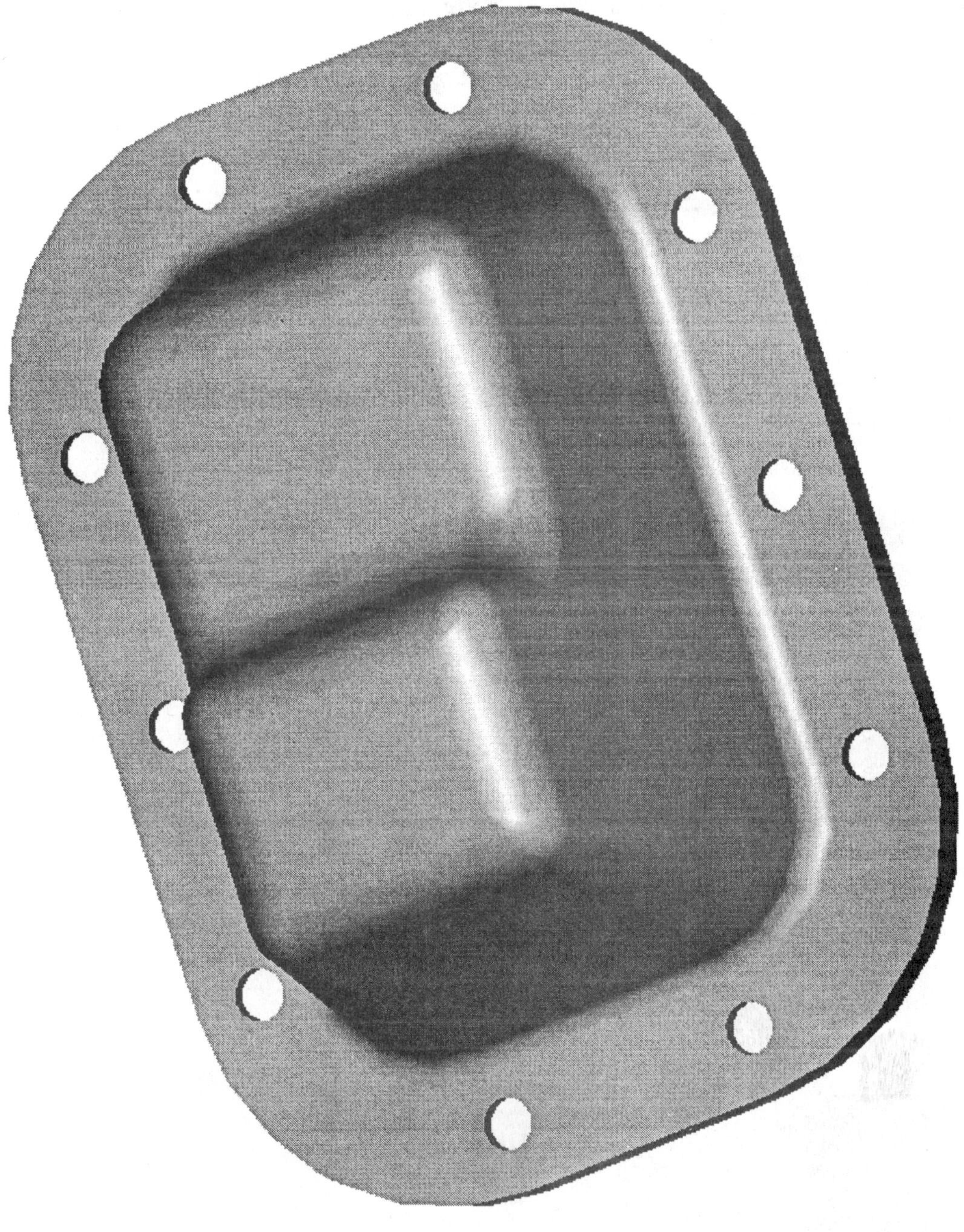

Questions:

1. Describe the method to create *Draft Angle* features.

2. Keeping the *History Tree* in mind, what is the difference between *Cut with a Pattern* and *Cut Each One Individually*?

3. What is the main advantage of using *Relations ON*?

4. What are the advantages and disadvantages of using *Edge Chaining ON* under the *Fillet* command?

5. How do we modify the pattern parameters after the model is built?

6. Identify the following commands:

(a)

(b)

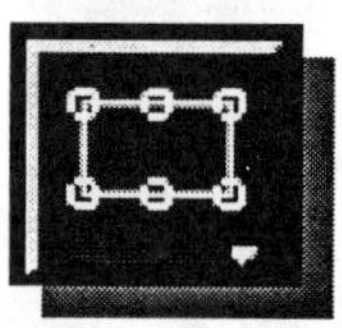

(c)

(d)

(e)

Exercise: (Wall-thickness: 0.125)

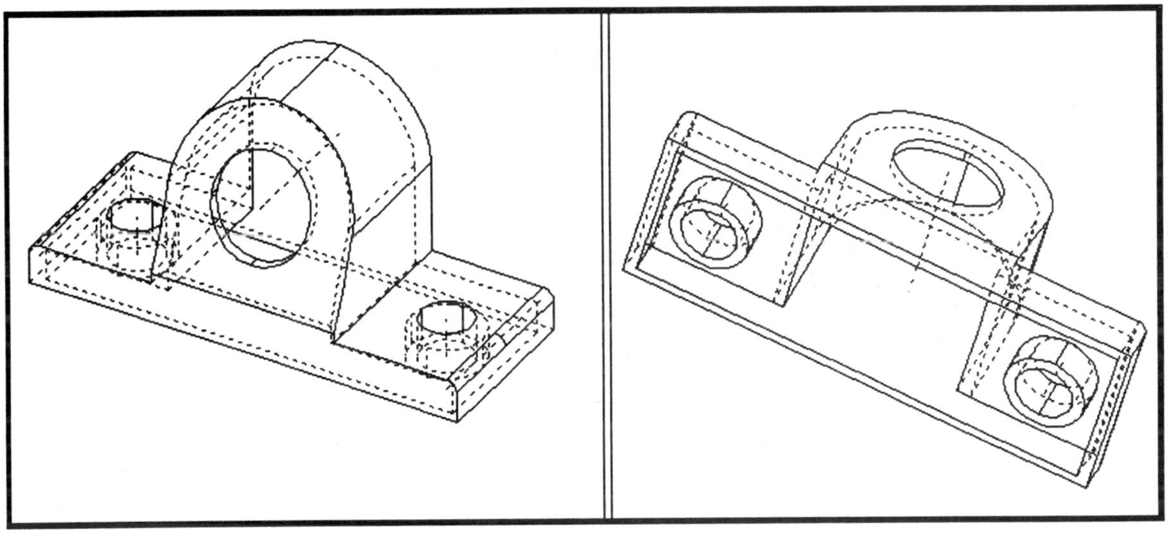

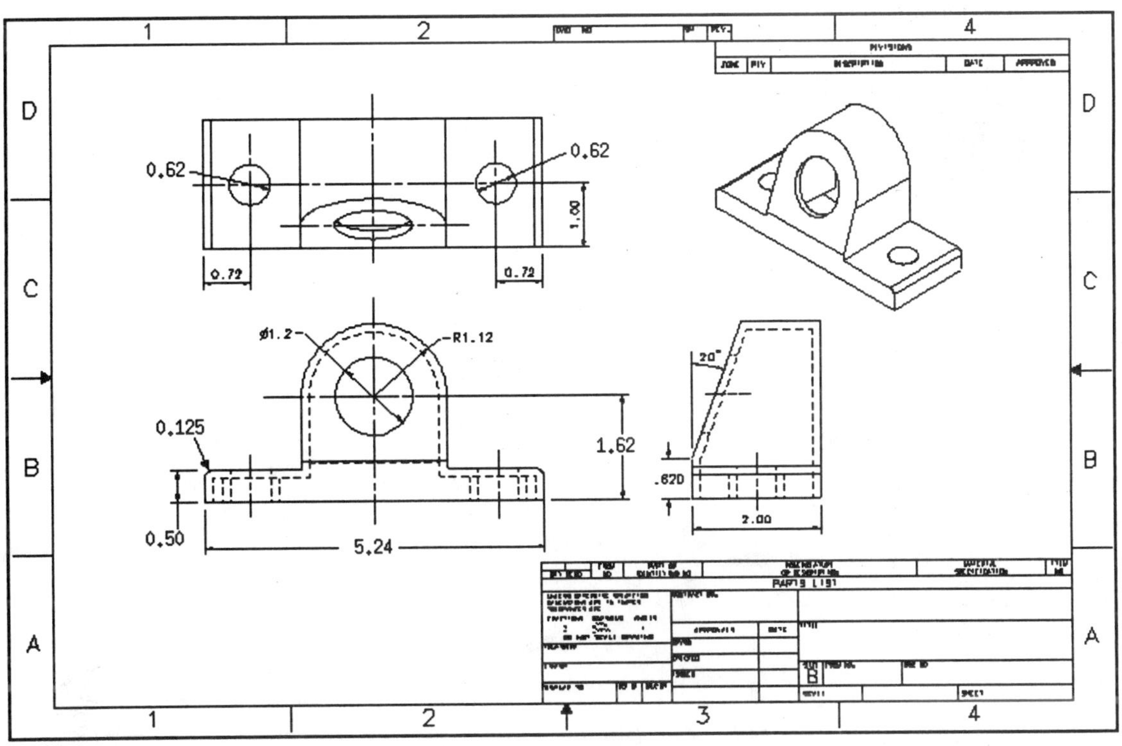

NOTES:

Chapter 11
Part Modeling - Finishing Touches

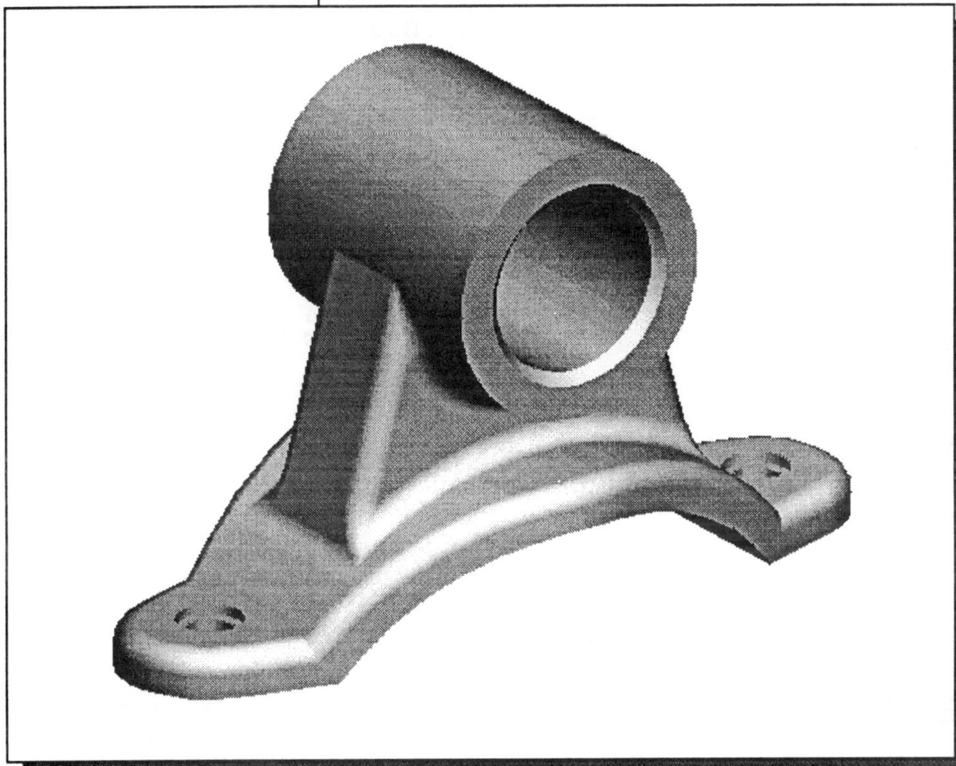

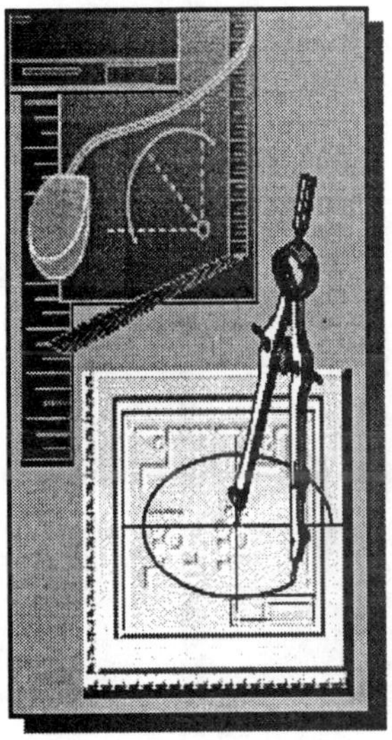

Learning Objectives

When you have completed this lesson, you will be able to:

- ♦ Apply the BORN techniqe.
- ♦ Use the CHAMFER command.
- ♦ Perform the Intersect - Boolean Operation.
- ♦ Understand the different aspects of Part Modeling.
- ♦ Review of Part Modeling Techniques.

Introduction

This chapter is intended to provide a summary of the construction techniques presented in the previous chapters. In this chapter, we will also illustrate variations of using the basic techniques introduced in the previous chapters. We will demonstrate, using the *BORN technique*, the *Intersect-Boolean Operation*, the *3-D Fillets* command, the *Chamfer* command, and other commands that you have already learned to create a design involving more complex geometry.

Summary of Modeling Considerations

- **Design Intent** – Determine the functionality of the design and select features that are central to the design.
- **Order of Features** – Consider the parent/child relationships necessary for all features.
- **Dimensional and Geometric Constraints** – The way in which the constraints are applied determines how the components are updated.
- **Relations** – Consider the orientation and parametric relationships required between features and in an assembly.

The BRACKET Design:

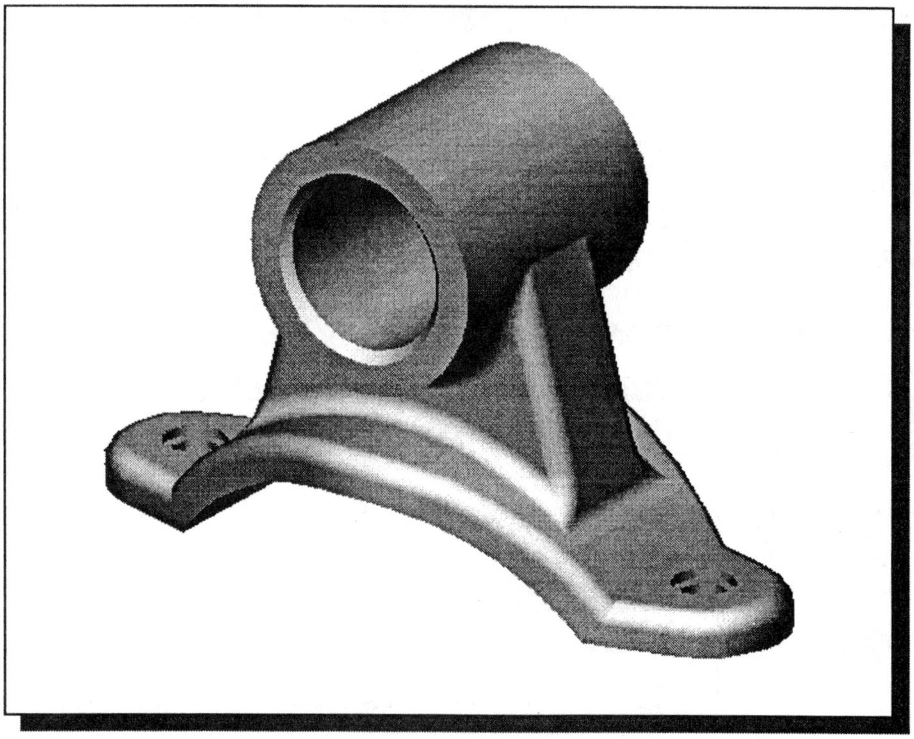

Modeling Strategy

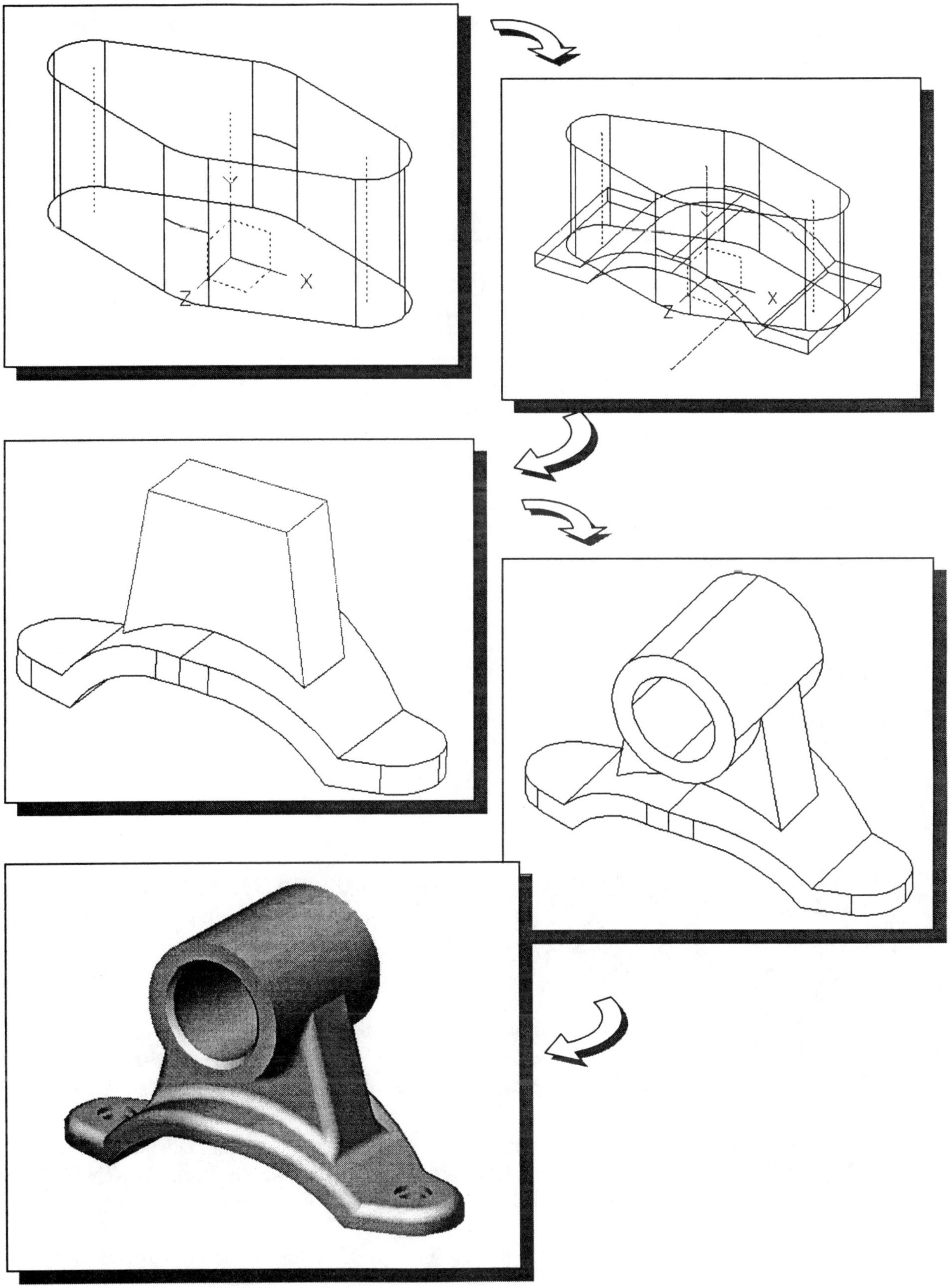

Starting I-DEAS

1. Login to the computer and bring up I-DEAS. Start a new model file by filling in the form items as shown below in the *I-DEAS Start* window:

Project Name: **(Your account Name)**
Model File Name: **Bracket**
Application: **Design**
Task: **Master Modeler**
OK

2. After you click on the **OK** button, a *warning window* will appear to tell you that a new model file will be created. Click **OK** to continue.

I-DEAS Warning
! New Model File will be created
OK

3. Select the **Options** menu in the icon panel.

4. Select the **Units** option in the pull-down menu.

5. Set the unit to **Inch (pound f)** by selecting from the pop-up menu.

Applying the BORN Technique

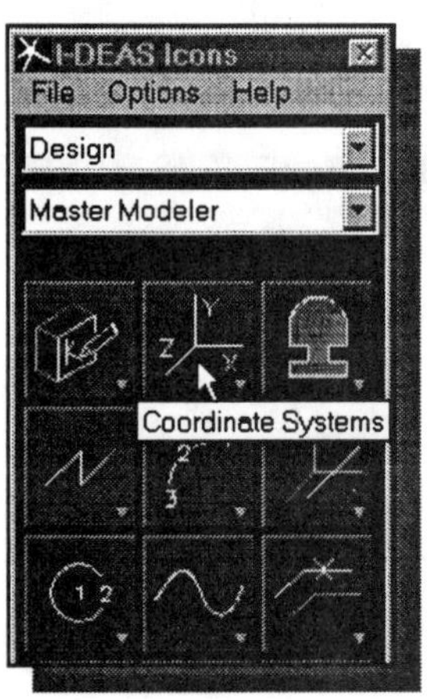

1. Choose **Coordinate Systems** in the icon panel. (The icon is located in the first row of the task icon panel.)

2. In the prompt window, the message "*Pick entity for coordinate system to reference*" is displayed. Select the **workplane** by left-clicking once on any of the edges.

3. In the prompt window, the message "*Select coordinate system component to define (Done)*" is displayed. Press the **ENTER** key or the **middle-mouse-button** to accept the default settings.

❖ By default, the user coordinate system is aligned to the world coordinate system.

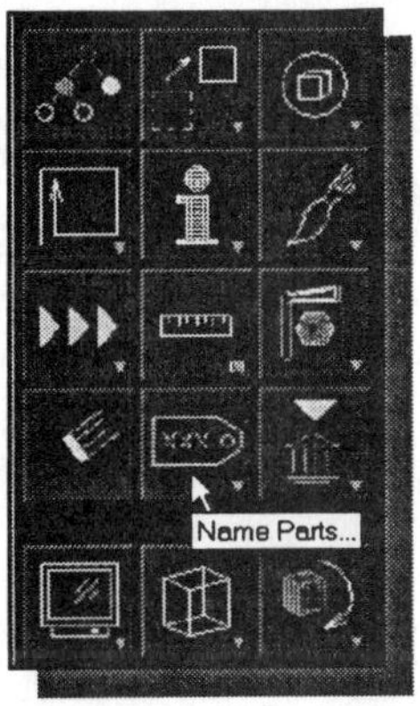

4. Choose **Name Parts...** in the icon panel. (The icon is located in the last row of the application specific icon panel.)

5. The message "*Pick part to name*" is displayed in the prompt window. Pick any edge of the coordinate system we just created. The *Name* window appears.

6. In the *Name* window, we can assign or change the name, number, and bin of a part. In the *Name* box, type in "**Bracket**" as the part name

7. Click on the **OK** icon to proceed.

8. The message "*Pick part to name (Done)*" is displayed in the prompt window. Press the **ENTER** key or the **middle-mouse-button** to end the *Name Parts* command.

Creating the Base Feature

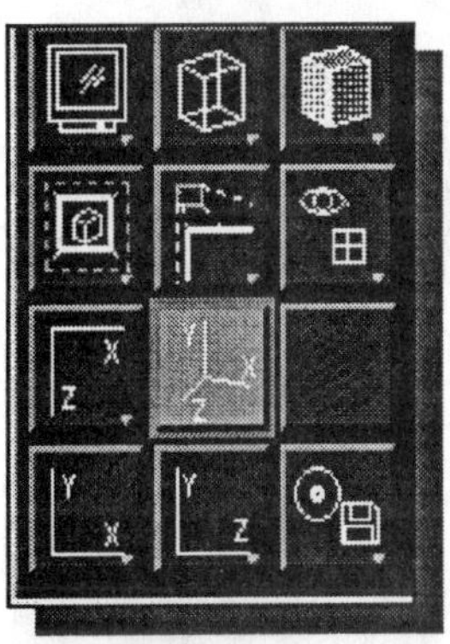

1. Choose **Isometric View** in the display viewing icon panel.

2. Choose **Zoom-All** in the display viewing icon panel.

3. Choose **Sketch in Place** in the icon panel. In the prompt window, the message "*Pick plane to sketch on*" is displayed.

4. Pick one of the edges of the **XZ plane** of the coordinate system. Note that the workplane is aligned with the *XZ-plane* of the coordinate system. Selecting the *XZ-plane* assures the sketch is attached to base node, the established part.

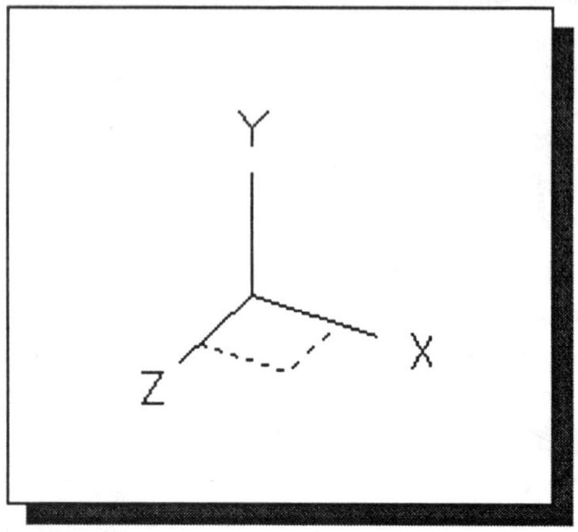

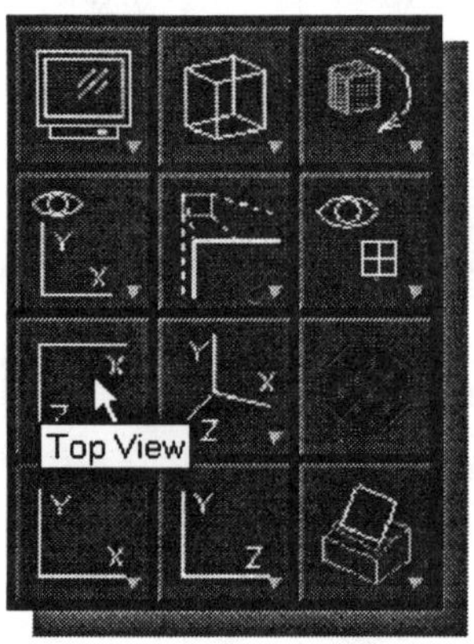

5. Choose **Top View** in the display icon panel.

6. Create the sketch as shown. Align the center of the 2-inch circle to the origin. (Hints: 1. Use dimensional constraints to control the alignment of the three circles. 2. *Zoom-In* to assure the proper *Tangent* constraints; if necessary apply the constraints manually.)

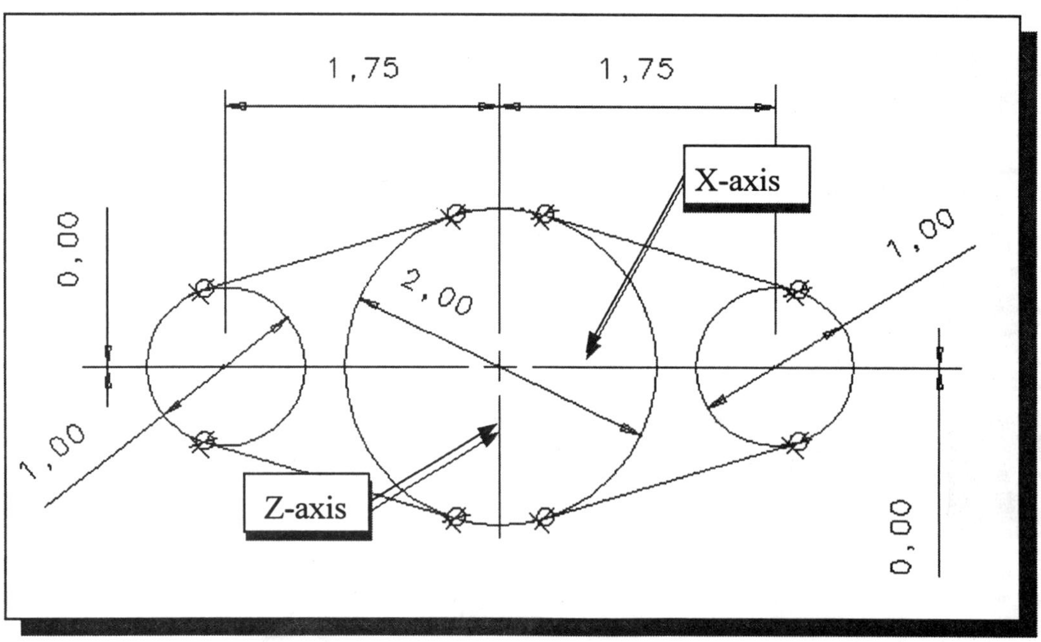

7. Use the **Build Section** command to create the section as shown below.

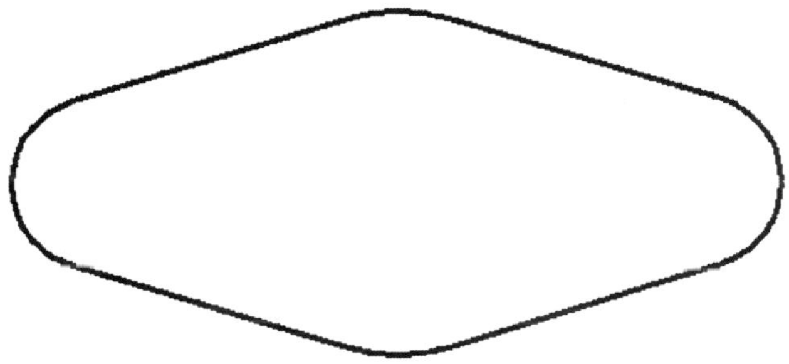

8. Choose **Extrude** in the icon panel. Extrude the section 2 inches in the positive Y-direction to create a protrusion.

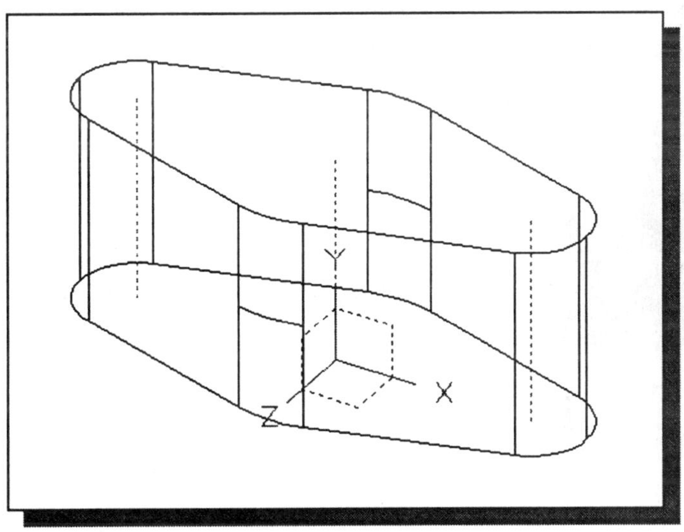

Creating the Second feature

To complete the base of the solid model, we will perform a *Boolean- Intersect* operation by using the cutout command. Currently, the workplane is reset to the world coordinate system. We will create the sketch of this second feature on the XY plane.

1. Choose **Sketch in Place** in the icon panel.

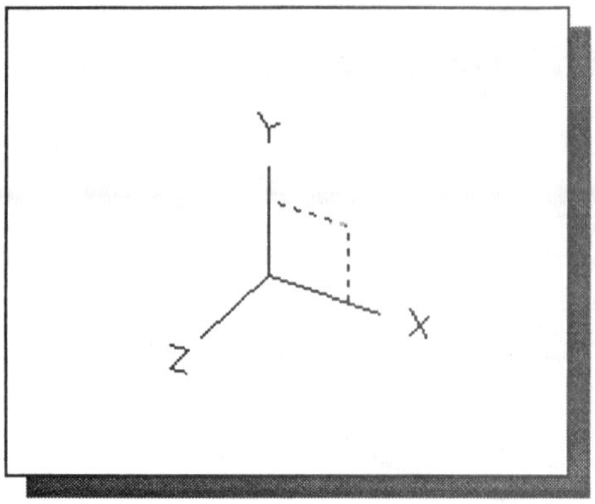

2. In the prompt window, the message "*Pick plane to sketch on*" is displayed. Pick one of the edges of the **XY plane** of the coordinate system.

3. Choose **Rectangle by 2 Corners** in the icon panel.

4. The message "*Locate first corner*" is displayed in the prompt window. Create a rectangle of arbitrary size near the center of the screen. (Do not be overly concerned with the actual size of the rectangle.)

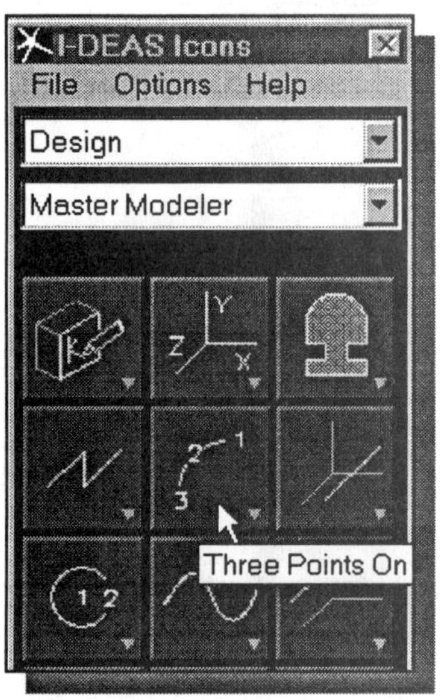

5. Choose *Arc* – **Three Points On** in the icon panel.

6. Create an arc with the endpoints on the top-edge of the rectangle as shown in the below figure.

7. On your own, add/modify the dimensions as shown below.

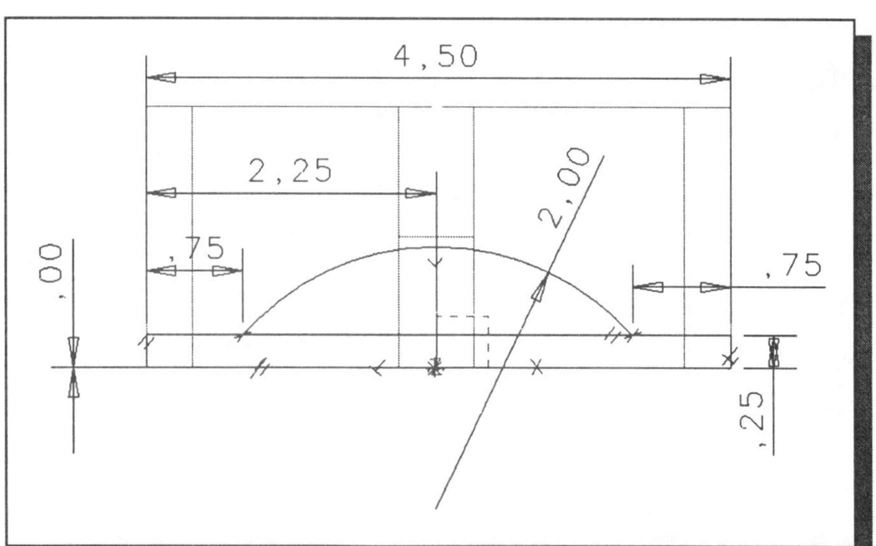

8. Choose *Circle* – **Center Edge** in the icon panel.

9. Create a **3.50-inch circle** in which the center coincides with the center of the arc as shown.

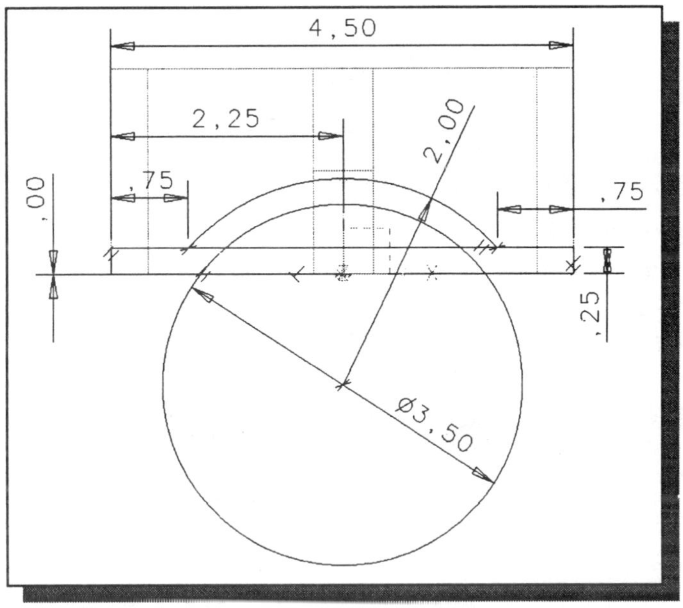

10. Choose **Rectangle by 2 Corners** in the icon panel.

11. The message "*Locate first corner*" is displayed in the prompt window. Create a rectangle and modify the size and location dimensions as shown.

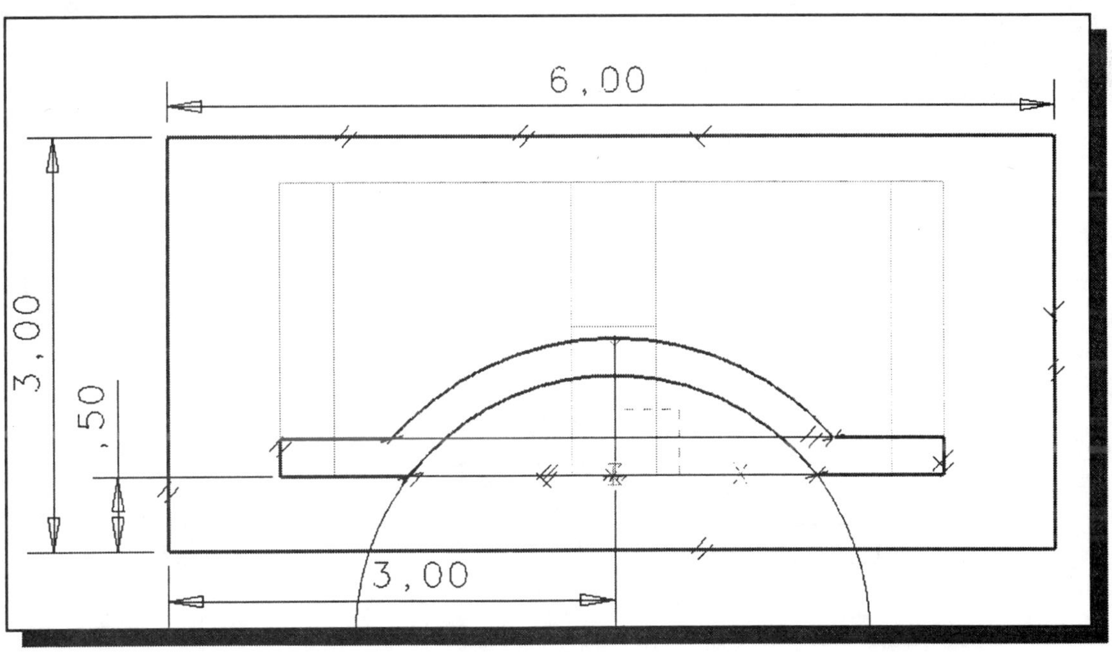

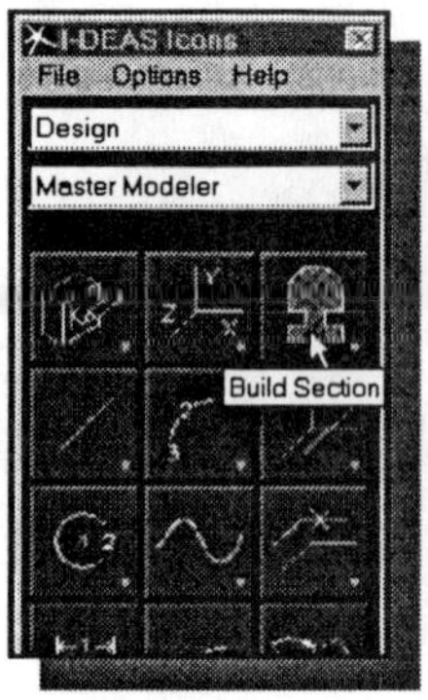

12. Select the **Build Section** icon. The message "*Pick curve or section*" is displayed in the prompt window.

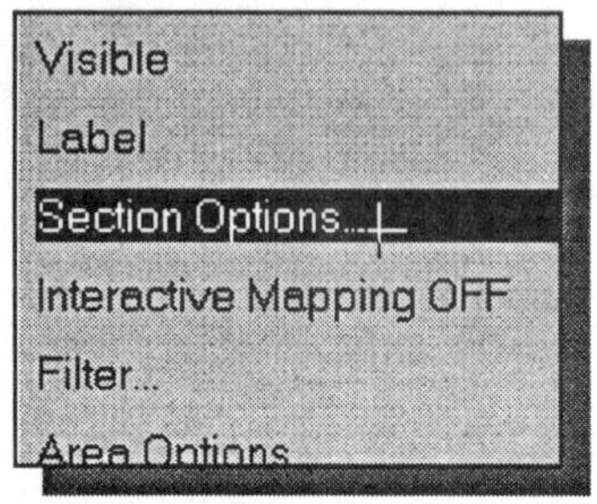

13. Move the cursor inside the graphics window. Press and hold down the right-mouse-button to select the **Section Options...** option. The *Section Options* window appears.

14. Switch on the **Stop at intersections** option so that all options in the *Section Options* window are turned on as shown.

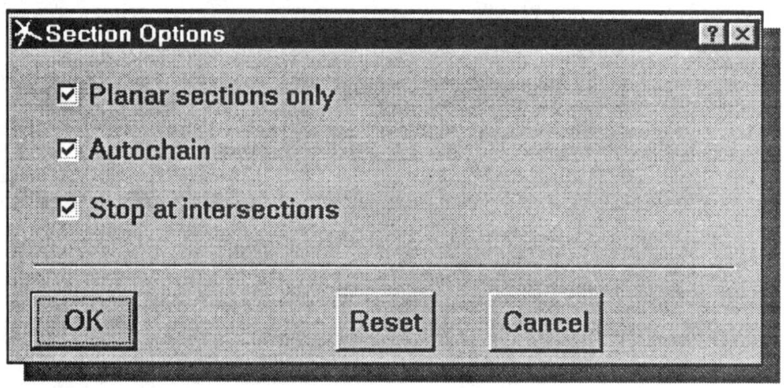

15. Select the **OK** icon to exit the *Section Options* window.

16. Create a section consisting of the two loops as shown below.

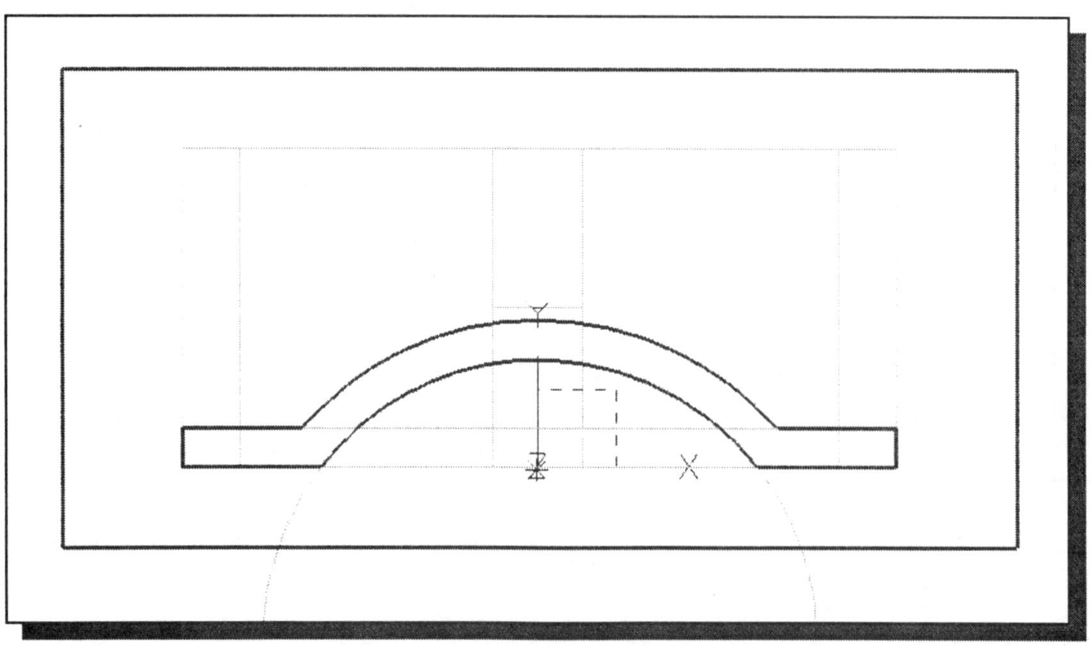

17. Choose **Extrude** in the icon panel.

18. Pick any edge of the section we just created.

19. Press the **ENTER** key or the **middle-mouse-button** to accept the selection.

20. The *Extrude Section* window will appear on the screen. Fill in the items as shown below.

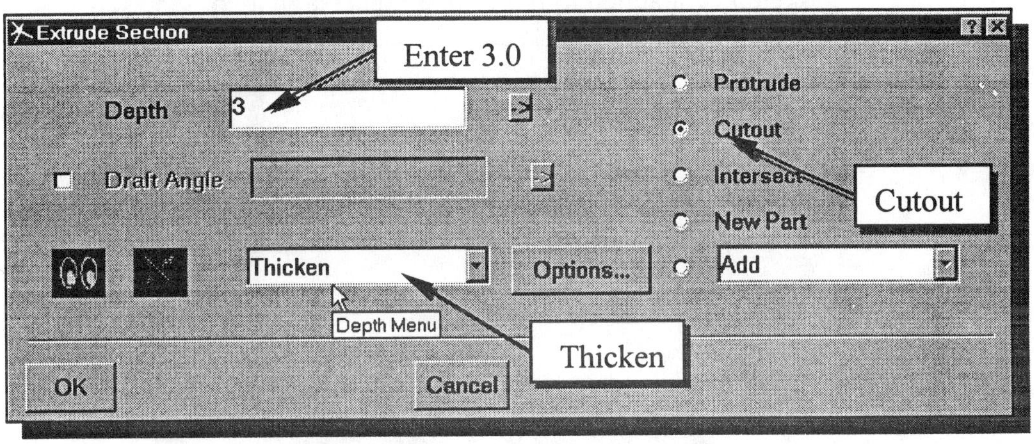

21. Click on the **OK** icon to accept the settings and complete the cut feature.

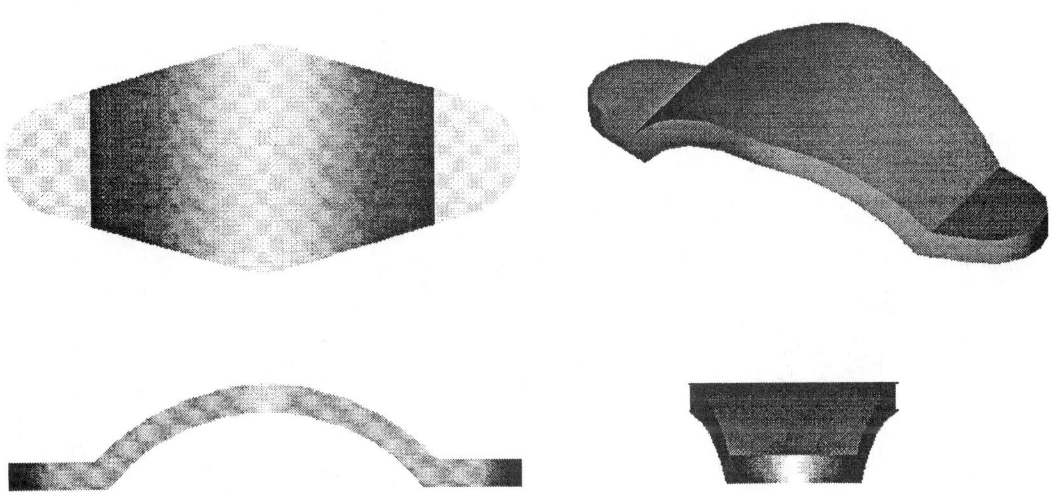

Create a 2-D Sketch of the next feature on the XY-plane

1. Choose **Sketch in Place** in the icon panel. In the prompt window, the message "*Pick plane to sketch on*" is displayed.

2. Pick one of the edges of the **XY plane** of the coordinate system. Note that even though the workplane was at the same orientation of the XY-plane of the coordinate system, selecting the XY-plane assures the sketch is attached to base node, the established part.

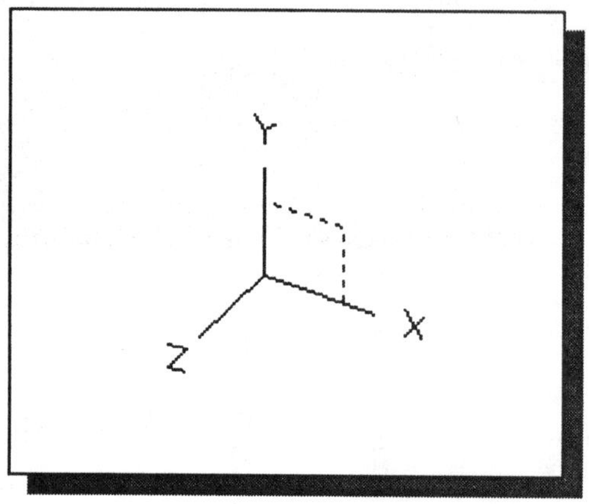

3. On your own, create the 2-D sketch as shown below. (Hint: use the ***Focus*** option to assure the alignment to the 3-D base.)

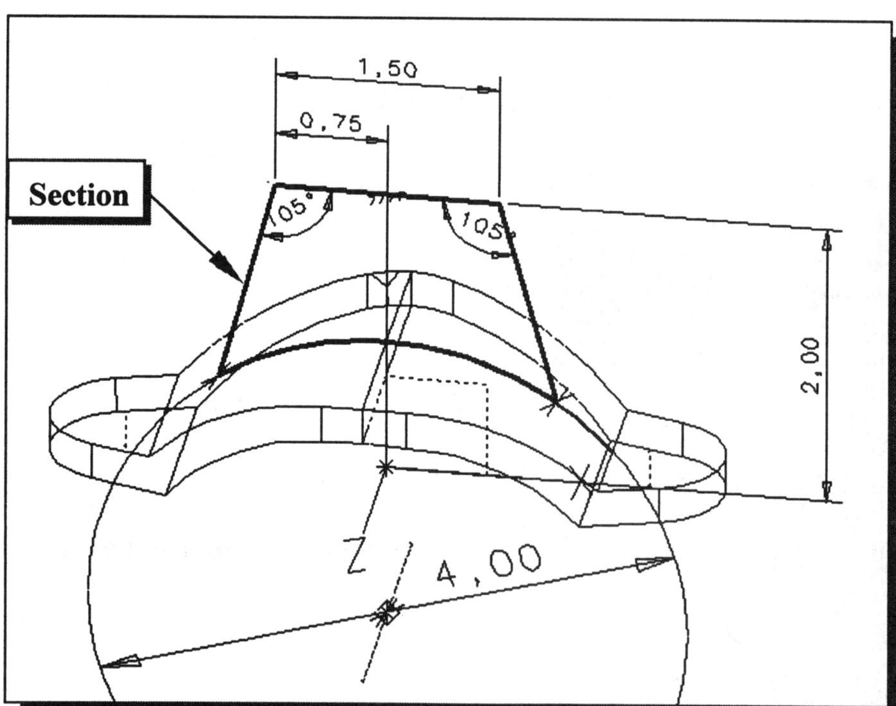

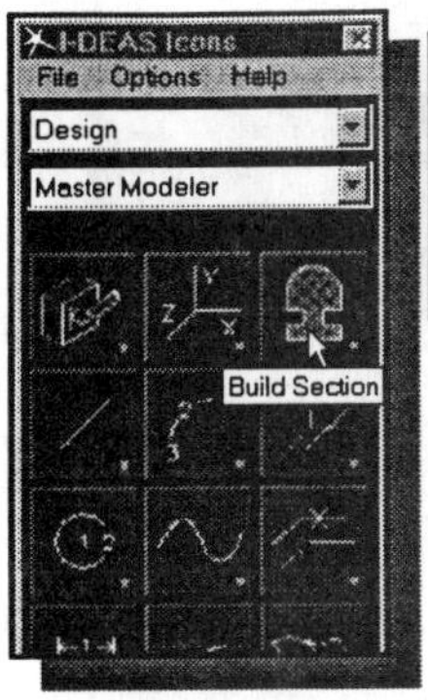

4. Choose **Build Section** in the icon panel. (The icon is located in the first row of the task specific icon panel.) The message "*Pick curve or section*" is displayed in the prompt window.

5. On your own, confirm the section options are all switched on as shown below.

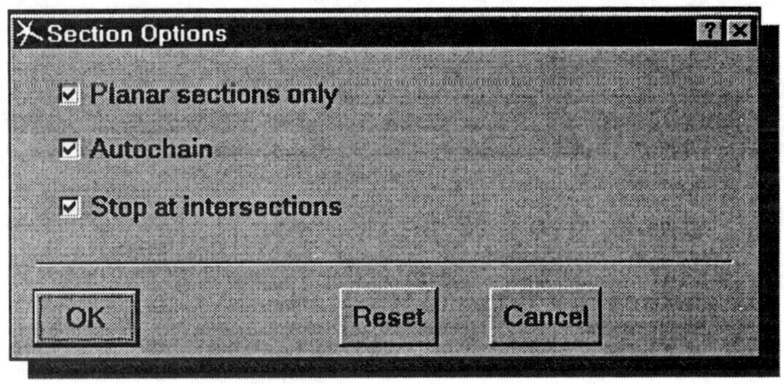

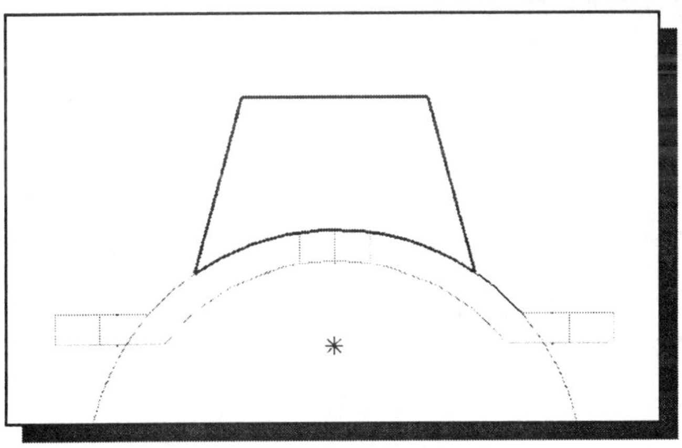

6. Create the section as shown in the figure (the thicker line denotes the desired section).

Extrude – *Thicken* Option

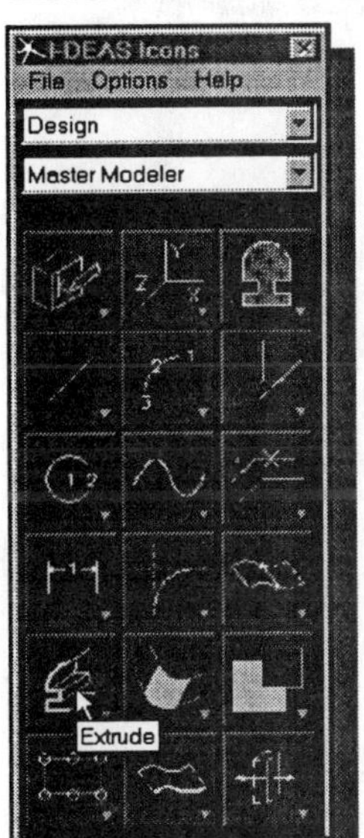

1. Choose the **Extrude** icon in the icon panel.

2. Select the section we just created.

3. Press the **ENTER** key or the **middle-mouse-button** to accept the selection.

4. In the *Extrude Section* window, fill in the items as shown below.

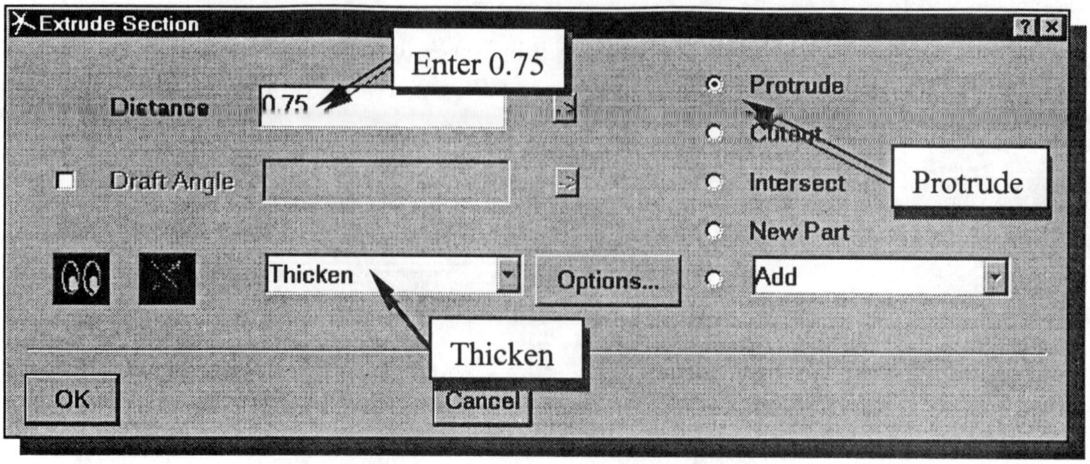

5. Click on the **OK** button to create the protrusion.

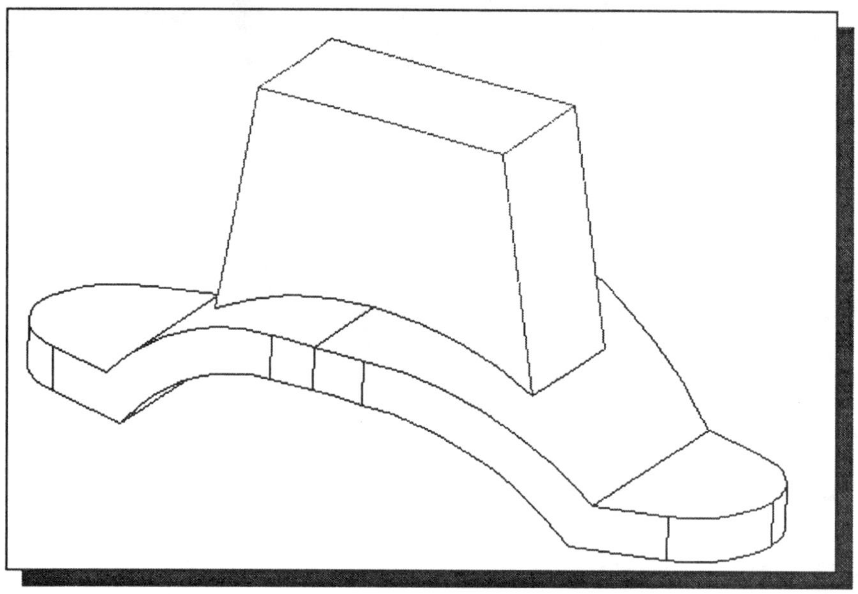

Create a Cylindrical Feature

1. Choose **Sketch in Place** in the icon panel. In the prompt window, the message "*Pick plane to sketch on*" is displayed.

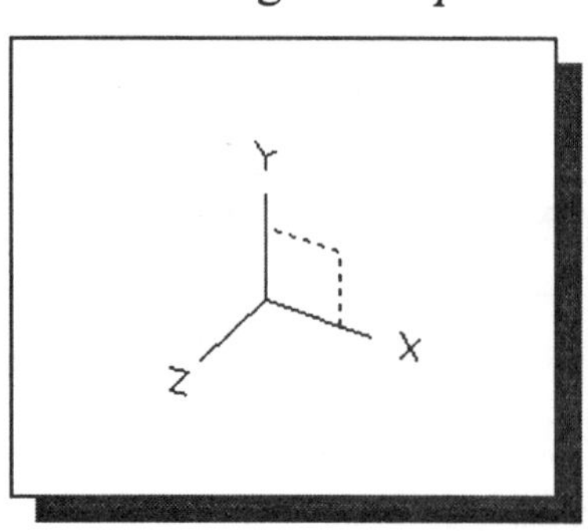

2. Pick any edge of the **XY-plane**.

3. Choose *Circle* – **Center Edge** in the icon panel. The message "*Locate center*" is displayed in the prompt window.

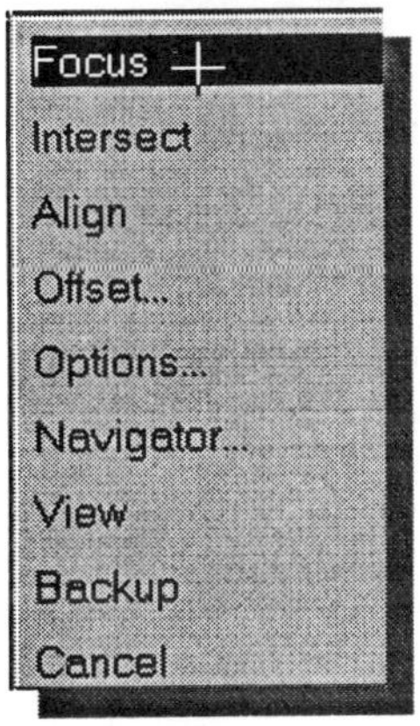

4. Move the cursor inside the graphics window. Press and hold down the right-mouse-button to display the option menu. Choose **Focus** in the option menu. The message "*Pick entity*" is displayed in the prompt window.

5. Click on the top-front edge of the 3-D solid.

6. Pick the midpoint on the focus line.

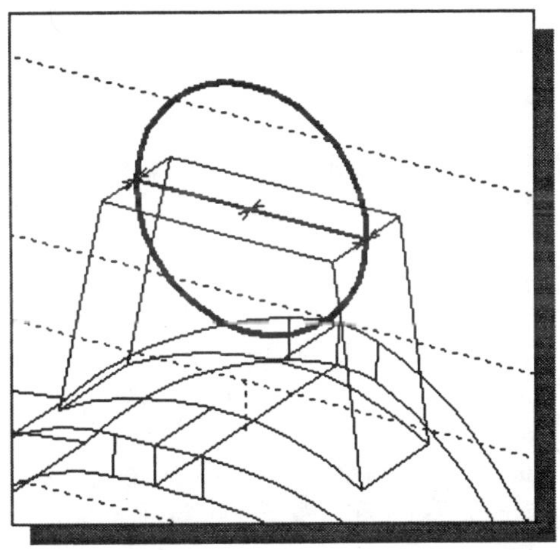

7. Pick either endpoint of the focus line to create the circle as shown.

8. Use the **Extrude** command. Select the sketched circle. Accept the selection and fill in the items as shown below.

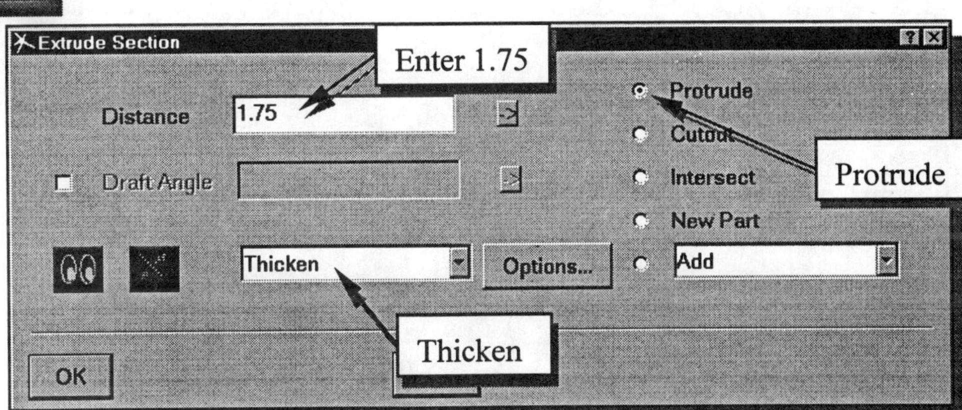

9. Click on the **OK** button to create the feature.

Create the Hole through the Cylinder

1. Choose **Sketch in Place** in the icon panel.

2. In the prompt window, the message "*Pick plane to sketch on*" is displayed. Pick the front surface of the newly created cylinder.

3. Choose *Circle* – **Center Edge** in the icon panel.

4. The message "*Locate center*" is displayed in the prompt window. Pick the front center of the cylinder.

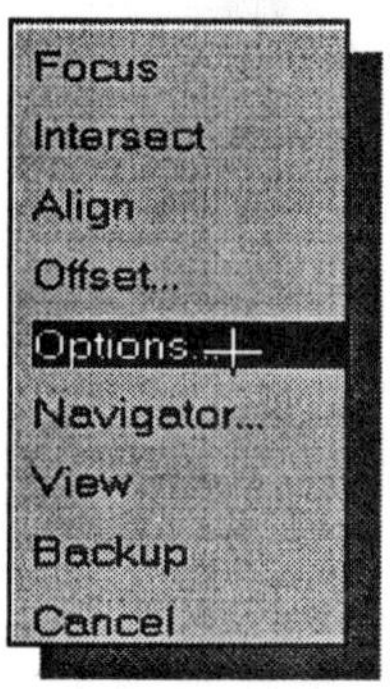

5. Move the cursor inside the graphics window. Press and hold down the right-mouse-button to choose the **Options** option.

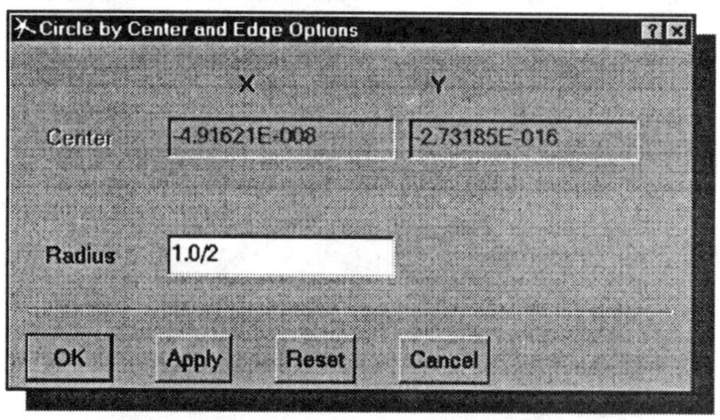

6. In the *Radius* box, enter **1.0/2.**

7. Click on the **OK** button to create the circle.

8. Use the **Extrude** command. Select the sketched circle. Accept the selection and fill in the items as shown below at the *Extrude Section* window:

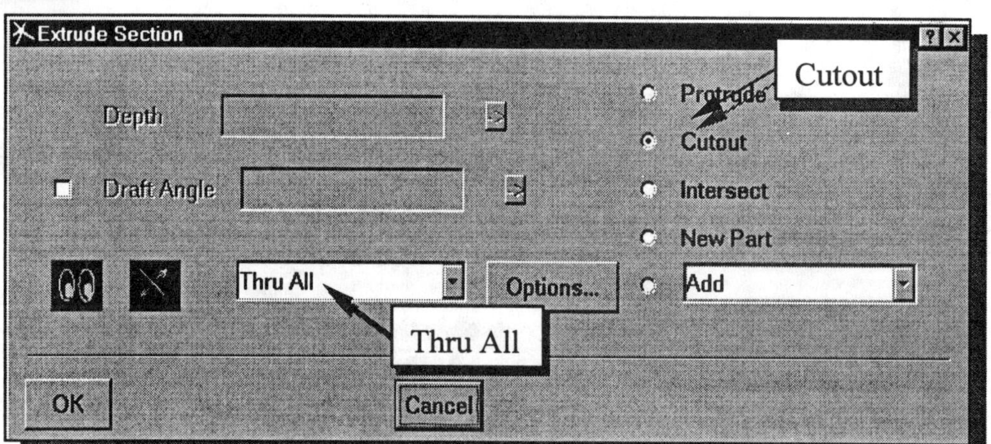

9. Click on the **OK** button to continue.

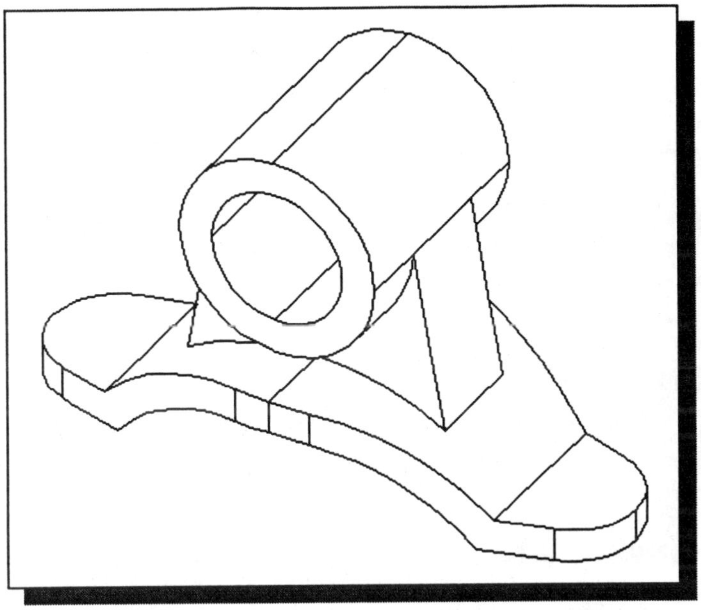

Create the Holes in the Base

1. Choose **Sketch in Place** in the icon panel. In the prompt window, the message "*Pick plane to sketch on*" is displayed.

2. Pick the top surface of the base as shown.

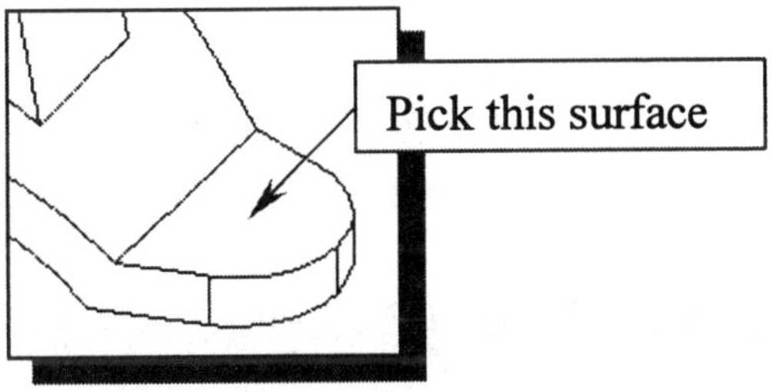

3. Choose *Circle* – **Center Edge** in the icon panel. The message "*Locate center*" is displayed in the prompt window.

4. Pick the center point on the sketch plane.

5. Move the cursor inside the graphics window. Press and hold down the right-mouse-button to choose *Options*.

6. In the *Radius* box, enter **0.25/2**.

7. Click on the **OK** button to continue.

10. Use the **Extrude** command. Select the sketched circle. Accept the selection and fill in the items as shown below at the *Extrude Section* window:

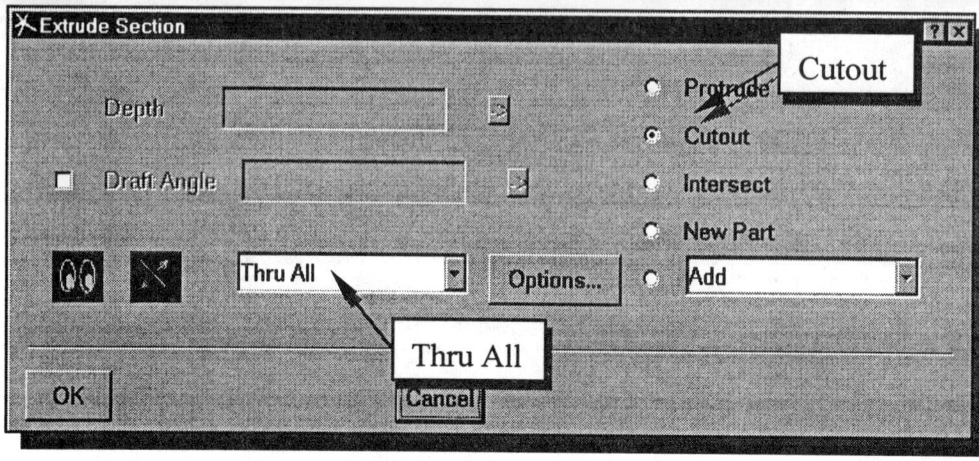

11. Click on the **OK** button to continue.

➢ On your own, repeat the above steps and create the same sized hole on the other side of the base.

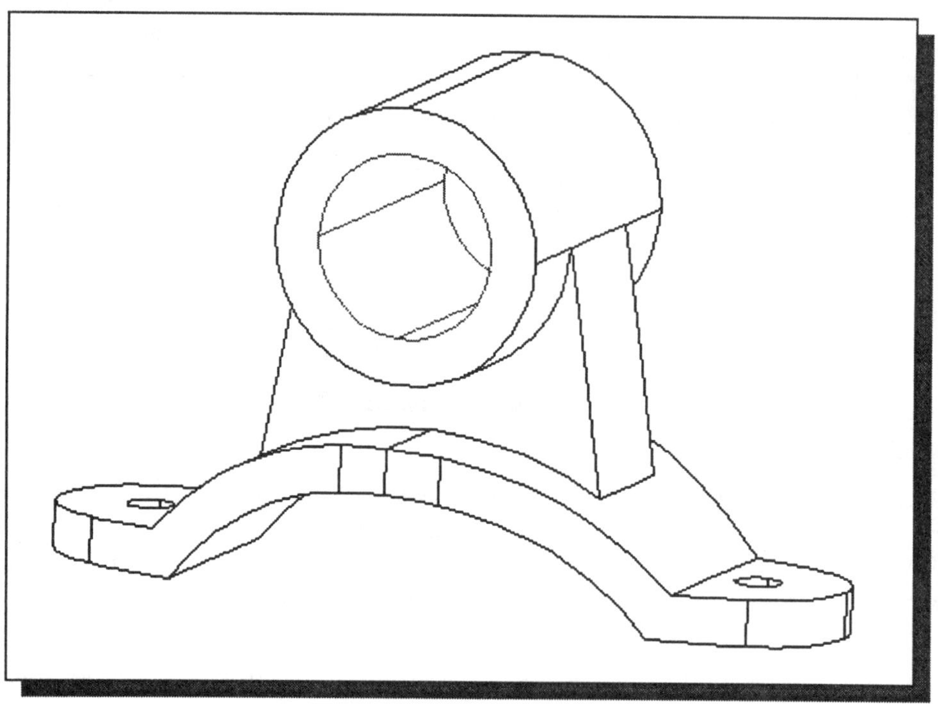

Adding 3-D Rounds and Fillets

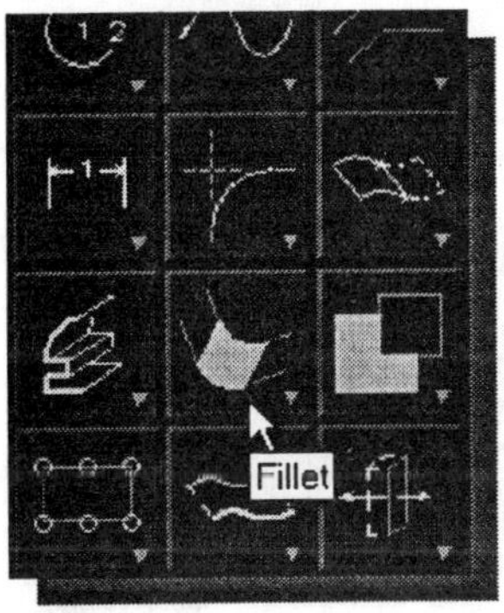

1. Choose **3-D Fillets** in the icon panel. (The icon is located in the fifth row of the task specific icon panel.)

2. The message "*Pick edges, vertices or surface to fillet/round*" is displayed in the prompt window. Pick the four faces of the vertical feature as shown.

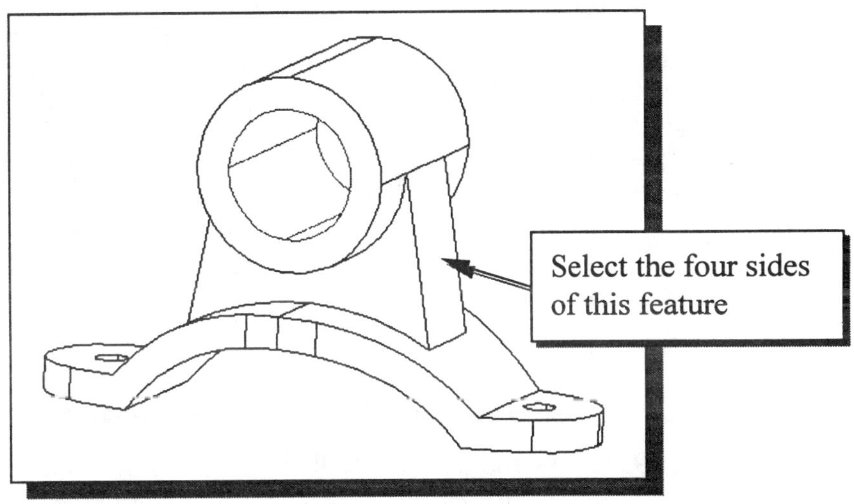

3. Press the **ENTER** key to accept the selections.

4. In the *prompt* window, enter the value of **0.125** for the radius of the round. A preview of the new radius for the rounds is displayed.

5. Press the **ENTER** key to complete the 3D fillets feature.

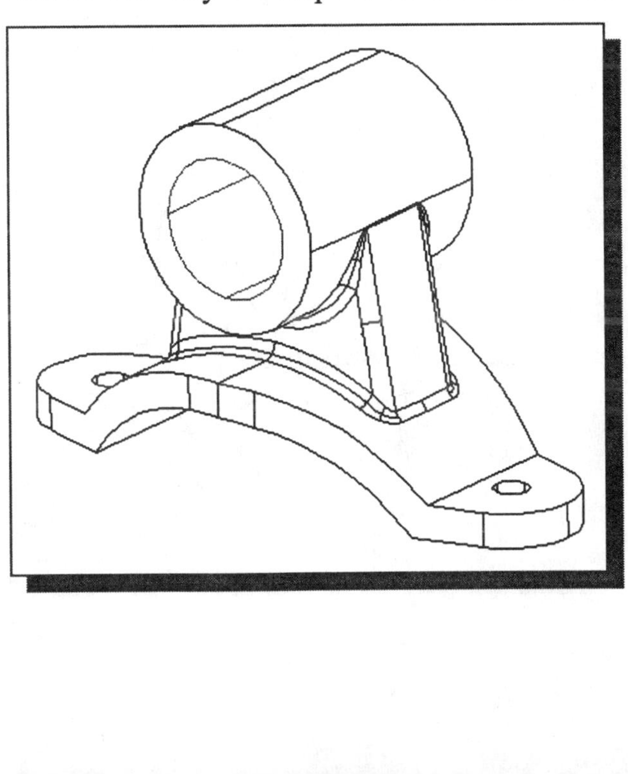

6. Pick **Fillets** again.

7. On your own, confirm *Edge Chaining* is switched *ON*.

8. Select the edge as shown.

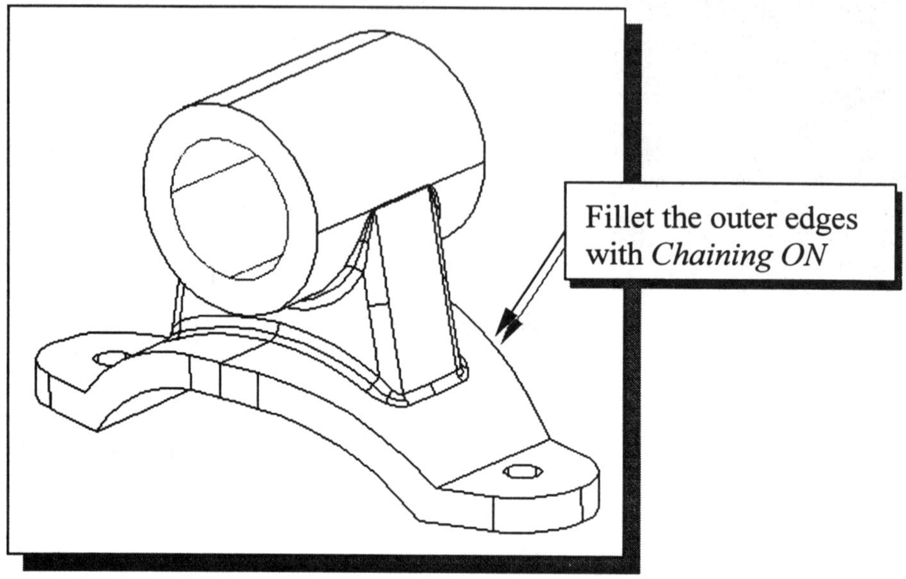

9. Press and hold the **SHIFT** key and left-click on the adjacent edges. (Refer to the figure below to determine the edges to be filleted.) Press the **ENTER** key to continue.

10. In the prompt window, enter the value of **0.125** for the radius of the round. A preview of the new radius for the rounds is displayed.

11. Press the **ENTER** key to accept the setting and create the fillets.

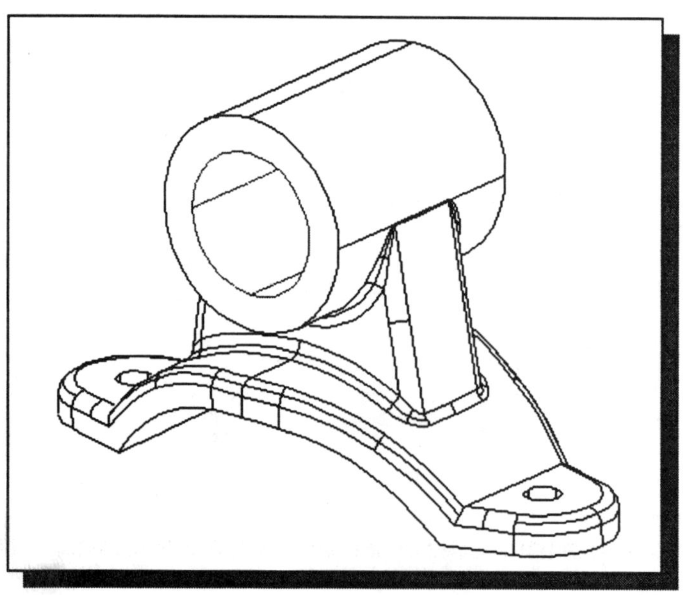

Creating Chamfers

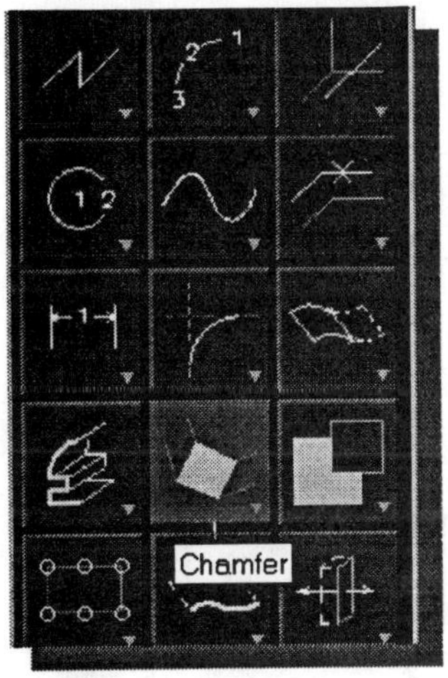

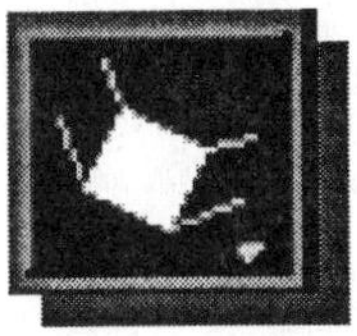

1. Choose **Chamfer** in the icon panel. The prompt window displays the message "*Pick edges, vertices or surfaces to chamfer.*"

2. Pick the two circles as shown.

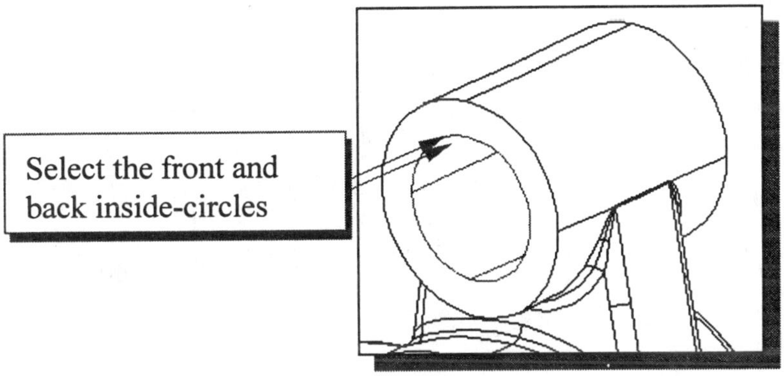

3. Press the **ENTER** key to continue.

4. In the prompt window, enter the value of **0.0625** as the chamfer dimension. A preview of the chamfers is displayed.

5. Press the **ENTER** key to create the chamfer feature and complete the model.

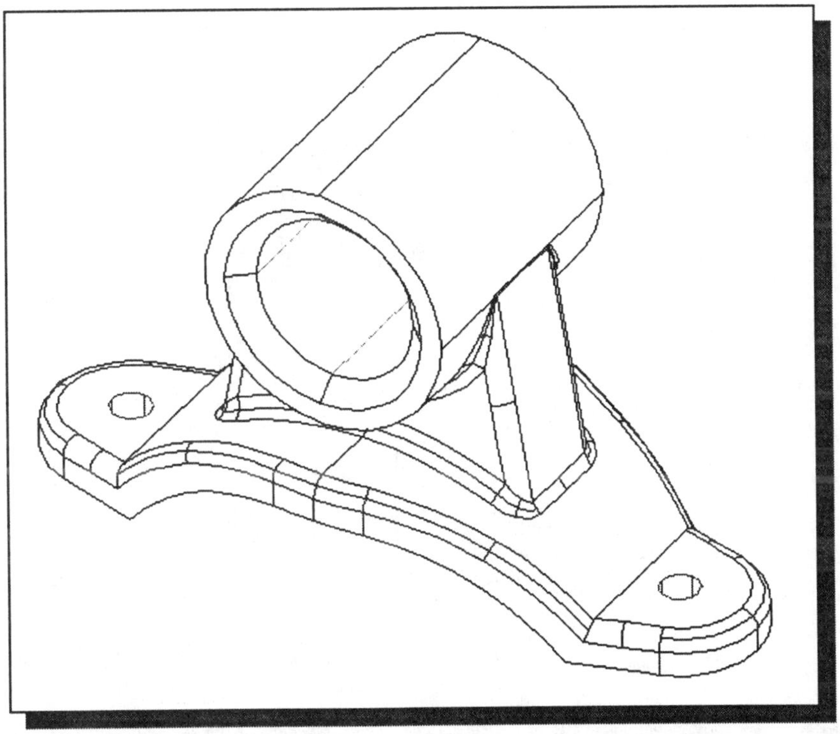

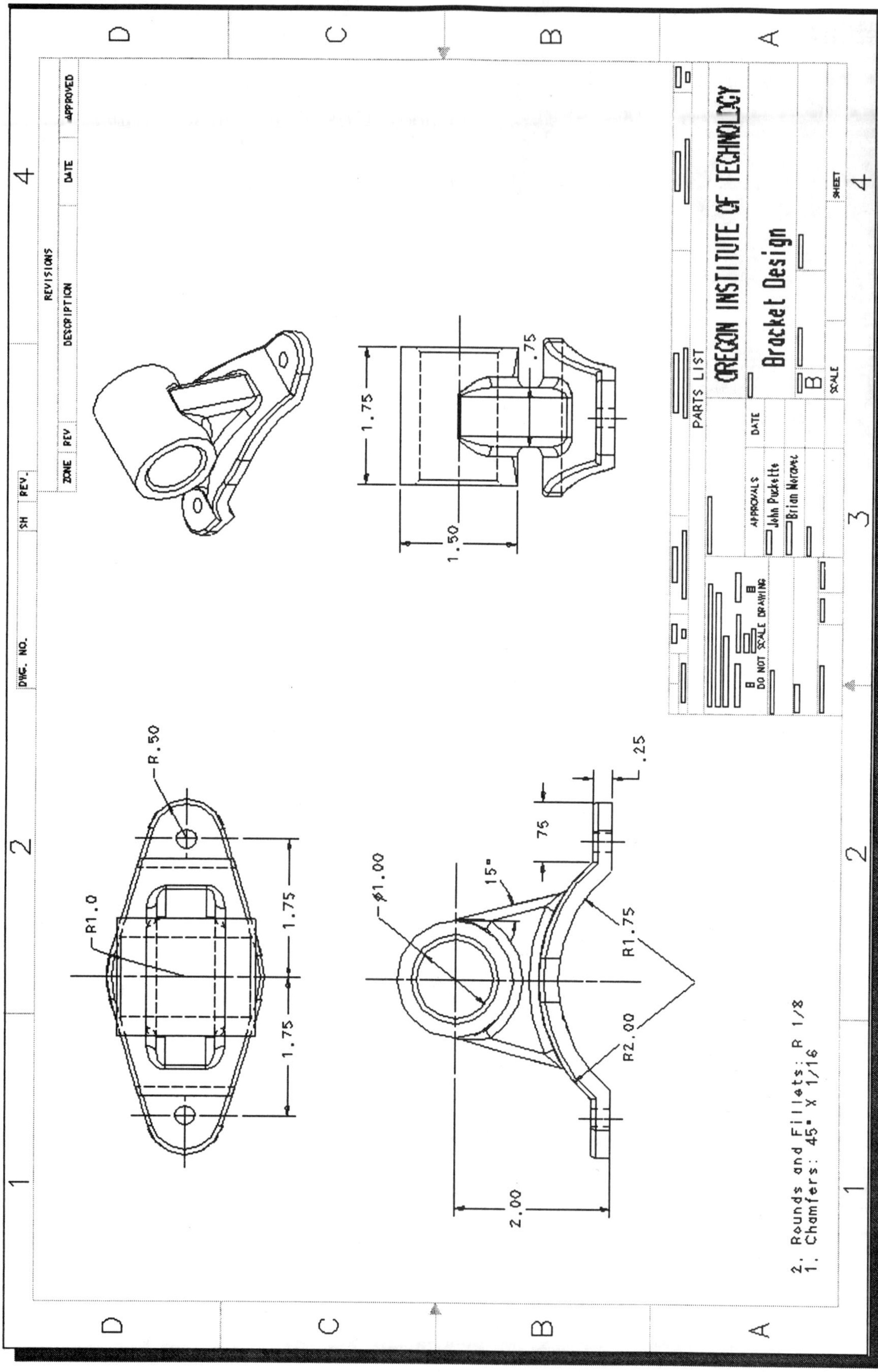
OREGON INSTITUTE OF TECHNOLOGY
Bracket Design
PARTS LIST
APPROVALS
John Puckette
Brian Moravec
DO NOT SCALE DRAWING
REVISIONS
ZONE REV DESCRIPTION DATE APPROVED
DWG. NO.
SH REV.
SCALE
SHEET
R1.0
R.50
1.75
1.75
⌀1.00
15°
.75
.25
R1.75
R2.00
2.00
1.50
.75
1. Chamfers: 45° X 1/16
2. Rounds and Fillets: R 1/8

Questions:

1. How can you distinguish dimensions that were derived from other dimensions from those that were not?

2. Will the dimensions be updated in the *Master Drafting* application when the geometry is modified in the Master Modeler?

3. Describe the *Intersect Boolean operation.*

4. How do you modify the arrowheads of a dimension?

5. What are the main differences between *Master Drafting* and *3D annotation*?

6. Can we change the direction of an extruded feature?

7. When extruding, what is the difference between *Through All* and *Thicken*?

8. Identify and describe the following commands:

(a)

(b)

(c)

(d)

Exercises:

1.

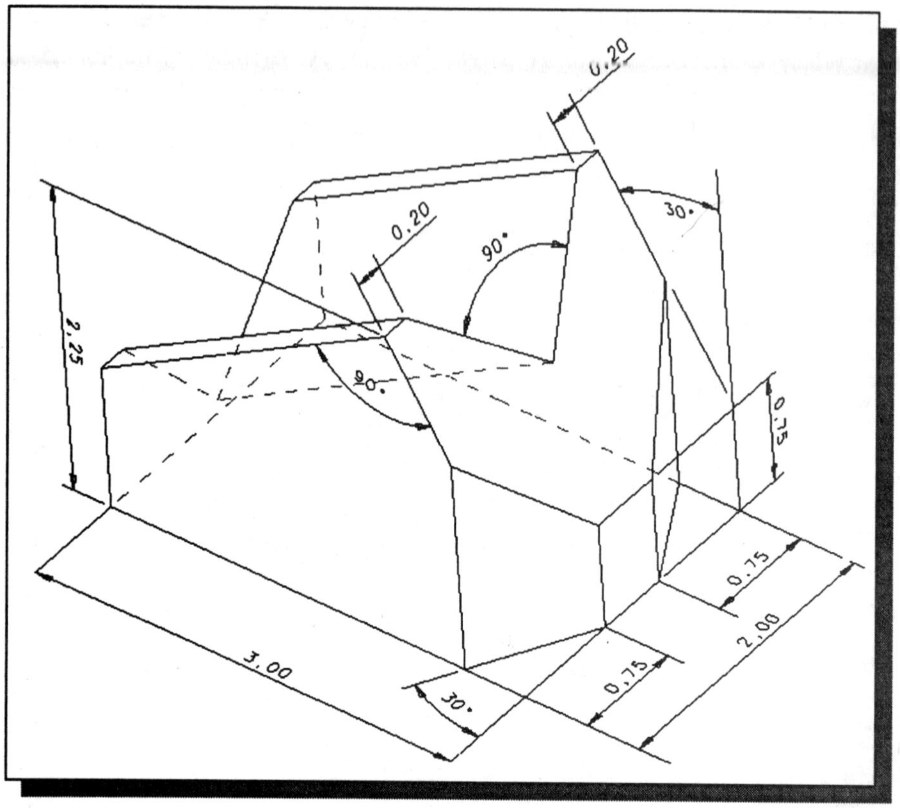

2.

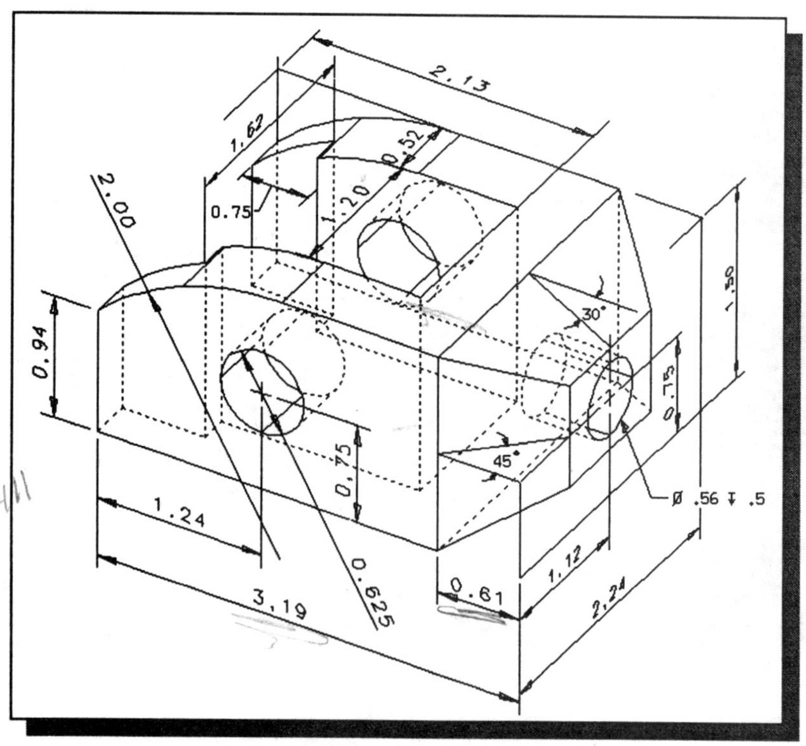

Chapter 12

Assembly Modeling - Putting It All Together

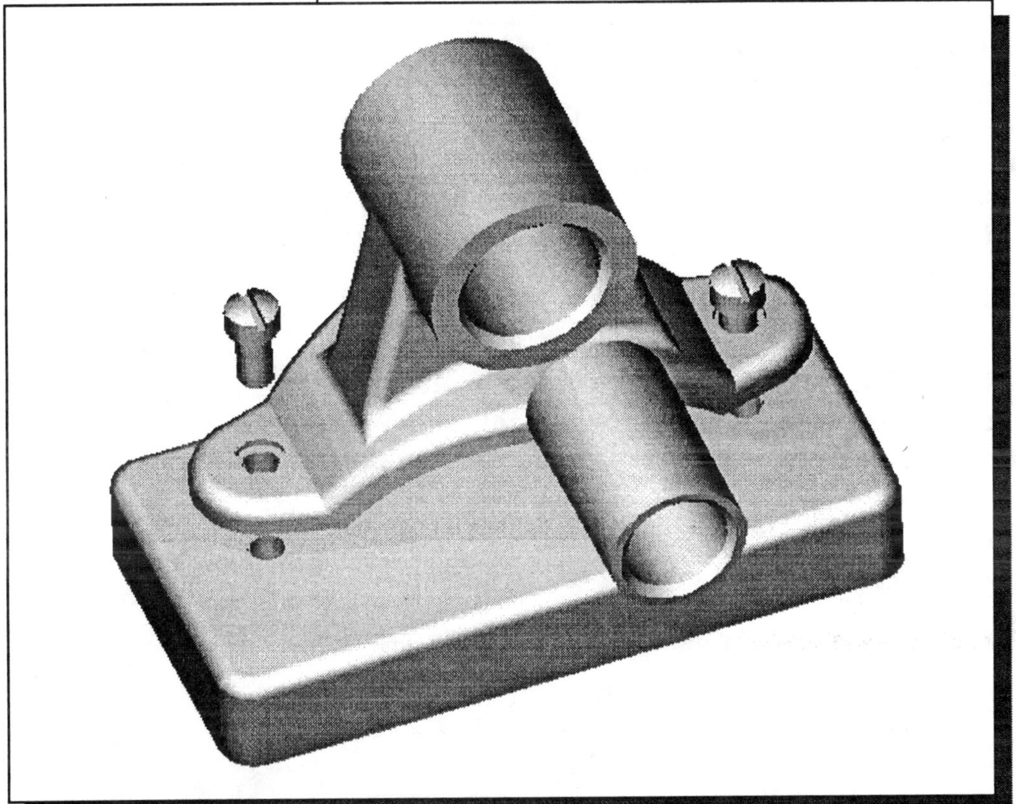

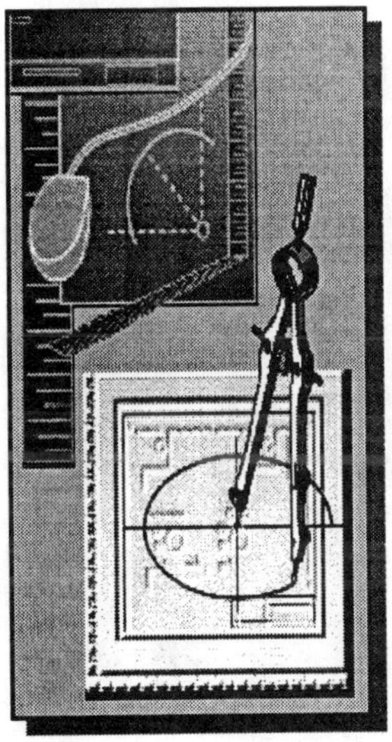

Learning Objectives

When you have completed this lesson, you will be able to:

- ♦ Understand the Assembly Modeling Methodology
- ♦ Acquire Parts in the Master Assembly Mode
- ♦ Understand and Utilize Assembly Constraints
- ♦ Understand the I-DEAS DOF Display
- ♦ Utilize the I-DEAS Assembly Modeling Hierarchy
- ♦ Create Exploded Assemblies

Introduction

In the previous chapters, we have gone over the fundamentals of creating basic parts and drawings. In this chapter, we will examine the functionality of *I-DEAS Master Assembly*, the assembly-modeling module of *I-DEAS*. We will start with a demonstration on how to create and modify assembly models. The main task in creating an assembly is establishing the assembly relationships between parts. To assemble parts into an assembly, we will need to consider the assembly relationships between parts. It is a good practice to assemble parts based on the way they would be assembled in the actual manufacturing process. We should also consider breaking down the assembly into smaller subassemblies, which helps the management of parts. In *I-DEAS*, a subassembly is treated the same way as a single part during assembling. Many parallels exist between assembly modeling and part modeling in parametric modeling software such as *I-DEAS*.

I-DEAS provides full associative functionality in all design modules, including assemblies. When we change a part model, *I-DEAS* will automatically reflect the changes in all assemblies that use the part. We can also modify a part in an assembly. **Bi-directional full associative functionality** is the main feature of parametric solid modeling software that allows us to increase productivity by reducing design cycle time.

The *BRACKET* Assembly:

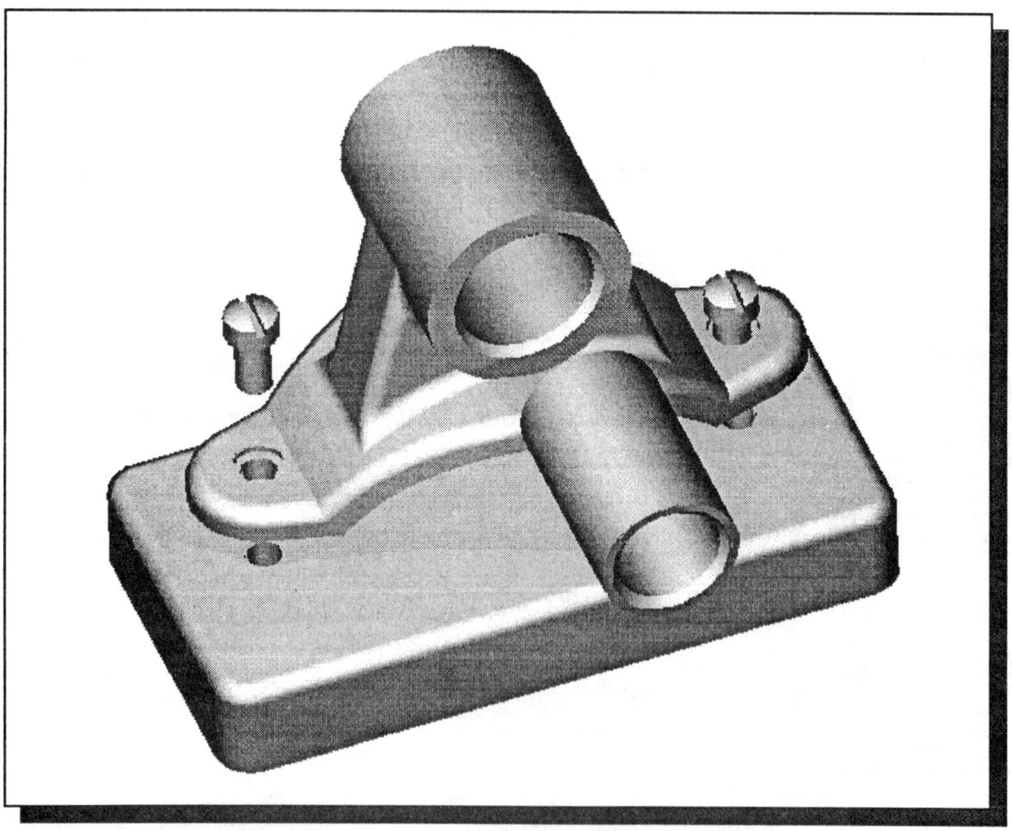

Assembly Modeling Methodology

The *I-DEAS* assembly modeler provides tools and functions that allow us to create 3D parametric assembly models. An assembly model is a 3D model with any combination of multiple part models. *Parametric Assembly constraints* can be used to control relationships between parts in an assembly model.

I-DEAS can work with any of the assembly modeling methodologies:

The Bottom Up approach

The first step in the *bottom up* assembly modeling approach is to create the individual parts. The parts are then pulled together into an assembly. This approach is typically used for smaller projects with very few team members.

The Top Down approach

The first step in the *top down* assembly modeling approach is to create the assembly model of the project. Initially, individual parts are represented by names or symbolically. The details of the individual parts are added as the project gets further along. This approach is typically used for larger projects or during the conceptual design stage. Members of the project team can then concentrate on the particular section of the project to which he/she is assigned.

The Middle Out approach

The *middle out* assembly modeling approach is a mixture of the bottom-up and top-down methods. This type of assembly model is usually constructed with most of the parts already created and additional parts are designed and created using the assembly for construction information. Some requirements are known and some standard components are used, but new designs must also be produced to meet specific objectives. This combined strategy is a very flexible approach to creating assembly models.

The different assembly modeling approaches described above can be used as guidelines to manage design projects. Keep in mind that we can start modeling our assembly using one approach and then switch to a different approach without any problems.

In this chapter, the *bottom up* assembly modeling approach is illustrated. All of the parts (components) required to form the assembly are created first. *I-DEAS*'s assembly modeling tools allow us to create complex assemblies by using components that are created in separate part files or in the same part file. A component can be a subassembly or a single part, where features and parts can be modified at any time. The sketches and sections used to build part features can be fully or partially constrained. Partially constrained features may be adaptive, which means the size or shape of the associated parts are adjusted in an assembly when the parts are constrained to other parts. The basic concept and procedure of using the adaptive assembly approach is demonstrated in the tutorial.

Additional Parts

Besides the ***Bracket***, we will need three additional parts: (1) ***Base Plate***, (2) ***Bushing*** and (3) ***Cap-screw***.

(1) Base Plate

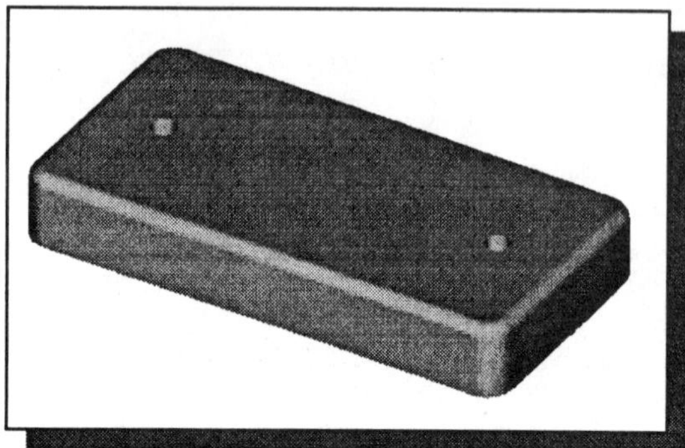

Hole sizes: Ø 0.25 and 0.6 deep. Center to center distance of the two holes: 3.5.
Rounds: R 0.125

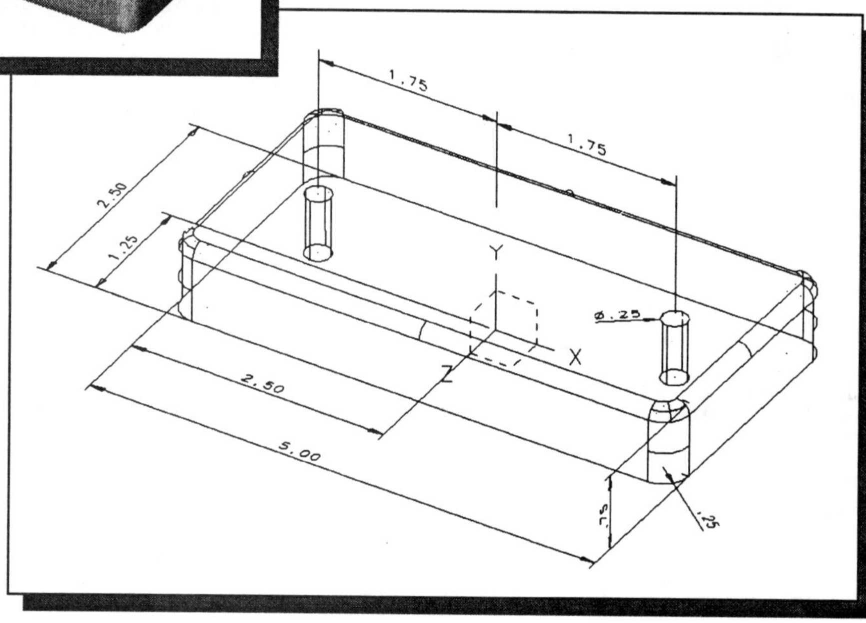

Starting I-DEAS

1. Login to the computer and bring up I-DEAS. Start a new model file by filling in the form items as shown below in the *I-DEAS Start* window:

   Project Name: **(Your account Name)**
   Model File Name: **Bracket**
   Application: **Design**
   Task: **Master Modeler**
   OK

2. Click on the **OK** button to accept the settings, I-DEAS will retrieve the *Bracket* model on the screen.

Applying the BORN Technique

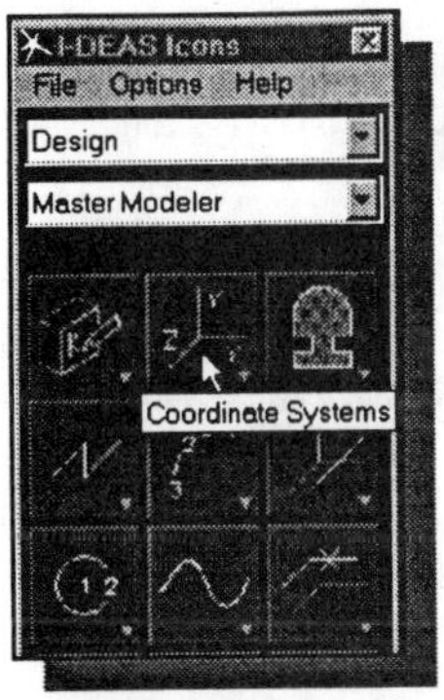

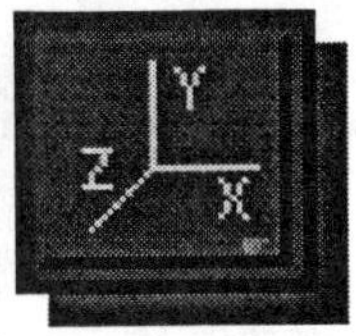

1. Choose **Coordinate Systems** in the icon panel. (The icon is located in the first row of the task icon panel.)

2. In the prompt window, the message "*Pick entity for coordinate system to reference*" is displayed. Select the default **workplane** (Blue color) by left-clicking once on any of the edges.

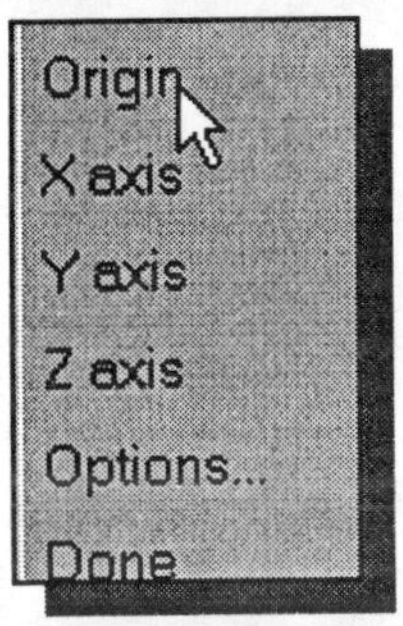

3. In the prompt window, the message "*Select coordinate system component to define (Done)*" is displayed. Select **Origin** in the popup menu.

❖ The *Origin* option allows us to define the location of the origin of the new coordinate system relative to the world coordinate system.

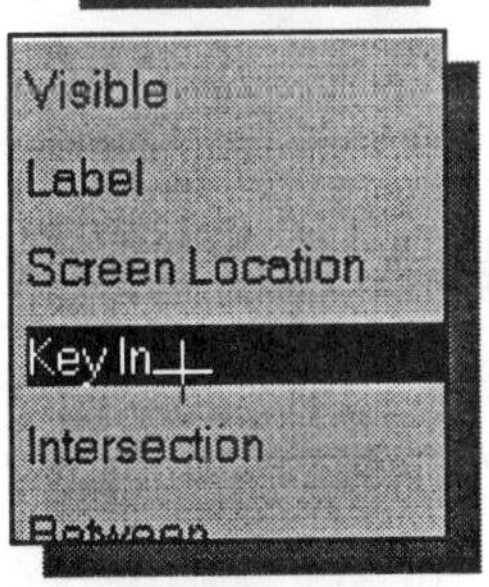

4. Inside the graphics window, right-mouse-click to bring up the option menu and select **Key In** as the method of identifying the location of the origin of the new coordinate system.

5. In the prompt window, the message "*Enter X, Y, Z of origin definition (Done)*" is displayed. Enter **6,0,0** to position the origin of the new coordinate system so that it is away from the ***Bracket*** part.

6. Select **Done** in the option menu or press the **ENTER** key to accept the settings and proceed with the creation of the new coordinate system.

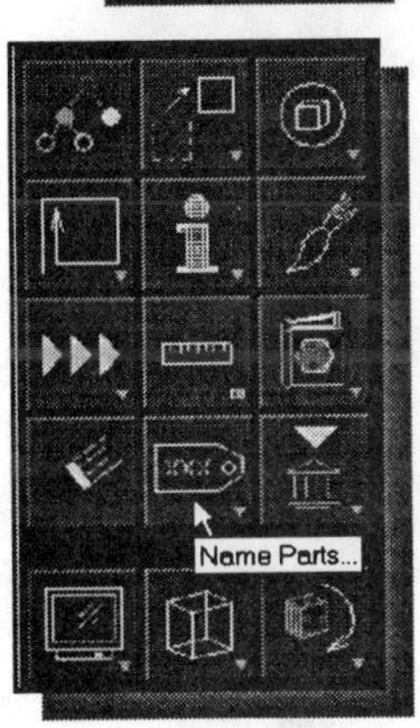

7. Choose **Name Parts...** in the icon panel. (The icon is located in the last row of the application specific icon panel.)

8. The message "*Pick part to name*" is displayed in the prompt window. Pick any edge of the coordinate system, the coordinate system that is toward the right side of the screen, which we just created. The *Name* window appears.

9. In the *Name* window, we can assign or change the name, number, and bin of a part. In the *Name* box, type in "**Base_Plate**" as the part name

10. Click on the **OK** button to accept the settings and proceed with naming the part.

11. The message "*Pick part to name (Done)*" is displayed in the prompt window. Press the **ENTER** key or the **middle-mouse-button** to end the *Name Parts* command.

❖ To avoid any confusion in the following steps to create the ***Base Plate*** part, we will first *PUT AWAY* the ***Bracket*** model.

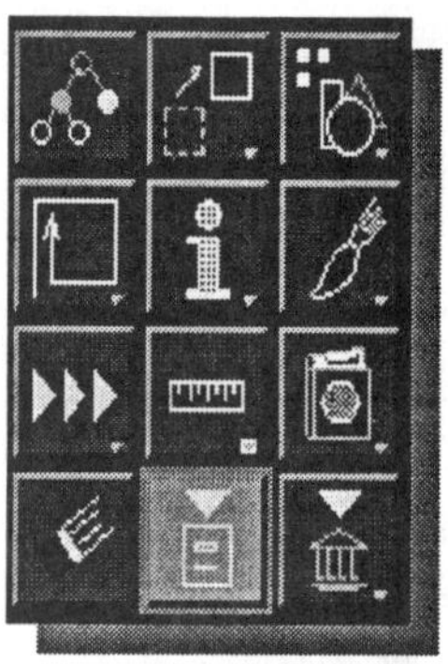

12. Choose **Put Away** in the icon panel. The icon is located in the fourth row of the application icon panel. (The icon is located at the same stack as the *Name Part* icon.)

13. In the prompt window, the message "*Pick part to put away*" is displayed. Pick any edges of the 3-D solid part. The part is now put into the *I-DEAS BIN* and disappears from the screen.

14. In the prompt window, the message "*Pick part to put away (Done)*" is displayed. Press the **ENTER** key or the **middle-mouse-button** to end the current command.

Creating the Base Plate part

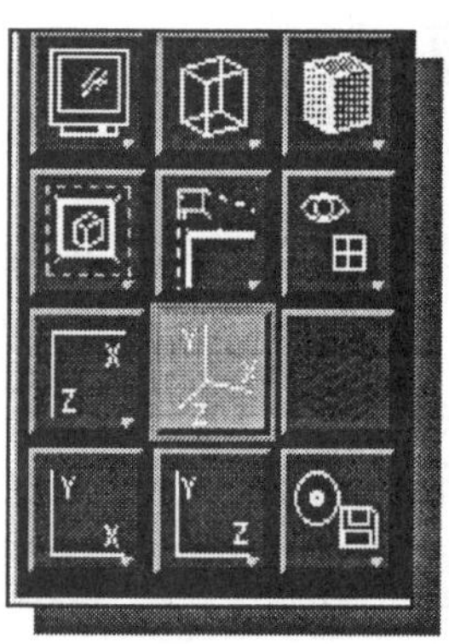

1. Choose **Isometric View** in the display viewing icon panel.

2. Choose **Zoom-All** in the display viewing icon panel.

3. Choose **Sketch in Place** in the icon panel. In the prompt window, the message "*Pick plane to sketch on*" is displayed.

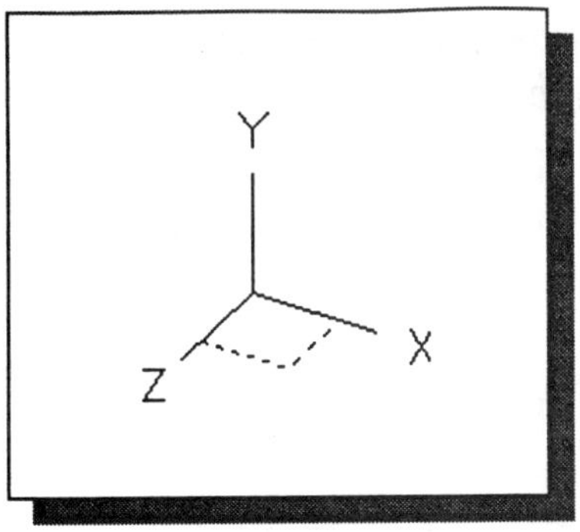

4. Pick one of the edges of the **XZ plane** of the coordinate system. Note that the workplane is aligned with the *XZ-plane* of the coordinate system. Selecting the *XZ-plane* assures the sketch is attached to base node, the established part.

5. On your own, construct a 2D sketch as shown in the figure below. Note that a *reference point* is placed at the origin of the part coordinate system, using the *Focus* option, to assure the alignment of the edges.

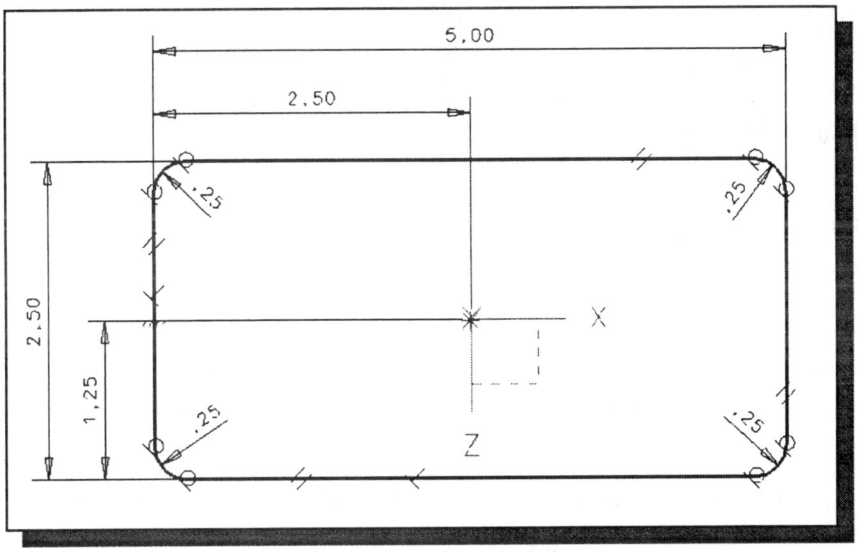

6. Complete the part by performing an extrusion in the *Y-direction.* Create the two holes at the center and use the *3D-fillets* command to add the *R .125* rounds on the top edges as shown.

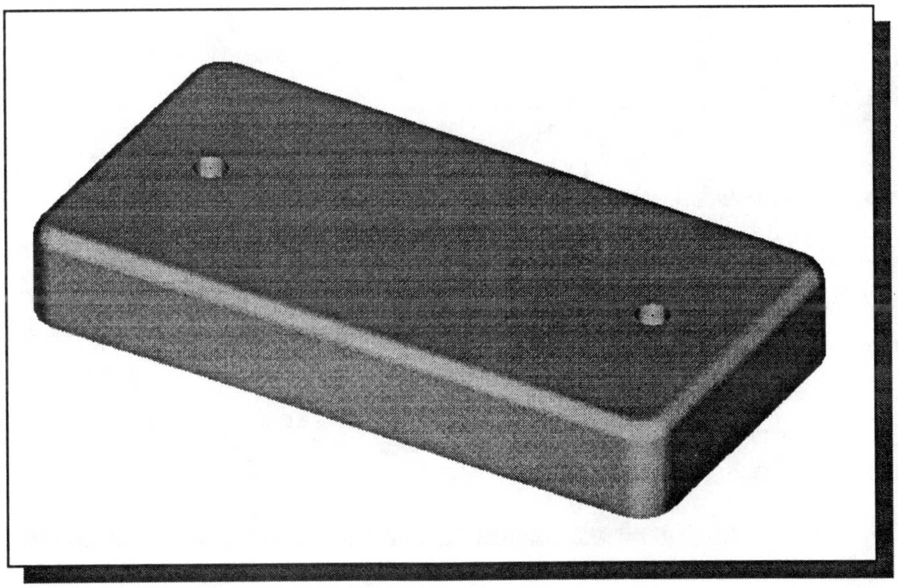

❖ On your own, create the ***Bushing*** and the ***Cap-screw*** parts as shown in the figures below. Note the position of the part coordinate systems in relation to the part.

(2) **Bushing**

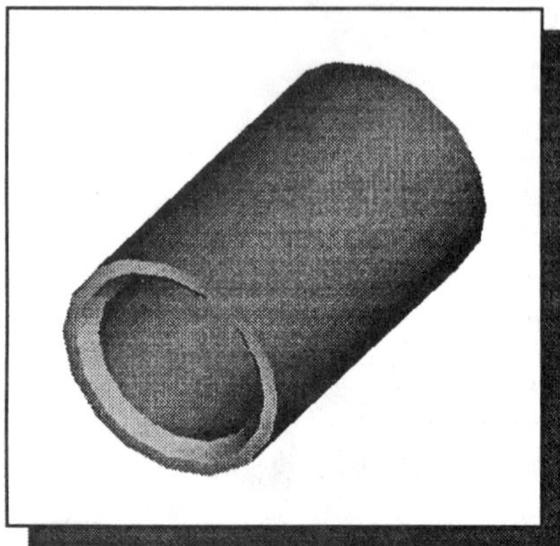

ID: Ø 0.75, OD: Ø 1.00, Length: 1.625
Chamfers: 45° X 0.0625

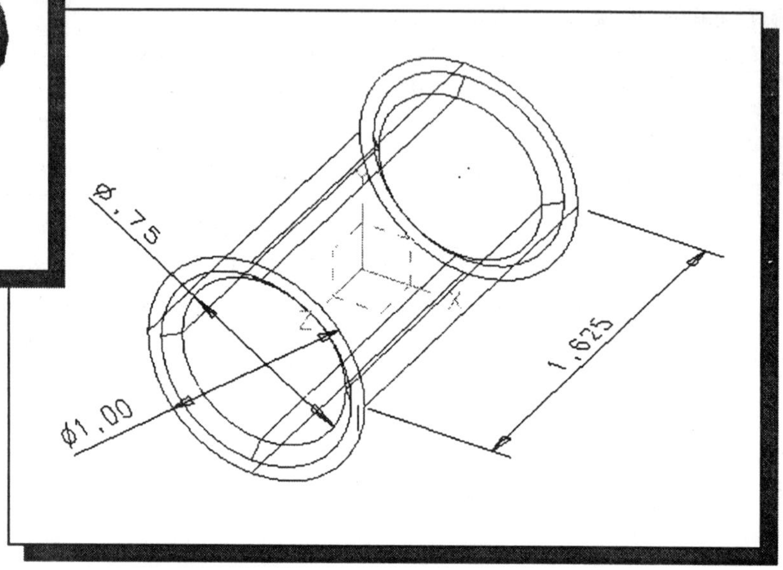

(3) **Cap Screw**

We will omit the threads in this model. Threads are complex three-dimensional curves and it will slow down the display considerably.

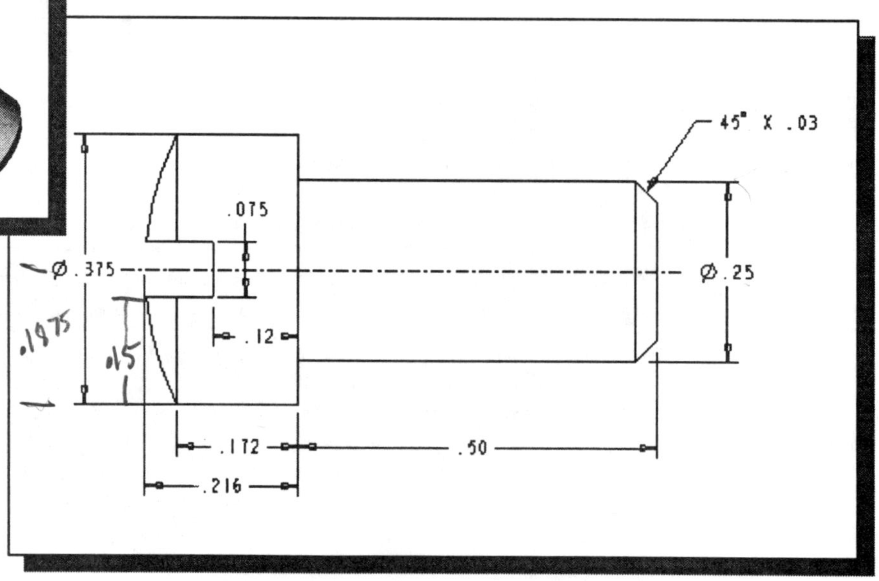

Retrieve the Solid Objects from the BIN

We will next retrieve all of the parts from the BIN.

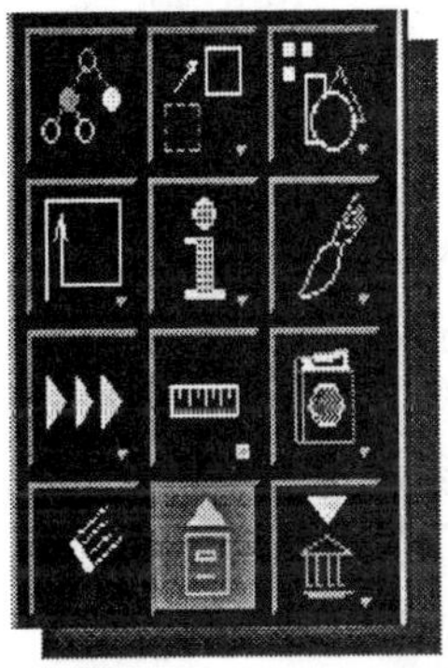

1. Choose **Get** in the icon panel. The icon is located in the fourth row of the application icon panel. (The icon is located in the same stack as the **Put Away** icon.) The *Get* window appears.

2. Pick the ***Bracket*** part in the *Main Bin* part list.

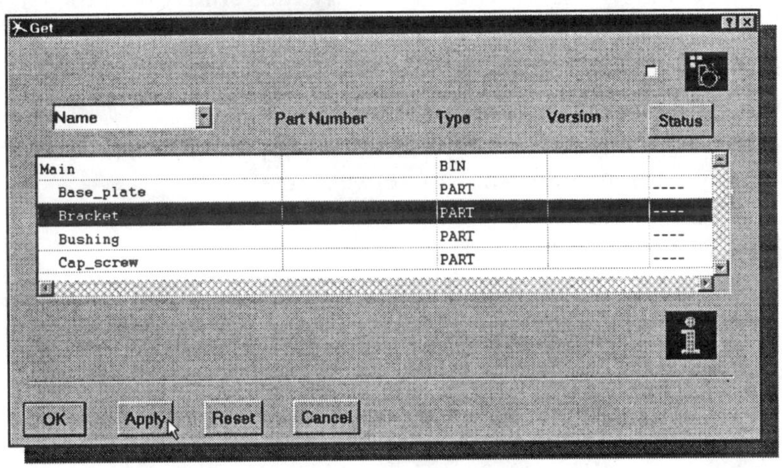

3. Click on the **Apply** button to place the part back on the workbench.

4. Repeat the above steps until all parts are displayed on the screen.

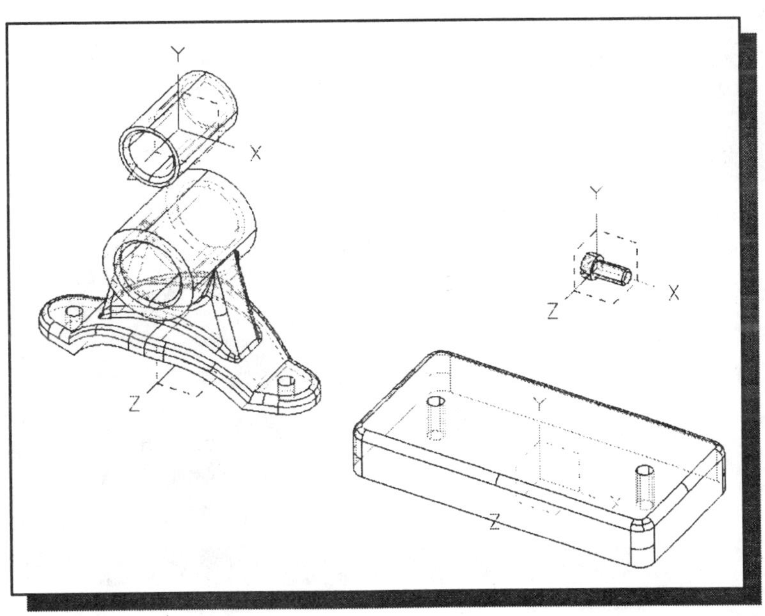

The I-DEAS Master Assembly Application

❖ The main function of the Master Assembly application is allowing the user to assemble models in a 3D environment. Once the parametric relations are established, we can also examine the design by performing operations such as interference checks or animations, or by transferring the assembly to the *I-DEAS Mechanism Design* application to perform kinematics analysis. In this example, all parts are stored in the same model file. To create assemblies with parts created in separate files, *place* the parts into the *I-DEAS library* and/or *catalog*. The I-DEAS data management system is designed to handle a concurrent engineering environment, where multiple groups all share the same database. The procedure illustrated in this chapter is applicable to both scenarios in creating assembly models.

The general procedure in creating an assembly model involves the following steps:

1. Acquire the necessary parts and/or subassemblies from the model file, library, or catalog.
2. Define the hierarchy, or order, of assembling parts for the assembly model.
3. Define the parametric relations in between parts.

1. Click with the **left-mouse-button** in the *Task* toolbar area to display the options list and select the ***Master Assembly*** task.

❖ The screen arrangement of the *Master Assembly* application remains the same as that of the *Master Modeler*, but you will see a different set of icons in the icon panels

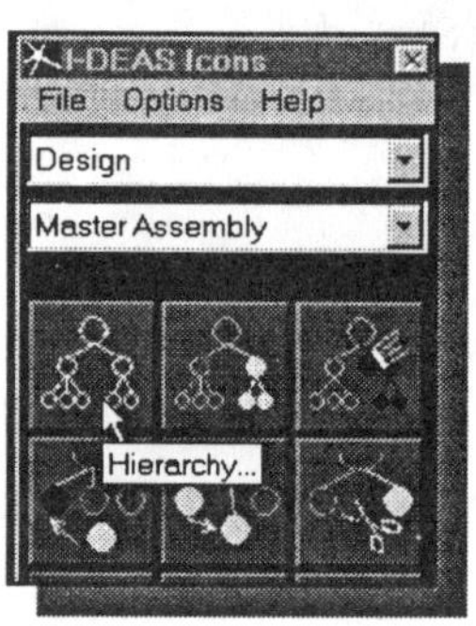

2. Choose **Hierarchy** in the icon panel (the first icon in the icon panel).

❖ Note that many of the commands displayed in the icon panel are also available in the *Hierarchy* window.

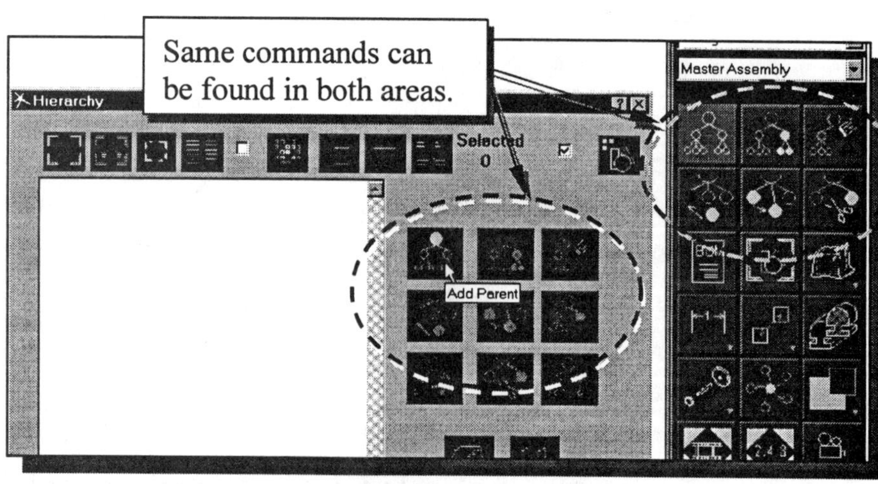

Acquiring parts from the model file and establish a hierarchy

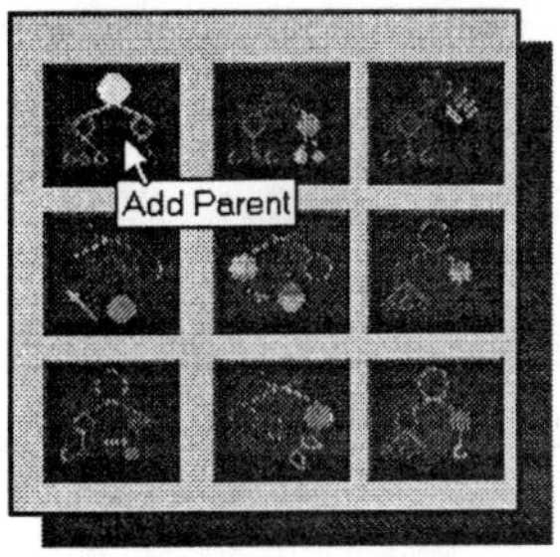

1. Click on **Add parent** in the *Hierarchy* window.

2. In the *Name window*, enter **Bracket_Assembly** as the name of the assembly to create.

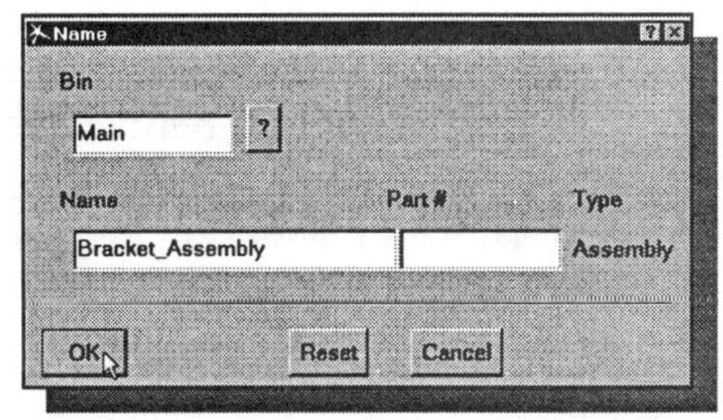

3. Click on the **OK** button to accept the settings.

4. Click on the assembly model name, **Bracket_Assembly,** in the *Hierarchy* list. Notice some of the grayed options are available once an assembly is identified.

5. Click on the **Add to** button in the *Hierarchy* window.

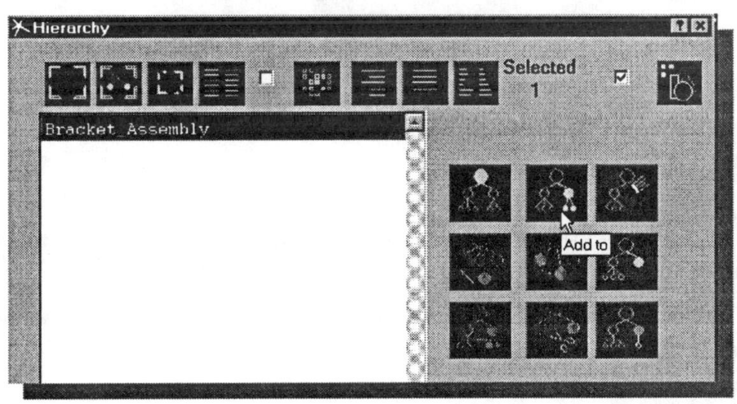

❖ The *Add to* command is used to add **instances** of parts or subassemblies to the selected assembly. An **instance** is referred to as the placement of a part in an assembly. If a second copy of the same part is placed in the assembly again, I-DEAS does not make another copy of the geometry. Each instance of a part gets its geometry from the part stored in the *Bin*. The concept of *instances* is similar to the **pointer** concept found in most computer programming languages.

6. In the prompt window, the message "*Pick part or assmebly to add*" is displayed.

7. Press and hold the **SHIFT** key and select all parts by left-clicking once on any edges of the displayed parts.

8. Press the **ENTER** key or the **middle-mouse-button** to accept the selections and end the *Add* command.

9. Click on the **Dismiss** button to close the *Hierarchy* window.

Placing the First Component in the Assembly model

- The first component placed in an assembly should be a fundamental part or subassembly that serves as a foundation, which is used to set the orientation of all subsequent parts and subassemblies. The first component is usually **grounded**, which means the part is prevented from moving in all directions within the assembly. The rest of the assembly is built on the first component, the **base component.** In most cases, this *base component* should be one that is **not likely to be removed** and **preferably a non-moving part** in the design. Note that there is no distinction in an assembly between components; the first component we place is usually considered as the *base component* because it is usually a fundamental component to which others are constrained. We can change the base component to a different base component by placing a new base component, specifying it as grounded, and then re-constraining any components placed earlier, including the first component. For our project, we will use the ***Base Plate*** as the base component in the assembly.

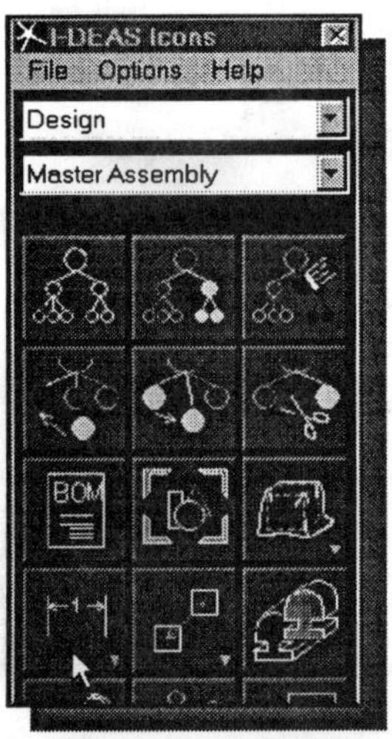

1. Press and hold down on the **Dimension** icon to display the other choices. Select the **Constrain & Dimension...** option.

- The *Constrain* window appears on the screen. Note that most of the assembly constraints are identical to the geometric constraints we have used in the *Master Modeler*.

2. In the *Constrain* window, select the ***Lock constraint*** command by left-mouse-clicking the icon.

3. In the prompt window, the message "*Pick part or assembly to add*" is displayed. Select the **Base Plate** in the display window.

4. Press the **ENTER** key or the **middle-mouse-button** to accept the selection.

5. In the prompt window, the message "*Pick second part or assembly instance to constrain (Bracket_Assembly_0)*" is displayed. Press the **ENTER** key or the **middle-mouse-button** to accept the selection.

❖ Note a *lock* symbol is placed at the origin of the default workplane.

Assembly Constraints

- We are now ready to assemble the components together. We will start by placing assembly constraints on the ***Bracket*** and the ***Base Plate***.

  To assemble components into an assembly, we need to establish the assembly relationships between components. It is a good practice to assemble components the way they would be assembled in the actual manufacturing process. **Assembly constraints** create a parent/child relationship that allows us to capture the design intent of the assembly. Because the component that we are placing actually becomes a child to the already assembled components, we must use caution when choosing constraint types and references to make sure they reflect the intent.

➢ The ***Bracket*** part will be the positioned and constrained relative to the ***Base Plate*** part.

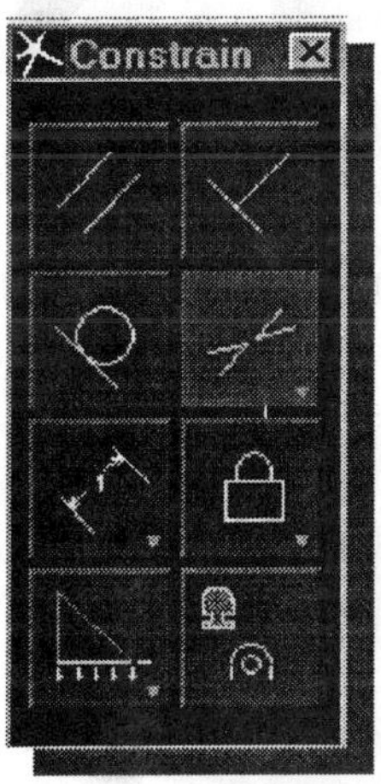

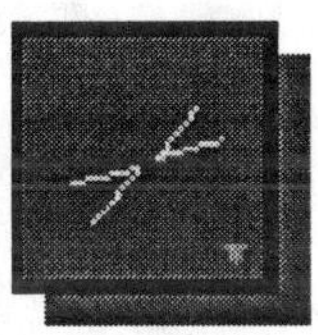

1. In the *Constrain* window, select the ***Coincident, Collinear constraint*** command by left-mouse-clicking the icon.

❖ The *coincident constraint* can be used to constrain entities to be coincident, collinear, or coplanar. The way we select entities determines the type of constraint that is applied.

2. In the prompt window, the message "*Pick the first entity to constrain*" is displayed. Select the top face of the ***Base Plate*** in the graphics window.

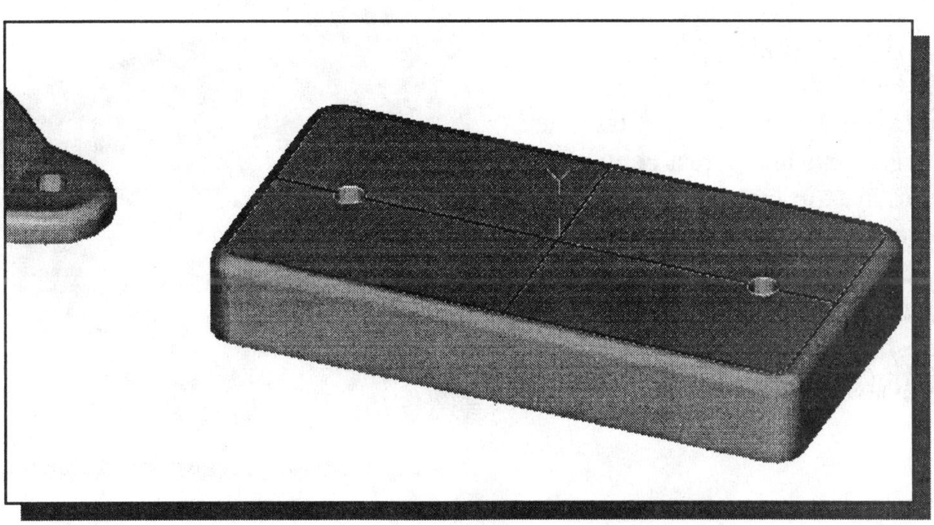

3. In the prompt window, the message "*Pick the Second entity to constrain*" is displayed. Dynamically rotate the displayed parts and select the bottom face of the ***Bracket*** in the graphics window.

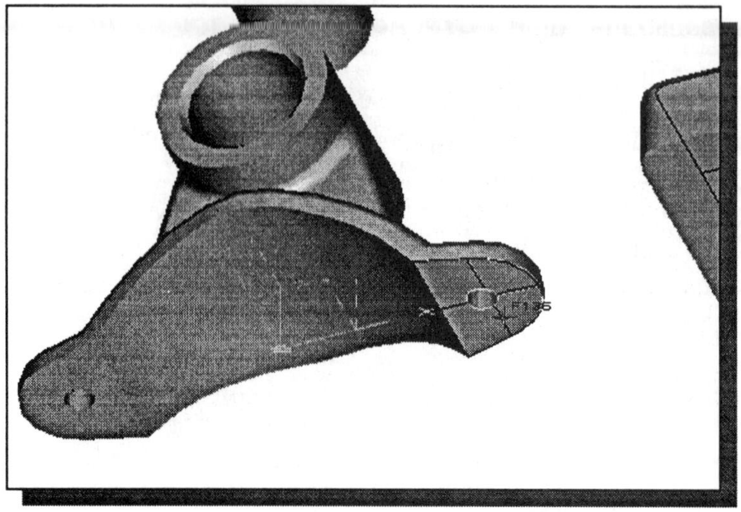

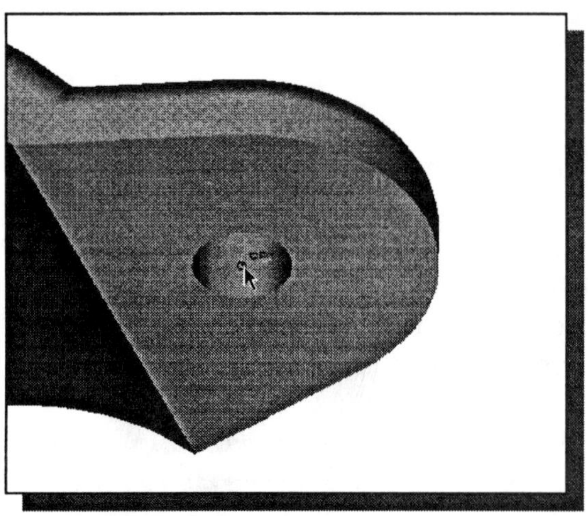

4. In the prompt window, the message "*Pick the first entity to constrain*" is displayed. Dynamically zoom in and select the center-point on the bottom face of the ***Bracket*** in the graphics window as shown.

5. Press the **ENTER** key or the **middle-mouse-button** to accept the selection.

6. In the prompt window, the message "*Pick the Second entity to constrain*" is displayed. Dynamically rotate the displayed parts and select center-point on the top face of the ***Base Plate*** in the graphics window.

7. Press the **ENTER** key or the **middle-mouse-button** to end the coincident constraint command.

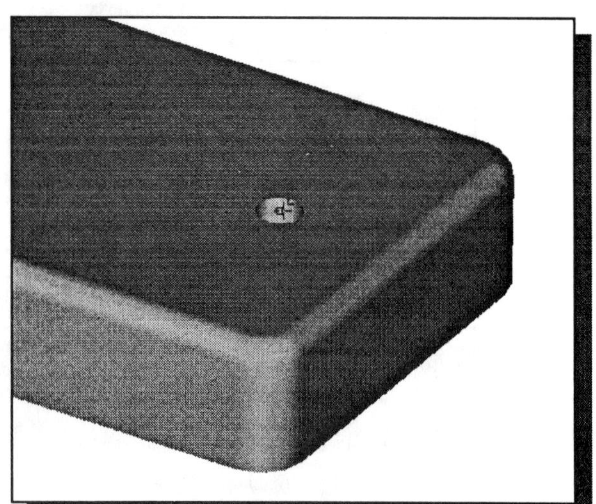

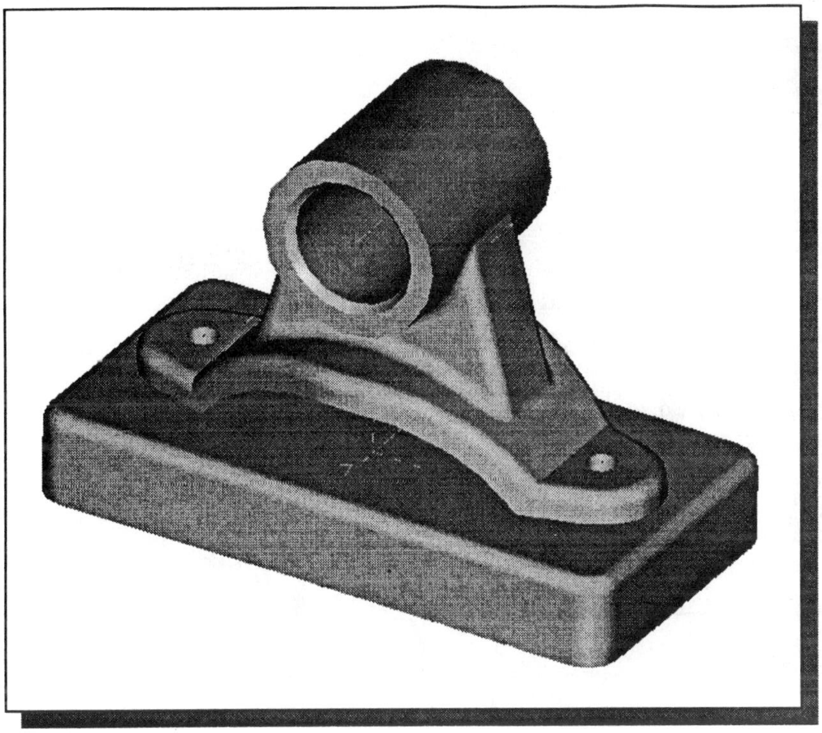

❖ Notice the different colors displayed as the constraints are applied by selecting the different types of entities. Is the ***Bracket*** part fully constrained?

Degrees of Freedom and Constraints

- Each component in an assembly has six **degrees of freedom (DOF)**, or ways in which 3D rigid bodies can move: move along X, Y, and Z axes (translational freedom), plus it can rotate around the X, Y, and Z axes (rotational freedom). Translational DOFs allow the part to move in the direction of the specified vector. Rotational DOFs allow the part to turn about the specified axis.

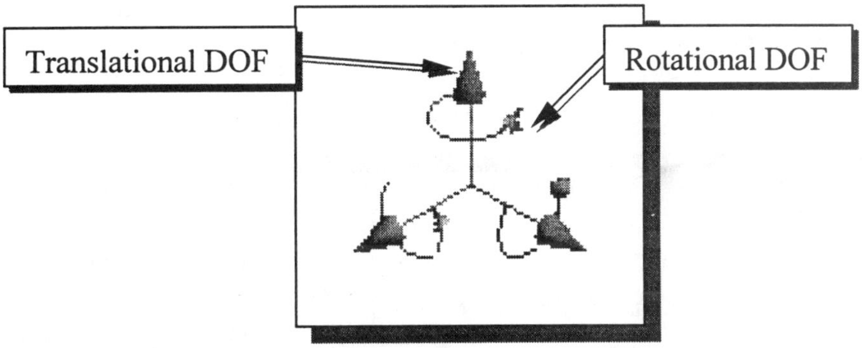

❖ **The I-DEAS constraint color-codes:**

- **Blue indicates fully constrained.**
- **Green indicates unconstrained.**
- **Other colors indicate partially constrained.**
- **Arrows indicate the direction of movement.**

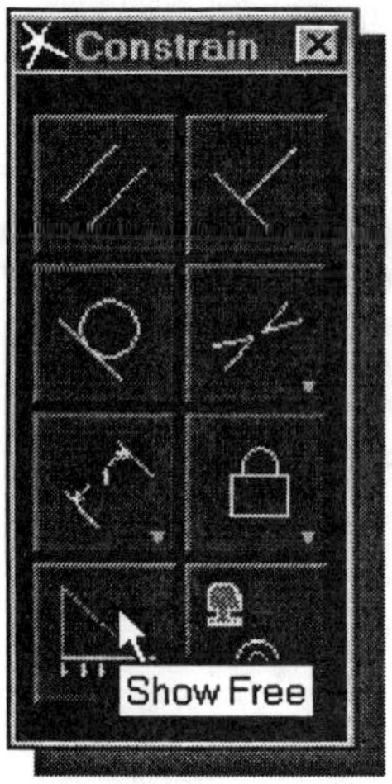

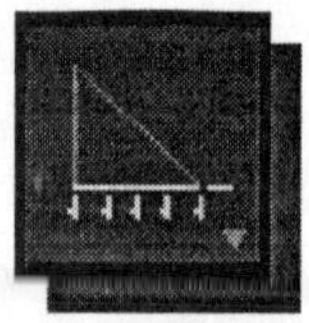

1. In the *Constrain* window, select the ***Show Free*** command by left-mouse-clicking the icon.

❖ The *Show Free* command is used to display the degrees of freedom (DOF) of any parts in an assembly.

2. In the prompt window, the message "*Pick Entity*" is displayed. Select the ***Bracket*** part by clicking twice on any surface of the part.

3. Press the **ENTER** key or the **middle-mouse-button** to accept the selection.

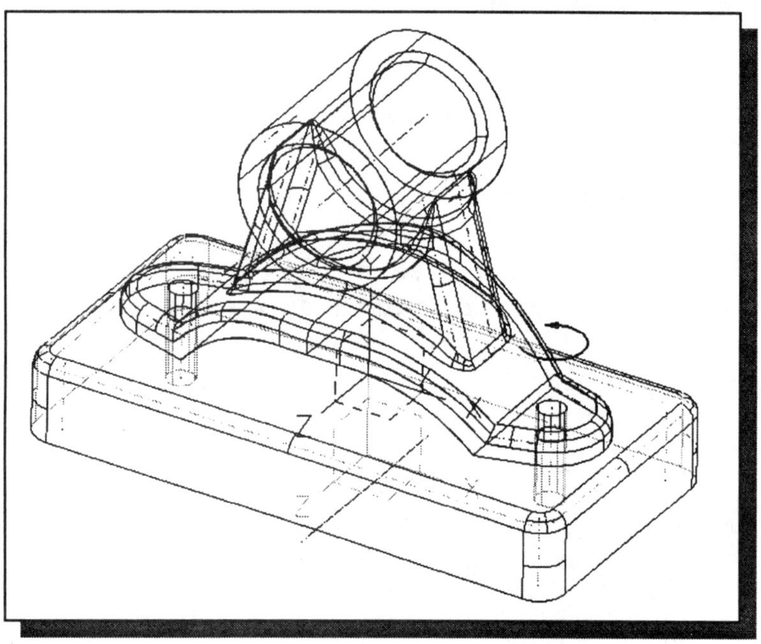

❖ With the *Show Free* command, I-DEAS displays the directions the part is free to move or rotate. Two constraints are applied to the ***Bracket*** part that removed five degrees of freedom of the part. The ***Bracket*** part is still free to rotate about the Y-axis as shown in the figure.

4. In the prompt window, the message "*Pick Entity*" is displayed. Select the ***Bushing*** part by clicking twice on any edge of the part.

5. Press the **ENTER** key or the **middle-mouse-button** to accept the selection. I-DEAS displays six arrows next to the part, the part can move in all three directions and rotate about the three axes.

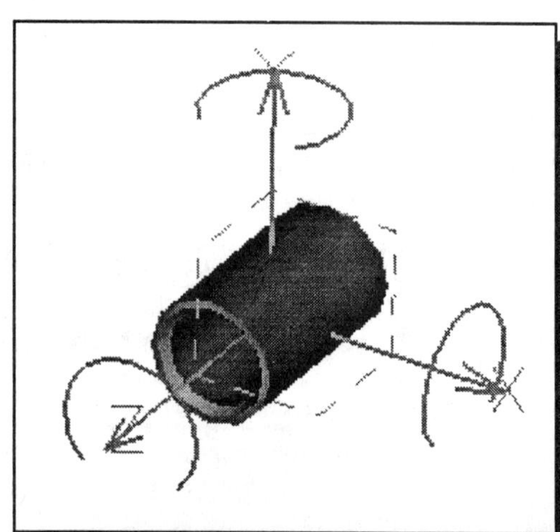

❖ In *I-DEAS*, the degrees-of-freedom symbol shows the remaining degrees of freedom (both translational and rotational) for the selected component. When a component is fully constrained in an assembly, the component cannot move in any direction. The position of the component is fixed relative to other assembly components. All of its degrees of freedom are removed. When we place an assembly constraint between two selected components, they are positioned relative to one another. Movement is still possible in the unconstrained directions. Assembly models are created by applying proper *assembly constraints* to restrict and control the movement between parts. Constraints eliminate rigid body degrees of freedom (**DOF**). A 3D part has six degrees of freedom since the part can rotate and translate relative to the three coordinate axes. Each time we add a constraint between two parts, one or more DOF is eliminated. The movement of a fully constrained part is restricted in all directions. Two basic types of assembly constraints are available in *I-DEAS*: geometric constraints and dimensional constraints; the applications of these constraints are parallel to the 2D constraints we have used in the *Master Modeler* application. Five geometric constraints are available in I-DEAS: *parallel*, *perpendicular*, *tangent*, *coincident*, and *lock.* The results of the applied geometric constraints depend on the selections of the different types of geometric entities. For example, as illustrated in the above procedure, applying the *coincident constraint* by selecting two planar surfaces results in the two surfaces being coplanar, thereby eliminating three degrees of freedom. Selecting two points joins the two points at the same location, also eliminating three degrees of freedom. Each constraint removes different combinations of rigid body degrees of freedom. Note that it is possible to apply different constraints and achieve the same results.

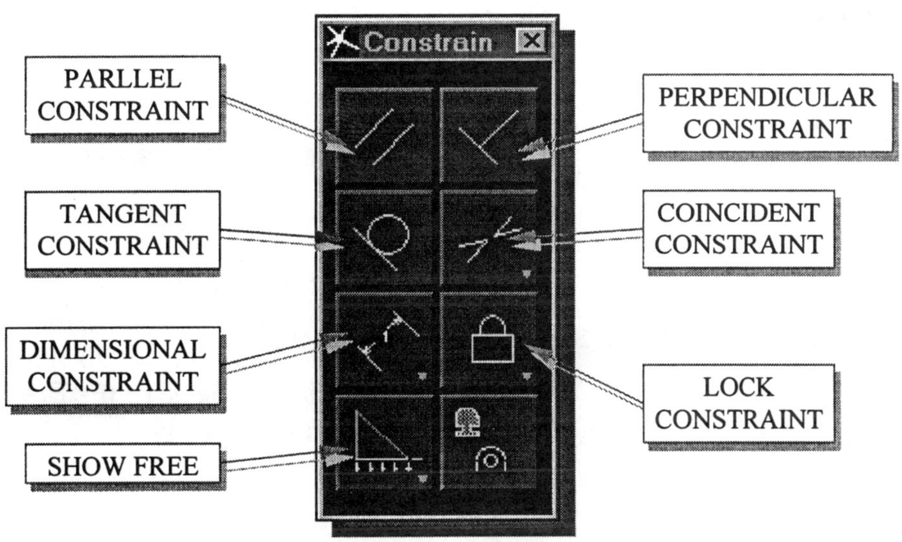

➢ It is usually a good idea to fully constrain components so that their behavior is predictable as changes are made to the assembly. Leaving some degrees of freedom open can sometimes help retain design flexibility. In some cases, it might be necessary to leave some degrees of freedom open to assure all components are assembled correctly. As a general rule, we should use only enough constraints to ensure predictable assembly behavior and avoid unnecessary complexity. For designs involving moving parts, a fully constrained assembly model is most desirable.

Fully Constrained Component

- Besides selecting the surfaces of solid models to apply constraints, we can also select the established part coordinate systems to apply the assembly constraints. This is an additional advantage of using the *BORN technique* in creating part models. For the ***Bracket*** part, we will apply another *coincident constraint* to two of the work planes and eliminate the last rotational DOF.

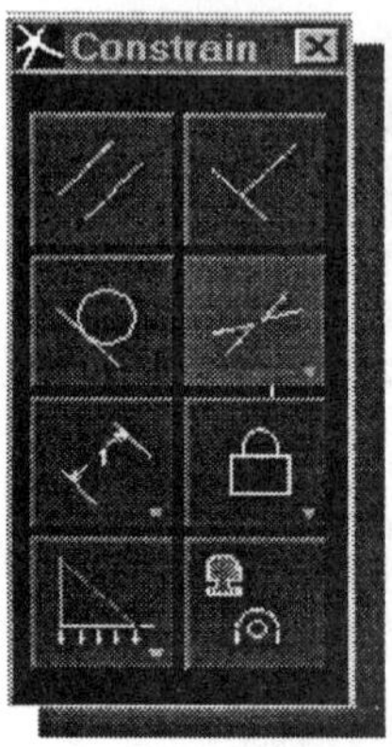

1. In the *Constrain* window, select the ***Coincident, Collinear constraint*** command by left-mouse-clicking the icon.

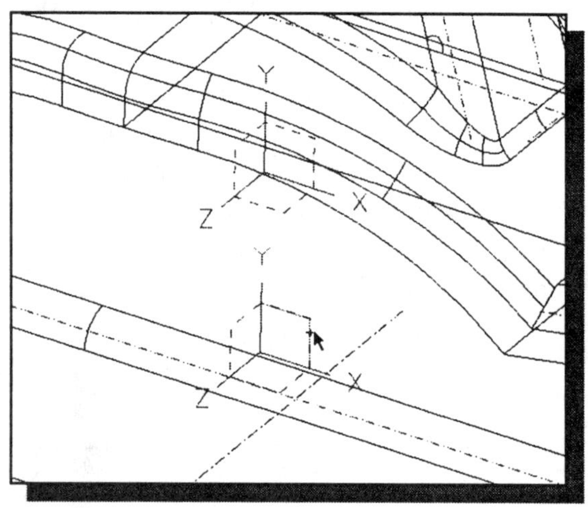

2. In the prompt window, the message "*Pick the first entity to constrain*" is displayed. Dynamically zoom-in and select the XY-plane of the ***Base Plate*** part in the graphics window.

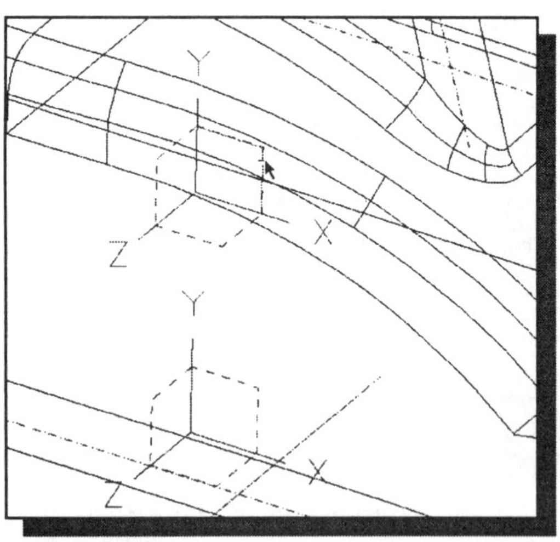

3. In the prompt window, the message "*Pick the Second entity to constrain*" is displayed. Dynamically rotate the displayed parts and select the XY-plane of the ***Bracket*** in the graphics window.

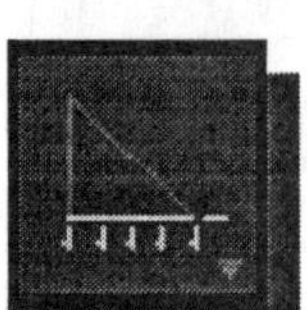

➢ On your own, use the *Show Free* command to confirm the ***Bracket*** part is fully constrained.

Placing the Bushing

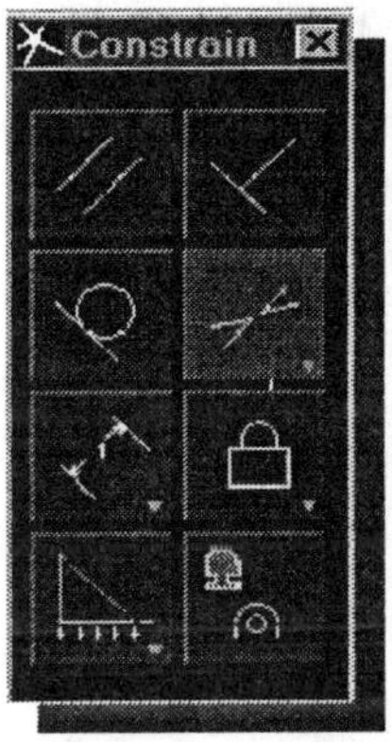

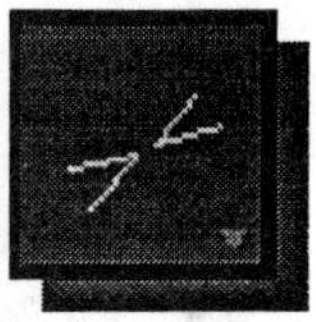

1. In the *Constrain* window, select the ***Coincident, Collinear constraint*** command by left-mouse-clicking the icon.

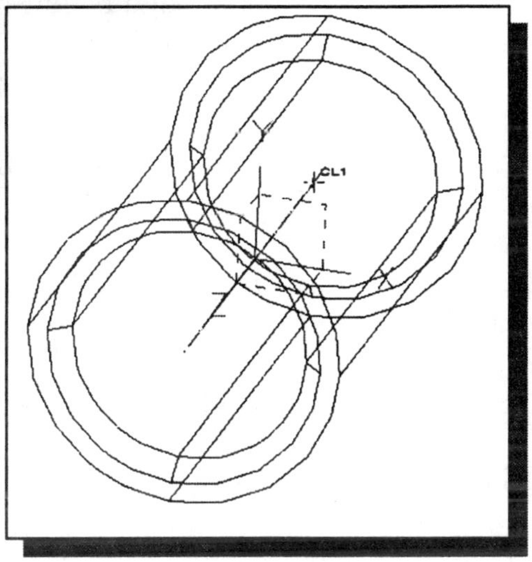

2. In the prompt window, the message "*Pick the first entity to constrain*" is displayed. Dynamically zoom-in and select the center axis of the ***Bushing*** part in the graphics window. (Note the **CLx** symbol signifies the high-lighted entity is a centerline.)

3. Press the **ENTER** key or the **middle-mouse-button** to accept the selection.

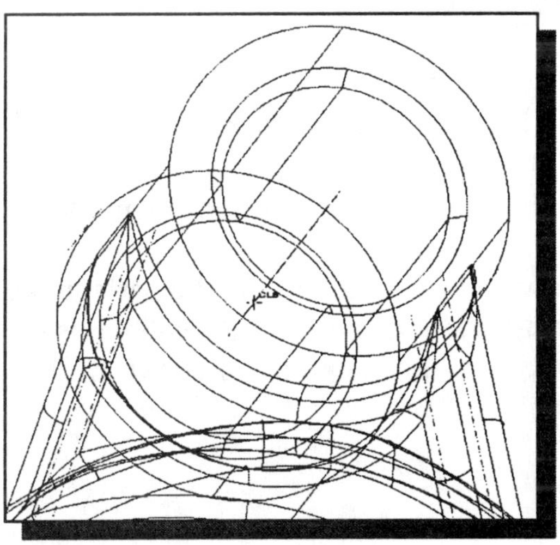

4. In the prompt window, the message "*Pick the Second entity to constrain*" is displayed. Dynamically zoom-in and select the center axis of the ***Bracket*** part, as shown in the figure, in the graphics window. (Note the CLx symbol signifies the highlighted entity is a centerline.)

5. Press the **ENTER** key or the **middle-mouse-button** to accept the selection.

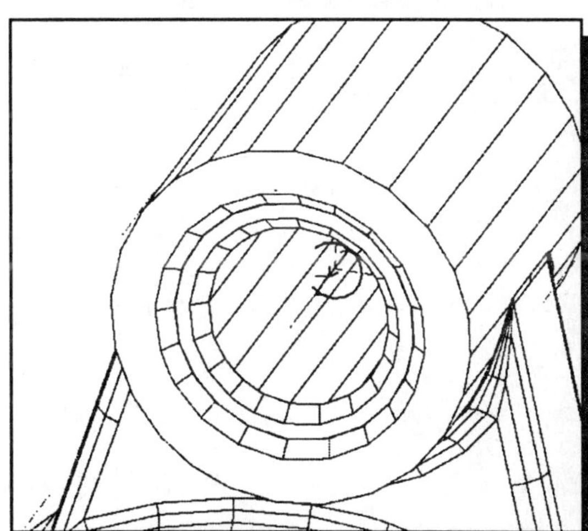

➢ On your own, use the *Show Free* command to examine the directions of free movement of the ***Bushing*** part.

Changing the Orientation of the Bushing Part

➢ Next, we will reposition the ***Bushing*** part to illustrate the effects of the applied constraints in the assembly model.

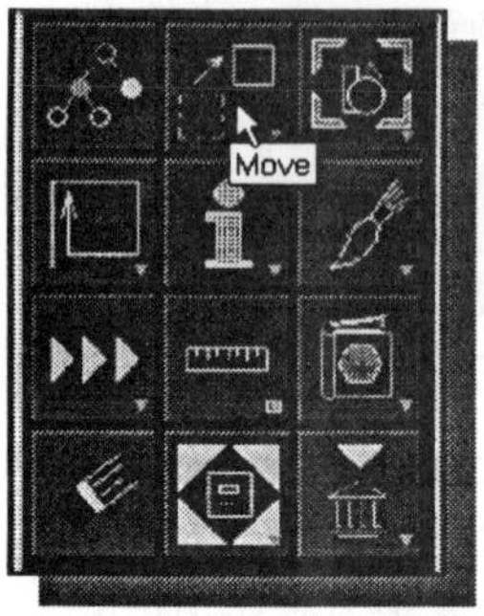

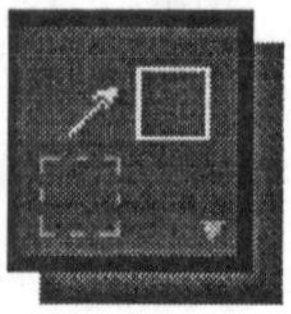

1. Select the **Move** command by left-mouse-clicking once on the icon in the icon panel.

❖ The *Move* command can be used to reposition parts in the unconstrained directions.

2. In the *prompt* window, the message "*Pick entity to move*" is displayed. Select the ***Bushing*** part in the graphics window.

3. Press the **ENTER** key or the **middle-mouse-button** to accept the selection.

4. In the *prompt* window, the message "*Enter Translation X,Y,Z (0.0,0.0,0.0)*" is displayed. Enter **1.0,1.0,3.0** as the distances to move the ***Bushing*** part in the X,Y,Z directions relative to its current location.

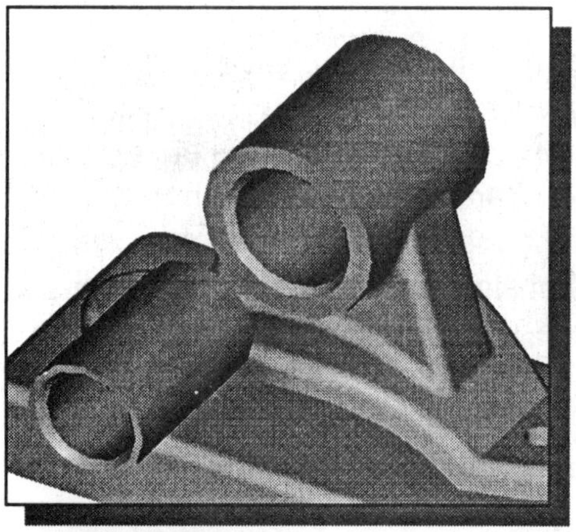

❖ Notice the ***Bushing*** part is moved only in the Z direction. The applied collinear constraint is maintained at all times in the assembly model.

➢ On your own, dynamically rotate the parts in the graphics window and confirm the center axis of the ***Bushing*** is aligned to the center axis of the ***Bracket*** part.

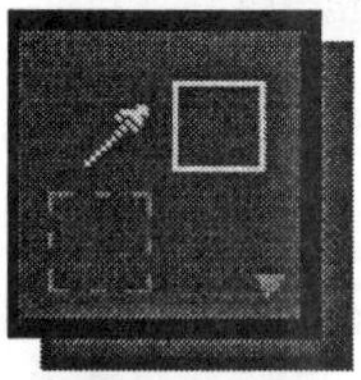

5. Select the ***Move*** command by left-mouse-clicking once on the icon in the icon panel.

6. In the *prompt* window, the message "*Pick entity to move*" is displayed. Select the ***Bushing*** part in the graphics window.

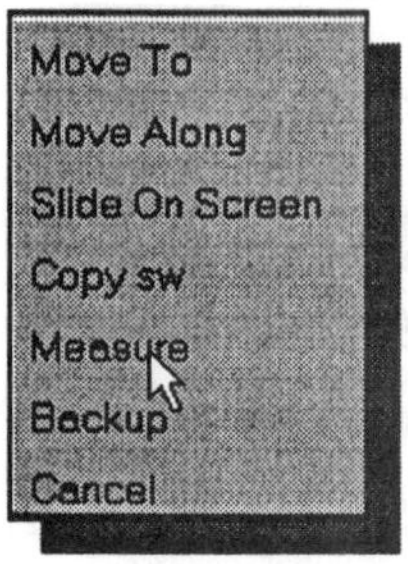

7. Press the **ENTER** key or the **middle-mouse-button** to accept the selection.

8. Inside the *graphics* window, press and hold down the **right-mouse-button** to display the option menu and select **Measure**.

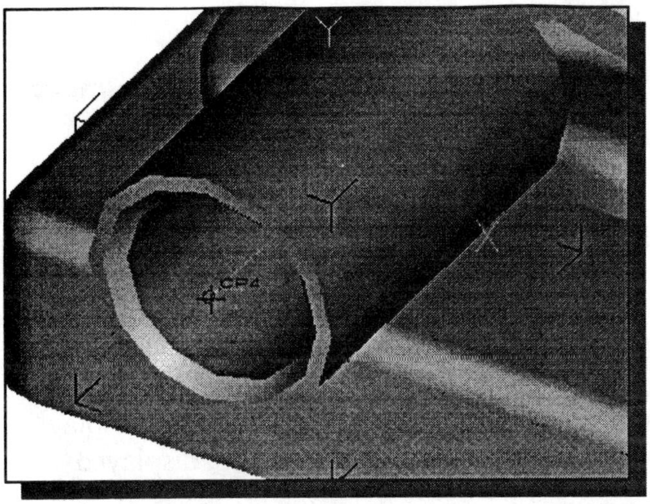

9. Select the front center point of the ***Bushing*** part. (Move the cursor along the axis to view the different center points available.)

10. Press the **ENTER** key or the **middle-mouse-button** to accept the selection.

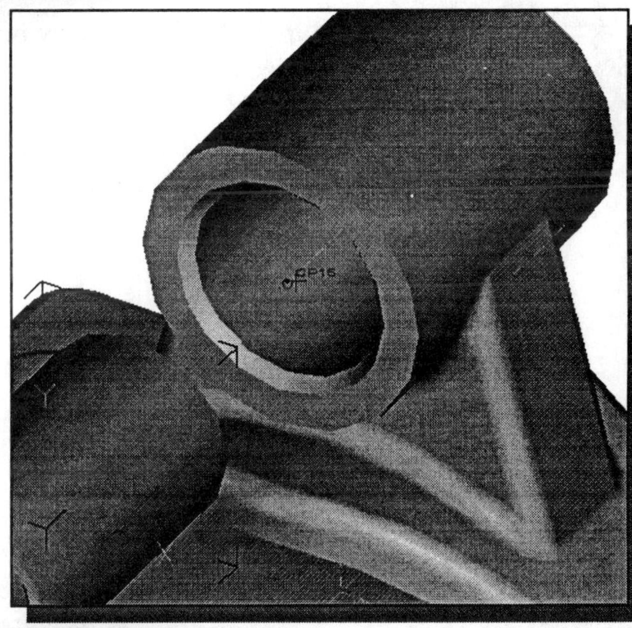

11. Select the front center point on the smaller circular surface of the chamfer feature of the ***Bracket*** part as shown. (Move the cursor along the axis to view the different center points available.)

12. Press the **ENTER** key or the **middle-mouse-button** to accept the selection.

13. Press the **ENTER** key or the **middle-mouse-button** to end the *Measure* option.

I-DEAS List

```
Proj. YZ      : DYZ1 =  3.000000
Proj. ZX      : DZX1 =  3.000000
Delta X       : DX1  =  0.0
Delta Y       : DY1  = -5.463696D-16
Delta Z       : DZ1  = -3.000000
Total         : D1   =  3.000000
```

➢ In the *I-DEAS List* window, the measured distance is displayed. Note that the zero distances in the X and Y directions.

14. In the prompt window, the message "*Enter Translation X,Y,Z (0.0,-5.463D-16,-3.0)*" is displayed. Press the **ENTER** key or the **middle-mouse-button** to accept the displayed values.

❖ The movement of a part is restricted in the unconstrained directions. The applied constraints are maintained at all time in the assembly model.

Locking the Bushing part

❖ In the actual manufacturing process, the ***Bushing*** part is pressed-fit into the ***Bracket*** part. We will therefore apply a ***Lock* constraint** to the ***Bushing*** and the ***Bracket***.

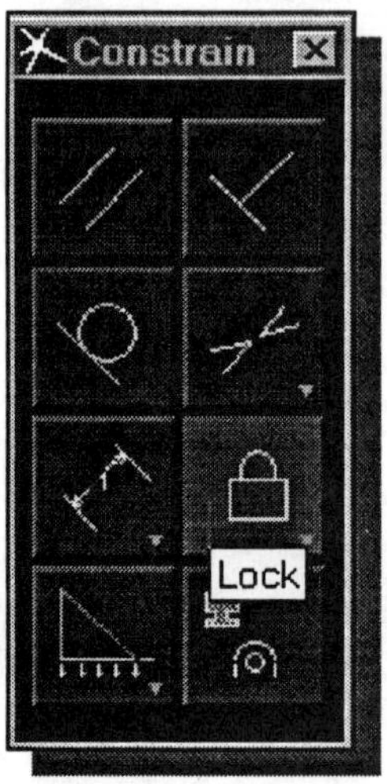

1. In the *Constrain* window, select the ***Lock* constraint** command by left-mouse-clicking once on the icon.

2. In the *prompt* window, the message "*Pick part or assembly to constrain*" is displayed. Select the ***Bushing*** part in the display window. Note the two degrees of freedom symbol displayed.

3. Press the **ENTER** key or the **middle-mouse-button** to accept the selection.

4. In the prompt window, the message "*Pick second part or assembly instance to constrain (Bracket_Assembly_0)*" is displayed. Select the ***Bracket*** in the display window.

5. Press the **ENTER** key or the **middle-mouse-button** to accept the selection.

❖ Notice the displayed color of the ***Bushing*** part, indicating the part is fully constrained.

6. Press the **ENTER** key or the **middle-mouse-button** to end the *Lock constraint* command.

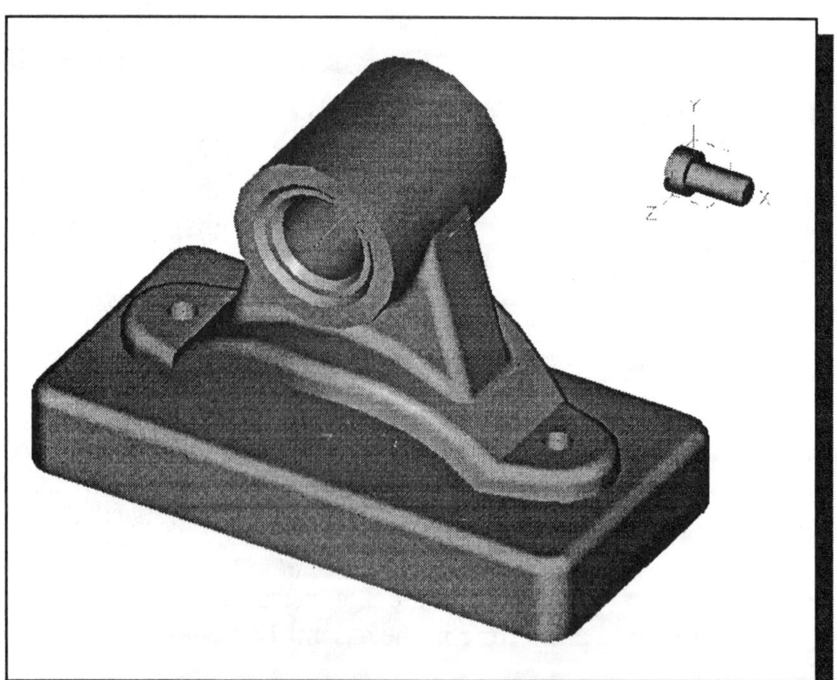

Adjusting the Orientation of the Cap-Screw

❖ As a general rule, parts should be oriented in the assembled directions to simulate the actual assembly process. In I-DEAS, we can use the ***Move*** and ***Rotate*** commands to adjust the orientations of parts.

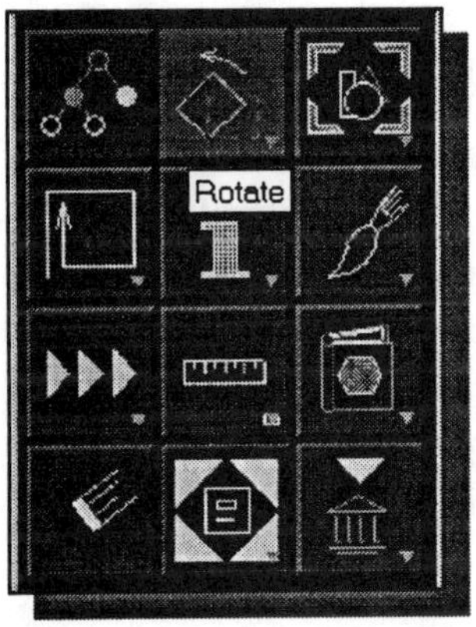

1. Select the ***Rotate*** command by left-mouse-clicking once on the icon in the icon panel.

❖ The *Rotate* command can be used to rotate parts in any unconstrained directions.

2. In the *prompt* window, the message "*Pick entity to move*" is displayed. Select the ***Cap-screw*** part in the graphics window.

3. Press the **ENTER** key or the **middle-mouse-button** to accept the selection.

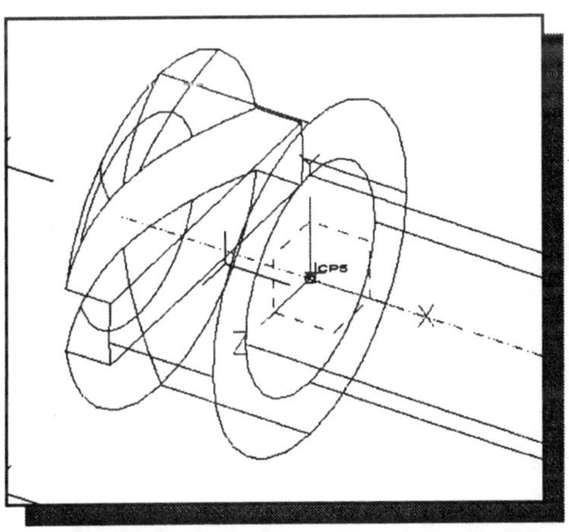

4. In the prompt window, the message "*Pick pivot point (origin)*" is displayed. Choose the origin of the ***Cap-screw*** part as the pivot point. Select the origin when the CPx symbol is displayed, as shown.

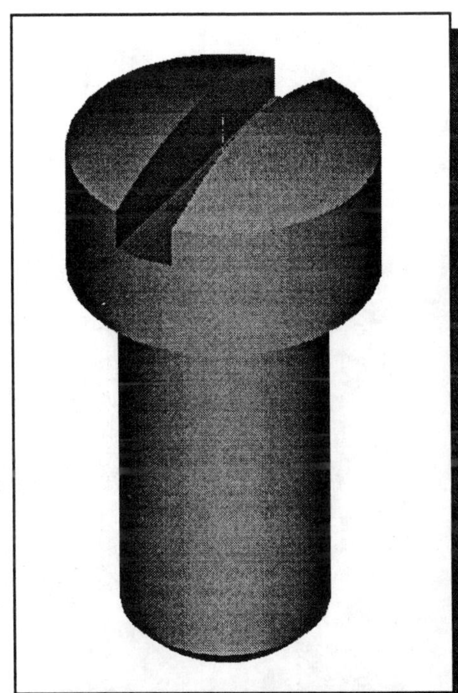

5. In the *prompt* window, the message "*Enter Rotation angles (0.0,0.0,0.0)*" is displayed. Enter **0.0,0.0,90** to rotate the part clockwise about the Z-axis.

➢ On your own, use the ***Rotate*** command to orient the ***Cap-screw*** in the vertical direction as shown. Position the ***Cap-screw*** near the right side of the ***Bracket*** part.

Assemble the Cap-Screw

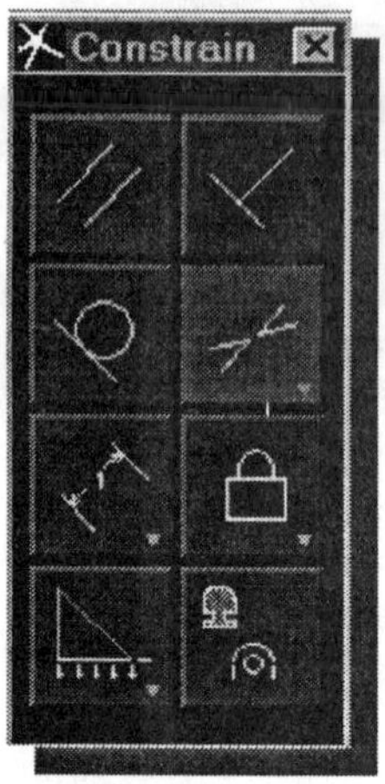

1. In the *Constrain* window, select the ***Coincident, Collinear constraint*** command by left-mouse-clicking the icon.

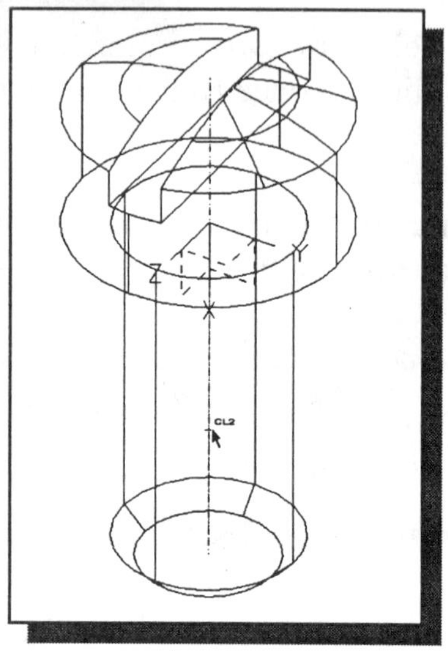

2. In the *prompt* window, the message "*Pick the first entity to constrain*" is displayed. Dynamically zoom-in and select the center axis of the **Cap-screw** part in the graphics window. (Note the CLx symbol signifying the highlighted entity is a centerline.)

3. In the *prompt* window, the message "*Pick the Second entity to constrain*" is displayed. Dynamically zoom-in and select the center axis of the right drill hole of the **Bracket** part, as shown in the figure, in the graphics window. (Note the CLx symbol signifies the highlighted entity is a centerline.)

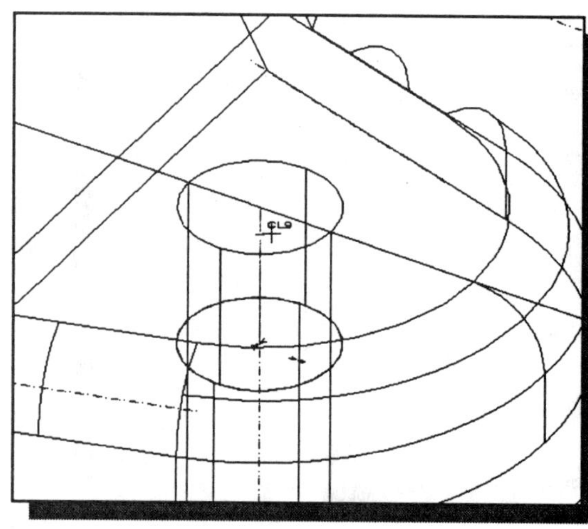

❖ On your own, examine and confirm the alignment of the **Cap-screw** part (in relation to the **Bracket** part.) Besides using the *coincident constraint* in the Y direction, we can also apply dimensional constraints to control the placement of the part. In most cases, the dimensional constraints allow us great flexibility in constraining components in an assembly.

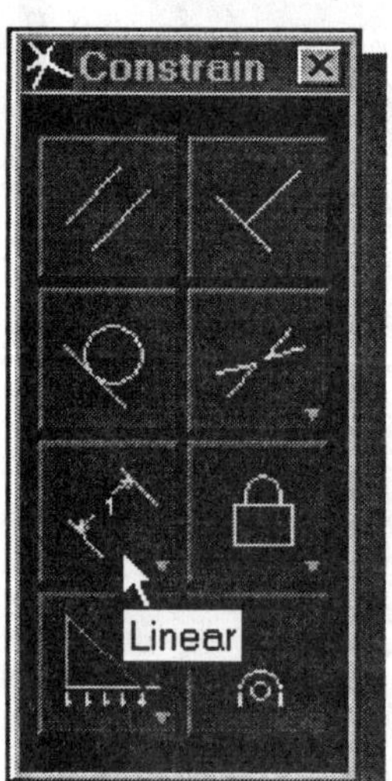

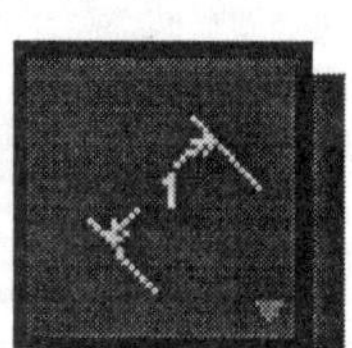

4. In the *Constrain* window, select the ***Coincident, Collinear constraint*** command by left-mouse-clicking the icon.

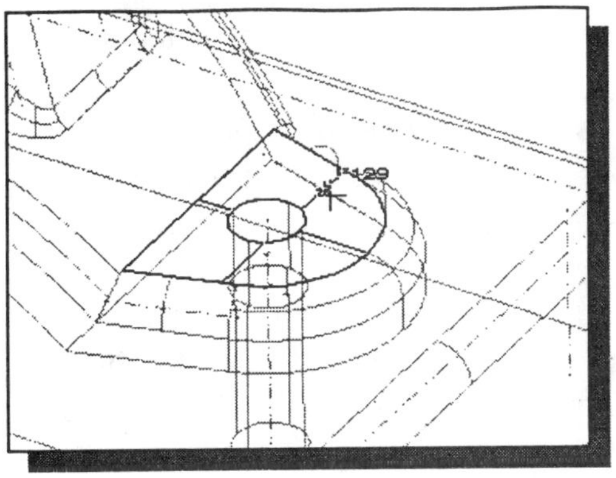

5. In the *prompt* window, the message "*Pick the first entity to Dimension*" is displayed. Select the top face of the ***Bracket*** part as shown in the figure.

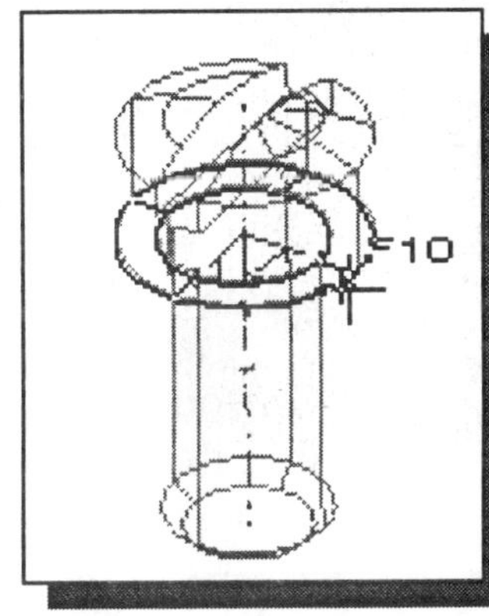

6. In the *prompt* window, the message "*Pick the second entity to Dimension*" is displayed. Select the circular surface of head of the ***Cap-screw*** part as shown in the figure.

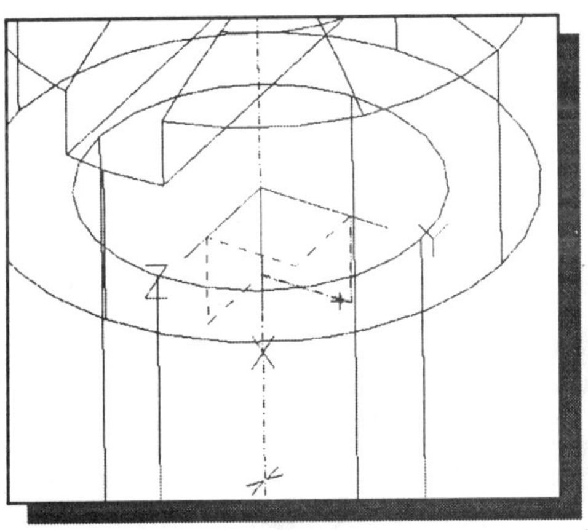

7. In the prompt window, the message "*Pick Dimension Plane*" is displayed. Select the **XY Plane** of the ***Cap-screw*** part coordinate system as shown in the figure.

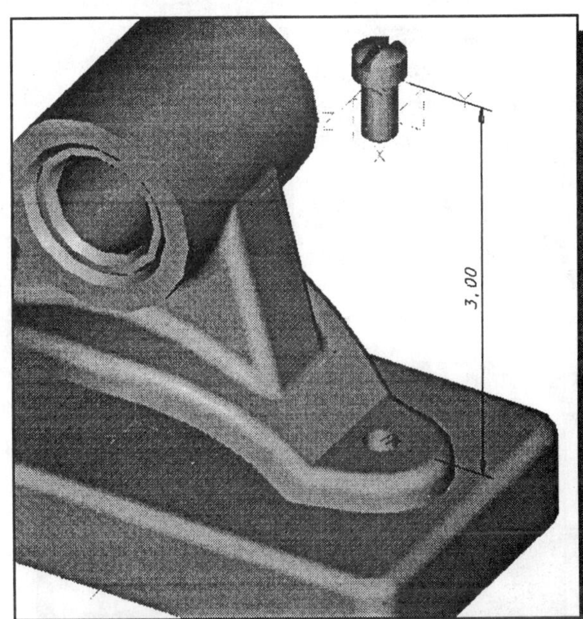

8. Place the dimension text toward the right side of the graphics window as shown.

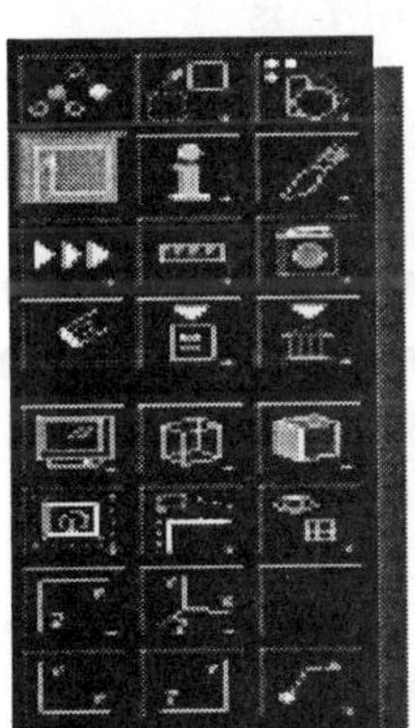

9. Choose **Modify** in the icon panel. (The icon is located in the second row of the application icon panel.)

10. The message "*Pick entity to modify*" is displayed in the prompt window. Pick the dimension we just created.

11. Press the **ENTER** key or the **middle-mouse-button** to accept the selection.

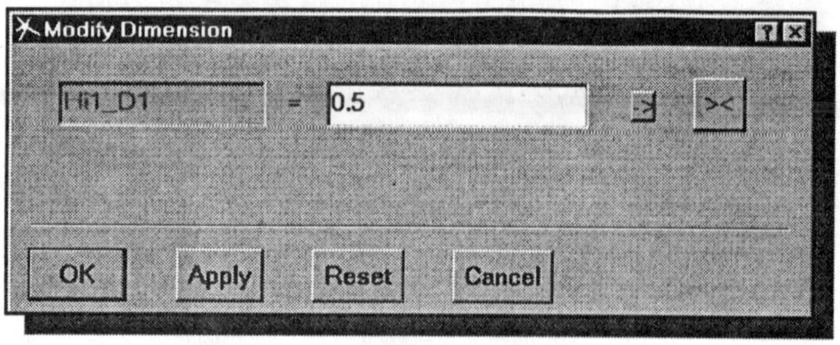

12. In the *Modify Dimension* window, click inside the value input box and change the dimension value to **0.5**, which will adjust the vertical alignment of the ***Cap-screw***.

13. Click on the **OK** button to accept the settings and adjust the size of the geometry.

14. On your own, repeat the above steps and adjust the above dimension value to **0.0**; the dimension constraint acts as a control for the vertical alignment of the ***Cap-screw***. Is the ***Cap-screw*** part fully constrained now?

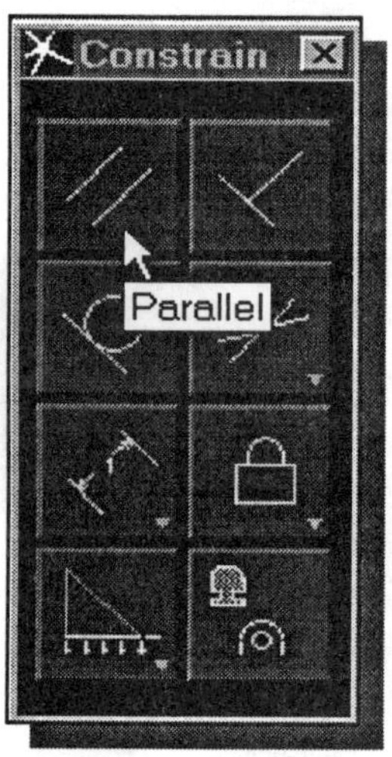

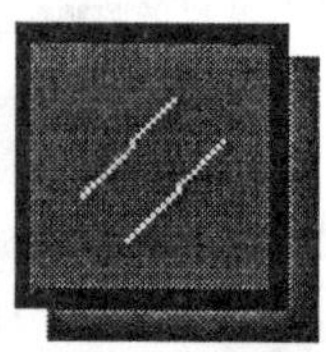

15. Select **Parallel** in the *Constrain* window.

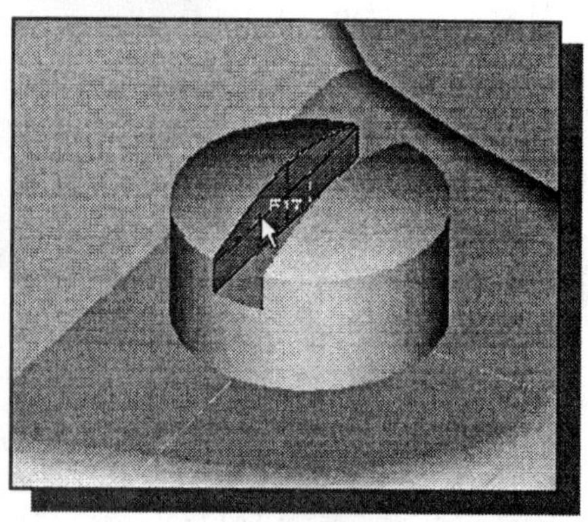

16. In the prompt window, the message "*Pick the first entity to constrain*" is displayed. Select one of the vertical surfaces of the ***Cap-screw*** part in the graphics window. (Note the Fx symbol signifies the highlighted entity is a face.)

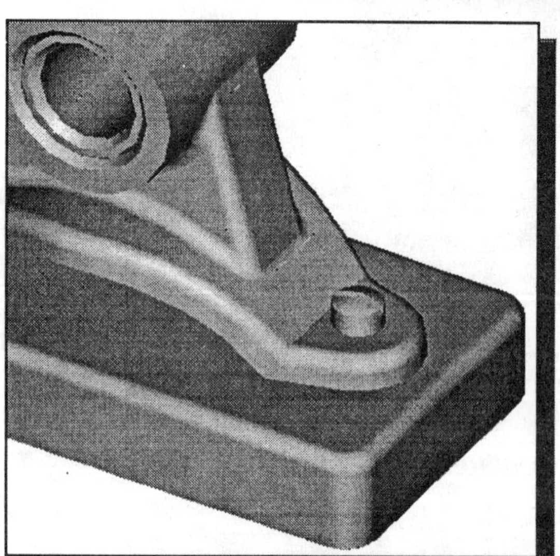

17. In the prompt window, the message "*Pick the Second entity to constrain*" is displayed. Select the front face of the ***Base Plate*** part in the graphics window.

➢ What other combinations of constraints can we apply to the ***Cap-screw*** and achieve the same results?

Duplicating an instance

- For the ***Bracket*** assembly, we need two copies of the ***Cap-screw*** part. The ***Duplicate*** command can be used to quickly create copies of any assembly components.

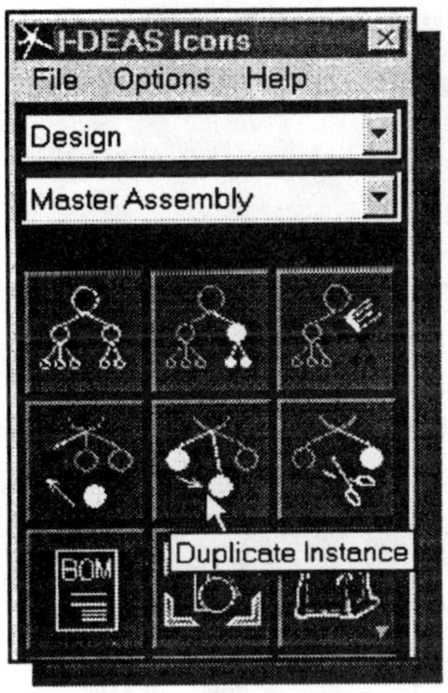

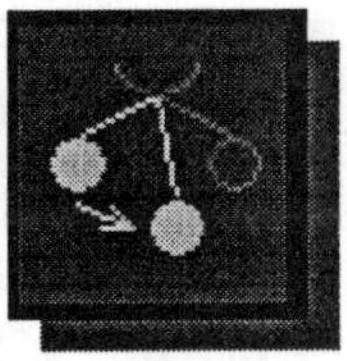

1. Select **Duplicate Instance** in the icon panel.

2. In the prompt window, the message "*Pick instances to duplicate*" is displayed. Select the ***Cap-screw*** part in the graphics window.

3. In the prompt window, the message "*Pick Assembly to add instance to (Hierarchy...)*" is displayed. Select the ***Bracket Assembly*** by clicking on any of the components in the graphics window.

4. Inside the graphics window, hold down the **left-mouse-button** on top of the ***Cap-screw*** part and drag to the left side of the ***Bracket Assembly***.

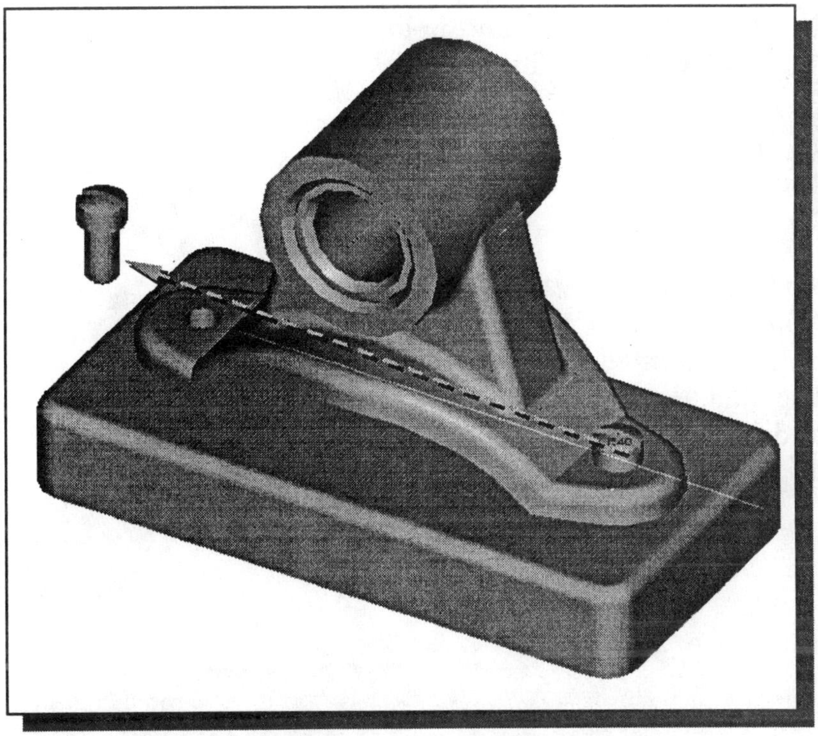

❖ The second copy of the ***Cap-screw*** is placed in the new location, oriented in the same directions as the original part.

➢ On your own, apply proper constraints to the second copy of the ***Cap-screw*** part.

Exploded View of the Assembly

- Exploded assemblies are often used in design presentations, catalogs, sales literature and in the shop to show all of the parts of an assembly and how they fit together. In *I-DEAS*, an exploded assembly can be created by two methods: (1) Apply proper dimensional constraints to control the movement in a specific direction, as it was illustrated in the previous section. (2) Use the ***Explode Linearly*** and ***Explode Radially*** commands.

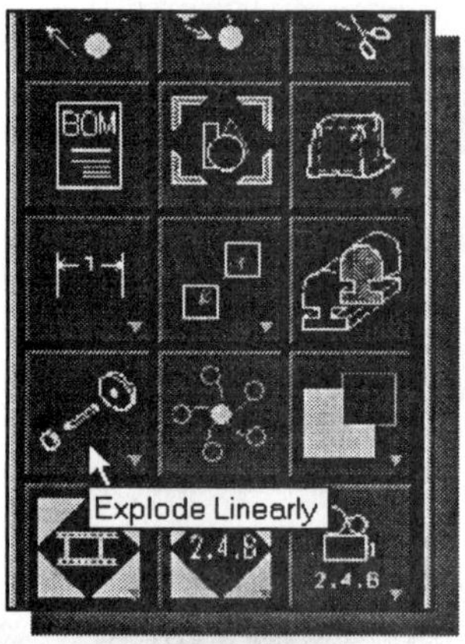

1. Select **Explode Linearly** in the icon panel.

2. In the *prompt* window, the message "*Pick assembly to explode*" is displayed. Select the ***Bracket Assembly*** by clicking on any components of the assembly in the *graphics* window.

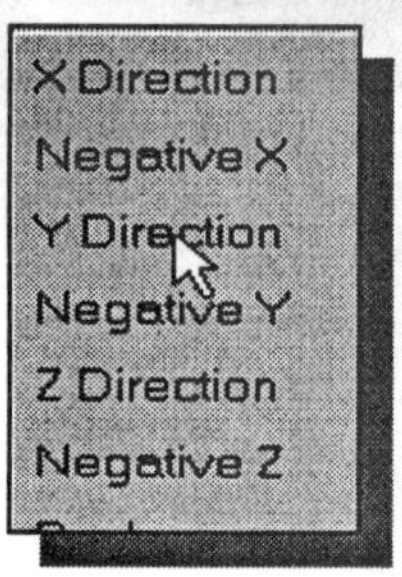

3. Move the cursor inside the graphics window. Press and hold down the **right-mouse-button** to display the option menu and select the **Y Direction** option.

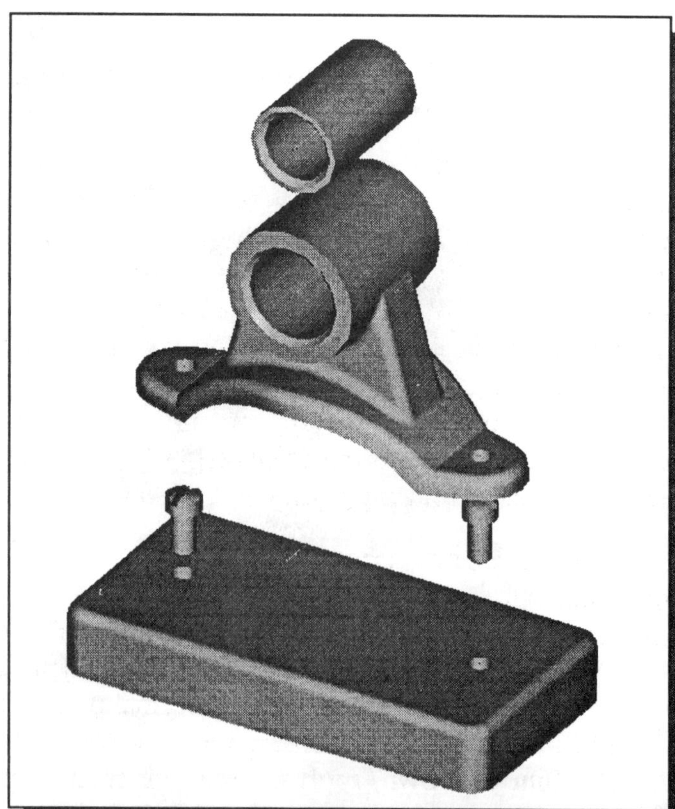

4. In the prompt window, the message "*Enter minimum distance between entities (0.0)*" is displayed. Enter **0.25** as the distance to move in the positive Y direction.

➢ On your own, repeat the above steps and adjust the distances in between the components of the assembly in the X and Z directions. You are also encouraged to experiment with the ***Explode Radially*** command to create an exploded view of the assembly.

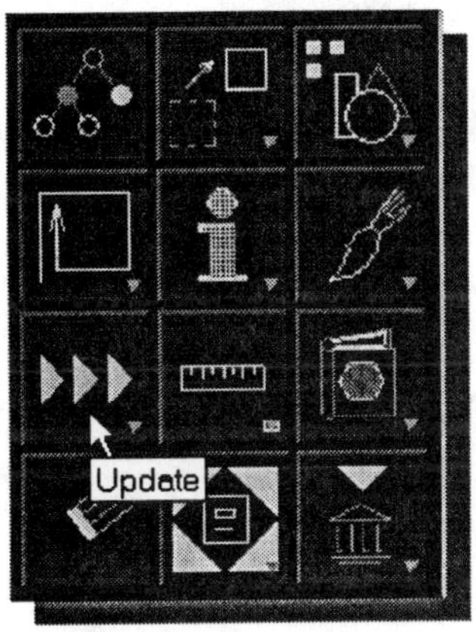

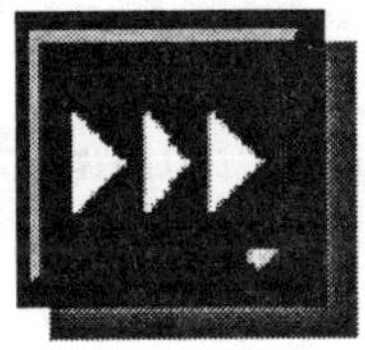

5. Pick **Update** in the icon panel. (The icon is in the third row of the application specific icon panel.) I-DEAS will reestablish the applied constraints to the assembly model.

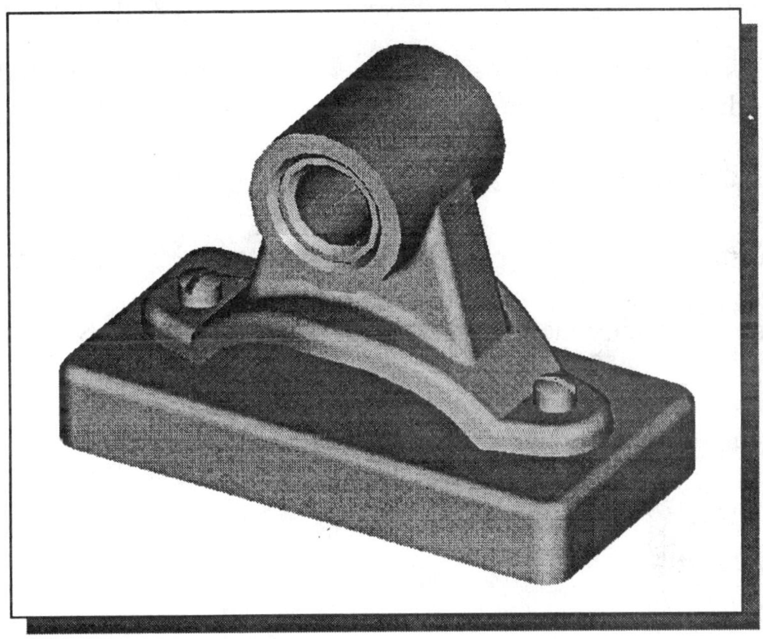

Conclusion

Design includes all activities involved from the original concept to the finished product. Design is the process by which products are created and modified. For many years designers sought ways to describe and analyze three-dimensional designs without building physical models. With the advancements in computer technology, the creation of parametric models on computers offers a wide range of benefits. Parametric models are easier to interpret and can be easily altered. Parametric models can be analyzed using finite element analysis software, and simulation of real-life loads can be applied to the models and the results graphically displayed. The finalized solid models can also be used directly by manufacturing equipment to manufacture the product.

Throughout this text, various modeling techniques have been presented. Mastering these techniques will enable you to create intelligent and flexible solid models. The goal is to make use of the tools provided by *I-DEAS* and to successfully capture the **DESIGN INTENT** of the product. In many instances, only a single approach to the modeling tasks was presented; you are encouraged to repeat all of the chapters and develop different ways of thinking in accomplishing the same tasks. We have only scratched the surface of *I-DEAS*'s functionality. The more time you spend using the system, the easier it will be to perform parametric modeling *with I-DEAS.*

Questions:

1. What is the purpose of using **Assembly constraints**?
2. List and describe three of the commonly used **Assembly constraints**.
3. Describe the difference between the **coincident** constraint and the **collinear** constraint.
4. In an assembly, can we place more than one copy of a part? How is it done?
5. How should we determine the assembly order of different parts in an assembly model?
6. How do we create an exploded assembly in *I-DEAS*?
7. In *I-DEAS*, how do we delete an applied assembly constraint?
8. Can we modify the dimensions of a part in the I-DEAS Master Assembly application?
9. Create sketches showing the steps you plan to use to create the four parts required for the assembly shown on the next page:

Ex.1)

Ex.2)

Ex.3)

Ex.4)

Exercise:

Leveling Device

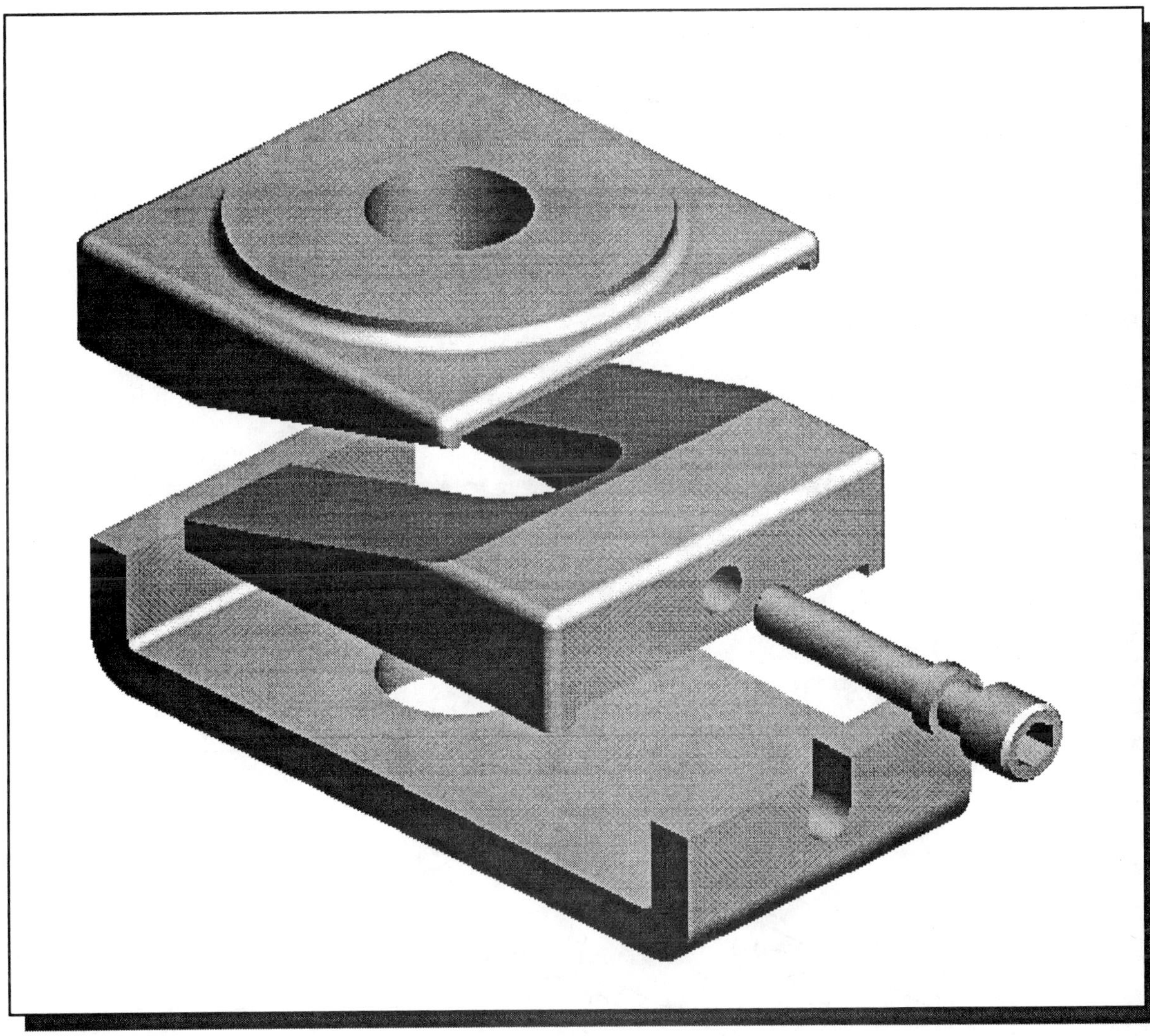

1. Base Plate (Units: mm)

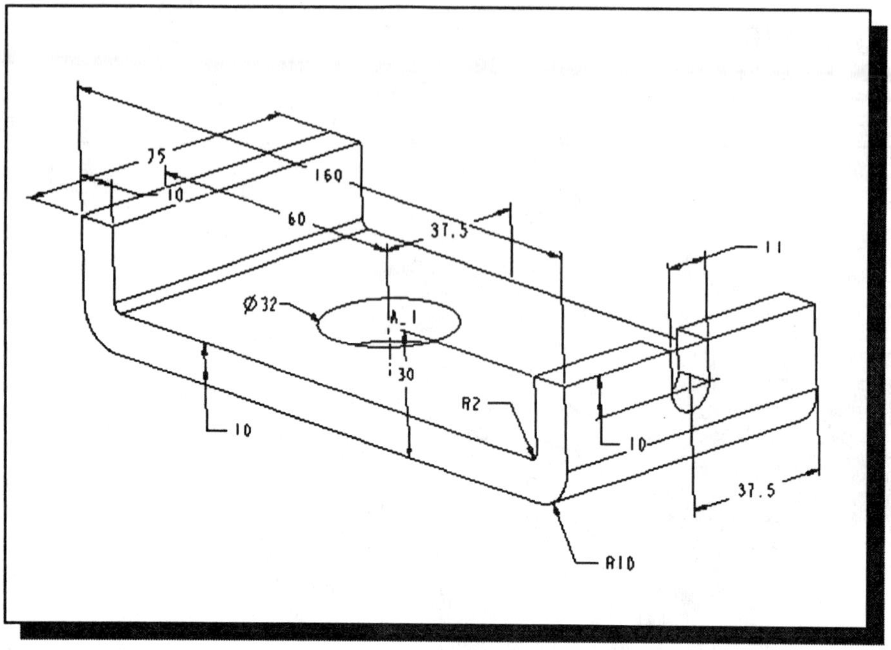

2. Sliding Block

(Rounds & Fillets: R3)

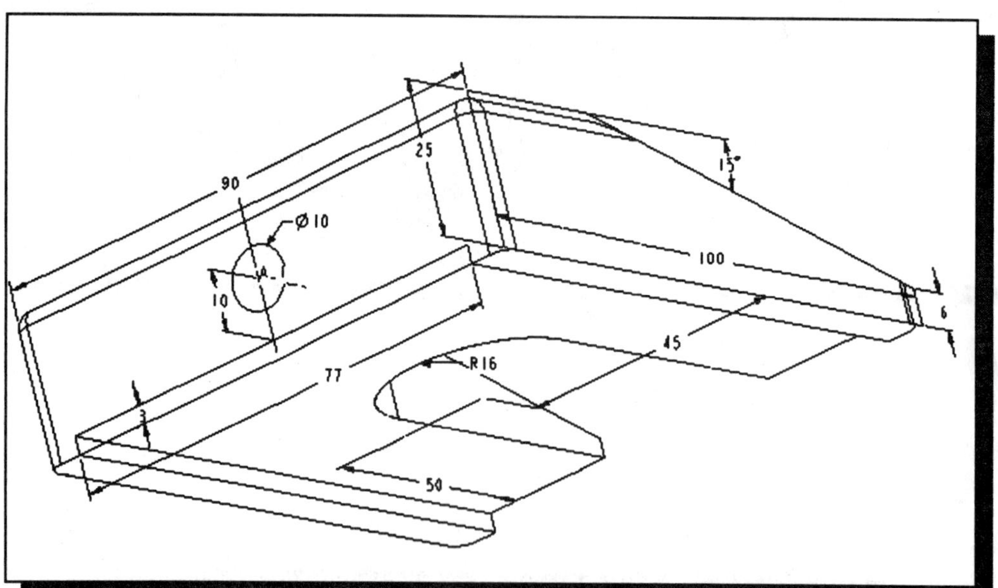

3. *Lifting Block*

(Rounds & Fillets: R3)

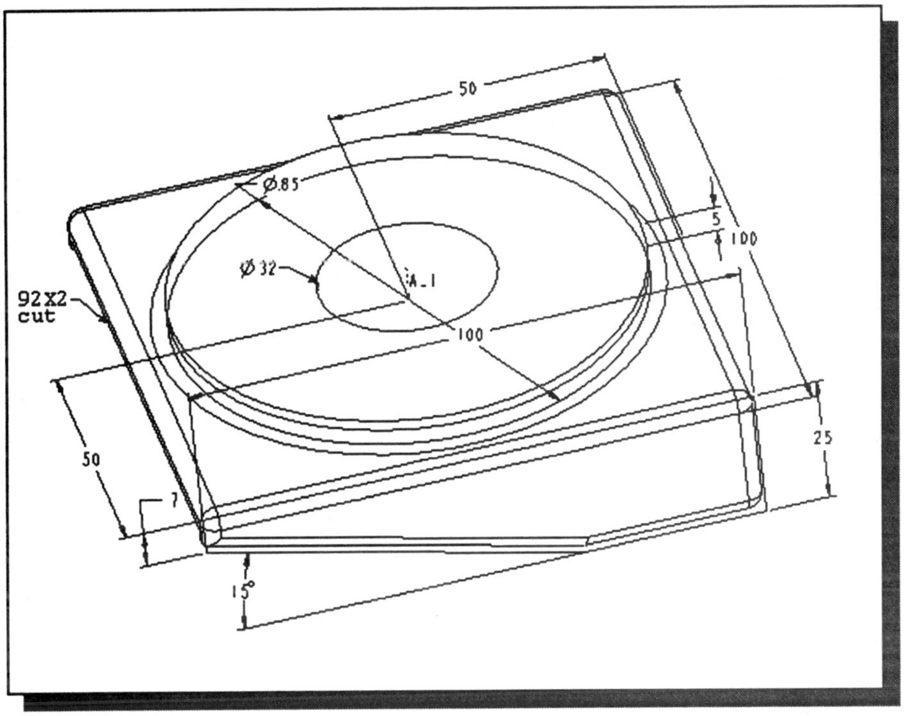

4. *Adjusting Screw*

(Threads Omitted)

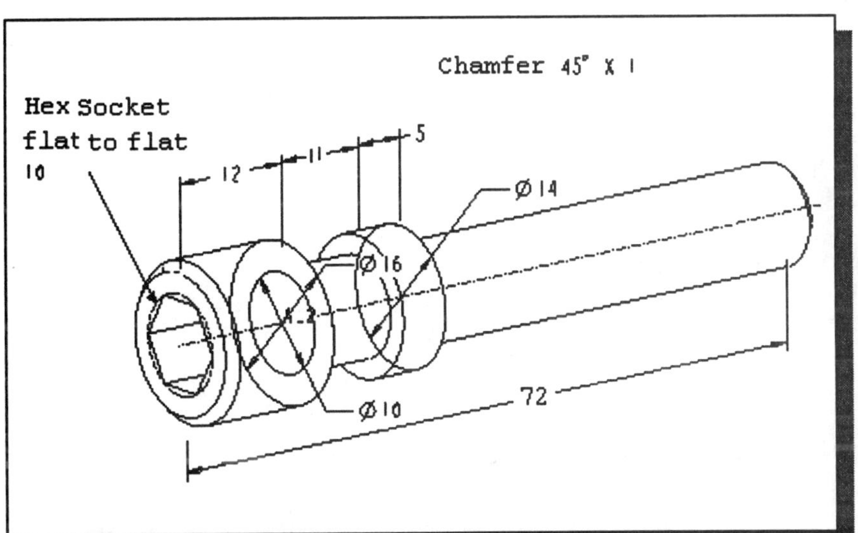

Notes:

INDEX

X

Y

Z